George Whitefield's Ministry
in New England, 1740-1770

George Whitefield's Ministry
in New England, 1740–1770

KENNETH LAWSON

Ambassador International
Greenville, South Carolina & Belfast, Northern Ireland
www.ambassador-international.com

GEORGE WHITEFIELD'S MINISTRY IN NEW ENGLAND, 1740-1770
©2024 by Kenneth Lawson
All rights reserved

Hardcover ISBN: 978-1-64960-310-4
Paperback ISBN: 978-1-64960-797-3
eISBN: 978-1-64960-332-6

Cover Design by Hannah Linder Designs
Interior Design by Dentelle Design

No part of this publication may be reproduced, distributed, or transmitted in any form or by any means, including photocopying, recording, or other electronic or mechanical methods, without the prior written permission of the publisher, except in the case of brief quotations embodied in critical reviews and certain other noncommercial uses permitted by copyright law. For permission requests, contact the publisher using the information below.

Ambassador International titles may be purchased in bulk for education, business, fundraising, or sales promotional use. For information, please email sales@emeraldhouse.com.

AMBASSADOR INTERNATIONAL
Emerald House
411 University Ridge, Suite B14
Greenville, SC 29601, USA
www.ambassador-international.com

AMBASSADOR BOOKS
The Mount
2 Woodstock Link
Belfast, BT6 8DD, Northern Ireland, UK
www.ambassadormedia.co.uk

The colophon is a trademark of Ambassador, a Christian publishing company.

CONTENTS

PREFACE 1

INTRODUCTION 5

CHAPTER 1
THE REVEREND GEORGE WHITEFIELD 9

CHAPTER 2
NEW ENGLAND BEFORE WHITEFIELD 15

CHAPTER 3
WHITEFIELD'S TOUR IN RHODE ISLAND 25

CHAPTER 4
WHITEFIELD'S FIRST VISIT TO BOSTON 33

CHAPTER 5
WHITEFIELD IN NORTHERN NEW ENGLAND 45

CHAPTER 6
WHITEFIELD IN BOSTON 59

CHAPTER 7
WHITEFIELD'S TOUR IN CENTRAL MASSACHUSETTS 67

CHAPTER 8
WHITEFIELD'S TOUR IN CONNECTICUT 83

CHAPTER 9
BOSTON AND EASTERN NEW ENGLAND AFTER WHITEFIELD'S DEPARTURE 103

CHAPTER 10
WHITEFIELD'S LIFE AND MINISTRY 113

CHAPTER 11
WHITEFIELD'S SECOND TOUR IN NORTHERN NEW ENGLAND 119

CHAPTER 12
WHITEFIELD'S VISIT TO BOSTON 127

CHAPTER 13
WHITEFIELD'S TOUR NORTH OF BOSTON, DECEMBER 13-19, 1744 137

CHAPTER 14
OPPOSITION AND OPPORTUNITY IN BOSTON 143

CHAPTER 15
A RESPITE FROM BOSTON: WHITEFIELD'S TOUR IN SOUTHERN MASSACHUSETTS. 153

CHAPTER 16
WHITEFIELD'S TOUR NORTH OF BOSTON 165

CHAPTER 17
WHITEFIELD'S TOUR INTO NEW HAMPSHIRE AND SOUTHERN MAINE 181

CHAPTER 18
WHITEFIELD'S MINISTRY IN EASTERN MAINE 199

CHAPTER 19
WHITEFIELD'S TOUR IN NEW HAMPSHIRE, NORTHERN MASSACHUSETTS, AND BOSTON 209

CHAPTER 20
WHITEFIELD IN RHODE ISLAND 217

CHAPTER 21
WHITEFIELD IN AND AROUND BOSTON AND A PREACHING CIRCUIT TO THE NORTH AND WEST 225

CHAPTER 22
WHITEFIELD'S MINISTRY IN WESTERN MASSACHUSETTS 243

CHAPTER 23
WHITEFIELD'S TOUR FROM WESTERN RHODE ISLAND THROUGH CONNECTICUT 257

CHAPTER 24
WHITEFIELD'S LIFE AND MINISTRY 275

CHAPTER 25
WHITEFIELD'S MINISTRY IN NEW ENGLAND 281

CHAPTER 26
A COMMUNITY IN TRANSITION 301

CHAPTER 27
WHITEFIELD'S TOUR IN EASTERN NEW ENGLAND 315

CHAPTER 28
WHITEFIELD'S TOUR IN NEW HAMPSHIRE AND MAINE 327

CHAPTER 29
WHITEFIELD'S PREACHING IN BOSTON AND WESTERN COMMUNITIES 335

CHAPTER 30
WHITEFIELD'S MINISTRY IN SOUTHERN MASSACHUSETTS, RHODE ISLAND, AND CONNECTICUT 347

CHAPTER 31
WHITEFIELD'S LIFE AND MINISTRY 361

CHAPTER 32
WHITEFIELD'S TOUR IN SOUTHERN NEW ENGLAND 367

CHAPTER 33
WHITEFIELD'S TOUR IN EASTERN AND SOUTHERN NEW ENGLAND 379

CHAPTER 34
NEW ENGLAND IN TRANSITION AND TURMOIL 397

CHAPTER 35
THE PROSPEROUS MINISTRY AND FAILING HEALTH OF GEORGE WHITEFIELD 407

CHAPTER 36
WHITEFIELD'S MINISTRY IN WESTERN NEW ENGLAND 415

CHAPTER 37
WHITEFIELD'S MINISTRY IN SOUTHERN NEW ENGLAND AND BOSTON 429

CHAPTER 38
THE FINAL VISIT TO NORTHERN NEW ENGLAND AND WHITEFIELD'S DEATH 441

CHAPTER 39
THE LEGACY OF WHITEFIELD IN NEW ENGLAND 463

APPENDIX A
SIGNIFICANT NEW ENGLAND MINISTERS WHO PUBLICLY SUPPORTED
GEORGE WHITEFIELD AND/OR THE AWAKENING   483

APPENDIX B
SIGNIFICANT NEW ENGLAND MINISTERS WHO PUBLICLY DID NOT SUPPORT
GEORGE WHITEFIELD AND/OR THE AWAKENING   485

SELECT BIBLIOGRAPHY   489

INDEX OF SIGNIFICANT PEOPLE   509

ABOUT THE AUTHOR   521

PREFACE

THIS TRAVELOGUE OF GEORGE WHITEFIELD in New England began in 1991 as a thesis for the Master of Arts degree in church history from the Cincinnati Bible Seminary in Ohio. Dr. James North served as my advisor for the project, providing encouragement and assistance. My original thesis concerned Whitefield's ministry only in northern New England and only through the Great Awakening of the 1740s. I was satisfied with the results of that research, yet believed someday I would expand and elaborate on this topic. Then the responsibilities of family, civilian ministries, and military chaplaincy obligations postponed my further research. For the next twenty-plus years, I read everything I could find on Whitefield, filing away copious notes and expanding my Whitefield library for further use. After a two- decades-plus delay, I was again able to concentrate on organizing my extensive notes, cross referencing research, visiting dozens of Whitefield sites in New England, writing new chapters, and then rewriting the text. My original thesis consists of about one-fifth of this present document. New material in this book concerns Whitefield's travels throughout all New England, over seven preaching tours, from 1740 to his death in Newburyport, Massachusetts in 1770.

For me, Dallimore's 1980 two volume text on Whitefield remains the standard biography on the popular itinerant evangelist, and is still in print. Over the last two decades there has been a resurgence of interest in Whitefield. The remarkable life and ministry of this evangelist still captivates attention. There was something unique, remarkable about him. Some loathed him and opposed his ministry at every opportunity. A few saw him as a nut, a lunatic. Others eagerly supported Whitefield, sometimes unto their own detriment. Some considered Whitefield an egomaniac, while others saw in him a model of humility. Whether in the mid-1700s, or today, it remains difficult to remain neutral about Whitefield's ministry.

Some recent scholarship has taken a different course than the hagiographies that often describe Whitefield scholarship. For example, in 1991 Harry Stout of Yale University wrote the controversial text, *The Divine Dramatist: George Whitefield and the Rise of Modern Evangelicalism*. Stout broke new ground when he stated that Whitefield's success in ministry was due to his showmanship and his manipulation of the masses through publications and private correspondence. Stout presented Whitefield as one who "lived his life almost exclusively for public performance," and as one who had "unprecedented success in marketing religion."[1] Stout presents Whitefield as a man with a tremendous ego, who practiced "theater-driven preaching" and as one who "strove to achieve the actor's command performance on center stage."[2] Stout called Whitefield "the proud performer" and a "self-made hero" whose itinerant ministry was similar to "an actor on tour."[3] Clearly Stout did not see a supernatural element in Whitefield's preaching and ministry. As Whitefield was ill and near death, Stout wrote that Whitefield was a "preacher-actor seizing the last moment in the limelight and giving the show of his life."[4]

---

1 Harry S. Stout, *The Divine Dramatist: George Whitefield and the Rise of Modern Evangelicalism*, (Grand Rapids, MI: Eerdman's Publishers, 1991), pp. xv, xviii.
2 Ibid., pp. xix, xxi.
3 Ibid., pp. 106, 252, 271.
4 Ibid., p. 278.

Another scholar who has taken an anti-supernatural view of Whitefield was Frank Lambert in his 1994 book, *Pedlar in Divinity: George Whitefield and the Transatlantic Revivals.* Lambert credits Whitefield with being a genius publicist, a commercial mastermind who utilized marketing techniques to generate large crowds and excite public interest. He credits Whitefield with "adapting commercial strategies for his own ends" and with "the commercialization of religion."[5] Lamberts asserts that Whitefield treated revival as a "commodity" that could be marketed like other commodities bought and sold in a marketplace.[6] He speaks of Whitefield as "organizing a revival" like one would organize a commercial marketing campaign to sell a new product.[7] Primarily through aggressive use of newspapers, Lambert asserts that Whitefield "would distinguish himself as an advertiser of divinity."[8] Indeed, much of Lambert's assessment of Whitefield's success can be attributed to the skillful use of marketing, the commercialization of religion, and promotion of the awakening through innovative advertising.[9]

Recent American scholarship related to Whitefield has sought to make a connection between his inter-colonial itinerant ministry and the founding of the United States as an independent nation. I alluded to this in the first edition of my Whitefield text,[10] and others have taken this theme and expanded it into a current scholastic trend in American church history and political studies. Stephen Mansfield was the first author to write a book length study on Whitefield as a founding father of the United States.[11] A more compelling book on this same theme was written by Jerome Mahaffey in 2007 which traced Whitefield's oratorical skills in relation to the rising American independence movement.[12] Mahaffey followed this book up with another more readable and shorter text on the same theme in 2011.[13] A thorough and recent book that discusses the nuances of Whitefield as a founding father of the United States was written by Thomas Kidd and published by Yale University Press.[14] I just completed reading a recent book by Nigel Scotland, *George Whitefield: The First Transatlantic Revivalist.*[15]

In the over twenty years gap in my writing about Whitefield, from 1996 to 2020, there have been numerous advances in research technologies. The speed of inter-library loans has dramatically increased. Libraries and historical societies nationwide have progressed in their computer cataloging systems, making cross referencing of sources simpler to accomplish. Many historic works related to Whitefield in America are now available on-line at a desktop computer, a concept foreign to me in the 1990s. Various historic newspapers are now available to read on a home computer. However, I still have found that the best, original research still happens when the scholar gets out of the library and walks the locations of historical events. In my doing so, I have met numerous local historical societies, church representatives, and regional history experts that have helped illuminate Whitefield's many travels and adventures in New England. For me, there is still a thrill in literally beating back the brush to discover a historic plaque or locate an overgrown, forgotten historical marker. There is a special sense of accomplishment in walking into a neglected historical society or

---

5   Frank Lambert, *Pedlar in Divinity: George Whitefield and the Transatlantic Revivals,* (Princeton, NJ: Princeton University Press, 1994), pp. 8, 9.
6   Ibid., p. 13.
7   Ibid., p. 14.
8   Ibid., p. 34.
9   Ibid., pp. 51, 229.
10 Kenneth E. Lawson, *George Whitefield's Ministry in Northern New England,* (Dracut, MA: Northeastern Bible Institute, 1996), pp. 223-226.
11 Stephen Mansfield, *Forgotten Founding Father: The Heroic Legacy of George Whitefield,* (Nashville, TN: Highland Books, 2001).
12 Jerome D. Mahaffey, *Preaching Politics: The Religious Rhetoric of George Whitefield and the Founding of a New Nation,* (Waco, TX: Baylor University Press, 2007).
13 Jerome Dean Mahaffey, *The Accidental Revolutionary: George Whitefield and the Creation of America,* (Waco, TX: Baylor University Press, 2011).
14 Thomas S. Kidd, *George Whitefield: America's Founding Father,* (New Haven, CT: Yale University Press, 2014).
15 Nigel Scotland, *George Whitefield: The First Transatlantic Revivalist,* (Oxford, England: Lion Hudson Publishers, 2019).

church library in a basement and blowing dust off a shoebox, opening the box and discovering documents overlooked for centuries. Due to recently discovered Whitefield documents in New England, and some new understandings of his influence, I have done some editing in select places of my 1996 Whitefield text.

I would like to thank my wife, Vera, for typing the original MA thesis in Cincinnati back in 1991. After expanding that research in the mid-1990s, Karen Holmes proved to be a capable typist and helpful editor. Years later, when I was able to recommit valuable time for further Whitefield research, I was assisted by various librarians, church pastors and deacons, historical society volunteers, and local history experts scattered throughout New England. Thank you all.

It is not my intent to create a hagiography of Whitefield. Admittedly, Whitefield intrigues me. How he did what he did, in preaching to millions in America over the exhausting course of his lifetime, is a remarkable achievement. Then and today, Whitefield has his critics.[16] While in his day some reviled him for his methods, none but the most hardened skeptic questioned his individual faith and devotion to Jesus Christ. While Harry Stout and Frank Lambert attributed Whitefield's success to pragmatic creativity and persuasive marketing, Whitefield attributed his power to God and his success in preaching to the blessings of the Lord. Stephen Mansfield stated,

> George Whitefield lived only fifty-six years and ministered publicly for only thirty-four of those years. Yet during that time, he changed the course of nations, founded institutions that survive to this day, and dug wells of revival that refresh even now. All this was possible because Whitefield believed that to lose one's life for Jesus meant surrendering every moment of the time in which that life is measured. It is why he always said to those who urged him to slow down, "It is better to wear out than to rust out."[17]

There were numerous historical societies throughout New England that assisted me in this research. Often staffed by volunteers, these societies are a treasure grove of local history that are often undiscovered. Numerous historic local churches shared with me their unpublished histories. Public libraries in various communities had local, unpublished resources that greatly added to the details of this research project. Thank you to Arthur Lawson, who created all the maps. I am especially thankful to the American Antiquarian Society in Worcester, Massachusetts; the Newport Historical Society Library in Newport, Rhode Island; The Connecticut Historical Society in Hartford, Connecticut; and the Peabody Essex Museum Library in Salem, Massachusetts. Their abundant primary source materials related to Whitefield's ministries throughout New England were valuable and appreciated.

Shortly after George Whitefield died in 1770, his longtime friend Benjamin Franklin of Philadelphia wrote, "I knew him intimately upward of thirty years. His integrity, disinterestedness, and indefatigable zeal in prosecuting every good work I have never seen equaled, I shall never see so excelled."[18] It is this interesting and complicated man whose steps we follow in this travelogue of Whitefield's ministries in New England.

DR. KENNETH LAWSON
North Andover, Massachusetts
2023

---

16 David C. Jones, "So Much Idolized by Some, and Railed by Others: Towards Understanding George Whitefield," *Wesley and Methodist Studies*, (2013), pp. 3-29.
17 Stephen Mansfield, *Forgotten Founding Father*, p. 133.
18 Joseph B. Wakeley, *Anecdotes of the Rev. George Whitefield, M.A.*, (London: 1772), p. 122.

George Whitefield as a boy helping in the family inn.

A sketch of George Whitefield working as a servant in the family inn, Gloucester, England, by Valerie Borgal.

INTRODUCTION

ABOUT TWO HUNDRED AND FIFTY-FIVE years ago, George Whitefield died in northern New England. His tomb is easily accessible and well preserved beneath the Old South Presbyterian Church in Newburyport, Massachusetts, a few miles northeast of my childhood home. In addition to being an active church congregation, several hundred tourists per year visit this historic meeting house, originally built in 1756.

Compared to the millions who were affected by Whitefield during his life, he is not well-remembered today. Whitefield has never been fully understood, even in his own lifetime. He was frequently accused of thievery, showmanship, and of an arrogance from the pulpit that shocked the eighteenth-century English-speaking world. Others perceived Whitefield as an apostle, a herald from God that was above human reproach and who did no wrong. The truth, of course, lies somewhere between these diverse opinions. Whitefield remains today a misunderstood person in the history of Christianity.

Of the several biographies of Whitefield written over the past 250-plus years, I found that three are particularly helpful. The first, written by his friend John Gillies in 1772 shortly after Whitefield's death in 1770, has served as a starting point for all other research on Whitefield's life.[1] Unfortunately, in his haste to print Whitefield's history for the public, Gillies left out large portions of Whitefield's life. The second major biography on Whitefield by Luke Tyerman appeared in 1876.[2] This massive work covers two large volumes and provides many details omitted from Gillies' work. Tyerman's biography is an excellent study. The third Whitefield biography that has been especially helpful is the two-volume work by Arnold Dallimore.[3] In this text, Dallimore uses both Gillies and Tyerman as a base, then expands and elaborates on events in Whitefield's life that previously had been unexplored. Further, Dallimore discovered numerous documents and articles pertaining to Whitefield that had been overlooked for many years.

Recently there has been a rediscovery of the life and ministry of George Whitefield. For those interested in a detailed study of Whitefield's ministry, Dallimore's book is still in print and is perhaps the most helpful. Smaller books on Whitefield's life, intended for a more general audience, are also available.[4] For the casual reader, Dallimore has abridged his massive two-volume study in a slim, convenient summary.[5] Further, Whitefield's *Journals* have remained in print for years, providing a first-hand narration of his ministry.

---

1 John Gilles, *Memoirs of the Life of the Reverend George Whitefield*, (London, England: E & C Dilly, 1772).
2 Luke Tyerman, *The Life of the Rev. George Whitefield*, (London, England: Hodder and Stoughton Publishers, 2 vols., 1876).
3 Arnold Dallimore, *George Whitefield: The Life and Times of the Great Evangelist of the Eighteenth Century Revival*, (Carlisle, PA: Banner of Truth Trust, 2 vols., 1980).
4 John Pollock, *George Whitefield and the Great Awakening*, (Belleville, MI: Lion Publishing Company, 1982). Bruce and Becky Durost Fish, *George Whitefield: Pioneering Evangelist*, (Uhrichsville, OH: Barbour Books, 2000). Michael A.G. Haykin, *The Revived Puritan: The Spirituality of George Whitefield*, (Dundas, Ontario: Joshua Press, 2000). Lucille Travis, *George Whitefield: The Voice that Shook the World*, (Fearn, Ross-Shire, Scotland, UK: 2011). Steven J. Lawson, *The Evangelistic Zeal of George Whitefield*, (Orlando, FL Reformation Trust, 2013). Dan Nelson, *A Burning and Shining Light: The Testimony and Witness of George Whitefield*, (Somis, CA: LifeSong Publishers, 2017).
5 Arnold Dallimore, *George Whitefield: God's Anointed Servant in the Great Revival of the Eighteenth Century*, (Westchester, IL: Crossway Books, 1990).

Unfortunately, these journals are brief and cover only the early years of Whitefield's ministry.[6] Interest in Whitefield has developed to the point that even John Gillies' work on Whitefield is now back in print, and compilations of Whitefield's sermons have been often reproduced.[7]

The Harvard academic Perry Miller (d.1963) was a virulent critic of George Whitefield's influence in Colonial America. Miller considered Whitefield "too shallow to respect and too facile." He declared Whitefield "reckless and irresponsible, whining and sanctimonious."[8] But more recent scholars of Whitefield have a mostly different perspective.

In 2008, E.A. Johnston published a two-volume work on Whitefield's life, called *George Whitefield: A Definitive Biography*. Johnston had access to numerous primary documents that were not utilized by previous Whitefield biographers.[9] This is a welcome addition to the Whitefield literature. Some more recent Whitefield books are by Dan Nelson, *A Burning and Shining Light: The Testimony and Witness of George Whitefield*; and a book by Tim McKnight, *No Better Gospel: George Whitefield's Theology and Methodology of Evangelism*. The Nelson book's best contribution is the chapter on "Lasting Contributions of George Whitefield."[10] The McKnight book is helpful in that it the first extended attempt to create a systematic theology of Whitefield's teachings.[11]

The focus of this text is on Colonial New England in the eighteenth century. There are several reasons for this emphasis. First, there is no detailed study on Whitefield's ministry in a particular community, tracing local responses and reactions over an extended period. Secondly, the amount of primary source material related to Whitefield is abundant, yet mostly unexplored, and poorly disseminated. Third, Whitefield experienced sensational success in these New England coastal cities and rural inland villages, often preaching to thousands in open fields. But he also experienced significant and enduring opposition. This focused research will help to fill in the many gaps in Whitefield's life that history has not yet discovered.

I have used as many original sources as possible in this book. Journals, diaries, pamphlets, newspapers, and references to private correspondence are numerous. I want to allow Whitefield, his friends, and his opponents to speak for themselves.

The outline of this book is logical and chronological. It is, essentially, a travelogue. Every effort has been made to try and track Whitefield's daily activities in New England over a thirty-year period. Inevitably there will be small gaps or mistakes in the detailed day-by-day chronology. Whitefield is introduced to the reader in small, orderly segments coinciding with the changing religious and political climate in New England. Colonial New England is described before, during and after Whitefield's seven successful visits to the area, tracing the footsteps of this itinerant minister over thirty years until his death in Newburyport, Massachusetts, in 1770.

---

6 George Whitefield, *George Whitefield's Journals*, (Carlisle, PA: Banner of Truth Trust, 1960. Reprinted from the 1756 edition).
7 George Whitefield: *Sermons*, (New Ipswich, NH: Pietan Publications, 1991, 1993, 1994, vols. 1-3). In 2000 Quinta Press of Oswestry, Shropshire, England collected all of Whitefield's journals, letters, and several biographies and made them available on a compact disc (CD).
8 Perry Miller, *Jonathan Edwards*, (Lincoln, NE: University of Nebraska Press, 1949), p. 143.
9 E.A. Johnston, *George Whitefield: A Definitive Biography*, (Stoke-on-Trent, Great Britain: Tentmaker Publications, 2008).
10 Dan Nelson, *A Burning and Shining Light: The Testimony and Witness of George Whitefield*, (Somis, CA: LifeSong Publishers, 2017), pp.255-268.
11 Tim McKnight, *No Better Gospel: George Whitefield's Theology and Methodology of Evangelism*, (Timmonsville, SC: Seed Publishing Group, 2017).

This portrait of Whitefield as a younger minister was painted by an unknown artist and is in the possession of Pembroke College, University of Oxford.
Source: www.bbc.co.uk.

CHAPTER 1

THE REVEREND GEORGE WHITEFIELD

THE LIFE AND MINISTRY OF George Whitefield is no less an enigma today than it was at the time of his public ministry over 250 years ago. To some, Whitefield was a hero, a messenger from God. Others saw him as meddlesome and conceited—a mere showman. These various opinions of Whitefield were often the causes of schisms in churches, dismissals of ministers, and volatile ecclesiastical councils. Wherever Whitefield preached, people were noticeably moved and compelled to action, either as advocates or adversaries of the revivals he instituted. Few characters in the history of American Christianity have achieved the level of controversy that surrounded the evangelist George Whitefield. He was a man out of his time, preaching a vital faith that had mostly vanished from the people he addressed. When he visited New England, no small stir surrounded his presence. He could arguably be called the most popular Englishman alive during the years of his ministry, 1738-1770.

The native New Englander Williston Walker (1860-1922) taught at both Hartford Theological Seminary and Yale University, both in Connecticut. He was a well-known church historian and frequently published author. Walker was no supporter of George Whitefield's message or methods. Yet he wrote of Whitefield, "On his last visit [to New England] he died at Newburyport, Mass., September 30, 1770; and his memory is that of one who with many faults of temper and of method yet with many virtues of heart and deep consecration of spirit was a prime human factor in the greatest religious overturning that New England has ever experienced."[1]

George Whitefield was born in December 1714, in Gloucester, England. The four family generations preceding him had personal relations with both the University of Oxford and the priesthood of the Church of England. His father, Thomas Whitefield, at age 19, began a prosperous business at the Bell Inn of Gloucester. His mother, Elizabeth Edwards Whitefield, also came from a reasonably successful but not wealthy background. Numerous relatives on her side of the family held positions of local civil leadership and authority. George Whitefield's early years were spent in the middle class. His parents, proprietors of a successful inn, were among the more noteworthy of Gloucester's citizens.[2]

Thomas Whitefield died in 1716, at the age of thirty-five, leaving his wife Elizabeth with seven children, the youngest of which was George. Despite numerous years of service as a laborer in the family business, George Whitefield was able to maintain the family tradition of attending Oxford University in 1732. He became a servitor, a type of errand-boy or assistant to older students, in exchange for free tuition. This humbling service would accompany his classroom training for three years. Although he stated that in his early years, "I was so brutish as to hate instruction, and used purposely to shun all opportunities of receiving

---

1 Williston Walker, *A History of the Congregational Churches in the United States*, (New York: Charles Scribner's Sons, 1916), p. 266.
2 Arnold Dallimore, *George Whitefield: The Life and Times of the Great Evangelist of the Eighteenth Century Revival*, (Carlisle, PA: Banner of Truth Trust, 1980), vol. I, p. 44.

it," such was not the case at Oxford.[3] He earned his degree in 1736, though little is known of his academic progress at the school.

The instruction Whitefield craved more than academics was in personal religion. He became more outwardly pious at the university than he had been prior. He recorded, "I now began to pray and sing psalms thrice every day, and to fast every Friday, and to receive the Sacrament at a parish church near our college . . . once a month."[4] Because of his refusal to join in the adolescent amusements of his peers, Whitefield found himself often alone and at the mercy of his cruel classmates. He longed to be acquainted with a group on campus known for their strict living and methodical behavior, i.e., the Methodists. The contact came through Charles Wesley, who was a member of the "Holy Club." He noticed Whitefield's devotion and separation from the distractions of the world. Whitefield said, "My soul, at that time, was athirst for some spiritual friends to lift up my hands when they hung down, and to strengthen my feeble knees."[5]

Whitefield enthusiastically joined the society of Methodists. He read numerous books on Christian topics, received instruction from both John and Charles Wesley on personal piety, and often practiced benevolent acts to his classmates and needful members of the local community. However, amidst such frenzied activity, Whitefield finally understood that he "must be a new creature."[6] The members of the Holy Club sought to earn or merit their salvation by personal duty, honesty and devotion. "Its members knew nothing of the inward miracle of the new birth, and in their search for spiritual satisfaction, turned increasingly to outward ritual."[7]

Whitefield became increasingly dissatisfied with the Oxford Holy Club. He earnestly sought even further to try to merit his salvation. He increased his bodily deprivations, he became prone to fits of emotional anxiety, and he even sought to separate himself from his spiritual peers in the Holy Club.[8] Upon coming to the end of his human abilities and resources, and in utter helplessness, God revealed himself by grace to George Whitefield, freely giving him what he had for years been trying to earn. The exact date of his conversion is uncertain. We do know, however, that by February of 1735 he fully understood salvation by grace and not of human effort. In a letter to a friend, Whitefield asserted that "True religion does not consist in anything besides an entire renewal of our natures into the image of God . . . How wretchedly most people do err . . . who suppose it to be nothing else . . . but a mere model of outward performances . . . "[9] In recalling this event, he wrote:

> The spirit of mourning was taken from me, and I knew what it was to rejoice in God my Savior; and, for some time, could not avoid singing psalms wherever I was; but my joy gradually became more settled, and, blessed be God, has abode and increased in my soul, saving a few casual intermissions, ever since.[10]

The newly converted Whitefield immediately showed benevolent works which verified his call to new life in Christ. He quickly told friends and acquaintances of his conversion, made restitution for petty crimes committed as a boy, and vigorously structured his time to allow for proper hours for prayer and Bible study. The blessedness of his new life, he knew, should not be kept to himself. He promptly began personal evangelism work and experienced immediate results. "Some people treated him with scorn, but many

---

3 George Whitefield, *George Whitefield's Journals*, (Carlisle, PA: Banner of Truth Trust, 1960), p. 37.
4 Ibid., p. 46.
5 Ibid.
6 Ibid., p. 47.
7 Arnold Dallimore, *George Whitefield*, vol. I, p. 71.
8 For more insights into Whitefield's struggles in this period, see Harry D. Rack, "Religious Societies and the Origins of Methodism," Journal of Ecclesiastical History, vol. 38, no. 4, (October 1987), pp. 582-595.
9 George Whitefield, "George Whitefield's Letters," *Works of George Whitefield*, (Carlisle, PA: Banner of Truth Trust, 1976), vol. I, p. 6.
10 George Whitefield, *George Whitefield's Journals*, p. 58.

regarded him with an overwhelming admiration and began to urge that he apply for ordination right away."[11] He assumed leadership positions in the Oxford Holy Club. He began publicly practicing what was called "exhorting," as only ordained ministers of his Anglican Church were allowed to preach. Finally, on June 20, 1736 George Whitefield was ordained as a priest of the Church of England. He promptly began to perform his ministerial duties. That afternoon, he ministered to prisoners in a local jail. The same evening, he read prayers at a church service. During the following week, he christened an infant, performed a marriage, and read prayers in public services.[12]

On Sunday June 27, 1736, Whitefield preached his first official public sermon at the age of twenty-two. The response of the large congregation gathered in his hometown of Gloucester was overwhelmingly favorable. This was the first of his thousands of sermons preached to millions of people through the next thirty-four years, over much of the English-speaking world. The day after his first sermon, in private correspondence, Whitefield stated:

> Tomorrow I am to preach at Crypt (the Church of St. Mary de Crypt) but believe I shall displease some, being determined to preach against their assemblies. But I must tell them the truth, or otherwise I shall not be a faithful minister of Christ.[13]

Preaching is what made Whitefield live. He feasted upon the public proclamation of the Word of God. It was an all-consuming passion for him to preach to the lost, that they, too, might experience new life in Christ. As one student of the art of preaching stated, "The history of preaching since the apostles does not contain a greater or worthier name than George Whitefield."[14]

The legacy of Whitefield is not maintained by the memory of his philanthropic work, though it was unique and significant. Nor is he remembered for being a great denominational leader, or as an international traveler. Rather, Whitefield is remembered as a Bible preacher. From the time the ordaining bishop laid his hands on his head in 1736, to the time he was laid in the tomb under the pulpit of a revivalist church in Newburyport, Massachusetts in 1770, Whitefield was totally consumed with the spreading of the gospel.

> In preaching he was terribly earnest. He spoke as if he believed the truths he uttered . . . that there was a heaven and a hell; as if he stood between them listening to the groans of the damned on the one hand, and the songs of the redeemed on the other.[15]

Another testimony to the effectiveness of Whitefield's ministry asserted, "Sacred oratory was the luminous center of the genius of Whitefield. In natural gifts of thrilling and persuasive address he was one of the most remarkable men that ever lived . . . He seemed to speak from the border of the spiritual world."[16]

The stage was well set for the appearance of Whitefield in both England and the American Colonies. The soul-winning fire of evangelism had all but extinguished. The inner devotion to God instituted by the indwelling Holy Spirit was excluded from most preaching, replaced by outward piety and church attendance. England responded to Whitefield's preaching at the Chapel of the Tower of London with curious support. A number were drawn to him, both leading citizens in the city and students, as well as the general populace.

---

11   Arnold Dallimore, *George Whitefield . . . , vol. I*, p. 86.
12   Ibid., p. 96. Luke Tyerman, *The Life of the Rev. George Whitefield*, (London, England: Hodder and Stoughton Publishers, 1876), vol. I, pp. 48-52.
13   George Whitefield, *Works, vol. I*, p. 17.
14   Edwin C. Dargan, *A History of Preaching*, (Grand Rapids, MI: Baker Book House, 1954), vol. II, p. 307.
15   J.B. Wakeley, *The Prince of Pulpit Orators: A Portraiture of Rev. George Whitefield*, (New York: Carleton & Lanahan Publishers, 1871), p. 27.
16   Henry C. Sheldon, *History of the Christian Church*, (Peabody, MA: Hendrickson Publishers, 1988. Reprinted from the 1898 edition.), vol. III, p. 55.

Invitations began to appear from various pulpits throughout the city. His work at the Oxford Holy Club also consumed his time. He was approached by the Bishop of London to accept a leading ministerial post in the city. His time was busy, and his labors in this period in his life were overwhelmingly successful.

During his noteworthy ministry in his native England, Whitefield learned of the spiritual need in the American Colonies, particularly in Georgia. The enormity of the religious challenge abroad at first overwhelmed the successful minister. Upon learning the needs of the colonies, he stated:

> Their account fired my soul, and made me even long to go abroad for God too; but having no outward call, and being, as I then thought, too weak in body ever to take a voyage by sea, I endeavored to lay aside all thought of going abroad. But my endeavors were all in vain; for I felt at times such a strong attraction in my soul towards Georgia, that I thought it almost irresistible.[17]

By January 1737, Whitefield had made up his mind. His shocked and disappointed admirers in England could only say, "The will of the Lord be done!" After saying his farewells and administrating his affairs in London, he departed on December 28, 1737 for the first of several journeys to the American Colonies.

The Georgia which received Whitefield was a pioneer outpost, a crude and undeveloped society. Although there were some English gentlemen that settled along the coast, most of the citizens were released debtors from British prisons. Savannah, the largest settlement in the colony, was little more than a clearing in the woods, and the population in the entire colony was probably less than a thousand.[18]

There was not as yet a church building in all of Georgia. Whitefield left the thousands that came to hear him preach in England to minister to this small, forgotten band in the wilderness. In addition to his evangelical labors, he also addressed himself to the temporal needs of the people. Schools were founded, a church meeting house constructed, and the Bethesda orphanage was planned. In a letter written from Savannah, dated June 10, 1738 Whitefield summarized his ministry in Georgia and his future plans:

> As for my ministerial office, I can inform you, that God (such is his goodness) sets his seal to it here, as at other places . . . The people receive me gladly, as yet, into their houses, and seem to be most kindly affected toward me . . . Blessed be God, I visit from house to house, catechize, read prayers twice and expound the two second lessons every day; read to a houseful of people three times a week; expound the two lessons at five in the morning . . . What I have most at heart, is the building of an orphanage, which I trust will be affected at my return to England.[19]

Whitefield had a strong desire to build an orphanage for boys and girls as a ministry to these forgotten or abandoned children in America. Creating and then maintaining such an orphanage would follow Whitefield for the rest of his life.

After a turbulent and uncomfortable journey across the Atlantic which lasted nine weeks, Whitefield returned first to Ireland and then to his native England. He had been away for eleven months. The news that he was back in England caused his enemies grief and his friends overwhelming joy. He saw the results of his former preaching endeavors all around him. He said at this time, "About noon I reached London; was received with much joy by my Christian friends . . . I perceive God has greatly watered the seed sown by my ministry when last in London. The Lord increase it more and more."[20]

---

17 George Whitefield, *Journals*, pp. 77-78.
18 Arnold Dallimore, *George Whitefield . . .* , vol. I, p. 201. Mary B. Warren, British Georgia: The First Settlers, 1733-1740, (Athens, GA: Heritage Papers, 2015).
19 George Whitefield, *Works, vol. I*, p. 44. Edwin J. Cashin, *Beloved Bethesda: A History of George Whitefield's Home for Boys*, (Atlanta, GA: Mercer University Press, 2001), pp. 1-23.
20 George Whitefield, *Journals*, p. 193.

If the signs of his former ministry were favorable, there were also indications that opposition had developed as well. Two days later, December 10, 1738, Whitefield recorded:

> When I was on board the *Mary*, those particular parts of the book of Jeremiah, which relate to the opposition he met from the false prophets, were deeply impressed upon my soul. Now I begin to see the wisdom of God in it; for five churches have already denied me, and some of the clergy, if possible, would oblige me to depart out of these coasts.[21]

Though the clergy in many instances forbade Whitefield to preach from their pulpits, his popularity with the people was not significantly affected. Clerical pamphlets against him reinforced his enemies but were of no importance to his followers. Many of his fellow ministers in the Church of England opposed his insistence on the new birth and his teaching on the indwelling presence of the Holy Spirit. Dallimore summarized the tension Whitefield felt at this time:

> The realization that deep doctrinal differences exist between himself and the majority of the clergy was of grave significance to Whitefield. These men were the officers of the church he respected so highly, yet allegiance to what he knew to be the truth of God separated him from them and required that he stand against them.[22]

Whitefield began to consider preaching outside the confines of a single church building. To an established and sedate clergy, such an idea bordered on insanity. Even Whitefield's supporters were hesitant, "who looked upon it as a mad notion."[23] Not only were many churches closed to him, but those that did allow him to preach could not hold the thousands which desired to hear him speak. After careful consideration, Whitefield decided to preach in the open air. His first open-air sermon was delivered on February 17, 1739 to coal miners in the Kingswood area of England. He recorded,

> My bowels have long since yearned toward the poor colliers, who are very numerous, and as sheep having no shepherd. After dinner, therefore, I went upon a mount, and spoke to as many people as came unto me. There were upwards of two hundred. Blessed be God that I have now broken the ice! I believe I was never more acceptable to my Master than when I was standing to teach those hearers in the open fields. Some may censure me; but if I thus please men, I should not be the servant of Christ.[24]

Whitefield's second open-air meeting for the people of Kingswood was attended not by two hundred, but by two thousand. He was a sensation not only among the people of Kingswood, but to all who supported his preaching of the gospel. The hundreds turned to thousands, and then to tens of thousands. The novelty of outdoor preaching, the unusual oratory skills of the preacher, and the message itself, made Whitefield's ministry an overwhelming success. One particular meeting of this sort deserves special attention. Whitefield wrote:

> At four in the afternoon, I went to the mount on Rose Green, and preached to about fourteen thousand souls, and so good was my God, that all could hear. I spoke, with great freedom, but thought all the while, as I do when I ascend the mount, that hereafter I shall suffer as well as speak for my Master's sake . . . My preaching in the fields may displease

---

21 Ibid.
22 Arnold Dallimore, *George Whitefield . . .*, vol. I, p. 227.
23 George Whitefield, *Journals*, p. 200.
24 Ibid., p. 216.

some timorous, bigoted men, but I am thoroughly persuaded it pleases God, and why should I fear anything else?[25]

Since his open-air preaching ministry had been so successful in England, every indication pointed to similar success in the American Colonies as well. Shortly before his second journey to America, Whitefield recorded the following assessment in a personal correspondence, dated August 3, 1739:

> The word runs very swift, and Satan falls like lightning from heaven. God has sent me into the highways and hedges, to compel poor sinners to come in; many are left to water what God hath been pleased to plant; I doubt not of his giving a substantial increase.[26]

The American Colonies had already, before Whitefield's second visit in 1740, experienced isolated outbreaks of revival preaching and awakenings. Pennsylvania's German people, made up of Lutherans, Baptists, Quakers, Moravians and others, were experiencing large conversions and rededications among their people. Much of New Jersey and New York, under the preaching of Theodorus Frelinghuysen and others, experienced revival among the Dutch Reformed Churches. Presbyterianism was experiencing new life under William Tennent, and later under his sons William and Gilbert, primarily in the central colonies. Lastly, the Congregationalists under Jonathan Edwards experienced revival in Connecticut and Massachusetts. Yet, each of these movements were geographically isolated from one another, and were denominationally distinct, so that they had little to do with each other. They were individual movements within their respective contexts and not a unified inter-colonial revival. It was while these conditions appeared in the colonies that the people heard of Whitefield's successes in England. Dallimore states that the ministries of Whitefield in England, which resulted in overwhelming numbers of eager listeners, were reported in colonial newspapers with great interest.[27]

Though only a young man in his twenties, Whitefield's name became a household word both in England and in America. New England eagerly anticipated a possible visit from this illustrious minister. Boston and some of its neighbors to the north, namely Salem, Marblehead and Portsmouth, constituted one of the most economically prosperous and densely populated regions in America. Newport, Rhode Island grew to become a major colonial city in Southern New England. Whitefield was preaching in America's deep south when he complied with the pressing invitations of the Reverends Coleman and Cooper of Boston to visit New England. This would be the first of seven visits by the famous evangelist to New England. He arrived in Newport, Rhode Island in mid-September 1740. The details of these visits constitute a large portion of Whitefield's public ministry, yet many of the specifics of his work in these areas are not known today. Here he found little initial opposition and made loyal and devoted lifelong friends. Here he would preach to the fourth generation from the founding fathers, descendants from the Puritans whom Whitefield read and enjoyed. And here would be the place of the evangelist's last sermon, and his untimely death and burial at age fifty-six, in the year 1770.

---

25 Ibid., p. 227.
26 George Whitefield, *Works* . . . , vol. I, p. 58.
27 Arnold Dallimore, George Whitefield . . . , vol. I, p. 429. Frank Lambert expands on the theme of Whitefield using newspapers effectively in *Pedlar in Divinity: George Whitefield and the Transatlantic Revivals*, (Princeton, NJ Princeton University Press, 1994). See also Peter C. Hoffer, *When Benjamin Franklin Met the Reverend Whitefield: Enlightenment, Revival, and the Power of the Printed Word*, (Baltimore, MD: The Johns Hopkins University Press, 2011).

CHAPTER 2

NEW ENGLAND BEFORE WHITEFIELD

1623-1740

THE MAJORITY OF THE FIRST European settlers of New England were English Puritans. Puritanism arose in England because of an intense dissatisfaction with the speed and depth of the English Reformation. The Puritans wanted more. Carefully controlled by the government, the Protestant Reformation in England never achieved the successes of those in Luther's Germany or Calvin's Geneva. Religious liberty in England depended on the whims of various monarchs, leaving the Puritans dissatisfied. Practices of the established church, such as the use of the *Common Prayer Book*, clerical vestments, and a formal liturgy, made the Puritans believe that the English church was a poor imitation of the Roman Church and needed to be purified at all costs.[1] Although not a Puritan, Captain John Smith of Virginia did much to influence the planting of Puritanism in the New World. In 1616, he published *A Description of New England* which quickly became a bestseller and stimulated the interest of both Puritans and others in their quests for a home where they could worship in peace. Other literature appearing in England that influenced settlement in the New World were works about the Plymouth Pilgrims, such as *Relation* (1622) and *Good News from New England* (1624).

In November 1620, the first settlers from England arrived in New England on Cape Cod, and were later called Pilgrims.[2] Through circumstances beyond their control, they left England five months late, missing the planting season. These Pilgrims of Plymouth were, in reality, Puritans who separated from the Church of England, having no patience or confidence in its potential reform. They were, in general, less educated, and not as well organized as the Puritans who would settle in and north of Boston. The Pilgrims were poorly equipped, overcrowded on ship, and had little chance of surviving in the New World. Upon their arrival, death quickly captured nearly half of the one hundred or so settlers, including their newly elected governor, John Carver. Many of these settlers did, however, survive their first trials in the New World, developing an orderly ecclesiastical and social /civil system of government, as revealed in the writings of their second governor, William Bradford. They lacked everything: money, supplies, supporters, even a charter. They believed that by trusting in their God and working hard, they would survive.[3]

For simplicity's sake, the Pilgrims were strict separatists who could no longer worship within the Church of England. The Puritans were those who decided to stay within the Church of England and seek to reform or purify the Church.

---

1 Jerald C. Brauer, "Conversion: from Puritanism to Revivalism," *Journal of Religion*, vol. 58 (July 1978), pp. 228-229.
2 David Beale, *The Mayflower Pilgrims*, (Greenville, SC: Emerald House Group, 2000). Rod Gragg, *The Pilgrim Chronicles: An Eyewitness History of the Pilgrims and the Founding of Plymouth Colony*, (Washington, DC: Regency History, 2014).
3 George F. Dow, *Everyday Life in the Massachusetts Bay Colony*, (New York: Dover Publications, 1988). For a case study, see Thomas F. Waters, *Ipswich in the Massachusetts Bay Colony*, (Ipswich, MA: Ipswich Historical Society, 1905).

The original Puritan settlements around Boston had little in common with their earlier, mostly working-class Pilgrim neighbors to the south. Under the increasingly unfavorable circumstances in England, a few of the more adventurous Puritans looked toward Boston and the New World as a place where they could practice their religion in ways denied them in Europe. Concerning the original Puritan settlers:

> Their leaders were from good station in England, many of them from the country gentry, men of wealth, character and education. Their ministers . . . were the peers in learning and ability of any in the Puritan wing of the Church of England . . . Probably no colony in the history of European emigration was superior to that of Massachusetts in wealth, station or cupidity.[4]

In 1626, several merchants, under the guidance of the Rev. John White, took out a patent from the Council of New England to establish a fishing settlement in the New World. They landed in Cape Ann, an outcropping of land some twenty-five miles north of Boston. The original intent was for the men to combine both fishing and farming for survival. However, they quickly found their dual obligations incompatible and abandoned their plan. Several of the fishermen/farmers remained in the area, led by the capable Roger Conant. With the continued support of Rev. White, they sought to form a colony where religion would be given prominence over trade. Conant led his men to a spot just south of Cape Ann, which would later be called Salem. The Scriptures say, "Gather my saints together unto me; those that have made a covenant with me by sacrifices" (Psalm 50:5). And on that injunction, these thirty settlers in Salem gathered together to announce: "We covenant with the Lord and with one another and do bind ourselves in the presence of God to work together in all his ways according as He is pleased to reveal Himself unto us in His blessed word of truth."[5] With these words, the Puritans of Salem put behind centuries of Christian tradition. This covenanted community was linking itself directly to God, not through an officially established church or formal liturgical ceremony.[6]

In the Connecticut Colony, the first English settlers arrived in 1634 in Wethersfield. The next year settlers founded Saybrook. In 1636, dissatisfied Massachusetts colonists travelled to central Connecticut and founded Hartford. In 1638, New Haven was founded and quickly became a major port along the extended Connecticut coastline. These Connecticut settlers were a serious-minded and hearty bunch, dedicated to God and committed to carve communities out of the wilderness.[7]

In 1628, the Massachusetts Bay Colony was established, as additional Puritan settlers arrived from England under the leadership of John Endicott. The next year nearly 400 well-provisioned settlers arrived from England, charter in hand, as part of an extremely well-planned expedition. Thousands of Puritans followed the leadership of the Massachusetts Bay Colony and came to New England. Early Puritan churches were founded in communities north of Boston such as Lynn (1632), Ipswich (1634), Newbury (1635) Hampton (1638), Dover (1638) and Rowley (1639). Cape Ann was resettled by the Puritans in 1642. The County of Essex was incorporated in 1643. In Cape Ann or Gloucester, a town was chartered, a meeting house constructed, canals built, and a mill developed. The founding of this settlement was a particularly enlightening example of the careful and diligent planning which the Puritans exercised in establishing themselves in the New World.[8]

Elsewhere in New England, during the mid-1600s, Connecticut continued to grow. In 1644 the Saybrook and Connecticut colonies merged. In 1646 New London was established as a fishing and shipbuilding center. In

---

4   Williston Walker, *History of Congregationalism in New England*, (New York: Charles Scribner's Sons, 1716), p. 98.
5   David Hawke, *The Colonial Experience*, (New York: MacMillan Publishing Company, 1985, p. 134.
6   James D. Phillips, *Salem in the Eighteenth Century*, (Boston, MA: Houghton Mifflin Company, 1937), pp. 1-36.
7   Jackson T. Main, *Society and Economy in Colonial Connecticut*, (Princeton, NJ: Princeton University Press, 1985), pp. 3-28.
8   M.T. Scopeland, *The Saga of Cape Ann*, (Freeport, ME: The Bond Wheelright Company, 1960), p. 237.

1665, the New Haven Colony merged with the Connecticut Colony. Indian wars or threats of war plagued Connecticut through much of the later seventeenth century. In 1717, the Collegiate School moved to New Haven and later became Yale College. Puritanism still permeated Connecticut, but a rising secularism was noticeable among merchants and businessmen.

New Hampshire was a deliberately planned colony, not for religious reasons, but for fishing. In 1623 Dover was founded. The colony grew slowly as early settlers

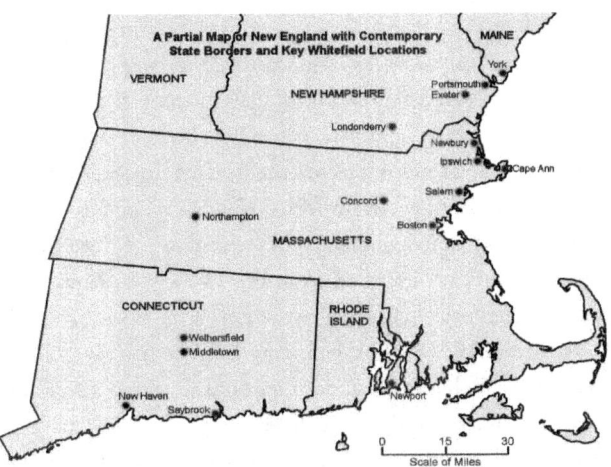

stayed by the coastline. The first generations of settlers were dependent on Massachusetts for civil support. By 1630 the first settlers of Portsmouth arrived, and in 1638 settlers went inland several miles to found Exeter. In 1691, New Hampshire permanently separated from Massachusetts. It was not until the later eighteenth century that New Hampshire experienced significant growth. This was not a Puritan community.[9]

Although the primary intent of the Puritans in New England was religious, secular interests were not excluded. Hopes of advantageous trade and prospects of opening new fishing territories were always present. Converting and civilizing the Indians was also the intent of some, as well as succeeding financially from the abundance of fir pelts, lumber, and raw materials in New England. Also, some were simply adventure seekers who sought to explore an unknown land. Yet, it remained true that the vast majority in this early period arrived in the New World for religious reasons.[10] One historian asserted that "The hope for profit had not been discarded . . . but it had been subordinated to another goal—the creation of a refuge for beleaguered Puritans."[11] Another well-known purpose for Puritan migration to the New World was to be free from the oppression of English civil magistrates. As C. P. Smith said: "There was, to be sure, a strong political element in the motive of the Puritans for leaving England, namely the necessity to escape from the repressive measures of (King) Charles and influential Bishop—now Archbishop—Laud."[12]

With all these varied purposes for settlement—religious, economic and political—the Puritan idea of creating a kingdom of God on earth was doomed from the beginning. Even within the first leaders of the settlements, tensions and anxieties existed. For example, Roger Conant and other refugees from the Massachusetts Cape Ann settlement, resided peacefully in Salem until the arrival of John Endicott in 1628. C. P. Smith is merciless in his criticisms of Endicott, referring to him in derogatory terms such as egocentric, possessing bigoted cruelty, a self-centered Arminian, one "in whom the light of religion had turned to the fire of self-assertiveness."[13] The behavior of Endicott in question centered on his displacement of Conant and the other original settlers of New England upon his arrival. As the holder of the official charter, Endicott possessed the homes of the prior English settlers of Salem, forcing them to move to an inferior location a short distance south. However, this relocation by Conant in the immediate vicinity could optimistically be understood as the two groups working together, not separating.[14] Furthermore, both Endicott and Conant remained members of the First Church of Salem all their lives without incident.

---

9   Jere R. Daniell, *Colonial New Hampshire: A History*, (Hanover, NH: University Press of New England, 1981), pp. 133-190.
10 D. Hamilton Hurd, *History of Essex County*, (Philadelphia, PA: F.W. Lewis & Company, 1888), vol. I, p. 18.
11 David Hawke, *The Colonial Experience*, p. 131.
12 C.P. Smith, *Yankees and God*, (New York: Hermitage House, 1954), p. 135.
13 Ibid., pp. 134-138, 173.
14 Clifford K. Shipton, *Roger Conant: A Founder of Massachusetts*, (Cambridge, MA: Harvard University Press, 1944), pp. 70-71.

Whatever the pressures and tensions experienced by the political leaders of the Massachusetts Colony, ecclesiastical controversies immediately began upon settlement. The First Church of Salem was founded in 1629. It was Congregational in polity, Puritan in theology. Its first elected leaders were Samuel Skelton as pastor and Francis Higginson as teacher, both of whom had prior ordination from the Church of England. Two prominent newcomers in the church in 1629 were Samuel and John Brown. They were quickly dissatisfied with the Puritan form of worship in the church and began holding their own services with a few like-minded malcontents. They chose to use both the *Prayer Book* and the liturgy of the English church. They were quickly expelled from the Colony by Endicott before their objections became too serious.[15] A second ecclesiastical controversy centered on Rev. Nathaniel Ward, pastor of the First Church of Ipswich. He arrived in 1634, but by February 1637 he had resigned his pulpit to explore and create new towns, such as Haverhill. What the abandonment of the sacred pulpit for such secular work meant to the Puritan settlers of Ipswich, we can only conjecture.

A third and the most well-known source of ecclesiastical conflict for the first generation of New England Puritans concerned Roger Williams and Anne Hutchinson. Williams was invited to Salem to assist the Rev. Samuel Skelton in 1631. The Massachusetts Court intervened and refused his admittance to the pulpit in Salem. In 1633, Williams did become Skelton's assistant, but remained unordained. Though Williams was repeatedly censured by the Governor and the Massachusetts Bay Company for offensive writings and publications, he was invited and ordained by the church at Salem to succeed Rev. Skelton upon his death. Roger Williams pastored in Salem from August 1634 until October 1635, when he was expelled from Massachusetts. While remaining essentially a Puritan in theology, he had enormous differences with the leadership of the Colony in relation to church/state affairs.[16] Although Williams remained a Puritan in theology, Anne Hutchinson certainly did not. She was summoned before the Colony's General Court in 1637 for encouraging erroneous opinions, antinomianism, conducting unauthorized meetings, and for claiming to have personal revelations from God. She was banished and excommunicated from the colony shortly thereafter.[17] Both Williams and Hutchinson settled in Rhode Island.

Rhode Island was first settled in 1635. Roger Williams brought a group in 1636 and founded Providence. In 1637, Ann Hutchinson arrived with settlers and founded Portsmouth. Newport was founded in 1639 and quickly became a significant maritime center. In 1647, Providence and Rhode Island merged to form one Colonial government, with an official charter granted in 1663. As with Connecticut, Indian wars plagued the colony in the later seventeenth century. The first Rhode Island census was taken in 1708, listing 7,181 residents. This was adamantly not a Puritan community. European rationalism was the talk of the town, not Puritan theology. While churches were founded and influenced their communities, this was not a Puritan theocracy. Free thinkers, secular merchants, whalers and other mariners, Quakers, and a significant Jewish population were all welcomed in Rhode Island.

With such a diverse foundation laid by the first generation of settlers in New England, it should be no surprise that the second generation had controversies unique to their day. John Endicott, as civil leader of the Massachusetts Colony, set himself against the Anabaptists as disturbers of the peace and disrupters of the affairs of the churches. Some Anabaptist were publicly punished, others were confined, while many more were placed under humiliating prohibitions. Quakers appeared in Salem by 1657. An entire shipload of Quakers arrived in Salem in 1660. Eighteen Quakers were publicly punished in Salem in 1661, while others were quietly oppressed and persecuted.[18]

---

15 Williston Walker, *History of Congregationalism in New England*, p. 107.
16 Perry Miller, *Roger Williams: His Contribution to the American Tradition*, (New York: Bobs-Merrill Company, 1953), pp. 22-48.
17 Marylin J. Westerkamp, "Ann Hutchinson, Sectarian Mysticism, and the Puritan Order," *Church History*, vol. 54, no. 4, (December 1990), pp. 482-496.
18 D. Hamilton Hurd, *History of Essex County, vol. I*, pp. 32-33.

The main threat to New England religious society did not come from such outside groups as the Anabaptists and Quakers, but from within their own local congregations. A Boston newspaper, which appeared during the Great Awakening in the 1740s, recalled the tensions which existed within the second generation Puritans:

> A little after 1660 there began to appear a decay: and this increased to 1670, when it grew very visible and threatening, and was generally complained of and bewailed bitterly by the pious among them: and yet much more to 1680, when but a few of the first generation remained.[19]

The religion of the New England Puritan founders was based on individual conversion. This consisted of a conscious and literal change of position from sinner to saint, from death to life, from being lost and bound for hell to being eternally secure in Christ. Salvation was a gift from God. Some in the second generation, however, downplayed the need for personal conversion. To many of the children of the founders, outward morality and acts of benevolence was true Christianity. Although the extent of this theological change differed from place to place, it occurred enough to warrant serious attention from the clergy. Individuals who believed they were saved began to see little need of faithful church attendance. Soon after, the outward works of moral behavior began to decline as well.

As early as 1642, ministers were rebuking outward piety and secret immorality among those who professed Christ. The Rev. Samuel Willard, of Boston's Third Church, exclaimed:

> How few thorough conversions to be observed, how scarce and seldom?—It hath been a frequent observation, that if one generation begins to decline, the next that follows usually grows worse, and so on, until God pours out His Spirit again among them.[20]

Increasingly, the children of the first generation of New Englanders failed to show the evidences of conversion which their parents experienced. Fewer and fewer of the second generation saw the need or had the desire for church membership. Both the civil and religious leaders of the Colonies could see their decreasing influence over the settlers, as well as increasing secularization. Meeting in the Synod of 1662, New England clergymen proposed the Half-Way Covenant. The idea of this decree was to maintain influence over the unregenerate by allowing them to attend the Puritan churches. Although they would be excluded from the Lord's Supper, they would still be under the influence of preachers and the converting influence of the word of God. In their attempt to maintain control, the Synod of 1662 decided that supervision of the unregenerate was more essential than the purity of each local church.[21]

The Half-Way Covenant helped to preserve a unified society for the second generation. Yet the vigorous Puritanism of many of the founders was declining fast. In 1679, a reforming synod of Massachusetts clergy met to note the causes of God's displeasure upon the colony, acknowledging that God had reason to be disappointed with their society. Civil leaders, clergymen, and the community were often called upon to seek God's face in repentance, praying for a fresh outpouring of the Spirit. The synod observed with distress that "ungodliness, worldliness, profanity, Sabbath-breaking, intemperance, strife among church members and laxity in family discipline were mounting."[22]

---

19 Thomas Prince, editor. *The Christian History*, (Boston, MA: 1743), p. 94.
20 H.F. Uhden, *The New England Theocracy: A History of Congregationalists in New England*, (Boston, MA: Gould and Lincoln Publishers, 1859), p. 227.
21 Robert G. Pope, *The Half-Way Covenant: Church Membership in Puritan New England*, (Eugene, OR: Wipf and Stock Publishers, 1969).
22 E. Oberholzer, *Delinquent Saints: Disciplinary Action in the Early Congregational Churches of Massachusetts*, (New York: Columbia University Press, 1966), p. 235.

As the second generation began to pass away and the clergy's concern for true piety remained, the Salem witch hysteria of 1692 spread throughout much of New England. From a combination of declining morality, frustration by civil leaders, and lack of options from the clergy, the witch trials became a vain attempt to stop the growth of apathy among the people and to reinforce the respect still demanded by the leaders of the Colony. Communities throughout New England attempted to explain the failure of the Puritan ideal as the work of the Devil.[23] The subsequent retractions by those officials who condemned the victims only added further spiritual uncertainty to a declining Puritanism. Connecticut also had a witch hysteria that predated the turmoil in Salem, lasting from 1647 to 1697.[24]

The ecclesiastical climate which surrounded the third generation of colonists in New England was permeated with increasing apathy, controversy, and general indifference. There were essentially four factors involved which caused the decline of the Puritan ideal. First, there was economic security, as New England was developing into a major trade area with the Old World. Next, the immigration of non-Puritans, especially wealthy merchants who frequently possessed low moral behavior, changed the culture. Third, the rise of "experimental science," or critical thinking from the European Enlightenment was transplanted from Europe and directly challenged New England Puritanism. Finally, the frequency of local calamities, and hostilities with Indians, made the Puritans realize that their attempt to create a kingdom of God on earth had failed. For example, in 1660 there was an epidemical cold, 1667 saw a smallpox epidemic, and in 1672 was the first of several great fires in Boston. Between 1675-1676, the scourge of King Philip's Indian War resulted in numerous rural communities in northern and central New England being destroyed. Also, in 1684 the charter of Massachusetts was revoked, while 1688 saw both a measles epidemic and the building of a dreaded Anglican church in Boston, King's Chapel, called by the Puritans the Temple of Antichrist. Finally, in 1689 war broke out with France, creating tension for northern New Englanders near French territory, while in 1692 a new Massachusetts charter was granted which required toleration of Quakers, Baptists, Anglicans, Anabaptists, and others.[25]

By the end of the second and the beginning of the third generation of New Englanders, many were living comfortably in the New World. This recent photograph is of a restored 1675 home in Sandwich, Massachusetts. Families that lived in homes like this lived as well as they did in England.
Source: https://www.thoughtco.com/colonial-houses-in-new-england-178009

---

23   Enders A. Robinson, *Andover Phase of the Salem Witch Trials*, (Goose Pond Press, 2020), pp. 106-170.
24   There are numerous books on the New England witch trials. I recommend Frances Hill, *A Delusion of Satan: The Full Story of the Salem Witch Trials*, (Cambridge, MA: DaCapo Press, 2002). A more recent text is by Emerson W. Baker, *A Storm of Witchcraft: The Salem Witch Trials and the American Experience*, (New York: Oxford University Press, 2014). The Connecticut witch trials are not as well-known as the trials in Salem. See John M. Taylor, *The Witchcraft Delusion in Colonial Connecticut, 1647-1697*, (1908: reprinted by The Grafton Press, 1974). Cynthia W. Boynton, *Connecticut Witch Trials: The First Panic in the New World*, (Charleston, SC: The History Press, 2014).
25   C.P. Smith, *Yankees and God*, pp. 187-192. "Religion in Colonial America: Trends, Regulations, and Beliefs," Facing History and Ourselves, https://www.facinghistory.org/nobigotry/religion-colonial-america-trends-regulations-and-beliefs. John Brown, *The English Puritans: The Rise, Growth, and Decline of the Puritan Movement*, (Warrendale, PA: Ichthus Publications, 2015), pp. 131-155.

At first, however, the difference between the present clergy and their predecessors manifested itself, for the most part, only in formality and coldness in the duties of their office. But with the lively intercourse constantly maintained with England, influences from the latter soon made themselves apparent, and Arminianism, which, in the preceding century had spread from the high church into the ranks of the Dissenters, now visited North America also. Here, it was precisely from the standpoint of indifference, that it made its first appearance. It manifested itself particularly in the view now current, that observance of outward religious ordinances joined with a moral and sober life is all that is needed for Christians. These opinions, in the condition of the church which has been described, found quick and easy entrance: and the spread of unbelief was, in general, much earlier than its decided manifestation.[26]

Perhaps the person who best illustrates the tensions which permeated the third generation of New Englanders is the Rev. Cotton Mather. Mather saw Massachusetts change during his lifetime, from being primarily Puritan to being interdenominational and increasingly secular. As pastor of the North Church in Boston from 1683 to his death in 1727, he saw the Puritanism of his father and grandfather threatened by the new ideas coming out of Europe. By the late 1600s, Mather was publishing numerous works on theology, religion, and history. As the most influential man in Massachusetts during his lifetime, he publicly lamented the decline of personal religion in New England. He complained shortly before the turn of the century that swearing, intemperance, the selling of liquor to Indians, vanity, sorcery, contention, sexual impurity and other such sins were common.[27] Cotton Mather sought to promote a balanced orthodoxy, while resisting the drift toward liberal and rational thought. While being thoroughly Calvinistic and opposed to the secular enlightenment in Europe, he did not turn away from the expanded intellectual opportunities the Enlightenment brought. He was a wide-ranging scholar who used the new ideas and information to expand his biblical faith.[28]

Not all New England ministers had Mather's ability to choose and select only the appropriate elements of the newly developed thinking. The father of Cotton Mather, the Rev. Increase Mather, in 1700 published a work entitled *Vindication of the Order of the Gospel in New England*. In this he stated:

> The congregational church discipline is not suited for a worldly interest, or a formal generation of professors. It will stand or fall, as godliness, in the power of it, does prevail or otherwise. That there is a great decay in the power of religion throughout all New England is lamentably true; if that revive, there will be no fear of departing from the holy discipline of the churches of Christ. If the begun apostasy should proceed as fast the next thirty years, as it has done these last, surely it will come to that in New England . . . the most conscientious people therein will think themselves concerned to gather churches out of the churches.[29]

By 1715, specifically in Connecticut, numerous Half-Way Covenant members were attached to virtually every Puritan church, and few congregations could claim to be the sacred and separated institutions described in the Scriptures.[30] A dismaying number of baptized persons, failing to receive saving grace in their lives, remained half in and half out of the churches.[31] Although some pockets of Puritan orthodoxy remained in various local assemblies, there was a general reaction in the early eighteenth century against Puritanism's

---

26 H.F. Uhden, *The New England Theocracy*, pp. 236-237.
27 Cotton Mather, *Diary of Cotton Mather*, (1724: reprinted New York: Fredrick Ungar Publishing Company, 1911), pp. 214-215.
28 Robert Middlekauff, *The Mathers*, (New York: Oxford University Press, 1971), pp. 262-319.
29 H.F. Uhden, *The New England Theocracy*, p. 226. For a thorough study, see Harry S. Stout, *The New England Soul: Preaching and Religious Culture in Colonial New England*, (New York: Oxford University Press, 2012).
30 Richard L. Bushman, *From Puritan to Yankee: Character and the Social Order in Connecticut, 1690-1765*, (Cambridge, MA: Harvard University Press, 1967), p. 153.
31 Ibid., p. 148.

rigid cultural order. The anxiety of soul of these Colonists who were changing, as Bushman says, from "Puritan to Yankee," created a religious order labeled superficial, or perhaps necessary when convenient. Prayer, Bible study and attendance in church meetings might result from worldly motives, to avoid disgrace, or to pacify a guilty conscience.[32]

In 1725, Cotton Mather of Boston presented a petition to the Legislature in the name of the Assembled General Convention of Ministers. In this petition, the clergy desired that a synod might be called for the remedy of the existing unhappy condition of the churches, in view of the great and visible decline of piety in the country. During the extended proceedings on the matter, Anglican clergymen in Boston attempted to hinder the work of the synod. They reported the affair to London, with the response that the calling of synods pertains to the King alone and the affair must end. The matter was therefore terminated.[33]

Because the Puritans were only human, they could not help but bring to the New World an element of sin, which they had sought to leave behind, and thus their potential Utopia shared the common fate of all such attempts to establish a perfect society with imperfect men.[34] By the fourth generation, a century after settling, the religion of the American settlers had, in most cases, reverted to many practices the Puritans had sought to escape. In 1724, years before the traditional 1738 date assigned to the Great Awakening and the soon arrival of George Whitefield, the Rev. Solomon Stoddard, grandfather of Jonathan Edwards, blamed the ministers for the spiritual lassitude of the people. Stoddard taught:

> There was a great want of good preaching; whence it came to pass, that among professors a spirit of piety runs exceedingly low . . . Every learned and moral man is not a sincere convert, and so not able to speak exactly and experimentally to such things as souls want to be instructed in.[35]

The cry by some New England preachers, for a return to the religion of the founding fathers, was repeatedly expressed in some pulpits and by many common people. Yet society was changing, and the majority of colonists did not know the personal conversion that their grandparents and great-grandparents knew. In time, the New Englanders realized that they were no longer the righteous remnant running from an apostate church; they were an establishment. "This drift from spiritual to material interests is not difficult to understand," according to Lang and Noll. "New Englanders were farmers and made an adequate living. Industries: lumbering, fishing, ship-building and others—did well, and artisans earned a good living."[36] This materialism drove many from the church.

Philip Greven's study of Andover, Massachusetts verifies these statements well. Puritan Andover had relatively quickly become a prosperous rural community, originally settled in 1635. After four generations, the town had come to resemble many old England communities, with extended family networks, stability, and a familiar social world.[37] Religious appearances were expected, but the vitality and stiff social structure of Puritanism had faded away. Around 1720, noticeable changes occurred in the attitudes and patterns of behavior of many of the town's inhabitants. Without in any way ceasing to be deeply religious, people living in towns like Andover found that their religious experiences, as fourth generation Colonists, had changed from those of their Puritan forefathers.[38]

---

32 Ibid., p. 193. H.F. Uhden, *The New England Theocracy*, p.236.
33 E. Oberholzer, *Delinquent Saints*, p. 250
34 Richard L. Bushman, *From Puritan to Yankee*, p. 178.
35 Stephen J. Lang and Mark A. Noll, "Colonial New England: An Old Order, a New Awakening," *Christian History*, vol.11, no. 4 (1985), p. 9.
36 Ibid.
37 Philip J. Greven, *Four Generations: Population, land and Family in Colonial Andover, Massachusetts*, (Ithaca, NY: Cornell University Press, 1970), p. 141.
38 Ibid., pp. 175, 278. Joseph Tracy, *The Great Awakening: A History of the Revival of Religion in the Time of Edwards and Whitefield*, (Carlisle, PA: Banner of Truth Trust, 1989), pp. 1-34. Richard L. Bushman, *From Puritan to Yankee*, pp. 135-146.

The Rev. Jonathan Webb, pastor of the new North Church in Boston, addressed his concerns about the so-called "new thinking" in a sermon preached before the House of Representatives in 1730. The title of his message was, "The Great Concern for New England." His text was I Kings 8:57; "The Lord our God be with us, as he was with our fathers, let him never leave us nor forsake us."[39] In this discourse, Webb addressed the need for personal dedication, separation from evil, and the maintenance of good works. But the flow of thought towards materialism and liberalism had by now become a flood.

There were occasional revivals of religious interest and devotion during this fourth generation. Other churches were focused on what seems like petty issues. For example, the Second Parish in Beverly, Massachusetts, experienced congregational disruption and tension in 1730 on whether or not songs should be "lined out," or sung according to written notes.[40] Other assemblies were experiencing serious seasons of renewed devotion to the faith of the Puritan founding fathers. For example, Northampton, Massachusetts had religious stirrings under Rev. Solomon Stoddard in 1679, 1683, 1696, 1712, and 1718. There was a renewal of piety in Hartford, Connecticut in 1696, and at Taunton, Massachusetts in 1705. A brief widespread stirring followed the great earthquake of 1727. Some of these movements were of lasting consequence.[41]

In December 1734, revival broke out in Jonathan Edward's church in Northampton, Massachusetts as he was preaching a series of sermons on justification by faith alone. In preaching this series of messages, Edwards was also addressing the notion popular in the fourth generation, that a person could by "means" prepare himself for conversion. By "means"—good works, church attendance, etc.,—a man could supposedly place himself in a more worthy position to receive saving grace from God. Edwards believed that the converted man will show good works as evidence of his salvation, not that good works and outward piety lead a person to conversion. Soon the whole community came under spiritual concern.

By May 1735, as the movement began to decline, more than 300 people apparently experienced rebirth around Northampton. The impulse of this local revival spread up and down the Connecticut River Valley, affecting thousands. The Rev. Benjamin Coleman of Boston, an avid supporter of revival, helped spread news of the awakening through Boston and New England. The revival quickly spread through Massachusetts, Connecticut, New Hampshire, and parts of Rhode Island. Edwards was encouraged by Christians on both sides of the Atlantic to record the event. He responded by writing, *A Faithful Narrative of the Surprising Work of God in the Conversion of Many Hundred Souls in Northampton and Neighboring Towns and Villages, in a letter to the Rev. Benjamin Coleman of Boston*. This work was printed and read throughout much of the English-speaking world in 1737 and 1738. While in England, George Whitefield read of the revival in Colonial New England and longed for the time he could meet Jonathan Edwards face-to-face.

Among the often ritualistic, stale, and sedate churches of New England in the early-to-mid 1700s, these revivals jarred many of the clergy out of their dreary homiletical rut. Such revival movements were "a welcome relief to people accustomed to sermons read from closely written manuscripts held in the hand of the preacher, and upon themes as bland as the droning voice in which they were uttered."[42] Others opposed the revival as a disturbance of the standing order. However, these sporadic revivals could not have indicated the extent of awakening and renewal in the fourth generation that occurred in New England under the ministry of George Whitefield. Various revivals had predated Whitefield's arrival in 1740. In some instances, New England clergymen had pleaded for renewal from their pulpits and had success. But there was nobody

---

39   John Webb, *The Great Concern for New England*, (Boston: 1730). William B. Sprague, *Annals of the American Pulpit: Congregational*, (New York: Robert Carter & Brothers, 1859), vol. I, p. 267.
40   D. Hamilton Hurd, *History of Essex County, vol. I*, p. 696.
41   Williston Walker, *History of Congregationalism in New England*, pp. 251-252. Edwin S. Gaustad, *The Great Awakening in New England*, (Gloucester, MA: Peter Smith Printer, 1965), pp. 16-41.
42   William Warren Sweet, *Religion in Colonial America*, (New York: Charles Scribner's Sons, 1942), p. 286.

who could have predicted the tidal wave of religious upheaval which engulfed New England beginning with Whitefield's arrival in Rhode Island in September 1740.

The Hazadiah Smith house in Beverly, Massachusetts was built in the mid-to-late 1600s, and is a good example of the comfortable lifestyle many colonists enjoyed.

Source: First Period Houses of Essex County.

CHAPTER 3

WHITEFIELD'S TOUR IN RHODE ISLAND

SEPTEMBER 14-17, 1740

WHITEFIELD FIRST ARRIVED IN NEW England on September 14, 1740, at Newport, Rhode Island. His few weeks at sea, travelling from Charleston, South Carolina, were on board a coastal trading sloop, a vessel that routinely made stops in major ports. Whitefield wrote in his *Journal*:

> Sunday, September 14. Was sick part of the voyage, but, afterwards the sea air, under God, much improved my health. Arrive at Newport just after the beginning of the evening service. We came purposely thither first with our sloop. Almost all the morning the wind was contrary. With a strong assurance that we should be heard, we prayed that the Lord would turn the wind, that we might give Him thanks in the great congregation; and, also, that he would send such to us, as He would have us to converse with, and who might shew us a lodging. Though the wind was rough when we began; yet, when we had done praying, and come up out of the cabin, it was quite fair. With a gentle breeze, we sailed pleasantly into the harbor; got to public worship before they had finished the Psalms, and sat, as I thought, undiscovered. After service was over, a gentleman asked me whether my name was Whitefield? I told him yes; he then desire me to go to his house, and he would take care of providing lodgings for me and my friends. I went silently admiring God's goodness in answering my prayer so minutely.[1]

Newport, Rhode Island was settled in 1639 by Puritans who were not comfortable with the civil and ecclesiastical situation in the Massachusetts Bay Colony. From its origins, this seaport community was far more eclectic than other Puritan settlements in New England. About 1643, the First Society of Friends (Quakers) organized in Newport. Both Jews and Baptists were early arrivals in this growing and diverse community. By the early 1700s, Newport had a Friends meeting house, a Baptist Church building, a Jewish synagogue, and a Congregational meeting house. The Episcopalians gathered about 1686, and in 1726 they constructed Trinity Church, which still stands today. Newport was a maritime center connected by ships to the West Indies, Africa, other American colonies, and Europe. The city thrived from commercial activities. Whaling developed into a major industry. A person who walked the streets of Newport, when Whitefield arrived in 1740, would immediately notice people dressed in the simple clothing of Quakers, or in elegant European fashions, or in worn, working class clothing associated with the trades.[2] This was clearly a diverse and prosperous English port.

---

1 George Whitefield, *George Whitefield's Journals*, (1747; reprinted, Carlisle, PA: Banner of Truth Trust, 1985), pp. 451-452.
2 For an interesting account of the rise of Newport, see Deborah Davis, *Gilded: How Newport became America's Richest Seaport*, (Hoboken, NJ: John Wiley & Sons, Publishers, 2009). For a broader view, see Richard V. Simpson, *Historic Tales of Colonial Rhode Island*, (Charleston, SC: The History Press, 2012).

Upon arriving in Newport on a Sunday evening, Whitefield wrote about going to "public worship before they had finished the Psalms." This refers to an Episcopal Church service, based on the Church of England liturgy, at Trinity Church. The walk to the church building was a few hundred feet from the harbor. No doubt, after spending weeks cramped on a sloop on the Atlantic Ocean, Whitefield was stunned by the spacious and elegant beauty of Trinity Church. This thriving congregation was composed of merchants, bankers, sea captains, tradesmen, and government officials. They sat in boxed pews of various shapes and sizes which reflected the status of the families that purchased the pews. The large sanctuary was almost surrounded with balconies. The acoustics of the building were excellent. The minister of Trinity Church was Rev. James Honeyman, who arrived in Newport in 1704 and served this church until his death in 1750. After this Sunday evening Episcopal Church service in Newport, Whitefield wrote:

> Several gentlemen of the town soon came to pay their respects to me, amongst whom was Mr. Clap, an aged dissenting minister, and the most venerable man I ever saw in my life. He looked like a good old Puritan, and gave me an idea of what stamp those men were, who first settled New England. His countenance was very heavenly, and he prayer most affectionately for a blessing upon my coming to Rhode Island.[3]

Rev. Nathaniel Clapp was the minister of the First Church Congregational. He arrived in Newport in 1696 and stayed until his death in 1745. The church officially organized in 1720. Throughout his many years of ministry, Clapp was known as a serious and severe minister. His church was embroiled in controversy in the 1720s, as Clapp, uneasy about the low spiritual state of his congregation, refused to serve communion. Many parishioners did not like this church discipline, and departed the First Church to form the Second Congregational Church in Newport, in 1728, under Rev. John Adams. Nathaniel Clapp held "rigid views of duty" expected of all Christians, and was "spoken of by his contemporaries as an eminently holy man."[4] When the twenty-six-year-old Whitefield met Clapp in 1740, Clapp was still active in ministry at about seventy-three years old, thus explaining why Whitefield called him, "an aged dissenting minister."

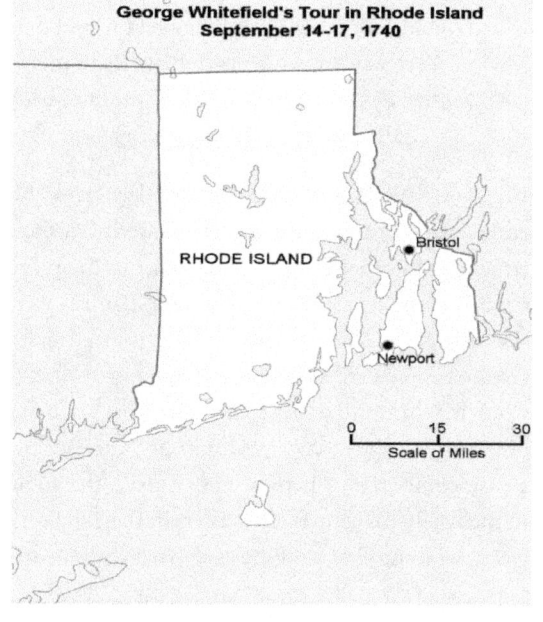

After settling in for a day, Whitefield made a social call to the Episcopal Church minister, Rev. James Honeyman. As a Church of England (Episcopal) priest, Whitefield thought it right and proper that he be allowed to preach in the Episcopal Church in Newport. Whitefield noted the reluctance of Honeyman to allow him access to the Episcopal pulpit in Newport.

> In the evening, with him [Rev. Nathaniel Clapp] and some more friends, I waited on Mr. H_n, the minister of the Church of England, and desired the use of his pulpit. At first he

---

3 George Whitefield, *Journals*, p. 452.
4 *American Quarterly Register*, vol. XII, no. 3 (February 1840), p. 267.

seemed a little unwilling, and wished to know "what extraordinary call I had to preach on week-days," which he said, "was disorderly?" I answered, "St. Paul exhorted Timothy to be instant in season and out of season; that, if the Orders of the Church were rightly complied with, our ministers should read public prayers twice every day, and then it would not be disorderly at such times, to give them a sermon." As to an extraordinary call, I claimed none otherwise than the Apostle's injunction, "as we have opportunity let us do good unto all men." He still held out, and did not give any positive answer; but, at last, after he had withdrawn and consulted with the gentlemen, he said, "If my preaching would promote the glory of God, and good of souls, I was welcomed to his church, as often as I would, during my stay in town." We then agreed to make use of it at ten in the morning, and three in the afternoon . . . Monday, September 15 . . . At ten in the morning, and three in the afternoon, according to appointment, I read prayers and preached in the [Episcopal] church. It is very commodious, and will contain three thousand people. It was more than filled in the afternoon, persons of all denominations attending. God assisted me much. I observed numbers affected, and had great reason to believe the Word of God had been sharper than a two-edged sword in some of the hearer's souls.[5]

George Whitefield would return to Newport many times over the next three decades, but this was the one and only time he was allowed to preach in Trinity Church. Whitefield's evangelical Calvinism did not sit well with the congregation, nor with their minister, James Honeyman. The theology of the Westminster Confession, eagerly embraced by Whitefield, was not taught, or welcomed at Trinity Church. As a Church of England congregation, Trinity Church appealed to the wealthy, aristocratic citizens of Newport. Parishioners took comfort in the church rituals and liturgy, which provided an outward religious experience. Whitefield's preaching of sin, repentance, and the desperate need of all men for the new birth was offensive to Honeyman and his congregation.

In Newport, the Congregationalist Rev. Nathaniel Clapp eventually served for fifty years at the First Church Congregational. Clapp was a serious and studious minister who also at times had a playful, approachable disposition. Whitefield was obviously impressed by the wisdom and experienced of the aged Nathaniel Clapp. After sharing a meal with him, Whitefield wrote:

Monday, September 15. Breakfasted this morning with old Mr. Clapp, and

An interior view of Trinity Church (Episcopal) in Newport, Rhode Island. Constructed in 1726, the pulpit and the sounding board above the pulpit were the same ones used by George Whitefield when he preached here in September 1740. Source: www.panoramio.com.

---

5 George Whitefield, *Journals*, pp. 452-453.

was much edified with his conversation. I could not but think, whilst at his table, that I was sitting with one of the patriarchs. He is full of days; a bachelor, and has been minister of a congregation in Rhode Island upwards of forty years. People of all denominations respect him. He abounds in good works; gives all away, and is wonderfully tender of little children; many of different persuasions come to be instructed by him.[6]

After preaching in the morning and the afternoon at Trinity Episcopal Church, Whitefield preached an evening sermon for Nathaniel Clapp at the First Congregational Church in Newport. He wrote in his *Journals*,

In the evening, I went to the venerable Mr. Clapp's, and exhorted and prayed with a great multitude, who, not only crowded into the house, but thronged every way about it. The dear old man rejoiced to see the things which he saw; and after my exhortation was over, dismissed me with his blessing. Lord Jesus, do Thou say Amen to it. Amen and Amen.[7]

Mrs. Sarah Osborn (1714-1796) heard Whitefield preach at the First Congregational Church in Newport in 1740. Her notes, letters, and journals consist of thousands of pages. Her handwriting is clear but has many punctuation and spelling errors. Sarah was born in London and immigrated to Newport with her parents. Her father was a leatherworker, a tanner. She married at age seventeen to a sailor and had a son, but her husband died two years later. She remarried to a widower named Henry Osborn, who had three children and who was old enough to be her father. Sarah was never wealthy. He husband was not healthy, so she taught school to earn an income. Sarah was raised in Puritanism and had deep spiritual convictions. She struggled with what she considered her own wickedness and unworthiness. In the late 1730s, as awakenings stirred various parts of New England, she was very supportive. When Whitefield came to Newport, Rhode Island in September 1740, she fully endorsed his preaching. The exact moment of Sarah's conversion is unclear, but she gave great praise to the New Light preaching of George Whitefield, Gilbert Tennent, and Ebenezer Wheelock. By 1742 she was an outspoken, born-again evangelical member of the First Church in Newport.[8] "She joined the throngs of people

Trinity Episcopal Church in Newport was built in 1726 and is a National Historic Landmark. George Whitefield preached here in 1740. Photograph by Ken Lawson.

---

6 George Whitefield, *Journals*, pp. 453.
7 Ibid., p. 454.
8 Catherine A. Brekus, Sarah Osborn's World: *The Rise of Evangelical Christianity in Early America,* (New Haven, CT: Yale University Press, 2013), p. 128.

who went to hear Whitefield preach."⁹ Sarah Osborn wrote, "God in mercy sent his dear servant Whitefield here which something stirred me up."¹⁰

Whitefield's schedule in Newport was relentless. Not only was he preaching at least once a day in church buildings; he also preached and prayed at spontaneous outdoor gatherings. This began to affect his health. He recorded,

Tuesday, September 16. Although a little low in the morning, I was enabled to read prayers and preach [in Trinity Episcopal Church, Newport] to still greater auditories than yesterday. It being assembly time, the gentlemen adjourned in order to attend the service, and several invitations were given to me to come to other adjacent places. The people were exceedingly attentive; tears trickled down their cheeks; and they so far prevailed with me by their importunity, that I promised, God willing, to call upon them in my return from Boston . . . In the evening I went, privately as I thought, to a friend's house; but the people were so eager to hear the Word, that in a short time, I believe, more than a thousand were before the door, besides those that were within, and filled every room in the house. I stood therefore upon the threshold, and spake for near an hour on these words, "Blessed are they that hunger and thirst after righteousness, for they shall be filled." It was a very solemn meeting. Glory be to God's great Name! Before I retired to bed, I went to take leave of Mr. H., [Rev. James Honeyman] and had some talk with him about the new birth. He was very civil, and would have liked for me to stay with him longer; but, having to go on a journey on the morrow, I took my leave, after we had conversed near half an hour. At my return to my lodgings, good old Mr. Clapp went with me into a private room, gave me something for my orphans, and spoke many kind things to me.¹¹

A sketch of Rev. Nathaniel Clapp, minister 1696 to 1745 of the First Congregational Church, Newport, Rhode Island. Public domain image.

Newport was and is a hilly community with narrow streets and winding roads. A few hundred feet up a small hill from the former First Congregational Church building is Touro Park. As overflow crowds packed the church to hear Whitefield, Rev. Nathaniel Clapp moved the meeting outside, up the hill to the park. Here Whitefield preached to a large crowd. His pulpit was a table donated from a local home. In 1891, this table was still used for teaching at the United Church in Newport.¹²

Whitefield had made previous plans with several ministers to preach in Boston. As he departed Newport, he was contemplative about the religious life of this city. He noted that they were "plain people in general,"

---

9   Catherine A. Brekus, Sarah Osborn's World: *The Rise of Evangelical Christianity in Early America,* (New Haven, CT: Yale University Press, 2013), p. 120.
10   Ibid.
11   George Whitefield, *Journals,* pp. 454-455.
12   Charles E. Hammett, *A Sketch of the History of the Congregational Churches of Newport, Rhode Island, from the Records and Other Sources,* (Newport Historical Society, 1891), 86.

A contemporary image of Touro Park, Newport. In September 1740, Whitefield held an outside preaching event at this location. Photograph by Ken Lawson.

no doubt from the Quaker influence. He wrote disapprovingly about those who came to church meetings "covered all over with the pride of life," a despairing reference to expensive, outward attire. Whitefield was dismayed by the fact that there were four Baptist Churches in Newport, and two Congregational meeting houses, evidence that the people could not get along in ecclesiastical issues. He certainly made no friends with the Episcopalians in Newport when he wrote that the externals of the church were in good order, "but many of the chief members were bigots."[13]

In 1740, Newport did not have a newspaper. But a summary of Whitefield's ministries in Newport was written and shared with other colonial newspapers. For example, the following account appeared in a Philadelphia newspaper:

> Newport, Rhode-Island, Sept 19. Last Lord's Day arrived here the Rev. Mr. George Whitefield, from South-Carolina, who preached two excellent sermons on Monday in the Church of England, in the forenoon from those Words in Rom. 14:17. And in the Afternoon from John 17:3. On Tuesday he preach'd twice in the Forenoon from the 2 Cor 5:17, in the Afternoon from Luke 18:14. And in the Evening of both the Days, he entertain'd a vast Number of People of several Denominations with Exhortations in private. Great Numbers of people flock'd from all Quarters both in Town and Country to hear his Sermons and Exhortations, and many of them could not refrain shedding Tears. He set out from hence for Boston on Wednesday Morning.[14]

From Newport, Whitefield's next stop, on his way to Boston, was in Bristol, Rhode Island. The town of Bristol is a peninsula surrounded on three sides by water. Located halfway between Newport and Providence, Bristol was a shipbuilding and light manufacturing center. Taverns along the well-travelled road brought money and gossip into town. Some residents became very wealthy through commerce, their large estates still standing in Bristol today. Whitefield wrote of his time in Bristol as follows:

---

13 George Whitefield, *Journals*, p. 455.
14 *The Pennsylvania Gazette*, October 2, 1740, p. 3.

> Wednesday, September 17. Left Newport in Rhode Island about nine in the morning, and reached Bristol, a town twelve miles distant, about noon. Several friends from Rhode Island accompanied me, and before we came to the town, a Dissenting minister (as I afterwards found) met me, and in the name of the Court, which was then sitting at Bristol, invited me and my friends to dine with them, and also desired me to give them a sermon. I complied. The gentlemen received us with much civility; and, after dinner, I preached in the meeting-house to more people than might have been expected on such sudden notice. My heart was much shut up in the exercise. However, the gentlemen seemed very thankful. I took my leave about four in the afternoon, and lay at an inn about ten miles further on the road. Thanks be to God for His unspeakable mercies.[15]

One account of Whitefield's preaching in Bristol stated, "Mr. Whitefield had preached in Bristol. The great preacher was detained by the rain, and that on this account he desired the shelter of a roof."[16]

Quoted above, Whitefield wrote that he was met by a "Dissenting minister," and that he preached in "the meeting-house." These remarks refer to Rev. John Burt, who served as the pastor of the First Church Congregational in Bristol. In 1740, Burt was a candidate for the ministry at Bristol. He was a Harvard graduate in 1736, and was ordained at the Congregational Church in Bristol in 1741.[17] Of John Burt's long ministry in Bristol, it was stated:

> His ministry was eminently successful. A faithful, bold, and earnest preacher, and judicious counselor and friend, he won the respect of all classes, and enjoyed, in a marked degree, the confidence and affection of his people. This period was emphatically one of peace and prosperity.[18]

An apparent discrepancy appears between Whitefield's *Journal* account in Bristol and the official history of the town. The apparent contradiction is resolved in that Whitefield was initially refused use of the Congregational meeting house to preach in the afternoon but was allowed to do so in the evening. In the afternoon he preached at the courthouse. Whitefield recorded that he dined with the dissenting minister, and was allowed to preach an afternoon sermon in the dissenting or Congregational meeting house.[19] Yet the official Bristol town history recorded, "On his arrival in Bristol, Mr. Whitefield was refused permission to preach in the meeting-house or the church, but through the exertions of Lydia, the wife of Hopestill Potter, the use of the court house was allowed him."[20] This reference identifies correctly that, in 1740, there were two church buildings in Bristol, the "meeting-house," and "the church." The meeting house was Congregational, and "the church" referred to Saint Michael's Episcopal Church in Bristol.

As previously stated, the Congregational minister in Bristol was Rev. John Burt. The Episcopalian minister in Bristol in 1740, was Rev. John Usher. Usher served the Episcopal Church in Bristol for fifty-two years, from 1723 to his death in 1775. A Harvard graduate in 1719, he served as a missionary pastor in Bristol for the Church of England. Usher was known as a stickler for formality and order. One report commented, "Mr. Usher's ministry seems to have been characterized by great diligence and fidelity, rather than by any very striking demonstrations or results."[21] Whitefield was not allowed to preach for Burt, even though they shared Church of England ordination.

---

15 Ibid., p. 456.
16 Wilfred H. Munro, *The Story of Mount Hope Lands: The History of Bristol, Rhode Island*, (Providence, RI: Reid Publishers, 1880), p. 263.
17 *Manual of the First Church in Bristol, Rhode Island, 1687-1872*, (Providence, RI: 1873), pp. 120-124.
18 James P. Lane, *Historical Sketches of the First Congregational Church, Bristol, Rhode Island, 1689-1872*, (Providence, RI: Providence Pres Company, 1872), p. 77.
19 George Whitefield, *Journals*, pp. 456.
20 Wilfred H. Munro, *The Story of Mount Hope Lands*, pp. 262-263.
21 William B. Sprague, *Annals of the American Episcopal Pulpit*, (New York: Robert Carter & Brothers Publishers, 1859), p. 48.

The exact details of Whitefield's brief visit to Bristol, Rhode Island, on September 17, 1740, may never be known. It is clear that Rhode Island was not as religiously divided as were its neighboring colonies. Rhode Island did not have a legally established Congregational church, as did Connecticut and Massachusetts. Therefore, there was more allowance for various religious views, or to have no religious preferences at all. Speaking about Whitefield, "His preaching in Newport and Bristol did not seem to have the same emotional impact as it was to have in Boston."[22]

Whitefield departed Bristol on September 17. He travelled a few hours that afternoon and rested. The next morning he woke up, long before sunrise, and departed for Boston, arriving at his destination after dark, on September 18, 1740.

A sketch of George Whitefield preaching outdoors.
Source: https://beliefitornot.wordpress.com/2018/04/29/ep-1-the-great-awakening.

---

22   William McLoughlin, *Rhode Island: A History*, (New York: W.W. Norton & Company, 1986), pp. 76-77.

CHAPTER 4

WHITEFIELD'S FIRST VISIT TO BOSTON

SEPTEMBER 1740

THERE CAN BE LITTLE DOUBT that George Whitefield was an English Puritan at heart. The individual piety, emphasis on repentance, conversion, and the practice of good works preached by New England's founding Puritan fathers were in perfect harmony with Whitefield's life and message. Furthermore, Whitefield openly praised the founding fathers of New England for their honest devotion to God. He said that the Puritans of the previous century were "burning and shining lights."[1] He further spoke of the Puritans,

> They wrote and preached as men having authority. Though dead, by their writings, they yet speak: a peculiar unction attends to them this very hour; and for these thirty years past I have remembered that the more, true and vital religion hath revived either at home or abroad, the more of the good old Puritanical writings, or the authors of a like stamp who lived and died in communion with the Church of England, have been called for.[2]

One of Whitefield's supporters in his 1740 visit to New England stated that Whitefield was "full of zeal to promote the Kingdom and interests of our Lord Jesus, and in the conversion of souls. His preaching seems to be much like that of the old English Puritans."[3] It should be no surprise that Whitefield identified himself with Puritanism. One author related that Whitefield's theology was developed as he read "the Scriptures, the Reformers and the Puritans," and that his concept of revival preaching was intended to bring people back to Puritanism.[4]

Whitefield's message was in harmony with those Puritans who settled in Boston a century before his arrival. If his New England preaching was opposed by his contemporaries, it was because they had changed their theology, values, and priorities, not because he preached a gospel they knew nothing about. In a book on Newburyport, Massachusetts, Labaree mentioned the decline of traditional values held by the founding Puritan fathers. He stated that deviations from traditional Puritanism was an occurrence before the revival controversies, and that religious turmoil was the norm before Whitefield made this first of several visits.[5] Yet,

---

1   George Whitefield, *Works of George Whitefield*, (1771: reprinted by Quinta Press, Shropshire, England, 2000), vol. iv, p. 306
2   Ibid.
3   Joseph Stafford, "A Lover of Truth," (Boston, MA: 1740). Reprinted in *The New England Historical and Genealogical Register*, (Boston, MA: Samuel G. Drake, 1871), vol. xv, p. 58.
4   Iain Murray, "Prefatory Note," *George Whitefield's Journals*, (1756; reprinted by Banner of Truth Trust, 1985), pp. 564-567.
5   Benjamin W. Labaree, *Patriots & Partisans: The Merchants of Newburyport, 1764-1815*, (New York: M.M. Norton & Company,

there were occasions when Whitefield found remnants of Puritanism during his 1740 visit to New England. For example, upon landing in Newport, Rhode Island, on September 14, Whitefield recorded:

> Several gentlemen of the town soon came to pay their respects to me, among whom was R. Clap, an aged Dissenting minister, and the most venerable man I ever saw in my life. He looked like a good old Puritan, and gave me an idea of what stamp those men were like who first settled New England. His countenance was very heavenly, and he prayed most affectionately for a blessing on my coming to Rhode Island.[6]

George Whitefield's mind was far from free of outside distractions when he reached Boston on September 18, 1740. His personal correspondence, just before his arrival, reveals the outside pressures he was feeling from his prior ministerial labors. In a letter to the Lord Bishop of London, who was no supporter of the revivals, Whitefield asked legal advice about his opposition from the Commissary of South Carolina. He also explained to the bishop that he had appeared recently before an ecclesiastical court for not following the proper order of worship in a service.[7] In another letter to a friend, Whitefield addressed the theological controversies that were developing concerning sinless perfection and eternal security for believers.[8] Furthermore, one of the societies which formed because of the revival in England was distancing itself from Whitefield. He wrote, "Some of the Fetter Lane Society, I fear, are running into sad errors . . . those that before, I suppose, would have plucked out their eyes for me, now I suspect I shall see very shy and avoiding me."[9] Lastly, the ongoing controversy or rivalry Whitefield had with John Wesley was developing in full force. Wesley had recently preached and published a sermon opposing various doctrines Whitefield supported. "It hath set the nation a disputing," Whitefield concluded.[10] The full force of Wesley's harm to Whitefield's work could not be realized until Whitefield's return to England several months later.[11]

When Whitefield arrived in Boston in the fall of 1740, he entered one of the most important cities in the world. In 1606, King James I of England claimed the region from Nova Scotia to the Carolinas as his domain. In 1614, Captain John Smith, of the Plymouth Company, explored North Virginia from central Maine to Cape Cod, and named the area New England. The year 1630 saw the first successful English settlers arrive in Boston. They were distinctly English Puritans. They quickly built homes and established the First Church. Boston was originally called Tri-Mountain by the first English settlers due to its topography. In June and July 1630, a great number of English immigrants arrived at Massachusetts, with John Winthrop as the first Governor. In 1632, Boston became the capital of the Massachusetts Bay Colony. The city thrived. There was plenty of fresh water, excellent coastal and deep-water fishing, fertile soil, and a deep harbor surrounded by thick forests. Boston quickly became a transplanted English village with artisans working out of their clapboard homes, creating everything from metal cooking utensils, to wooden roof shingles, to leather products for horses and home.[12]

The first generation of Bostonians rapidly organized themselves as a Puritan and an enlightened community. In 1634 the Boston Common was designated as open land for the growing city. In 1635 the

---

1975), p. 8.
6 George Whitefield, *George Whitefield's Journals*, (1756; reprinted by Banner of Truth Trust, 1985), p. 452.
7 George Whitefield, *Works, vol. I*, pp. 206-207.
8 Ibid., p. 209.
9 Ibid., p. 210.
10 Ibid., p. 212.
11 Susan F. Harrington, "Friendship under Fire: George Whitefield and John Wesley, 1739-1741," *Andover Newton Quarterly*, vol. xv, no. 3, (January 1975), pp. 167-181.
12 Michael Rawson, *Eden on the Charles: The Making of Boston*, (Cambridge, MA: Harvard University Press, 2010), pp. 24-31.

Boston Latin School was founded to educate the male youth of Boston. A representative style of government was elected. Every able Englishman was allowed two acres, and each able young male one acre, for planting crops. On May 6th, a beacon was built on top of Sentry Hill (Beacon Hill), with a man stationed there to light a warning fire in case of danger. Although Boston had little fear of attacks from the French or Spanish, outlying settlements feared attacks from Indians. Able bodied men were expected to serve in the militia. In 1637 the Ancient and Honorable Artillery Company was founded, even while Boston men deployed west and south in military actions against the Pequot Indians.

Early Bostonians were dedicated to the Puritan ideal of theocracy, meaning God was their ruler and the Bible was their guidebook. This quickly created problems. Those who did not conform to the Puritan way were not recognized as full members of the community. Merchants, traders, civil leaders, mariners, intellectuals, craftsmen, and others who lived and worked in Boston may or may not have accepted Puritanism, but they generally conformed for expediency's sake. Those who did not outwardly conform were dealt with harshly. In the late 1630s, Anne Hutchinson was publicly at odds with Boston's Puritan leaders, resulting in her 1637 banishment from the colony and her 1638 excommunication. In 1648, Margaret Jones was hanged for witchcraft, as was Anne Hibbons in 1656. In 1660, William Leddra and Mary Dyer, both Quakers, were hanged in Boston.

The importance of the founding of New College in 1636, soon called Harvard College, cannot be overstated. Founded by capable and dedicated Puritans, Harvard became the educational standard throughout all thirteen American Colonies. As the first college in America, Harvard trained all the New England clergy. The school quickly developed a reputation for academic excellence, and trained the first American clergy, civil leaders, businessmen, and lawyers. The second college founded in America was the College of William and Mary in Virginia, established in 1693. Located within walking distance or a short carriage ride from colonial Boston, Harvard College in Cambridge helped make Boston a thriving city. The civil and ministerial leaders in Boston all became Harvard graduates. This created an educated, wealthy class in contrast with the middle-class merchants, skilled tradesmen, mariners, and common laborers. The Puritans believed that each person was made in the image of God and was therefore of exceeding value, but this egalitarianism was tempered by those in the city who had more wealth, education, resources, and influence on others. Boston's leadership was later called "the oligarchy of the magistrates."[13]

The second and third generations of Bostonians saw remarkable changes. The population of the city expanded rapidly, creating the need for more local churches. In 1649, the Second Church was established. In 1669, to accommodate a growing and spreading population, the Third Church in Boston was constructed. Amidst controversy, a Baptist meeting house was built in 1679. As a further sign that the Puritanism of the founding Bostonians was unraveling, in 1688 the King's Chapel, sponsored by the dreaded Church of England, was founded in Boston. The expanding city required various cultural adaptions. For example, in 1652 a mint was established at Boston, for the purpose for coining silver. In 1690 the first paper money in America was printed in Boston. By 1700 the North Writing School was established. In 1704 the *Boston News-Letter* began publication, followed by the *Boston Gazette* in 1719.

By the early 1700s, Boston was an eclectic, cosmopolitan city known throughout much of the world as a thriving port city. Numerous languages were spoken on the Boston waterfront, as merchants, sea captains, and traders from various countries came to Boston to ply their trades. As the capital city of the Massachusetts Bay Colony, Boston hummed with the traffic from civil leaders, political opportunists, and elected officials busy about the business of government. The city developed a noticeable stratification of society. The latest European fashions in carriages, clothing, furniture, cutlery, and dishware were all for sale. The very wealthy

---

13   Chard P. Smith, *Yankees and God*, (New York: Hermitage House, 1954), p. 25.

lived in elaborate homes, while the working poor resided in hovels. Middle class merchants, civil employees, mariners, and tradesmen were the most numerous, and built smaller homes in the ever-expanding Boston periphery. The growing population necessitated more churches. In 1699 the Brattle Street Church was built. Four churches were built in rapid succession; the Old North Church in 1723; the Old South Meeting House in 1729; the Hollis Street Church in 1732; and the Trinity Church on Summer Street in 1735.

A sketch of George Whitefield in prayer, by Valerie Borgal.

Early Boston was not without its challenges and tragedies. In 1699, Captain William Kidd, the notorious pirate, was arrested at Boston and sent to England. A fire in 1711 destroyed much of the city. In 1717, six pirates were executed at Boston. In 1721 the smallpox raged, and eight hundred and forty-four persons died. When she was twenty-six years old, unmarried Rebekah Chamblit lived in Boston and was tried and executed in 1733 for infanticide. Perhaps the greatest challenge to Bostonians was the change in culture, from dedicated Puritan to cosmopolitan and eclectic Englishmen in a successful city in a prosperous colony. Many of Boston's clergy saw the commercial and secular growth of Boston as a threat to the Puritan way of life, and as damning to the souls of Bostonians.

In the late 1730s, George Whitefield received numerous requests from Boston clergymen to visit the city, to help stem the tide of what was seen as a falling away from the faith. Local clergy saw Boston sliding away from its Puritan ideal. The city prospered to the point that it rivaled almost any city in the English-speaking world. Homes became more elaborate, decorated with expensive silks and linens with elaborate imported European furniture. Small homes expanded out and up, creating congested urban neighborhoods for both the wealthy and others.[14] In the early 1700s, Boston had a population of well over 10,000 people. Immigrants, traders, slaves, and others arrived from various European, African, and Caribbean locations with a wide variety of religious beliefs. The Puritan vision of the Kingdom of God on earth was being swallowed up by commercialism, intellectualism, and indifference.[15]

In September 1740, when Whitefield arrived in Boston, he walked the cobblestone streets of a bustling and prosperous port city. Puritanism was preached in some of Boston's pulpits but was generally overlooked in everyday life. The foundation of Puritanism was separation from the corrupt Church of England, yet when Whitefield arrived in Boston he observed large and prosperous Church of England churches in Boston, namely King's Chapel (f.1688), Christ Church (f.1723), and Trinity Church (f.1729). Baptists and Quakers, persecuted a few generations before in Boston by Puritans, now walked the streets unashamed and were even considered respectable members of the community. Boston was clearly a city in transition. But transitions can cause friction and controversy. Boston had a changing identity. Some clung to the old theocratic identity

---

14   George F. Dow, *Everyday Life in the Massachusetts Bay Colony*, (New York: Dover Publications, 1988), pp. 12-39.
15   Chard P. Smith, *Yankees and God*, p. 214.

of the Puritans, while most adhered to a more cosmopolitan, secular, commercial view of the world. There was an uncertainty, an apprehension, a sense of cultural displacement by many in Boston. This set the stage for Whitefield's arrival.

> The new clouds began gathering . . . when twenty-six year-old George Whitefield, semi-educated oratorical genius . . . moved toward Boston leveling the little towns as he passed. It broke and whirled cyclonic in Boston where he spent four weeks thundering from the pulpits of the churches, from perches on the Common, and in the assemblies at Harvard. New England had never seen anything like this man, unpresupposing in his appearance with his crossed eyes, unrestrained, short on doctrine, long on weeping and shouting, and possessed of unique magnetism of voice . . . But it made small difference what leaders were for or against Whitefield. This was a movement of the people, a release of that hunger for religion . . . that had been lying restless over New England during the autumn of Puritanism's year . . . Now they rose to Whitefield from every forest and field.[16]

September 18, 1740 was an eventful day in Boston's history. At a time when popular interest in revivals had already developed in parts of New England, Whitefield arrived in Boston. All of Massachusetts was full of excitement as they anticipated his arrival. His name was already a household word among New Englanders, due to his revival work in England, his previous preaching tour in the southern colonies, and the willingness of the Boston newspapers to announce Whitefield's ministerial successes. No source is as helpful as Whitefield's own *Journal* and letters in discovering the details of his labors in Boston.

> Friday, September 19. I was visited by several gentlemen and ministers, and went to the Governor's with Esquire Willard, the Secretary of the Province, a man fearing God, and with whom I have corresponded some time, though before unknown in person. The Governor received me with the utmost respect, and desired me to see him as often as I could.[17]

Governor Jonathan Belcher (1682-1757) became a devoted friend and admirer of Whitefield. Belcher was known throughout Massachusetts as a Christian Gentleman and a friend of the needy. A Harvard graduate, he was impeccably honest and widely respected as a civil leader. While it is not apparent which church the governor attended in Boston, time would reveal that he was obviously supportive of the awakening and sympathetic to the New Light followers of Whitefield. Whitefield's *Journal* continues,

> At eleven, I went to public worship at the Church of England, and afterwards went home with the Commissary, who had read prayers. He received me very courteously; and, it being a day whereon the clergy of the Established Church met, I had an opportunity of conversing with five of them together . . . Finding how inconsistently they were I took my leave, resolving they should not have an opportunity of denying me the use of their pulpits. However, they treated me with more civility than any of our own clergymen have done for a long while. The Commissary very kindly urged me to dine with them, but, being pre-engaged, I went to my lodgings, and in the afternoon, preached to about four thousand people in Dr. Coleman's meeting house; and afterwards exhorted and prayed with many who came to my lodgings, rejoicing at the prospect there was of bringing many souls in Boston to the saving knowledge of the Lord Jesus Christ. Grant this, O father, for thy dear Son's sake! Amen.

---

16   Ibid., pp. 252-253.
17   George Whitefield, *Journals*, pp. 457-474. The following Journal quotes all fall within these pages.

The afore-mentioned Church of England where Whitefield attended but did not preach could have been King's Chapel, founded in 1689. This church in 1740 was temporarily without a rector. Or it could be Christ Church Episcopal, founded in 1723, with Rev. Timothy Cutler as minister. Or Whitefield could have been referring to the Trinity Church (Episcopal), founded in 1729. The minister or rector at Trinity Church in 1740 was Rev. Addington Davenport, who proved to be no friend of Whitefield. One source stated that when Whitefield arrived in Boston, the next day he respectfully went to see fellow Church of England minister Timothy Cutler at Christ Church, but Cutler was "cold to him."[18] Mentioned in the above quote is Dr. Joseph Sewall, the minister of South Church in Boston. His assistant was Thomas Prince, who edited the revivalist paper, *The Christian History*. Sewall was a Harvard graduate who served at the church from 1713 to his death in 1769. As a prominent citizen in Boston, he wholeheartedly supported Whitefield. Continuing in Whitefield's *Journals*:

> Sunday, September 21. Went in the morning, and heard Dr. Coleman preach. Dined with his colleague, the Rev. Mr. Cooper. Preached in the afternoon, to a thronged auditory, at the Rev. Mr. Foxcroft's meeting-house. Immediately after, on the common, to about fifteen thousand; and again, at my lodgings, to a greater company than before.

Three clergymen are mentioned in this quote: Benjamin Colman, William Cooper, and Thomas Foxcroft. Remarkably, Whitefield mentioned only in passing that he preached to fifteen thousand people on the Boston Common. This was the first of dozens of sermons Whitefield preached on the Boston Common, for collectively over a hundred thousand people. Cooper assisted Coleman at the Brattle Street Church. Both supported the awakening, although Cooper was more willing to overlook extremes than was his colleague Coleman. The Brattle Street Church was founded by Puritans in 1698, and Colman was their first minister. Their wooden meeting house, in which Whitefield preached, was constructed in 1699. The aforementioned Rev. Thomas Foxcroft, a Harvard graduate, ministered at the First Church from 1717 to his death in 1769. Whitefield's *Journal* narrative continues:

> Monday, September 22. Preached this morning at the Rev. Mr. Webb's meeting house, to six thousand hearers in the house, besides great numbers standing at the doors. Most wept for a considerable time. In the afternoon I went to preach at the Rev. Mr. Checkley's meeting house; but God was pleased to humble us by a very awful providence.

Rev. Jonathan Webb of the New North Church in Boston was a devoted friend of Whitefield, and a thorough New Light. Although not as well-known as his contemporary pastors in Boston, Webb allowed thousands to hear Whitefield from his pulpit. He died in 1750. The Rev. Samuel Checkley was the first minister of the South Church in Boston, serving there from 1719 to 1769. In mentioning his preaching for Checkley at the South Church, Whitefield recorded:

> The meeting house being filled, though there was no real danger, on a sudden all the people were in an uproar; and so unaccountably surprised, that some threw themselves out the windows, others threw themselves out of the gallery, and others trampled upon one another so that five were actually killed, and others dangerously wounded. I happened to come in in the midst of the uproar, and saw two or three lying in the ground in a pitiable condition. God was pleased to give me presence of mind; so that I gave notice I would immediately preach upon the common. The weather was wet, but many thousands followed in the field, to whom I preached from these words, "Go out into the highways and hedges, and compel them to come in."

---

18 Charles L. Biggs, "When George Whitefield Came Through New Haven," unpublished manuscript, Connecticut Historical Society.

Tuesday, September 23. Went this morning, with Dr. Coleman and the Secretary to Roxbury, three miles from Boston, to see the Rev. Mr. Walter, a good old Puritan . . . At eleven we returned, and I preached in the Rev. Mr. Gee's meeting house, but not to a very crowded auditory, because the people were in doubt where I would preach. Dined at the Secretary's; preached in the afternoon at a thronged congregation, and exhorted and prayed at my own lodgings. Lord, let Thy Presence always follow me, or otherwise I shall be but as a sounding brass or a tinkling cymbal.[19]

The above-named Rev. Mr. Walter was Nathaniel Walter of the Second Church Congregational at Roxbury, a couple of miles west of Boston. Walter was a Harvard graduate, ordained in 1729, and settled at the Second Church in 1734 until his death in 1776.[20] Rev. Joshua Gee was the minister at Second Church of Boston. Gee had been a colleague of the then deceased Cotton Mather. Gee was an outspoken Whitefield supporter. In a personal letter dated September 23, Whitefield summarized his ministry in Boston, saying:

> Hither God brought me on Thursday evening. I preached once on Friday, and twice every day since. The power of the Lord advances sweetly. Our Lord, I believe, will revive his work in the midst of the years; he enables me to preach plainly. Some ministers, I hope, will be quickened, as well as people. They attend, and are exceedingly civil, as is the governor.[21]

The New North Church, now known as the Old North Church, is still standing in downtown Boston. George Whitefield preached here in 1740 to huge crowds. Photograph by Ken Lawson.

An eyewitness of Whitefield's success in Boston was Rev. Ebenezer Parkman of the Congregational Church in Westborough, Massachusetts. Parkman was a Congregational minister, a Harvard graduate in 1721, and was in Boston for whatever reason when Whitefield was preaching. Parkman wrote in his diary,

1740

Sept. 19. Mr. Whitefield came last Night to Boston.

Sept. 23. Mr. Whitefield preaches Twice every Day to the astonishment of all.

---

19 George Whitefield, *Journals*, pp. 461–462.
20 John McClintock & James Strong, *Cyclopedia of Biblical, Theological, and Ecclesiastical Literature*, (New York: Harper & Brothers Publishers, 1894), vol. x, p. 872.
21 George Whitefield, *Works*, vol. I, p. 208. The Massachusetts governor referenced here was Jonathan Belcher.

> Sept. 24. I went to [Harvard] College where Mr. Whitefield had been preaching . . . and thence went to Mr. Appleton's where Mr. Whitefield was.[22] The account which he gave of the Time and Manner of the Powerful working of the Spirit of God upon him. P.M. he preach'd in the College yard again . . . It was to incredible multitudes, and with wondrous power.

> Sept. 25. Mr. Whitefield preached the Public Lecture at Boston. His text was John 2,11. P.M. he preached at Charleston on John 3,3.[23]

News of Whitefield's successful ministry in Boston travelled fast. For example, Rev. Stephen Williams was serving almost one hundred miles away in Longmeadow, Massachusetts when he heard of Whitefield's preaching to large crowds in Boston. Williams was an active supporter of the revival sweeping through central Massachusetts. In his diary, Williams wrote:

> Sept. 23, 1740. This day I hear the Rev'd Mr. Whitefield is come to Boston—& his preaching is well approved of—Oh Lord, grant good may come by this, his visit to our Country, Oh Lord to pour out thy Spirit, upon ye land.

> Sept. 26, 1740. This Evening—I hear of the awful [awesome] Providence, at Boston—on a day ye Rev'd Mr. Whitefield preached there—ye Lord mercifully over rule & prevent his own name being dishonored—and his interest being wrong.[24]

Whitefield's *Journal* narrative continues:

> Wednesday, September 24. Went this morning to see and preach at Cambridge [Harvard] the chief college for training the sons of the prophets in New England. It has one president, four tutors and about a hundred students . . . A great number of neighboring ministers attended, God gave me great boldness and freedom of speech. The President of the college and minister of the parish treated me very civilly. In the afternoon, I preached again, in the court, when, I believe, there were about seven thousand hearers. The Holy Spirit melted many hearts.

Whitefield had already been successfully preaching in Boston for several days before he preached at Cambridge, across the Charles River from Boston, where Harvard College is located. This was the school for the education of Boston's clergy. Founded in 1636 by Puritans from Massachusetts Bay Colony, Harvard was the first school of higher learning in the American Colonies. The school was named after a local congregational minister who bequeathed his library to the fledgling college. The president of Harvard that greeted Whitefield in 1740 was Rev. Edward Holyoke, who served the college from 1739 to his death in 1769. Whitefield and Holyoke had an on-and-off relationship for decades, but in 1740, Whitefield was welcomed to speak at Harvard. Holyoke is the "one president" and the "President of the college" Whitefield mentioned above. Whitefield recorded in his *Journal*:

> Thursday, September 25. Preached the weekly lecture at Mr. Foxcroft's meeting house . . . After public worship, I went, at his Excellency's invitation, and dined with him. Most of the ministers of the town were invited with me. Before dinner, the Governor sent for me into his chamber.

---

22 Rev. Nathaniel Appleton was a Congregational minister in Cambridge and was influential at Harvard College.
23 Ebenezer Parkman, *The Diary of Ebenezer Parkman, 1739-1744*, (Worcester, MA: American Antiquarian Society), pp. 131-132.
24 Stephen Williams, *Diary of Rev. Stephen Williams, Longmeadow, Massachusetts*, (Longmeadow, MA: Richard S. Storrs Library, 2011), pp. 327-328.

He wept, wished me good luck in the Name of the Lord, and recommended himself, ministers and people to my prayers. Immediately after dinner, I prayed for them all; and then went in his carriage to the end of the town, crossed the ferry, and preached at Charleston, lying on the north side of Boston. The meeting house was very capacious, and quite filled. A gracious melting was discernible through the whole congregation.

Friday, September 26. Preached in the morning at Roxbury, to many thousands of people, from a little ascent. Several came afterwards to me, telling how they were struck at that time under the Word . . . In the afternoon, preached from a scaffold erected outside the Rev. Mr. Byle's meeting house, to a congregation nearly double that in the morning. Gave a short exhortation to a great crowd of people.

A contemporary photograph of Massachusetts Hall, built in 1720 as a student residence at Harvard College. The students who resided in this dormitory flocked to hear George Whitefield preach in Cambridge in September, 1740.
Source: www.historicbuildingsct.com.

The Rev. Mather Byles was the minister of Hollis Street Church in Boston. Founded in 1732, this church was begun to accommodate the shifting and growing population in Boston. Mather Byles was a direct descendant of the first generation of Puritans that settled Boston a century earlier. He earned degrees at Harvard in 1725 and again in 1728 and settled at the Hollis Street Church in 1733. His sermons were scholarly and well-written, often appearing in local Boston newspapers. He was a keen student of the Bible, and a Calvinist who was known for his poetry and whit. He was never called a great orator. His biographer said that Byles was an "old Calvinist" and that he made "no original contribution to New England theology."[25] It is unclear what Mather Byles thought of Whitefield. Initially, Byles was caught up in the excitement of having the famous Whitefield visit Boston. Yet the emotional, passionate, and aggressive preaching style of Whitefield may have been too much for Byles to accept, as his ministry was known "as on the whole one of comparative formalism and general lack of spiritual enthusiasm."[26] The following narrative describes the initial welcome Whitefield received from Byles, and the later distance Byles placed between himself and Whitefield.

That the "Great Awakening: of 1740-'42 influenced very deeply the Hollis Street Church we have no reason to think, for the records of the church during that time do not show

---

25 Arthur W.H. Eaton, *The Famous Mather Byles . . . , 1707-1788*, (Boston, MA: W.A. Butterfield, 1914), pp. 75, 77.
26 Ibid., p. 76.

any remarkable increase in the number of admissions to communion. When Whitefield first appeared in Boston in the middle of September, 1740, he was received generally among the Congregationalists, and no doubt by Dr. Byles as by other ministers, with great warmth and was heartily welcomed to the churches. On the 26th of the month he preached from a scaffold erected outside the Hollis Street meeting house, no doubt to accommodate a larger audience than could find room within the building. From a discussion in 1743 of the effects of the revival in which several ministers took an earnest part, some approving, some deprecating, Doctor Byles . . . stood entirely aloof.[27]

The next day, Whitefield's *Journals* continued:

Saturday, September 27. In the morning. Preached at the Rev. Mr. Welstead's meeting house; in the afternoon, on the common to about 15,000 people. Oh, how did the Word run! It rejoiced me to see such numbers affected; I could scarce abstain from crying out, "This is no other than the House of God and the Gate of Heaven."

The Rev. William Welstead was the minister of the New Brick Church, which formed from a separation out of the New North Church in 1719. He was a Harvard graduate in 1716, and was called "an excellent Christian gentleman, and an exemplary minister."[28] A comment must be made on the above mention of Whitefield preaching on the Boston Common to 15,000 people. Although the first U.S. Census was not done in Boston until the 1750s, an estimate of the city's population in 1740 is 16,400 people.[29] This means that the majority of Bostonians flocked to the spacious Common to hear the itinerant Whitefield preach in the open air, the crowd filled with interested listeners from surrounding communities. This was a remarkable and unprecedented preaching event in America. One account summarized Whitefield's ministry on Saturday,

A contemporary photograph of part of the large Boston Common. In 1740, George Whitefield preached here numerous times to tens-of-thousands of people. Photograph by Ken Lawson.

---

27 Ibid., pp. 82-83.
28 Ezra H. Bylngton, *The Puritan in England and New England*, (Boston, MA: Roberts Brothers, 1897), p. 353.
29 "Top 20 U.S. Metropolitan Areas by Population, 1790-2010, with Top 4 Metropolitan Areas 1680-1775," http://www.peakbagger.com/pdgoeg/histmetropop.aspx.

September 27, 1740 as follows: "On Saturday he preached in the morning at the New Brick Church pastored by Rev. Welsteed [Welstead]. In the afternoon, Whitefield again preached on the Boston Common to a huge audience of 15,000. Both sermons apparently had a powerful effect.[30] Another account summarized the amazing number gathered to hear Whitefield on Boston Common; "New England witnessed one of the most powerful phases of the awakenings of the 1740s . . . In Boston, on September 27, 1740, Whitefield preached on the common to a crowd estimated at 15,000. Many were deeply affected." The author stated, "Boston common has become a portal to divine glory."[31] One account summarized, "He preached in Boston to the greatest crowds ever assembled there to hear the gospel. Some 8,000 assembled in the morning and some 15,000 returned to the famous Commons in the evening.[32]

Whitefield kept a remarkably detailed account of his daily ministries in Boston. Clearly, he was thrilled to be preaching successfully in this city founded by Puritans. His *Journals* continued:

> Sunday, September 28. Preached, in the morning, at Mr. Sewall's meeting house, to very crowded auditory, and £555 currency were collected for the Orphan House. Was taken ill after dinner with a vomiting fit; but was enabled to preach, in the afternoon, at Dr. Coleman's, to as great, if not greater congregation than in the morning. Here £470 were collected. In both places, all things were carried out with great decency and order. People went slowly out, as though they had not a mind to escape giving; and Dr. Coleman said it was the most pleasant time they had enjoyed in the meeting house through the whole course of his life. After sermon, I had the honor of a private visit from the Governor, who came to take his leave of me for the present. At their request, I then went and preached to a great number of negroes on the conversion of the Ethiopian eunuch (Acts VIII); and, at my return, gave a word of exhortation to a crowd of people, who were waiting at my lodgings.

The above-mentioned Dr. Sewell was Rev. Joseph Sewell of the South Church Congregational, Boston. He was widely respected as a minister, theologian, and civil leader. Sewell was a 1707 graduate of Harvard, earning a second degree in 1710. He was ordained to serve the South Church in 1713, a ministry he successfully maintained until his death in 1769. Sewell was widely published on both sides of the Atlantic. In 1731, the University of Glasgow, Scotland, granted him the Doctor of Divinity degree.

Whitefield's first ministry in Boston in September 1740, was remarkable. He wrote to a friend in Great Britain during this period and concluded that, "God is working powerfully in America. He fills me with his presence and causes me to go away rejoicing. Grace! Grace![33] Whitefield had much to be thankful for in this initial visit to Boston. There was virtually no opposition to his ministry, except for the few Church of England ministers in the area. His correspondence, dated September 26, says "Almost all the ministers and vast bodies of the people, have been continually pressing to hear the Word of God, sometimes in the fields, and sometimes in the meeting houses."[34] The results of Whitefield's ministry during his 1740 Boston visit were so successful that he apologetically wrote to a friend on September 28, saying, "Excuse the brevity of this. So many persons come to me under convictions, and for advice, that I have scarce time to eat bread. Wonderful things are doing here. The word runs like lightening. Dagon daily falls before the ark."[35]

---

30 "History of Revivalism in Boston," Emmanuel Research Review, Emmanuel Gospel Center, Boston, (Issue 24, May 2010), p. 2.
31 "The Great Awakening 1730 Onward," http://culvercitygospelhall.com/amhist2010/GreatAwakening.pdf.
32 "George Whitefield," http://www.evanwiggs.com/revival/portrait/whitefie.html.
33 George Whitefield, *Works*, vol. I, p. 210.
34 Ibid., p. 213.
35 Ibid., p. 216.

A sketch of George Whitefield preaching outdoors.
Source: https://georgiainfo.galileo.usg.edu/gastudiesimages/George%20Whitefield%20Preaching.htm.

CHAPTER 5
WHITEFIELD IN NORTHERN NEW ENGLAND

1740

AFTER ONE WEEK OF MINISTRY in Boston, Whitefield departed for northern New England on September 29, 1740. He returned shortly thereafter, on October 6, to resume his ministry in Boston. Dallimore said of his northern preaching tour,

> Thus ended Whitefield's first week in New England. During the second week he followed a practice that we have seen him observing in old England—he made a seven day preaching tour to several outlying towns. This took him to Marble Head, Salem, Ipswich, Newbury, Hampton, and finally to York in what now is the state of Maine. On the journey back to Boston he preached again at these places—his custom to preach and return—and rejoiced to see that the seed sown the few days earlier was already bearing fruit.[1]

The time spent in these northern coastal cities of New England kindled a lifelong affection for this area towards Whitefield. As in Boston, these northern communities received Whitefield as a hero, with scarcely a single voice of opposition. Whitefield wrote,

> Monday, September 29. Set out at seven in the morning for Marble Head, a large town twenty miles from Boston. About eleven I preached to some thousands in a broad place in the middle of town. Dined with Rev. Mr. Barnard, one of the ministers of the place. Rode to Salem, four miles from Marblehead, and preached there also, to about two thousand. Here, one was struck down by the power of the Word; and in every part of the congregation, persons might be seen under great concern. Salem is the first settled and largest town (next to Boston) in all New England; and, as far as I could see and hear, rather exceeds it for politeness. I found the inhabitants had been sadly divided about their ministers and God be pleased, before I knew their circumstances, to direct me to a suitable subject. Lord, heal their divisions, and grant that with one heart and one mind, they may endeavor to glorify Thy Holy Name. After the exercise, I immediately set out for Ipswich, another large town, some sixteen miles (the way we went) distant from Salem. Two or three gentlemen came to meet me, and I and my friends were most kindly entertained at the house of the Rev. Mr. Rogers, one of the ministers of the place.[2]

Three towns are mentioned here—Marblehead, Salem, and Ipswich. Each deserves special attention.

---

1 Arnold Dallimore, *George Whitefield: The Life and Times of the Great Evangelist of the Eighteenth Century Revival*, (Carlisle, PA: Banner of Truth Trust, 1980), vol. II, p. 532.
2 George Whitefield, *Journals of George Whitefield*, (1756: reprinted by Banner of Truth Trust, Carlisle, PA: 1985), p. 465.

A large number of Colonial era homes still exist as residences in Marblehead, Massachusetts. Walking these streets gives an idea of what life was like in Colonial America.
Source: http://gadling.com/2012/03/23/marblehead-massachusetts-americas-best-preserved-historic-tow.

Marblehead was primarily a fishing and maritime community, prosperous and economically stable. Day fishermen worked along the coast, while others journeyed farther out to sea to catch cod, halibut, and haddock. Fish cutting and flaking operations caused the entire town to smell of fish. Shipbuilding activities lined the rocky shore, as maritime activities such as whaling, fishing, and coastal trading expanded. This was never a Puritan community, but the Puritan influence from Boston directly influenced Marblehead. In 1692, Marblehead resident Wilmott Redd was hanged as a witch in nearby Salem. By the early 1700s, Marblehead had an air of sophistication and affluence, as wealthy sea captains, merchants, and traders settled in the town and built larger homes, many of which are still standing today.[3] When Whitefield came to Marblehead in September 1740, there were two primary churches in town—the Congregational Church, founded in 1684; and the St. Michael's Episcopal Church, founded in 1714.

The two ministers in Marblehead in 1740 were the Congregationalist Rev. John Barnard, who served in the town from 1714 to 1770; and Rev. Alexander Malcom of the Church of England, St. Michael's Church, who served there from 1740 to 1749. It is interesting to note that Whitefield, as a Church of England minister, was not welcomed by Malcom, but instead was welcomed by the Congregationalist Barnard. Malcom represented the traditional Church of England establishment, with formal ceremonies, liturgical repetitions, and prayers read from the *Prayer Book*. Malcom perceived Whitefield as a dangerous novelty, an itinerant that would upset the normal religious life of Marblehead. Barnard was more evangelical, more in support of revival and awakening in the community.

The reception of Whitefield in Marblehead was remarkable. He wrote in his *Journals*, "About eleven I preached to some thousands in a broad place in the middle of town. Dined with Rev. Mr. Barnard, one of the ministers of the place." This broad location in the middle of town was on the large granite steps of the Old Town House, the civic building constructed in 1727. There is no longer a "broad space" around the building, but the structure is in beautiful condition.

Another town north of Boston mentioned by Whitefield in his September 29, 1740 *Journals* entry was Salem. First settled in 1626 and incorporated in 1629, Salem was originally much larger than it is today. The site was settled because of its proximity to fresh water and good fishing. However, the port of Salem quickly

---

3   Samuel Roads, *The History and Traditions of Marblehead*, (Boston, MA: Houghton, Mifflin and Company, 1881), p. 58. For a detailed study of early Marblehead see Lauren Fogle, *Colonial Marblehead: from Rogues to Revolutionaries*, (Charleston, SC: The History Press, 2008). Photographs of many colonial homes from Marblehead are found in John H. Wright, *Marblehead: Images of America*, vol. I, (Charleston, SC Arcadia Publishing, 1996).

became known as a shipping and trading center. In 1649 the first Salem Custom House was built, for the purpose of collecting taxes on maritime imports and cataloging exports. This was a Puritan settlement with a passion for business and commercial activities. The Salem Witch Trials of 1692 were a tragic and short-term distraction to the rising influence of this expanding city. Today, numerous homes from the mid-1600s through the 1700s still stand in Salem, a testimony to the prosperity and opulence gained by successful merchants, bankers, businessmen, ship builders, and sea captains. Throughout the 1700s, Salem vessels sailed to ports throughout the Americas, Asia, and Africa, bringing home exotic and valuable merchandise.[4] When Whitefield arrived in Salem in September 1740, he witnessed a growing city that would be one of the wealthiest New World cities by the turn of the century.

Several things are interesting about Whitefield's September 29, 1740, *Journals* entry related to Salem, as quoted above. First, it is telling that he did not name the minister who hosted him in Salem. Next, he noted that he preached "to about two thousand people." The location is unknown. Further, Whitefield commented that "in every part of the congregation, persons might be seen under great concern." That meant people were listening and attentive to his message, and were influenced by what he said. He then comments on the large size of the city and formal manners of the residents, and then remarks, "I found the inhabitants had been sadly divided about their ministers." Why were the people "sadly divided" over the ministers in Salem?

The three prominent ministers in Salem in 1740 were Rev. John Sparhawk of the First Church; Rev. Peter Clark of the Salem Village Church (now in Danvers); and Rev. Benjamin Prescott of the South Parish (now in Peabody). All three men were Harvard graduates and all were apparently of like faith and practice. This is evident in that Clark and Prescott officiated at the ordination and installation ceremony of Sparhawk to the First Church in 1736.[5] One author stated, "Rev. John Sparhawk [was] one of the early Puritan pastors of the historic First Church in Salem, Mass."[6] The fact that Salem was "sadly divided" over their ministers probably had a lot to do with finances. For example, Rev. Prescott at the South Church Congregational had a decades-long controversy with his congregation over his salary. His salary was set without consideration for

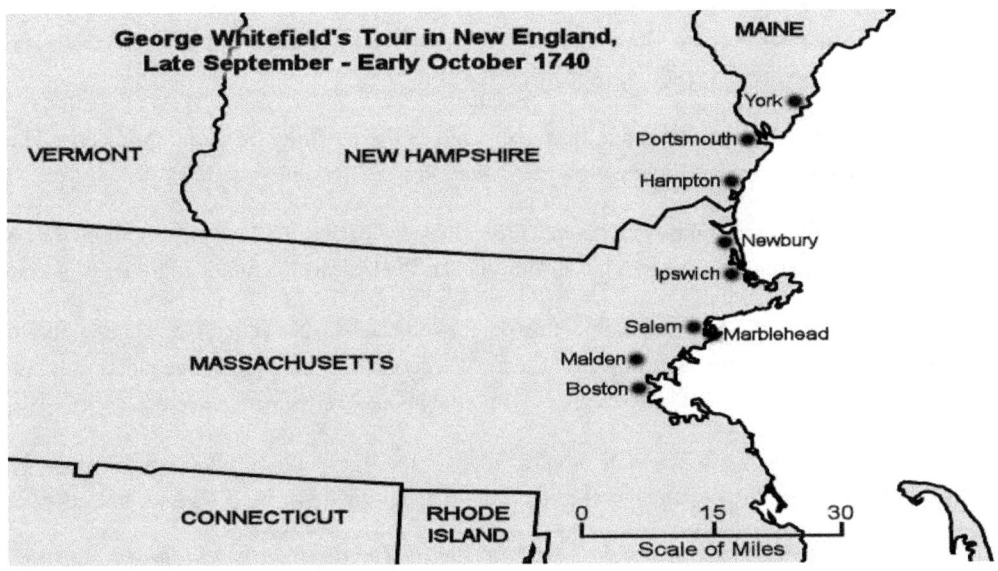

---

4   Robert Booth, *Death of an Empire: The Rise and Murderous Fall of Salem, America's Richest City*, (New York: St. Martin's Press, 2011), pp. xi-xvi.
5   Cecil H.C. Howard, *Materials for a Genealogy of the Sparhawk Family in New England*, (Salem, MA: Printed at the Salem Press, 1892), p. 14.
6   Ibid., p. 72.

the depreciation of paper currency, his expanding family, or the fact that Salem was a thriving commercial community that was expensive to live in. Further, his pay was often late or he was underpaid.[7]

We do not know which of the three Salem ministers invited Whitefield to speak. Perhaps all of them welcomed the itinerant preacher. But we do know that Whitefield preached with "power" to "about two thousand" with success. Whitefield's *Journals* continued:

> After the exercise [in Salem], I immediately set out for Ipswich, another large town, some sixteen miles (the way we went) distant from Salem. Two or three gentlemen came to meet me, and I and my friends were most kindly entertained at the house of the Rev. Mr. Rogers, one of the ministers of the place.[8]

Ipswich, Massachusetts was established in 1633. Located in a tidal marsh area, the community was well planned and prospered as a rural fishing and farming community. The first settlers traveled on small rafts, canoes, or other boats as well as by horseback or on foot. Food was abundant, fish were plenty, and the mud flats were abounding with clams. The small settlement quickly prospered, and by 1646 Ipswich had nearly 800 inhabitants. The first generations were farmers, fishermen, shipbuilders, and traders. By the mid-1700s, bridges crossed the Ipswich River, wharfs and storehouses aligned the shore of the deeper, navigable water, and small waterfront industries such as a salt works, a tannery, fish flaking operations, and a ship building yard were functioning. Fishing was the most profitable industry on the Ipswich River and its tidal estuaries. Occasionally, a ship from the West Indies unloaded molasses at the wharf. The barrels were rolled directly into a thriving distillery, the town's second largest commercial operation in Ipswich, after the fisheries.[9]

Whitefield wrote in his *Journals*, quoted above, that he was "most kindly entertained at the house of the Rev. Mr. Rogers, one of the ministers of the place." This is a reference to Rev. John Rogers, who was born in Ipswich in 1666. The Rogers family in Ipswich, and previously in England, had a long line of Puritan ministers. John Rogers graduated from Harvard in 1684, and settled as a minister in Ipswich and was ordained in 1692. He ministered in Ipswich at the First Church until his death in 1745.[10] Whitefield certainly had an ally in John Rogers. Both men longed for a revival of Puritanism to spread throughout the region. Whitefield wrote of his preaching in Ipswich as follows:

> Tuesday, September 30. Preached at Ipswich, at ten in the morning, to many thousands. The Lord gave me freedom, and there was a great melting in the congregation.

Another account of this preaching event stated, "From the ledge nearest the Meeting-House, as the tradition is, Whitefield preached to thousands, hushed to solemn silence."[11] His *Journals* continued his travel narrative.

> [Tuesday, September 30.] . . . After dinner set out for and reached, Newbury, twelve miles distant from Ipswich, about three. The power of the Lord accompanied the Word. The meeting-house was very large. Many ministers were present, and the people were greatly affected.

The minister in Newbury was Rev. Christopher Toppan, the son of a local physician. He was a Harvard graduate who served at the First Church Newbury from 1697 to his death in 1747. Like his father, Toppan

---

7   Duane H. Hurd, *History of Essex County, Massachusetts*, (Philadelphia, PA: W. Lewis & Company, 1888), vol. II, pp. 1030-1031.
8   George Whitefield, *Journals of George Whitefield*, p. 465.
9   "Ipswich, Massachusetts," http://www.ipswichma.com/directory/history.asp. For a detailed look at the trades and crafts of colonial Ipswich, see Robert Tarule, *The Artisan of Ipswich: Craftsmanship and Community in Colonial New England*, (Baltimore, MD: The Johns Hopkins University Press, 2004).
10 *Biographical Sketches of Representative Citizens of the Commonwealth of Massachusetts*, (Boston, MA: Graves & Steinbarger, Publishers, 1901), pp. 251-252.
11 Thomas F. Waters, *Ipswich in the Massachusetts Bay Colony*, (Ipswich Historical Society, 1905), p. 435.

practiced medicine, along with his ministerial duties.[12] Newbury was first settled by the English in 1635. The hay from the salt marshes supported thousands of cattle. Fishing was abundant, and the flat lands made for excellent farming. Fresh water from the Parker River provided drinking and washing water, as well as water power for grist and saw mills. In 1699, two years after Toppan settled in Newbury, a new and spacious meeting house was constructed. Whitefield preached here on September 30, 1740, and afterwards remarked, "The meeting-house was very large." It is interesting that Whitefield does not name his ministerial host in Newbury, Rev. Christopher Toppan, nor does he name the "many ministers [who] were present" at his preaching in Newbury.

From Newbury, Whitefield proceeded north, crossing the Merrimack River, and for the first time entered New Hampshire. The Colony of New Hampshire was settled in 1623 as a land grant from the Merrimack River to the Piscataqua River. Fishing was the primary industry. In 1630, a large group of English settlers arrived and founded Strawberry Bank, later called Portsmouth. The first settlements in New Hampshire were not successful, as a poor central government caused each town to act independently. The New Hampshire settlers came under the civil influence of Massachusetts from 1641 to 1679, and from 1686 to 1691. Until 1741, the governor of New Hampshire was but a lieutenant under the supervision of the governor of Massachusetts. New Hampshire grew very slowly for many years. The chief cause of this was disputes over the legality of land claims, and threats from hostile Indians. In 1719, a colony of Scotch-Irish immigrants settled in south-central New Hampshire and founded the town of Londonderry, named after the city in Ireland from which they came. The community thrived. When Whitefield arrived in New Hampshire in October 1740, the coastal settlements he visited were beginning to show initial signs of stability and prosperity. Whitefield wrote in his *Journal* of his arrival in New Hampshire as follows:

> [Tuesday September 30] Took ferry, immediately after sermon, and with the Rev. Mr. Cotton, minister of the place, who came to fetch me, went in a chaise to Hampton.

Rev. Ward Cotton met Whitefield at the ferry crossing the Merrimack River. Cotton, a Harvard graduate, was the minister of the North Hill Parish in Hampton, New Hampshire. Cotton served at the church from 1731 to 1765. When Cotton became pastor of the church in Hampton, there were 235 members in full communion—84 males and 169 females.[13] Originally, Hampton, New Hampshire, was a huge town, since divided up into eight smaller towns. The people farmed and lumbered. Whitefield spent an evening at the parsonage of Ward and Joanna Cotton and their three small children.[14] Apparently the domestic simplicity and tranquility of the Cotton household made an impression on the bachelor Whitefield. He wrote in his *Journals*, on September 30, 1740:

> I was pleased to see more plainness in Mr. Cotton's house, than I had seen in any minister's house since my arrival. His wife was as one that serveth. Oh, that all minister's wives were so! Nothing gives me more offense than to see clergy-men's wives dressed out in the pride of life. By this they bring a reproach upon religion . . .

Due to the vast size of Hampton, smaller communities grew up within the confines of the town and established their own local churches. An example of this is the church in Hampton Falls, a neighborhood of Hampton. The minister at the church in Hampton Falls was Rev. Joseph Whipple, a Harvard graduate who

---

12 Daniel L. Tappan, *Tappan-Toppan Genealogy of Newbury, Massachusetts, 1606-1672*, (Arlington, MA: Printed by the Author, 1915), pp. 54-56.
13 "Rev. Cotton Ward, Pastor," http://www.hampton.lib.nh.us/hampton/history/dow/chap22_1.htm. John A. Ross, "History of the Congregational Church in Hampton," Granite Monthly, Vol. 43 (1911), pp. 142-149.
14 Joseph Dow, *History of the Town of Hampton, New Hampshire, from its Settlement in 1638 to the Autumn of 1892*, (Salem, MA: L.E. Dow Printers, 1893), p. 648.

settled there in 1726. "Mr. Whipple disapproved of the course of Whitefield and was one of the ministers who cautioned the Boston ministers against admitting him to their pulpits."[15] Whipple and Cotton's disagreement regarding Whitefield divided the town. Whitefield preached in Hampton on a Wednesday morning, not a normal time to gather for church services. He preached outside, since no building in town could hold the crowd. Yet Whitefield felt constrained in his preaching, knowing that there was disunity in Hampton concerning his visit. He wrote in his *Journals*:

> Wednesday, October 1. Preached in the morning, though not with so much freedom as usual, at Hampton, to some thousands in the open air. The wind was almost too high for me. God's spirit bloweth when and where it listeth.

Whitefield's next preaching stop was in Portsmouth, New Hampshire. This area had an excellent harbor to protect its fisheries. Early Portsmouth was a remarkably successful cod and haddock fishing community, sending hundreds of thousands of tons of fish annually back to England for sale or trade. The first settlers in 1630 settled on the west side of the harbor among the wild strawberry fields. The Piscataqua River provided fresh water and excellent seasonal fishing for salmon, trout, and shad. By the 1670s, the town was a gathering place for disgruntled Puritans from Massachusetts. In June 1682, a supernatural phenomenon related to flying stones was explained as a "Rock Throwing Devil."[16] By 1690, Portsmouth was a major shipbuilding community for the British Empire. The community was constantly harassed by thieving Indians stealing cows, and an Indian attack was made on Portsmouth in 1696. In the early 1700s, the community thrived. While not reaching the size or influence of Boston or Salem, Portsmouth nevertheless was a vibrant colonial city with an eclectic and international population. It was the colonial capital of New Hampshire from 1679 to the Revolutionary War. Trade flourished, bringing money into the city that built private mansions, urban improvements, and a thriving waterfront with full warehouses and busy wharves.

In 1740, the influential churches in Portsmouth were the North Parish Church and the South Parish Church. These churches were originally one, but shifting population and controversy created the two congregations in 1713. A small group of Anglicans met in a meeting house built in 1732.[17] The North Parish constructed a large three-story meeting house in 1714. When Whitefield came to Portsmouth in the fall of 1740, he had a firm ally in Rev. William Shurtleff of the South Church. Writing of his welcome to Portsmouth, Whitefield recorded in his *Journals*:

> After dinner, rode in company with many to Portsmouth, fourteen miles from Hampton. Got thither in about an hour and a half, and preached to a polite auditory, and so very unconcerned, that I began

An undated painting of Rev. William Shurtleff of South Parish Church, Portsmouth, New Hampshire.

Source: www.findagrave.com.

---

15 Warren Brown, *History of Hampton Falls, N.H.*, (Concord, NH: The Rumford Press, 1918), vol. II, p. 18.
16 "Portsmouth Timeline," http://www.seacoastnh.com/timeline.
17 Richard M. Candee, *Building Portsmouth: The Neighborhoods and Architecture of New Hampshire's Oldest City*, (Portsmouth, NH: Back Channel Press, 2006), p. 1.

to question whether I had been preaching to rational or brute creatures. Seeing no immediate effects on the word I preached, I was a little dejected; but God, to comfort my heart, sent one young man to me, crying out in great anguish of spirit, "What shall I do to be saved?"

Whitefield saw limited immediate results from his preaching in Portsmouth. A few days later, after preaching in the north, he returned to Portsmouth to a larger and enthusiastic crowd. But for now, he departed Portsmouth, crossed the Piscataqua River on the ferry, and travelled on a winding, rocky road to the port of York.

In 1740, York was part of Massachusetts, but is now located in the state of Maine. York was first settled in 1624, eventually named after York, England. In 1636 a Church of England meeting house was constructed, but nothing is known of its dimensions. The First Church Congregational was organized in 1672. As a port on the Atlantic Ocean and on the York River, this small community survived through the fisheries, shipbuilding, and trade, as inland lumber, firs, and local crops were traded in England for manufactured products. York was the site of the British provincial capital and the British Royal Gaol (jail), in which Canadian and American convicts were interred. Indeed, in the early 1700s, York looked like a small but prosperous English village. Whitefield wrote on October 1, 1740, of his impressions of York in his *Journals*:

> Crossed the ferry, immediately after sermon, and went over a very stony way to York. As I came along, I was surprised to see such an improvement made in a place of a hundred years' standing, and could not but fancy myself in Old England. Surely, God is a covenant keeping God. He has blessed this generation for their fathers' sake, with all temporal blessings. Lord, with these temporal, give them spiritual blessings; otherwise, prosperity will destroy them.

From the ferry landing at York, Whitefield traveled uphill about a half-mile to the Congregational meeting house. Today the area has many colonial era homes from Whitefield's time. In York, Whitefield had a friend in Rev. Samuel Moody. A Harvard graduate in 1697, Moody was the son of a wealthy and influential member of the Massachusetts General Court. He began preaching in York in 1698 and was ordained at the First Church in York, in 1700. He ministered in York until his death in 1747. Affectionately known as "Parson Moody" or "Father Moody," he had a remarkable and enduring influence on York. "He was distinguished alike for his eccentricities, his zeal as a man of God, his remarkable faith and fervency in prayer, and his uncommon benevolence."[18] Moody served as a volunteer chaplain to the British garrison at York. He and his male parishioners were known to carry firearms with them to church services, as the Indian threat was real. Moody's pulpit at the First Church was open to Whitefield, and he preached with visible results. Whitefield wrote about York in his *Journals*:

> Thursday, October 2. Preached both morning and evening. Was comforted to hear good Mr. Moody tell me that he believed I should preach to a hundred new creatures this morning in his congregation. And, indeed, I believe I did. When I came to preach, I could speak little or no terror but almost all consolation. The hearts looked plain and simple; and tears trickled apace down most of their cheeks.

As an itinerant preacher, Whitefield sought to employ a sow now, reap later methodology. That meant he would preach in a community, sowing the gospel seed. Then he would try to return to that community shortly thereafter, to reap what had been sown earlier. This circuit riding technique was first practiced by Whitefield in New England in the communities north of Boston. In late September 1740, he departed Boston and preached north and east as far as York, Maine. He then backtracked his steps, returning to many

---

18 Charles C.P. Moody, *Biographical Sketches of the Moody Family . . .*, (Boston, MA: Samuel G. Drake, Publisher, 1847), pp. 54-55.

of the same pulpits he had visited days or weeks earlier. This was his spiritual follow-up, his watering of gospel seeds to see what would bring forth a spiritual harvest. As he began his route south, returning to Boston, Whitefield recorded in his *Journals*:

> [October 2, 1740] Left York at four in the evening, and reached Portsmouth by night. Conversed and sang psalms with my friends.

> Friday, October 3. Preached this morning, at Portsmouth, to a far greater congregation than before; but, instead of preaching to stocks, I had now reason to believe that I was preaching to living men. People began to melt soon after I began to pray, and the influence increased more and more during the whole sermon. The Word seemed to pierce through and through, and carried such conviction to it, that many, who before had industriously spoken evil of me, were ashamed of themselves. Mr. Shurtleff, the minister, when he afterwards sent me £97, collected at this time for the orphans, wrote thus: "You have left great numbers under great impressions, and I trust in God they will not wear off; but that the convictions of some will be kept up and cherished, till they have had the desired effect." Amen and Amen.

A minister near Portsmouth that heard Whitefield preach was Rev. William Allen of Greenland, who served a church a few miles west of Portsmouth. Whitefield did not visit rural Greenland, so Allen and an unknown number of parishioners went to listen to him. The Greenland town history states of Rev. Allen, "He certainly was friendly towards George Whitefield, and the number of admissions to his society in 1741-42 suggests that, rather than bringing about a schism in his church by opposing the Awakening, as some ministers did, Mr. Allen was able to accommodate himself and his parish to its call for less purely intellectual, and more emotional, religious expression." Some church growth resulted. "Six people were admitted to the church on Dec. 6, 1741; 17 on April 4, 1742; four on May 23; and six on Oct. 10."[19]

Rev. William Shurtleff of Portsmouth was an outspoken supporter of Whitefield and the awakening. Shurtleff was ordained at Newcastle, New Hampshire, in 1712. He married Mary Atkinson and did not have any children. He was installed at Portsmouth's South Church in 1733, serving there until his death in 1747. "He was eminent for piety and pastoral fidelity. During his ministry in Portsmouth, he baptized more than seven hundred, and admitted one hundred and thirty communicants to the church."[20] A later pastor of the South Church remarked that "his name will long be mentioned with respect, for his uncommon meekness and patience under great trials, and for his distinguished piety, talents and pastoral fidelity."[21]

Whitefield enjoyed a meal with Shurtleff and then proceeded on his return journey towards Boston. Whitefield's October 3, 1740 *Journals* narrative continued:

> After dinner I hastened to Hampstead and preached to several thousands of people with a great deal of life and power. Collected £41 for the orphan children . . . ;

Whitefield preaching in Hampstead, New Hampshire is an interesting highlight, since there was no finished church building in that community in 1740. Hampstead was first settled in 1728 as a farming community. These frontier settlers lived hard lives in log cabins, with little contact with the outside world. They hunted and farmed to survive, raised cattle, and were always on the alert for Indian attacks.[22] In 1733,

---

19 Paul C. Hughes, Anna Hughes, and Paul F. Hughes, *A Pleasant Abiding Place: A History of Greenland, New Hampshire*, (Greenland Historical Society, 2018), p. 95.
20 "South Church Papers—MS039," http://www.portsmouthathenaeum.org/findingains/ms039.htm.
21 Ibid.
22 Isaac W. Smith, *History of the Town of Hampstead, N.H.*, (Haverhill, MA: 1884), pp. 7-9.

a hearty group of twenty-five families lived in what is now Hampstead. They asked permission from their church in Haverhill, Massachusetts, to conduct Sunday church services themselves in homes in Hampstead, due to the great distance between their homes and the meeting house. They met "in a log house, probably patterned after the meeting houses of the early Puritans, with its thatched roof of hay or straw, and roughhewn logs for pulpit and seats."[23] Neighboring ministers probably preached on a rotating basis. When no minister was available, one of the men would read a previously published sermon. Since there were only a couple of hundred people living in this community in 1740, how is it that Whitefield could write in his *Journal*, "After dinner I hastened to Hampstead and preached to several thousands of people with a great deal of life and power." Where did the "several thousand people" come from?

On October 3, 1740, there was a huge outdoors preaching event in Hampstead that was the largest public meeting for many years in New Hampshire. The several thousand that heard Whitefield preach that day could never have fit within any building in Hampstead. Instead, Whitefield preached outside, probably in the field around the meeting house. The thousands of listeners must have come from Haverhill, about ten miles south of Hampstead, which was a much larger town and was the location of the original church members in Hampstead. Other listeners may have come from Londonderry, a Presbyterian settlement about fifteen miles west of Hampstead. Whitefield gives us very few details of this outdoors preaching event. He then continues his *Journals* account from Hampstead:

> set out directly for Newbury, which we reached at about eight at night; and was kindly entertained at a gentleman's house with all my friends. My heart was filled with joy.

The Toppan house was originally built in 1697. Rev. Christopher Toppan resided here. The home is on the main road from Newbury to Rowley. Whitefield rested here in October 1740.
Photograph by Ken Lawson.

Whitefield was now fully engaged in his circuit preaching, returning to locations he had previously visited. A few days prior he preached for Rev. Christopher Toppan of the First Church in Newbury. On Friday evening October 3, he reached Newbury, rested, and preached in the morning for Rev. John Lowell of the Third Church, now the First Church in Newburyport. Whitefield wrote of this as follows:

---

23 Harriett E. Noyes, *A Memorial History of Hampstead, New Hampshire*, (Boston, MA: George B. Reed, Publisher, 1903), p. 14.

> Saturday, October 4. Lay at the house of Mr. L, minister of the place. Preached in the morning to a very thronged congregation. Collected £80.

John Lowell of Newbury (later Newburyport) was ordained and installed as the first minister of the Third Parish, Newbury, in 1726. A Harvard graduate in 1721, he served in Newbury until his death in 1767. The official history of the church, written in 1933 after the congregation became Unitarian, speaks despairingly of Whitefield preaching in the church in 1740, calling him a "famous zealot" and "the foremost agitator" of the religious unrest of the Great Awakening. The author almost mocking stated that Whitefield "preached in barns." Yet the official church history of The First Religious Society in Newburyport, stated, "Mr. Lowell, usually most liberal, invited him [Whitefield] to preach in the meeting house. The invitation was never repeated, although, owing to Whitefield's flaming eloquence one hundred and forty-three souls were added to the parish list of communicants."[24] From Newbury, Whitefield had a short ride on a flat, well-travelled dirt road to Ipswich.

On October 4, 1740, Whitefield wrote in his *Journals*, "Hasted to Ipswich. Preached to a larger congregation than when there last. Collected £79 for the orphans." He had preached there a few days earlier, on September 30, sponsored by Rev. John Rogers. At his first visit to Ipswich, Whitefield wrote that he preached "to many thousands." Yet at his second visit he wrote that he spoke "to a larger congregation" than at his first visit.

An interesting legend developed related to Whitefield preaching in Ipswich in the fall of 1740. The fanciful account of "The Devil's Footprint" in Ipswich is marketed by the town as an intriguing tourist site.

This image is from a larger mural painted by Alan Pearsall at the Ipswich Riverwalk. Notice the Devil on the church steeple, and Whitefield preaching outside the meetinghouse on a large outcropping of rock. The "Devil's Footprint" in the rock is still visible today.

Source: "Devil's Footprint, Ipswich, Massachusetts," http://storiesfromipswich.org/2014/01/21/the-devils-footprint.

---

24 Minnie Atkinson, *A History of the First Religious Society in Newburyport, Massachusetts*, (Newburyport, MA: News Publishing Company, 1933), p. 22.

Imprinted into the rocks in front of the First Church in Ipswich is the footprint of the devil, left there forever in a legendary encounter with the traveling English evangelist George Whitefield in 1740. Young, energetic and extremely cross-eyed, the widely proclaimed Whitefield was on a tour of New England and this was his second trip to the church in Ipswich. On that early fall day he preached a long and energetic sermon of such great intensity that his voice could be heard for miles around. Thousands flocked to the Green. The church being insufficient in size for such a gathering, he made the ledge outside of the church his stage . . . What happened next has been told with infinite variations since that fateful day, but it is agreed by all that the devil and the young Reverend went right at it. They wrestled like maniacs, pushing and shoving each other back and forth. Whitefield gave chase and soon they were face to face at the pinnacle of the steeple with the horrified congregation watching below. The esteemed pastor uttered forth with his commanding voice accompanied by a mighty push. The devil was hurled to the rocks below, landed on one foot and scrambled down the hill in terrified leaps and bounds, never to return.[25]

This imprint in granite is located outside the current location of the First Church Congregational, Ipswich Massachusetts. Local tradition identifies this as the Devil's footprint. Photograph by Ken Lawson.

Whatever may be said about the Devil's footprint story, Whitefield was experiencing sensational results from his itinerant preaching.

There is a surviving account from Whitefield preaching in 1740 in Ipswich, outside on an outcropping of a ledge of granite near the Congregational meeting house. In an article titled, "The Old Man and Whitefield's Pulpit," the account states that a visitor to Ipswich on a Sunday morning was listening to the church bell ring and watching the townsfolk walk to the church building. The account is undated but probably occurred in the late 1700s. The visitor met an Ipswich old-timer who asked the stranger if he had ever heard of George Whitefield. When the visitor stated he had, the elderly gentleman stated:

> Well, I've seen Whitefield. George Whitefield stood on this very stone, [dropping his stick feebly from his shaking hands,] and I heard him preach here. And do you remember anything

---

25 "Devil's Footprint, Ipswich, Massachusetts," http://storiesfromipswich.org/2014/01/21/the-devils-footprint.

about him? I asked. Well, I guess I do. I was but a bit of a boy then; but here he stood on this stone, looking like a flying angel, and we call it Whitefield's Pulpit to this day . . . here were folks here from all parts to hear him, so he was obliged to preach outside; for the church wasn't half big enough for'em, and no two ways about it. I've heard many parsons since that time, but none of 'em could come nigh him any how they could fix it. Do you remember any thing of his sermon? I enquired. O, I was too young to notice aught, sir, but the preacher hisself and the crowds of people, but I know he had a very sweet voice, and, as I said, when he spread his arms out, with a little Bible in his hand, he looked like a flying angel. There never were so many people afore, nor since, in old Ipswich.[26]

On October 4, 1740, Whitefield wrote in his *Journals*, "Got to Salem about eight at night, where I was kindly received by Colonel P., and also favored with a visit from the minister belonging to the Church of England."

Colonel William Pepperell was a merchant and militia soldier, a native of Kittery, Maine, which was then part of Massachusetts. He became very wealthy through shipping and trading businesses. He served on the Massachusetts's Governor's Council from 1727 to 1759, and was a chief justice of the Court of Common Pleas. Pepperell was probably in Salem attending to his shipping and trading obligations. He was an active member of the First Church in York, under Rev. Samuel Moody. Previously, Whitefield had spoken outside in Salem on September 29, with two thousand in attendance. On Whitefield's return visit to Salem, Pepperell noted that he received "a visit from the minister belonging to the Church of England."

St. Peter's Episcopal Church in Salem was established in 1733, with a wooden church building constructed in 1734. The land was donated by a local merchant, Philip English. English and his wife had been falsely accused of witchcraft during the hysteria of the Salem witchcraft trials of 1692. The original church structure was taken down in 1833, replaced by a Gothic stone building that still stands today in downtown Salem. The Church of England minister who met with Whitefield in Salem was Rev. Charles Brockwell. A graduate of Cambridge in England, Brockwell came to America as a missionary to Salem in October 1738.[27] As the Rector of St. Peter's, Brockwell was concerned about Whitefield's preaching style and evangelical doctrines. Both men had Church of England ordinations and could readily communicate on church polity and theology. Brockwell was forty-four years old when he met the twenty-six year-old Whitefield. He was a cautious observer of Whitefield when the itinerant came through Salem several days prior. Brockwell had the chance to think through what he saw and heard, and he had the time to speak to others in Salem and at St. Peter's Church about Whitefield.

When he returned to Salem, Whitefield wrote in his *Journals* that he was "favored with a visit from the minister belonging to the Church of England." We do not have a record of the conversation between Brockwell and Whitefield, but we do know that Brockwell consented to have Whitefield speak at St. Peter's Church, twice on a Sunday. This was a clear, public endorsement of Whitefield by Brockwell. In his *Journals*, Whitefield wrote about his preaching at St. Peter's Church in Salem.

> Sunday, October 5. Preached at eight in the morning, in the meeting house, at the minister's request. Read prayers, and assisted in the Sacrament, in the Church of England; but thought matters were not at all carried on with decency and order. Preached again, in the afternoon, in the meeting house, and collected £72 for the orphans.

As a missionary with the Church of England, under the Society for the Propagation of the Gospel to Foreign Parts, Brockwell was well-received by his congregation in Salem. "In a letter to the Society in

---

26 Joseph B. Wakeley, *Anecdotes of the Rev. George Whitefield, M.A.*, (London: 1772), p. 387.
27 Charles S. Osgood, *Historical Sketch of Salem, 1626-1879*, (Salem, MA: Essex Institute, 1879), p. 87.

England, soon after this period, the wardens and vestry of the church expressed the highest satisfaction at the appointment of Mr. Brockwell, and spoke of him in the warmest terms of approbation."[28] As Whitefield wrote above, the "meeting house" was St. Peter's Episcopal Church. One wonders what the Congregational ministers in Salem thought of Whitefield preaching for them the week before, and then the next week preaching in the Episcopal Church.

Continuing his circuit riding route in revisiting places where he had previously preached, Whitefield returned to Marblehead. He wrote in his *Journals*:

> Monday, October 6. Set out from Salem at nine this morning. Preached in Marble Head about eleven; and the Lord attended His word with such power, that I trust it will be a day to be remembered by many souls. I was upon the mount myself. The two ministers presented me with £72 for the orphans, which they had voluntarily collected yesterday, in their own private meetings. Was most affectionately received and entertained by Col. M.

The two ministers that collected a generous offering for Whitefield's orphan house in Georgia were the Congregationalist Rev. John Barnard, and Rev. Alexander Malcom of St. Michael's Episcopal Church. A Monday morning sermon, in a working-class maritime community such as Marblehead, was a unique experience, but Whitefield did it, saying it was "a day to be remembered."

The final stop on Whitefield's itinerant preaching tour north of Boston was at Malden, Massachusetts. This was his first opportunity to speak in this historic town. Malden was founded by Puritans in 1640. Several years before Whitefield arrived, the town boundaries for Malden were rewritten because of expanding population. This divided longstanding parishes and discontent was common in the meeting houses.[29] Perhaps the unsettled religious state in Malden contributed to the weak reception Whitefield received. Whitefield recorded in his *Journals*:

> [October 6, 1740] At the request of the Rev. Mr. E., son-in-law of the dear Mr. Moody, we went to Maulden, fourteen miles from Marble Head, where I preached, but not with so much power as in the morning.

While in Malden, Whitefield was hosted by Rev. Joseph Emerson. Born in 1700, Emerson was a Harvard graduate in 1717. He taught school in York, Newbury, and Malden, Massachusetts. While in York he attended the First Church under Rev. Samuel Moody, and married Moody's daughter Mary in 1721. He was invited to preach at Malden, and was ordained there October 31, 1721. His pastorate there lasted forty-six years until his death. One account of Emerson stated, "His sermons were carefully prepared, written out, and delivered with earnestness and force; several of them were published."[30] On July 31, 1724, his parsonage was burned down. A public contribution was taken up, and within a short time a new parsonage was erected. A larger meeting house was built in 1730. He was respected as a man with "a reputation as a scholar, who delighted in scholarly studies." Further speaking of Joseph Emerson:

> Though a prolonged and fierce conflict raged in the town, during his ministry, respecting the location of the meeting house, yet he was not reproached by any as the cause. He was a positive man, spoke openly and preached faithfully, but appears to have retained the respect of both parties. He must have been a man of vigorous health, as during his long ministry of more than forty-five

---

28 *The Gospel Advocate . . . for the Year 1822*, (Boston, MA: Joseph W. Ingraham, Printer, 1822), pp. 341-342.
29 Deloraine P. Corey, *The History of Malden, Massachusetts, 1633-1785*, (Malden, MA: Printed by the Author, 1899), pp. 632-638.
30 "Family of Deacon Edward Emerson (12774) and Rebecca Waldo Emerson," Pane-Joyce Genealogy, http://aleph0.clarku.edu/~djoyce/gen/report/rr13/rr13/_018.html.

years, he lost but two Sabbaths by sickness. The town record of his death states that he had been in the Judgment of charity a faithful minister here, and that for the space of forty and five years, deceased in the evening very soon after lying down to sleep who was cheerily and in health before.[31]

Whitefield's 1740 preaching tour north of Boston lasted from September 19, when he arrived in Marblehead, to October 6, when he returned to Boston. For these seventeen days he preached one or twice daily, in meeting houses and in open fields. The weather appears to have fully cooperated. His *Journals* does not record any health issues. He received warm welcomes almost everywhere he preached. A few other locations were more cautious. Tens of thousands of northern New Englanders heard Whitefield preach in what are now the states of Massachusetts, New Hampshire, and Maine. In his *Journals*, Whitefield concluded his comments about his northern New England tour by writing,

> I set out with them, immediately after sermon, and got privately into Boston at about seven at night . . . Though I had ridden a hundred and seventy eight miles, and preached sixteen times, yet I was not in the least wearied. I went to rest, full of peace, and desiring to be thankful to the Lord, for causing me thus to renew my strength. Oh, what a good master is Jesus Christ!

---

31 Ibid. See also *Manual of the First Church, Malden. May 1878.* (Boston, MA: Beacon Press, 1878), p. 4.

CHAPTER 6

WHITEFIELD IN BOSTON

OCTOBER 1740

WHITEFIELD DEPARTED BOSTON ON SEPTEMBER 19 for a preaching circuit in the northeast. When he returned on October 6, the city was unsettled. Boston had never heard or seen such a preaching sensation. Whitefield's oratorical skills enamored Boston. Tens of thousands of Bostonians heard Whitefield preach for the first time. Then, as his manner was, he departed and later returned to sow the gospel seeds that he had previously watered. Now, upon his return to Boston, the crowds thronged to hear him. As he reentered Boston, he wrote in his *Journals*, "My health has much improved since I left Boston."[1]

Boston was enamored by Whitefield. Some went to hear him under deep spiritual conviction. Others were simply curious. Some only wanted to be part of the huge assemblies on the Boston Common, as unprecedented tens of thousands flocked to hear his outdoors preaching. A few mocked him. In the mid-eighteenth century, Boston was an educated, cultured, and wealthy city. The port bustled with activity. European cultural refinements in dress and household comforts were common among the wealthy. A distinct merchant middle class prospered, while an underside of the city was known for stealing, corruption, prostitution, and assaults. After his tour of New England's northern port cities, Whitefield resumed his overwhelmingly successful ministry in Boston. In his *Journals*, Whitefield wrote:

> Tuesday, October 7. Preached, both morning and evening, in Dr. Coleman's meeting house, with much power. People seemed greatly rejoiced at my arrival, it being reported that I had died suddenly, or was poisoned.

An undated woodcut image of a younger Whitefield, from Justin Winsor, The Memorial History of Boston . . . 1630-1880, p. 238.

---

1 George Whitefield, *George Whitefield's Journals*, (1756; reprinted by Banner of Truth Trust, Carlisle, PA, 1985), p. 468. All the Journal entries in this chapter fall between pages 469-474.

59

Dr. Benjamin Colman was the senior pastor of the Brattle Street Church. A few weeks earlier, Whitefield preached "to about four thousand"[2] for Colman. He also attended a service on a Sunday morning at Brattle Street, but he did not preach. After that service, Whitefield had a meal with Colman and his assistant, Rev. William Cooper. Apparently, Colman needed some personal assurances from Whitefield related to doctrine and ministerial practices. Now, a few weeks later, Whitefield was invited to preach in the Brattle Street Church, twice on a Tuesday, to a large and receptive audience. Whitefield was a sensation. Capitalizing on Whitefield's popularity, in early October 1740, the *Boston News-Letter* printed an advertisement for a just published two-volume collection of Whitefield's sermons.[3] Whitefield's *Journals* continued:

> Wednesday, October 8. Went with the governor in his coach, to Mr. Webb's meeting house, where I preached both morning and evening, to very great auditories. Both times, Jesus Christ manifested forth His glory. Many hearts were melted down. I think I never was so drawn out to pray for little children, and invite little children to Jesus Christ, as I was this morning. I had just heard of a child, whom after hearing me preach, was immediately taken sick, and died. This encouraged me to speak to little ones; but, oh, how were the old people effected, when I said, "Little children, if your parents will not come to Christ, do you come, and go to heaven without them. There seemed to be but few dry eyes. I have not seen such a great commotion since my preaching at Boston. Glory be to God, who has not forgotten to be gracious! Went with the governor, in his coach, to my lodgings. Gave a word of exhortation to a great crowd of people, and afterwards slipped out privately, by a back door, and went to a man's house, whose wife and sister, as well as himself, I trust the Lord will visit with His salvation. Amen.

Rev. Jonathan Webb was the first minister of the New North Church, on Hanover Street in Boston. He served there from 1714 to his death in 1750. The church met in a wooden building first constructed in 1714. Webb was a British military chaplain stationed in Boston when he accepted the call to serve at the New North Church. Whitefield previously spoke for Webb at his meeting house on September 22, to thousands. Whitefield was invited again to preach. But no revival occurred in this church, and no significant increase in church memberships was noted. For the 1740 period, a history of the New North Church spends several pages discussing ministerial controversies with no mention of Whitefield's two visits and no mention of an awakening.[4] As noted in the quote above, Massachusetts Governor Jonathan Belcher continued to support Whitefield. The next entry in Whitefield's *Journals* states:

> Thursday, October 9. Every morning, since my return, I have been applied to by many souls under distress, and was grieved that I could not have more time with them. Gave, this morning, the public lecture at Dr. Sewall's meeting house, which was very much crowded. When I came near the meeting house, I found it much impressed upon my heart that I should preach upon our Lord's conference with Nicodemus. When I got into the pulpit, I saw a great number of ministers sitting around and before me. Coming to these words, "art thou a master in Israel, and knowest not these things?" the Lord enabled me to open my mouth boldly against unconverted ministers; for, I am persuaded, the generality of preachers talk of an unknown and unfelt Christ. The reason why congregations have been so dead is, because they had dead men preaching to them. O that the Lord may quicken and revive them! How can dead men beget living children?

---

2   George Whitefield, *George Whitefield's Journals*, p. 459.
3   Boston News-Letter, October 7, 1740, p. 2.
4   Arthur Fuller, *An Historical Discourse Delivered in the New North Church, October 1, 1854*, (Boston, MA: Crosby, Nichols & Company, 1854), pp. 5-6.

The above-mentioned Rev. Samuel Sewell of the South Church was one of the most widely respected ministers in New England. His endorsement of Whitefield carried a lot of weight in the Boston community. One person greatly influenced by Whitefield in Boston in 1740 was Samuel Adams.

Samuel Adams had just graduated from Harvard when Whitefield preached in Boston. As an infant, Adams was baptized by Rev. Samuel Checkley at the New North Church. Adams was deeply moved by hearing Whitefield preach, and he was among the throngs on the Boston Common to listen to the eloquent itinerant. Three decades later, Samuel Adams would be a household name in the American Colonies as a patriot leader in Boston against the British. But in 1740, Adams was an impressionable eighteen-year-old that accepted Whitefield's message. Adams was never an outspoken evangelical Christian, but shortly after hearing Whitefield preach, he became a full member of the Brattle Street Church. At that time, church membership required a conversion testimony, and Adams was accepted as a church member by Rev. Benjamin Colman. A biographer of Adams stated, "It is unquestionable that Whitefield's visit to Boston left a lasting impression on Samuel Adams. Forty years later, in December of 1780, Adams wrote to a friend how Whitefield 'Thundered in the pulpit against Assemblies & Balls.'"[5] Whitefield's *Journals* narrative continued:

> Thursday, October 9. In the afternoon, I preached, on the common, to about fifteen thousand people, and collected upward of £200 for the orphans . . . .I went to the almshouse, and preached on these words, "The poor received the gospel," for near half an hour; then I went to the work-house, where I prayed with and exhorted a great number of people, who crowded after me, besides those belonging to the house, for near an hour more; and then, hearing there was a considerable number waiting at my lodgings, God strengthened me to give them a spiritual morsel. Soon after, I retired to rest.

> Friday, October 10. Was still busied, from the very moment I arose until I went out, in answering those that had come to me under great distress. About nine, went with Mr. Cooper over Charleston ferry, where I preached with much freedom of spirit, and collected £156 for the orphans. I dined at Mystick, at the house of Mr. R, a rich young man, who has seemed much affected for some time. O that he may not lack one thing! Immediately after dinner, we hastened to Reading, twelve miles from Charleston, where I preached to many thousands, and collected £51 for the orphans. A considerable moving was discernible in the congregation.

After a remarkable preaching event on the Boston Common to fifteen thousand people, Whitefield again hit the road as an itinerant preacher. The above quote states that Whitefield crossed the ferry and preached in Charlestown "with much freedom of spirit." It was only a few miles to the ferry that crossed the Charles River. Charlestown was a Puritan enclave founded just outside of Boston in 1628. Charlestown was a fishing and farming community, currently confined to a peninsula, but in the early eighteenth century the town was massive. Many wealthy and influential colonial leaders lived in Charlestown. When Whitefield arrived in October 1740, the ministers in Charlestown were the elderly Rev. Simon Bradstreet, and his associate, Rev. Thomas Prentice.

Born in New London, Connecticut, Bradstreet was a Harvard graduate in 1693, who was ordained in Charlestown in 1698. As he got older, Bradstreet developed some eccentricities. One account stated, "Simon Bradstreet . . . minister of Charlestown, Mass., was a man of great classical attainments, but of an infirm constitution and desponding temperament."[6] Another account of his infirmities as an older

---

5   Ira Stoll, *Samuel Adams: A Life*, (New York: Free Press, 2008), p. 21.
6   Francis M. Caulkins, *History of New London, Connecticut* . . . , (New London, CT: Published by the Author, 1860), p. 17.

man stated, "He was very learned, with a tenacious memory and lively imagination, but of melancholy disposition. He was considered one of the first literary characters and best preachers in America. For some years prior to his death he was afraid to preach from his pulpit, and delivered his sermons from the deacon's seat, using no notes."[7]

Whitefield was met in Charleston by the elderly Bradstreet and his associate, Thomas Prentice. Beginning at the church in 1739, Prentice spent decades in Charlestown. He died in 1782. One report of Whitefield preaching in Charlestown said, "Here the Rev. George Whitefield preached to crowded congregations, and the great revival of [1740] ensued, where there were sixty-six admissions to the church—the largest number in any year. The chair and the Bible that he used are still preserved."[8]

In this journal, Whitefield wrote, "immediately after dinner, we hastened to Reading, twelve miles from Charleston, where I preached to many thousands, and collected £51 for the orphans. A considerable moving was discernible in the congregation." The First Church in Reading, Massachusetts, was founded in 1645. The church slowly grew as the town developed. During the 1692 Salem witch hysteria, Reading was deeply affected, with eight women accused of sorcery and one who died in jail. Rev. William Hobby was the sixth minister of the First Church. He was installed in 1733 and served there until his death in 1765. Hobby was one of the "many thousands" who heard Whitefield preach in Reading on October 10, 1740.

William Hobby was born in Boston in 1707 and was a Harvard graduate in 1725. Apparently, when Whitefield came to Reading to preach, Hobby was not initially a supporter. But hearing Whitefield changed his mind. One account stated:

> Rev. William Hobby . . . In 1733, the town of Reading invited him to settle as minister of the First Parish . . . Mr. Hobby was ordained in that town in September 1733 . . . In 1741 [actually 1740] Rev. Whitefield preached on Reading Common. Mr. Hobby went to hear him, and it is said that he afterwards remarked, "that he went to pick a hole in Whitefield's coat, but that Whitefield picked a hole in his (Hobby's) heart."[9]

For the rest of his life, Hobby would be an outspoken advocate of Whitefield, often ridiculed for his support of the itinerant evangelist. Hobby was described as follows; "He was distinguished for his natural endowments . . . He preached with great fluency, copiousness and unction, and was a staunch advocate for the doctrines of Calvinism."[10] Another account stated that Hobby "was a learned and pious man, an able writer and forceful speaker." On the Sabbath it was said that he wore "showy sacerdotal vestments" and that "he entered the temple of the Lord and ascended to the pulpit with dignity and majesty. He died, June 18, 1765, in Reading, after a ministry of thirty-two years."[11] Whitefield's *Journals* narrative continued:

> Saturday, October 11. Was weak in body, having taken cold. But preaching, I find, is a constant remedy against all indispositions. Went again to Cambridge, four miles from Mystick, and preached, at the meeting-house door, to a great body of people, who stood very attentively (though it rained), and were much affected. It being a university town, I discoursed on these

---

7 James G. Wilson & John Fiske, editors, Appleton's *Cyclopedia of American Biography*, (New York: D. Appleton & Company, 1887), vol. I, p. 354.
8 James F. Hunnewell, *A Century of Town Life: A History of Charlestown, Massachusetts* . . . , (Boston, MA: Little, Brown & Company, 1888), p. 184.
9 Oliver A. Roberts, *History of the Military Company of the Massachusetts, now called the Ancient and Honorable Artillery Company, 1637-1888*, (Boston, MA: Alfred Mudge & Son, Printers, 1888), vol. II, p. 48.
10 William B. Sprague, *Annals of the American Pulpit: Unitarianism Congregational*, (New York: Robert Carter & Brothers, 1865), vol. III, p. 132.
11 Oliver A. Roberts, *History of the Military Company*, p. 48.

words, "Noah, the eighth person, a preacher of righteousness;" and endeavored to shew the qualifications for a true evangelical preacher of Christ's righteousness. I spoke very plainly to tutors and pupils.

As stated, Whitefield preached in Cambridge "at the meeting-house door" of the First Church Congregational. Founded in 1633, the First Church was meeting in its third meeting house, built in 1706. When Whitefield arrived in 1740, this church ministered both to the Cambridge community and to Harvard College. It had an educated, wealthy, and cultured membership. The minister of the First Church was Rev. Nathaniel Appleton, who was born in Ipswich, Massachusetts, and was a Harvard graduate in 1712. Initially, Appleton was swept up in the Whitefield phenomena, and allowed the itinerant to preach on the meeting house steps, as the crowd was too large to all fit inside. But Appleton was clearly not a supporter of Whitefield. Shortly after Whitefield departed New England, Appleton would take to his study to write various pamphlets against Whitefield's methods and theology. One writer stated, "Although Calvinistic in persuasion and sincerely pious in conviction and practice, Appleton was not a real friend of the Great Awakening. In fact, his position was without question anti-revival."[12]

This 1767 sketch by Paul Revere of Harvard College is a view from the west.
Source: "List of Colonial Colleges," https://enacademic.com/dic.nsf/enwiki/11563792.

Whitefield wrote of Cambridge, that it was "a university town" and that he "spoke very plainly to tutors and pupils." The president of Harvard College in Cambridge was Edward Holyoke, who served from 1739-69 until he died in office. As was Appleton of the First Church, so was Holyoke caught up in the Whitefield sensation, and he allowed Whitefield to preach to the college faculty and students. Also like Appleton, Holyoke proved later not to be a supporter of the awakening, and he likewise wrote pamphlets critical of Whitefield's theology and methodology. Appleton and Holyoke saw the revival movement as a disturbance of the established church order, as a disorderly movement of sensationalism and misguided theology, and as a detriment to the student life at Harvard. But for now, in the fall of 1740, Whitefield was welcomed to Cambridge with no apparent reservations. In fact, about seven months after Whitefield departed, Holyoke wrote a pamphlet defending Whitefield, calling him a "pious and valuable" man of God who has been "greatly instrumental in the hands of God, in reviving His blessed work; and many, no doubt, have been savingly converted from the errors of their ways, many more have been convicted, and

---

12 Richard O. Roberts, *Whitefield in Print*, (Wheaton, IL: Richard Owen Roberts Publishers, 1988), p. 70.

all have been in some measure roused from their lethargy."[13] But Holyoke's approval of Whitefield would later change.

A Harvard College tutor who heard Whitefield in 1740 was Mr. Henry Flynt. His extensive diary is a key document recording daily activities in pre-Revolutionary War Cambridge and Boston. Flynt wrote of Whitefield,

> He appears to be a good man, and sincerely desirous to do good to the souls of sinners; he is very apt to judge harshly, and censure, in the severest terms, those that differ from his scheme . . . I think he is a composition of a great deal of good and some bad; and I pray God to grant success to what is well designed and acted by him.[14]

After preaching in Cambridge to the residents and the Harvard faculty and students, Whitefield re-crossed the Charles River on a ferry and returned to Boston. His *Journals* continued,

> [October 11] About four we reached Boston, where I preached immediately, in Dr. Sewall's meeting-house. I exhorted a great number afterwards at my lodgings; and then was employed, till near midnight, in settling my private affairs, answering letters, and speaking to those under conviction.

Rev. Joseph Sewell of the South Church was a leading minister in Boston. He was the son of Chief Justice Samuel E. Sewall and Hannah Hull. His family genealogy was directly in line with the Puritan founders of Massachusetts. It was unusual to have a Saturday afternoon preaching event, but Sewell opened the doors of his meeting house to allow Whitefield to preach. The above quote shows another side of Whitefield. Most people saw him as an eloquent preacher, a public figure that could draw the masses and keep their attention with his oratory skills. But another side of Whitefield was his personal work with individuals, his meeting with people face-to-face for religious counseling, or as he put it above, "speaking to those under conviction." This often consumed many hours of his time late into the night. In addition, Whitefield was a prolific correspondent and journalist. Hundreds of his letters survive, and his *Journals* narrated his daily activities:

> Sunday, October 12. Spoke to as many as I could, who came for spiritual advice. Preached, with great power at Dr. Sewall's meeting-house, which was so exceedingly thronged, that I was obliged to get in at one of the windows . . . .Went with the Governor in his coach, to the common, where I preached my farewell sermon to nearly twenty-thousand people—a sight I have not seen since I left Blackhearth—and a sight, perhaps never seen before in America. It being nearly dusk before I had done, the sight was more solemn. Numbers, great numbers, melted into tears, when I talked of leaving them. I was very particular in my application, both to rulers, ministers and people, and exhorted my hearers steadily to imitate the piety of their forefathers; so that I might hear, that with one heart and mind, they were striving together for the faith of the Gospel.

It seems almost unimaginable today that a church meeting would be so crowded, that the minister had to climb through a window to enter the building to preach to the masses. But this is what happened to Whitefield at the South Church in Boston. Further, the 20,000 people that attended Whitefield's farewell sermon in Boston is a stunning number. Dallimore stated, "Apparently the vast majority of the inhabitants of Boston were there and many from outlying towns."[15] Philip wrote, "The effect at Boston was amazing . . . Such was

---

13 Edward Holyoke, *The Duty of Ministers of the Gospel to Guard Against the Pharisaism and Sadduceeism of the Present Day*, (Boston, MA: Printed by Thomas Fleet, 1741).
14 Quoted in Justin Winsor, *The Memorial History of Boston . . .* , (Boston, MA: Ticknor and Company, 1881), vol. II, p. 234.
15 Arnold Dallimore, *George Whitefield: The Life and Times of the Great Evangelist of the Eighteenth Century Revival*, (Carlisle, PA: Banner of Truth Trust, 1979), vol. I, p. 533.

the interest excited by his preaching, that his farewell sermon was attended by 20,000 persons. And, during his visit, it was testified by the first authorities in the city, that many of the careless were awakened, and more of the lukewarm quickened."[16] Stout recorded, "In this case, the audience at his farewell sermon on Boston Common—estimated at twenty thousand—was all inclusive. Magistrates and Harvard students, almshouse residents and slaves, friends and enemies all attended. None could stay away . . . In fact, there had never been a larger crowd in America to that date."[17] Whitefield gave a summary of his Boston experience in his *Journal*:

> Sunday, October 12. Boston is a large, populous place, and very wealthy . . . One thing Boston is very remarkable for, *viz.*, the external observance of the Sabbath. Men in civil offices have a regard for religion. The Governor encourages them; and the minister and magistrates seem to be more united than in any other place where I have been. Both were exceedingly civil during my stay . . . They were greatly affected by the Word, followed night and day, and were very liberal to my dear orphans. I promised, God willing, to visit them again when it shall please Him to bring me again from my native country.

News of Whitefield's preaching success spread rapidly. Invitations to preach came to him from various locations. For example, Rev. Stephen Williams of the Congregational Church in Longmeadow, Massachusetts, about one hundred miles from Boston, heard of Whitefield's preaching and desired the evangelist to preach in Longmeadow. Williams wrote in his diary:

> Oct. 11, 1740. I hear of ye Extraordinary Labors & Services of the Rev'd Mr. Whitefield in one place & another—Ye Lord Grant yet much good may be done by his servant—to ye Souls of his people. I pray God, to prepare me for his holy day.

> Oct. 14, 1740. I have wrote a letter, to the Rev'd Mr. Whitefield to desire him to preach among us, if he does come—I desire it may be to our Edification & real benefit & advantage.[18]

Many eyewitnesses recorded their thoughts on Whitefield's 1740 Boston ministry, and a few will now be considered. Bostonian Paul Dudley wrote:

> Mr. Whitefield is without doubt a very extraordinary man, full of zeal . . . His preaching seems to be much like that of the old English Puritans. It was not so much the matter of his sermons, as the very serious, earnest, and affectionate delivery of them without notes, that gained him such a multitude of hearers. The main subject of his preaching while here were the nature and necessity of regeneration, or conversion, and justification by the righteousness of Christ by faith alone.[19]

Another eyewitness of Whitefield's preaching tour in and around Boston was from Rev. Thomas Prince, of the Old South Church in Boston. Prince recorded:

> Upon Mr. Whitefield leaving us, great numbers in this town were so happily concerned about their souls, as we had never seen anything like it before . . . And their desires were excited to hear ministers more than ever; so that our assemblies, both on lectures and Sabbaths, were

---

16   Robert Philip, *The Life and Times of George Whitefield*, (1837: reprinted by Banner of Truth Trust, Carlisle, PA: 2007, p. 152.
17   Harry Stout, *The Divine Dramatist: George Whitefield and the Rise of Modern Evangelicalism*, (Grand Rapids, MI: Eerdman's Publishing, 1991), p. 125.
18   Stephen Williams, *Diary of Stephen Williams, Longmeadow, Massachusetts*, (Longmeadow, MA: Richard S. Storrs Library, 2011), p. 330.
19   Justin Winsor, *The Memorial History of Boston . . .* , p. 233.

surprisingly increased. And now the people wanted to hear us oftener, in consideration of which a public lecture was proposed to be set up at Dr. Colman's church, near the midst of the town, on every Tuesday evening . . . When the evening came, the house seemed to be crowded as much as if Mr. Whitefield was there. It was the first stated evening lecture in these parts of the world.[20]

Zaccheus Collins of Lynn, Massachusetts was a farmer and a merchant. Born in 1689 in Lynn, he was a married Quaker with seven children, not all of whom lived to adulthood. Collins was a selectman in Lynn. In 1740 in his *Diary,* he made the following eyewitness remarks on George Whitefield. "October 22. At Boston round through Charleston, heard the Great Preacher George Whitefield preach on the Common at Boston." His *Diary* then has several daily entries related to town business, cleaning out his well, deaths in town, family news, and the weather. His next Whitefield reference stated; "October 29. The Great preacher George Whitefield preached in the training field at Marblehead in the fore noon & likewise at Salem in the after noon to a great number of hearers."[21]

As his ministry around Boston came to an end, Whitefield recorded in his *Letters,* "God works by me, I think, more than ever. I am quite well in bodily health. Ministers as well as people are stirred up, and the government is exceedingly civil. In short, God is doing greater things than can be expressed."[22]

By Tuesday, October 14, 1740 Whitefield left Boston. A few weeks after Whitefield departed the Boston area, Rev. Samuel Dexter of Dedham recalled Whitefield's visit. Dedham is about twelve miles southwest of Boston. A Harvard graduate in 1720, Dexter served in Dedham from 1724 to 1755. Dexter wrote in his diary,

October 23, 1740. I have lately enjoyed ye Ministry of ye Dear Servant of Christ Mr. Whitefield, by whose ministry I was greatly Affected, & I humbly hope greatly benefited. Ten Thousand, Thousands Worlds would I give, if I had them, to feel & Experience what I believe ye Man of God does.[23]

At first, it appeared that Whitefield's labors were overwhelmingly successful. However, such was not always the case. Many that remained silent upon his initial visit to Boston later began to preach and write against Whitefield. The religious fervor which remained in Boston and much of New England after October 1740 divided churches, instigated public riots, caused ministers to be expelled from their pulpits, and created an enormous gulf between the advocates of the revival and those who supported established approaches to religion. Congregations split. New churches were founded in numerous communities, and hundreds were added to those congregations that supported Whitefield. Yet, to others the awakening was merely an emotional disturbance to be avoided at any cost. Once Whitefield left, the pamphlet war began.

An image of Rev. Thomas Prince of the Old South Church, Boston, c. 1745.

Source: www.christianitytoday.com.

---

20 Ibid., pp. 233-234.
21 Zaccheus Collins, *Diary of Zaccheus Collins of Lynn, 1726-1769,* (original manuscript courtesy of the Peabody Essex Museum, Phillips Library, Rowley, MA), vol. I, p. 229.
22 George Whitefield, *Works of George Whitefield,* (1771: reprinted by Quinta Press, Shropshire, England: 2000), vol. I, p. 217.
23 Samuel Dexter, "Diary of Rev. Samuel Dexter," *The New England Historical and Genealogical Register for the Year 1860,* (Boston, MA: Samuel G. Drake, Publisher, 1860), vol. xiv, p. 205.

CHAPTER 7

WHITEFIELD'S TOUR IN CENTRAL MASSACHUSETTS

OCTOBER 13-21, 1740

FOR THE PREVIOUS FOUR WEEKS, Whitefield had a remarkable ministry in Boston and locations north and northeast of the city. He had the unqualified support of Massachusetts Governor Jonathan Belcher. Whitefield preached for the leading ministers at the largest churches in Boston, almost always to overflow crowds. He preached at the influential Harvard College, where most of the clergy of Massachusetts were trained. Then Whitefield completed a preaching tour into northeast Massachusetts, into New Hampshire, and into what would eventually be called the state of Maine. Circling back, he returned to Boston. Then it was time for another preaching tour.

One of the western Massachusetts Colony ministers who supported Whitefield, and hoped for a visit from the traveling preacher, was Rev. Stephen Williams of Longmeadow. In his 1740 *Diary*, Williams wrote, "October 11. I hear of ye extra ordinary labors—& services of the Rev. Mr. Whitefield in one place and another—the Lord grant much good may be done by His servant . . . ." A few days later he wrote, "October 14. "I have wrote a letter, to the Rev. Mr. Whitefield to desire him to preach among us, if he does come—I desire it may be to our sanctification & real benefit & advantage . . . ."[1]

Before Whitefield departed the Boston area for a westerly preaching tour, he preached at the First Church in Newton. This community was originally part of Cambridge, but growing populations meant a new town was designated in 1681. Rev. John Cotton (1693-1757) served the church from 1714 to his death. He came from four generations of Puritan ministers in Boston, his great grandfather being the patriarch Rev. John Cotton of the First Church, Boston. "George Whitefield preached in Newton, in November [October] 1740, to a crowded audience."[2] Over the next eighteen months, Rev. Cotton saw rapid growth in his congregation. With the approval of Cotton, Whitefield "preached in Newton before crowded and attentive audiences." Specifically, from June 1741 to April 1742, there were one hundred and four new members added to the First Church in Newton.[3]

Rev. John Cotton was initially happy to have Whitefield preach in his church. On July 3, 1743, he sighed a ministerial declaration in support of Whitefield.[4] But ongoing rivalries and dissensions caused him to reconsider. Even with tremendous church growth, in January 1745, Cotton signed a petition

---

1 Stephen Williams, *Stephen Williams Diary*, (transcribed and printed by the Town of Longmeadow, MA), vol. 4, p. 330.
2 Francis Jackson, *A History of the Early Settlement of Newton . . . Massachusetts . . . from 1639 to 1800*, (Boston, MA: Stacy and Richardson Printers, 1854), p. 131.
3 Samuel F. Smith, *History of Newton, Massachusetts: Town and City, from its Earliest Settlement to the Present Time, 16330-1880*, (Boston, MA: American Logotype Company, 1880), p. 219.
4 Joseph Tracy, *The Great Awakening: A History of the Revival of Religion in the Time of Edwards & Whitefield*, (1842: reprinted by Banner of Truth Trust, Carlisle, PA, 1989), p. 295.

denouncing Whitefield and the ongoing disputes within churches.[5] One example of these church disputes was evidenced by Mr. Nathan Ward of Newton. Ward was a member of Cotton's church. As a Whitefield convert, Mr. Ward gathered townsfolk around him and hosted church meetings in his home. This small but zealous New Light group ordained Ward and considered him their minister, much to the ongoing discomfort of Rev. Cotton.[6]

Whitefield began a Fall, 1740 preaching tour towards towns in western Massachusetts. On October 13, Whitefield preached in Concord, almost twenty miles west of Boston, to thousands in the open air. He wrote in his *Journals*:

> Monday, October 13. Took an affectionate leave of many dear friends, especially of my kind host and hostess, who have been exceedingly kind to me and mine, and wept at my departure from them. Went with the Governor, in his Coach, to Charleston ferry, where he handed me into the boat, kissed me, reached Concord, eighteen miles from Boston, where I preached to some thousands in the open air. The hearers were melted down. About £45 were collected for the orphans. The minister of the town being, I believe, a child of God, I chose to stay all night at his house, that we might rejoice together.[7]

The minister in Concord that hosted Whitefield was Rev. Daniel Bliss. A Yale College graduate in 1732, Bliss served the First Church in Concord from 1739 to 1764. Bliss was widely known as a "New Light" minister, as one who fully endorsed the revivals spreading throughout New England in the 1740s. Whitefield preached for Bliss in the meeting house that was constructed in 1711. The official church history of the First Parish Church in Concord states:

> Mr. Bliss was most earnest in his dedication to God and truth as he saw it. His was the era of the Great Awakening and evangelists, and Rev. Bliss was becoming a crusading evangelist himself, to the disdain of some parishioners. He invited the British evangelist George Whitefield to come here and preach. He [Whitefield] held outdoor mass meetings and preached such a dynamic sermon on one occasion that they all ended up "weeping on each other's shoulders."[8]

After Concord, Whitefield then headed west into central Massachusetts, intent on meeting the well-respected Rev. Jonathan Edwards of Northampton. Whitefield's *Journals* notes:

> Tuesday, October 14. Reached Sudbury, six miles from Concord, about ten. Preached to some thousands, and observed a considerable commotion in the assembly. Got to Marlboro, eight miles from Sudbury, about four, where I preached to a large congregation. At first my heart seemed dead, and I had but little freedom; but before I had finished, the Word came with such demonstration of the Spirit, that great numbers were melted down.[9]

Two towns are mentioned in Whitefield's *Journals* entry, namely Sudbury and Marlboro. Sudbury was an early inland Puritan settlement from 1638. The first meeting house was built in 1643. By the time of Whitefield's arrival in Sudbury in October 1740, there were two Congregational Churches in Sudbury. Their ministers were Rev. Israel Loring and Rev. William Cook. Of Loring it was stated:

---

5   Ibid., p. 346
6   Samuel F. Smith, *History of Newton, Massachusetts*, pp. 290-292.
7   George Whitefield, *George Whitefield's Journals*, (1756: reprinted by Banner of Truth Trust, Carlisle, PA: 1985), p. 474.
8   Marian Wheeler, "Ministers of First Parish Church in Concord, 369 Years of Ministry," http://www.firstparish.org.
9   George Whitefield, *George Whitefield's Journals*, pp. 474.

Mr. Loring was a strong Calvinist, an earnest preacher and [a] somewhat noted minister. It is said he did not like the ways of Mr. Whitefield, the evangelist, and the excitement attendant upon his revivals; and this, together with some other matters, led to some unpleasantness for a time.[10]

Rev. William Cook, of the East Parish Congregational Church, supported Whitefield in Sudbury. Cook was a Harvard graduate who ministered in Sudbury from 1723 to his death in 1760. With the endorsement of Cook, Whitefield wrote, as noted above, that he "Preached to some thousands," in Sudbury.

Rev. Israel Loring of Sudbury kept a detailed journal of his everyday experiences. His notes on colonial Massachusetts makes for fascinating reading. He wrote of family concerns, community news, church matters, legal disputes, and larger issues concerning Colonial America and Europe. Loring made notations of Whitefield's 1740 visit to his general community:

Sept. 18. Mr. Whitefield came to Boston.

Oct. 13. I went over to Concord to hear Mr. Whitefield. His sermon was from Jon. 12.21, Sir, we would see Jesus. The second was from Mark 5.34, And he said unto her, Daughter, thy faith had made thee whole.

Oct. 14. Mr. Whitefield preached at Sudbury, from Rom. 14.17, For the kingdom of God is not meat and drink, but righteousness, and peace, and joy in the holy ghost. On same evening, he preached at Marlborough on the pharisee and the publican, but I was not there.[11]

These journal entries show that Israel Loring was interested in Whitefield, and was not at this time opposed to the itinerant preacher in Sudbury. But his opinion of Whitefield would change over the next few years.

Another town Whitefield mentioned in his October 14, 1740, *Journals* entry, was Marlborough, Massachusetts. Whitefield simply stated, "Got to Marlboro, eight miles from Sudbury, about four, where I preached to a large congregation."[12]

The Congregational Church in Marlboro, founded in 1662, was recovering from several recent years of turmoil. Upon the death of a longtime and faithful minister, a new minister was called but ultimately rejected. Accusations of Arminianism swirled throughout the town, as civil and ecclesiastical groups could not agree upon the selection of a new minister. Candidates were scrupulously interviewed, with some refusing to accept a call to preach in the troubled town. Rivalries, disorders, and divisions abounded. As the Great Awakening spread throughout central Massachusetts, the Congregational Church in Marlboro desired a conservative, Trinitarian, Calvinistic minister. Mr. Aaron Smith was approved by the church on December 24, 1739 and was ordained in Marlborough on June 11, 1740.[13] It was with the approval of Rev. Smith that Whitefield was allowed to preach "to a large congregation," as he wrote in his *Journals*, in Marlboro. Whitefield may have preached in the Congregational meeting house while it rained outside. He may also have preached outside in front of the meeting house because the building was denied him. Governor Jonathan Belcher was in the audience.[14] Shortly thereafter, the ministerial association around

---

10 Alfred S. Hudson, *The History of Sudbury, Massachusetts, 1638-1889*, (Published by the Town of Sudbury, 1889), p. 355.
11 Israel Loring, *The Journal of Rev. Israel Loring (1682-1772) of Sudbury, Massachusetts, Covering his Early Life and the Years 1704-1745*, L.P. Thomas, editor (Sudbury, MA Public Library), 32.
12 George Whitefield, *George Whitefield's Journals*, p. 474.
13 Charles Hudson, *History of the Town of Marlborough, Middlesex County, Massachusetts . . .*, (Boston, MA: T.R. Marvin & Son, Publishers, 1862), pp. 127-128.
14 George Whitefield, *George Whitefield's Journals*, p. 474.

Marlboro met and drew up a testimony against Whitefield. Rev. Aaron Smith signed it. "Mr. Smith had little sympathy with the awakening."[15]

A Congregational minister in nearby Westboro was happy to seek out Whitefield and hear him preach. Rev. Ebenezer Parkman had heard Whitefield preach in Boston a few weeks earlier. Now that Whitefield was on an itinerant preaching tour in central Massachusetts, Parkman happily welcomed Whitefield. Parkman wrote in his diary:

> Oct. 14, 1740. Notwithstanding that it was somewhat rainy my wife and I rode down to Marlborough to attend upon the preaching of the Reverend Mr. George Whitefield . . . Mr. Whitefield preached at Sudbury in the forenoon, and came about ½ after 3 this afternoon. He preached to a great assembly from Luke 18,14. Governor Belcher present. In Dr. Gott's name I asked Mr. Whitefield and his fellow travelers to his House and they accordingly went, but could not be persuaded to make any stay nor to lodge short of Worcester, even altho the weather was rainy.[16]

Whitefield continued his journey west, to the significant central Massachusetts town of Worcester. Located half-way between Boston and Springfield, Massachusetts, Worcester was first settled in 1674. The town was abandoned and burned several times from Indian wars, and was finally incorporated in 1722. In 1731, Worcester was chosen as the county seat for the newly formed Worcester County government. Rev. Isaac Burr, the Congregational minister in Worcester from 1725 to 1745, welcomed Whitefield to Worcester. One report narrated:

> The celebrated Whitefield, whose splendid eloquence seemed almost the gift of inspiration, controlling the judgment, and swaying the feelings of men at pleasure, went through New England . . . preaching to congregations gathering, by the acre, beneath the open sky, in numbers no house could contain. On his way to New York, this powerful exhorter arrived in Worchester, Oct. 14, 1740, accompanied by Governor Belcher . . . [17]

Whitefield wrote about his ministry in Worcester, as follows:

> Tuesday, October 14 . . . [We went] . . . as far as Worcester, fifteen miles from Marlboro, wither we got about eight at night. Here we were kindly entertained . . . Wednesday, October 16 . . . I preached in the open air to some thousands. The Word fell with weight: it carried all before it. After sermon, the Governor remarked, "I pray God, I may apply what has been said to my own heart. Pray, Mr. Whitefield, that I may hunger and thirst after righteousness."[18]

Governor Jonathan Belcher referred to this occasion in his personal correspondence among the Belcher papers:

A painting of Governor Jonathan Belcher.

Source: www.masshist.org

---

15 *History of the First Church in Marlborough (Congregational), United Church of Christ on the Occasion of its Three Hundred and Fiftieth Anniversary, 1666-2016*, (Marlborough, MA: Printed by the First Church Congregational, 2017), p. 15.
16 Ebenezer Parkman, *The Diary of Ebenezer Parkman, 1739-1744*, (Worcester, MA: The American Antiquarian Society), p. 136.
17 William Lincoln, *History of Worcester, Massachusetts, from its Earliest Settlement to September, 1836*, (Worcester, MA: Charles Hersey, Publisher, 1862), pp. 107-108.
18 George Whitefield, *George Whitefield's Journals*, pp. 474-475.

> What crowned the pleasure of the journey was my unexpectedly meeting on the road, the excellent, lovely, heavenly Whitefield, whom I had often heard at Boston without weariness, and wherefore eagerly heard him again at Marlborough and Worcester; and although I greatly approve and admire his matter and manner of preaching, yet having an opportunity in this journey of considerable conversation with him, by his piety, meekness, humility, innocence and great simplicity, he has most of all enamored me.[19]

The October 14, 1740 reference to Whitefield's *Journal* speaks of him preaching in Worcester "in the open air to some thousands." This outside preaching is elaborated upon by Caleb A. Hall, in *Reminiscences Of Worcester*, where he wrote of "the distinguished and eloquent revivalist preacher, Whitefield, who went through Worcester on his New England tour in the fall of 1740, preaching in the open air to such numerous congregations that no house could contain them. He was in Worcester, Oct. 15, when he exhorted to an immense congregation on the common . . . ."[20]

The Worcester common was created in 1669 on twenty acres of land for common public use. The Congregational Church served by Rev. Isaac Burr was located on the common. Thousands of people gathered here to hear Whitefield preach outside. Today the common has been reduced by urban growth to 4.4 acres.

Although the location is the same, today the Worcester Common has few similarities to the common where Whitefield preached in mid-October 1740. Photograph by Ken Lawson.

Isaac Burr ministered in a Congregational meeting house built in 1719. By 1733, the town spent money to paint and beautify the building. As the town of Worcester grew, so did this Puritan congregation. A Yale College graduate, Burr had a steady, harmonious, uneventful ministry until Whitefield came to town in October 1740. The sensational oratory of Whitefield amazed the Worcester Congregationalists. A historian of church life in Worcester wrote,

> Preaching so impassioned, eloquence such as never before had entranced the people, stirred the emotive nature to its centre. Waves of feelings were raised, which could not at once subside. Numbers were stimulated to crave a more animated and rousing style of address

---

19 Caroline V.D. Chenoweth, *History of the Second Congregational Church and Society in Leicester, Massachusetts*, (Worcester, MA: Commonwealth Press, 1908), pp. 32-33.
20 Caleb A. Wall, *Reminiscences of Worcester from the Earliest Period, Historical and Genealogical . . .* , (Worcester, MA: 1877), p. 119.

than they had before been accustomed to, and, not being gratified, were not slow to express dissatisfaction. Mr. Burr was too quiet and conservative to suit them.[21]

Isaac Burr struggled with the Great Awakening. He approved of the theology but not of the methodology. Although Burr welcomed Whitefield to Worcester, he did not welcome the numerous Whitefield imitators who traveled from place-to-place, often unwelcomed and uninvited. These bombastic itinerant preachers stirred up emotions, divided congregations, and harangued all who paused to consider their legitimacy. By 1742, Isaac Burr was refusing his pulpit to all itinerants, even though his congregation desired otherwise. The contention in Worcester caused Burr to become ill. He resigned from the church in 1744 in broken health, to retirement in Windsor, Connecticut.[22]

A sketch of the home of Rev. Isaac Burr in Worcester, Massachusetts. Here Burr entertained the traveling evangelist Rev. George Whitefield in October 1740.

Source: Collections of the Worcester Historical Museum and Library.

After departing Worcester, Whitefield preached in two small towns on his journey west, namely Leicester and Brookfield. These inland towns were not founded by Puritans. Leicester was first settled in 1713, in an area of hilly terrain and thick forests. As the community grew along a postal road from Boston to Albany, New York, several taverns appeared over the years for travelers. This was a poorer, working-class community in which all families had a farm or large garden, and most men were bi-vocational. It was common for people to wear homespun clothing. The first schoolhouse was built in 1738, and a Society of Friends (Quakers) meeting house was constructed in 1739.[23] The largest church in Leicester, the First Congregational Church, was founded in 1719. When Whitefield arrived in the fall of 1740, the Congregational meeting house was under construction, as the awakening in central Massachusetts brought more people into the church. This created the need for galleries to be built within the meeting house.

Whitefield was welcomed to Leicester by the Congregational Church minister, Rev. David Goddard. A Harvard graduate, Goddard served in Leicester from 1736 to his death in 1754. Because of poverty, the townsfolk could not always pay his salary, or pay him on time. Of Goddard it was stated:

> He was a man of devoted piety, morbidly conscientious, sympathized with the people in their financial straits, and was in full sympathy of the great religious movements of his time. In the afternoon of October 15, 1740, Rev. George Whitefield preached in Leicester . . . In connection with this work there were evidently some extravagances.[24]

Whitefield succinctly wrote of his brief time in Leicester, "Preached, in the afternoon, at Leicester, six miles from Worcester."[25] But there was much more going on in Leicester that Whitefield's brief note reveals. Before Whitefield arrived, Rev. Goddard was deeply grieved over the low spirituality of his community,

---

21 E. Smalley, *The Worcester Pulpit with Notices, Historical and Biographical*, (Boston, MA: Phillips, Sampson and Company, 1851), p. 46.
22 E. Smalley, *The Worcester Pulpit with Notices*, pp. 47-48. *Early Records of the Town of Worcester*, (Book II, 1740-1753: Worcester, MA: 1880), p. 52.
23 Mark K. Burnett, editor. *Handbook of Historical Data Concerning Leicester, Massachusetts*, (Leicester, MA: 190), pp. 15-24.
24 A.H. Coolidge, *A Brief History of Leicester, Massachusetts*, (Leicester, MA: 1890), p. 18.
25 George Whitefield, *George Whitefield's Journals*, p. 475.

and his Congregational Church in particular. When revival swept through central Massachusetts in the late 1730s, Goddard rejoiced. He was in full sympathy with the awakening, and he happily welcomed Whitefield to Leicester. But not all welcomed Whitefield. Some were offended by Whitefield's preaching and writings, particularly when he denounced ministers as unconverted or unfaithful. One account commented about the revival in and around Leicester.

> The revivals of this period were probably not without their infelicities. Whitefield was charged, probably with some reason, with harsh denunciations of ministers . . . There were afterward, much discussion and wide differences of opinion upon the value of the labors of Whitefield . . . [26]

After departing Leicester, Whitefield arrived at Brookfield, Massachusetts. Incorporated as a town in 1718, the minister of the town was Rev. Thomas Cheney, who served in Brookfield from 1717 to his death in 1747. A Harvard graduate in 1711, Cheney was concerned about the disruptions that resulted from itinerant revival preachers. He did not allow Whitefield to preach in the Congregational Church in Brookfield. Interestingly, it is not evident from Whitefield's *Journals* that he was refused the pulpit in Brookfield. Whitefield wrote,

> Wednesday, October 15 . . . Got to Brookfield by night . . . Oh what precious hours are those, when we are thus strengthened, as it were, to lay hold on God . . . Thursday October 16. Preached, with little freedom at first; but, at the last, many were melted down. After dinner, was much enlarged and strengthened to wrestle strongly with God, for a revival of His work in these parts . . . [27]

Whitefield described this event in Brookfield as he preached "with little freedom at first." This is a veiled reference to the initial opposition he received in Brookfield. The fuller account is that Whitefield was denied the pulpit of the Congregational Church by Cheney, so he preached outside to a significant gathering from a large stone in an open field. Since 1740, this stone has been called the "Whitefield Rock." A plaque on the bolder commemorates the date and time when Whitefield preached outdoors to several hundred people in the small town of Brookfield. The official town history of Brookfield calls this place, "Whitefield Rock, near the top of Foster's Hill, from which Mr. Whitefield preached in October 1740."[28]

The rock from Whitefield preached in Brookfield is about as tall as an average man. The granite rock protrudes out at the edge of a farmer's field, near an apple orchard today. A tree-lined suburban road on Foster Hill takes visitors to the spot of the boulder and the plaque. There are several local history accounts of Whitefield preaching in Brookfield. For example,

> Mr. Cheney's pastorate lasted thirty years, during which he labored faithfully for the spread of the Gospel and the upbuilding of Christ's kingdom. It was while he was pastor that the famous Methodist preacher, George Whitefield, came to this town on his way to visit Jonathan Edwards at Northampton, October 16, 1740. There was some hesitancy about letting him occupy the pulpit for fear he might utter some heretical statements, but the pastor finally consented when it was found that the crowd was so large that it was impossible to seat them in the church, and tradition says he preached from the rock which is inscribed with his name.[29]

---

26   Amos H. Coolidge, *The Religious History of the First Congregational Church in Leicester*, (Worcester, MA: Charles Hamilton, Printer, 1887), p. 21.
27   George Whitefield, *George Whitefield's Journals*, p. 475.
28   J.H. Temple, *History of North Brookfield, Massachusetts*, (Published by the Town of Brookfield, 1887), p. 17.
29   Charles B. Toleman, *An Historical Sermon Delivered in the First Church of Christ (of the Old Town of Brookfield) at West Brookfield, Mass. Sunday, September 18, 1910*, (Ware, MA: Ware River News Print, 1911), p. 12.

A woman present in Brookfield when Whitefield began to preach from the rock in the field recalled that he stated, "Some of you come to hear what the babbler will say."[30] As a result of that sermon, a revival broke out in the town, which Rev. Cheney encouraged for years afterwards. The influence of Whitefield's one sermon in Brookfield endured. The last person who heard Whitefield preach in Brookfield and was converted was Mrs. Mercy Banister, who died in 1819. Her conversion to Christ was well-known in town, that she was born-again after hearing Whitefield preach on October 16, 1740.[31]

The "Pulpit Rock" used by George Whitefield on his visit to Brookfield, MA. The memorial plaque says, "George Whitefield early Methodist Evangelist preached from this rock October 16, 1740 on his first tour of America . . . Plaque provided by the New England Methodist Historical Society, 1960." Photograph by Ken Lawson.

Another anecdote from Whitefield's preaching in Brookfield names Captain and Mrs. Thomas Hale as eager to hear Whitefield preach. "The Captain and his wife were church members, and they with two boys rode on one horse six miles to Foster's Hill to hear Whitefield preach from the rock."[32] The town history of Brookfield recorded significant events on an annual basis. The only notation for 1740 states, "1740. Oct. 16, Rev. George Whitefield preached in Brookfield, from the large rock on the top of Foster's Hill."[33] One historian has identified "Whitefield Rock" as a notable location in American Christian history:

> On October 16 he [Whitefield] stood in the center of the Quaboag Plantation in West Brookfield, Massachusetts with a crowd of at least 500 standing about him and there he preached the gospel of Jesus Christ. As he preached, he stood upon a great rock, known today—appropriately—as Whitefield Rock . . . While Whitefield and other revivalists were overwhelmingly popular, they were also regarded with distrust and suspicion by many church leaders. These leaders saw that the revivalists could preach anywhere they wanted, rather than only in established church buildings. Not only that, but they could preach for a time and then go on their way. Division soon followed, with some clergy distancing themselves from Whitefield and others . . . And this is why, on October 16, 1740, Whitefield found himself outdoors, on Foster Hill, outside the town of West Brookfield, Massachusetts. This was a rough, hilly and sparsely populated region and the crowd of nearly 500 people marked this as a major event for the area.[34]

---

30 Lyman Whiting, *A Bi-Centennial Oration made in West Brookfield, July 4, 1860, at the Celebration of the Two Hundredth Anniversary of the Settlement of the Town of Brookfield*, (West Brookfield, MA: Thomas Morey, Printer, 1869), p. 38.
31 Samuel Dunham, *An Historical Discourse delivered at West Brookfield, Mass. On the Occasion of the One Hundred and Fiftieth Anniversary of the First Church in Brookfield, October 16, 1867*, (Springfield, MA: Samuel Bowles & Company, Printers, 1867), p. 13. *Manual of the Congregational Church, West Brookfield, Mass.*, (West Brookfield, MA: Steam Press of O.S. Cooke & Co., 1853), p. 9.
32 J.H. Temple, *History of North Brookfield, Massachusetts*, p. 611.
33 Ibid., p. 202.
34 Tim Challies, "The History of Christianity in 25 Objects," http://www.challies.com/articles/the-history-of-christianity-in-25-objects-whitefield-rock.

After preaching in Brookfield, Whitefield preached at a private home fifteen miles away in a village called Cold Spring (now Belchertown), "to three of four hundred people."[35] He was in good health, the colorful New England fall foliage was beautiful, and invitations for him to preach were ongoing. Whitefield's next stop on his westward preaching tour was in Hadley, Massachusetts.

Hadley was first settled in 1659 by disgruntled Puritans from Connecticut. These early settlers could not accommodate the rules related to communion, church discipline, baptism, and the overall leadership of various Connecticut Puritans. Hadley was a heavily wooded wilderness, connected to the outside world by the Connecticut River. Once cleared, the rolling hills and rich soil made ideal farmlands. Shortly before Whitefield arrived in 1740, the town was overwhelmed by revival. The late 1730s in Hadley was a time that townsfolk flocked to the Congregational Church for extended preaching and additional services. Upon the death of their minister, the Congregational Church in Hadley called Mr. Chester Williams to be their pastor. Williams began his ministry in Hadley in September 1740 and was ordained there on January 21, 1741. He was a Yale College graduate in 1735. On the tombstone of Williams in Hadley, it was written:

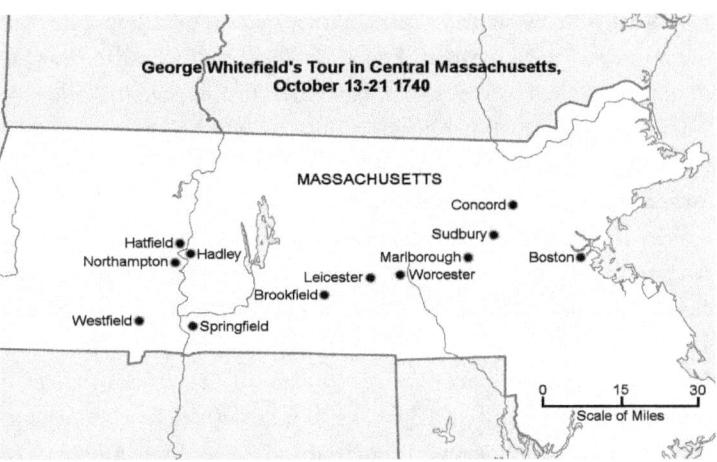

> Here rests the body of the Rev. Mr. Chester Williams, in whom bright parts, solid learning, unfeigned piety, happy elocution, universal benevolence, hospitality and Christian love, combined to form the exemplary pastor, the kind husband, the tender parent, the delightful companion, and the faithful friend, who departed this life, 13th October, 1755, aged 36.[36]

When Whitefield arrived in Hadley on October 17, 1740, Williams was serving in the Congregational Church, awaiting ordination. One account recorded, "Mr. Whitefield preached once at Hadley and perhaps more than once. He first came to Northampton on the evening of Oct. 16, 1740, having preached at Hadley along the way."[37] In his *Journals*, Whitefield wrote:

> Friday, October 17. Set out as soon as it was light, and reached Hadley, a place where a great work was carried on some years ago; but lately, the people of God have complained of deadness and losing their first love. As soon as I mentioned what God had done for their souls formerly, it was like putting fire to tinder. The remembrance of it caused many to weep sorely . . .[38]

One of the ways Whitefield determined where to preach was from letters of invitation. On February 12, 1740 Jonathan Edwards invited George Whitefield to preach in Northampton. In his one-page invitation, Edwards wrote, "from what I have heard, that you are the one that has the blessing of heaven attending you

---

35 George Whitefield, *George Whitefield's Journals*, p. 475.
36 Stephen Williams, *The Genealogy and History of the Family of Williams in America . . .*, (1847: reprinted by the University of Wisconsin Press, 2008), p. 128.
37 Sylvester Judd, *History of Hadley . . . , Massachusetts*, (Springfield, MA: H.R. Hunting & Company 1905), p. 330.
38 George Whitefield, *George Whitefield's Journals*, pp. 475-476.

wherever you go."³⁹ Now, six months later, Whitefield was in Northampton. Several days before Whitefield arrived in Northampton, Edwards wrote a letter to Rev. Ebenezer Wheelock. Edwards discussed the revival, thanked Wheelock for his role in the awakening, and prayed that the Lord would continue to empower men like Whitefield to continue to do great things for God.⁴⁰

No doubt, Whitefield eagerly anticipated his next stop. Northampton, Massachusetts was the home of the renowned Rev. Jonathan Edwards. These two men had heard of each other through printed sermons in newspapers and by theological pamphlets that crossed the Atlantic. They had exchanged correspondence. Whitefield was a young minister in England when he first heard and read of Edward's remarkable ministry in Northampton. Not only was Edwards a keen theologian, he was also the key human element in the Great Awakening in the northern American Colonies.

In 1740, when Edwards and Whitefield first met, Edwards was thirty-seven years old, as Whitefield was twenty-six years old. Edwards came from a distinguished ministerial family, as did his wife. The Edwards' had eleven children, and Sarah Edwards was known as a radiant Christian wife and mother. Whitefield came from a middle-class home, as his parents were the successful proprietors of a well-respected inn located in Gloucester, England.⁴¹ Whitefield's marriage in November 1741, was not a model union, and he and his wife did not have any children that survived. Edwards had heard of Whitefield's remarkable oratory skills, and the revivals that often followed his preaching in England and in the other American colonies. Edwards was Congregationalist, Whitefield was Anglican, but both were Calvinists. Certainly, both men were happily anticipating meeting for the first time. One writer stated:

> Edwards and Whitefield shared many similarities. They were both highly respected Christian leaders, they both had a reputation as powerful preachers, they were both Calvinistic in their theological outlook. But there, the similarities ended. Their style of preaching was very different. Edwards was a careful, logical teacher. Whitefield was all life and fire, thunder and lightning. Edwards was a meticulous writer, crafting pamphlets for publication. Whitefield barely had the time to check the proof copies of manuscripts of his sermons and had the disappointment of seeing very poor versions of his sermons in print without his permission. Edwards was a settled Pastor overseeing a local congregation, and very much a responsible Pastor of one parish. Whitefield, on the other hand, had declared that the whole world was now his parish and lived a life of itinerant preaching. Edwards was a family man, with a godly wife and several children. Whitefield was still single [in 1740], and still waiting for the love of his life to come along.⁴²

Rev. Jonathan Edwards of Northampton, Massachusetts. Public domain image.

---

39 Jonathan Edwards, *Letters and Personal Writings of Rev. Jonathan Edwards*, (New Haven, CT: Yale University Press), vol. 16, p. 80.
40 "Letter from Rev. Jonathan Edwards to Rev. Ebenezer Wheelock, October 9, 1740," (History Room, Forbes Library, Northampton, MA).
41 Arnold Dallimore, George Whitefield, *The Life and Times of the Great Evangelist of the Eighteenth Century Revival*, (Carlisle, PA: Banner of Truth Trust, 1979), vol. I. pp. 37-43.
42 Adrian Warnock, "George Whitefield meets Jonathan Edwards," http://www.pathos.com/blogs/adrianwarnock/2009/11/george-whitefield-meets-jonathan. Ava Chamberlain, "The Great Sower of the Seed: Jonathan Edwards' Critique of George Whitefield, *The New England Quarterly*, Vol. 70, No. 3 (September 1997), pp. 368-385.

An early biographer of Whitefield stated, "He next went to Northampton, having an earnest desire to see the Rev. Jonathan Edwards, and to receive from the mouth of that eminent divine, an account of a remarkable conversion there."[43] Another Whitefield biographer noted the Whitefield-Edwards meeting as follows:

> On his arrival at Northampton, that cradle of revivals, he was at home at once with Jonathan Edwards . . . But whilst these two eminent ministers esteemed, and even loved each other, as servants of God, Edwards did not think that Whitefield regarded him as a confidential friend exactly. The fact is, Edwards had cautioned him upon the subject of impulses and guarded him against the practice of judging others to be unconverted. This was touching sore places, at the time. Whitefield seems to have winced a little, with impatience, under the metaphysical probe of Edwards; but to have conceded nothing then. They parted, however, with mutual love; and whatever differences existed between their theories of impulses, both soon rejoiced equally in "a glorious progress of the work of God," at Northampton, that year.[44]

This image is of the third congregational meeting house in Northampton, built under Rev. Jonathan Edward's pastorate in 1737. This building was replaced in 1812.

Source: Historic North Hampton Museum & Education Center.

Whitefield recorded his historic meeting with Edwards in his *Journals*.

> Friday, October 17 . . . After a little refreshment, we crossed the ferry to Northampton, where no less than three hundred souls were saved about five years ago. Their pastor's name is Edwards . . . Mr. Edwards is a solid, excellent Christian, but, at present, weak in body. I think I have not seen his fellow in all New England. When I came into his pulpit, I found my heart drawn out to talk of scarce anything besides the consolations and privileges of saints, and the plentiful effusion of the Spirit upon Believers. When I came to remind them of their former experiences, and how zealous and lively they were at that time, both minister and the people wept much. In the evening, I gave a word of exhortation to several who came to Mr. Edwards' house. My body was weak, and my appetite almost gone; but my Lord gave me meat, which the world knows nothing of. Lord, evermore give me this bread! Amen and Amen.[45]

Sarah Edwards was an active, studious, and benevolent mate for her husband Jonathan. She helped her husband entertain Whitefield in their home and she was very capable in theological discussions. A few days after Whitefield departed Northampton and the Edwards' home, Sarah wrote a letter to her brother, James Pierpoint of New Haven, Connecticut. The letter is as follows.

---

43   John Gilles, *Memoirs of George Whitefield*, (1774: reprinted by Hunt & Noyes Publishers, Middletown, CT: 1838), pp. 50-51.
44   Robert Philip, *The Life and Times of George Whitefield*, (1837: reprinted by Banner of Truth Trust, Carlisle, PA: 2007), pp. 188-189
45   George Whitefield, *George Whitefield's Journals*, p. 476.

October 24, 1740.

Dear Brother James,

I want to prepare you for a visit from the Rev. Mr. Whitefield, the famous preacher of England. He has been sojourning with us, and after visiting a few of the neighbouring towns, is going to New Haven, and from thence to New York. He is truly a remarkable man, and during his visit, has, I think, verified all we have heard of him. He makes less of the doctrines than our American preachers generally do and aims more at affecting the heart. He is a born orator. You have already heard of his deep-toned yet clear and melodious voice. O it is perfect music to listen to that alone!

And he speaks so easily, without any apparent effort. You remember that David Hume thought it was worth going twenty miles to hear him speak; and Garrick said, 'He could move men to tears or make them tremble by his simple intonations in pronouncing the word Mesopotamia.' Well, this last was a mere speech of the play actor; but it is truly wonderful to see what a spell this preacher often casts over an audience by proclaiming the simplest truths of the Bible. I have seen upwards of a thousand people hang on his words with breathless silence, broken only by an occasional half-suppressed sob.

He impresses the ignorant, and not less, the educated and refined. It is reported that while the miners of England listened to him, the tears made white furrows down their smutty cheeks. So here, our mechanics shut up their shops, and the day-labourers throw down their tools, to go and hear him preach, and few return unaffected. A prejudiced person, I know, might say that this is all theatrical artifice and display; but not so will anyone think who has seen and known him.

He is a very devout and godly man, and his only aim seems to be to reach and influence men the best way. He speaks from a heart aglow with love, and pours out a torrent of eloquence which is almost irresistible. Many, very many persons in Northampton date the beginning of new thoughts, new desires, new purposes, and a new life, from the day on which they heard him preach of Christ and this salvation. I wish him success in his apostolic career; and when he reaches New Haven, you will, I know, show him warm hospitality.

Yours in faithful affection,

Sarah[46]

Whitefield preached for Edwards in Northampton four times, once on Friday, once on Saturday, and twice on Sunday, October 19. On Saturday, October 18, Edwards took Whitefield to nearby Hatfield, to preach. Hatfield, Massachusetts, was founded in 1660, and quickly became a dairy and agricultural center known for its healthy cattle and sheep, as well as its corn, tobacco, and various other crops. In 1740, the Congregational minister in Hatfield was the elderly Rev. William Williams, a 1683 graduate of Harvard College. Williams was born into a wealthy, aristocratic family, and was known to possess "brilliant intellectual gifts." Williams won

---

[46] "Sarah Edwards on George Whitefield," Banner of Truth, https://banneroftruth.org/us/resources/articles/2012/sarah-edwards-on-george-whitefield.

"the implicit confidence of the people of Hatfield. He possessed a power of persuasive utterance and was tactful in his dealings with men. As a preacher he was noteworthy . . . ."[47] Williams was a rigid Puritan, and Whitefield was not welcomed by Williams to preach in the Congregational meeting house in Hatfield. Therefore, Edwards accompanied Whitefield to Hatfield as a sponsor to facilitate Whitefield preaching outdoors. Whitefield wrote briefly of his preaching in Hadfield. "Saturday, October 18 . . . Preached at Hadfield, [Hatfield] five miles from Northampton, but found myself not much strengthened."[48] A detailed history of the town of Hatfield stated,

> The movement known as the "Great Awakening" in the eighteenth century, which caused considerable controversy in parts of Massachusetts and Connecticut, seems to have had little effect in Hatfield. George Whitefield preached in Hadley, but was not invited to Hatfield, where the Rev. William Williams, though seventy-five years old, still ruled with a firm hand and was opposed to such revivals . . . It is reported that Whitefield's stentorian tones were heard across the river. Some of Mr. Williams' parishioners took the opportunity to hear him in Hadley and Northampton.[49]

The place where Whitefield preached outside in Hatfield was probably in the open space behind the Congregational Church building, where today there is an elementary school, public gardens, open space, and a cemetery. It was not that the older Williams opposed Whitefield's message, but he saw Whitefield as a disrupter of the Puritan establishment that he tried to maintain in Hatfield. As evidence that Williams did not oppose the awakening, Rev. Jonathan Edwards was designated to preach the funeral sermon for Rev. Williams in 1741.

It would be more than four years before Whitefield and Edwards would meet again face-to-face. Whitefield must have been pleased by the letter he received from Edwards two months after the itinerant departed Northampton. In a letter dated December 14, 1740, Edwards thanks God for the recent Whitefield visit, and said to Whitefield, "a blessed work seems now to be going on in this place."[50]

Whitefield departed the Hadley-Hatfield-Northampton area on Monday evening, October 20. He wrote in his *Journals*, "Monday, October 20. Left Northampton in the evening, and rode eighteen miles to Westfield . . . Preached the next morning to a considerable congregation."[51]

Westfield was a settlement in the rolling hills of western Massachusetts. First settled in 1660, the first church was founded in 1679. A new Congregational meeting house was under construction for much of the 1720s. This was a small, rural farming community composed mostly of pioneers. Whitefield was only about ninety miles from urban, articulate, cosmopolitan Boston, but the difference between remote Westfield and Boston was severe. John Ballentine, a Harvard graduate in 1735, arrived in Westfield in December 1740. He was ordained by the Congregational Church here in 1741 and died in Westfield in 1776.[52] One author noted, "Mr. Ballentine was a man of respectable talents, and excelled I should judge in his knowledge of the ancient languages. He was attentive to the spiritual interest of his peoples, always present to administer council to the sick, and to offer his prayers on their behalf."[53]

Whitefield arrived in Westfield on October 21, 1740. Rev. Ballentine arrived about two months later. That means Whitefield preached to a large group in Westfield with an unfinished meeting house and no minister. "Prior to Mr. Ballentine's arrival, George Whitefield visited the area, preaching before a large

---

47 Daniel and Ruben Wells, *A History of Hatfield, Massachusetts, 1660-1910*, (Springfield, MA: F.C.H. Gibbons, Printer, 1910), pp. 113.
48 George Whitefield, *George Whitefield's Journals*, p. 476.
49 Daniel and Ruben Wells, *A History of Hatfield, Massachusetts, 1660-1910*, (Springfield, MA: F.C.H. Gibbons, Printer, 1910), p. 170.
50 Jonathan Edwards, *Letters and Personal Writings of Rev. Jonathan Edwards, vol. 16*, p. 87.
51 George Whitefield, *George Whitefield's Journals*, p. 477.
52 John H. Lockwood, *A Sermon Commemorative of the Two Hundredth Anniversary of the First Congregational Church of Westfield, Mass.*, (Westfield, MA: Clark & Story Printers, 1879), p. 21.
53 Emerson Davis, *A Historical Sketch of Westfield*, (Westfield, MA: Joseph Root Publishers, 1826), p. 30.

congregation in Westfield. The effects of the Great Awakening were still being felt in the church upon Mr. Ballentine's arrival, and ninety persons were admitted to full communion in the first two years of his pastorate."[54] Ballentine was not a supporter of the awakening spreading throughout much of New England. However, in 1741, the Congregational Church in Westfield added sixty-nine people to their membership rolls, based on new professions of faith.[55] This is a remarkable fact, based on the small, rural population of Westfield. Obviously, Whitefield's revival preaching had its intended effect in Westfield. Ballentine benefited from the awakening while not supporting it. He was at constant odds with Jonathan Edwards, and he considered those who followed Whitefield and Edwards troublemakers.[56]

Eagerly waiting for Whitefield in Westfield was Rev. Stephen Williams of nearby Longmeadow. As a child he was captured by Indians and held prisoner for over one year. In his extensive diary, the Harvard-trained Williams wrote about daily news and weather, as well as his spiritual struggles as an evangelical minister eager to see revival. His *Diary* reads like a prayer journal or a spiritual autobiography, as he pled to God for the souls of the townsfolk in Longmeadow. On October 11, 1740 Williams wrote in his *Diary* that he heard of Whitefield's success in preaching in New England, recording, "I hear of ye extra ordinary labors—& services of the Rev. Mr. G.W. in one place & another—ye Lord grant yet much good may be done by his Servant to ye souls of his people."[57] On October 14, Williams wrote in his *Diary*, "I have wrote a letter, to the Rev'd Mr. Whitefield to desire him to preach among us, if he can come—I desire it may be to our edification & real benefit & advantage."[58] Williams described meeting Whitefield as follows.

> Oct. 20, 1740. This day I went to Westfield where I met the Rev'd Mr. Whitefield & company & proceeded with him, to Town—& then to ye West Parish—& so to Suffield at Each of which places I heard him preach to great Auditory—he is a warm fervent preacher—has an inimitable faculty of touching ye affections & passions—I pray God to bless the labors of his Servant for Saving good to many.[59]

Here Rev. Stephen Williams stated that he accompanied Whitefield and heard him preach in three places—"to Town—& then to ye West Parish—& so to Suffield." The "Town" mentioned here is Springfield. The "West Parish" is the Springfield community on the west side of the Connecticut River.[60] And "Suffield" was a small town in Northern Connecticut on the Massachusetts border. After Williams travelled with Whitefield for a day or so, he wrote in his *Diary*, "October 21. I returned home & found all well—blessed be God."[61] Rev. Williams soon realized that there was a diversity of opinion in his church related to Whitefield. On October 22 he wrote in his *Diary*, "Various are ye sentiments of people, respecting Mr. W. [Whitefield] & his performances—oh yet God would appear and advance his own kingdom amongst this people."[62]

Whitefield's next stop that we know about on this central Massachusetts tour was in the larger town of Springfield. Located at an ideal spot on the Connecticut River, the first settlers arrived in 1636. The community thrived as an agricultural and trading center, with easy access to markets by the Connecticut River, and from a good north-south road that connected Springfield to Hartford, Connecticut. The

---

54 *History of the First Congregational Church of Westfield, Mass.*, (Printed for the church, 1979), p. 6.
55 John H. Lockwood, *A Sermon Commemorative . . .*, p. 22.
56 Wilma Pappalardo, "Reverend John Ballentine: A Profile of the Complete 18th Century Minister," Westfield Athenaeum—Westfield History Room, April 6, 1990), p. 1-3.
57 Stephen Williams, *Diary of Rev. Stephen Williams, Longmeadow, Massachusetts*, (Longmeadow, MA: Richard S. Storrs Library, 2011), Vol. III, p. 330.
58 Ibid., Vol. III, pp. 330-331.
59 Ibid., Vol. III, p. 331.
60 Correspondence from Elizabeth Hoff, Longmeadow Historical Society, July 5, 2019.
61 Stephen Williams, *Diary of Rev. Stephen Williams, Vol. III*, p. 331
62 Ibid., Vol. III, p. 331-332.

Congregational Church in Springfield dates to 1636. The minister who met Whitefield in Springfield was the controversial Rev. Robert Breck.

The most noteworthy event of Breck's forty-nine-year ministry in Springfield was the fierce debates that surrounded his call and ordination to the Congregational Church in Springfield. He served this church from 1734 to his death in 1784.[63] A contentious debate raged over his orthodoxy and the legalities related to his call to the church. Admittedly, Breck stated, in his years before arriving at Springfield, he made some unwise theological statements and speculations about the inspiration of the Bible, and the final destiny of the heathen. Clearly, he had Universalist tendencies as a young minister.[64] In these earlier sermons his theology was not yet established, and his first sermons did not reveal his later more Calvinist orthodoxy. His ordination council consisted of all orthodox clergymen, though some were more supportive of the awakening than others. Not all the men on this ordination council supported the itinerancy and sometimes bombastic statements of Whitefield. Insightfully, one historian noted about Robert Breck, "Jonathan Edwards and he belonged to the same association, and sometimes shot barbed arrows at each other."[65]

Whitefield wrote about his ministry in Springfield, under the watchful eyes of Breck, as follows.

> Monday, October 20 . . . Hastened to Springfield, ten miles from Westfield, crossed a ferry, preached to a large auditory, and then returned and preached to those who could not get over the ferry, by reason of the wind. The meeting-house was full.[66]

The fact that Whitefield preached in the Congregational meeting house, and that the "meeting-house was full," means that Breck allowed Whitefield the use of the building, and he endorsed the itinerant preacher to minister among his church members. Under Breck's leadership, the Congregational Church in Springfield never experienced a revival. Robert Breck was known as a serious thinker, a dedicated scholar, and as a man who prayed deliberate prayers and who carefully examined the scriptures.[67] No records exist of his face-to-face interaction with Whitefield.

Whitefield departed Boston on October 13, and completed his western Massachusetts preaching tour on Tuesday morning, October 21, 1740. His somewhat inglorious departure from Massachusetts is recorded in his *Journals*.

> Monday, October 20 . . . After I left Springfield, my horse, coming over a broken bridge, threw me over its head, directly upon my nose. I was stunned for a while, my mouth was full of dust, and I bled a little; but, falling upon soft sand, I got not much damage. After I had recovered myself, and mounted my horse . . . We stopped at a friend's house, about four miles from Springfield; and, after refreshment, went to rest, desiring to be thankful for the peculiar favors conferred upon me the past night . . . Tuesday, October 21. Set out for Suffield, [Connecticut] which is about eight miles from the place where I lay . . . .[68]

---

63 Henry M. Burt, *The First Century of the History of Springfield, Massachusetts, the Official Records from 1636 to 1736*, (Springfield, MA: Henry M. Burt, Printer, 1898), p. 23.
64 Theo W. Ellis, *Manual of the First Church of Christ and Names of all the Members: from the Year 1735 to Nov. 1, 1885*, (Springfield, MA: Springfield Printing Company, 1885), p. 72.
65 William B. Sprague, *Annals of the American Pulpit, or Commemorative Notices of Distinguished American Clergymen*, (New York: Robert Carter & Brothers, Printers, 1866), p. 385.
66 George Whitefield, *George Whitefield's Journals*, p. 477.
67 Ezra H. Byington, *The Puritan in England and New England*, (Boston: Roberts Brothers Printers, 1896), pp. 367-368.
68 George Whitefield, *George Whitefield's Journals*, pp. 477-478.

CHAPTER 8

WHITEFIELD'S TOUR IN CONNECTICUT

OCTOBER 21-30, 1740

IN THE 1630S, ENGLISH COLONISTS settled in various locations along the coastline and inland rivers that would eventually become the state of Connecticut. Significantly, Thomas Hooker founded Connecticut Colony in 1636, John Winthrop founded the Saybrook Colony in 1644, and John Davenport founded New Haven Colony in 1662. These men were important leaders in the English Puritan movement. These merged colonies refused to cooperate with the 1686 Dominion of America, which was an attempt to administer American colonial activities under English rule, with one colonial government, covering what are today the states of Maine to New Jersey. Church records from those early years are a rich source of ecclesiastical, civil, and social information. Like Massachusetts, colonial Connecticut was created by devout Puritans, Congregationalists, for the distinct purposes of religious and civil freedoms.[1]

In 1638, the *Fundamental Orders of Connecticut* was written. This document was a constitution. It is considered by many as the first written Constitution in America, thus earning Connecticut the label of "The Constitution State." This was an ecclesiastical and civil document that regulated the Connecticut Colony. The *Fundamental Orders* were transcribed into the official Connecticut Colony records by the colony's secretary, Thomas Welles, to serve as a constitution for the colonial government located in Hartford.[2]

The Puritan viewpoint guided many of the concerns of the Connecticut colonial legislature. These early colonists fled the Church of England, and sought to establish a theocentric world in America. The Connecticut colonial legislature, for example, controlled church growth and restricted or excluded other churches. A church could not be organized unless it had permission from the legislature and the surrounding churches. Many new churches were created as cooperative break-away churches from an older church, as new settlements created the need for new local Congregational churches. Each church raised taxes for its minister and the maintenance of the meeting house from all residents in the town, church members or not. The interconnected nature of church and government was assumed and accepted. The *Fundamental Orders*, which served as the first constitution of the colony, mandated that the Congregational churches and the civil government would go about their activities independently but cooperatively.[3]

Until 1818, Connecticut's history was closely connected to the Congregational Church. It was only at that late date, long after the United States Bill of Rights removed the idea of a government

---

1 For a thorough study, see Benjamin Trumbull, *A Complete History of Connecticut, Civil and Ecclesiastical . . .* , (Hartford, CT: Hudson & Goodwin Printers, 1797).
2 "The Fundamental Orders of Connecticut," http://connecticuthistory.org/the-fundamental-orders-of-connecticut. David M. Roth, Connecticut: A History, (New York: W.W. Norton & Company Publishers, 1979), pp. 34-65.
3 Barbara J. Matthews, "Congregational Church Records in Connecticut," http://www.americanancestors.org/Congregational_Church_Records_in_Connecticut, p. 1.

sponsored church, that Connecticut's Congregational churches were disestablished by the new state constitution. After 1708, the Act of Toleration prevailed in Connecticut. This act permitted citizens to declare themselves non-Congregationalists. They could then attend religious services of their own choosing, but they still had to pay taxes to support the Congregational minister. Beginning in 1727, Episcopalians could opt out of taxes, and Baptists and Quakers in Connecticut could do so starting in 1729. Nevertheless, until 1818, Connecticut citizens still had to pay taxes to support Congregational ministers, unless they could show they were financially committed to supporting ministers from another denomination.[4]

The decline in piety among the second generation of Puritans, which stemmed from economic changes, political transformations, and secular Enlightenment rationalism, was the primary cause of civil and ecclesiastical unrest. Devout Puritans were distracted from religious obligations. The standard of living for many Puritan merchants and manufacturers elevated in Connecticut towns and villages, causing many to devote more time to physical necessities that to spiritual pursuits. There was a noticeable decline in piety and a laxity of morals within the Congregational Churches.

In addition, accommodations, or compromises within the Congregational churches of Connecticut contributed to religious doubts and the weakening of religious dedication. To compensate for the decline, the Congregational churches of Connecticut and Massachusetts in 1662 adopted the Halfway Covenant. Prior to 1662, membership in the church required a personal conversion account and a credible testimony of a changed life. Practicing typical Puritan reformed or covenant theology, churches baptized the second generation of Puritan children with the expectation that they would be regenerated later in life. However, as politics and economics competed with religion, the second generation of Puritans often failed to live up to the expectations of their parents of maintaining a regenerated society. Attendance at Congregational churches plummeted.[5]

To sustain the population and influence of individual congregations, Congregational Churches adopted the Halfway Covenant. This allowed the children of Puritans, church members or not, to be baptized, but forbid them to partake of communion until a public profession of faith was demonstrated. This Halfway Covenant furthered the degeneration of the church, almost isolating the third generation of Puritans. The second and third generations of Connecticut Puritans failed to demonstrate the same devotion and discipline that the original Puritans had practiced.[6]

In an attempt to restore discipline and promote growth in the Congregational churches of Connecticut, ministers and others selected by the Connecticut General Court, drafted the Saybrook Platform. Approved by Governor Gurdon Saltonstall in 1708, the Saybrook Platform administrated order over the churches, establishing consociations in each Connecticut county to oversee ecclesiastical decisions such as the purchase of property, licensing of candidates, ordinations, installations, and dismissals of Congregational ministers.

The elimination of local church control, and the creation of a religious hierarchy upon the previously autonomous Congregational churches, created outrage in some communities. Outspoken ministers saw the Saybrook Platform as the first step towards a reinstitution of ecclesiastical hierarchy, which their forefathers fled from in the Church of England. The Saybrook Platform created bitter controversies and caused divisions throughout the Connecticut Colony.

---

4   For an overview of civil and ecclesiastical relationships in colonial America, see James H. Hutson, *Church and State in America: The First Two Centuries*, (New York: Cambridge University Press, 2014). For a specific study on this issue in Connecticut, see Paul R. Lucas, *Valley of Discord: Church and State along the Connecticut River, 1636-1725*, (Lebanon, NH: University Press of New England, 1976).

5   A detailed study of the results of these changes is found in Richard L. Bushman, *From Puritan to Yankee: Character and the Social Order in Connecticut, 1690-1765*, (Cambridge, MA: Harvard University Press, 1967), pp. 3-221.

6   "1740s—Jonathan Edwards and the Great Awakening," The Society of Colonial Wars in the State of Connecticut, http://colonialwardct.org/1740_s.htm, pp. 4-5.

To further disrupt church affairs, in the early eighteenth century, other Protestant churches made gains in Connecticut. For example, the first Anglican (Episcopal) Church was established at Stratford in 1707. The first Methodist Episcopal missionary appeared in Connecticut in 1767. The first Baptist church was established in Groton in 1704. Although Scottish ministers were found in early Congregational churches, the first church established in Connecticut as a Scott-Presbyterian church was founded much later in 1839 in Thompsonville. Unitarian and Universalist ideas spread in eighteenth century Congregational churches, with the first Unitarian Church in Connecticut founded in Brooklyn in 1731, and the first Universalist Church established in 1792 in Southington.[7]

In the 1730s and early 1740s, the Great Awakening began as a spiritual revival in the Connecticut River Valley of Massachusetts and Connecticut. The excitement, called in a derogatory way "enthusiasm," split towns, disrupted churches, and divided civil colonial assemblies. Initially, this was a movement within Congregational Churches. The Awakening resulted in doctrinal changes and influenced social and political thought. Jonathan Edwards is typically credited as the human catalyst of this spiritual movement.[8] Those who preferred the older, established ways were called Old Lights. Those who supported the awakening were described as New Lights. Bitter doctrinal disputes were fought in local newspapers, in Sunday preaching services, and with printed sermons and religious pamphlets. New Light theology was an evangelical Calvinism outside denominational boundaries. Old Light theology developed into a mix of mild Calvinism, Anglicanism, Unitarianism, or Universalism.[9]

In Connecticut, the Great Awakening spread quickly and was very popular. Civil as well as religious leaders got caught up in the movement. The Connecticut Colony enjoyed strong governors in the eighteenth century, many who served multiple terms in office. Upon the death of Fitz-John Winthrop in 1707, Gurdon Saltonstall, Winthrop's minister in New London, was elected governor. Saltonstall was the only clergyman to serve as governor of Connecticut. He supported the awakening. Governor Saltonstall was in office when George Whitefield first came to Connecticut in 1740.

George Whitefield came to Connecticut in October 1740. His eight-day visit permanently changed the ecclesiastical history of the Connecticut Colony. He was not uninvited. For example, the Fairfield East Association recorded, "1740, October.—The consociation resolved to endear to secure the labors of Rev. George Whitefield for this district."[10]

Whitefield entered Connecticut on October 21, 1740. Having spent the previous night near Springfield, Massachusetts, he travelled on a good road south to Suffield called the Hampton Path. The town of Suffield started in 1670. It was carefully planned, with land reserved for a central common area and designated locations for a school, a Congregational meeting house, and land for the Congregational minister. The first minister arrived in Suffield in 1679. The meeting house was constructed in the early 1680s, and the site of this first meeting house is now designated by a monument on the town common. Residents of Suffield were farmers, woodsmen, fishermen, and merchants who utilized the adjoining Connecticut River to facilitate trade and other commercial activities. Tobacco was the most valuable crop. Life in early Suffield consisted of hard work, humble living, and a society governed by

---

7   Barbara Jean Matthews, "Congregational Church Records in Connecticut," p.1. For a case study of religious changes and controversies in a colonial Connecticut town, see Peter J. Malia, *Visible Saints: West Haven Connecticut, 1648-1798*, (Monroe, CT: Connecticut Press, 2009).

8   There are a multitude of books about Jonathan Edwards and the Great Awakening. A good place to start is with Jonathan Edwards, *Jonathan Edward's Writings from the Great Awakening*, (New York: Library of America, 2013), and Robert D. Smart, *Jonathan Edward's Apologetic for the Great Awakening*, (Grand Rapids, MI: Reformation Heritage Books, 2011).

9   For a survey, see Andrea Greenwood and Mark W. Harris, *An Introduction to Unitarian and Universalist Traditions*, (New York: Cambridge University Press, 2011).

10 William L. Kingsley, *Contributions to the Ecclesiastical History of Connecticut*, (New Haven, CT: William L. Kingsley, Publisher, 1861), p. 298.

the *Fundamental Orders of the Congregational Church*. Calvinism was the rule for both ecclesiastical and civil life, as church and local government were one. It was not until the Great Awakening period in the 1740s, that religious and cultural changes occurred in Suffield. For example, in 1740 the Second Congregational Church was formed, with its meeting house constructed in 1743. Shortly thereafter, Baptists came to Suffield, with the First Baptist Church in Suffield founded in 1769. Whitefield wrote of his arrival in Suffield as follows:

> Tuesday, October 21. Set out for Suffield, which is about eight miles from the place where I lay. Reached thither, and preached at eleven o'clock to several thousands of people. Meeting with a minister in the way who said, "it was not absolutely necessary for a Gospel minister, that he should be converted," I insisted much in my discourse upon the doctrine of the new birth, and also the necessity of a minister being converted, before he could preach aright. The word came with great power, and a strong impression was made upon the people in all parts of the assembly. Many ministers were present . . . .[11]

Whitefield's host for his first preaching experience in Connecticut was Rev. Ebenezer Devotion, minister of the First Church of Christ, the Congregational Church in Suffield. This church was the focal point of all activities in the town. Rev. Devotion served in Suffield from 1710 to 1741, and was greatly respected and loved by the townspeople. He was a 1707 graduate of Harvard College. On his tombstone in Suffield it states:

> Here lies the body of the Rev. Mr. Ebenezer Devotion, late minister of the Gospel in this Town, who died April the 11th, 1741, in the 31st year of his ministry. At age 57. He was a man of Sound Judgment, great Stability of Mind & singular Modesty and Humility, a True Friend and Faithful Minister, steady upon his attendance upon the altar, close and pungent in his preaching and very exemplary in his life, a Pattern of Industry and Resignation and of all Christian Graces. As while living he was greatly beloved, so his death was very much lamented.[12]

From Suffield, Whitefield was off for an afternoon preaching appointment in Windsor, just south of Suffield. Windsor was the original English settlement in Connecticut. Located at the confluence of the Farmington and Connecticut Rivers, Windsor was famous for producing tobacco crops and for its dozens of small brick-making factories. The port of Windsor connected the community to other American colonies. The First Parish Congregational Church in Windsor is the oldest church in Connecticut, dating to 1630 when it was organized in England. Whitefield wrote of his experiences in Windsor as follows:

> As I was riding to Windsor, after dinner, an old man came up to me, saying he "knew what I had preached in the morning was true," for he had felt it. "I was under the spirit of bondage twenty years," he said, "and have received the

Rev. Ebenezer Devotion, Suffield, CT. Public domain image.

---

11 George Whitefield, *George Whitefield's Journals*, p. 478.
12 Cameron H. King, *The King family of Suffield, Connecticut*, (San Francisco, CA: Cameron H. King, Publisher, 1908), p. 102.

spirit of adoption twenty-three years." The people of God seemed much revived at Windsor, where a converted man is minister.[13]

The minister who welcomed Whitefield to Windsor was Rev. Jonathan Marsh of the First Parish Church. He was a 1705 graduate of Harvard College, and settled in the ministry at Windsor in 1710. Marsh was a full supporter of Jonathan Edwards and the awakening in the Connecticut River Valley. Under Marsh's ministry in Windsor, it was stated that there was "a very great ingathering of souls to Christ." Of Marsh it was recorded that "he possessed great amiability of temper, with strong powers of mind; and fervent piety was happily blended with sound judgment."[14] Related to Rev. Jonathan Marsh and Whitefield's visit to the church in Windsor:

> About this time the celebrated Whitefield preached, at least once, in Windsor. The meeting-house . . . was very large and had two galleries, yet it could not accommodate the hundreds who came to listen to the burning eloquence of the Man of God.[15]

After preaching in Windsor, Whitefield immediately departed for another preaching appointment a few miles away in East Windsor (modern South Windsor). Whitefield's host in East Windsor was Rev. Timothy and Esther Edwards, the parents of the celebrated Jonathan Edwards of Northampton, Massachusetts. Travelling with Whitefield was Jonathan Edwards, who was happy to engage in conversation with Whitefield and was glad to be able to visit his parents in East Windsor. Whitefield wrote of preaching for Timothy Edwards and departing Windsor as follows:

> As soon as sermon was over, I rode a mile and a half, and preached to a thronged congregation belonging to old Mr. Edwards, father of Mr. Edwards of Northampton. After exercise, we supped at the house of old Mr. Edwards. His wife was as aged, I believe, as himself, and I fancied that I was sitting in the house of a Zacharias and Elizabeth. I parted from him and his son (who came with me thus far) with regret; but, blessed be God, we shall meet in eternity! Lord, grant that I may always comfort myself with this thought![16]

Whitefield's next stop, the following morning, was at Wethersfield, Connecticut. The town of Wethersfield was one of the first settlements in Connecticut, dating to 1634. The Congregational minister in Wethersfield was Rev. James Lockwood, who was a Yale graduate in 1735. He began his ministry in Wethersfield in 1738. Lockwood was a scholarly man who was widely appreciated. He had many sermons published and was the eleventh minister of the First Ecclesiastical Society of Wethersfield, Congregational. Lockwood was so widely respected, that he was offered the presidency of Yale College and the College of New Jersey in Princeton. But his congregation was reluctant to allow him to depart, and Lockwood stayed in town. In gratitude, the church built Rev. Lockwood a home and gave it to him. The house was completed in 1767 and is still standing today in Wethersfield. Lockwood was:

> among the ministers most favorable to Whitefield's movements; and there is a tradition at Wethersfield, that the great itinerant made several visits there; and that, as the meeting house was unable to accommodate the multitudes who thronged to hear him, he held a meeting, at least on one occasion, in the open air. There is no doubt that Mr. Lockwood not only fully sympathized with, but cooperated with him to the extent of his ability.[17]

---

13 George Whitefield, *George Whitefield's Journals*, pp. 478-479.
14 Henry R. Stiles, *The History of Ancient Windsor, Connecticut*, (New York: Charles B. Norton Publisher, 1859), p. 360.
15 Ibid.
16 George Whitefield, *George Whitefield's Journals*, p. 479.
17 Henry R. Stiles, editor. *The History of Ancient Wethersfield, Connecticut . . .*, (New York: The Grafton Press, 1904), vol. I, p. 333.

Whitefield preached twice in the same day at Wethersfield. He wrote succinctly of his preaching in Wethersfield, with the endorsement of Rev. Lockwood, as follows:

> Wednesday, October 22. Preached, in the morning, to many thousands, with much freedom and power; and, in the afternoon, to about the same number, at Wethersfield, three miles from Hartford.[18] [Hartford]

Hartford, Connecticut was here mentioned by Whitefield. Rev. Daniel Wadsworth of the First Church of Christ (Congregational) in Hartford did not support Whitefield. Born into an upper middle-class family in Connecticut and a Yale College graduate in 1726, Wadsworth was married to a daughter of the Governor of the Connecticut Colony. A steady and unremarkable minister, Wadsworth kept a diary from 1732 to his death in Hartford in 1747. Under his leadership, the First Church experienced slow but steady growth, this at a time when churches were disrupted over the Great Awakening. No such divisions or controversies affected the First Church in Hartford, and a new church building was constructed under his tenure. David Wadsworth was described as "a timid, cautious, sincere-hearted pastor . . . His time, however, was a rather dull one in his church's history."[19]

At first, Wadsworth did not know what to make of the awakening and itinerant preachers like George Whitefield. His diary reveals that he initially interacted with both New Light and Old Light ministers. "Personally, Mr. Wadsworth was very clearly a man of kind heart and strong pastoral and family affections. He was nervous and as he himself says, bashful . . . Though apparently a dyspeptic and semi-hypochondriac he was after his method a laborious and industrious man." Wadsworth showed "his timidity in apparently on no occasion speaking without fully written notes."[20] It must have been a shock to Wadsworth's sensibilities, to learn of an extroverted, itinerant preacher like Whitefield, with a sensational voice, preaching out-of-doors to thousands, with emotionally charged evangelistic sermons, all the time preaching without notes. To his credit, Wadsworth did not immediately dismiss Whitefield. Instead, he read letters for and against Whitefield and he went at least twice to hear the itinerant preacher. Wadsworth's *Diary* is insightful as he determines whether he will support Whitefield and allow him to preach in his Congregational pulpit in Hartford.

1740

> April 30. This day reading, visiting &. Went to Weathersfield & heard yet Mr. Whitefield is arrived at New York.

> October 11. This day in study. At night received a letter from Dr. Colman concerning Mr. Whitefield . . .

> October 21. This day went to Farmington, my uncle Hez. interred. A sorrowful day: at night ye famous Mr. Whitefield came to town.

> October 22. This day Mr. Whitefield preached in ye forenoon to a vast Concourse of people here from Romans 14:17th verse, and in ye afternoon at Weathersfield from 2 Corinthians

---

18 George Whitefield, *George Whitefield's Journals*, p. 479.
19 Daniel Wadsworth, *Diary of Rev. Daniel Wadsworth, Seventh Pastor of the Church of Christ in Hartford*, (Hartford, CT: Press of the Case, Lockwood, & Brainard Company, 1894), p. 3
20 Ibid., p. 6.

5, latter part of ye 14th verse, Old things are past away &. What to think of ye man and his itinerant preachings I scarcely know: ye things which I know not I pray God to teach me, wherein I am in error I pray God to discover it to me, wherein I have embraced ye truth I pray God yet I might hold fast to ye end.[21]

Wadsworth was genuinely seeking how he could support the revival. After Whitefield's departure from Connecticut in 1740, roving evangelists came and spoke harshly to the people. Imitators of Whitefield tried to copy his style of preaching, but instead they insulted the congregations and made wild accusations and bombastic threats of divine judgment that recoiled many of the people and their ministers. This eventually caused Daniel Wadsworth of the First Church in Hartford to speak against Whitefield and the revival. Wadsworth publicly expressed a "conservative attitude" towards the awakening, meaning he supported the traditional beliefs and practices of the Connecticut clergy, and came out against the revival movement. "Mr. Wadsworth was only one among many who were not able to sympathize with the new measures introduced by the Great Awakening."[22] Later, when Whitefield returned to New England to begin his 1745 preaching tour through the area, Wadsworth publicly endorsed a ministerial association that denounced Whitefield and the revival movement. In his *Diary*, Wadsworth made the following brief notation:

1745.

February 5. This day went to ye association at Windsor. Ye association agreed upon a Testimony against Mr. Whitefield."[23]

As noted above, Rev. Daniel Wadsworth of Hartford made a note on October 22, 1740, stating that Whitefield preached that afternoon at Weathersfield (Wethersfield). He was welcomed there by Rev. James Lockwood, who served the First Church of Christ Congregational in Wethersfield from 1739 to 1772. The current church building dates from 1761-1764 but the pulpit was used in the previous church building from the 1680s. The church pulpit still used today was there when Whitefield arrived in the fall of 1740. Whether Whitefield used this pulpit is unknown, since his preaching in Wethersfield was

The current church pulpit in the First Congregational Church, Wethersfield, Connecticut was used in 1740 when George Whitefield came to Wethersfield. Photograph by Ken Lawson.

---

21 Ibid., pp. 50-56.
22 Ibid., pp. 3-4.
23 Ibid., p. 120.

probably outside due to the size of the crowds.[24] But this was the pulpit of Whitefield's host in Wethersfield, Rev. Lockwood. A Yale graduate in 1735, he was supportive of the revival on the Yale campus during his student years. The official history of the Congregational Church in Wethersfield states:

> Lockwood welcomed Whitefield to preach at Wethersfield on at least one occasion and tradition holds that the meeting was held out-of-doors, possibly at the meeting house square or on the Broad Street Green. Whitefield's preaching did have an effect on the Wethersfield church, for in 1741 and 1742, forty-three and twenty-five new members were received. For all the other years of Mr. Lockwood's ministry the average number of new members a year was seven or eight.[25]

Although Whitefield had been in Connecticut only a few days, news of his large and successful preaching events travelled fast. Both written and personal invitations asked Whitefield to come to various towns and preach. He was undecided which direction to go. Whitefield wrote about his indecision, and his arrival at his next destination in Middletown, as follows:

> . . . after prayer and consultation with my friends, I resolved to proceed directly to New York. Accordingly, at night, I rode to Middletown, ten miles from Wethersfield, and was entertained at the house of Mr. Russell, the minister of the place.[26]

The community of Middletown, Connecticut, traces its origins to 1650. Located twenty-eight miles from the ocean, Middletown was located at the only major bend in the Connecticut River. The shallow waters at this bend created the need for a port at which goods could be loaded and unloaded. Yankee sea traders used the inland port of Middletown as a center of operations. Farmers, merchants, and mariners gathered here to conduct business. Mansions built in the eighteenth century are still standing in Middletown, a testimony to the historic prosperity of the city. Goods from the West Indies, Europe, and other American colonies arrived in Middletown, making this city, in the 1700s the wealthiest, and most populated city in Connecticut. The First Church of Christ, Congregational, was founded in 1669.[27]

On October 22, 1740, Whitefield arrived in Middletown and was welcomed by Rev. William Russell, minister at the First Church of Christ, Congregational. Russell was a Yale graduate who was ordained at the church in 1715. He became minister of this church after his father, Noadiah Russell, the previous minister, died in 1713. The first two decades of his ministry in Middletown were uneventful, but in 1736 things changed, as revival swept through central Connecticut. The published sermons of Jonathan Edwards were the main catalyst for this initial awakening in Middletown. In 1737, Rev. William Russell welcomed nineteen new members to the church, an almost unheard of growth spurt. In 1738, there were eighteen additions to the church. The church welcomed thirty-five new members in 1741 and a remarkable sixty-eight new members in 1742. In speaking of the years 1740 to 1742 and the Congregational Church in Middletown:

> The abundant fruitage of these last two years was doubtless owing in large measure, on the human side, to the mighty influence of George Whitefield. This eloquent preacher came to New England in 1740, and went through its length and breadth conquering and to conquer . . . On his way thence to New Haven, the superb orator thrilled the people of Middletown and its

---

24 Thomas F. Walsh, "Whitefield in Wethersfield," www.weathersfieldhistory.org/articles/george-whitefield-the-billy-graham-of-colonial-america.
25 Lois M. Wieder, *A Pleasant Land—A Goodly Heritage*, (Wethersfield, CT: First Church of Christ, 1986), p. 61.
26 Daniel Wadsworth, *Diary of Rev. Daniel Wadsworth*, p. 120.
27 *Middletown, Connecticut: A Progressive Community of Modern New England*, (Middletown Chamber of Commerce, 1923), pp. 1, 9. Robert and Kathleen Hubbard, *Middletown: Images of America*, (Charleston, SC: Arcadia Publishing, 2009), p. 7.

vicinity with his fiery eloquence, bringing not a few of them to his own claims of Christ. A warm friendship is said to have sprung between Mr. Whitefield and the pastor of this church.[28]

Not all in Middletown appreciated Whitefield's message and methods. A local physician named John Osborn considered Whitefield an egotistical, bombastic intruder into the peacefulness of Middletown's society. He stated Whitefield made "a great stir and noise," and that his message was like a disease that spread throughout the community. Osborn called Whitefield's time in Middletown "a heap of confusion, railing, bombast, fawning, and nonsense." After hearing Whitefield preach in Middletown, Dr. Osborn noted that his sermon was full of "distorted motions, grimaces, and squeaking voices."[29]

William Russell was pastor of the Congregational Church until his death in Middletown in 1761. He married Mary Pierpont, the daughter of an influential Congregational Church pastor in New Haven. The Pierpont family was intimately associated with leadership positions at Yale College. Russell was related by marriage to Jonathan Edwards, as Edward's wife Sarah Pierpont was from the same family. Russell successfully served as a minister in Middletown from 1721 to 1761. He was lured away from this ministry by an offer to become the rector or president of Yale, but the townspeople in Middletown would not let him go. William Russell was considered, "A gentleman of great respect—ability for knowledge, experience, moderation, and for pacific measures on all occasions."[30]

With the full support of his host, William Russell, Whitefield had a remarkable preaching experience in Middletown. In his *Journals*, Whitefield wrote:

> Thursday October 23. I was much pleased with the simplicity of our host, and the order wherewith his children attended their family devotions. Preached to about four thousand people at eleven o'clock.[31]

One of the four thousand people who heard Whitefield preach in Middletown was a twenty-nine-year old farmer and carpenter named Nathan Cole. A highly literate tradesman for his day, Cole provides a fascinating and extended account of Whitefield preaching in the open air on the South Green at Middletown.[32] Excerpts from Cole's account are as follows:

> Now it pleased God to send Mr. Whitefield into this land . . . Then on a Sudden, in the morning about 8 or 9 of the Clock there came a messenger and said Mr. Whitefield preached at Hartford and Wethersfield yesterday and is to preach at Middletown this morning at ten of the Clock. I was in my field at Work, I dropped my tool and I had in my hand and ran home to my wife telling her to make ready quickly to go and hear Mr. Whitefield preach at Middletown. Then run to my pasture for my horse with all my might; fearing that I should be too late; having my horse I wish my wife soon mounted the horse and went forward as fast as I thought the horse could bear, and when my horse got much out of breath I would get down and put my wife on the Saddle and bid her ride as fast as she could and not Stop or Slack for me except I bad her and so I would run until I was much out of breath; and then mount my horse again, and so I did several times to favor my horse; we improved every moment to get

---

28 Azel W. Hazen, *A Brief History of the First Church of Christ in Middletown, Connecticut, 1668-1918*, (Middletown, CT: Russell Library, 1918), p. 44.
29 *Letter from John Osborn to Samuel Osborn*, November 17, 1740. Courtesy of the Boston Public Library.
30 William R. Cutter, editor. *New England Families, Genealogical and Memorial*, (New York: Lewis Historical Publishing Company, 1913), vol. III, p. 1428. In historical documents, the name Russell is sometimes spelt as Russel.
31 George Whitefield, *George Whitefield's Journals*, p. 479.
32 Leonard Labaree, "George Whitefield comes to Middletown," *William and Mary Quarterly*, vol. 7, no. 4 (October 1950), pp. 588-591.

along as if we were fleeing for our lives; all the while fearing we should be too late to hear the Sermon, for we had twelve miles to ride double in little more than an hour and we went round by the upper housen parish.

And when we came within about half a mile or a mile of the Road that comes down from Hartford, Wethersfield and Stepney to Middletown; on high land I saw before me a Cloud or fogg rising; I first thought it came from the great River, but I came near the Road, I heard a noise something like a low rumbling thunder and presently found it was the noise of Horses feet coming down the Road and this Cloud was a Cloud of dust made by the Horses felt. It arose some Rods into the air over the tops of Hills and trees and when I came within about 20 rods of the Road, I could see men and horses Slipping along in the Cloud like shadows. And as I drew nearer it seemed like a steady Stream of horses and their riders, scarcely a horse more than a length behind another, all of a Lather and foam with sweat, their breath rolling out of their nostrils every Jump; every horse seemed to go with all his might to carry his rider to hear news from heaven for the saving of Souls; it made me tremble to see the Sight, how the world was in a Struggle; I found a Vacancy between two horses to Slip in me and my wife said all our cloths will be all spoiled see how they look, for they were so Covered with dust, that they looked almost all of the same Colour—Coats, hats, shirts, and horses.

We went down in the Stream but heard no man speak a word all the way for 3 miles but every one pressing forward in great haste. And when we got to Middletown old meeting house there was a great multitude it was said to be 3 or 4000 of people Assembled together; we dismounted and shook off our Dust; and the ministers were then Coming to the meeting house; I turned and looked towards the Great River and saw the ferry boats Running swift backward and forward bringing over loads of people and the Oars rowed nimble and quick; every thing, men, horses, and boats, seemed to be Struggling for life; The land and banks over the river looked black with people and horses all along the 12 miles I saw no man at work in his field, but all seemed to be gone.

When I saw Mr. Whitefield come upon the Scaffold he looked almost angelical; a young, Slim, slender, youth before some thousands of people with a bold undaunted Countenance, and my hearing how God was with him every where he came along it Solemnized my mind; and put me into a trembling fear before he began to preach; for he looked as if he was Cloathed with authority from the Great God; and a sweet sollume solemnity sat upon his brow. And my hearing him preach, gave me a heart wound; By God's blessings: my old Foundation was broken up, and I saw that my righteousness would not save me; then I was convinced of the doctrine of Election and went right to quarrelling with God about it; because that all I could do would not save me; and he had decreed from Eternity who would be saved and who not.[33]

In speaking of the Congregational Church in Middletown, it was stated of Whitefield, "the superb orator thrilled the people of Middletown and its vicinity with his fiery eloquence."[34] The phrase related to the "vicinity" of Middletown deserves some recognition. Two towns adjoining Middletown on the south are Haddam and

---

33 Nathan Cole, *The Spiritual Travels of Nathan Cole, 1761.* http://www.learnnc.org/lp/editions/nchist-colonial/4213. Reprinted with permission from the Connecticut Historical Society. To facilitate reading, I have made only minor corrections to the original text.
34 Azel W. Hazen, *A Brief History of the First Church of Christ in Middletown, Connecticut, 1668-1918*, p. 44.

Durham. Although these towns are not mentioned in Whitefield's *Journals*, his influence in these communities was significant.

For example, in Haddam, the minister of the Congregational Church was Rev. Aaron Cleveland, a Harvard College graduate in 1735. Cleveland began serving in Haddam in 1739, in the midst of a revival of which he was fully supportive. Cleveland was a firm advocate for Whitefield, which caused disharmony in

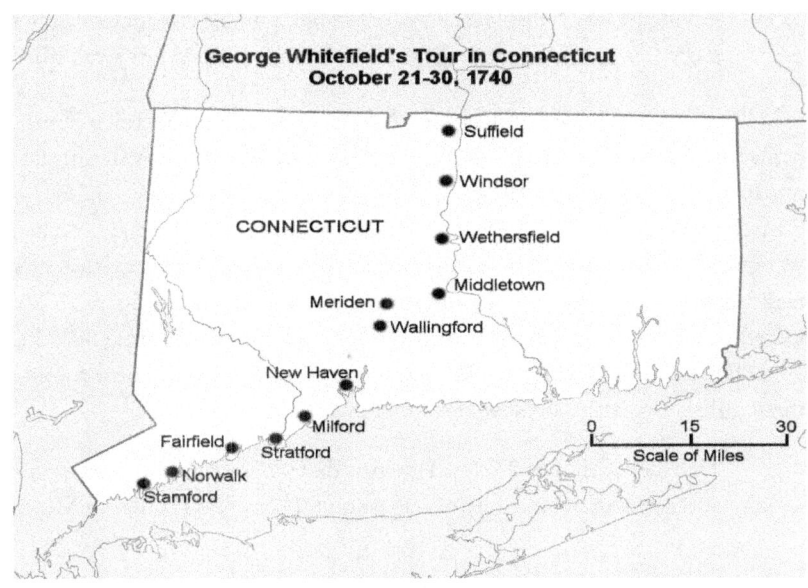

his church. He even copied the extemporaneous and emotional preaching style of Whitefield, to the chagrin of many of his church members. In the midst of several controversies, Cleveland departed the Congregational Church in Haddam to serve churches in Massachusetts and then in Nova Scotia.[35] Another example of Whitefield's influence in the vicinity of Middletown was in Durham. Rev. Nathaniel Chauncey served the Congregational Church in Durham from 1706 to his death in 1756. Chauncey was, like Whitefield, a Calvinist. But unlike Whitefield, Chauncey did not advocate itinerant preaching, he did not support open invitations for sinners to come to faith in Christ, and he resented the sometimes emotional outburst from Whitefield's listeners. While Chauncey generally supported revivals, he did not support Whitefield. Chauncey was a confirmed Old Light, an advocate of sustaining the religious norms in Connecticut society. To him, Whitefield was a disturbance.[36]

After departing Middletown, Whitefield next preached in Wallingford, fourteen miles to the southwest. Whitefield was now leaving the Connecticut River Valley on his way to New Haven and eventually New York. Whitefield wrote briefly in his *Journals*, "Thursday, October 23 . . . Preached . . . in the afternoon at Wallingford, fourteen miles from Middletown."[37]

Wallingford, Connecticut, was founded in 1667 and quickly became a local center for pewter and silver industries. Whitefield's host in Wallingford was Rev. Samuel Whittlesey, senior, called "a man of marked ability."[38] The Congregational stronghold on almost all Connecticut towns was less apparent in Wallingford, as an Episcopal Church started in the town in 1740. An account of Whitefield preaching in Wallingford recorded,

> He preached in Wallingford in Mr. Whittlesely's church about the middle of October, 1740, and also in Mr. Hall's church in Meriden parish. Our records of that date inform us of considerable accessions to the church. From Wallingford Mr. Whitefield proceeded to New Haven . . . While in Wallingford his wife joined him, having come from Hartford. Before

---

35 Everett E. Lewis, *Historical Sketch, First Congregational Church, Haddam, Connecticut*, (Middletown, CT: Pelton & King Printers, 1879), p. 23.
36 A helpful essay on Nathaniel Chauncey is found in William B. Sprague, *Annals of the American Pulpit*, (Trinitarian Congregational), (New York: Robert Carter, Publisher, 1866), vol. I, pp. 263-266.
37 George Whitefield, *George Whitefield's Journals*, p. 479.
38 "Rev. Samuel Whittlesey, 1686-1752," http://strongfamilyofamerica.org/genealogy/getperson.php?personID=1201299&tree=strong.

leaving the town he preached while standing in his chariot to a large multitude, and soon after leaving the town he started for New Haven, large multitudes following him several miles on foot or on horses.[39]

The previous quotation mentions "Mr. Hall's church in Meriden parish." The town of Meriden is not named in Whitefield's *Journals*, but his influence in Meriden was significant. Whitefield's host in Meriden was Rev. Theophilus Hall. He was a 1727 graduate of Yale College and was ordained at the Congregational Church in Meriden in 1729. The above quote states that Whitefield preached in Meriden in October, 1740. Whitefield preached for Hall in the Congregational meeting house that was built in 1727. Of Theophilus Hall is was stated, "The good parson . . . was faithful and unremitting in his attention to his duties and his forceful character made a great and enduring impression on his little flock . . . "[40]

After his brief ministries in Wallingford and Meriden, Whitefield continued to travel southwest towards the significant port city of New Haven. He wrote in his *Journals*:

> Thursday, October 23 . . . I then rode to New Haven, fourteen mile further, where I was affectionately received by Mr. Pierpoint, [Pierpont] brother to Mr. Edwards in Northampton.
>
> Friday, October 24 . . . I declined preaching in the morning, because it was wet, the people had no notice of my coming, and I had much private business on my hands. Preached in the afternoon, and it being the time in which the Assembly met, the Governor, the Council, and the members of the Lower House were present. After sermon, two young ministers came to converse with me; and, in the evening, I expounded at my lodgings to a room full of people. Oh, who would but travel for Christ![41]

The aforementioned Mr. Pierpont was Rev. James Pierpont, a Congregational minister in New Haven. His father, James senior, was a physician, congregational minister, and a founder of what would later be Yale College. The younger James was a 1718 graduate of Yale and was a leader of the separatist movement during the Great Awakening, splitting the Congregational Church in New Haven. The younger James was a tutor at Yale from 1722 to 1724, and then for a few years was engaged in the apothecary business in Boston, but he returned to New Haven and occupied his father's residence at Elm and Temple Streets.[42] James the younger was a brother-in-law to Jonathan Edwards, not a brother, as Whitefield noted above. The Governor named by Whitefield was Connecticut Colony Governor Joseph Talcott, who served as governor from 1724 to 1741.

Whitefield was enthusiastically welcomed in New Haven. Newspaper accounts and word-of mouth testimonies spread the word about his visit. Awakenings had preceded his arrival. The town and Yale College were happy to receive him. One account stated:

> Late in October he [Whitefield] reached New Haven, and was affectionately welcomed and entertained at the house of Mr. James Pierpont, a brother-in-law of Edwards, and a sympathizer with his religious views. People came in from the country at a distance of twenty miles to hear him, and many neighboring ministers also sought the opportunity of personal intercourse with a clergyman whose zeal and eloquence were so widely known.[43]

---

39 Charles H.S. Davis, *History of Wallingford, Connecticut* . . . , (Meriden, CT: Published by the Author, 1870), p. 301.
40 C. Bancroft Gillespie, compiler. *An Historical Record and Pictorial Description of the Town of Meriden, Connecticut*, (Meriden, CT: Journal Publishing Company, 1906), p. 143.
41 George Whitefield, *George Whitefield's Journals*, pp. 479-480.
42 "James Pierpont," http://www.wikitree.com/wiki/Pierpont-280-#Biography. For more details see Michael Sletcher, *New Haven: From Puritanism to the Age of Terror*, (Charleston, SC: Arcadia Publishing, 2004), pp. 20-39.
43 Charles H.S. Davis, *History of Wallingford, Connecticut* . . . , (Meriden, CT: Published by the Author, 1870), pp. 301-302.

The maritime city of New Haven was founded in 1638, as was the Congregational Church. The city was very well planned, centered on a sixteen-acre common. The influence of Yale College was significant. New Haven prospered from trade with the West Indies, England, and other American colonies. The community had a wealthy and educated political class, a middle class of merchants and businessmen, and a large working class of men who worked as fishermen, farmers, whalers, dock laborers, and warehouse workers. Whitefield wrote in some detail about his experience at New Haven and Yale College:

> Saturday, October 25. Was refreshed this morning by the sight of Mr. Jedediah Mills, the minister at Ripton near Stratford. He wrote to me some time ago. I felt his letter, and now also felt the man. I could not help thinking God would do great things by him. He had a remarkable work in his parish some time ago, and talked like one who was no novice in Divine things. With him I dined at the Rev. Mr. Clap's, Rector of New Haven College, about one-third part as big as that of Cambridge. It has one Rector, three Tutors, and about a hundred students. I hear of no remarkable concern among them regarding religion. I preached twice, and there were sweet meltings discernible both times. I spoke very closely to the students, and shewed the dreadful ill consequences of an unconverted ministry. Oh, that God may quicken ministers! Oh that the Lord may make them a flaming fire! Amen and Amen.[44]

The two men named by Whitefield in the above *Journals* entry deserve attention. Rev. Jedediah Mills was a Yale graduate in 1722. He began serving a church in Ripton, in a village north of Stratford, Connecticut, in 1723. This was a small, poor Congregational Church that could not pay their minister a living wage. To supplement his income, Mills worked as a tutor at Yale College. A firm supporter of Whitefield, Mills served the Congregational Church in Ripton until his death in 1776. The other person named was "Rev. Mr. Clap's, Rector of New Haven College." Rev. Thomas Clap was newly appointed as rector or president of Yale when Whitefield came to New Haven. Clap was a Harvard graduate in 1722 and a Congregational minister. He was a firm Calvinist, a skilled administrator and librarian, and he was known to firmly oppose Arminianism. Clap welcomed Whitefield to Yale.

> Like most New England ministers, Clap had at first been delighted by the reawakening of religious interests produced by Whitefield. He too had been worried by the declining religiosity of the people, so he welcomed Whitefield and brought him to the college to preach to the students.[45]

When Yale College moved to New Haven in 1718, the College House was built at the corner of College and Chapel Streets. This was a wood-framed structure that contained all the major departments of the college, with student rooms, a library, and a combined chapel and dining hall. Other smaller buildings housed support staff. Falling into disrepair, College House was taken down in 1782. It was in the College House that Whitefield preached to overflow crowds in October 1740. He recorded:

> Sunday, October 26. Preached both morning and evening to much larger congregations than before; and in the afternoon especially was the presence of God felt in the assembly. Many, I believe, were comforted and quickened by the Holy Ghost. I trust this will be an acceptable year of the Lord. After sermon, I waited on the Governor, whom I had observed much affected under the Word. When I came in, he said, "I am glad to see you, and heartily glad to hear you." His heart was so full that he could not speak much; and tears coursed down his aged cheeks.

---

44 George Whitefield, *George Whitefield's Journals*, p. 480.
45 Brooks M. Kelley, *Yale: A History*, (New Haven, CT: Yale University Press, 1999), p. 52.

He also said he was "thankful to God for such refreshing in our way to our rest. Food does us good, when we eat it with an appetite;" and, indeed, I believe he had fed upon the Word. The Lord support him when his strength fails, and bring his grey hairs with comfort to the grave! In the evening, I expounded to a great number of people at my lodgings, and collected upwards of £35 for the orphans.[46]

In October 1740, Samuel Hopkins was a student in his last year at Yale College. He heard Whitefield preach at a large assembly and at a smaller evening meeting, and he "highly approved of him." Hopkins wrote that thousands heard Whitefield in New Haven and at Yale, and that some came from twenty miles away to hear the itinerant preacher, writing "the people flocked to hear him, when he came to New Haven." Hopkins recorded, "The assemblies were crowded and remarkably attentive, and people appeared generally to approve."[47]

While in the New Haven area, Whitefield preached in Branford for Rev. Philemon Robbins. This event was not recorded in Whitefield's *Journal*. Bordering New Haven to the east, Branford was founded in 1638 as part of the New Haven Colony. This agrarian and maritime community survived through shipbuilding and coastal trading. An iron furnace began in Branford in 1655, the first in Connecticut. In 1701, a group of ministers met to found a school to train ministers, which would eventually become Yale College. Philemon Robbins was a Harvard trained minister who served in Branford from his ordination in 1732 to his death in 1781. Robbins was a passionate admirer of Jonathan Edwards and George Whitefield. He invited Whitefield to preach in Branford, and the itinerant accepted.[48]

A sketch of the College House at Yale. This four stories wood-framed structure contained all the academic and social activities of the college.

Source: https://en.wikipedia.org/wiki/Old_Campus_(Yale_University)

Robbins was a New Light but not a fanatic. Following the example of Whitefield, Robbins did some itinerant preaching, much to the annoyance of some of his ministerial associates. The grandson of Philemon Robbins, Rev. Thomas Robbins, wrote in his diary his recollections of his grandfather's interactions with Whitefield. He noted that the elder Robbins was steadfast in support of the awakening and Whitefield, even while opposed by civil and ecclesiastical authorities. The diary further describes Philemon Robbins as follows.

> He was naturally of a remarkably mild and benevolent spirit, and reprobated many of the extravagancies of the times . . . He was distinguished rather for activity and readiness of mind,

---

46 George Whitefield, *George Whitefield's Journals*, p. 480.
47 Samuel Hopkins, *The Works of Samuel Hopkins*, (Boston, MA: 1852), vol. I, p. 15.
48 J. Rupert Simonds, *A History of the First Church and Society of Branford, Connecticut, 1644-1919*, (New Haven, CT: Tuttle, Moorehouse & Taylor Printers, 1919), p. 88.

and for a quick and retentive memory . . . He had a strong and pleasant voice, and his manner was free and engaging, and breathed much of the natural benevolence of his spirit. He preached from short notes, and had a ready command of language in extemporaneous speaking.[49]

Whitefield departed the New Haven and Yale College area unaware that the results of his visit would permanently divide the churches of Connecticut. For now, all seamed positive and encouraging. Whitefield wrote of his departure from New Haven as follows.

> Sunday, October 26 . . . After I had given a word of exhortation, that they should study to adorn the Gospel of our Lord in all things, we went forward on our journey, and got to Milford, ten miles from New Haven, about ten at night. The Lord's name be praised from the rising of the sun unto the going down of the same! Amen.[50]

Nearby, Milford, Connecticut traces its Puritan origins to 1639. The town was based on agrarian and maritime industries, supported by various trades and laborers. Milford had several water-powered grist and lumber mills. Mounds of oyster shells were scattered around the fourteen-mile ocean coastline. A thriving tavern welcomed travelers along the road from New Haven to New York. The Congregational Church was the center of the community, and needed to expand its building in 1728. Milford was a working-class town, that by 1740 was gathering resources to open its first library.[51] The town was deeply divided over the Awakening in Connecticut. Many in Milford wanted to welcome Whitefield, but Rev. Samuel Whittlesey, Junior, would not comply. One report stated,

> George Whitefield, whom the dissenters wished to hear, was denied the use of the church by Reverend Whittlesey, and conducted service from the doorstone to what must have seemed a multitude, for a thousand people gathered to hear him.[52]

Rev. Samuel Whittlesey of Milford was the son of Rev. Samuel Whittlesey, senior, from nearby Wallingford. The younger Whittlesey was an Old Light, a minister set in the established civil and ecclesiastical routine in historical Congregational Connecticut. This caused serious tensions in Milford. Whittlesey was ordained in Milford in 1737, much to the consternation of the more Calvinistic residents in town. A vocal minority in Milford resisted him, based on suspicion that he was not an orthodox Christian. Whittlesey was accepted as an assistant minister at the Congregational Church only from a compromise with the more Calvinistic members. The accusations against him were "on the ground that he did not preach the gospel but rather a system of morals."[53] The Congregational meeting house in Milford was constructed in 1728, eighty feet by forty-five feet, with two galleries and a bell tower. Whittlesey did not allow Whitefield to preach in this building.

In Whitefield's *Journals*, he did not mention that he was opposed by Rev. Whittlesey in Milford. Instead, Whitefield emphasized the success of his outdoors preaching in Milford and his reuniting with Rev. Jedediah Mills of neighboring Stratford. Whitefield wrote,

> Monday, October 27. Preached this morning at Milford to a large assembly. Many ministers were present, and they could not help glorifying God. Mr. Mills, who came again to meet me this morning, was much affected; and, as I was riding out of town, a gentleman met me,

---

49 Thomas Robbins, *Diary of Thomas Robbins, D.D.*, (Boston, MA: Beacon Press, 1887), vol. II, pp. 1092-1093.
50 Ibid.
51 *History of Milford, Connecticut*, written by the Federal Writer's Project, (Bridgeport, CT: Braunworth Press, 1939), pp. 42-58.
52 Ibid., p. 54.
53 Ibid.

and with tears said, "I never felt God's Presence in the Sanctuary like this before; it has been a blessed time to my soul." In the afternoon, I preached at Stratford, four miles from Milford.[54]

Whitefield was introduced to Rev. Jedediah Mills by correspondence. They first met a few days prior to this time, in New Haven. Mills was present to support Whitefield when the pulpit of the Congregational Church in Milford was closed to him. When Whitefield wrote, "In the afternoon, I preached at Stratford," he preached with the full support of Mills, who served at the Congregational Church, Ripton Parish, in Stratford.

Stratford, Connecticut, was founded by Puritans as a community based on the teachings from the Bible as interpreted and applied by the Congregational Church. In the one hundred or so years from the founding of the town in 1639, to Whitefield's visit in 1740, Stratford had transformed from a Puritan stronghold to a more eclectic, egalitarian, and pragmatic society. Nevertheless, the Congregational Church was still a primary force in all town civic, cultural, and religious issues. This maritime community had two nearby harbors and easy access inland from the Pequonnock and Housatonic Rivers. Hunting was good, fishing was abundant, and the flat terrain encouraged farming.

Whitefield preached on Monday afternoon, October 27, 1740, in Stratford, Connecticut. His host was Rev. Hezekiah Gold of the First Church, Congregational. The official history of the town of Stratford states,

> Whitefield's stay in Stratford extended to a few hours only. He preached in New Haven on Sunday, and on Monday morning came to Stratford, preached at the meeting-house, probably outside, in the open air; dined with the Rev. Mr. Gold, then went to Fairfield, where he preached in the afternoon of the same day.[55]

The meeting house associated with Rev. Hezekiah Gold was the Congregational Church, dating back to 1639. Gold was a 1719 graduate of Harvard College. He began at the church in 1722, and served there for thirty years. There was slow but consistent growth in the Congregational Church until shortly before Whitefield arrived. In the late 1730s the church had stirrings of revival, with increases in membership. Gold was fully like-minded to Whitefield, welcoming the itinerant evangelist to Stratford with the overwhelming support from most of the townspeople. One account stated, "Mr. Gold, then pastor at Stratford, was cordially interested in the work of grace attending Mr. Whitefield's preaching.[56] Another report said, "Mr. Whitefield preached for Mr. Gold. His sermon was blessed to the conversion of several souls."[57]

Two interesting accounts have survived from women who heard Whitefield preach in Stratford. Mrs. Ann Brooks walked from her home with an infant in her arms, to hear Whitefield preach in Stratford. She was very interested, so much so that she travelled to hear him preach again the next day at another place, at Fairfield. Her conversion was dated to this time, after which she joined the Congregational Church in Stratford.[58] Another woman who heard Whitefield preach in Stratford was a Mrs. Burritt. Her experience states,

> Mrs. Burritt, who lived on the wood end road below Main Street, as being in the yard of her dwelling, farther down, than any house now stands, and a mile nearby from the meeting house hill, where she distinctly heard Mr. Whitefield name his text from Zechariah IX.12: "Turn ye to the stronghold, ye prisoners of hope," and repeated it to her husband on his return home. Hence, it is probable, that this sermon was delivered in the open air.[59]

---

54 George Whitefield, *George Whitefield's Journals*, p. 481.
55 Samuel Orcutt, *A History of the Old Town of Stratford* . . . , (New Haven, CT: Fairfield County Historical Society, 1886), p. 347.
56 Ibid., p. 305.
57   Theodore S. Gold, *Historical Records of the Town of Cornwall, Litchfield County, Connecticut*, (Hartford, CT: Case, Lockwood & Brainard Press, 1877), p. 290.
58 Samuel Orcutt, *A History of the Old Town of Stratford* . . . , pp. 305-306.
59 Ibid., p. 306.

An interesting legend arouse related to George Whitefield in Stratford. Historically, the salt marshes around Stratford was considered valuable in feeding cattle. Farmers and laborers would harvest the salt marsh hay for winter feed. Somehow, the salt marsh became infested with mosquitoes. The legend says that Whitefield was poorly treated by the Church of England people in Stratford.[60] In response, when Whitefield departed, he cursed the salt marsh and the town with mosquitoes.[61]

Whitefield's next preaching appointment was a few miles west from Stratford, at Fairfield. After riding on horseback through the snow, he wrote,

> Tuesday, October 28. Got to Fairfield, eight miles from Stratford, about ten last night. The weather was very cold, having snowed a great part of the afternoon; but the Lord brought us on in safety. Preached, in the morning, to a considerable congregation, and in the prayer after the sermon, I scarce knew how to leave off.

Fairfield, Connecticut was founded in 1639. The Congregational Church formed here in 1644. Not much is known about Whitefield's preaching in Fairfield beyond him writing that he preached "to a considerable congregation," as noted above. The official history of Fairfield simply records about Whitefield, "Leaving New Haven, he preached at Milford, Stratford, Fairfield, Norwalk, Stamford, and other places, arriving in New York on the 13th of October."[62]

Whitefield was denounced as an enthusiast, a fanatic, by an Episcopal minister in Fairfield named Rev. Henry Caner. As a Yale graduate, Caner served as a missionary with the Society for the Propagation of the Gospel, an Episcopal Church mission sponsored by the Church of England. The fact that an Episcopal mission was formed in Fairfield in 1737 under Henry Caner, infuriated most of the civil and ecclesiastical residents of this Congregational community. As the Great Awakening spread through Connecticut, Caner resisted the movement. He was a confirmed anti-revival minister who denounced the awakening as enthusiasm, irreverent, and contrary to the teachings of the Church of England. The fact that Whitefield was an ordained Church of England clergyman, who was a catalyst for the revival, infuriated Henry Caner. Caner was indignant against Whitefield. Because of Caner's influence in Fairfield, there was no large revival in this town. Caner happily reported, "Enthusiasm made no progress in Fairfield," and that his intention was, "the reconciling [of] many sober & considerate people to the Communion of our church," meaning the Episcopal Church.[63]

Rev. Henry Caner served an Episcopal congregation in a wooden building in Fairfield, until a more permanent stone meeting place was constructed in 1742. As a committed Old Light, traditional clergyman, he opposed Whitefield's itinerant preaching and his denouncing of unregenerate clergy.[64] Caner took deliberate steps to oppose the awakening in Fairfield. He wrote,

> In order to prevent as much as possible the spreading of enthusiasm, both now & hereafter among us, I have applied myself closely to catechizing both young & old, who do not appear to have sufficiently digested the grounds of our most holy faith; the catechumens being divided

---

60 The Church of England in Stratford, Connecticut was served by Rev. Samuel Johnson from 1723 to 1754. Now called the Christ Episcopal Church, this is the oldest Church of England congregation in Connecticut, founded in 1707.
61 *The Bridgeport Telegraph* (Bridgeport, Connecticut), August 13, 1925, p. 5.
62 Elizabeth H. Schenck, *The History of Fairfield, Fairfield County, Connecticut, from 1700 to 1800*, (Mew York: Published by the Author, 1905), vol. II, p. 130. While this text states that Whitefield arrived in New York "on the 13th of October," the actual date was closer to October 30.
63 Ibid., p. 131.
64 *Norwalk after Two Hundred and Fifty Years*, Norwalk Historical and Memorial Library Association, (South Norwalk, CT: C.A. Freeman, Publisher, 1901), p. 268.

into three classes, are examined & instructed according to their several improvements every Lord's day after sermon in the afternoon.⁶⁵

Whitefield spent only a few hours in Fairfield. He arrived, preached outdoors, ate supper, and travelled to his next appointment, in Norwalk, Connecticut, an easy ride west from Fairfield. Whitefield wrote in his *Journals*:

> Tuesday, October 28 . . . In the afternoon at Newark, [Norwalk] twelve miles from Fairfield, I was much restrained both in prayer and preaching. It rained greatly, so that we had not a very large congregation. However, some were affected. I believe my Lord never lets me preach in vain.⁶⁶

When Whitefield arrived in Norwalk, he observed a small maritime and agricultural community with an excellent harbor. The Congregational Church was founded in 1652, with its first meeting house constructed in 1657. Norwalk had a large farming community that harvested corn, wheat, rye, barley, and oats. There was also a healthy dairy business, and the fisheries excelled. Whitefield's host in Norwalk was Rev. Moses Dickinson of the First Church, Congregational.

Moses Dickinson graduated from Yale in 1717. His ordination was with the Presbyterian Church, where he previously served in Maidenhead, New York. In 1727 he became a Congregationalist and accepted a call to the church in Norwalk. In his *Journals*, Whitefield admitted that there was a low turnout for his preaching due to foul weather. While we do know that Dickinson supported Whitefield, and allowed the itinerant preacher to speak at the Congregational meeting house, no details of this event have survived. The records of the Congregational Church in Norwalk were destroyed by insects in 1806.⁶⁷ Of Dickinson it was stated that he was held in "high veneration . . . in all the surrounding region," and that "he was a man of superior learning and capacity, of earnest and uniform piety, of sound judgment and strong common sense . . . looked up to as a beloved minister of Christ."⁶⁸

From Norwalk, Whitefield travelled to nearby Stamford, Connecticut. This would be his last stop on his 1740 tour through Connecticut. Stamford was a farming and maritime community. The town was founded in 1640, and its first schoolhouse was constructed in 1671, a small wooden building about twelve-feet square. Norwalk was the home of the controversial revival preacher, Rev. James Davenport. When Whitefield spoke in the Congregational Church in Stamford, he spoke in an older, smaller meeting house constructed in 1705. Extra galleries were added to the building in 1723, and the first church bell was installed in 1735. Whitefield's host in Stamford was Rev. Ebenezer Wright of the First Church, Congregational. Whitefield wrote of his time in Stamford as follows:

> Wednesday, October 29. Came hither last night in safety, though dark and rainy. Was somewhat dejected before I went from my lodgings, and distressed for a text after I got up into the pulpit. But the Lord directed me to one, and, before I had preached half an hour, the Blessed Spirit began to move the hearer's hearts in a very awful manner. Young, and especially many old people were surprisingly affected. At dinner, I spoke with such vigor

---

65 Elizabeth H. Schenck, *The History of Fairfield, Fairfield County, Connecticut,* p. 132.
66 George Whitefield, *George Whitefield's Journals,* p. 481.
67 There are two books written in the nineteenth century that cover the history of Norwalk in detail. Edwin Hall, *The Ancient Historical Records of Norwalk, Connecticut . . . ,* (New York: James Mallory & Company Printers, 1847). Nathaniel Bouton, *An Historical Discourse in Commemoration of the 200th Anniversary of the Settlement of Norwalk, Connecticut, in 1651 . . . ,* (New York: S. W. Benedict Printer, 1851). While both of these texts are thorough, they are hindered from a detailed history of the Norwalk Congregational Church due to the loss of church records. There is no mention of Whitefield's visit in these texts.
68 Frederick W. Loetscher, editor. *Papers of the American Society of Church History,* (New York: G. P. Putnam's Sons—Knickerbocker Press, 1921), pp. 311-312.

against sending unconverted ministers into the ministry, that two ministers with tears in their eyes, publically confessed, that they had laid hands on two young men without so much as asking them, "whether they were born again of God, or not?" After dinner, I prayed, and one old minister was so deeply convicted . . . with great difficulty (because of the weeping), he desired our prayers, "for," said he, "I have been a scholar, and have preached the doctrines of grace a long time, but I believe I have never felt the power of them in my own soul." Oh, that all unconverted ministers were brought to make the same confession! After having by prayer recommended him to God, I took horse, rejoicing exceedingly in spirit, to see how our Lord was getting Himself the victory, in a place where Mr. Davenport, a native of Stamford, a minister of the blessed Jesus, had been slighted and despised.[69]

This *Journals* entry by Whitefield is insightful for several reasons. First, he gives testimony that the young and old were spiritually stirred by his preaching in Stamford. Next, he gives some details about the many private meetings he had with clergymen, and how these personal interviews with Whitefield deeply influenced other ministers. Also, Whitefield mentions Rev. James Davenport of Stamford as a minister whom he can support. A few years after his 1740 tour through Connecticut, Whitefield would distance himself from Davenport. In the late 1730s and early 1740s, Davenport was a popular, emotional, and flamboyant preacher who defied and antagonized many New England clergymen. Eventually, both Old Lights and New Lights disassociated themselves from Davenport. While the New Lights agreed with his preaching on the new birth and the spiritual lethargy of most churches and their ministers, Davenport was by most accounts excessive, erratic, and insulting. Eventually, Whitefield separated from Davenport. But in 1740, Whitefield defended and endorsed the increasingly unstable Davenport.

The well-travelled and energetic Whitefield was concluding his New England tour. One account summarized his last days on this 1740 New England trip as follows; "On the 23d of October, he reached New Haven . . . After the Sabbath, he preached at Milford, and prosecuting his journey to New York, and the southern colonies, he preached with his usual popularity and success, at Stratford, Fairfield, Norwalk, and Stamford."[70] After his meal with Rev. Ebenezer Wright and the other ministers in Stamford, mentioned above, Whitefield took the time to pen an extended account of his previous travels throughout New England.

Wednesday, October 29 . . . Here I think it proper to set up my Ebenezer, before I enter the Province of New York, to give God thanks for sending me to New England. I have now had an opportunity of seeing the greatest and most populous part of it. On many accounts, it certainly excels all other provinces in America; and, for the establishment of religion, perhaps all other parts of the world. The towns all through Connecticut, and eastward toward York, in the Province of Massachusetts, near the riverside, are large and well peopled. Every five miles or perhaps less, you have a meeting-house; and, I believe, there is no such thing as a pluralist or non-resident minister in both provinces. Many, nay most that preach, I fear, do not experimentally know Christ . . . Few country ministers, I have been informed, have sufficient money allowed them to maintain a family. God has remarkably, at sundry times and in divers manners, poured out His Spirit in several parts; and it often refreshed my soul to hear of the faith of their good forefathers, who first settled in these parts. Notwithstanding they had their foibles, surely they were a set of righteous men. They certainly followed our Lord's rule, "by seeking first the Kingdom of God and His Righteousness," and all other things God added unto them. I think the ministers almost universally preaching by note, is

---

69 George Whitefield, *George Whitefield's Journals*, pp. 481-482.
70 Benjamin Trumbull, *A Complete History of Connecticut, Civil and Ecclesiastical . . .* ,vol. II, p. 153.

a mark that they have, in a great measure, lost the old spirit of preaching. Though all are not to be condemned who use notes, yet it is a symptom of the decay of religion, when reading sermons becomes fashionable where extempore preaching did once almost universally prevail. When the spirit of prayer began to be lost, then forms of prayer were invented, and, I believe, the same observation will hold good as to preaching. The civil government of New England seems to be well regulated; and, I think, at the opening of all their courts, either the judge or a minister begins with a prayer. Family worship, I believe, is generally kept up: and the Negros are better used than in any other province I have yet seen. In short, I like New England exceedingly well. Send forth, Oh Lord, Thy light and Thy truth, and for Thy infinite mercy's sake, shew Thou hast a peculiar delight in these habitable parts of the earth. Amen![71]

A painting of George Whitefield preaching, by John Wollaston, about 1742. Recently married, the woman listening affectionately to his preaching is undoubtedly his new wife Elizabeth.

Source: www.tracts.ukgo.com/george_whitefield.htm.

---

71 George Whitefield, *George Whitefield's Journals*, pp. 482-483. Several comments in this extended quote by Whitefield deserve further comments. The phrase, "set up my Ebenezer," refers to a biblical text in I Samuel 7:12, when the prophet Samuel set up an Ebenezer stone, a memorial marker, to commemorate defeating the Philistines in battle. An Ebenezer became known in church history as a physical act to commemorate a spiritual victory. His comment that "the establishment of religion," related to Massachusetts and Connecticut laws requiring local civil authorities to tax citizens for the support of Congregational churches. The phrase, "there is no such thing as a pluralist or non-resident minister" emphasized that each meeting house had a designated minister, and that a minister did not have to serve more than one church. Whitefield spoke of "the faith of their good forefathers," as a compliment to the original Puritans who settled New England. Whitefield perhaps overstated his case when he referred to ministers who preach with notes as "a symptom of the decay of religion."

CHAPTER 9

BOSTON AND EASTERN NEW ENGLAND AFTER WHITEFIELD'S DEPARTURE

1740-1744

A FEW WEEKS AFTER WHITEFIELD departed New England, an insightful letter was written by William Gaylord of Norwalk, Connecticut to Rev. Eleazer Wheelock of Lebanon, Connecticut. Both men supported Whitefield. Gaylord wrote, "I really desired his coming and was heartily glad to see him, because I believe he excels in that which we (especially in these parts) want most, I mean zeal for God and compassion for immortal souls." Gaylord writes of Whitefield's powerful speaking voice and of the vast crowds who came to hear him preach. He also stated, "You know there is a mixture of Wisdom and Folly [,] Good and Evil in the best men we meet with." Then Gaylord wrote that Whitefield "lays vastly too much weight upon the affection, tears, and meltings, etc. that appear in the face of the assembly, as an argument of his success."[1]

Whitefield was cautious about the initial favorable response to his ministry in Boston and its surrounding communities. It is as if he understood, as in prior ministries in England, that some dissention and controversy would inevitably result from his preaching. He was able to see through the thin veneer of tolerance granted him by some local Massachusetts clergy, as his following *Journals* entry indicates:

> Boston is a large, populous place, and very wealthy. It has the form of religion kept up, but has lost much of its power. I have not heard of any remarkable stir for many years. Ministers and people are obliged to confess, that the love of many is waxed cold. Both seem to be too much conformed to the world. There is much of the pride of life to be seen in their assemblies . . . I never saw such little scoffing, and never had so little opposition. Still, I fear, many rest in head knowledge, are close to Pharisees, and have only a name to live. It must needs be so, when the power of godliness is dwindled away, where the form only of religion is become fashionable amongst the people.[2]

In November 1744, Whitefield returned to Boston. Four years would separate his visits. The controversies and turmoil which consumed the people during his absence was previously unknown in any of the American Colonies. All aspects of religious life came under new criticism—the deadness of worship, lack of discipline, ostentation in dress, the questionable piety of the clergy, and the general inadequacy of the whole religious establishment.[3]

During Whitefield's absence, the revival in New England continued under the leadership of men motivated by Whitefield's message of salvation and his method of itinerancy. The Presbyterian Gilbert Tennent from New

---

1 Richard Bushman, *The Great Awakening: Documents on the Revival of Religion, 1740-1745*, (Chapel Hill, NC: North Carolina Press, 1969), pp. 39-40. The letter was dated November 24, 1740.
2 George Whitefield, *Journals of George Whitefield*, (1756: reprinted by Banner of Truth Trust, Carlisle, PA: 1985), p. 473.
3 Jerald C. Brauer, "Conversion: From Puritanism to Revivalism," *Journal of Religion*, (July 1978), p. 239.

Jersey accepted Whitefield's invitation to continue the work in New England. Initially, the ministry proceeded smoothly with no notable disturbances. Rev. Thomas Prince of the Old South Church in Boston reported:

> In the year 1741, the very face of the town seemed strangely altered. Some who had not been here since the fall before, have told me of their surprise at the change in the general look and carriage of the people . . . and thus successfully did this divine work . . . go on in town, without any lisp, as I remember, of a separation, wither in this town or province, for above a year and a half after Mr. Whitefield left us.[4]

In Gloucester, Massachusetts is the small community called Annisquam. The community was served by Rev. Benjamin Bradstreet and his assistant, Moses Parsons of the Third Parish. Bradstreet and Parsons were New Light ministers who endorsed Whitefield and the awakening. A revival started in the church in January 1741. Moses Parsons was teaching the children when religious excitement began. The usual children's lessons were given up, and Pastor Bradstreet was called to assist. The spiritual awakening in the children quickly spread to their parents. Eighteen months later, evidence of genuine revival remained in the Annisquam church. Bradstreet wrote in 1743, "Thanks be to God, we have no divisions, nor separations among us . . . I freely confess that I verily believe, there has been of late and now is, a blessed work on God going on in many parts of this land, and divine influence the spring of it."[5]

The message of the revival was carried primarily through publishing and preaching. Many ministers of local congregations were forced to increase the number of public services to accommodate the needs of the people. Joseph Tracy's study of primary source documents for this period shows us that Boston was fully absorbed in the revival. For example:

> The weekly Tuesday evening lectures at the church in Brattle Street were much crowded and not sufficient. April 17, 1741, another lecture was therefore opened every Friday evening at the South Church: and soon after, another lecture every Tuesday and Friday evening was opened at the New North; three of the most capacious houses of public worship in town, the least of which I suppose will hold three thousand people; besides the ancient lecture every Thursday noon at the Old Church, and other lectures in other churches.[6]

In addition to the increase in the number of church services, numerous unordained men began to gather followers as they preached the salvation message. These men were known as "exhorters," as preaching in the colonies at this time was restricted to the ordained.[7] The names of these men, who were largely responsible for spreading the revival to remote villages in New England, are largely lost to us. In addition, men educated as ministers left the comfortable confines of their meeting houses and began itinerant preaching. One example of this that has survived is that of Nathaniel and John Rogers, fourth-generation Puritan preachers in Ipswich, Massachusetts. Not only did the Rogers brothers heartily support Whitefield, they also personally followed his example of itinerancy, preaching up and down the Merrimack River Valley.[8]

After Whitefield's departure from New England, there was some benefit in the sincere efforts of itinerant preachers that followed his example. But certain elements entered the work which were destructive. One issue was over the nature of itinerant ministry, and its relationship with the established churches. A second topic of

---

4 Thomas Prince, editor, *The Christian History,* (Boston, MA: 1744), pp. 395-397.
5 "Benjamin Bradstreet," https://www.wikitree.com/wiki/Bradstreet-347. See also, *The Testimony and Advice of an Assembly of the Pastors, July 7, 1743*. (Boston: 1743), pp. 39-41.
6 Joseph Tracy, *The Great Awakening*, (Carlisle, PA: Banner of Truth Trust, 1976), p. 118.
7 Arnold Dallimore, *George Whitefield: The Life and Times of the Great Evangelist of the Eighteenth Century Revival*, (Carlisle, PA: Banner of Truth Trust, 1979), vol. II, pp. 181-182.
8 Christopher Jedrey, *The World of John Cleveland*, (New York: W.W. Norton & Company, 1979), p. 47.

discussion was centered on "enthusiasm," or fanaticism with emotional extremes in response to the preaching of the itinerants. There were cases when crowds were almost overtaken with emotion, leading to fainting, shouting, and other outbursts. The revival work always had its silent critics while Whitefield was present. For as long as a year and a half after his departure, the revival work progressed somewhat smoothly. Yet the issues of itinerancy and fanaticism became causes of turmoil within the church life of New England.

Whitefield departed New England the end of October 1740. Over the following year, nominal doctrinal and pragmatic differences became intensified. Revival supporters became known as "New Lights" and those who resisted the revival were called "Old Lights."[9] It is wrong to assume that the "Old Lights" opposed Whitefield's message—many did not. However, they were offended at such things as outdoors or field preaching, interdenominational services, itinerancy, and the pluralistic spirit of Whitefield and the itinerants. Also, there were theological differences over the nature of man's sin and the extent of Christ's atonement. Whitefield remained a firm Calvinist and an advocate of the Westminster Confession, but many clergymen in New England were drifting away from these Puritan beliefs into what would later be identified as Unitarianism and Universalism.

The antagonism between Old Lights and New Lights became incendiary. At that tense time in the religious life of New England, the Rev. James Davenport of Long Island, New York took up the work of itinerant evangelism. The tension which existed between the New and Old Lights before his appearance exploded into an irreconcilable division after his wild and fanciful exploits in the name of revival. What Whitefield had begun in 1740, James Davenport poorly imitated in 1741. "Everywhere he aroused resentment and opposition by his fanatical harangues and his arrogant attacks on 'unconverted' ministers."[10] Although Davenport came from an old and respected New England family, he had in his youth suffered an emotional breakdown. When Whitefield met Davenport in 1740, he thought highly of him. Yet, as Davenport commenced his itinerant evangelism, he soon proved that his unstable constitution could not cope with the pressures and excitement of the ongoing revival ministry. In 1742, Davenport was arrested in Connecticut, but later released, because he was considered mentally disturbed. The same happened to him in Boston in 1743. After a frenzied book-burning ceremony, and some sage advice by two New Light ministers, Davenport apparently regained his senses.

While excesses related to Davenport were newsworthy, smaller, quitter results of the awakening surfaced throughout New England. For example, in the Ipswich-Chebacco parish in what is now Essex, Massachusetts, a prominent citizen named Mary Dodge wrote, "In the later end of the year 1741, began a gloris reviel [glorious revival] of the work of God," which "was at first begun by the rev. Mr. Whitefield and Mr. Tennant as the means."[11]

The harm Davenport caused the revival in New England was extreme. Those who moderately supported or opposed the revival had reason to turn from it completely. Other silent opponents had opportunity to express their true dispositions. Davenport printed a retraction in 1744, and never again partook of such extremes. He was even elected in 1754 to moderate the New York Presbyterian Synod. In his confession to the public, Davenport confirmed that the awakening was indeed a work of God, and that God appointed him to preach the gospel. On these counts he made no excuses.[12] After considering his past ministry, he admitted to several excesses and unnecessary additions to his preaching ministry, such as "misguided zeal," being influenced by a "false spirit" and practicing "misconduct."[13] Although his confession and subsequent behavior re-established Davenport in the gospel ministry, dreadful damage had been done to the work advanced by Whitefield.

---

9 It would be an over-simplification to assert that all New England churches consciously chose to be "New Light" or "Old Light." A great number of ministers were neither, or both. See David H. Harlan, "The Travail of Religious Moderation: Jonathan Dickson and the Great Awakening," *Journal of Presbyterian History*, vol. 61 (1983), pp. 411-426.
10 Sydney E. Ahlstrom, *A Religious History of the American People*, (New Haven, CT: Yale University Press, 1972), p. 285.
11 *Mary (Dodge) Cleveland Papers, Diary 1742-1762*, (box 2, John Cleveland Papers, Essex Institute, Salem, Massachusetts).
12 James Davenport, *The Reverend Mr. James Davenport's Confession*, (Boston, MA: 1744), p. 1.
13 Ibid., pp. 3-4.

During this period of religious turmoil, there were impassioned pleas by the clergy of New England for peace and unity in the churches. We will consider several, chronologically. The Rev. Nathaniel Appleton was born in Ipswich in 1693, graduated from Harvard in 1712, and pastored the First Church in Cambridge until his death in 1784. He was a Calvinist and supported evangelism, while opposing excesses promoted by itinerants. He preached a sermon in 1741, as converts began swarming into his congregation after a visit from Whitefield. He warned of divisions and affirmed that God should receive all the glory, by asserting:

> It hath been but a dead and dull time with us upon spiritual accounts of late, but small additions made to the church, but few coming in to own the covenant, and give themselves up to God. But blessed be God, there seems some Revival among us, there are more affected, awakened and convinced, and put upon their duty, than is common among us. The word preached seems to have come with greater power upon the souls of people, especially of the younger sort. I have planted, Mr. Whitefield has watered, but God has given some increase. I mention the name of that young Apollos, because most of those, that are to be received to the communion and fellowship of the saints, have declared to me, what powerful influence his fervent preaching had upon them. And surely we ought to rejoice and give God the glory, whenever he accompanies his preached work, or any of his ordinances, with power unto the souls of many.[14]

Rev. Eleazar Wheelock was born into a prosperous farming family in Windham, Connecticut in 1711. He graduated from Yale College in 1734, was married in 1735, and began serving as the pastor of the Second Congregational Church in Lebanon, Connecticut from 1735 to 1769. Eventually, Wheelock would get involved with missions to American Indians and would be a founder of Dartmouth College in New Hampshire in 1769, serving as its first president. But in the early 1740s, Wheelock was simply a Congregational pastor in Lebanon and an itinerant preacher. He was fully supportive of the Great Awakening and Whitefield. The diary of Eleazar Wheelock gives a fascinating view of the turmoil in New England churches caused by the awakening and the travels of Whitefield. Excerpts are from Wheelock's itinerant preaching trip from Connecticut to Boston.

> October 21, 1741. Rode to Voluntown [Connecticut] . . . Went to meeting at ten . . . There is a great work in this town; but more of the footsteps of Satan than in any place I have yet been in: the zeal of some too furious . . .
>
> October 22. Preached twice with enlargement . . . many cried out; many stood trembling . . . four or five converted.
>
> October 23. Left Voluntown about seven, accompanied by a great number of wounded and comforted. Came to . . . Situate [Rhode Island]. Preached to a considerable assembly.
>
> October 26. Returned with a great number to Providence [Rhode Island]. Preached to a full assembly: many scoffers present; one man hired for twenty shillings to come into the meeting house and fall down; which he did, and made a great disturbance . . .
>
> October 29. Came with . . . many others to Attleborough [Massachusetts] . . . a great deal of affection and sobbing through the whole assembly . . .
>
> October 30. Rode with . . . many others to Norton . . . Preached to a full assembly; much affection and sobbing through the whole assembly. Rode to Raynham.

---

14 Nathaniel Appleton, *God, and not Ministers to Have the Glory of All Successes Given to the Preached Gospel*, (Boston: 1741), p. 21.

> November 1. Preached in the forenoon to a full assembly. Went . . . to Taunton Preached there. One or two cried out. Appointed another meeting in the evening. I believe thirty cried out. Almost all the negroes in the town wounded; three or four converted.
>
> November 5. Came to . . . Braintree. Preached with great freedom.
>
> November 6. Set out for Boston. Met by dear Mr. Prince . . . about eight miles from Boston.[15]

A widely distributed sermon by Rev. Joseph Seccombe was preached in 1741 which called for sober-minded evaluation of an individual's salvation. This was significant in relation to the rampant emotionalism of the time. Seccombe was born in Boston in 1706, graduated from Harvard in 1732, and ministered in Kingston, New Hampshire until his death in 1760. Seccombe preached and published a sermon entitled, "Reflections on Hypocrisy," which emphasized personal examinations of belief, the need for conversion, and submission to the plan of God. He challenged his people, saying:

> Have you ever taken pains to examine yourselves to discover your sins and humble yourselves before God? And do you plead the merits of Christ for pardon of sin and reconciliation to God? Have you been very earnest in your prayers to God that he would pour out his spirit upon you to work all graces in you, to put your graces in lively exercise, and enable you to mortify your lusts and corruptions?[16]

In 1742, Seccombe again preached a sermon which directly addressed the needs of his people.[17] In this highly logical, organized, and scholarly work, in which he freely quotes Jonathan Edwards to support the revivals, he does not hesitate to rebuke emotionalism and deviant behavior. In his preface, he asserts:

> It is the view of the writer, and his hope, under God, to promote the progress of reformation, and Revival of religion among us, by removing some misapprehensions, which might be prejudicial to the reception or continuance of the Divine influence.[18]

If all New England ministers of that time were as sensible as Seccombe, unwarranted tensions might have subsided. However, some seemed determined to spread their personal frustrations over the revival from their pulpits. One such minister was Jonathan Ashley from Deerfield, west of Boston, in the territory where Jonathan Edwards was helping to spread the revival in western Massachusetts. In a sermon preached as a guest speaker in the Brattle Street Church in Boston, Ashley almost exclusively pointed out the negative aspects of the revival, such as religious debates among people, divisiveness and man-following, and the public exhortation by unordained clergy.[19] Furthermore, he stated that "There is a greater backwardness to the support of ministers than ever; as though an extraordinary degree of zeal excused people from supporting their ministers."[20] His sermon in 1742, preached in Boston, was his personal and public declaration of opposition to the awakening, and it was widely circulated.

---

15 "Extracts from the Private Journal of the Rev. Eleazer Wheelock," in Joseph Tracy, *The Great Awakening: A History of the Revival of Religion in the Time of Edwards & Whitefield*, (1842: Carlisle, PA: Banner of Truth Trust, 1989), pp. 201-203.
16 Joseph Seccombe, *Reflections on Hypocrisy*, (Boston, MA: 1741), p. 12.
17 Joseph Seccombe, *Occasional Thoughts on the Influence of the Spirit with Seasonable Cautions Against Mistakes and Abuses*, (Boston, MA: 1742).
18 Ibid., p. 1.
19 Jonathan Ashley, *The Great Duty of Charity*, (Boston, MA: 1742), pp. 2-4.
20 Ibid., p. 4.

While ministers like Jonathan Ashley of Deerfield publicly deplored the excesses of the revival, men like the Rev. Peter Brockwell of St. Peter's Episcopal Church in Salem openly named individuals in his criticism of the revival work. Brockwell wrote,

> The Wesleys and Whitefield are expected here in the fall. We universally dread the consequence of their coming . . . Whitefield is destitute [of learning], and therefore the victory over him is neither difficult nor glorious, however he may boast in his lying and scandalous Journals. Whitefield is . . . an enemy to our church and constitution.[21]

Men like the Rev. Thomas Barnard of Newbury chose to leave their pulpits rather than fight the revival work or mediate the resulting disputes. After graduation from Harvard in 1732, and his ordination in Newbury in 1738, Barnard shortly thereafter departed the ministry on account of difficulties with Whitefield's preaching. Barnard was a man of questionable orthodoxy and was known as a poor public speaker.[22] "He left Newbury on account of opposition from the friends of Whitefield; studied and practiced law after his dismission; but afterwards returned to the ministry and was settled at Salem, September 18, 1755."[23] Thomas Barnard remained at the First Church in Salem until his death in 1775.

The unorganized protests which surfaced after Whitefield's 1740 departure gained a united and authoritative spokesman in 1743, when the Rev. Dr. Charles Chauncey, of the prestigious First Church in Boston, published his *Seasonable Thoughts on the State of Religion in New England*. Dr. Chauncey had been a critic of Whitefield before the publication of this important work. In a letter by Chauncey to an area minister, dated March 16, 1742, Chauncey speaks of Whitefield as "vain," hoping he will "meet with disappointment," and that Whitefield was of "smaller talents" than the clergymen of Boston.[24] He consistently named Whitefield as a disturbing and unscriptural influence on the churches of New England.[25] After the influential Chauncey publicly and eloquently opposed Whitefield, New England speedily divided into two open and antagonistic parties. The New Lights maintained their support of Whitefield, while the Old Lights, under Dr. Chauncey's example, published and preached openly against the revival.

Charles Chauncey was born in 1705 in Boston. He was named after his great-grandfather, who was the second president of Harvard College. His father was a successful Boston merchant, a member of the wealthy Puritan merchant class. Chauncey earned degrees at Harvard, and later in life was awarded a Doctor of Divinity degree from the University of Edinburgh. He was ordained as minister of Boston's First Church (Congregational) in 1727 and served there until his death sixty years later. Later in life, Chauncey would be known for his patriotic response towards American liberty, his opposition to an Anglican bishop in America, and as a patriarch of religious liberalism in America. But in the 1740s, Chauncey was simply the minister of an important and historic church in a thriving city, but with only local recognition.

A painting of Rev. Dr. Charles Chauncey, c.1780.
Source: www.firstchurchboston.com.

---

21 Harriet S. Tapley, "St. Peter's Church in Salem before the Revolution," *Essex Institute Historical Collections*, (vol. 80: 1944), pp. 258-259. The quoted letter from Brockwell is dated June 15, 1741.
22 *The First Centenary of the North Church and Society in Salem, Massachusetts*, (Salem, MA: Printed for the Society, 1873), p. 171.
23 Ibid.
24 Charles Chauncey, "Original Letters of Charles Chauncey," *The New England Historical and Genealogical Register*, vol. X (1859), p. 333.
25 Ibid., *Seasonable Thoughts on the State of Religion in New England*, (Boston, MA: Rogers and Fowle Printers, 1743), pp. 35-48.

His aggressive, articulate, and ongoing opposition to Whitefield made Chauncey a household name in much of the American Colonies and in Great Britain. Chauncey waited almost two years before publishing against Whitefield. No doubt this senior clergyman in Boston was offended by references in Whitefield's 1740 first edition of his *Journals*, in which the itinerant made various references to the low spiritual state of many of Boston's ministers. Further, the imitators that followed Whitefield caused more harm than good in Boston, and Chauncey could not remain silent.[26]

Although students of American church history may be familiar with Chauncey, many lesser known ministers in New England also opposed the methods and/or message of Whitefield and the revival. For example, the Rev. John Barnard of Marblehead, while being polite and cordial to Mr. Whitefield face to face, secretly opposed his itinerant evangelism. John Barnard was the pastor of the First Church Congregational in Marblehead, Massachusetts. Whitefield recorded in his *Journals*, in his visits to Marblehead, that he was treated cordially by Barnard. Barnard, no friend of revivalism, later recorded:

> In the time of the Whitefieldian ferment, in 1741, I was enabled, by the grace of God, so to conduct as not only to preserve my own flock in peace and quietness, but to prevent the other church in town, and their minister, from being thrown into like disorders and confusions in which so many towns and churches in the country were involved.[27]

To the advocates of formal ecclesiastical order, the very idea of itinerant evangelism was obnoxious, appearing to be a disruptive agent and a source of schism and sectarianism. John Barnard of Andover (cousin to John Barnard of Marblehead) had a supreme regard for order and propriety. John was opposed to itinerant evangelism and was no supporter of "enthusiastic" preaching.[28] In her book, *The History of North Parish in North Andover*, Mofford speaks of the itinerant preaching of Whitefield as "unheard of . . . threatening the entire church order of the colony."[29]

In 1743, local councils were formed throughout New England that attempted to present a united voice opposing the revival in general and Whitefield in particular. Exeter, New Hampshire, was the site of a small council created to resolve tensions within a particular church torn apart by the issues of Whitefield and itinerant preaching. Rev. Woodbridge Oldin, of the First Church in Exeter, refused to allow his pulpit to be used by itinerants, while his parishioners supported the idea. Pastors and elders came from numerous churches in the vicinity—Kittery, Salem, Andover, Bradford, Dover, and Rye, to list only a few—for the purpose of settling the dispute. Oldin would not allow itinerants to use his pulpit because, "He himself judged it would not be to the edification and peace of his flock committed to his care to admit them."[30] The council supported Oldin, declaring:

> We find . . . that a considerable number of the brethren are withdrawn from the communion of this church. And having duly weighed the reasons given by them for their withdrawal . . . we judge they are utterly insufficient to justify that point of their conduct.[31]

Another little-known consortium of opinion was presented by a group of laymen for the general public in 1743. This shamelessly unobjective pamphlet referred to Whitefield sarcastically as "The Grand Itinerant" and "the Rev. Bachelor of Arts," and spoke of him as:

---

26   Edward M. Griffin, *Old Brick: Charles Chauncey of Boston, 1705-1787*, (Minneapolis, MN: University of Minnesota Press, 1980), P. 53.
27   John Barnard, "Autobiography of John Barnard," *Massachusetts Historical Society Collection*, III series, (September 5, 1836), pp. 229-230.
28   Sarah L. Bailey, *Historical Sketches of Andover, Massachusetts*, (Boston, MA: Houghton, Mifflin, and Company, 1880), p. 434.
29   Juliet H. Mofford, *The History of North Parish in North Andover*, (Lawrence, MA: Namian Press, 1975), p. 73.
30   *The Result of a Council of Ten Churches Convened at Exeter*, January 31, 1743, (Boston, MA: 1744), p. 4.
31   Ibid.

A man but of a weak mind, little learning, and no argument, yet by means of a somewhat crafty improvement of the advantageous circumstances and character under which he arrived, and by his being somewhat of an orator and assuming an over-sanctified behavior by great diligence, and by preaching frequently by memory, and with a vehemence unusual to the people of this province, he gained upon their passions, and thereby wheeled himself into their good affections.[32]

A prestigious and influential ministerial council opposed to Whitefield met in Boston on May 25, 1743. The state of religion in the land was the dominant issue, with both sides of the revival being supported by those in attendance. The Old Lights, who did not advocate revivalism, were accused of political maneuvering and misrepresentation. The council produced a document condemning the revival movement, with the support of many ministers who had no personal contact with the revival. Those who supported Whitefield and the awakening were interrupted, treated poorly, and formally opposed.[33] On May 27, those outraged at the bias of the council met and agreed to hold another council to show their support for the revival. This second convention met a few weeks later, on July 7, 1743, to credit and praise God for "a happy revival of religion," and to speak against "those errors in doctrine and disorders in practice" which accompanied some of the lay itinerant preachers. The official declaration of this convention says, in part:

> More particularly, when Christ is pleased to come into his church in a plentiful effusion of his Holy Spirit, by whose powerful influences the ministration of the Word is attended with uncommon success, salvation—work carried on in an eminent manner and his kingdom, which is within men, and consists of righteousness and peace and joy in the Holy Ghost, is noticeably advanced, this is an event which, above all others, invites the notice and bespeaks the praises of the Lord's people, and should be declared abroad for a memorial of the divine grace . . . but if it is justly expected of all who profess themselves in the discipline of Christ, that they should openly acknowledge and rejoice in a work of this nature, wherein the honor of the divine Master is so much concerned, . . . for these and other reasons, we, whose names are hereunto annexed, pastors of churches in New England, we together in Boston, July 7, 1743, think it our indispensable duty, (without judging or censuring such of our brethren who cannot at present see things in the same light as us,) in this open and conjunct manner to declare, to the glory of sovereign grace, our full persuasion, either from what we have seen ourselves, or received upon credible testimony, that there has been a happy and remarkable Revival of religion in many parts of this land . . .[34]

The Rev. Joshua Gee of the Second Church, located on Hanover Street in Boston, was a Whitefield supporter and an opponent of the manipulative aspects of the May 25, 1743 council. He personally wrote of his disappointment with the anti-revival stance of this council. Gee asked, in writing a pamphlet for publication, "Whether this testimony of the late convention, taken in the full view of it, is likely to have a good effect for the revival and advancement of real, vital and practical religion."[35] Other lesser-known ministers also supported Whitefield and the revivals, in spite of the May 25, Boston ministerial council. For example, in *Salem in the Eighteenth Century,* Phillips mentions both the Rev. Peter Clark of Salem Village and the Rev. John Cleveland of Ipswich—Chebacco as clergymen who fully "took up the enthusiasm."[36] Further, the Rev. John Rogers of Ipswich, in a letter to the May 25 convention of ministers, stated:

---

32 *The Testimony and Advice of a Number of Laymen,* (Boston, MA: 1743), pp. 2-3.
33 Joseph Tracy, *The Great Awakening,* pp. 290-292.
34 *The Testimony and Advice of an Assembly of Pastors and Churches in New England, at a Meeting in Boston. July 7, 1743, Occasioned by the Late and Happy Revival of Religion in the Land,* (Boston, MA: 1743), pp. 1-2.
35 Joshua Gee, *A Letter to the Rev. Mr. Nathaniel Fells, Moderator of the Late Convention of Pastors in Boston,* (Boston, MA: 1743), p. 1.
36 James D. Philips, *Salem in the Eighteenth Century,* (Salem, MA: Essex Institute, 1969), p. 164.

I have the utmost reason to bless God, who has given me to see a day of such marvelous power and grace, particularly in this place . . . since the Rev. Whitefield . . . came among us. Wherein great numbers of our young people and others of more advanced age give evidence of a saving change wrought in them, and, by the fruits of the Spirit, show that they are born of the Spirit.[37]

In February 1743, Rev. Jonathan Edwards was asked to sit on a Westfield church council concerning the itinerant exhorter Mrs. Bathsheba Kingsley. Her husband Hains Kingsley asked for the council of ministers to meet, because his wife's church activities were neglecting her duties at home. She claimed to receive divine dreams and impulses, and would take her husband's horse from town to town exhorting small groups and criticizing local clergy. These types of excesses were what the Old Lights used to criticize the awakening.[38] The council met with the couple. The results of the meeting, written in Jonathan Edwards' handwriting, admonished Bathsheba for "exhorting, censoriousness, and enthusiasm," and instructed her to be more diligent in her wifely and domestic responsibilities. Interestingly, the council also stated that Hains Kingsley should make accommodations for his wife to attend religious meetings in Westfield and nearby towns, and for her to continue her home meetings.[39]

Nathaniel Ames of Dedham, Massachusetts was a physician, a tavern keeper, and an amateur astronomer. He was most famous for his annual almanacs in which he recorded the weather and commented on civil, religious, and other subjects. Dr. Ames was highly critical of the Great Awakening and the excesses that he thought were an integral part of the movement. In his Almanac for 1744, Ames wrote, "There is not a more melancholy Object, than a Man who has his head turned with Religious Enthusiasm. A Person that is crazed, tho' with Pride of Malice, is a Sight mortifying to human nature . . . we should be particularly careful to keep our reason as cool as possible, and to guard ourselves in all parts of life, against the influence of Passion, Imagination, and Constitution . . . ."[40]

The ministers who publicly supported Whitefield and the revival movement came from as far north in New England as settlement reached at that time. Yet Whitefield had visited only a portion of those churches whose ministers supported the declarations of the pro-Whitefield July 7, 1743 second council. For example, Rev. Joseph Adams of Newington, James Pike of Somersworth, Rev. Amos Main of Rochester, and Rev. Joshua Tufts of Litchfield, all of whom were from New Hampshire, had not yet experienced a personal visit from Whitefield.[41] Yet, all these men, and numerous others, had either experienced personal revival, or heard from other nearby parishes which had. They did not hesitate to sign the petition supporting revival. Whitefield would visit these areas in the future. The initial 1740 awakening had spread through New England through printed sermons, individual eyewitness accounts, and itinerant evangelists. The opposition to the revival was strong in isolated pockets, and often led by the most educated members of society. The awakening eventually found limited support in towns like Marblehead, whose clergy was divided over Whitefield. For example, Samuel Roads wrote in *The History and Traditions of Marblehead*,

---

37   Joseph Felt, *History of Ipswich, Essex and Hamilton*, (Cambridge, MA: Folson Printers, 1834), p. 214. The letter from Rev. John Rogers is dated July 2, 1743.
38   George Hammond and David C. Jones, *George Whitefield: Life, Context, and Legacy*, (Oxford University Press, 2016), p. 122.
39   Stephen J. Stein, editor, *Jonathan Edwards' Writings: Text, Context, Interpretation*, (Bloomington, IN: Indiana University Press, 1996), p. 16.
40   Nathaniel Ames, *Almanac for 1744*, (Boston, MA: R&S Draper, Printers, 1745), n.p. Original at the American Antiquarian Society, Worcester, MA.
41   In addition to these New Hampshire ministers who had not yet met Whitefield, numerous pastors in Maine also endorsed Whitefield, sight unseen. These Maine ministers were from such towns as Berwick, Falmouth, Scarborough, Wells, and others. A full listing of the 133 New England clergymen who supported the revivals can be seen in Joseph Tracy, The Great Awakening, pp. 209-302.

During the year 1743 the religious movement known as the Great Awakening swept like a whirlwind through every town in the province . . . Hundreds were brought into the churches, and the result was a controversy which long agitated the colony.[42]

Perhaps no area in the American Colonies was more affected by the revivals of 1740-1743 than eastern New England. The resulting opposition in Boston and local communities was also significant. When Whitefield returned to the Boston area for his second itinerant preaching tour in 1744, he did not find the cordial welcome which had accompanied his first visit. Whitefield received the challenge of his life when he returned. His enemies were outspoken, bold, and united against him personally, against his theology, and opposed to his method of ministry. But before Whitefield returned to New England for his second visit in 1744, he had various experiences elsewhere that helped to shape his life and mold his ministry.

A sketch of Whitefield preaching in a large New England meeting house.

by Valarie Borgal.

---

42 Samuel Roads, Jr., *The History and Traditions of Marblehead*, (Boston, MA: Houghton, Osgood & Company, 1880), pp. 57-58.

CHAPTER 10

WHITEFIELD'S LIFE AND MINISTRY

1741-1744

THIS CHAPTER WILL NARRATE THE events surrounding Whitefield's life between his first and second visits to New England. No attempt has been made at an exhaustive study of his career and activities during these formative years. For our present purpose, only those events and issues which weighed heavily on Whitefield's mind, and which may have influenced his second visit to New England, are included.

Unfortunately, the years 1741 to 1744 have not been carefully preserved in Whitefield's personal *Journals*. This is a significant loss. However, there is numerous Whitefield correspondence from these years. Many of his letters are somewhat autobiographical. This overview of these maturing years in Whitefield's life will center on his personal, ecclesiastical, and legal issues before evaluating his ministry during this formative period.

Whitefield sailed for England, from Boston, on January 17, 1741.[1] Although he was suspicious of the outward piety of the Bostonians, his optimism for his labors in England was running high. In a letter to a Bostonian written two days before his departure, he wrote:

> I cannot but think our Lord will let his word run, and be abundantly glorified in America. Boston people are much upon my heart. The memory of their forefathers is precious to my soul. May you live to see the spirit of scriptural Puritanism universally prevail.[2]

Over twenty-five letters from his ocean journey back to England have survived. Their tone is consistently positive and affectionate. At times he appears overwhelmed and at awe, as he recalls the success of his gospel ministry in America. Although still a young man in his late twenties, his advice to others was often seasoned, mature, and fatherly. He had been used of God in America over several months, more than many men together experience in a lifetime. Yet he cannot have overlooked the fact that he was sometimes harsh, judgmental, and almost arrogant against those who disagreed with him.

Numerous personal issues faced Whitefield upon his arrival in England. His bodily health, even as a young man, was erratic and often poor. His personal correspondence reveals a continuing struggle against weakening health. This was a situation he would have to live with his entire life. Whitefield was not above romance, either. Through personal correspondence and a prior meeting, he had become attached to a Welsh widow named Elizabeth James. He was looking for a woman who could encourage and support his itinerant evangelism, and also oversee the orphanage in Georgia. Elizabeth James' life had been confined

---

1 John Gilles, *Memoirs of Rev. George Whitefield*, (1772: reprinted by Hunt & Noyes Publishers, Middletown, CT: 1836), pp. 50-102. Luke Tyerman, *The Life of the Rev. George Whitefield*, (New York: Anson D.F. Randolf & Company, 1877), vol. I, pp. 523-561. Arnold Dallimore, *George Whitefield, The Life and Times of the Great Evangelist of the Eighteenth Century Revival*, (Carlisle, PA: Banner of Truth Trust, 1979), vol. II, pp. 43-176.

2 George Whitefield, *Works of George Whitefield*, (1771: reprinted by Quinta Press, Shropshire, England: 2000), vol. I, p. 233.

to Wales, she had not attended a university, and she was uncomfortable in upper-class company. But her Christian piety and godly character made her a suitable wife for George Whitefield. Dallimore concluded that, "Whitefield's proposal consisted of a challenge to assist the ministry of a mighty man of God, and she was the kind of woman who would feel the attraction of that challenge and would want to accept it, no matter what difficulties it might entail."[3] They were married on November 14, 1741.

In addition to inconsistent health and a new marriage, another issue confronting Whitefield in the British Isles was the abuse he received from those who opposed his message. Almost immediately upon his arrival from America, he began preaching in England. On April 8, 1742 Whitefield recorded that the work in London grew steadily during his preaching. On April 22, he spoke of the ministry in London doing "wonderfully well," with many conquests being made for Christ.[4] Yet by May 11, a noticeable change had overcome many of his listeners in the open fields of London. Routinely, numerous vendors and comedians used the open city parks as areas of worldly amusement and carnal activities. The preaching of Whitefield in the city parks was a direct and ongoing threat to these merchants and hucksters, and some responded violently. Whitefield recorded in some detail the action-packed events of his London ministry on May 11-12, 1742:

> You may easily guess that there was some noise among the craftsmen, and that I was honored with having a few stones, dirt, rotten eggs and pieces of dead cats thrown at me . . . God's people kept praying, and the enemy's agents made a kind of roaring at some distance . . . At length they approached nearer . . . and advancing near the pulpit, attempted to slash me with a long and heavy whip several times, but always with the violence of his motion tumbled down . . . . Finding these efforts to fail, a large body . . . assembled together, and having got a large pole for their standard, advanced toward us with heavy and formidable steps . . . Just as they approached us with looks full of resentment, I know not by what accident, they quarreled among themselves, threw down their staff, and went away . . . . A number of enemies strove to push my friends down . . . I narrowly escaped with my life: for as I was passing from the pulpit to the coach, I felt my wig and hat to be almost off. I turned about, and observed a sword just touching my temples.[5]

The English monarch was King George II, who ruled 1727 to 1760. His reign was marred by ongoing European wars and civil conflicts at home. He survived various coup attempts and was not known as an exceptionally moral man, even by the low standards of that time. He had several mistresses and was known to frequent prostitutes. George II was the last British monarch to lead troops in battle, at the 1743 Battle of Dettingen in Bavaria. As king, George II was the titular head of the Church of England, and he remained unmoved by the Great Awakening in England led by George Whitefield and John Wesley.

During his 1741-1744 years in England, Whitefield was surrounded by consistent threats of persecution or a violent death. Dallimore quoted an eyewitness source from the summer of 1743, which found Whitefield the object "for gathering the mob" into uncivil behavior. He was, in this instance, personally insulted to his face, yet continued preaching well into the evening in a private residence, surrounded by an abusive mob.[6] Near the eve of his 1744 return journey to America, Whitefield suffered from an attack in which he was nearly murdered in bed. He was beaten unmercifully with a gold-headed cane, and only the arrival of his hostess saved him from an apparent brutal death. Methodists in Great Britain became a despised class that often suffered persecution from Roman Catholics, Church of England ministers, and the general rabble of the population.[7]

---

3   Arnold Dallimore, *George Whitefield, vol. II,* p. 108.
4   George Whitefield, *Works, vol. I,* pp. 382-383.
5   Ibid., pp. 385-386.
6   *A Brief Account of the Late Persecution and Barbarous Usage of the Methodists at Exeter,* (Oxford: Andrew Brice Printer, 1745). Arnold Dallimore, *George Whitefield,* vol. II, p. 164.
7   Ibid., p. 14

Whitefield understood that as a minister, he should marry. Unfortunately, his emphasis on self-denial had left him unprepared to know how to deal with romance. A first attempt at marriage in 1740 resulted in the prospective bride refusing Whitefield's advances. Later, he met a widow, Mrs. Elizabeth James and her teenage daughter, through their mutual friend Howell Harris of Wales. When he proposed to Elizabeth, he made clear that his arduous itinerant ministry would continue unabated even after marriage. The couple had difficulty finding a minister who would marry them, as their Methodism was not accepted by all. They were married on November 14, 1741. One writer stated, "George Whitefield married a woman he barely knew. Though he and his bride corresponded, they had probably spent less than a week together before marrying. As many as four different ministers refused to marry the couple."[8] Another stated of Elizabeth Whitefield, "While she did not possess any true intellectual culture or breadth of reading, she nevertheless was superior to most Welsh women of those times in education and general knowledge."[9] Whitefield maintained a schedule of preaching twice a day during their honeymoon. Most of his married life was spent away from home on his various itinerant preaching tours.

A personal issue surrounding Whitefield that influenced his thinking before his return to America, was the birth of his son, John. John Whitefield was born on or about October 5, 1743, in London. As a new father, Whitefield eagerly and publicly presented his son to England as a future preacher of the gospel. However, such was not to be. The child died early in February 1744, only eight months before Whitefield's return to America. The inner disappointment and pain of the evangelist is recorded in his private correspondence. One way he worked through his grief was to relentlessly preach. "When his 4-month old son died, Whitefield did not stop preaching; he preached three times before the funeral and was preaching as the bells rang for the service itself."[10]

The personal matters so far highlighted—poor health, a new marriage, physical abuse, and now the death of his son—were only some of the issues which confronted Whitefield upon his 1744 return to New England. In addition to these personal issues, there were also the ongoing ecclesiastical controversies Whitefield confronted in Great Britain with the Church of England.

As an ordained Anglican priest, certain expectations of methodology and doctrine were expected upon Whitefield by the Anglican bishops. Although he never broke ties with his ordaining church, Whitefield's message, as well as his methods, were virtually unheard of in many of the Anglican churches of his day. Tension and controversy were inevitable. Sometimes, Whitefield was impulsive and overstated his arguments. Other times his youthful exuberance grated against the more experienced clergy.

Early in his public ministry, an obvious mistake Whitefield made was to speak unfavorably of the Church of England Archbishop John Tillotson, a well respected Anglican churchman of a prior generation. Whitefield made the following unwise statement regarding Tillotson, which cost him many friends in the Anglican Church: "Archbishop Tillotson knew no more about true Christianity than did Mohammed."[11] Whitefield's opposition to Tillotson was often bombastic and was eagerly gossiped about by the public.[12] Whitefield saw theological ambiguities in Tillotson's writings, but as he addressed these concerns his manner was abrupt. In Philadelphia on April 15, 1740, Whitefield concluded a sermon by reading extracts of a letter written by Rev. Jonathan Edwards of Northampton, Massachusetts, repudiating the teachings of Tillotson.[13] Also, when Whitefield realized that Tillotson was read by ministerial students at Harvard, he responded by saying, "Bad

---

8 "George Whitefield—Did You Know?" *Christian History,* http://www.christianitytoday.com/ch/1993/issue 38/3208.html.
9 Arnold Dallimore, *George Whitefield, vol. II,* p. 102.
10 "George Whitefield—Did You Know?", p. 1.
11 Luke Tyerman, *The Life of the Rev. George Whitefield, vol. I,* p. 360.
12 The reasons for Whitefield's opposition to Archbishop Tillotson was based on Tillotson's apparently weak view on justification by faith alone, his seeming denial of the eternal punishment in hell of the unconverted, and his apparent lack of the new birth through Jesus Christ. The youthful Whitefield saw in Tillotson the fledgling doctrines of Unitarianism and rebuked him sharply. See Luke Tyerman, *The Life of the Rev. George Whitefield,* pp. 360-362.
13 George Whitefield, *Journals of George Whitefield,* (1747: reprinted by Banner of Truth Trust, Carlisle, PA, 1985), p. 407.

books are becoming fashionable among the tutors and students."[14] Although Whitefield later apologized for the abrasive language he had used against Tillotson, the damage was done. Many New England clergymen read about Whitefield's harsh remarks and did not eagerly anticipate the itinerant's return.

Unrelated to the Tillotson controversy, there were other ecclesiastical groups which attacked Whitefield and his ministry. One opponent was the Associate Presbytery in Scotland, which called a public fast and published a destructive pamphlet which personally attacked Whitefield. He was accused of being a "scandalous idolater," of having "foul, prelative, sectarian hands" and of being a "limb of anti-Christ; a boar, and wild beast of the field."[15] Although no formal reply came, Whitefield did record in personal correspondence; "Dear men, I pity them. Writing I feel will be in vain. Surely they must grieve the Holy Spirit much. Oh for a mind divested of all sects and names and parties."[16]

A second unrelated ecclesiastical confrontation in England was a series of well-written, anonymous pamphlets attacking both Whitefield and the revival movement in general. In addition to portraying Whitefield as a fanatic, the pamphlets sought to show that the Methodist movement was disloyal to the Crown and should be outlawed. Because of potential danger resulting from such a serious accusation, Whitefield's second trip to New England was postponed. His published reply is an articulate defense of the revival movement, the patriotism of the Methodists, and the legality of open-air preaching.[17] His remarks were never answered publicly.

A most distressing ecclesiastical issue burdening Whitefield was the ongoing controversy with John and Charles Wesley. Whitefield and the Wesley brothers were co-workers in the awakening but did not agree on several theological issues. While all three were preachers of the new birth and were Methodists, tension existed over doctrinal differences. While Whitefield was away in the American Colonies, John Wesley's controversial sermon on *Free Grace* had been deliberately circulated among Whitefield's converts. Dissension resulted, which Whitefield had to address. In a letter to Gilbert Tennent, Whitefield wrote,

> I found when I came at first, I had all my work to begin again. Brother Wesley had so prejudiced the people against me, that those who were my spiritual children would not so much as come and see me; they have gone by me while preaching in Moorfields, and stopped their ears.[18]

Because of the confused state of Whitefield's converts, and the need for a definitive statement, Whitefield published the document he had previously published in America, called *A Letter to the Rev. Mr. Wesley in Answer to His Sermon Entitled 'Free Grace'*.[19] The controversy between John Wesley and George Whitefield was more than Calvinism verses Arminianism. The control of the revival movement among the Methodists was a key factor in Wesley's opposition to Whitefield. The fact is they were rivals. Success had influenced both Whitefield and John Wesley. There was a certain amount of pride, or the desire for control, in both men. It grated against Wesley that Whitefield was successful in America, whereas he was not. Whitefield was always forced to admit that he was invited into the Oxford Holy Club, in which the Wesley's were leaders before him. And Wesley had to admit that Whitefield was the initiator in open air preaching in the British Isles.[20]

---

14 Ibid., p. 462.
15 Luke Tyerman, *The Life of the Rev. George Whitefield*, vol. II, p. 11.
16 George Whitefield, *Works, vol. I*, p. 446.
17 Ibid., An Answer to the First Part of an Anonymous Pamphlet entitled 'Observations upon the Conduct and Behavior of a Certain Sect Usually Distinguished by the Name of Methodists,' *Works*, vol. IV, pp. 123-140.
18 Ibid., vol. I, p. 362.
19 Although lost for many years, Whitefield's letter to John Wesley was reprinted in 1960 as an appendix to George Whitefield's *Journals, pp. 569-588.*
20 For an overview of the relationship between Whitefield and John Wesley, see Kenneth E. Lawson, "Who Founded Methodism? Wesley's Dependence upon Whitefield in the Eighteenth Century Revival, *Reformation and Revival Journal*, (Summer 1995), pp. 39-57. For a more detailed study see Ian J. Maddock, *Men of One Book: A Comparison of Two Methodist Preachers, John Wesley and George Whitefield*, (Cambridge, Great Britain: The Lutherworth Press, 2011).

During the first few months after Whitefield's 1740 return to England, John Wesley printed or reprinted sermons, essays and hymns which supported his theological ideas, to the detriment of Whitefield.[21] Some of the literature was reprinted two or three times in the first months after Whitefield's return. In addition to using a printing press, the Wesley brothers "exercised a direct opposition to Whitefield in their daily ministries."[22] This was done by following behind Whitefield's meetings in order to steal converts, passing out opposing literature at the door of Whitefield's congregation, and claiming physical property owned or managed by Whitefield and his followers for use by the Wesleys. One letter of private correspondence between Charles and John Wesley has survived, showing the disrespectful attitudes they had toward Whitefield. Calling Whitefield a plague, the note states,

> Stop the plague just now, or it will be too late. Send me word, first post, that you have warned our flock from going to hear the other's gospel. Regard not fair speeches: renounce your credulity and George Whitefield, till he renounces reprobation. Send me word, I say, by next post, that you have restrained the unwary; or I shall, on the first preaching night, renounce George Whitefield on the house-top.[23]

It was difficult, but by 1743 there was a more cordial relationship between Whitefield and the Wesleys. Although it was several years before fellowship was fully restored, the pamphlet wars and rivalries slowly diminished. By 1744, as Whitefield prepared for another trip to America, numerous ecclesiastical crises had been confronted and, for the most part, successfully diffused.[24]

Another issue which weighed heavily on Whitefield's mind was the legal status of his Bethesda orphanage in Georgia. Dallimore stated,

> He was deeply in debt for the Orphan House, and was beginning to realize still more clearly that due to its locality its expenses would always be exorbitantly high and that the great burden the institution posed would probably last throughout his lifetime.[25]

Because of his indebtedness, the threat of debtor's prison was a constant reality to Whitefield. Three months of ministry in England elapsed before financial help was provided, though temporarily. In a letter on June 8, 1741, Whitefield spoke of the tension he felt from his legal indebtedness. He stated, "You know how I was threatened to be arrested, soon after my arrival, for above three hundred pounds, due on account of the Orphan House in Georgia . . . This drove me to my knees."[26] During the totality of his life, Whitefield was never free from the pressures of providing for the orphans and staff of the Orphan House.

This chapter has surveyed the personal, ecclesiastical, and legal controversies which surrounded Whitefield's ministry in the years between his first two visits to New England. To prevent a wrong impression, one further issue needs to be addressed—the remarkable successes Whitefield achieved during his 1741 to 1744 ministry through the British Isles. His London congregation built Whitefield an enormous meeting house, called the Tabernacle, so that the immense congregations which met in the open fields could be protected from the weather. Also, new preaching opportunities were open to him, and invitations were sent to him from many places

---

21 Arnold Dallimore, *George Whitefield*, vol. II, p. 68. Dallimore stated that Wesley released anti-Whitefield literature on a monthly basis.
22 Ibid., p. 69.
23 Luke Tyerman, *The Life of the Rev. George Whitefield*, vol. I, p. 482.
24 The theological differences and resulting rivalries between Whitefield and Wesley have been frequently studied by scholars. A good example is by Irwin W. Reist, "John Wesley and George Whitefield: A Study in the Integrity of Two Theologies of Grace," *The Evangelical Quarterly*, vol. 47, No. 1 (January-March 1975), pp. 26-40.
25 Arnold Dallimore, *George Whitefield*, vol. II, p. 46.
26 George Whitefield, *Works*, vol. I, p. 271.

where he had previously never been. His twice-per-day itinerant preaching in new cities produced outdoors congregations that approached 10,000 persons, with large numbers of souls under conviction.[27] Scotland was a key area for Whitefield, with whole towns coming under conviction, thousands making professions of faith in Christ, and numerous churches and societies of believers being formed. In spite of the controversies mentioned above, Whitefield's ministry, on the eve of his return to New England, was going very well.

Amidst the revival work in Scotland and England, publications from America began to reach Whitefield concerning the state of revival in the American Colonies. These pamphlets and newspaper articles reported and exaggerated certain isolated fanatical practices that had developed, especially in New England. Although it had been a few years since he left the colonies, the blame for the emotionalism and fanatical behavior was placed on Whitefield. A senior clergyman in Boston, Rev. Charles Chauncey, wrote a pamphlet that was widely distributed, a publication that opposed Whitefield's message and his methods. Whitefield answered the charges in a pamphlet entitled, *Some Remarks on the Late Pamphlet 'The State of Religion in New England Since the Rev. Whitefield's Arrival There.'* Nevertheless, without personally confronting the situation in New England, he had little chance of healing the wounds or effectively answering his critics. In the minds of his enemies, as well as in some supporters, the flamboyant itinerant ministry of men like Rev. James Davenport, and others, discredited Whitefield's ministry. By early 1744, Whitefield made plans to return to America, this time in the company of Mrs. Whitefield. He needed to pacify many people upon this journey, and he knew it. Yet, he could never have realized the polarization and sectarianism that so dominated New England a few years after his first visit. Here he had to use all his gifts and abilities in order to prevent the revival from declining to complete chaos and failure.

A woodcarving image of George Whitefield preaching outside.

Source: *Memoirs of Rev. George Whitefield*, by John Gillies.

27 Ibid., p. 276.

CHAPTER 11

WHITEFIELD'S SECOND TOUR IN NORTHERN NEW ENGLAND

OCTOBER–NOVEMBER 1744

To the Publisher of the Evening Post

Boston, October 27, 1744

The Arrival of Mr. Whitefield again in these Parts, has [become a] Matter of great Joy to the Leaders of his Party, and raised the drooped Spirits of all his Followers. They, no doubt, expecting, that at his second coming, he will carry on to greater Degrees of Perfection, the Confusions begun by him at his first Appearance.

On the other Hand, I believe the sincere lovers of the Peace, Order and Safety of our Churches, have Reason to deprecate his coming; especially considering that he has been the instrumental Cause of those Divisions and Contentions which have rent to Pieces so many Churches in this and the neighboring Governments; and that it is more than probable he will come again in the same Spirit, and prosecute the same Design. It is therefore, I think, highly incumbent on Ministers and People, in their respective Capacities, to oppose his Measures, and Discountenance him to the utmost of their Power.[1]

Whitefield boarded a ship in Plymouth, and departed England with his wife Elizabeth about August 10, 1744, for America. Behind him in England he left a revival work fragmented but healing. The Awakening in the British Isles was simply remarkable, but the complications and rivalries from the work were daunting. The Atlantic Ocean passage was long, rough, and dangerous. The weather was dreadful, contrary winds delayed the Atlantic crossing, and at one point Whitefield's vessel was accidentally rammed by another ship at sea. In late October 1744, Whitefield returned to New England, landing in York, presently in the state of Maine. He was almost thirty years old. His *Journals* narrative stated:

> Friday, October 26. Through the good hand of our God upon us we arrived at port this morning after a long and perilous sea passage of twelve weeks, lacking about two or three days. Our putting in at York was somewhat remarkable.[2]

---

1   *Boston Evening Post*, October 29, 1744, p. 4.
2   George Whitefield, *George Whitefield's Journals*, (1747: reprinted by Banner of Truth Trust, Carlisle, PA: 1985), p. 516. The narrative of his second journey around Boston and northern New England is found in pp. 516-528, 533-534, 543-558.

The long, turbulent ocean journey took its toll on Whitefield's health. His "putting in at York" was nearly fatal, as Whitefield was tossed about in a dory in high seas. Later, in his private correspondence, dated October 30, 1744, Whitefield recorded that on the ship he heard scuttlebutt about much of New England turning New Light, and that the itinerant evangelist Whitefield was due to arrive soon. Remaining undetected, Whitefield wrote:

> I continued undiscovered; and in a few hours, in answer I trust to new light prayers, we arrived safe at York, a few miles off Piscataqua, the place to which we were bound . . . In about an half hour after my arrival, I was put to bed, racked with a nervous colic . . . Though I was so sick as to not be able to bear the sound of the tread of a foot . . . yet my heart was kept in perfect peace.[3]

After several days of recuperation, Whitefield's health returned, and he was ready to commence his ministry. Jonathan Edwards of Northampton wrote of Whitefield's reception in New England by the clergy; "Many ministers were alarmed at his coming . . . They soon began to preach and write against him . . . It was a kind of miracle that Mr. Whitefield should appear so little moved by all that he met with, and should in the midst of all possess himself with so much courage and calmness . . . [4]

The people of York were very dear to Whitefield. He was told that on his prior visit to York, new converts abounded, and hearts were melted by his preaching.[5] Here he began his 1744 New England ministry. Whitefield wrote in his *Journals*:

> Sunday, November 4. Rode out in a chaise for the first time this day and perceived my natural appetite to return. In the afternoon I had the pleasure of seeing the Reverend Mr. Moody, just returned from Cape Ann—He saluted me in the following manner: "Sir, first you are welcome to America, second to New England, third, to all the good people in New England, fourth to all the faithful ministers in New England, fifth you are welcomed to York, and sixth, you are welcome to me who am less than the least of these all."

Rev. Samuel Moody of the First Church in York was an active supporter of Whitefield, though he did oppose unnecessary separations within churches and emotional excesses from the revival. Moody was the most influential person in the coastal community of York, widely respected and appreciated for his religious and civic activities. Interestingly, no emotional extremes or deviant behavior accompanied Whitefield's 1744 preaching tour in northern New England. In York, the sickly Whitefield was greeted as a returning hero.

> Sunday, November 5. Preached this day twice in Mr. Moody's pulpit, with freedom and power, and was enabled to answer several letters . . . In the afternoon praiseworthy Mr. Moody gave thanks for our remarkable deliverance, and enumerated what great blessings his congregation had enjoyed. I find they were favored with some glorious gales of the blessed Spirit about three years ago and other adjacent places catched the flame; numbers were savingly converted and enjoyed uncommon manifestations of divine love. Some that appeared to be wrought upon have apostatized and there was a general complaint of a withdrawal of the remarkable outpouring of the Spirit of God. The general language was, favor thy work, O Lord, in the midst of the years. May the Lord say Amen.

---

3   George Whitefield, *Works of George Whitefield*, (Shropshire, England: Quinta Press, 2000), vol. II, pp.69-70.
4   Iain Murray, *Jonathan Edwards: A New Biography*, (Carlisle, PA: Banner of Truth Trust, 2000), p. 247.
5   Ibid., *Journals*, p. 467.

> Monday, Nov. 6. Preached this morning by nine o'clock at the desire of Mr. Moody. The Lord was with us. Was very ill both before and after dinner; but having engaged myself to Mr. Chandler; the minister of Scotland, about four miles from York, I went thither and through the divine assistance was strengthened to preach with sweetness and freedom to a very crowded auditory, and, blessed be God in and through Christ Jesus, for this and all his tender mercies.[6]

Scotland, Maine, was a community a few miles west of York on the north side of the York River. This was a small waterfront settlement for fishing, clamming, farming, and shipbuilding. Whitefield mentioned "Mr. Chandler, the minister of Scotland." This refers to Rev. Samuel Chandler of the Second Church in York. Due to changes in population, the Second Church separated from the First Church in 1730. Chandler came to the Second Church in the Scotland community near York, in 1742. A Harvard graduate in 1735, Chandler came to York to serve as the second pastor of the church and as a schoolteacher. His grammar school operated year-round, in a rural community that fully supported his ministry.[7] Whitefield wrote that he preached for Chandler, "to a very crowded auditory." The *Journals* narrative of Whitefield continued:

> Tuesday, Nov. 7. Went in a chaise with Mr. Henry Sherburn, an eminent and wealthy merchant, to Portsmouth, on Piscataqua, where we designed to land. This Mr. Sherburn is a glorious instance of rich and sovereign grace. He told me he received one of his first impressions under my first sermon at Piscataqua, four years ago, but afterwards was effectually wrought of God, by Mr. Gerring and other (faithful) ministers who went about preaching the everlasting gospel. A notable and evident change has been wrought in him . . . About three in the afternoon we reached Piscataqua. The two ministers of the place and many others came to the River's side to give us the meeting. Mr. Sherburn and his wife gladly received us into their house. About six I preached to a large and effected auditory, but perceived my disorder of a nervous cholick [colic] returning fast upon me as soon as I had done. Lord, let thy will be done in, by, and upon me, whether thou hast designed for me life or death . . .

Portsmouth, New Hampshire was a thriving port city. The community prospered from various maritime industries. The Piscataqua River abounded with flat bottomed skiffs and shallops that transported supplies from local craftsmen in the town to various larger vessels that sought Portsmouth as a safe harbor. Enormous New Hampshire white pines were floated down the river to Portsmouth for use as ship masts and construction material for the sturdy homes in Portsmouth, Boston, Salem, and elsewhere. Wealthy merchants dwelt in the city, building large brick homes, many of which still stand today. Elegant clothing fashions and delicate household items came from Europe. Local wealthy families intermarried, creating an elite class in Portsmouth.[8]

Whitefield specifically mentioned "Mr. Henry Sherburn, an eminent and wealthy merchant" in Portsmouth. Sherburne was a descendant of the original 1632 settlers. He was born into the Portsmouth aristocracy. He began his young adult life as a mariner and shipmaster, thereafter becoming a successful merchant. Sherburne served as a local selectman, as a Representative to the General Assembly, and as a member of the King's Council from 1728 to his death in 1757. "He was a man of great wealth and lived in almost Royal style in the first brick mansion built in Portsmouth at the head of the Pier."[9] Henry Sherburne

---

6   Ibid., p. 523.
7   George Chandler, *The Chandler Family: The Descendants of William and Annis Chandler . . .*, (Worcester, MA: Press of Charles Hamilton, 1883), p. 191.
8   Thomas B. Aldrich, *An Old Town by the Sea*, (Boston, MA: Houghton Mifflin & Company, 1894). John & Nancy Grossman, *Portsmouth: New Hampshire's Colonial Capital*, (Portsmouth, NH: Back Channel Press, 2007).
9   Edward R. Sherburne, *Some Descendants of Henry and John Sherburne of Portsmouth, N.H.*, (Boston, MA: The New England Historical and Genealogical Society, 1904), p. 5.

was converted in the Great Awakening and became an avid supporter of Whitefield. As he wrote in the above *Journals* quote, George and Elizabeth Whitefield were entertained in the mansion of Henry Sherburn in Portsmouth. Whitefield wrote of "The two ministers of the place and many others came to the River's side to give us the meeting." This likely refers to Rev. William Shurtleff of the South Church, and either Rev. Samuel Chandler of the Second Church, or perhaps the elderly Rev. Jabez Fitch, or his assistant Rev. Samuel Langdon, of the North Church.

Health issues plagued the relentless Whitefield. He received the best medical attention available in Portsmouth, but fatigue overwhelmed him. At one preaching event in Portsmouth, the

In early November 1744, George Whitefield and his wife stayed in this home as the guests of Henry Sherburne in Portsmouth, New Hampshire. It is on the National Register of Historic Places.

Source: https://www.luxuryportfolio.com/ Property/ portsmouth-properties-the-henry-sherburne-house/LKIT.

congregation was astonished at how sickly the thirty-year old minister looked. Whitefield preached for an hour, exhausted, and collapsed. Whitefield was now thoroughly disabled.[10] Yet great crowds thronged to hear him. Whitefield wrote in his *Journals*:

> Wednesday, Nov. 8. I intended to preach in the evening but was unable, however there being great crowds come out of the country, and God being pleased for a while to suspend my pain, I ventured out in the afternoon and preached with great power to a large congregation, till the cries of the people, albeit I begged them to refrain themselves, drowned my voice (indeed the Savior's presence was amongst us) a more visible alteration I never saw in any people, and I could scarce believe I was preaching to the same persons that behaved like rocks and stones four years earlier, and I saw and felt so much of the divine presence that I could contentedly have went to my lodgings and died. Oh that I may be ready at whatever hour my Lord shall come!

Whitefield's first visit to the Portsmouth / Piscataqua area in 1740 was initially uneventful. At that time, he called them "a polite auditory, and so very unconcerned, that I began to question whether I had been preaching to rational or brute creatures."[11] The revival was slow to begin but eventually thrived. By the time of Whitefield's second visit in 1744, the awakening had fully consumed the city. Scarcely a voice was raised against Whitefield. The day before he left Portsmouth, Rev. William Shurtleff wrote:

> The prejudices of most that set themselves against him before his coming, seem to be in a great measure abated, and in some, to be wholly removed; and there is no opposition made to him. I have frequent opportunities of being with him, and there always appears in him such a concern for the advancement of the Redeemer's Kingdom and the good of souls, such a care to employ

---

10 Luke Tyerman, *The Life of the Rev. George Whitefield*, (New York: Anson D.F. Randolph & Company, 1877), vol. II, p. 122.
11 George Whitefield, *Journals*, p. 466.

his whole time to these purposes, such sweetness of disposition, and so much of the temper of his great Lord and Master, that every time I see him, I find my heart drawn further towards him.[12]

Shurtleff's affectionate summary of Whitefield's ministry and personality may lack objectivity. Yet it is true that Shurtleff remained a firm supporter of Whitefield after his second visit ended, when enemies preached and printed against the revival. Shurtleff's support of the awakening was both scholarly and defensible. For example, after Whitefield departed Portsmouth, Shurtleff wrote a twenty-three-page scholarly and devotional pamphlet to his fellow New England ministers, defending Whitefield. The pamphlet was printed in Boston and widely distributed.[13]

After this short but successful preaching ministry in the York and Portsmouth areas, Whitefield again became sick. After November 8, we have no record of any preaching activity until November 22. Additional physicians were summoned for assistance in treating Whitefield's failing health. A few weeks of rest resulted in a suitable recovery. During his recovery time, Mrs. Elizabeth Whitefield wrote a letter from Portsmouth, dated November 14. She wrote of her husband,

> As soon as he was able to go about, he went out and preached twice a day, which was too much for him. We came from York here; and, in the way, he preached in the rain. On reaching Portsmouth, he preached at candle-light. This laid him up again, and the next day he was judged to be dangerously ill; but, when the time he had proposed to preach arrived, finding himself free from pain, he went out and preached. This had like to have cost him his life, for he became as cold as a clod. But the Lord was pleased to hear prayer from him, and he is now in a fair way.[14]

In a letter dated November 16, 1744 from Portsmouth, Whitefield wrote that he left his sick bed to preach. Although he was pale and weak, he preached, then he collapsed. He wrote,

> All seemed to be melted, and were drowned in tears. The cry after me, when I left the pulpit, was like the cry of sincere mourners when attending the funeral of a dear friend. Upon my coming home, I was laid on a bed upon the ground near the fire, and I heard them say, "He is gone;" but still you find by this I am alive, and if spared to be made instrumental in making any poor dead soul alive to God, I shall rejoice that the all-wise Redeemer has kept out of heaven a little longer, your, G.W.[15]

Several miles inland, to the northeast of Portsmouth, was the farming community of Somersworth, New Hampshire. Rev. James Pike, a Harvard College graduate in 1725, was ordained in Somersworth (now Rollinsford) in 1739. Pike was a multi-talented minister who served a large geographic but sparsely populated area. Pike was the most influential person in his community. He died in Somersworth in 1792. Speaking of Pastor James Pike:

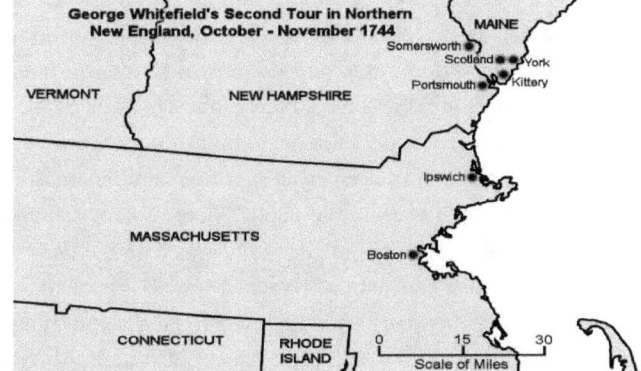

George Whitefield's Second Tour in Northern New England, October – November 1744

---

12 Joseph Tracy, *The Great Awakening*, (1842: reprinted by Banner of Truth Trust, Carlisle, PA: 1989), p. 342.
13 William Shurtleff, *A Letter to those of His Brethren in the Ministry who Refuse to Admit the Reverend Mr. George Whitefield into their Pulpits . . .* , (Boston, MA: Kneeland & Green, Printers, 1745).
14 Quoted in Luke Tyerman, *The Life of the Rev. George Whitefield*, vol. II, pp. 122-123.
15 George Whitefield, *Works*, vol. II, pp. 71-72.

> His parish was very large, extending throughout what is Somersworth and Rollinsford, and it was his custom to visit every home in the whole town, of whatever denomination of belief . . . He was the common scrivener for the whole parish; when they wanted any legal papers drawn they called on him to write them . . . When Whitefield came to this country in 1744 he was the guest of Mr. Pike for several days and preached in the meeting house one Sunday.[16]

The next preaching event recorded by Whitefield was for Rev. Jabez Fitch of the North Church in Portsmouth. Fitch was born in Connecticut, the son of a minister. He graduated Harvard College in 1694 with both a bachelor's degree and a master's degree. While at the North Church he also served on the faculty at Harvard as a tutor and was a fellow of the college. When Whitefield preached in the North Church for Fitch in November 1744, the elderly Fitch was seventy-two years old, assisted by the younger Rev. Samuel Langdon. The church meeting house was constructed in 1712. It was a three-decked building with two tiers of balconies and a 150-foot steeple. The building was replaced in 1835. Whitefield simply wrote of his preaching at the North Church in Portsmouth, noting in his *Journals*:

> Thursday, Nov. 22. Preached in Mr. Fitche's meeting house this afternoon with a sweet sense of the divine presence.

For the previous month or so, Whitefield had been preaching in the Kittery and York, Maine, and Portsmouth, New Hampshire areas. His health was delicate, as thousands came to hear the famous itinerate evangelist and orator. In keeping with his methodology of revisiting areas where he had already preached, Whitefield would return to this area in a few months. He headed south, towards Boston, traveling through Essex County, Massachusetts, where he was so eagerly received on his 1740 tour. Whitefield wrote in his *Journals*:

> Saturday, Nov. 24. Set out this morning from Portsmouth in a coach sent for that purpose by Mr. Sherburn, and Mr. John Rogers, Minister of Kittery, who tho' he has been in the ministry these 30 years, told me as we rode in the coach, he was not acquainted with real religion, till I was last in New England. The words that struck him were these, "If I was to draw the picture of a natural man I must go to Hell for a picture to draw him by." This I think was at Hampton. At York, in my discourse upon the Prodigal, he told me I pulled him all to pieces, and razed his false foundation and led him to a sin forgiving God. He thought I aimed at and spoke particularly to him, and said he should have cried out, only pride prevented him; but he could not refrain after he had come out of the meeting house. Ever since he has fought the good fight and appeared boldly in defense of the late great and glorious work of God in New England, and even before his conversion was so eminent for his good sense and rational powers that one said, if Mr. John Rogers should become a New Light he should think there was something in it. And yet, when he did become one, that would not do . . . Got over Newbury ferry between four and five in the afternoon and perceived near two hundred on the shore to see us land. The coachman being not ready, I went to the publick house. Many crowded in after me and I gave them as I stood a word of exhortation. The Lord was with me. Several wept, and the woman of the house was very much affected . . . Reached Ipswich about nine at night and was to preach on the Lord's Day following my arrival but was so fatigued with my journey that I could scarce move off the bed all day and was in great danger of relapse. Abundance of Dear Souls came from Newbury and other parts to hear me, but God's thoughts are never our thoughts. However I was made

---

16 John Scales, *History of Strafford County, New Hampshire and Representative Citizens*, (Chicago, IL: Richmond-Arnold Publishing, 1914), p. 220.

abundantly to rejoice in the Good News. Mr. Rogers, the minister of the place, told me what had been done in the parish both for his own heart and the other Souls. He is a brother of Mr. John Rogers that came with me and has also a new heart given him too in these and years past. He has had glorious harvest . . . .At night the people flocked round my room door full of love and exceedingly desirous to see me, but my illness did not admit of it, however one Gracious Man desired me he might sit up and watch with me. I accepted the offer and was refreshed with his conversation. He told me he believed a hundred were converted by the sermons I preached at Newbury when last at New England, that his wife lately deceased was one, and himself another.

Monday, November 25th. Left Ipswich by seven in the morning and called as I went by his house on the Rev. Mr. Rogers, Father to the person where I lay and senior Pastor of the Church.

The Rogers family of Ipswich were a stellar example of the remnant of orthodox Puritanism in select areas of New England. John Rogers, who met and welcomed Whitefield in Ipswich, was of the fourth generation of Puritan preachers in the Rogers family. Whitefield called him, "the senior pastor of the church" in Ipswich. His three sons were all New Light revival preachers: John in Kittery, Nathaniel assisting his father in Ipswich, and Daniel in Exeter, New Hampshire. Located a convenient distance between Portsmouth and Boston, Ipswich was deeply moved by the Great Awakening. When Whitefield preached there in 1740, thousands gathered to listen. During this 1744 visit to Ipswich, Whitefield was too ill to preach. His *Journals* narrative, on November 25, 1744 from Ipswich, continued.

The Lord was good to me in the way and brought me according to my desire, in a private manner to Boston, just as it began to grow duskish . . . A whole room full of friends that had notice of my coming were ready to welcome me to Boston, which they did in a cordial and affectionate manner. I spent some time with them, as my health would permit, prayed, and retired to rest, blessing God that He had visited me with sickness in order to prepare me for the mercies he had in store for me.

The Rev. Nathaniel Rogers home as it appears today in Ipswich. The house was originally built in 1727 and has been slightly altered over the years. George Whitefield was a frequent guest in this home.

Photograph by Ken Lawson.

CHAPTER 12

WHITEFIELD'S VISIT TO BOSTON

NOVEMBER-DECEMBER 1744

DRAMATIC CULTURAL AND ECCLESIASTICAL CHANGES had occurred in Boston. The awakening of 1740 only amplified numerous transformations in the culture of New England. The Puritan stronghold in many New England communities had collapsed. No longer did most New Englanders consider themselves "a city upon a hill" to shine as a witness to the world, as wrote the future Massachusetts Bay Colony Governor John Winthrop in 1630.

While never ceasing to remain a religious people, Bostonians became experts in shipping, trading, urban planning, and commercial development. A common fisherman could become a sea captain, then a wealthy merchant. A simple bookkeeper could become a prosperous entrepreneur. A cooper or a shoemaker might become a school committeeman or a selectman in local government. The Congregational churches in New England had long taught egalitarianism, that all church members were equal and as one before God. But the prosperity of Boston, coupled with waves on non-Puritan immigrants, created a society in which anyone could potentially become successful. One author called this "an expansion of Congregational Equality to Secular Equality."[1] By the mid-eighteenth century, over 100,000 people lived in New England, and the region no longer considered itself inferior to Great Britain. The larger New England cities saw an increase in new Anglican churches, a rise in secular or humanistic preaching from the European Enlightenment, a proliferation of new churches formed from expanding populations, and numerous controversies related to George Whitefield and the Great Awakening.[2]

Two influential sermons from this period greatly affected the churches of the American Colonies, New England in particular. One was by Rev. Gilbert Tennent, an itinerant New Jersey minister and ally of Whitefield. Preached and published in 1740, the sermon was called, *The Danger of an Unconverted Ministry*. In twelve pages, Tennent explains that a natural, unconverted man cannot effectively serve as a minister of the Lord, since his unregenerate state places him as an alien and enemy to God. Both Tennent and Whitefield believed much of the New England clergy was unconverted, and the publication of this sermon infuriated many Boston preachers and others. The second significant sermon, preached and published in 1741, was by Rev. Jonathan Edwards, called *The Distinguishing Marks of a Work of the Spirit of God*. This thirteen-page pamphlet credited the physical manifestations seen in revival meetings as outwards signs of inner spiritual struggles. Edwards did not advocate for emotional extremes in the awakening, but he was not opposed to the idea that, at times, distinguishing appearances of the work of the Spirit of God could be evidenced in the

---

1   Chard P. Smith, *Yankees and God*, (New York: Hermitage House, 1954), p. 225
2   Harry S. Stout, *The New England Soul: Preaching and Religious Culture in Colonial New England*, (New York: Oxford University Press, 1986), pp. 185-232. Edwin S. Gaustad, *The Great Awakening in New England*, (Gloucester, MA: Peter Smith Publisher, 1965), pp. 61-101.

behaviors of people under spiritual convictions. This was rejected by many of the clergy who saw the revival as disorderly, carnal, or a harmful distraction to their routine ministries.

Whitefield arrived in northern New England in late October 1744. He preached in what are now the states of Maine and New Hampshire, with great success. He then worked his way south into Massachusetts, destined for Boston, arriving on November 25, 1744. Here he was reacquainted with men who firmly supported his revival work and encouraged the awakening. The most notable was Dr. Benjamin Coleman, who was largely responsible for inviting Whitefield to Boston in 1740. Coleman was pastor of the Brattle Street Church. Dr. Joseph Sewall was the respected Puritan pastor of the Old South Church. Rev. Thomas Foxcroft of the First Church, though a colleague of Whitefield's enemy Dr. Charles Chauncey, was a firm supporter of Whitefield. It must have been interesting to be a member of the First Church in Boston in the 1740s, with the senior minister, Charles Chauncey an outspoken critic of Whitefield, and his assistant minister, Thomas Foxcroft a vocal and prominent advocate of Whitefield and the awakening. Coinciding with Whitefield's visit to Boston in 1744 and 1745, Foxcroft wrote a thirty-eight-page defense for Whitefield, entitled *An Apology in Behalf of Mr. Whitefield*, which clearly stated his support of the revival and his personal endorsement of Whitefield.

The First Church in Boston dates to 1630. The building constructed in 1713 is pictured here. This is the meeting house where Rev. Charles Chauncey and Rev. Thomas Foxcroft served. Chauncey opposed Whitefield but Foxcroft endorsed Whitefield. Source: www.firstchurchbostonhistory.org.

Various Boston ministers recalled with affection the historic days of the Puritans and their doctrinal orthodoxy. Boston had become a prosperous and eclectic city with streets crowded with people who did not go to church on Sundays. "Colonial preachers never tired of referring to the good old days of the founders, when people kept to their covenant with God—in contrast to the lukewarm and lackadaisical people of their own day, the early eighteenth century. Someone had to rekindle the fires."[3]

Whitefield remained in Boston from November 25 to December 13, 1744. His *Journals* relate many details from this brief period.[4]

> Monday, November 25 [1744]. The Lord was good to me in the way and brought me according to my desire, in a private manner, to Boston, just as it began to grow duskish. I was met by and received into the home of Mr. John Smith, a Merchant, a true Disciple of the Lord Jesus. He was the chief instrument under God of bringing me at this time to New England, and gave me an invitation to his house before we embarked.

---

3 Martin E. Marty, *Strangers in their Own Land: Five Hundred Years of Religion in America*, (New York: Penguin Books, 1984), p. 107.
4 George Whitefield, *Journals of George Whitefield* (1756: reprinted by Banner of Truth Trust, Carlisle, PA: 1985). Whitefield's 1744 Boston ministry is recorded on pages 527-533.

It is interesting to note Whitefield's strategy upon his arrival in Boston. It was late, it was getting dark, and there was no large reception. This was deliberate. He knew that he had to tread lightly and carefully in this city, as he had many potential enemies in Boston. His *Journals* continued,

> A whole room full of friends that had notice of my coming were ready to welcome me to Boston, which they did in the most cordial affectionate manner. I spent some time with them, as my health would permit, prayed, and retired to rest, blessing God that He had visited me with sickness in order to prepare me for the mercies He had in store for me.
>
> Tuesday, November 27th. Had the pleasure of dining today at my lodging with the Rev. Dr. Sewell, Doctor Coleman, Mr. Foxcroft, and Mr. Prince, four of the senior Ministers in Boston and very worthy men who have distinguished themselves in the late.
>
> Before dinner we had some free conversation together in relation to some passages in my journals and the present posture of religious affairs in New England.

The four clergymen listed here in Whitefield's *Journals* were his avid supporters. Rev. Joseph Sewell was from a distinguished Puritan family tracing its roots to the first generation of New Englanders. His assistant minister at the Old South Church was Rev. Thomas Prince, who chronicled eyewitness accounts of the awakening in articles that became a book called *Christian History*. Benjamin Coleman was the minister of the Brattle Street Church. Coleman supported the awakening but was critical of some extremes. Thomas Foxcroft was the assistant minister of the historic First Church, Boston.

A Harvard student named Edward Holyoke heard Whitefield preach in Cambridge near Boston in 1744. There was an older elm tree under which Whitefield preached to multitudes. When almost one hundred years old, Holyoke returned to Cambridge and saw that elm for the last time, recalling "while he passed this tree with a friend, remarked that he had, when a student in Harvard College, heard the sermon Whitefield delivered under that tree."[5]

Boston was geographically confined to a peninsula that jutted out into Massachusetts Bay. All the ten or so church buildings in Boston were within a mile of each other. Many were within sight of one another. The Boston skyline in the 1740s was dominated by a scattering of church steeples. All enjoyed the fresh ocean breezes in the summer, and all suffered from the cold winter winds. Many Bostonians attended the same church as their parents and grandparents, while recent immigrants often initially struggled to find their place in society. All ministers of that day wore a clerical wig and black robes when preaching, with the Anglican ministers more liturgical and formally arrayed.

Whitefield mentioned above that he and four ministers in Boston, "had some free conversation together in relation to some passages in my journals and the present posture of religious affairs in New England." This was a shrewd move by Whitefield, to gather the support of his friends and answer their questions before preaching in a city that had developed some animosity towards the awakening. There is no doubt that Whitefield regretted some of the wording he used in his *Journals*. His youthful zeal was evident in often antagonistic, overgeneralized statements that appeared more bombastic that reasoned critiques. This was especially true about his accusatory comments to the two New England colleges, Harvard and Yale. He intended to manage the damage he already caused, while healing divisions and preaching the Gospel. His *Journals*, dated November 27, 1744 continues discussing his meeting with Reverends Sewell, Coleman, Foxcroft, and Prince:

---

5   Joseph B. Wakeley, *Anecdotes of the Rev. George Whitefield, M.A.*, (London: 1772), p. 310.

I found by what they said and by what I had heard by letters that the work of God had went on in a most glorious manner for near two Years after my departure from New England, but then a chill came over the work, through the imprudence of some Ministers who had been promoters and private persons who had been happy subjects of it.

They were apprehensive, I found too, that I would promote or encourage separations, and that some would have been encouraged to separate by my saying in my journal that I found the generality of Preachers preached an Unknown Christ, that the Colleges had darkness in them, even darkness that might be felt, and that speaking of the dangers of an Unconverted Ministry, I said, How can a dead man begat a living child? . . .

I said, I was sorry if anything I wrote had been a means of promoting separations for I was of no separating principles, but came to New England to preach the Gospel of peace to all that were willing to hear in my way to Georgia, and promote charity and love among all.

We talked freely and friendly about several other things and dined very comfortably by which their jealousies they had entertained concerning me seemed to be in a great measure ended, and Dr. Coleman invited me to preach the next day at his Meeting house.

Benjamin Coleman of the Brattle Street Church was a careful, reasonable minister with an evangelical passion for Calvinistic orthodoxy. Not physically imposing, as a Harvard trained young man, he travelled in 1699 to England to further prepare for the ministry. On the way his ship was attacked by French privateers. Coleman manned a weapon and fought the French with small arms and assisted with the cannons. He was a prisoner in France for two months before being released to England. He returned to Boston in 1699 and became pastor of the Brattle Street Church. He received an honorary Doctor of Divinity degree from the University of Glasgow in 1731. When he and Whitefield collaborated in 1744, Coleman was seventy-two years old, Whitefield was thirty years old. Yet the older, more experienced Coleman saw something in the youthful, often rash, and exuberant Whitefield that he could support. One author noted:

Built in 1729, the Old South Meeting House is still standing as a National Historic Site and a tourist destination. George Whitefield preached here numerous times from 1740 to 1770. Photograph by Ken Lawson.

Dr. Coleman was regarded in his day as a man possessing all those traits which constitute goodness of disposition, in its most comprehensive meaning. In the pulpit he was distinguished for his grace and dignity of manner, as well as for his powers of persuasion and argument. In the private walks of life, he was hailed as one gifted in an eminent degree with the nobler qualities of our nature. His interest in public business brought upon him the blame of many, and he was charged with an officious intermeddling in civil and secular affairs . . . Among the worthies of the Massachusetts clergy, we can perhaps select no character, which we may regard with more thorough esteem, than that of Dr. Coleman; and not much more may be said of any man. If his mind was not of that class, by which great revolutions are produced in the intellectual or social world, it was still one of uncommon comprehensiveness, penetration, wisdom, and activity; and it had been cultivated by an enlarged acquaintance with books and men.[6]

Coleman was a reconciler. He was a man gifted in mediating disputes. Deeply influenced by the historic Puritan Mather family in Boston, Coleman was orthodox in theology but practical and accommodating in non-essential issues. He supported the awakening, but he refrained from its extreme elements. "Benjamin Colman was one of the most prominent ministers of his generation." As a Congregational minister, he supported Whitefield, a Church of England minister, an Anglican priest. "Though Colman advocated a strict separation between Anglicans and Congregationalists, he maintained a sympathetic and mutually supportive relationship with the Church of England." In 1740 and again in 1744 and 1745, Coleman endorsed Whitefield, and encouraged his fellow Boston clergymen and Harvard College to open their pulpits to the itinerant evangelist. "When Whitefield alienated and angered many Boston clergy with his criticisms, Colman successfully mediated the disputes that arouse."[7] Whitefield's *Journals* narrates his preaching for Benjamin Coleman at the Brattle Street Church.

An undated portrait of Rev. Benjamin Colman

Source: www.www.studyblue.com

Wednesday, November 28th. Opened my public administration at Boston this afternoon at Dr. Coleman's meeting house from Rom. 1st, 16th. I am not ashamed of the Gospel of Christ for it is the power of God unto salvation to everyone that believeth. The congregation was very large, several ministers were present and the word was attended with sweet power . . . My heart, whilst I was preaching, leaped for joy to think what God had done for Dear New England since I spoke from that pulpit last . . . made me cry out with greater vigor, I am not ashamed of the Gospel of Christ, for there were many living witnesses that it had been the power of God unto the salvation of souls.

Blessed be God for such an entrance into Boston! How does the Lord delight to disappoint fears and overcome hopes! O blessed is the man, O Jesus, that putteth his trust in thee!

Saturday, November 30th. Preached a preparation sermon, yesterday in the afternoon for the Rev'd Doctor Coleman, and again in the afternoon for the Rev'd Dr. Webb at his meeting house, where it was observed the gracious God generally appeared most when I was last in New England.

Whitefield mentioned "Rev'd Dr. Webb." This was John Webb, minister of the New North Church. On September 22, 1740, Whitefield preached for Webb to over 6,000 listeners, and a few weeks later October

---

6   "Benjamin Coleman (1673-1747): Critical and Biographical Notice," http://www.bartleby.com/96/11.html.
7   "Benjamin Coleman Papers," Massachusetts Historical Society, http://masshist.org/collection-guides/view/fa0288.

8, twice on a Wednesday to "very great auditories."[8] Now in 1744, Whitefield was back. Webb was the first minister at New North Church, serving there from his ordination in 1714 to his death in 1750. Before the awakening of the 1740s, Webb's ministry at New North Church was consistent but uneventful. He exchanged pulpits with other ministers in Boston, and was well known and respected in the city. He was called "a very popular preacher and greatly beloved."[9] Webb was one of the Puritan New England ministers who pleaded with the city for a return to the faith of the founding fathers. In 1730, John Webb preached and published a sermon called *The Great Concern of New England*, emphasizing the need for renewal and repentance. In 1734 he preached and published a message with the compelling title, *The Duty of a Degenerate People to Pray for the Reviving of God's Work*. During and after the revival, Webb was a straightforward promoter of Whitefield and the awakening. Whitefield's *Journals* speaks about his preaching for Benjamin Coleman and John Webb.

> Saturday, November 30, 1744 . . . The congregations were very large at both places, and many people's prejudices, which had been raised in their minds upon a surmise that I would encourage separations and countenance disorders, I found wore away apace. I preached on Fryday upon Christ's love to us and today upon the marks of our love to him. Sweet was the power that attended the word preached, and my soul was delighted to hear worthy Mr. Webb (an Israelite indeed) inform me how full his hands were for fiveteen months successively in speaking to souls under concern and how many had been added to his Church during the late Revival of Religion in New England. Surely God has done for them great things. Holy and Reverend be His Name!

> Sunday, December 1st. Heard the Rev'd Mr. Coleman preach a sweet sermon this morning upon these words, "Behold I bring forth my servant the branch," and after sermon the Doctor having notified to the congregation that he had asked me to assist him and nobody making any objection, I administered the holy sacrament, and many, I believe, set under the shadow of God's Servant the Branch with great delight and his fruit was pleasant to taste.

Here at the Brattle Street Church in Boston, an unusual event took place. The church was Congregational but allowed Whitefield, as an ordained priest of the Church of England, to assist with the celebration of communion. Knowing the Congregationalist history in Boston of animosity towards the Anglican Church, this was a remarkable event. The awakening in general, but Whitefield in particular, was breaking down denominational barriers and ecclesiastical distinctions. Less than two weeks later, Whitefield would help celebrate communion in a Presbyterian Church in Boston. Historically, Congregationalism and Presbyterianism were reactions to and rejections of the Anglican Church of England. Whitefield's preaching essentially ignored denominational distinctions as he presented gospel-centered sermons on Jesus Christ and the need for the new birth. In this Christological and soteriological focus, man-made ecclesiastical practices faded by the wayside, replaced by the simple message of Holy Scripture.[10] Boston Congregationalists and Presbyterians welcomed the preaching of this Anglican priest. Whitefield's *Journal* continues.

---

8 George Whitefield, *Journals*, pp. 460, 469.
9 New North Religious Society, *Historical Notices of the New North Religious Society, Boston*, (Boston, MA: 1822), p. 13.
10 George Whitefield was an ordained and dedicated Anglican priest of the Church of England. In that capacity he recognized the vast and crucial influence of the Protestant reformers. These reformers came from various denominational backgrounds, but Christ was their central focus. Whitefield was an Anglican who respected Protestants of various denominations. For him, denominational distinctives and peculiarities of church polity were secondary issues to the preaching of Christ and the new birth. See Dan Nelson, *A Burning and Shining Light: The Testimony and Witness of George Whitefield*, (Somis, CA: LifeSong Publishers, 2017), pp. 255-257. Michael A.G. Haykin, *George Whitefield*, (Grand Rapids, MI: EP Books, 2014), pp. 105, 109. Nigel Scotland, *George Whitefield: The First Transatlantic Revivalist*, (Oxford, England, 2019), p. 271. Whitefield's trans-denominational view is summed up in one of his letters, where he asserted, "I wish all names among the saints of God were swallowed up in that one word Christian. I long for professors to leave off placing religion in saying, 'I am a

[Sunday December 1st] After having dined with Dr. Coleman I went and heard Dr. Sewell upon the Divinity of Jesus Christ. Blessed be God who has yet left unto his people so many Defenders of the faith once delivered to the saints.

The Puritan Rev. Joseph Sewell, of the Old South Church, was an orthodox Calvinist minister. He was a member of the propagation of the Gospel in New England, and a corresponding member of the Scottish Society for Promoting Christian Knowledge, a missionary organization. He was a fellow of Harvard College from 1728 to 1765. The honorary degree of Doctor of Divinity was bestowed on Sewell by the University of Glasgow in 1731. Many of his sermons were published in Boston newspapers and reprinted throughout the Colonies. Whitefield noted above that he considered Sewell a defender of the faith. When he and Whitefield met in 1744, Sewell was fifty-six years old. He served at Old South Church until his death in 1769. Whitefield's *Journals* continues:

An undated sketch of Rev. Joseph Sewell.
Source: sewellgenealogy.com/p524.htm

> Sunday, December 8th. Preached four times this last week in several meeting houses to very crowded auditories, and once on Thursday afternoon to the poor people in the Work-House, and had the pleasure of finding that the prejudiced persons were more and more reconciled to me, especially by the sermon I preached at Worthy Doctor Sewell's on Tuesday on walking with God . . . A fire happening in the town I preached on Fryday on Lot's delivery out of Sodom.

> Waited Yesterday as I rode along to Esq'r Ryall's, who sent his chariot for me, to the aged and venerable Mr. Walter of Roxbury, who I heard had some way or another imbibed [received or assimilated] prejudices against me. He received me civilly but did not expostulate with me upon any particular nor mention anything to me that was the cause of offense to him I suppose on account of the shortness of my visit, being in haste.

Whitefield wrote of "the aged and venerable Mr. Walter of Roxbury." Whitefield and Rev. Nathaniel Walter first met when Whitefield preached in Boston in September 1740, but their meeting was brief and insignificant.[11] Walter was a former missionary to the Indians, who occasionally left his pulpit in Roxbury for missionary work with the tribes in western Massachusetts. Now in December 1744, Nathaniel Walter was hesitant to fully endorse Whitefield, and when the two met face-to-face, Whitefield wrote above that their conversation was brief and civil, not confrontational. Whitefield's *Journals* narrative continues on December 8, 1744.

> Preached twice and administered the Holy Sacrament at good old Mr. Chivers the most aged, and perhaps the most hearty minister of his age in all New England. I think he told me he was 87 years of age, and had now and then a little pain in his leg, but not so much He said as He had twenty years ago . . . Jesus was with us both in preaching and in administration of the

---

Churchman, I am a Dissenter.' My language to such is, 'Are you of Christ? If so, I love you with all my heart.'" George Whitefield, *Works of George Whitefield*, (London: 1771), Vol. I, p. 115.

11 George Whitefield, *Journals*, p. 461.

Lord's Supper, and though it was the first time I had ventured to preach twice in a day, since my sickness yet the Lord was pleased to strengthen and comfort me very much and we closed our Sabbath very sweetly at Esq'r Ryall's.

Whitefield wrote of "good old Mr. Chivers." This was Rev. Thomas Cheever of the First Church in Chelsea, Massachusetts. Cheever was born in Ipswich, Massachusetts in 1658, making him a remarkable seventy-six years old when Whitefield met him in 1744 and called him "old." Harvard educated, Thomas Cheever began preaching in nearby Malden in 1679, and was ordained there in 1681. In 1686 he had a falling out with the church, charges were exchanged, and Cheever was dismissed. For the next thirty years he maintained schools in the Chelsea and Malden areas. He was later installed as the minister of the First Church in Rumney Marsh (Chelsea) in 1715, a position he held until his death in 1749. Cheever was respected by townsfolk and clergy, and faithfully served the only church in Chelsea, an area much larger than the city of Chelsea today.[12] Cheever kept a large garden and had geese, cows, sheep, and pigs. His was called "a very able pastorate" in Chelsea.[13] Whitefield wrote above that he preached twice in one day for Cheever in Chelsea, and the two shared the administration of the Lord's Supper.

At this point in Whitefield's *Journals*, he no longer recorded his daily activities. Instead, he wrote weekly summaries of his ministry experiences. At times the exact dates are confused, and at other times the exact dates are unknown. His *Journals* continued:

Preached on Monday [December 9] to a large auditory for the Rev'd Mr. Emerson of Maulden, who has appeared and continued singularly steady and zealous in the late revival of Religion.

Rev. Joseph Emerson served as the pastor of a Congregational Church in Malden, Massachusetts, from 1721 to 1767. Born in Chelmsford, Massachusetts, Emerson was a 1717 graduate of Harvard College. Thereafter he taught school nearby in York, Newbury, and Malden. In York he met his wife Mary, the daughter of Rev. Samuel Moody. He was ordained as a Congregational minister in Malden in 1721, and served there for 46 years until his death. His sermons were written out, and his preaching style was forceful. Over many years he and the town bickered over the condition of the parsonage, but no animosity was evident between both parties.[14] Emerson "labored with great fidelity and acceptance" in Malden. He was a confirmed New Light preacher, balanced and unemotional but eager to promote the awakening. Previously, Whitefield preached for Emerson in October 1740, and the two became longtime friends. Malden was divided over the revival, and the town had numerous ecclesiastical controversies in the mid-1740s.[15] Whitefield's *Journals* narrative then names some familiar and trusted ministerial friends in Boston:

On Tuesday [December 10] at the desire of Rev. Mr. Foxcroft, I ventured to preach in his evening Lecture at Doctor Coleman's Meeting and, blessed be God, found it not so prejudicial to my health as was feared it would be.

On Wednesday [December 11] I preached in the forenoon at Mr. Webb's, and in the afternoon for the Rev. Mr. Gee, a dear minister of Jesus Christ.

---

12 John L. Sibley, *Biographical Sketches of Graduates of Harvard University*, (Cambridge, MA: C.W. Sever, Printer, 1881), vol. II, pp. 501-506. Isaac P. Langworthy, *A Historical Discourse delivered at Chelsea, Mass., Sept. 20, 1866, at the Twenty-Fifth Anniversary of the Winnisimmet Congregational Church*, (Chelsea, MA: 1866), pp. 9-11.
13 Mellen Chamberlain, *A Documentary History of Chelsea . . . 1624-1824*, (Boston, MA: Massachusetts Historical Society, 1908), p. 158.
14 "Family of Deacon Edward Emerson & Rebecca Waldo," http://aleph0.clarku.edu/~djoyce/gen/report /rr13/rr13_018.html. Frank Russell, *An Early History of Malden*, (Charleston, SC: The History Press, 2018), pp. 18-21.
15 Deloraine P. Corey, *The History of Malden, Massachusetts 1633-1785*, (Malden, MA: Published by the Author, 1899), p. 641.

Tens-of-thousands of Bostonians, and those from neighboring towns, heard Whitefield preach. Some went to hear him out of spite or ridicule, and were changed by his message. The following account is an illustration:

> When Whitefield visited Boston in 1744, a number were converted; among others a man of brilliant wit and racy humor, who delighted to preach over a bottle to his boon companions. Having gone to hear Whitefield in order to get up a new "tavern harangue," and having, as he thought, heard enough of the sermon for his purpose, he was about leaving the church for the inn, when "he found his endeavors to get out fruitless, being so pent up." While thus fixed, and waiting for "fresh matter of ridicule," he was arrested by the power of the Gospel. That night he went to Mr. Prince, a preacher in Boston, full of horror, and earnestly desiring to beg Mr. Whitefield's pardon. Mr. Prince encouraged him to visit Mr. Whitefield. He did so with fear and trembling. Whitefield says of him, "By the paleness, pensiveness, and horror of his countenance, I guessed he was the man of whom I had been apprised. "Sir, can you forgive?" I smiled and said, "Yes, Sir, very readily." "Indeed, you cannot," he said, "when I tell you all." "I then asked him to sit down, and, judging that he had sufficiently felt the lash of the law, I preached to him the gospel. The man was converted, and consecrated his wit, genius, and talents to God." This and other remarkable conversions gave to Mr. Whitefield preaching in Boston increased power and influence.[16]

Talk in Boston was rife with discontent against Whitefield, the revival, and the excesses demonstrated by some itinerant preachers. With Reverends Foxcroft, Colman, Webb, and Gee, Whitefield had sober and enduring ministerial allies. But others in Boston and nearby Cambridge were openly antagonistic to Whitefield. A few weeks later, in December and January 1745, significant publications against Whitefield appeared in Boston and surrounding communities. But for now, Whitefield continued preaching in Boston. His *Journals* stated:

> On [December 12] Thursday [preached] for the Rev'd Mr. Morehead, the Presbyterian minister, a hearty Friend to the late work, and whose people spent a whole night in prayer for my recovery from sickness.

This is the first account we have of Whitefield interacting with Rev. John Moorhead. Born in Northern Ireland in 1703 and educated in Scotland, Moorhead immigrated to Boston as a Presbyterian missionary. He arrived in 1727 and took classes at Harvard. Beginning in 1730 he served at the Scotch-Irish Presbyterian Church on the corner of Federal and Channing Streets in Boston. This church has been variously known as The Church of the Presbyterian Strangers; The Long Lane Church; The Federal Street Church; and, most recently, The Arlington Street Church. The Scotch-Irish Presbyterian Church initially met in a barn. A Harvard graduate, John Moorhead was well received, and his preaching brought in new members. In 1735, the congregation numbered 250. One source stated:

> Very few men have left behind them a fairer or better character, — charitable and liberal to the poor, with a hearty disposition to render them every service in his power, — industrious and faithful in the dispensation of the word, and a most earnest desire for the good of souls which was the actuating and ruling principle of his life. His mind was deeply impressed with the importance of the truth of the atonement of Jesus Christ as the only well-grounded hope of salvation and happiness in a future state; this made him anxiously desirous to communicate

---

16 Joseph B. Wakeley, *Anecdotes of the Rev. George Whitefield, M.A.*, pp. 143-144.

that impression to others. With this view his labors were incessant. In all his discourses from the sacred desk he held up this grand truth as the only principle upon which depended the very existence of Christianity; also frequently visiting the families of his flock, and endeavoring to inspire them to practice as well as believe the Gospel. His honesty of heart, open and frank manner of address, rendered him at all times an able and faithful adviser.[17]

Moorhead was a devout Presbyterian and confirmed Calvinist, with an evangelical zeal that made him and Whitefield close friends. When the awakening reached Boston, Moorhead was fully supportive. His congregation quickly outgrew its meeting space in a barn, and in 1744, constructed a new meeting house for the growing congregation.[18] Moorhead and Whitefield appear to have been very likeminded. John Moorhead was described as follows:

> Mr. Moorhead was a plain, evangelical and practical preacher . . . He insisted principally on the peculiar doctrines of the Gospel—the deep depravity of human nature; the Divinity of Jesus Christ, and the efficacy of the atonement; the special agency of the Divine Spirit in regeneration; the necessity of repentance, of faith in Jesus Christ, and of good works.[19]

Moorhead served the Scotch-Irish Presbyterian Church until his death in 1773. The church had the tradition of celebrating the Lord's Supper four times per year. At these solemn and highly anticipated events, the church often asked a neighboring minister of like faith to participate in the sacred service. On at least one occasion, George Whitefield was the invited minister who assisted in the communion celebration. When Whitefield spoke at the communion service at the Scotch-Irish Presbyterian Church in Boston, "every heart was moved by his solemn and enrapturing performance."[20]

Having completed several weeks of preaching in Boston, Whitefield decided to depart the city for a brief preaching tour to the suburbs north and east of the city. This was familiar and friendly territory, as he had just preached through this area a few months prior. In keeping with his itinerant circuit riding methodology, Whitefield preached, departed, and returned to re-water gospel seeds previously planted. Boston newspapers ignored his preaching in the surrounding communities. He may have been unaware of the opposition he would receive in various communities.

---

17 "Rev. John Moorhead," https://familysearch.org/photos/stories/3221672. Kim K. Crawford Harvie, "Arlington Street Church," Lecture at the Unitarian Universalist General Assembly in Boston, Massachusetts, June 29, 2003.
18 "Arlington Street Church," http://www.acsboston.org/about/history.html#highlights. https://www.ascboston.org/about/history-minns.html.
19 William B. Sprague, *Annals of the American Pulpit, vol. III Presbyterian*, (New York: Robert Carter & Brothers Publishers, 1859), p. 46.
20 Ibid.

CHAPTER 13

WHITEFIELD'S TOUR NORTH OF BOSTON, DECEMBER 13-19, 1744

AFTER SEVERAL WEEKS OF PREACHING in Boston to large crowds, Whitefield left the city to preach in neighboring communities. This was his model—preach in an area, depart, and then return to preach again to those who were previously influenced by his ministry. This preaching circuit would be only five days, in which he preached at least twelve times in five towns. Whitefield could have preached through a local circuit to the north, west, or south. He decided to preach on a tour to the north and east of Boston. The reasons for this are unclear. Perhaps he saw the need to solidify the revival work in these exact locations. He might have had written invitations to visit and preach. Perhaps his allies in these towns needed his encouragement, as local opposition to the awakening was firm in many areas, especially in Lynn. Whitefield's *Journals* describes his account of departing Boston for a brief preaching circuit.[1] He wrote:

> On Friday [December 13] I went to Lyn[n] and preached to a large auditory for the Rev. Mr. Chivers, grand-son to old Mr. Chivers of Chelsea and I trust likeminded with him.

Lynn, Massachusetts is located along the coastline, about 12 miles northeast of Boston. The community was torn apart by controversies related to the awakening. Whitefield above mentioned a "Rev. Mr. Chivers." This was Rev. Edward Cheever of the Third Congregational Church in Lynn (now Saugus), Massachusetts. Cheever was relatively new to the ministry, a Harvard graduate in 1737 and ordained at the Third Church in 1739. Coming from a family with Puritan and Calvinist leanings, Cheever welcomed Whitefield and the revival in Lynn. The senior minister in Lynn was Rev. Nathaniel Henchman of the First Church of Christ Congregational. The older Henchman made life miserable for the younger Cheever. Around 1747, Cheever severed his connection to the Third Church and departed Lynn.[2] Henchman remained in Lynn until his death in 1761.

Nathaniel Henchman was born in 1700 in Boston. He was a Harvard graduate in 1717, and at age twenty, in 1720, he became the minister of the First Church in Lynn. From its first settlement in 1629, the community later called Lynn was involved in maritime activities and the leather trades. Lynn was named in 1637 and did not prosper as quickly as its neighbors in Salem or Boston. When Henchman arrived in Lynn, he met initial success as a minister. "His learning was extensive, and his integrity and virtue entitled him to high respect."[3] He was a stickler for propriety and order. He was cordial in his manners and is said to have treated Whitefield with civility when they met face-to-face. But during the awakening, Henchman refused to add more church

---

1 George Whitefield, *George Whitefield's Journals*, (1756: reprinted by Banner of Truth Trust, Carlisle, PA: 1985), p. 533.
2 Alonzo Lewis & James Newhall, *History of Lynn, Massachusetts*, (Boston, MA: 1865), pp. 325, 328.
3 Alonzo Lewis, *The History of Lynn; Including Nahant*, (Boston, MA: Samuel N. Dickinson Printer, 1844), p. 207.

services, and opposed guest speakers in his pulpit, which caused dissension in his church.[4] Henchman and his relationship to Whitefield is described as follows:

> The pastor of the Lynn church was Nathaniel Henchman. He was not in sympathy with the new movement. During the Great Awakening he would not admit to his pulpit the neighboring ministers who sympathized with Edwards [Rev. Jonathan Edwards of Northampton, MA]. His people wanted to hear them. But he would not. Then began a controversy which lasted twenty-three years,—until his death. It was nominally about salary, but back of that was his attitude toward the new preachers. When Whitefield came the second time [December 1744], Henchman's pulpit was closed against him. The people desired to hear him [Whitefield], took a door off a neighboring barn, put it on barrels on the Common and made a platform from which Whitefield preached to hundreds of eager hearers. Henchman wrote a pamphlet explaining his attitude. This was replied to in a Christian spirit by the minister in Reading [Rev. William Hobby]. Henchman replied to this. His reply was sarcastic, satirical, and bitter. The air was full of invective.[5]

Clearly, Whitefield targeted Lynn as a place where his presence was needed. Pastor Edward Cheever was overwhelmed with antagonism from the older Henchman, and the revival in Lynn was suffering. When Henchman publicly opposed Whitefield, the itinerant simply preached out of doors on the common near the meeting house to a large congregation.[6] Obviously this defiance infuriated Henchman.

The public animosity of Henchman towards Whitefield and the awakening is evident in his pamphlets written from 1743-1745. Henchman wrote a letter to a neighboring minister, Rev. Stephen Chase of Lynn End (now Lynnfield) in which he explained his opposition to Whitefield.[7] Henchman and Chase had a cordial relationship, as Chase was simply curious as to why Henchman was so adamant against Whitefield and the revival. Chase was a Harvard graduate in 1728 and began his ministry in Lynn End in 1731, remaining there until he resigned to accept a call to a church in New Castle, New Hampshire in 1755. Chase appears to have gotten along with Henchman. One correspondent who publicly opposed Henchman was Rev. William Hobby of nearby Reading, Massachusetts.

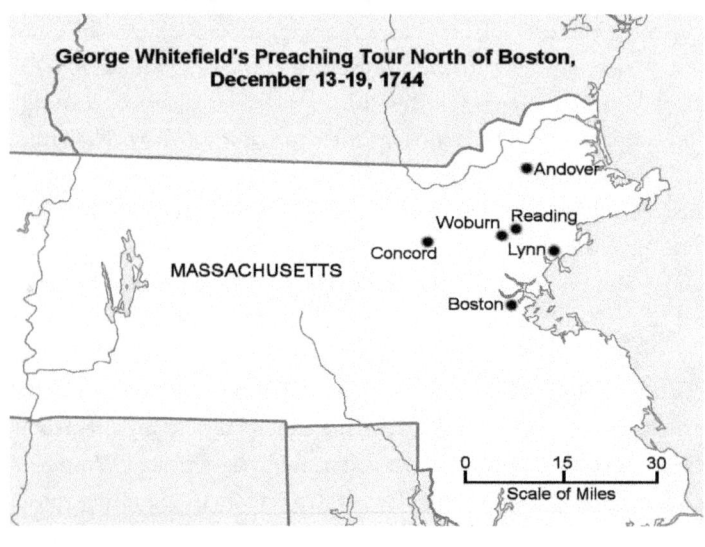

William Hobby became a Whitefield admirer after the evangelist preached outside in Reading in 1740. As Henchman printed against Whitefield, Hobby responded in support of the awakening. The pamphlets published by Henchman are bitter and antagonistic, while Hobby's pamphlets are kinder and more reasonable. In a few days, Whitefield would be in Hobby's church, preaching to encourage the beleaguered Hobby and to support the awakening in Reading. In the

---

4   Ibid.
5   *The Register of the Lynn Historical Society . . . for the Year 1912*, (Lynn, MA: Frank S. Whitten, Publisher, 1913), p. 60.
6   D. Hamilton Hurd, *History of Essex County, Massachusetts*, (Philadelphia, PA: J.W. Lewis & Company, 1888), vol. I, p. 266.
7   Nathaniel Henchman, *A Letter from the Rev. Nathaniel Henchman, Pastor of the First Church in Lynn, to the Rev. Stephen Chase, of Lynn End, giving his reasons for Declining to admit the Rev. George Whitefield into His Pulpit*, (Boston, MA: 1744).

meantime, Henchman in Lynn remained antagonistic to the revival. The effect of Whitefield's December 13, 1744 visit to Lynn is summarized as follows, with particular reference to Nathaniel Henchman and the First Church.

> Whitefield went, but he left seeds of bitterness which bore fruit later. A wide breach had been opened between pulpit and people in Lynn. The people had a taste of live preaching and they never again could be satisfied with the old kind. Membership in the [First Congregational] Church dropped to a very low point.[8]

After preaching outdoors in Lynn, no small feat in December in chilly Massachusetts, Whitefield travelled northwest several miles to Concord. His *Journals* narrative stated,

> In the evening I returned and expounded at Mr. Ryall's and this afternoon came to Concord where I had a kind reception from Mr. Bliss and where with some other Boston friends we began the Sabbath, as is customary in New England, with praising and blessing God for all past mercies, for the outpouring of the Spirit, since we saw one another last, and in praying that we might yet see greater things than ever we saw or heard yet. Even so Lord Jesus, come quickly. Amen and Amen.

The "Mr. Ryall" mentioned above is unidentifiable. The name could be misspelt or misunderstood by Whitefield. The "Mr. Bliss" of Concord was Rev. Daniel Bliss, pastor of the First Parish Church Concord. He graduated from Yale in 1732 and was ordained March 7, 1739. Bliss was pastor of the Congregational Church of Concord from 1738 to his death in 1764. He was a New Light minister and a full supporter of the Great Awakening in New England. Because of his support of Whitefield and the revival, many townsfolk in Concord were offended. Charges were brought against Bliss, and a dispute raged for a few years. Mutual councils were called, and charges were exchanged, on issues from everything to the minister's salary, to the concept of itinerant ministry, to the length and content of his prayers. Bliss and Whitefield had met in 1740. Now Whitefield had returned to support the beleaguered Daniel Bliss and conduct damage control for the church in Concord. Whitefield wrote in his *Journals:*

> Preached thrice on Lord's Day [December 15] and once on Monday [December 16] with great sweetness and freedom to large and very affected auditories in Concord. Had much of the divine presence in private conversation both days, and near access to God in our social addresses to Him.

A few miles away in Sudbury, Rev. Israel Loring wrote in his *Journal*, "This Lord's Day Mr. Whitefield preached at Concord. A considerable number went from us to hear him on that day, and again on Monday, when he preached in the forenoon, and then went off to Reading."[9]

An undated image of Rev. Daniel Bliss of Concord.

Source: https://www.geni.com/people/Rev-Daniel-bliss/6000000003940284745

---

8   *The Register of the Lynn Historical Society*, p. 61.
9   Israel Loring, *The Journal of Rev. Israel Loring (1682-1772) of Sudbury, Massachusetts Covering his Early Life and the Years 1704-1745*, edited by L.P. Thomas, (Sudbury, MA Public Library), 28.

Meanwhile, Whitefield's critics began to surface. For example, the November 19, 1744 issue of the *Boston Evening Post* listed several recurring themes of opposition to Whitefield. The *Post* mentioned his itinerancy, his slander directed to local respected ministers, his alleged improper financial records of his offerings, his opposition to the faculty and curriculum at Harvard, and his opposition to Archbishop Tillotson.[10] The December 17 issue of the *Boston Evening Post* said of Whitefield:

> Indeed, he seems to be more cautious than formerly, and so refrains his lips from speaking all the gross things, which were so shocking to serious and thinking persons; and he insists something more upon the substantial and useful doctrines and duties of religion. But an express and full acknowledgement of his faults, and an honest testimony against bad principles and uncharitable speeches and disorderly walking, is still all together wanting, and therefore everything else he says or does can have little or no effect: the evil will still remain the same that it was.[11]

Whitefield's *Journals* entry continued from Concord.

> [Dec 16] I scarce knew how to go away, but having engaged myself before, I rode after sermon in a chaise, about 14 miles, to Reading to the house of the Rev'd Mr. Hobby, a person of great abilities, but one that is not ashamed to own (and which indeed is visible to all his friends) that he has been greatly changed for the better both as to principles and practice, in the glorious visit of God's Spirit to New England, and who declared, before I came, that if no other minister would invite me to preach, his pulpit would be open.

Whitefield had a firm friend in Rev. William Hobby of the First Church in Reading, Massachusetts. Few men in New England were persecuted for their support of Whitefield to the extent as was Hobby. Rev. Nathaniel Henchman of Lynn singled out Hobby for public ridicule. This belligerent anti-Hobby literature, published in Boston, had a wide circulation. In 1745, Hobby wrote an articulate response to Henchman that was widely distributed, called *An Inquiry into the Itinerancy, and the Conduct, of the Rev. Mr. George Whitefield* . . . This twenty-nine-page pamphlet addressed both doctrinal and practical issues in support of the revival and in defense of Whitefield. Hobby was in a difficult situation, and Whitefield came to his defense. In his *Journals*, Whitefield wrote of preaching in the First Church in Reading for Hobby.

> On Tuesday afternoon [December 17] and again in the evening I preached in it to large auditories. On Wednesday [December 18] my last sermon was very awakening.

The relentless Whitefield continued his brief itinerant preaching tour in the towns north and east of Boston. His next stop was in Woburn.

> On Wednesday [December 18] I preached twice at Woburn, 5 miles from Reading, for the Rev. Mr. Jackson. It was a snowy day but the congregation was large. My Lord helped me in delivering His word and there seems to be a stirring among the dry bones. After the sermon we went to the seat of Mr. Ryall's who came with some friends to hear me at Woburn. I expounded at his house as usual and went to Boston the next day . . .

---

10   Joseph Tracy, *The Great Awakening*, (1842: reprinted by Banner of Truth Trust, Carlisle, PA: 1989), p. 344.
11   It should be noted that the *Boston Evening Post* was never a supporter of Whitefield or the Awakening. The preaching events at which thousands gathered to hear Whitefield in and around Boston in 1744 and 1745 were virtually ignored in this newspaper. The November 19 and December 17, 1744 *Boston Evening Post* articles quoted above were front-page stories merciless in their criticism of Whitefield.

As far as we know, this was Whitefield's first visit to Woburn. The town of Woburn, located about twelve miles north of Boston, was founded in 1640 by Puritans expanding settlements out from Boston. The town grew slowly, but by 1700 Woburn was a small but successful town with about 1,000 residents. Initially, the community educated its children through their ministers, and in 1713 the first school house was built. In 1719, Woburn had its own physician. New roads were constructed which formed neighborhoods, connecting the community south to Boston and in other directions to local farmlands. When Whitefield came to Woburn in December 1744, he preached at the First Parish Church. The ministers were Rev. John Fox, assisted by Rev. Edward Jackson. The two ministers had a contentious relationship. They had disputes over finances, theology, and practical issues. The tension between Fox and Jackson was so rife that they "would not speak to each other in the pulpit."[12] After years of rivalry and litigation, a group under Jackson separated from the First Church in 1746, called The Third Parish Congregational Church. But in 1744, Whitefield preached for a congregation in deep turmoil, in a town divided over their ministerial controversy. Whitefield wrote above that he "preached twice at Woburn . . . for the Rev. Mr. Jackson." He wrote that "the congregation was large" and that "there seems to be a stirring among the dry bones." Jackson served in Woburn until his death in 1754.

Rev. Jonathan Barnard of Andover, North Parish had a fulfilling ministry as the successful pastor in a community that was founded by Puritans in 1646. His parsonage was comfortable, his farmlands were fertile supplied by a small stream, and he had a short walk up the hill past the cemetery to the meeting house. Rev. Barnard and his wife were highly respected members of the Andover (later North Andover) community. Barnard thought it his duty to protect his flock from the Whitefield hysteria. He signed the 1743 *Testimony* against Whitefield and did not advocate Whitefield's peaching style or itineracy. In December 1744, Whitefield was in the next town to Andover, in Reading. But Whitefield avoided an unfriendly reception in Andover by preaching in other nearby towns where he was welcome.

This several-day preaching tour by Whitefield was a quick damage-control trip to support several of his beleaguered friends. He returned to Boston in mid-December 1744 and was in for the fight of his life.

The Parson Jonathan Barnard house in North Andover, Massachusetts. From here Rev. Barnard organized his thoughts against Whitefield. Photograph by Ken Lawson.

---

12 Samuel Sewell, *The History of Woburn, Middlesex County, Mass., from 1640 to the Year 1860*, (Boston, MA: Wiggin and Lunt, Publishers, 1868), p. 267.

CHAPTER 14
OPPOSITION AND OPPORTUNITY IN BOSTON

DECEMBER 1744 TO FEBRUARY 1745

IN MID-DECEMBER 1744, WHITEFIELD RETURNED to Boston from his brief damage-control tour in several communities just outside the city. These smaller communities he had just visited—Lynn, Reading, Concord, and Woburn—were quaint colonial towns with a village common and smaller single-family homes. The townsfolk embraced a mostly agrarian lifestyle.

In contrast, Boston was a thriving maritime city with a commercial center and booming industrial and manufacturing areas. With its excellent deep and sheltered harbor, Boston was becoming a leading commercial center in all America. Shipbuilding thrived, overseas trade with Europe and the Caribbean prospered, and various trades such as ironworks, tanneries, and the various fisheries made the Boston waterfront and warehouse areas bustle with activity. The growing city had dozens of churches, taverns, trade shops, social parlors, and equestrian stables. Except for the main routes, almost all roads were crooked, narrow, dirty, and rutted from wagon wheels. Only the significant streets were paved with cobblestones. Traffic in Boston was a problem, as horses, pedestrians, venders, wagons, carriages, and herds of animals all competed for space. Issues in the city were sanitation, maintaining accessibility to fresh water, crime, threats of fire, disease, poverty, and meeting the insatiable demand for firewood from the ever-expanding population. In 1742, the spacious Faneuil Hall was constructed to help organize the multitude of farmers and tradesmen who came to Boston to sell their goods. While the elite of Boston in 1745 were preparing to hear the first lectures on electricity from thunderstorms, the Boston poor house overflowed with destitute recent immigrants, a disheveled underclass, and displaced mariners.[1] In 1750 the population of Boston was 15,000 people and growing.

Whitefield returned to the city and immediately met with his ministerial friends. After departing nearby Woburn and upon entering Boston, Whitefield wrote on or around December 19, 1744 in his *Journals*,

> [W]ent to Boston the next day and preached at three o'clock in the afternoon at the Meeting house of the Rev'd Mr. Checkly and again in the evening at the Rev'd Doctor Coleman's.
>
> The Lord was with me in both seasons as well as also on Fryday evening at the Rev'd Doctor Sewell's. The congregation as well as a sense of the Divine presence seemed to increase more and more; and good Dr. Sewell, after sermon, said to me, "Vive et vige" Holy Father set thy Almighty fiat to it for Jesus Christ's sake.[2]

---

1   Caleb H. Snow, *A History of Boston, the Metropolis of Massachusetts . . .* , (Boston, MA: Munroe & Francis Printers, 1825), pp. 225-230. Marjorie D. Ross, *The Book of Boston, the Colonial Period, 1630-1775*, (New York: Hastings House Publishers, 1960).
2   George Whitefield, *Journals of George Whitefield*, (1756: reprinted by Banner of Truth Trust, Carlisle, PA: 1985), p. 534.

Although Whitefield's chronology is sketchy, it appears these two days described above were on or around December 19-20, 1744. Boston had numerous churches, but Whitefield was content to concentrate his efforts in the city at familiar meeting houses with allied ministers. The above named "Rev'd Mr. Checkly" was Samuel Checkly of the New South Church. "Rev'd Doctor Coleman" was Benjamin Colman of the Brattle Street Church. Also named was the "Rev'd Doctor Sewell," referring to Joseph Sewell of the South Church. The Latin expression "Vive et vige" quoted by Sewell, loosely translated means "Alive and flourish."

It is not surprising that Whitefield concentrated his efforts in Boston at familiar places among his supporters. This was a definite strategy. All Boston was in dispute over the December 28, 1744 letter from Harvard College denouncing Whitefield. "The workings and ferments of the intense religious excitement caused by the visit and preaching of Whitefield, which stirred the people with a new sensation, led to a deluge of polemical pamphlets."[3] One of the most substantial and damaging of these polemical or highly critical pamphlets, came from the Harvard president. Preceding the harmful Harvard pamphlet were a series of ministerial councils and resulting publications in newspapers and in pamphlet forms, highly critical of Whitefield.

For example, a group of ministers from northern New England met in mid-December, and published a pamphlet denouncing Whitefield and his itinerancy on December 26, 1744. These ten clergymen served churches in Salisbury, Newbury, and Amesbury, Massachusetts; and in Hampton Falls, Kensington, North Hampton, Kingston, and South Hampton, New Hampshire. These ten clergymen saw Whitefield as one who created "great and grievous disorders" and as one who made "wicked and slanderous" remarks about unconverted ministers in New England. They accused him of being unwilling "to heal the unhappy divisions occasioned by his former visit" and that Whitefield had done "more harm than good."[4] They were especially incensed by what appeared to be Whitefield's arrogance or presumption, as he simply appeared in a community unannounced and expected the use of the meeting house pulpit. When it was refused, he preached outdoors, much to the irritation of the local ministers.[5] This eight-page pamphlet was directed to clergymen in Boston, suggesting to them that they disallow Whitefield the use of their meeting houses.

Another example of a ministerial declaration against Whitefield came from a group of clergymen that met in Cambridge, in the shadow of Harvard College, on January 1, 1745.[6] These nine ministers were from the suburbs of Boston, namely Lexington, Weston, Newton, Cambridge, Waltham, Watertown, Medford, and Bedford. Rev. Nathaniel Appleton

A South East View of the Great Town of Boston in New England in America, 1743. Sketch by William Burgis and William Price. Source: http://www.loc.gov/pictures/item/2004671510/. Notice the numerous church steeples that adorn the skyline of the town.

3   Justin Winsor, *The Memorial History of Boston . . .*, 1630-1880, (Boston, MA: James R. Osgood & Company, 1882), vol. II, p. 61.
4   *A Letter from Two Neighboring Associations of Ministers in the Country, to the Associated Ministers of Boston and Charles-Town, Relating to the Admission of Mr. Whitefield into Their Pulpits*, (Boston: Rogers & Fowle, 1745), pp. 2-7.
5   Joseph Tracy, *The Great Awakening*, (Carlisle, PA: Banner of Truth Trust, 1989), pp. 345-346. Richard O. Roberts, *Whitefield in Print*, (Wheaton, IL: Richard Owen Roberts Publisher, 1988), p. 445.
6   *The Testimony of the President, Professors, Tutors and Hebrew Instructor of Harvard College in Cambridge, Against the Rev. Mr. George Whitefield and his Conduct*, (Boston: Heart & Crown Publishers, 1744).

of the Congregational Church in Cambridge was also pastor to students at Harvard. Appleton asked his ministerial colleagues whether he should allow Whitefield to preach from his pulpit to the Cambridge community and to the Harvard students. "It was unanimously voted, That it is not advisable, under the present situation of things, that the Rev. Mr. Appleton invite the Rev. Mr. Whitefield to preach in Cambridge. And they accordingly declared, each of them for themselves respectfully, that they would not invite the said gentleman into their pulpits."[7]

This influential letter from Harvard College against Whitefield was signed by Harvard President Edward Holyoke; Henry Flynt, college Secretary and Tutor; Edward Wigglesworth, Divinity Professor; Judah Mosis, Hebrew Instructor; Belcher Hancock, Tutor; Joseph Mayhew, Tutor; Thomas Marsh, Tutor and Librarian; and John Winthrop, Professor of Mathematics and Natural Philosophy.[8] This well-written fifteen-page pamphlet sets the tone for the rest of the document by stating, "We look upon his going about in an itinerant way, especially as he hath so much of an enthusiastical turn of mind, utterly inconsistent with the peace and order, if not the very being, of these churches of Christ." Then the pamphlet lists four major objections against Whitefield.[9]

Harvard's first objection against Whitefield was that they charged him with "enthusiasm." This was the heretical idea that a person could receive dreams, impressions, or impulses from the Holy Spirit giving instructions or guidance. They criticized Whitefield for "feeling" the leading of the Holy Spirit, attributing to him delusional ideas and unbiblical characteristics. The second accusation against Whitefield was that he was "an uncharitable, censorious and slanderous man." This accusation was made as a result of Whitefield's renouncing of Archbishop Tillotson, his criticism of the Harvard faculty, and his belief that many New England ministers were unconverted.

Harvard's third charge against Whitefield was that he was "a deluder of the people" in relation to his orphan house in Georgia. They thought Whitefield was sloppy in his financial records of the orphan house, and they did not approve of the caretaker of the institution. The final Harvard accusation against Whitefield was his "extempore manner of preaching" and his "itinerancy." This meant that they considered Whitefield a lazy expositor of the scriptures, and shallow in theology, because he did not write out his sermons and read them from the pulpit. They also disliked the fact that Whitefield did not have a settled parish, but wandered around preaching wherever he liked, regardless of ministerial parish boundaries or permissions from local ministers. Speaking of this *Testimony from the President and Professors* at Harvard, Dallimore wrote, "Probably nothing has been so effective in molding a derogatory concept of Whitefield on the American continent as the Testimony; not on account of its contents, for they have been but little known, but merely by reason of the fact that Harvard published against him."[10] Whitefield replied to this damaging pamphlet about a month later.

Most of the common people received Whitefield with joy. But many ministers, influenced by Harvard College, were hesitant, even resistant to Whitefield. He preached in the largest meeting houses in Boston to big crowds, but there was an underlying resistance by some to his ministry. The crowds were large, but not excessively large, as in his 1740 tour in Boston. The publication of his *Journal*, with his unguarded and hasty remarks about unregenerate clergy and false teaching at Harvard, turned away influential and prominent people in the city, many of whom were loyal Harvard graduates. Many blamed Whitefield for the contentious spirit in numerous churches. "Whitefield spent about three months in Boston and its vicinity on his second visit," that being late 1744 into 1745.[11] That included his brief preaching tours in the suburbs

---

7 Joseph Tracy, *The Great Awakening*, p. 346.
8 Richard O. Roberts, *Whitefield in Print*, p. 371.
9 Joseph Tracy, *The Great Awakening*, pp. 348-350.
10 Arnold Dallimore, *George Whitefield: The Life and Times of the Great Evangelist of the Eighteenth Century Revival,* (Carlisle, PA: Banner of Truth Trust, 1980), vol. II, p. 197.
11 Justin Winsor, *The Memorial History of Boston . . .* , 1630-1880, p. 239.

of Boston. Specifically, for this chapter, his short December to February ministry in Boston was a brief stop before he headed south for another short New England preaching tour.

At the start of the New Year 1745, Boston newspapers kept their readers aware of the Whitefield phenomena. The *Boston Evening Post* advertised for sale, "Just printed and sold by the Publisher of this paper. The Testimony of the President, Professors, Tutors, and Hebrew Instructor of Harvard College in Cambridge, against the Rev. Mr. George Whitefield, and his conduct."[12] A few weeks later the *Post* promoted a letter published, "To the Rev. Mr. George Whitefield, urging upon him the Duty of Repentance, and returning unto the Bosom of that Church to which he professes himself a member and minister, by Canonicus."[13] The anonymous author this letter, using the pseudonym Canonicus, disapproved of Whitefield preaching outside the confines of the Anglican Church, the denomination by which Whitefield "professes himself to be a member and minister." The *Boston Evening Post* was anti-Whitefield, and the number of letters, articles, and advertisements by the *Post* against Whitefield were overwhelming. However, an exception to the newspaper's bias against the itinerant preacher was shown in the January 21, 1745 edition of the *Post*, when a pro-Whitefield advertisement was printed. The advertisement was for an apologetic or defensive pamphlet written by Whitefield's firm ally at the First Church Congregational in Boston, Rev. Thomas Foxcroft. It was called, *An Apology in behalf of the Rev. Mr. Whitefield: Offering a fair Solution of certain Difficulties, objected against some Parts of his publick Conduct in Point of moral Honestly, and Uniformity with his own Subscriptions and Ordination vows*.[14]

In Boston, Whitefield preached again to large crowds. But his opposition became entrenched, and he was forced to respond. His *Journals* stated,

> Tuesday, January 8th [1745]. Reached Boston this afternoon and preached in the Evening lecture for the Rev'd Mr. Coleman, and Hearing that notwithstanding both my conduct and preaching breathed nothing but love, that many would harp upon the things; I thought it my duty to publish a letter which I had written in the time of my sickness to the Rev'd Dr. Chauncey. May God give it his blessing.[15]

In 1743, the influential Rev. Charles Chauncey of the First Church in Boston wrote a widely distributed 424-page book against Whitefield and Jonathan Edwards in particular, and against the revival in general.[16] This thoughtful and well-written document had much of Boston abuzz with rumors, accusations, and innuendoes against Whitefield and the awakening. Chauncey's book was divided into five main parts. First, he wanted to point out the "bad and dangerous tendencies" of the movement. Next, he wrote to encourage pastors "to suppress prevailing disorders." Third, Chauncey stated that those who opposed the revival had been poorly treated by some in Boston. Then he wrote to expose what had to be "corrected or avoided." Finally, Chauncey stated his ideas on how to promote true religion in Boston and elsewhere.[17]

Chauncey mentioned Whitefield's name sixteen times in *Seasonable Thoughts*. He wrote that Whitefield's itinerant ministry was neither "from Scripture or reason," and that Whitefield encouraged the itinerant troublemakers that followed him in Boston.[18] Chauncey criticized Whitefield for his financial indiscretions related to the orphanage in Georgia, and his neglect of the orphans.[19] In a subjective critique of Whitefield,

---

12 *Boston Evening Post*, January 7, 1745, p. 2.
13 *Boston Evening Post*, January 21, 1745, p. 2.
14 Ibid.
15 George Whitefield, *Journals of George Whitefield*, (1756: reprinted by Banner of Truth Trust, Carlisle, PA: 1885), p. 543. The Whitefield Journal quotes in this chapter are from pp. 543-545.
16 Charles Chauncey, *Seasonable Thoughts on the State of Religion in New England*, (Boston, MA: Rogers & Fowle Printers, 1743),
17 Ibid., p. iii.
18 Ibid., pp. 36, 38.
19 Ibid., pp. 37, 48.

Chauncey remarked that he opposed the fact that Whitefield often smiled when he preached, and that he rejoiced when a person was visibly under spiritual distress, seeing this as "too much levity" and "a want of due reverence."[20] Chauncey thought Whitefield wrote "with rashness and indiscretion" from his youth, and that he had "a monstrous spirit of censorious judgment."[21] Whitefield had written some unwise and insensitive words about Church of England Archbishop of Canterbury John Tillotson, which Chauncey noted as improper and untrue.[22] Chauncey also rejected the idea that Whitefield could receive "impulses and impressions" directly from God,[23] and he opposed the Whitefield idea that unconverted clergy were unable to do spiritual good.[24]

In his *Journals*, Whitefield wrote, "I thought it my duty to publish a letter which I had written in the time of my sickness to the Rev'd Dr. Chauncey." This letter from Whitefield to Chauncey was 14 pages long. It was originally written while he was sick in Portsmouth, New Hampshire, on November 19, 1744, but was edited and released to the public under the date of January 18, 1745.[25] Chauncey was one of the most influential men in all New England. In this brief but courteous reply to Chauncey, Whitefield quoted scripture to defend his itinerant practices. He defended himself against the charges of financial indiscretions and abandonment of the Georgia orphans. Whitefield also apologized for stating that most New England ministers were unconverted, and he commented about Archbishop Tillotson, "I acknowledge that I spake of his person in too strong terms, and too rashly condemned his state, when I ought only to have censured his doctrine."[26] The following is Whitefield's concluding paragraph:

> I write this under the immediate views of a happy eternity and rejoice in the prospect of that day, wherein I shall appear before a compassionate Judge, who will cover all my infirmities with the mantle of His everlasting righteousness, and graciously accept my poor and weak efforts to promote His kingdom. I beg, reverend sir, an interest in your prayers, that I may glorify God, whether by life or death; and, praying that you may be taught of God to preach the truth as it is in Jesus, turn many to righteousness, and shine in the kingdom of heaven, as the stars in the firmament, for ever and ever, I subscribe myself, reverend and dear sir, your most affectionate servant, GEORGE WHITEFIELD.[27]

Chauncey continued to oppose Whitefield and the awakening, writing dozens of pamphlets and newspaper articles against the revival. In response to Whitefield's fourteen-page response to Chauncey's *Seasonable Thoughts*, the influential Chauncey wrote an eight-page rebuttal to Whitefield, which by 1745 had gone through three editions. Chauncey also engaged in an extended pamphlet war with Jonathan Edwards of Northampton, Massachusetts. By early 1745, the two opposing factions in Boston—Whitefield and Edwards and the awakening verses Chauncey and the status quo—were entrenched positions.

The Quaker Zaccheus Collins of Lynn appears to have been unshaken by the theological disputes of his day. In January 1745, he wrote in his extensive *Diary* about schooners in the harbor, the slaughtering of cows, receiving cords of firewood, and hosting various house guests. On January 12, Collins briefly wrote, "At home. George Whitefield preaches about in towns."[28]

---

20 Ibid., p. 127.
21 Ibid., p. 144.
22 Ibid., p. 146.
23 Ibid., p. 178.
24 Ibid., p. 242.
25 George Whitefield, *A Letter to the Rev. Dr. Chauncey, on Account of some Passages Relating to the Rev. Mr. Whitefield*, in his book entitled, *Seasonable Thoughts on the State of Religion in New England*, (Boston: January 18, 1745).
26 Luke Tyerman, *The Life of the Rev. George Whitefield*, (New York: Anson D.F. Randolph & Company, 1877), vol. II. p. 129.
27 Ibid., pp. 129-130.
28 Zaccheus Collins, *Diary of Zaccheus Collins of Lynn, 1726 to 1769*, (original manuscript at the Peabody Essex Museum, Phillips Library, Rowley, MA), vol. I, p. 305.

The influential ministers in Boston, as well as the anti-Whitefield account from Harvard, had a direct influence on many ministers who initially supported or tolerated Whitefield. Many were turned against the traveling preacher, as was Rev. Israel Loring of Sudbury, Massachusetts. In October 1740, Loring heard Whitefield preach and noted the sermon texts in his *Journal*. He made no negative notations. But in the few years between that time and Whitefield's return to New England in 1744-1745, Loring changed his mind. The pamphlet wars between Whitefield and his enemies soured Loring against Whitefield and the awakening. Loring's 1745 *Journal* comments are insightful:

> Jan. 13. Began to preach against Mr. Whitefield, and shewed the unsoundness of his doctrine . . . He is guilty of irregularity in his life and [his] conduct remains yet to be spoken unto. May a gracious God add his blessing to what has been said.

> Jan. 20. Lord's Day . . . P.M. Finished my discourse against Mr. Whitefield and [his] conduct. Some are greatly disturbed. The Lord forgive what he has seen me guilty of in preparing & preaching it. Defend & Protect me from those that are greatly enraged at me for preaching as I have done, and Lord follow it with thy blessing.[29]

Many in Israel Loring's church in Sudbury were pro-Whitefield and opposed their minister in his anti-Whitefield preaching. Loring's *Journal* has accounts of church members denouncing him, and even asking to see his sermons before they were preached, to insure there were no anti-Whitefield remarks in the sermon text. Several church folks were especially vocal and dissatisfied. The following Loring *Journal* entry is of note:

> Feb. 22. The first person that had assaulted me after [I] had preached my first sermon against Mr. W____d, on Jan. 13, was Mr. Dakin. He was greatly disturbed, and asked me whether I intended to preach against Mr. W_____d the next Lord's day, and when I told him he might depend upon it, he said ye reason of his asking was because he did not intend to be there, to Whom I replied, that he might go away for good and all.[30]

Despite stiff opposition in Boston, Whitefield decided to extend his stay in the city, continuing his very public ministry. He wrote in his *Journals*:

The Rev. Israel Loring house is still standing in Sudbury. The original house is to the left of the photograph. Here Loring wrote against Whitefield in 1744-1745. Photograph by Ken Lawson.

> [Saturday, February __, 1745] Continued preaching for near a month at Boston, sometimes once, sometimes twice a day, to very crowded and affected auditories, and with much of the Divine Presence, and notwithstanding I preached so often, besides exhorting several times a week in my own Lodging and at private houses, yet the people crowded more and more and would my private business have admitted, I might have spent whole days in talking with souls; but I generally sent them to their own Ministers. We had two remarkable Sunday Evening Lectures. In the day I attended on

---

29 Israel Loring, *The Journal of Rev. Israel Loring (1682-1772) of Sudbury, Massachusetts Covering his Early Life and the Years 1704-1745*, edited by L.P. Thomas, (Sudbury Public Library), p. 32.
30 Israel Loring, *The Journal of Rev. Israel Loring*, p. 35.

stated sermons, and felt much of the Divine Presence, especially under the Ministry of Mr. Webb, and could not help blessing God who had yet left himself so many faithful Witnesses in Boston, who preached the truth as it is in Jesus.

One wonders what attracted so many thousands to hear Whitefield day after day, week after week. Perhaps such attendance resulted from the pamphlet wars between Whitefield and his detractors, as controversy often increases interest. Certainly, the support of senior ministers in Boston, like Rev. John Webb named above, contributed to Whitefield's legitimacy, as these clergymen encouraged their congregations to attend various meetings at different meeting houses, and in open areas. Whitefield's reputation as an orator certainly drew crowds. Twice in the above quote Whitefield attributed his preaching success to "much of the Divine Presence."

January and February of 1745 were difficult months for Whitefield to minister in Boston. A distraction to his preaching ministry were the numerous pamphlets from regional ministers and various associations that published against him. For example, on January 3, Rev. Nathaniel Henchman published a letter to Rev. Stephen Chase of Lynn End (now Lynnfield, Massachusetts) giving his reasons for declining Whitefield the use of his pulpit. On January 15, a council of ministers met in Weymouth, south of Boston, to write a pamphlet opposing Whitefield's theology and itinerancy. On January 22, a bitter and antagonistic pamphlet was printed by a group of clergymen that convened in Marlboro, Massachusetts, about 35 miles west of Boston, denouncing Whitefield personally for his deviant and disorderly behavior in the New England churches.[31]

The distractions from his opponents did not hinder Whitefield from his relentless preaching ministry in Boston. There was even a demand for a morning lecture before the city went to work. Whitefield recorded in his *Journals*:

> About the last week [of February 1745] I opened a 7 o'clock morning Lecture at the Rev'd Moorhead's meeting house, which to my great surprise and the surprise of hundreds more, was so crowded that numbers were obliged to return home because they could not come in. People came from all quarters, some 4 or 5 miles off, and it seems very delightful to see those who had been used to lie in bed till 8 or 9 in the morning, running to hear the word in a cold winter season, by break of day, and hearing a sermon before the time they usually got up.

Whitefield mentions the support he received from Rev. John Moorhead of the Scotch-Irish Presbyterian Church in Boston. There was something remarkable, something unusual happening in Boston at that time. To have hundreds of people turned away from an early morning lecture because of overcrowding, on dark, cold winter mornings, when people were used to sleeping in, was clearly a unique event.

Much of Boston was dominated by Harvard College. The leading men of the city were almost unanimously faithful alumni of the college. Virtually all the prominent ministers in Boston were graduates of Harvard, as were the leading political figures of that time. The influence of Harvard permeated all New England. It was a great obstacle for Whitefield to have Harvard publish against him. As already stated, in 1744, the college published *The Testimony of the President, Professors, Tutors, and Hebrew Instructor of Harvard College, against the Rev. Mr. George Whitefield and his Conduct*. This fifteen-page pamphlet was devastating to Whitefield's credibility and reputation in New England. Many of the same charges against Whitefield were made previously by Rev. Charles Chauncey of Boston's First Church, charges such as enthusiasm, uncharitable accusations, financial improprieties, extemporaneous preaching, and itinerancy. During his Boston preaching tour, on January 23, 1745, Whitefield responded to the Harvard *Testimony*.

---

31 Joseph Tracy, *The Great Awakening*, (1842: reprinted by Banner of Truth Trust, Carlisle, PA: 1898), pp. 353-263. *The Testimony of an Association of Ministers Convened at Marlboro, Jan. 22, 1744-45, against the Rev. Mr. George Whitefield and His Conduct . . .*, (Boston, 1745).

Whitefield's response to the Harvard *Testimony* was called, *A Letter to the Reverend President and Professors . . . of Harvard-College in Cambridge; in Answer to A Testimony published by them Against the Reverend Mr. George Whitefield and His Conduct*. This twenty-three-page document was delivered to the publisher in Boston on January 23, 1745. In this pamphlet, Whitefield is courteous, but then restates the validity of his positions. Whitefield used the example of the Apostle Paul in the book of Acts, as an illustration of a traveling preacher harassed by local authorities. He then responded to the charge of "enthusiast," an accusation made because Whitefield believed in the indwelling of the Holy Spirit within all true Believers, with this indwelling guiding, correcting, and leading a Christian.[32] Whitefield clarified some principles on Bible interpretation and application, and then addressed the issue of his "uncharitable, censorious, slanderous" speech against religious leaders.[33] He stated that he was justified in using such language against false teachers since Jesus and the Apostles had done likewise. Whitefield defended his remarks about the low spirituality at Harvard, and he restated that all finances related to the orphan house were accountable.[34] The Harvard faculty were indignant against Whitefield for his extempore preaching and his itinerancy, both which he claimed were biblical and historical.[35]

Several letters written by Whitefield from this period in Boston have survived. On January 18, Whitefield wrote that he had previously arrived in the city from the north "in a coach and four," meaning he travelled in a comfortable carriage pulled by four horses. He wrote that many of the Boston clergy that were once polite and cordial to him had turned to be "open and avowed enemies." He admitted that in times past he had written and spoken things that were objectionable. Then he analyzed his current situation in Boston, writing, "My poor labors are yet attended with unusual blessings, and therefore I must entreat you as usual to pray and give thanks."[36] Another letter from Whitefield was written in Boston dated February 6, 1745. This letter remarked that he was receiving notes from Christians requesting that he preach in their churches, since their ministers were hesitant to ask Whitefield themselves. He wrote of a six o'clock in the morning lecture at which he was asked to preach, stating, "Such great numbers flocked to hear, that I was obliged for the future to make use of two of their very largest places of worship, where I believe seldom less than two or three thousand attentive hearers hung as it were upon me, to hear the word preached . . . one morning the crowd was so great, that I was obliged to go in at the window."[37]

After a brief several days preaching tour nearby in communities north and east of Boston, Whitefield wrote a letter from Boston dated February 17, 1745. In this letter he wrote about a personal encounter with a Bostonian who was deeply convicted by his preaching:

> Our good friend Mr. S____ tells me, while I am here he looks upon his house as not his own, but mine. His parlour is large, and I sit there to receive gospel visitations. Good Mr. P___ told me some time ago, that I should shortly be favored with the company of a very pensive and uncommon person; a man of good parts, ready wit, and lively imagination, and who had made it his business, in order to furnish matter for preaching over a bottle, to come and hear, and then carry away scraps of my sermons, which it seems were to serve as texts or these for his tavern harangues. A few nights ago he came for this purpose to Dr. S___'s meeting; upon my coming in, he crowded after amongst the people, and having got sufficient matter to work upon as he thought, attempted to go out; but being pent in on every side, he found his endeavors fruitless.

---

32 George Whitefield, *A Letter to the Reverend President and Professors . . . of Harvard-College in Cambridge . . .*, (Boston, MA: 1745), pp. 203-207
33 Ibid., p. 212.
34 Ibid., pp. 213-214.
35 Ibid., p. 218.
36 George Whitefield, *Works of George Whitefield*, (1772: reprinted by Quinta Press, Shropshire England, 2000), vol. II, p. 73.
37 Ibid., pp. 73-74.

Obliged thus to stay, and looking up to me, waiting for some fresh matter for ridicule, God was pleased to prick him to the heart. He came to Mr. P___ full of horror, confessed his crimes, and longed to ask my pardon, but was afraid to see me. Mr. P___ encouraged him to venture. This morning hearing somebody knock at the parlour door, I arose, and upon opening the door, by the paleness, pensiveness, and horror of his countenance, guessed I had met with the person of whom Mr. P___ had apprized me. Immediately he cried with a low but plaintive voice, "Sir, can you forgive me?" I smiled and said, "Yes, Sir, very readily." Indeed, replied he, Sir, you cannot when I tell you all. I then asked him to sit down; and judging that he had sufficiently felt the lashes of the law, I preached to him the gospel. That it may be the power of God through faith unto his eternal salvation, will you join in praying dear madam.[38]

In the above Whitefield letter, Mr. S___ is unidentifiable. Mr. P___ is Rev. Thomas Prince of the Old South Church.[39] Dr. S__ is clearly Rev. Dr. Joseph Sewell of the Old South Church in Boston, who was an avid Whitefield supporter. This personal testimony clearly states the mocking Whitefield sometimes experienced from those more interested in ridicule than salvation. Whitefield wrote that so many individuals came to him for personal counseling, that a parlor room had to be designated for that purpose.

A Whitefield letter written from Boston on February 19, 1745, made note of the clerical opposition he received by some in Boston and at Harvard. Whitefield wrote,

The clergy, amongst whom are a few mistaken, misinformed good old men, are publishing halfpenny testimonials against me. Even the president, professors, and tutors of Harvard College where I was, as you know, some few years ago received with so much uncommon respect, have joined the confederacy. Good Mr. C_, that venerable, truly primitive, good old Puritan, as I am informed, had many of these testimonials brought him, in order to judge of their importance. He took them, weighed them in his hand, and having read them before, returned them immediately, saying, "They did not weigh much."[40]

Here Whitefield makes note of the pamphlet war that existed in Boston at that time, a publishing feud between those in support and those opposed to the awakening. He mentions the influential Harvard testimony against the revival in general and Whitefield in particular. This was especially concerning, since in Whitefield's 1740 visit to Boston and Harvard, the college received him openly. Now they were antagonistic towards him. The above mentioned "Good Mr. C__, that venerable, truly primitive, good old Puritan," was Rev. Dr. Benjamin Colman of the Brattle Street Church in Boston. Whitefield's February 19, 1745 letter from Boston continued,

Amidst all, the word runs and is glorified, and many are so enraged at the treatment I meet with, that they came to me lately, assuring me, that if I'll consent, they will erect in a few weeks time, the largest place of worship that was ever erected in America; but you know ceiled houses were never my aim. I therefore thanked them for, but at the same time begged leave to refuse the accepting of their kind offer.[41]

Whitefield's late 1744 and early 1745 ministry in Boston was remarkable. The city was polarized by his presence. A small but significant number of ministers and educators published against him. Some Bostonians

---

38 Ibid., pp. 75-76.
39 Robert Philip, *The Life and Times of George Whitefield*, (1837: reprinted by Banner of Truth Trust, Carlisle, PA, 2007), pp. 323-324.
40 George Whitefield, *Works, vol. II*, p. 76.
41 Ibid., pp. 76-77.

made Whitefield the butt of their saloon jokes. But thousands came to hear him preach and were deeply affected. As he prepared to leave Boston for a preaching tour to the southeast, Whitefield wrote in his *Journals*,

> Several other testimonies were published against me; but one or two being downright scurrilous, and others founded merely upon hearsay and only idem for idem with that from the College, I did not think myself called from more important affairs to answer them . . . Thanks be to God for this unspeakable mercy. Left Boston last Saturday after having preached upon these words, "Put on, therefore, as the elect of God, Holy and Beloved, bowels of Compassion, meekness, longsuffering, humbleness of mind, forgiving one another, if any man have a quarrel against any, as God for Christ's sake, hath forgiven you, so also do ye."

During his months of ministry in Boston, Whitefield felt the urge to travel as an itinerant preacher to surrounding communities. Leaving the city, he made such a trip for a few weeks in southeastern Massachusetts, late December to early February 1745.

CHAPTER 15

A RESPITE FROM BOSTON: WHITEFIELD'S TOUR IN SOUTHERN MASSACHUSETTS

DECEMBER 21, 1744 TO JANUARY 8, 1745

AMID A SUCCESSFUL MINISTRY IN Boston, Whitefield began a preaching tour to a new area. He had never visited southern Massachusetts, in the Massachusetts Bay Colony. Here Whitefield would preach in the oldest English settlements in Massachusetts, in towns where the descendants of the original English Pilgrims and Puritans landed in the early-mid 1600s. He travelled in the snow and cold of a New England winter, in a carriage or on horseback. This tour is the last in which he kept a random account in his *Journal*. During this southern Massachusetts tour, there is no surviving correspondence from Whitefield in his *Collected Works*. Whitefield's *Journals* states, after departing Boston,

> Saturday, December 21 . . . Set out this morning in a great storm of snow in order to go to Weymouth, but was obliged to stay on the way on account of the weather . . . Sunday, December 22nd. Had a sweet opportunity for a little-wished-for retirement last night at Milton. Publick notice being give and the morning being fair I thought it my duty to go on to Weymouth where I was engaged to preach for the Rev. Mr. Bayly.[1]

The Town of Weymouth is the second oldest town in Massachusetts, dating from 1622. The early settlement slowly grew as a fishing and agricultural community. By the time of Whitefield's 1744 visit, the town may have had 1,000 residents. Weymouth maintained an important connection to the sea. The town was connected to nearby communities by a network of horse and cart paths and roads that wound through the varied inland terrain. Whitefield would spend the next 18 or so days on these roads on his preaching tour.

As pastor of the Second Church Congregational in Weymouth, Rev. James Bayley was ordained at the church in 1723, and served here until his death in 1766. The Second Church was formed as the town expanded. When Whitefield arrived in December 1744, there was an ongoing debate with the town about who owned the church parsonage, with the town and the Second Church in disagreement.[2] Generally speaking, the town was small but prospered. Whitefield wrote in his *Journals*:

> I rode on horseback, a thing I had not done before for near six months. The weather was very sharp; but the Good Lord preserved me from hurt. When I came to Weymouth I found that yesterday's violent storm made people think that I would not come. The congregation was

---

1 George Whitefield, *George Whitefield's Journals*, (1740: reprinted by Carlisle, PA: Banner of Truth Trust, 1985), p. 535. Rev. James Bayly has his name spelt several ways in the historical records. The most common spelling is Bayley.
2 Gilbert Nash, *Historical Sketch of the Town of Weymouth, Massachusetts, 1622-1884*, (Weymouth, MA Historical Society, 1885), p. 50.

small, but there seemed to be a very considerable melting and moving among them. After sermon one came to be under awakenings and in the afterpart of the Evening I was sweetly entertained by Mr. Bayly's giving me an account, not only of what the Lord had done for his people, but also a gracious turn he himself had met with from the most High about three years ago. Though he had been settled and reckoned a pious Minister near twenty years.[3]

Of Rev. James Bayley of Weymouth, it was recorded, "During his extended ministry there were added to the church in all two hundred and seven persons. He seems to have been much beloved by his people, and was held in estimation by the neighboring parishes."[4] Whitefield's next stop was in Duxbury, Massachusetts Bay Colony. He wrote:

Thursday, December 26. Rode on Monday to Duxbury, 16 miles from Weymouth, wither I was invited by the Rev'd. Mr. Veisy, Minister of the place, and who also dates his conversion about four years back. There I preached in the evening but to a very small congregation, because I was not expected on account of the storm, and many have looked at Mr. Veisy as their Enemy since his awakening He has told them the truth.[5]

Duxbury, Massachusetts was founded in 1632. The minister at the First Church Congregational in 1744 was Rev. Samuel Veazie, who was a 1736 Harvard College graduate. Veazie was in a difficult situation, as his fellow Congregational ministers in the nearby towns of Hingham and Scituate had publicly spoken and written against Whitefield, and on this 1744 tour, they refused to allow Whitefield into their pulpits. Veazie was an outspoken Whitefield supporter. He had a contentious relationship with the Duxbury Congregational Church and the town council. By 1743, a tense division existed in the church and town against Veazie. Most of Duxbury remained Old Light. "Nevertheless, Whitefield visited, converted, and made Mr. Veazie a complete fire brand or new light; and . . . if it never so happened to any one else, he was evidently made a worse man by his conversion."[6]

It appears that Rev. Veazie lost his spiritual balance or perspective. He was described as "morose, dogmatic, and furious." Veazie "waged a fierce and bitter war" against the Duxbury townsfolk who did not support him, and he began to promote erratic and inconsistent theological ideas that both New Lights and Old Lights could not accept.[7] He accused his detractors as being demon possessed, and his ministry degenerated into a series of belligerent and chaotic confrontations. This antagonistic atmosphere was unknown to Whitefield when he arrived in Duxbury in December 1744. On December 26, Whitefield wrote that he preached to a "small congregation," due to inclement weather. He recorded in his *Journal*, "The next morning I preached again to a larger and more affected Auditory . . . [8] Whitefield preached twice, over two days, for Veazie in Duxbury. Most of the townspeople were not impressed with Whitefield. In fact, about two months after Whitefield departed, the town of Duxbury passed an interesting resolution: "1744-45. Mar. 18th. At a meeting of the town on this date, they voted to choose some persons to take care of their meeting house to keep out of it itinerant preachers."[9] Obviously, Veazie and the town of Duxbury were at an impasse. After several more years of bitterness and disharmony, Veazie resigned, under pressure, from the First Church pulpit in 1750.

---

3 George Whitefield, *Journals*, p. 535.
4 Gilbert Nash, *Historical Sketch of the Town of Weymouth*, Massachusetts, p. 109.
5 George Whitefield, *Journals*, pp. 535-536.
6 Justin Winsor, *History of the Town of Duxbury, Massachusetts* . . . , (Boston, MA: John Putnam Printer, 1849), pp. 192-193.
7 Ibid., p. 193.
8 George Whitefield, *Journals*, p. 536.
9 Justin Winsor, *History of the Town of Duxbury, Massachusetts* . . . , p. 195.

A town not named in Whitefield's *Journals* is Kingston. This community is located directly between Duxbury and Plymouth, Massachusetts Colony. The Congregational Church in Kingston was disrupted by Whitefield's 1744 tour through the area. Although Whitefield did not preach in Kingston, he traveled through the town on his way to Plymouth. The minister in Kingston, Rev. Thaddeus Maccarty, was a New Light and eager to promote Whitefield. Trouble developed between the First Church and Maccarty, who was newly arrived in Kingston in 1742. In 1744, the majority of the church opposed Whitefield's preaching in the meeting house, and he passed them by.

An undated painting of Rev. Thaddeus Maccarty, who served in Kingston when Whitefield arrived in December 1744.

Source: American Antiquarian Society.

> Later . . . it was rumored that Mr. Maccarty had invited Mr. Whitefield, in spite of the wishes of the parish, to deliver a Thursday lecture, and the committee, to prevent his occupying the pulpit, had the church fastened against him. This caused a bitter feeling, and Mr. Maccarty immediately asked for his dismission. The church soon granted it . . . [10]

Another source recorded the people of Kingston as opposed to Whitefield, calling him "the obnoxious individual." With the townsfolk moving against him, "Much excitement arose, and effectual care was taken to prevent the exercises of the obnoxious individual, by closing and fastening the meeting house, nailing the doors, and covering the windows with boards."[11] Pastor Maccarty was so furious he resigned and became a longtime pastor in Worcester, Massachusetts.

After his stop in Duxbury, bypassing Kingston, Whitefield next preached in Plymouth. Upon leaving Duxbury, Whitefield wrote, "I . . . went afterwards in company with several Dear Ministers to Plymouth, 6 miles from Duxbury, where I was enabled to preach an evening Lecture in loving labor with Freedom and power to a numerous and attentive congregation."[12]

Plymouth, Massachusetts Bay Colony, was the site of the famous 1620 landing of the Pilgrims from England. It is the oldest municipality in Massachusetts and one of the oldest in the United States. The First Parish Church was formed in England in 1608, and transferred many of its members to America in 1620. When Whitefield arrived in 1744, Plymouth was rife with controversy. The new minister, Rev. Nathaniel Leonard, arrived in 1742. The church constructed a new meeting house, completed in 1744. Much to the chagrin of many in Plymouth, Leonard was an avowed Whitefield supporter. Those who were bitterly opposed to Mr. Leonard withdrew from the church, and in 1744, organized the Third Congregational Society within the town of Plymouth.[13] Not afraid to be outspoken, Leonard signed, with numerous local ministers, *The Testimony of a Number of Ministers* . . . , in early 1745, fully endorsing the revival and supporting Whitefield.[14]

An anecdote has survived from Whitefield's Plymouth visit. Of this stop in Plymouth, Whitefield wrote, "I was enabled to preach an evening Lecture in loving labor with Freedom and power to a numerous and

---

10 D. Hamilton Hurd, *History of Plymouth County, Massachusetts, with Biographical Sketches* . . . , (Philadelphia, PA: J.W. Lewis & Co., 1884), p. 260.
11 William Lincoln, *History of Worcester, Massachusetts: From its Earliest Settlement to September, 1836* . . . , (Worcester, MA: Moses D. Phillips and Company, 1837), p. 175.
12 George Whitefield, *Journals*, p. 536.
13 "Plymouth Town Records," *Publications of the Colonial Society of Massachusetts*, vol. xxii, Collections, (Boston, MA: Published by the Society, 1920), pp. xxxiv-xxxv.
14 *The Testimony of a Number of Ministers Convened at Taunton, in the County of Bristol, March 5, 1745, In Favor of the Rev. Mr. Whitefield, & c. Giving Reasons of their Inviting Him into their Pulpits* . . . , (Boston, 1745).

attentive congregation." Mr. Francis Barker of Pembroke, just west of Duxbury and north of Plymouth, heard Whitefield preach in Plymouth. Mr. Barker "went to Plymouth to hear Whitefield preach, and became religiously insane, and was chained to a sill in the south front room for the rest of his life."[15]

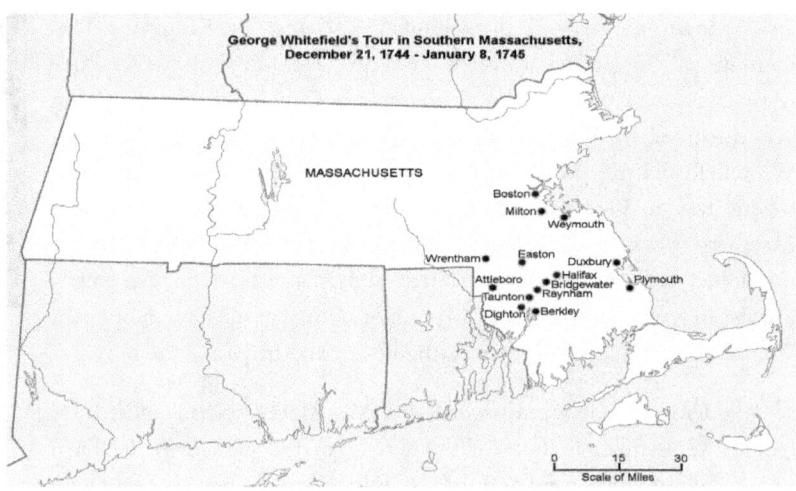

Whitefield stayed in Plymouth for three days, supporting Rev. Nathaniel Leonard. The dates were probably December 24 to 26, 1744. Speaking of Plymouth, Whitefield wrote in his *Journals*, "On Wednesday I preached thrice and on Thursday twice, to yet larger and larger auditories. Many ministers were present, and He that holds the stars in his right hand, was peculiarly present also."[16] Then Whitefield wrote an extended comment of the revival in Plymouth with an endorsement of Leonard:

> A time of refreshing came from the presence of the Lord. The cup of some of God's people almost run over. Dr. Leonard was highly delighted. He is a choice, humble, Judicious, Minister of Christ . . . and seems to be placed in these parts by the Great Head of the Church to stand in defense of the power of religion and strengthen the hands of several Young Witnesses that have already been converted and called to settle in some Adjacent Parishes. The share that Plymouth has had in the late outpouring of the Spirit was not small. It was delightful to hear of it. A surprising alteration hath been made both in the principles and conduct of Mr. Leonard . . . This stirred up the Old Man [the sin nature] in many and together with his openly owning the work of God, and opening his Pulpit to itinerant preachers, so irritated a part of his congregation that they asked a dismission (which was granted them) and they have since joined in a separate congregation, built a new meeting-house, and have lately had a minister ordained over them . . . [17]

The ministry of the First Church in Plymouth had grown to the point where Pastor Leonard and his deacons began discussing plans to construct a new meeting house for the church. This building would be owned by the church, separate from the town, a first for this congregation. This would be the third church building in the history of this church. The building was nearly completed when Whitefield preached in the new church building in late December 1744.

From these days of excitement in Plymouth, Whitefield went northwest a few miles to the nearby town of Halifax. Founded in 1669, Halifax was a lumbering and agricultural community. The minister was Rev. John Cotton, grandson of the famous Rev. John Cotton of Boston. Cotton served in Halifax from 1735 to 1756, when he was forced to resign due to a throat ailment. He taught school in Halifax, and preached in an unplastered meeting house for all of his twenty years in the town. Cotton was no theological novice.

---

15 Duane H. Hurd, *History of Plymouth County, Massachusetts: with Biographical Sketches* . . . , (Philadelphia, PA: J.W. Lewis & Co., 1884), p. 233.
16 George Whitefield, *Journals*, p. 536.
17 Ibid.

He thoughtfully analyzed the religious trends of his day. He was concerned by the widening or liberalizing of classic Calvinism. This theological broadening was accepted throughout much of early eighteenth-century New England.[18] Often called Arminianism, this alteration of historic Calvinism disturbed Cotton. When Whitefield came to Halifax in December 1744, he found a theological ally in Cotton. In Whitefield's published sermons, in his *Journals*, and in his correspondence published in newspapers, Cotton saw in Whitefield a classic Calvinist, one who affirmed the traditional doctrines of the Protestant Reformation. Whitefield wrote of his meeting with Cotton:

> Saturday, December 29th. Went on Thursday, after having preached, and had my soul greatly delighted at Plymouth, to Halifax, 6 miles from thence, to the house of Mr. Rev. Cotton, who dates his first turn from Arminianism and a state of nature, from his hearing me at Dr. Sewell's about 4 years ago, (O free Grace), when I remember I was very explicit in showing the danger of preaching an unfelt Christ. He seemed to be a settled solid, devout soul . . . On Friday I preached twice to a Crowded Auditory in his meeting-house and great were the outgoings of the Lord in his Sanctuary.[19]

A 1744 sketch of the First Church Congregational, Plymouth.
Source: https://en.wikipedia.org/wiki/First_Parish_Church_in_Plymouth.

The Great Awakening in general, and the ministry of Whitefield in particular, had a deep influence on the Congregational Church in Halifax. Church memberships soared. One source stated:

> Halifax seemed to be trying to tighten its theological values in the early 1740s towards a more classic Calvinism. The response of this and the fervor of the Great Awakening was a massive influx of members, some of which had been in the area for some time and in the vicinity of the church for some time, yet did not make a commitment. The fear of God was laid on their hearts and they responded.[20]

Bridgewater was founded from settlers of neighboring towns in 1645. Due to population shifts, the Second or South Congregational Church was founded in Bridgewater in 1716. Rev. John Shaw served this church from his ordination in 1731 to 1791, to his death at age 82. His extended time at South Church was a time when he was "much beloved and respected by his people."[21] Whitefield wrote of his time with Shaw at Bridgewater as follows:

> Saturday, December 29th. In the evening I went to Bridgewater to Rev'd Shaw's who had been one of my hearers at Halifax, and behaved with great civility. This day I preached twice for him, to very large Auditories, and the Power of God amongst the people seemed to increase also. I was more than happy in my soul and many of the Hearers by their behavior

---

18   Ernest Gordon, *The Leaven of the Sadducees*, (Chicago, IL: Bible Institute Colportage Association, 1926), pp. 7-20. Harry S. Stout, *The New England Soul: Preaching and Religious Culture in Colonial New England*, (New York: Oxford University Press, 1986), pp. 155-156, 180-181, 218-228.
19   Ibid., p. 537.
20   Joseph A.C. Wadsworth III, *The History of the Halifax Congregational Church of Halifax*, Massachusetts, (Halifax, MA: 2008), vol. I, p. 95.
21   Nahum Mitchell, *History of Bridgewater, Massachusetts*, (Bridgewater, MA: Henry T. Pratt, Publisher, 1897), p. 46.

seemed to give great proves they were indeed some of Christ's born babes that desired to be fed with the sincere milk of his most holy word.²²

It was somewhat unusual for Whitefield to preach at two different meeting houses in the same small town. Yet this is what happened in Bridgewater. Typically, these rural communities had one meeting house for the Congregational Church. However, because of population shifts and factions from the awakening, a second church, or additional churches, could be found in a small but growing rural New England town. As stated above, Whitefield preached for Rev. John Shaw at the Second or South Congregational Church in Bridgewater. But in the last few days of December 1744, Whitefield preached five times and assisted in the sacrament of communion for Rev. John Porter of the Fourth Congregational Church in North Bridgewater. Whitefield wrote about this briefly in his *Journals*.

> Monday, December 31. Preached twice this day and thrice yesterday and helped administer the holy sacrament at another Meeting-house in Bridgewater, for the Rev'd Mr. Porter, a Dear Young Witness to Jesus Christ who dates his awakening (as have many others) from my preaching in the Old Brick Church when last in Boston, 4 years ago . . . His parish has shared richly in the late outpouring of the Spirit and whilst I was preaching and assisting in the Sacrament Our Savior filled his people as with new wine. The arrows of conviction seemed also to fly about. There was much people and some crying out, and as it did not give offense and as I thought country people could not so well restrain themselves as those of a more polite Education in the Town, I did not so much insist upon them holding their peace, especially as they did not prevent my speaking so as to be heard.²³

Porter was able to balance and moderate the often excessive behaviors and bombastic accusations that sometimes accompanied New Light preaching. At a vulnerable time in his young ministerial life, and in a transition period for the church with its new minister, Porter and the Fourth Church remained united. One author wrote:

> Rev. Mr. Porter was a man of very respectable talent, distinguished for his prudence, fidelity, exemplary life, and holy conversation. The great doctrines of the gospel were prominent in all his preaching; and a crucified Redeemer was a theme on which he delighted to dwell with particular earnestness, interest, and satisfaction. He continued to preach for this society for sixty years . . . ²⁴

After a few days in Bridgewater with Revs. Shaw and Porter, the next town Whitefield visited, to the northwest, was East Town, called Easton today. Easton was settled in 1694 and incorporated as a town in 1725. The Congregational Church pastor was dismissed in April 1744, and the church had difficulty finding a new minister. When Whitefield came to Easton on New Year's Eve 1744-1745, the church was without a settled minister. Instead, several candidates came and preached for the church, but the new minister, Rev. Solomon Prentice, was not called to the church until September 1747. Whitefield wrote in his *Journal*:

> 1744/45. Tuesday, January 1st. Came last night to East Town. Ended the Old Year very happily and began the New Year very comfortably, and preached twice to crowded auditories for Mr. Pritt, a Young Zealous Candidate for the Ministry, who has been blessed much in late times.²⁵

---

22 George Whitefield, *Journals*, p. 537.
23 Ibid., p. 538.
24 Bradford Kingman, *History of North Bridgewater, Plymouth County, Massachusetts*, (Boston, MA: Published by the Author, 1866), p. 24.
25 George Whitefield, *Journals*, p. 538.

The identity of "Rev. Pritt" is uncertain. Knowing that Whitefield's *Journals* was, by this time, deteriorating in its reliability of names and dates, perhaps the "Rev. Pritt" was meant to be "Rev. Prent," as in Rev. Solomon Prentice. It is likely that Whitefield forgot the name of the temporary minister and wrote from memory as best he could remember the name. Solomon Prentice was installed as the pastor of the Congregational Church in Easton in 1747, but he had, for a few years prior, been in a strained relationship with his former church in Grafton, Massachusetts. Before any church called a minister, the candidate had to preach at the church and interview with the church elders and town council. Whitefield identified the minister of the church, in early January 1745, as "Mr. Pritt, a Young Zealous Candidate for the Ministry." It is more than likely that Whitefield misstated the name of the minister, as he did numerous times in his *Journals*. Prentice was dismissed from his previous church in Grafton because, "He was one of those ministers greatly moved by Whitefield," so much so, that the Old Lights in Grafton asked him to leave.[26] In the few years before he was finally dismissed from Grafton, things were tense at the church. Prentice may have travelled as a candidate looking for another ministry, and overlapped with Whitefield in Easton. Eventually, the Easton church did call Prentice to be their minister. Whitefield wrote of his preaching in Easton as follows:

This old photograph is of the Rev. John Shaw home in Bridgewater. Shaw maintained a day school here for children in the community. The home was built in 1740 and was taken down in 1904.

Source: www.digitalcommonwealth.org.

> The power of the Lord was indeed among the people. My heart as well as the hearts of others were filled with praise. We looked upon it as a token for good that we should have a happy new year, and the road from the meeting-house to the place where I lodged being pretty solitary, we gave vent to out Joy in singing a solemn hymn of praise.[27]

From Easton, Whitefield travelled south to the town of Taunton. Here he was among friends, as local ministers in and around Taunton wrote a testimonial later in 1745 in support of Whitefield and the awakening. Taunton was founded in 1637 by Pilgrims from Plymouth Bay Colony, who moved inland to hunt, farm, and lumber. The Taunton River provided plenty of fresh water for these industrious settlers. When Whitefield came to Taunton in January 1745, he was welcomed by the Congregational minister, Rev. Josiah Crocker. A Harvard graduate in 1738, Crocker began preaching in Taunton in 1741, was ordained there in 1742, and stayed until his dismissal in 1765. Before Whitefield arrived, the Congregational Church in Taunton was fully consumed in the Great Awakening of the late 1730s, with dozens converted and welcomed into church membership every year. Crocker was a popular preacher. One source stated, "He entered upon the work of a pastor at an early age, and was distinguished for his ador, pathos, persuasive powers, and warm-hearted devotion to his calling."[28] Whitefield wrote in *Journals* about his time in Taunton:

---

26   William Chaffin, *History of the Town of Easton, Massachusetts*, (Cambridge, MA: John Wilson & Son Printers, 1866), p. 104.
27   George Whitefield, *Journals*, p. 538.
28   Samuel H. Emery, *The Ministry of Taunton*, (Boston, MA: John P. Jewett Publisher, 1853), vol. I, p. 335.

Wednesday, January 2nd. Reached Taunton, twelve miles from East-town, last night and preached there for the Rev'd Mr. Crocker, another Young Zealous, Servant of the Glorious Jesus . . . He is a young man of pregnant parts and has been made instrumental of doing much good and bringing many souls to the Lamb's Blood since he has been called of God himself. The people under his care have been highly favored . . . Being led to discourse in the evening on Satan's tempting Christ, I could not help saying that they who would not pay their Minister unless He preached so as to please their corrupt hearts, were too much like the Devil . . . Our Lord was remarkably with us, the two first sermons. Several ministers from several other places attended as likewise some young Candidates for the ministry . . . [29]

Rev. Josiah Crocker received some opposition for his support of Whitefield. One source stated, "It is not strange that a world which hated Whitefield, should feel some measure of aversion towards one of his warmest friends," referring to Josiah Crocker.[30] Further speaking of Crocker, "It is well known that Whitefield had no sincerer friend in this part of the country than the then minister in Taunton."[31] Speaking of Josiah Crocker,

> The Taunton minister was a great friend of Whitefield . . . Mr. Whitefield preached in his pulpit, and . . . many were displeased with him for this. The people in Taunton, as elsewhere, were divided concerning what were called "new measures." But Mr. Crocker entered into them most heartily, and would be called at the present time a revival preacher. He was often invited to preach in neighboring towns and persons came from a long distance, even as far as Plymouth, to listen to his sermons. The story is told of a woman who quieted her baby, weary from the long march, by shouting, "Crocker is coming."[32]

Clearly, Whitefield had gained momentum on this preaching tour. There was little open hostility to him in southern Massachusetts. In winter weather, large crowds gathered in numerous meeting houses to hear the famous Whitefield. An example of this was his next stop, in Raynham:

> Thursday, January 3rd. Preached thrice at Raynham, about 5 miles from Taunton, for the Rev'd Mr. Wales, to very crowded Auditories and had as sweet appearances of the Divine Presence as in any place where I have yet been. After sermon, five or six Negroes desired to speak to me. One seemed to be filled with love of God, two had been Backsliders, and the other was slightly wounded. I was much helped in discoursing with them. Dear Mr. Wales stood by, and in prayer our hearts were melted much, hoping that the great God would revive his work in this and the other parishes which have been already favored with the outpouring of the Holy Spirit.[33]

Rev. John Wales was a Harvard graduate who came to the Congregational Church in Raynham when it was formed in 1731. Raynham, which was originally part of Taunton, was settled in 1639. Raynham was known for its shipbuilding along the Taunton River, and for its successful iron ore businesses. Wales ministered in Raynham until his death in 1765.[34] "He was blessed with talents which

---

29 George Whitefield, *Journals*, p. 539.
30 Samuel H. Emery, *The Ministry of Taunton, vol. II*, p. 382.
31 Ibid., p. 336.
32 D. Hamilton Hurd, *History of Bristol County, Massachusetts*, (Philadelphia, PA: J.W. Lewis and Company, 1883), vol. II, p. 788.
33 George Whitefield, *Journals*, pp. 539-540.
34 Enoch Sanford, *History of Raynham, Massachusetts, from the First Settlement to the Present Time*, (Providence, RI: Hammond, Angel & Co., Printers, 1870), pp. 7-9.

rendered him very amiable and entertaining in social life. In public prayer, his performances were eminent, and on some occasions, almost unequalled. He was a faithful, plain preacher . . . ."[35] Wales was an avid supporter of the awakening and he fully endorsed Whitefield. Under John Wales, the Congregational Church in Raynham had seasons of revival and times of normalcy. During his thirty-four-year ministry in Raynham, the church baptized 350 people of all ages, and admitted 126 to full membership and communion.[36]

Whitefield's next stop was in nearby Berkley. This was a tiny farming community, which became an independent town in 1735. The land was flat and the soil very rich. Agriculture was the main activity of the town, with supporting businesses such as a tanner, a blacksmith, a general store, a stable, as well as the Congregational Church. The first minister, Rev. Samuel Tobey, was called to Berkley when the town was formed in 1735, and he stayed until his death in 1781. Tobey taught the children of the town in the meeting house. Although he was described as firm and impartial, the schoolchildren loved him and flocked to him. "All revered him as a man of eminent abilities and great common sense."[37] Tobey kept meticulous church records, but none of his personal letters exist, and none of his sermons were published. He had scarcely completed his divinity studies at Harvard in 1733, when he was a candidate for the new church in Berkley. His parish consisted of farmers and tradesmen, widely scattered in a rural area. He and his wife Bathsheba had twelve children, and the Tobey family was a pillar in the community.[38] Whitefield wrote of his time in Berkley, and his support of Rev. Samuel Tobey, as follows:

> Fryday, January 4th. Preached yesterday twice at Barkly for the Rev'd Mr. Toby, whose parish has been also visited in the late season of peculiar grace . . . Both the fore and afternoon the Lord was with us and I spent the remainder part of the Evening in sweet fellowship with Mr. Toby and another humble follower and Minister of the Lord Jesus, who hath also met with some bad usage for his hearty adherence to the cause, work and truth of God.[39]

Whitefield was now fully involved in his southern Massachusetts Colony tour. Soon he would swing north, returning to Boston. His ministry in Raynham, Berkley, and Dighton was in newer communities recently settled. Among these ministers, Whitefield found friends. The town of Dighton became a town in 1712. Located at the tidewater mark of the Taunton River, Dighton soon developed various small industries related to textiles and manufacturing. Shipbuilding was a dominant trade. Farmers and herdsmen composed much of the community. Because the town was connected to the ocean by the Taunton River, the town of Dighton quickly became a major southern Massachusetts port. The first minister in Dighton was the Congregational pastor, Rev. Nathaniel Fisher. A 1706 graduate of Harvard College, Fisher came to Dighton while the community was still part of Taunton. He served the church in Dighton until his death in 1777, at the remarkable age of ninety-two. Fisher was called, "a good and worthy minister of the gospel."[40] Whitefield wrote in his *Journals* about his preaching in Dighton and meeting Fisher.

> Saturday, January 5th. Preached once this morning for the Rev'd Mr. Fisher, not to a very large Auditory, or so deeply an affected one as was to be seen elsewhere. However we could say, God was with us . . . .[41]

---

35 Samuel H. Emery, *The Ministry of Taunton, vol. II*, p. 215.
36 Ibid., p. 218.
37 D. Hamilton Hurd, *History of Bristol County, Massachusetts, with Biographical Sketches* . . . , p. 176.
38 Enoch Sanford, *History of the Town of Berkley, Massachusetts*, (New York: Kilbourne Thompkins Publisher, 1872), pp. 6-8.
39 George Whitefield, *Journals*, p. 540.
40 Samuel H. Emery, *The Ministry of Taunton* . . . , vol.II, p. 187.
41 George Whitefield, *Journals*, pp. 540-541.

After departing Dighton, Whitefield made a determined move to head back to Boston. His southern Massachusetts tour was coming to an end. About twenty miles northwest from Dighton, Whitefield stopped to preach in Attleboro. This community was overwhelmed with revival in 1740, under the ministry of their Congregational minister, Rev. Habijah Weld. Attleboro was settled in 1634, was slow to develop, and was resettled in 1694. The first schoolmaster arrived in 1698. Although located in Massachusetts, Attleboro was much closer to Rhode Island and the larger town of Providence. In 1728, the town had grown to the point that the Congregational meeting house was expanded. The awakening in the late 1730s shook the community, and by the 1740s, Attleboro was in the midst of a revival. In the few years prior to Whitefield's 1745 visit, the First Church Congregational in Attleboro had about 200 members added to the church.[42] In 1743, the Second Congregational Church formed in Attleboro, not from any religious disputes, but from population growth in the town and the influence of the awakening.

When Whitefield arrived in Attleboro, he was welcomed at the First Congregational Church by Rev. Habijah Weld. A Harvard graduate, Weld served this church for fifty-five years, until his death in 1782. Whitefield wrote,

> Sunday, January 6th. Reached Attleboro, near 20 miles from Deighton, about 8 last night. A place that has been most highly favored indeed, above many others in the present day . . . Preached twice and assisted the Rev'd Mr. Wells [Weld] in administering the Holy Communion of the body and blood of Christ. But a sweeter sacrament I scarce ever saw . . . The communicants seemed to be filled as with New wine, and I believe it was a feast of fat things to many souls.[43]

This must have been quite a sight—a Church of England priest (Whitefield) sharing communion with a Congregational minister (Weld) in a Congregational Church. Rev. Weld was known to be exact and precise in his theology and in his personal, practical activities. "He was rigidly precise in everything, not a bed was to be made or a room swept on the Sabbath and the food for that day was prepared on Saturday."[44] Yet Weld was able to overcome his predictability and preciseness to accommodate an itinerant Anglican evangelist, not only to preach in his Congregational church, but to share the administration of the communion sacrament with his congregation. Whitefield preached twice for Weld, and enjoyed his hospitality with Habijah and Mary Weld and their household that eventually had fourteen children. The large parsonage for the Weld family was made of wood and brick, and their small farm supplied the family with meat, dairy, and vegetables. A local Attleboro tale is that a prominent resident, Mr. Caleb Parmenter, hosted Whitefield for a meal and a small religious service; "Tradition says that he entertained Whitefield at his home here and that a religious service was held under the grand old elms."[45] Whitefield made no mention of this event in his *Journals*. Whitefield did write the following remarks on Attleboro.

> Under both sermons there was a very great concern and melting among the people, which, together with the account Mr. Wells [Weld] gave me of what God had done in his parish, was very comforting and confirming to my soul. After evening service and taking some bodily refreshment, I rode 6 miles to Wrentham . . . [46]

Wrentham, Massachusetts Colony was the last stop on Whitefield's southern Massachusetts preaching tour. Two Congregational ministers settled in this large, rural town, Rev. Henry Messenger at the First

---

42 John Doggett, *A Sketch of the History of Attleboro . . .*, (Boston, MA: Press of Samuel Usher, 1894), p. 257.
43 George Whitefield, *Journals*, p. 542.
44 John B. Hill, *Bi-Centennial of Old Dunstable . . .*, (Nashua, NH: E.H. Spalding Publisher, 1878), p. 183.
45 John Doggett, *A Sketch of the History of Attleboro . . .*, p. 681.
46 George Whitefield, *Journals*, p. 542.

Church, and, after the founding of the Second Church in 1738, Rev. Elias Haven. Both men were New Lights, both were Harvard graduates, and both ministers happily welcomed Whitefield to Wrentham. Prior to Whitefield's arrival in January 1745, Wrentham experienced an awakening that changed the culture of the town. Both Messenger and Haven are mentioned in Whitefield's *Journals* entry for Wrentham.

> Monday, January 7th. Reached Wrentham about ten at night and lay very comfortably at the house of the Rev'd Mr. Messenger, who . . . has been a Cordial promoter of the glorious work of God . . . I preached twice with but little interval, and I believe it was a convicting time for sinners as well as the day of consolation to the Saints. Many, very many, were deeply affected. Indeed the concern seemed to be general. There was a very great weeping and crying out, but nothing as I saw that was extravagant. One of the ministers told me, Our Lord has kept the good wine until the last, and Mr. Haven said he did not doubt but hundreds felt the power of the Everlasting God. To Him and Him alone be all the Glory.[47]

Wrentham was first settled in 1660, but the fledgling town was burned to the ground in King Philip's War, 1675-1676. The town had three lakes, good farmland, and was located on the Rhode Island boundary. By 1721, a larger Congregational meeting house was built, due to increased population. The following account states how Rev. Messenger and Rev. Haven guided the awakening in Wrentham.

> It was during the ministry of Messrs. Messenger and Haven that the Great Awakening took place in this country, commonly called the Whitefieldian Revival. It prevailed in Boston and in most of the adjacent towns. It prevailed extensively in both the parishes in Wrentham, and both the ministers were eagerly engaged in it. They prayed and labored assiduously for its advancement in their own parishes, and in other places, and more than two hundred in Wrentham made a public profession of faith.[48]

As Whitefield completed this seventeen-day tour of southern Massachusetts, all seemed well. The weather mostly cooperated, no small thing in Massachusetts in December-January. There were pockets of opposition, but mostly he was well received. Crowds that attended his preaching were large, especially considering the time of the year. His health remained good, and his preaching voice remained strong. Before Whitefield arrived, this part of Massachusetts Colony was overwhelmed by the awakening. Literally thousands of people flocked into several dozen churches in this region. Some of these new church members were recent converts. Others were backslidden individuals who had previously professed Christianity, wandered away from the faith, and were now compelled to repent and return. When Whitefield appeared in New England in 1744-1745, he preached in many churches and communities already spiritually excited. He promoted revival, but without any extremes in behavior or emotionalism. This preaching tour was an overwhelming success. On or around January 7, 1745, Whitefield departed Wrentham in a direct line to Boston. Because of the distance, he stopped along the way to sleep at a home in Milton. He wrote of his brief southern Massachusetts tour in his *Journals*.

> I do not remember I scarce had a pleasanter circuit since I have been a preacher. I do not know that we have had one dry meeting. Everywhere visible tokens of the Divine Presence attended the Word. My bodily strength was wonderfully kept up and renewed and my soul exceedingly happy. The congregations were large, notwithstanding it was winter. Generally we were remarkably favored with dry weather . . . what I saw myself in the Congregations and

---

47 Ibid.
48 Christopher Cushing, editor. *The Congregational Quarterly vol. xx*—New Series, vol. x, (Boston, MA: Congregational House, 1878), p. 325.

what I gathered by conversing with some people, and what I heard from their own minister's mouths, more and more convinced me that God had visited his Dear New England in a most Extraordinary manner.[49]

The new year 1745 began with Whitefield preaching to large crowds in the Boston area. He soon learned that a local and influential ministerial association around Boston had published against him. On January 1, 1745, several ministers met at Cambridge and published their declaration that their pulpits were closed to George Whitefield. These ministers who stood against Whitefield were John Hancock of Lexington; William Williams of Weston; John Cotton of Newton; Nathaniel Appleton of Cambridge; Warham Williams of Waltham; Seth Storer of Watertown; Ebenezer Turell of Medford; Nicholas Bowes of Bedford; and Samuel Cook of Cambridge. The initial purpose of this meeting was to advise Rev. Appleton of Cambridge, on how to handle the many requests from residents of his town to allow Whitefield to preach from his church pulpit. The ministerial report stated,

> The many weighty objections, which lie against the said Mr. Whitefield, with respect to his Principles, Expressions and Conduct, which are not yet answered, nor has any Christian Satisfaction been given by him for them; Considering also how much the Order, Peace, and Edification of the Churches of this Land are endangered, together with the unhappy, divided state of many of them;

> It was unanimously voted, that it is not advisable, under the Present Situation of Things, that the Rev. Mr. Appleton should invite the Rev. Mr. Whitefield to preach in Cambridge.

> And they accordingly declared, each of them for themselves respectively, that they would not invite the said Gentleman into their Pulpits.[50]

---

49 George Whitefield, *Journals*, pp. 542-543.
50 *The Boston Evening Post*, January 1, 1745, p. 2.

CHAPTER 16

WHITEFIELD'S TOUR NORTH OF BOSTON

MID-FEBRUARY TO EARLY MARCH 1745

MANY CHURCH HISTORIANS HAVE CONSIDERED Whitefield's 1744-1745 second tour of New England unsuccessful. This is inaccurate. It is often said that opposition was far greater than support, with the number of pulpits closed to him being the emphasis. For example, Williston Walker said Whitefield's visit had minimum influence when compared to his first ministerial tour.[1] H.F. Uhden asserted similar ideas when he stated,

> How greatly all had changed is most clearly seen in the cool way, nay, to some extent, the hostile reception experienced by Whitefield on his renewed visit in 1745 ... With the declining fellowship for the revivals vanished also the revived interest in religion.[2]

It is true that the Old Light ministers of New England were no longer silent. They publicly preached and published numerous pamphlets and newspaper articles against Whitefield. One clergyman supposedly met Whitefield in Boston and said, "I am sorry to see you here," to which Whitefield replied, "Aye, and so is the devil."[3] The Rev. Alexander Malcolm, of St. Peter's Episcopal Church in Marblehead, wrote on July 30, 1745 that his congregation had happily kept clear of the disorders sown by "the enthusiast" Whitefield.[4] Both in public newspapers and in local Old Light churches, opposition remained firm. Yet the crowds supporting Whitefield in Boston were sensational, and many ministers in the areas around Boston eagerly welcomed the itinerant evangelist to their pulpits.

Up to this point, Whitefield's 1744-1745 stay in Boston and areas around the city had lasted a few months. He supported the ministries of his allies, and he preached in some areas he had previously not visited. Inevitable controversies developed. Both opponents and supporters of Whitefield were polarized. Their positions were firm. The Great Awakening had become contentious and was settling into mutually exclusive camps that grew to dislike but eventually tolerate each other. Whitefield's ministry had not diminished, and revivals continued to spread.

Whitefield's tours through New England intensified the strain already existent between the established formal churches and the New Lights.[5] As the revival grew in size and influence, then stabilized, the Old

---

1   Williston Walker, *A History of the Congregational Churches in the United States*, (New York: Charles Scribner's Sons, 1916), p. 266.
2   H.F. Uhden, *The New England Theocracy*, (Boston, MA: Gould & Lincoln Printers, 1859), p. 279.
3   Quoted in Juliet H. Mofford, *The History of North Parish Church in North Andover*, (Lawrence, MA: Naiman Press, 1975), p. 73.
4   Samuel Roads, Jr., *The History and Traditions of Marblehead*, (Boston, MA: Houghton, Osgood & Company, 1880), p. 369.
5   A helpful study on the tensions within the clergy during the awakening is by James W. Schmotter, "The Irony of Clerical Professionalism: New England's Congregational Ministers and the Great Awakening," *American Quarterly*, vol. 31 (1979), pp. 148-168. Schmotter believes that "An underlying cause for many problems faced by ministers in the 1740s was a

St. Michael's Episcopal Church in Marblehead was constructed in 1714. There are many original features of this building inside and outside. This is the oldest Episcopal Church in New England on its original site and original building. The wooden panel behind the altar has inscribed the Ten Commandments, the Lord's Prayer, and the Apostle's Creed, and dates to 1714. In 1740, George Whitefield was denounced by Rev. Alexander Malcolm at this location. Photographs by Ken Lawson.

Lights, in reaction, took a firmer stand against what they called "emotional religion."[6] A few ministers were suspicious of Whitefield from the start, and their doubts easily turned to dislike. Rev. Caleb Cushing of Salisbury spoke of the New Lights as promoting "new doctrines, and corrupt errors."[7] Rev. John Barnard of Andover abhorred what he regarded as the "irreverence and impiety of the great evangelist."[8] Rev. Benjamin Prescott of Salem's South Congregational Church (now in Peabody) opposed the "disorders of the revival" and resisted Whitefield openly.[9] In February 1745, Whitefield was about to leave Boston on a preaching circuit into these various communities. His *Journals* stated:

> Saturday, February _ [1745]. Left Boston last Saturday after having preached upon these words, Put on, therefore, as the elect of God, Holy and Beloved, bowels of Compassion, meekness, longsuffering, humbleness of mind, forgiving one another, if any man have a quarrel against any, as God for Christ's sake, hath forgiven you, so also do ye.
>
> The same evening I preached at Esq'r Ryall's. On Lord's Day twice for Rev'd Mr. Chiver's of Lynn.
>
> On Monday once at Maulden and once at Esq'r Ryall's. On Tuesday twice at Lyn again.[10]

---

heightened sense of clerical self-interest best termed professionalism. Ironically, it was a concern for professional stability that produced conditions that led to the instability most pastors sought to avoid," p.149.

6   Richard Bushman, editor, *The Great Awakening: Documents on the Revival of Religion*, (Chapel Hill, NC: University of North Carolina Press, 1989), p. 197.
7   "Brief Memoirs and Notices of Prince's Subscribers," *The New England Historical and Genealogical Register, vol. 8*, (1854), p. 43.
8   Sarah L. Bailey, *Historical Sketches of Andover, Massachusetts*, (Boston, MA: Houghton, Mifflin, and Company, 1880), p. 434.
9   Joseph Felt, *Annals of Salem*, Boston, MA: James Monroe & Company, 1945), p. 594.
10 George Whitefield, *Journals of George Whitefield*, (1756: reprinted by Banner of Truth Trust, Carlisle, PA: 1985), p.545. The Journal quotes in this chapter are from pp. 545-551.

At this point in Whitefield's *Journals*, all semblance of chronology is lost. As stated above, on an undetermined Saturday in February 1745, he reflected upon his week of traveling and preaching with short, summary statements. He wrote that he departed Boston and travelled to preach for Esquire Ryall, who is unidentifiable. He then travelled to coastal Lynn, Massachusetts, to preach for Rev. Edward Cheever of the Third Congregational Church (now in Saugus). Cheever was in a longstanding controversy with Rev. Nathaniel Henchmen of the First Church Congregational in Lynn. Cheever and Henchmen conducted a pamphlet dispute over the awakening in general and Whitefield in particular. The fact that Whitefield preached "On Lord's Day twice for Rev'd Mr. Chiver's of Lynn," shows that the itinerant evangelist was not afraid to stand with those of like faith in the midst of heated controversy. In his typical preach-and-return circuit ministry, Whitefield wrote above that he returned to Lynn two days later and preached twice on a Tuesday for Edward Cheever. Also mentioned above in Whitefield's *Journals* is that he preached "On Monday once at Maulden." This preaching event was for the Congregational minister Rev. Joseph Emerson of Malden, Massachusetts. Emerson was from distinct Puritan heritage, was scholarly and reserved, and advocated revivals.[11] He and Whitefield were clearly allies. Whitefield's *Journals* continued:

> On Wednesday evening I reached Ipswich, where I preached twice on Thursday and on Fryday, and once on Saturday. But with what sweetness to my own soul and satisfaction to the souls of others I cannot easily tell. Everywhere and at every sermon the blessed Jesus vouchsafed to follow the word with very promising impressions and though at Lyn my body was but weak yet the Father of Mercies and God of all consolations strengthened me visibly by His power in the inner man.

Ipswich was completely shaken by the awakening. This rural farming and fishing community eagerly welcomed Whitefield on his many visits to their town. Despite the ongoing antagonism from Rev. Theophilus Pickering of the Chebacco Parish in Ipswich, the revival in Ipswich was remarkable. Whitefield wrote a letter from Ipswich dated February 7, 1745, in which he said, "we have been carried through various trials . . . He is pleased to bear me up on eagle's wings, and causes both sinners and saints to hear his voice."[12] The elderly Rev. John Rogers, the senior minister at the First Church, assisted by his son Nathaniel Rogers, were able and eager facilitators of the awakening in this rural town. Whitefield mentions the Rogers' family in his next *Journals* entry:

> Several ministers came to me at Ipswich to give me fresh invitations to preach in some Neighboring Parishes. Good old Mr. Rogers and his sons were much delighted and we had repeated reasons given us to lie low at the foot stool of free Grace and repeat our acts of praise

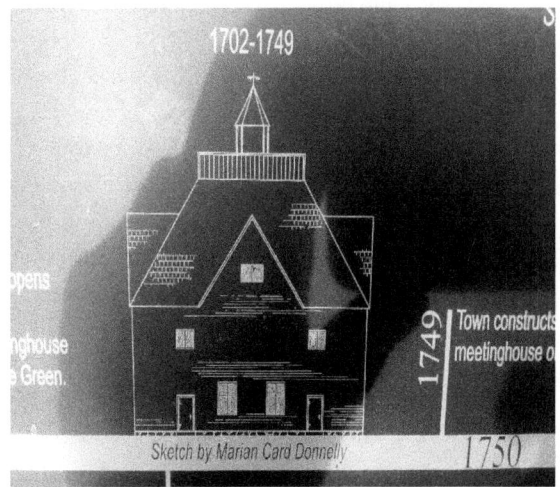

The meeting house for the First Church in Ipswich in 1745 was their third church building. This structure was built in 1702 and lasted until 1749. Sketch by Marian C. Donnelly, Ipswich Historical Society.

---

11   William B. Sprague, *Annals of the American Pulpit*, (New York: Robert Carter & Brothers, 1859), vol. I, p. 246.
12   George Whitefield, *Works of George Whitefield*, (1772: reprinted by Quinta Press, Shropshire, England, 2000), vol. II, pp. 74–75.

and thanksgiving. Accept them at our hand, Good and Gracious God, for the sake of Jesus Christ. Amen, and Amen.

Whitefield wrote a letter from Ipswich, Massachusetts, dated February 7, 1745. In this letter he wrote to a friend in England, stating:

> We have been carried through various trials; and can set up our Ebenezer, saying, "Hitherto hath the Lord helped us."—I cannot help thinking but that the Lord Jesus is about to triumph gloriously.—He is pleased to bear me as on eagle's wings, and causes both sinners and saints to hear his voice.[13]

Whitefield's use of the term "Ebenezer" is insightful. In Hebrew the word means "stone of help." It was used in the Bible in 1 Samuel 7:12, to commemorate a Hebrew military victory over the Philistines. In celebration, Samuel the prophet erected a stone monument and called it Ebenezer, meaning thus far has the Lord helped us. Whitefield used this biblical analogy to state that his preaching tour in the communities northeast of Boston, particularly in Ipswich, was going especially well with God's help.

Whitefield mentioned above that "both sinners and saints" were hearing the word of the Lord in Ipswich. Why visit Ipswich at this time? The rural fishing and farming community of Ipswich was deeply moved by the Great Awakening. Whitefield preached there in 1740, and thousands came to listen. During his 1744 tour in the area, Whitefield was too ill to preach in Ipswich, but the town was still disrupted from his visit four years earlier. Now, in February 1745, Whitefield may have stopped in Ipswich for damage control, as deep ecclesiastical, civil, and social divisions were created in this small Colonial Massachusetts village.

Ipswich had a long history of Puritanism. The minister of the Chebacco Parish in Ipswich, Rev. John Wise, maintained a small but growing Calvinistic and Puritan congregation until his death in 1725. Later that year, the church in Chebacco called Rev. Theophilus Pickering to be their minister, and he served in Ipswich until his death in 1746. Pickering was born in nearby Salem in 1700, and graduated from Harvard in 1719. Pickering was no friend of the awakening and no supporter of Whitefield. By 1745, disruptions in the Chebacco Parish were outrageous, as some in the church supported the revival and wanted itinerant preachers to speak, while Pickering and his followers resisted the revival. Whitefield's visit to Ipswich in February 1745 was intended to support the awakening. Pickering wrote against Whitefield in 1745, in an eight-page pamphlet that was circulated in Boston, called *Mr. Pickering's Letter to Mr. Whitefield,* in which he criticizes Whitefield for his itinerancy, his dreams and impressions, and his ordination with the Church of England.[14] Now Whitefield came to Ipswich to endorse the separatist group as it prepared to split from the Chebacco Church. This new congregation, officially formed in 1746, called a firm Whitefield ally, Rev. John Cleveland of Connecticut, to be their minister.

Another reason Whitefield may have visited Ipswich was because of the failing health and imminent death of Rev. John Rogers of the First Church in Ipswich. This congregation fully supported Whitefield and the awakening. John Rogers was the senior minister, assisted after 1727 by his son Nathaniel. Nathaniel tried to convince Pickering of the Chebacco Parish, of the legitimacy of the revival, but Pickering was not persuaded.[15] When John Rogers died in December 1745, Nathaniel Rogers continued in the ministry at the First Church until his death in 1775. During the peak years of the awakening, 1741 to 1746, there were 149 people added to the First Church membership,[16] with many hundreds becoming more regular attendees.

---

13 George Whitefield, *Works*, vol. II, pp. 74-75.
14 Theophilus Pickering, *Mr. Pickering's Letter to Mr. Whitefield . . .* , (Boston, MA: Rogers & Fowle Printers, 1745).
15 Thomas S. Kidd, *The Great Awakening*, (New Haven, CT: Yale University Press, 2007), pp. 175-177.
16 David T. Kimball, *A Sketch of the Ecclesiastical History of Ipswich, Massachusetts*, (Haverhill, MA: Printed at the Gazette and Patriot Office, 1823), p. 25.

Whitefield's presence in Ipswich, in February 1745, served as a respectful farewell to a friend of the awakening, John Rogers, and a public endorsement of his son, Nathaniel Rogers, as the minister of the church. Ecclesiastical feuding in Ipswich was prevailing, and Whitefield sought to support his allies in the revival by his visit to this rural, maritime colonial town.

After preaching in Ipswich, Whitefield headed east to the peninsula called Cape Ann. This was his first visit to this maritime community. Cape Ann now consists of the towns of Gloucester, Essex, Rockport, and Manchester-by-the-Sea. In the mid-1700s, the majority of the population of Cape Ann was located around the deep and wide Gloucester Harbor or in small nearby oceanfront villages. The first settlers survived by subsistence farming, fishing, and logging. Extensive logging revealed the often poor quality soil for farming. With its granite hills, Cape Ann was not well suited for large-scale agricultural pursuits. Small family farms, fresh fish, and livestock provided the bulk of the sustenance to the population. While always a fishing community, the first fisheries were limited to close-to-shore day fishing trips. By the time of Whitefield's visit to Gloucester-Cape Ann in February 1745, local shipbuilders were constructing vessels suitable for extended fishing trips far out to sea to Georges Banks. The growth of the fisheries

An undated sketch of Rev. John Rogers of the First Church, Ipswich, Massachusetts.
Source: www.findagrave.com.

was a boom to the area, and money slowly but consistently began to pour into Gloucester. Some became very wealthy, while others simply worked hard and steady in various fishing trades. Later, a thriving granite quarrying industry developed.

Gloucester grew, and the town population expanded, creating the need for divided parishes and new meeting houses. In 1718, the settlers on the western shore of the Annisquam River split off from the First Parish community and formed the Second Parish. In northern Gloucester, the Third Parish was formed in 1728. The Fourth Parish separated from First Parish in 1742. Later, in 1754, a group of people in Sandy Bay (later Rockport) grew tired of the long ride to the meeting house and split off from First Parish to found the Fifth Parish.[17] In February 1745, Whitefield spent several days on Cape Ann, meeting pastors and preaching in various churches. The senior minister in the area was the sixty-eight-year old Congregationalist Rev. John White. Whitefield wrote in his *Journals*:

> Wednesday, Feb: _. Went to Gloucester on Cape Ann, 13 miles from Ipswich, where I had promised to go when here last if ever I came to New England again. Was met on the road by the Rev'd and aged Mr. White, and the young Rev'd Mr. Rogers, the ministers of the town. The later told me my Journals were blessed to make the first abiding impressions on his heart, and the former is a Good Old Man that frankly told me, he wished one or two things cleared up to Him, which I accordingly did in a few minutes as we rode along, to his full satisfaction. O that all who have it in their power would take a like method!

---

17 For a thorough study of Gloucester history, see John J. Babson, *History of Gloucester, Cape Ann, Massachusetts*, (Gloucester, MA: Proctor Brothers Printing, 1860). A newer text is by John Morris, *Alone at Sea: Gloucester in the Age of the Dorymen, 1623-1939*, (Beverly, MA: Commonwealth Editions, 2010).

The Rev. John White house in Gloucester was built for him in 1710. It is on the National Register of Historic Sites. The interior of the house looks almost the same as when Whitefield stayed here in 1745. Photograph by Ken Lawson.

The above named "Rev'd and aged Mr. White," was Pastor John White of the First Congregational Church, a Harvard graduate. He arrived in Gloucester in 1702 and remained here until his death in 1760. His congregation was eclectic, composed of fishermen, warehouse workers, merchants, sea captains, skilled tradesmen, and wealthy businessmen. The parsonage for Rev. White, built in 1710, is still standing in Gloucester in pristine condition, now as a museum. White was married three times, having eleven children, all by his first wife. In addition to White, Whitefield was also greeted on the road to Gloucester by "the young Rev'd Mr. Rogers." This refers to Rev. John Rogers, formerly of Kittery, Maine. Rogers came to Gloucester in 1743 to be the first minister of the Fourth Parish Church. Rogers was there from 1743 to his death in 1782. He was related to the influential Rogers family of nearby Ipswich. Whitefield's *Journals* relates some of his activities in Gloucester:

> [Wednesday, Feb.:_]. On Lord's Day morning I preached for Mr. Rogers, in the afternoon for Mr. White, and in the Evening a third time, for Mr. Rogers.
>
> On Monday I preached for Mr. White.
>
> On Tuesday [preached] twice for the Rev'd Mr. Broadstreet at Squam, about 9 miles distant, and on Wednesday for the Rev'd Mr. Jacques. All within a few miles one of another.

Whitefield here mentioned "the Rev'd Mr. Broadstreet at Squam." This was Rev. Benjamin Bradstreet from the Gloucester community now called Annisquam. This village within Gloucester, was a hard-working fishing and lobstering community, later expanding into the granite quarry industry. This was the Third Parish. Bradstreet, a Harvard graduate in 1725, was formerly from Newbury, about twenty miles northwest of Gloucester. He arrived in Gloucester in 1728. Whitefield also wrote about preaching for "the Rev'd Mr. Jacques." This was Rev. Richard Jacques of Gloucester's Second Parish Church. Jacques came to Gloucester from nearby Newbury and served at the Second Parish from 1725 until his death in 1777.[18]

---

18   William B. Sprague, *Annals of the American Pulpit*, vol. I, p. 460.

The Gloucester that welcomed Whitefield in the cold month of February 1745, was a town experiencing vigorous growth. There was plenty of work for the able-bodied, and those less fortunate were often cared for by the community and the churches. There were about seventy large fishing vessels in the Gloucester fleet, designed and built locally for extended trips out to sea. Innumerable other smaller vessels traded with coastal communities from Portsmouth to the north, down to Boston in the south. One historian remarked that "a general air of content and prosperity prevailed on every hand."[19] An anecdote from Whitefield's 1745 visit to Gloucester has survived. In the mid-eighteenth century, the Eveleth family was prominent on Cape Ann. Joseph Eveleth was 105 years old when he met Whitefield in his home in Gloucester. The elderly Eveleth supported Whitefield, met the young itinerant, and blessed him with a prayer. An Eveleth family descendant, who was a little girl and a witness of this encounter, told of this event which was written down and preserved:

> Among her interesting recollections of her aged ancestor was that of a visit made to him [Joseph Eveleth], just before his death, by the celebrated Rev. George Whitefield. Her mind always retained a vivid impression of the solemnity of the scene that was presented, when Mr. Whitefield knelt upon the floor, and received, from the lips that could relate a Christian experience of a hundred years, a truly patriarchal blessing.[20]

Whitefield received no open opposition on Cape Ann. He summarized his few days at Gloucester in his *Journals*:

> Indeed they were most delightful seasons. All were extremely kind. The congregations were large, the weather uncommonly fair and pleasant. Many seemed to be brought under conviction and others to experience a refreshing time from the presence of the Lord, and I could have willingly complied with their invitation to have stayed with them longer would my calls to other places have permitted.

While Whitefield preached throughout Cape Ann and other areas northeast of Boston, theological disputes simmered in his wake. His preaching methods and evangelistic sermons mostly caused his opposition not to reconsider, but to be strengthened in their established ways. "The clergy who opposed the hellfire and brimstone preaching . . . were united as never before, forgetting small disagreements which formerly divided them."[21] Fuess speaks of the Episcopal churches in particular, as being separated further from the awakening because of Whitefield; "The churchmen did not go to the revival meetings, and some people were attracted to the Episcopal Church because it did not countenance such methods revival."[22] Whitefield's influence in Marblehead was

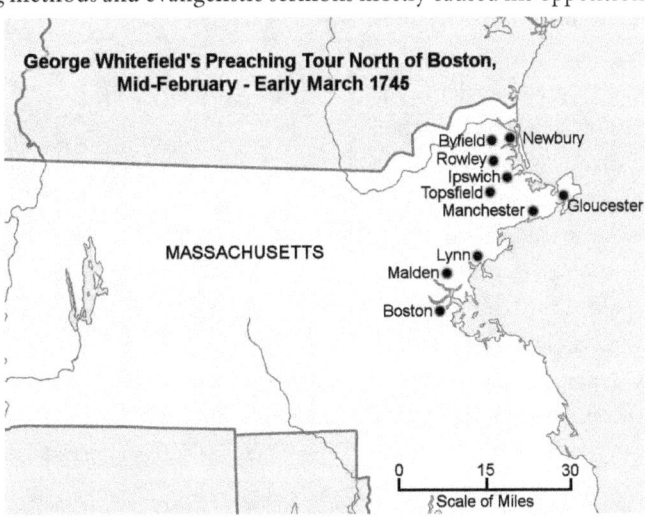

---

19 James R. Pringle, *History of the Town and City of Gloucester, Cape Ann, Massachusetts*, (Gloucester, MA: Published by the Author, 1892), p. 65.
20 John B. Babson, *History of Gloucester, Cape Ann, Massachusetts*, p. 92.
21 Juliet H. Mofford, *The History of North Parish Church in North Andover* p. 75.
22 Claude M. Fuess, *The Story of Essex County*, (New York: The American Historical Society, 1935), pp. 636-637.

"only to endear the church the more to its faithful children."[23] Rev. Peter Brockwell of St. Peter's Church in Salem, an opponent of Whitefield, spoke of the division and turmoil caused by the evangelist as having "opened the eyes of some so as to behold the beauty of our church, which has hitherto escaped the snares, laid by the great deceiver of mankind."[24] Rev. John Cleveland, a supporter of Whitefield from Ipswich, wrote, "The appeal of the old church was strongest among the oldest villagers. More than four-fifths of those aged sixty or older remained loyal to the church of their youth. The older people were either resistant to the appeal of the revivals or . . . still unable to break with the church."[25]

Departing Cape Ann, Whitefield traveled back to Ipswich, where he had been several days earlier. The well-worn dirt roads with deep wagon wheel ruts made for an easy ride of about twelve miles over numerous bridges covering small, tidal rivers. The scene was very rural. The date is mid-to-late February 1745. Whitefield's *Journals* stated:

> Thursday, Feb.: _. Returned last night to Mr. Rogers, his house at Ipswich, and preached twice today with much freedom at Manchester—miles from thence, to very crowded auditories, for Mr. Roberts, a choice Young Candidate for the Ministry and who has a call from Manchester people. He dates his awakening under God, from hearing me at Boston about four years agoe. His conversion was very clear and he was then made much use of in awakening and alarming his fellow students at Harvard College.

Again, the above named "Mr. Rogers" is Rev. John Rogers of the First Church in Ipswich. Whitefield had been with Rogers several days prior. He stayed at Rogers' home to rest and the next day preached in a new community, Manchester, Massachusetts.

The first worship service in Manchester was held under a tree on Gale's Point in 1630, as the first settlers landed in Manchester. From 1635 to 1716, they worshipped with the Salem and then with the Beverly churches. The Congregational Church was founded on November 7, 1716, with a membership of nine men and ten women. The church grew rapidly in the 1700s. This congregation currently meets in a beautiful church building, constructed in 1809.[26]

When Whitefield spoke in Manchester, he was welcomed by the Congregational minister, whom he identified above as "Mr. Roberts, a choice Young Candidate for the

An undated sketch of the Congregational meeting house in Manchester, Massachusetts. This was the third structure for the congregation. It stood from 1720 to 1809.

Source: D.F. Lamson, *History of the Town of Manchester, Massachusetts, 1645-1895*, p. 240.

---

23 Samuel Roads, Jr., *The History and Traditions of Marblehead*, p. 371.
24 Joseph Felt, *Annals of Salem*, pp. 599-600.
25 Christopher M. Jedry, *The World of John Cleveland*, (New York: W.W. Norton & Company, 1979), p. 52.
26 "First Parish Church Congregational," http://www.firstparishchurch.org/about/our-history. Stephen R. Holt, *Manchester-By-The-Sea*, (Charleston, SC: Arcadia Publishing, 2009), pp. 34-35.

Ministry and who has a call from Manchester people." This refers to Joseph Roberts, a Harvard graduate in 1741 who served at the church shortly after his graduation until 1754, when he went to a church in Leicester, Massachusetts. Roberts heard Whitefield preach at Harvard in 1740, and was converted and called into the ministry. The people of the Congregational Church in Manchester experienced a toilsome life in a small coastal village. Although shipbuilding and the fisheries dominated the community, other trades worked in the town, such as a grist mill, a brick making business, a saw mill, a blacksmith shop, and a leather shop that made everything from horse saddles to people's shoes. Manchester knew "nothing of the luxuries and little of what we consider the comforts of life."[27]

When Whitefield spoke in Manchester in February 1745, he preached in the village's third meeting house, which was built in 1720. His *Journals* continued:

> Fryday, Feb.:_. Returned to Manchester on Thursday night, and preached twice yesterday at Ipswich Hamlet, 4 miles from Ipswich Town, for the Rev'd Mr. Wigglesworth, who treated me with great civility and told me when I called on him last Wednesday, that there had been a gracious outpouring of the blessed Spirit in his congregation, and that my preaching some years agoe had been blessed to several of them.

> The meeting house was much thronged, some were obliged to stand without, and Our Savior was pleased to countenance our waiting upon him . . .

> Sunday, February _____: Preached once yesterday and thrice this day at Ipswich, where our Lord was pleased to bless and shine upon his congregation more and more. Never did I see people more attentive, solid, and serious.

> I took my leave of them by night by preaching on Joseph's blessing and indeed our parting was very solemn and affecting. Many came afterwards to me, weeping and wishing that the blessing of Him that was separated from his Brethren might rest upon me.

> O Ipswich, thou hast been highly favored. May the bow of thy Ministers and people abide in strength, and the arms of their hands be strengthened by the hands of the mighty God of Jacob.

It is apparent that one of Whitefield's favorite places to visit in New England was Ipswich, Massachusetts. No doubt he considered Ipswich "highly favored" for at least three reasons. First, he admired the fact that the community was founded by English Puritans, whom he greatly admired. Second, Whitefield was thrilled to discover ministers in Ipswich, namely John Rogers, John Cleveland, and Samuel Wigglesworth, who still preached the gospel of the Puritans. Also, Whitefield admired Ipswich because he saw enduring evidences of genuine revival in the community. The objections of Rev. Theophilus Pickering of Chebacco Parish in Ipswich notwithstanding, this community was deeply stirred by the awakening.

Whitefield mentioned above in his *Journals*, "Rev'd Mr. Wigglesworth" of Ipswich Hamlet. This refers to Rev. Samuel Wigglesworth, pastor of the Third Church in Ipswich, now in the town of Hamilton, Massachusetts. He was a 1707 graduate of Harvard College. "After practicing medicine, teaching school and preaching several years, he was ordained over the church at Ipswich Hamlet, now Hamilton, October 27,

---

27   D.F. Lamson, *History of the Town of Manchester, Massachusetts, 1645-1895*, (Manchester, MA: Printed by the Town, 1895), p. 53

1714."[28] Wigglesworth married twice, had thirteen children, and served the Congregational Church (Third Church) until his death in 1768. He was the brother of Rev. Edward Wigglesworth of the Harvard College faculty. A few years earlier, Edward was part of the Harvard faculty that rejected Whitefield and the awakening.

The cold, snowy February weather along coastal northern Massachusetts, appears to have not slowed Whitefield down. Meeting houses were full of his listeners, with times that people had to stand outside by the open windows and doors to hear him preach. In his *Journals*, Whitefield's writing becomes more erratic. On an unspecified Saturday in February 1745, he recollected events from the prior week. Whitefield wrote in his *Journals*:

> Blessed be God for this last week's mercies, for in it I have seen some sweet days of the Son of Man.
>
> On Monday I preached twice for the Rev'd Mr. Jewett of Rowley, 3 miles from Ipswich, an hearty friend to the late times.
>
> On Tuesday, for the Rev'd Mr. Chandler, 6 miles from thence, who is like minded.
>
> On Wednesday for the Rev'd Mr. Emerson of Topsfield, of the same stamp, and on Thursday for the Rev'd Mr. Parsons of Byfield, and on Fryday at Newbury.

These were easy days and celebratory times for Whitefield. His preaching was well-received. His travels every day were short, quick, and simple. The weather cooperated. And his physical stamina appears strong. Whitefield mentioned four ministers in the above *Journals* quotation. Rev. Jedediah Jewett was from the Congregational Church in the farming community of Rowley. Jewett was called "a noted congregational minister,"[29] and "was a man of broad character, highly esteemed and much beloved by his people. He was continually active in the ministry, and also in many business enterprises; owned considerable property and a man of influence."[30] Rev. James Chandler served at the Second Church in Rowley. A Harvard graduate in 1728, Chandler was the first minister of the church, installed as the pastor in 1732. The Rowley Parish (now Georgetown) built a new Congregationalist meeting house for their minister, who stayed at the church until his death in 1789. Chandler "was a man of sound doctrine, exemplary life and conversation, dignified deportment, and esteem both at home and abroad."[31] Rev. John Emerson came from a long line of New England ministers and civic leaders. He graduated from Harvard College in 1726 and was quickly thereafter installed as the minister of the Congregational Church in Topsfield, where he served until his death in 1774. "Rev. John Emerson was a pious clergyman of good attainments and his long ministry flowed on in quiet harmony."[32] During his long tenure as minister, the Congregational Church in Topsfield grew steadily, a product of the Great Awakening, with two hundred and seven names added to the official church membership rolls.[33]

The fourth minister mentioned above by Whitefield was Rev. Moses Parsons, pastor of the Congregational Church in the tiny farming community of Byfield, Massachusetts Colony. He was born and educated in nearby Gloucester as a member of the influential Parsons family of that town. He departed the fishing port of Gloucester to attend Harvard, graduated in 1736, and returned to Gloucester to teach school. In the evenings

---

28 John W. Dean, *Memoir of Rev. Michael Wigglesworth . . .* , (New York: Joel Munsell Printer, 1871), p. 20.
29 Evelyn L. Gilmore, Christ Church, Gardiner, *Maine: Antecedents and History*, (Gardner, ME: The Reporter-Journal Press, 1893), p. 66.
30 Frederic C. Jewett, *History and Genealogy of the Jewetts in America*, (New York: The Grafton Press, 1908), vol. I, p. 75.
31 *Contributions to the Ecclesiastical History of Essex County, Mass.*, (Boston, MA: Congregational Board of Publication, 1865), p. 59.
32 *Historical Manual of the Congregational Church in Topsfield, Massachusetts, 1663-1907*, (Topsfield, MA: Published by the Church, 1907), pp. 26-27.
33 Ibid., p. 27.

he studied theology. He was married in 1742, and ordained as the minister of the Congregational Church in nearby Byfield in June 1744. Whitefield had travelled through this area in 1740, and the previous minister of the church refused to allow Whitefield to preach from the Byfield Congregational Church pulpit. "Mr. Parsons had hardly been settled when his troubles with the Whitefield movement began."[34] In February 1745, Whitefield was back, and was welcomed by Moses Parsons to preach in Byfield. Parsons defended Whitefield when the itinerant was criticized, and said of him, "I look on Mr. Whitefield as a good man and a faithful minister and as one yet has been improved as an Instrument to do much good."[35]

The mostly rural communities that composed Essex County, Massachusetts, maintained enclaves of Puritanism four generations from the Puritan founding fathers. For example, Rev. John Emerson of Topsfield may have been the only Harvard educated citizen of his rural mostly Puritan community. His congregation were simple, God-fearing Christians of the Puritan persuasion. Mid-eighteenth century residents of Topsfield were farmers, herdsmen, tradesmen, or labors in equine or agrarian pursuits. Few ever made the day trip to cosmopolitan Boston. Instead, residents of Topsfield lived a cloistered and content life centered on God, family, and faith, with the meeting house as the center of their lives. Essex County in general, and Topsfield under Rev. John Emerson in particular, were deeply moved by the Great Awakening. Whitefield wrote of this in his *Journal*.

> At every place near 7 or 8 Dear Ministers of Jesus Christ accompanied me. Their presence strengthened me and greatly satisfied the people. Our Saviour fed us as well as marrow and fatness and caused us to praise him with joyful lips. Each of the ministers for who I preached gave me delightful accounts of what God had done for their people. Mr. Emerson in particular told me there had been more done for him and his flock in a year or two than for nearly twenty years before. At the same time they acknowledged there had been many imprudencies and I did not spare God's children in my sermons, but spoke home to them, and bid them beware that Jesus Christ was not wounded in the house of his friends. It seemed to cut them to the heart.

> I preached but little terror. It seemed best to tell them their Father would be angry with them. They looked, they heard, they sighd, and many wept bitterly.

Amid Whitefield's 1745 preaching circuit through northern New England, there remained cases of false accusations and innuendoes against him. For example, a farmer named Reuben Fletcher of Westford, about twenty-five miles northwest of Boston, was a man in his mid-twenties when Whitefield came through New England in 1745. Fletcher was described as "a man of high standing in the community, and a member of the Baptist Church."[36] Later in life, in 1772, Fletcher recalled the animosity and slander he heard against Whitefield during his 1744-1745 New England preaching circuit. Fletcher wrote,

> They lied about the orphan house, that Mr. Whitefield had built in Georgia, so much, that they contradicted themselves, for some said that not above half the money that he gathered went to support it, others said the orphan house was built and supported by gentlemen in England, others said there was no orphan house. They called Mr. Whitefield, and those that joined him, disorderly persons, who went about doing mischief, and poor preachers, and said they joined the pope.[37]

---

34 John L. Ewell, *The Story of Byfield: A New England Parish*, (Boston, MA: G.E. Littlefield Printer, 1904), p. 105.
35 Ibid., p. 107.
36 Edward H. Fletcher, *The Descendants of Robert Fletcher of Concord, Mass.*, (Boston, MA: Printed for the Author, 1881), p. 262.
37 Reuben Fletcher, *The Lamentable State of New England, being an Account of the Beginning, or Origins of the Separates in New England . . .*, (Boston, MA: Printed for the Author, 1772), p. 11.

Individual followers of Whitefield sometimes did more harm than good as they fervently supported New Light beliefs. Overzealous persons such as Mary Stedman of Chelmsford, held deviant New Light ideas, and was admonished by her church. She believed she "enjoyed such immediate revelations and communications from above as raised her to the privilege of exemption from all ecclesiastical authority and rule of the earth."[38] Her indecorous behavior resulted in her suspension from the church, until she confessed her errors eighteen years later. The harm that such a deviant New Light extremist did in a small town like Chelmsford can well be imagined. Similarly, Mofford spoke of religious tension in colonial Andover, when she stated, "The Great Awakening was a time when men searched their soul. Because of the conflict and fervor over religion, individuals were pressured to declare themselves theologically."[39] This pressure, caused by Whitefield, drove a wedge through New England congregationalism. His *Journals* narrates his continued travels in northeastern Massachusetts, and then into far northern New England. He was not always welcome. In Newbury, Massachusetts, there was a distinct disruption which Whitefield sought to address. His visit to Newbury was a damage control trip. Whitefield's *Journals* recorded:

> At Newbury I waited upon both the ministers, who treated me civilly but would not consent to my preaching in their pulpits. I was therefore Obliged because it snowed very much on Fryday, having first consulted the ministers that were with me, to preach in a New Meetinghouse belonging to an Incorporated Society, separated by Council from the Rev'd Mr. T_p. These men sent me an invitation, and the Rev'd Mr. Webb advised me to comply with it. Notwithstanding, before sermon, I declared that I did not preach in the congregation as a separate people, but only for convinency on account of the weather.

In the mid-1700s, Newbury was a large town, which eventually became the towns of West Newbury, Newbury, and Newburyport. This community was torn apart by controversy and rivalry related to the awakening. The two ministers of Newbury that Whitefield spoke to, and who denied him access to their pulpits, were Rev. Theodore Barnard of the Second Church, and Rev. John Lowell of the Third Church. Whitefield wrote above of a minister in Newbury referred to as "the Rev'd Mr. T p. If, in Whitefield's original handwriting, the designation was "the Rev'd C_t," that would designate Rev. Christopher Toppan of Newbury's First Church. The editors of Whitefield's *Journals* stated that this abbreviated name does refer to Rev. Christopher Toppan of the First Church (Congregational) in Newbury, Massachusetts.[40]

Long before the Great Awakening, in 1726 Toppan's First Church had a split which created the Third Church in Newbury, under Rev. Lowell. This was the "Incorporated Society, separated by Council from the Rev'd Mr. T_p." mentioned above, in which Whitefield preached. He was not welcomed in the First or the Second Church, and he was invited and tolerated to preach in the Third Church in Newbury, who were the "separate people," as noted above. But this only caused the Third Church to have another division, with a new group forming in 1745 as an independent, evangelical church in full support of Whitefield and the awakening. That church eventually became the Old South Parish Church, later the Old South Presbyterian Church of Newburyport. They called a firm Whitefield ally, Rev. Jonathan Parsons of Lyme, Connecticut to be their minister.[41] With Whitefield's encouragement, Parsons arrived in

---

38 *Chelmsford Town Records*, 1746-1762, vol. I, pp. 112-113, vol. II, p.294. Quoted in Emil Oberholzer, Jr., *Delinquent Saints*, (New York: Columbia University Press, 1956), p. 45.
39 Juliet H. Mofford, *The History of North Parish Church in North Andover* p. 75.
40 George Whitefield, *Journals*, p. 549.
41 John Greenleaf, "Memoir of Rev. Jonathan Parsons," (Boston, MA: 1841). Quoted in *American Quarterly Register, vol. xiv* (November 1841), p. 114.

the fall of 1745 to pastor this new separated congregation. When Parsons arrived, he found Newbury full of bitter disputes, low spirituality, and embroiled in civil and ecclesiastical controversies.[42]

In Newbury, many of the average citizens wanted to hear Whitefield preach, while ministerial opposition remained. He therefore went to an open field and preached to the masses from the various Newbury churches, from other nearby churches, and to the unchurched. Whitefield's *Journals* wrote of this outside preaching event in Newbury as follows:

> Accordingly on Saturday, the weather being fair, I preached twice in a field belonging to Colonel Pearse with whom I lodged, and the Lord was pleased to melt down the people much.

The "Colonel Pearce" here named was a reference to Mr. Charles Pierce, the grandson of Newbury patriarch Colonel Daniel Pierce. Charles Pierce "was a man prominent in church affairs. We find him a firm advocate of Whitefield, taking part in the great controversy which eventually divided the old town church and led to the establishment of the old South Society at the Port."[43] Charles Pierce was an outspoken New Light who was a wealthy Newbury resident with a large estate.[44] Pierce maintained a heated correspondence with Rev. Christopher Toppan of Newbury's First Church, as charges and countercharges were exchanged between the two.[45] Whitefield preached twice outside to large crowds in Newbury, on Charles Pierce's property. Whitefield wrote in his *Journals*, "This was my second time of preaching in the fields this winter. I do not remember that I ever was enabled to preach so frequently, with such short intermission before."[46]

A recent photograph of the current 1869 meeting house of the First Church, Newbury, Massachusetts. The earliest meeting houses were built in 1646, 1660, 1700, and 1806. This current building is only a few feet away from where the previous meeting houses were located. In 1745, Whitefield was not allowed to preach in the First Church Newbury by Rev. Christopher Toppan.

Photograph by Ken Lawson.

---

42 Ibid.
43 Mary H. Northend, *Historic Homes of New England*, (Boston, MA: Little, Brown and Company, 1914), p. 100.
44 John J. Currier, *Old Newbury: Historical and Biographical Sketches*, (Boston, MA: Damrell & Upham Publishers, 1896), pp. 35-36.
45 Joshua Coffin, *A Sketch of the History of Newbury, Newburyport, and West Newbury*, (Boston, MA: Samuel G. Drake, Publisher, 1845), p. 213.
46 George Whitefield, *Journals*, p. 549.

The oldest church in Newbury was the First Church, founded in 1635. When Whitefield came to town in 1745, the Rev. Christopher Toppan was the minister. Toppan, a Harvard graduate in 1691, was ordained in Newbury in 1696, serving the church until his death in 1747. Toppan was a theologian, a Latin scholar, and was a practicing physician. When the first stirrings of revival spread through New England around 1740, Toppan was skeptical. As the awakening spread throughout New England, Toppan remained hesitant, then openly opposed to the movement. While interest in the revival spread in Newbury, Toppan openly preached and wrote against it. In July 1744, a council composed of eight ministers met to help mediate the charges and countercharges between Toppan and Newbury residents. By the time of Whitefield's visit in February 1745, Toppan had been acquitted of most of the charges against him, and he remained at the First Church. But mental illness had affected Toppan's mind. He came to believe that he was directly attacked by the Devil, because he opposed the work of the Devil that was promoted by Whitefield and the awakening. Further, about the time Whitefield was in Newbury in 1745, "In the latter part of his life he [Toppan] was at times partially deranged, and on one occasion . . . carried a whip into the church under his cloak, in order, as he said, to scourge out the enthusiasts, or schemers as he called them, during the period of the excitement at the time of the great revival."[47]

While revival controversies tore apart towns such as Newbury, a bigger threat, the potential for international military hostilities, became a reality for New England. In 1744 the European War of the Austrian Succession began, eventually pitting Great Britain and her colonies against France and her colonies. This meant parts of North America would become a battlefield. In America, this conflict was called King George's War, which lasted from 1744 to 1748. New England maritime interests feared the large French fortress at Louisburg, Cape Breton Island, Canada, as a real threat to maritime commerce and the fisheries. Massachusetts Colonial Governor William Shirley led the way in organizing support for an attack on the Louisburg fortress. Massachusetts provided the most colonial troops, followed by Connecticut, New Hampshire, and Rhode Island. New York, Pennsylvania, and New Jersey provided material or financial support. A few thousand Colonial troops, supported by the British Navy, began leaving New England ports for the attack in March 1745. Mr. Thomas Smith, a Newbury resident, wrote of the turmoil in his town related to the simultaneous influences of Whitefield and the pending attack upon the French garrison at Louisburg.

> February 2d. [1745]. Great talk about Whitefield's preaching, and the fleet to Cape Breton. These two subjects, war and religion, were at this time in everybody's mouth. The enthusiasm in favor of the expedition against Louisburg was extraordinary, and almost unanimous, whilst on the subject of the religious tenents and practices of Whitefield and his adherents, the community was divided, and almost every man was either an ardent advocate, or a decided opponent.[48]

Whitefield appears to have been in good health. His stamina was robust, his energy level was sometimes drained, but he endured preaching twice a day for two weeks in rural towns a day's ride from Boston. He wrote in his *Journals:*

> For almost a whole fortnight [two weeks] together I preached twice every day, besides riding, with only about a half hours intermission. I found it hard for my body, but, as it seemed, better for the people's souls, and they could by this means return sooner to their families. Here I parted from my good friends, Mr. Jewett, Mr. Nathaniel Rogers, [Mr.] Emerson and old Mr. White, who went with me to the Newbury Ministers, and has favored me with his company ever since I came to Cape Ann. Our parting was very affectionate for our fellowship had been very sweet, and we rejoiced at the prospect of meeting never to part any more, in the presence

---

47 Joshua Coffin, *A Sketch of the History of Newbury, Newburyport, and West Newbury*, p. 377.
48 Ibid., p. 215.

of that God who made his angels spirits and his Ministers a flaming fire. Make these Thy Dear Servants, O Lord, more and more such, for Jesus Christ's sake. Amen and Amen.

From Newbury, Whitefield preached in several nearby towns, with some ministers traveling with him. They were Rev. Jedediah Jewett of the Rowley Congregational Church; Rev. Nathaniel Rogers of the First Church in Ipswich; Rev. John Emerson from Topsfield, and "old Mr. White," Rev. John White of the First Church in Gloucester. White was elderly, and he spoke of next seeing Whitefield in heaven in the presence of God, although he did not die until 1760 in Gloucester. Whitefield then returned to Newbury. He wrote in his *Journals,*

> Sunday, February: _. Went in the morning to public worship at the Rev'd Mr. T_p, and in the afternoon to hear the Rev'd Mr. Lowell and preached about 5 in the evening to a very large congregation in a person's Court Yard belonging to the Town, where the Lord met both preachers and hearers by his spirit. Afterwards I conversed with several at my lodgings, that had been greatly comforted, and from all I could hear, had reason to believe Our Savior had much people in and about Newbury who like new-born babes were desirous of being fed the sincere milk of the word. Lord give it to them for thy Dear Son's sake, and grant they may grow thereby.

Whitefield here stated there were two churches in Newbury that he attended but were closed to his preaching. The "Rev'd Mr. T____p" was Christopher Tappan of Newbury's First Church, and "Rev'd Mr. Lowell" was John Lowell of Third Church in Newbury. Not being welcomed in their meeting houses, Whitefield preached outside to "a very large congregation," as stated above. He had also preached outdoors in Newbury a few weeks prior. Whitefield's *Journals* continued.

> Saturday, February: _. Left Newbury on Monday morning, tho it was somewhat difficult to part with so many souls. Stopped two places on the way and gave an exhortation at each place at the earnest desire of several. God was with us and also brought me in good season to Portsmouth . . .

Whitefield's successful but controversial preaching tour through northern and eastern Massachusetts now comes to an end. Crossing the Merrimack River on a horse powered ferry, he passed from Newbury north into New Hampshire. He would preach throughout southeastern New Hampshire, in mostly familiar areas. Then his preaching tour would take him into a new area, into remote coastal Maine.

CHAPTER 17
WHITEFIELD'S TOUR INTO NEW HAMPSHIRE AND SOUTHERN MAINE

MARCH 1745

AS GEORGE WHITEFIELD DEPARTED MASSACHUSETTS for a preaching tour in northern New England, word reached him that Yale College had published against him. This 14-page pamphlet was titled, *A Declaration of the Rector and Tutors of Yale College in New Haven, against the Rev. Mr. George Whitefield, his Principles, and Designs*. Dated February 25, 1745, this forcefully written document supported the previously written anti-Whitefield documents from Harvard College, and from four ministerial associations around Boston. The Yale *Declaration* speaks against itinerant preachers, and against Whitefield's accusations that many New England ministers were unconverted. Whitefield is then criticized for supposedly encouraging separations and splits within individual churches. Further, he and Rev. Jonathan Edwards of Northampton are both rebuked for allegedly scheming to replace unconverted New England clergymen with converted clergymen from Scotland or Ireland. Whitefield is also accused of planning to train his orphans from the Georgia orphan house to become ministers, after which he will send them to New England to overthrow the established order of churches.[1]

It is significant to note that virtually all the New England clergy received a thorough ministerial education at either Harvard or Yale. Further, the leading civil and business leaders in New England were typically graduates of these schools. The influence of Harvard and Yale in eighteenth century New England was all-encompassing.

> Through the agency of Harvard and Yale, the region included over six hundred classically educated Congregational clergymen, placed in virtually every town throughout Massachusetts and Connecticut. The ratio of minister to population was the lowest in the Western world, and as public voices they had few competitors. Indeed, the ministers controlled public communications so effectively that in most communities they simply were the voice of authority and corporate meaning.[2]

As Whitefield headed into northern New England, he faced a daunting task—how could he preach as an itinerant evangelist in communities composed of ministers from Harvard and Yale, knowing that both colleges had denounced him? Ministers throughout New England were divided. Some pledged loyalty to their college, while others supported the revival in contradiction to the published statements

---

1   *The Declaration of the Rector and Tutors of Yale College in New Haven, against the Rev. Mr. George Whitefield ...*, (Boston, MA: T. Fleet Printer, 1745). Joseph Tracy, *The Great Awakening*, (1842: reprinted by Banner of Truth Trust, Carlisle, PA: 1898), pp. 367-368.
2   Harry S. Stout, *The Divine Dramatist: George Whitefield and the Rise of Modern Evangelicalism*, (Grand Rapids, MI: Eerdman's Publishing, 1991), p. 115.

of their colleges. The February 25, 1745 declaration from Yale against Whitefield did not hinder him from continuing his preaching circuit north into New Hampshire and Maine. Departing Newbury, Massachusetts, Whitefield travelled along the north coastal road to Portsmouth, New Hampshire. It was now the first week of March 1745. He recorded in his *Journals*, "God was with us and also brought me in good season to Portsmouth to dear Mr. S_'s where I expected to have been in a few days after I left Boston, little thinking of having so many invitations on the way. Speaking of Portsmouth, he wrote, "All received me with open hearts. I preached on Tuesday, and so every day, generally twice all the week, and redeemed as much time as I could to write to my dear friends at home."[3] The mentioned dear Mr. S_ was either Rev. William Shurtleff, minister of the South Church in Portsmouth, or Mr. Henry Sherburn, Whitefield's host while he ministered in Portsmouth.

Whitefield stated in his *Journals*, quoted above, that "he redeemed as much time as I could to write to my dear friends at home." No doubt he was assisted in this by his wife Elizabeth, who was travelling with him. Two letters written at this time from Portsmouth have survived. In a letter dated March 6, 1745 from Piscataqua, a region of Portsmouth, Whitefield wrote about his reply to Harvard College, his inability to find the time to write out his sermons, and his intent to write another journal for publication. While expecting news from the orphanage in Georgia, Whitefield wrote:

> America, I am afraid, begins to be too dear to me. The Lord smiles upon me and mine, and makes us very happy in himself, and happy in one another. Here is a very large field of action. A very fine and effectual door is opened; my bodily strength is recovered, and my soul more than ever in love with a crucified Jesus. I could write more to you and other dear friends, but if I do, I shall neglect things of a more public and immediate concern; neither can my dear wife write, because she is fully employed in copying my letters . . . [W]e do not forget our dear London and English friends. We pray for them often, and sometimes cannot help wishing some more may come over unto this delightful wilderness; it is a fruitful field. Jesus waters it with his blessings . . . Here are wars and rumors of wars, on this, as well as your side of the water. But Jesus' disciples may be at peace.[4]

This brief letter reveals several interesting facts. Whitefield was very content, even though he daily faced the results of both Harvard and Yale publishing against him. His physical strength had recovered. He obviously enjoyed travelling with his wife. He found he was without enough time in the day to complete his writing projects. Further, when he wrote, "Here are wars and rumors of wars, on this, as well as your side of the water," he was referring to the mustering of the colonial militia in New England for an attack upon the French fortress at Louisburg, Cape Breton Island, Canada.

In a second letter written by Whitefield from Portsmouth, New Hampshire, dated March 6, 1745, he wrote about the large amount of ministry work that faced him, as well as the success he experienced in preaching. Whitefield stated:

> Our Saviour wonderfully smiles on us here; several year's work I think lies before me. The Lord helps me to preach with the demonstration of the Spirit and with power, my strength is daily renewed, and my wife and I go like two happy pilgrims, leaning upon our beloved. O help us to adore and praise free grace.[5]

---

3   George Whitefield, *Journals of George Whitefield*, (1756: reprinted by Banner of Truth Trust, 1985), pp.550-551. The Journal quotations in this chapter are from pp. 550-558.
4   George Whitefield, *Works of George Whitefield*, (1772: reprinted by Quinta Press, 2000), vol. II, pp. 77-78.
5   Ibid., p. 78.

Whitefield had a firm ally in Rev. William Shurtleff, pastor of the South Church in Portsmouth. Shurtleff wrote numerous pamphlets in defense of the awakening and in support of Whitefield. In 1745 he published a twenty-three-page pamphlet, praising Whitefield and challenging all opponents to substantiate and defend their positions.[6] Shurtleff's document deserved close examination. He

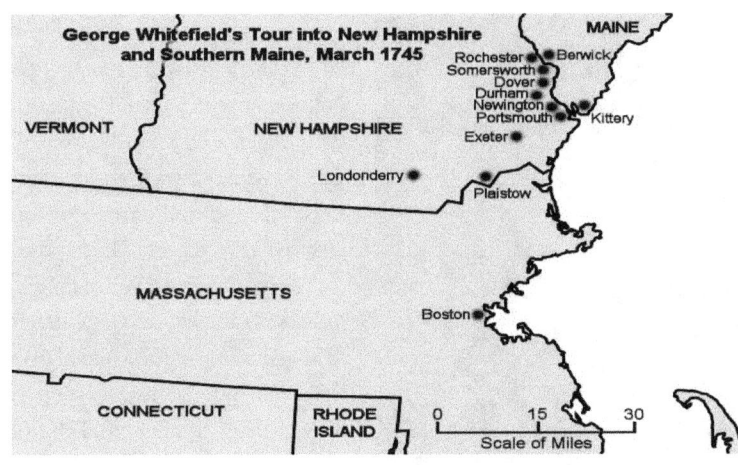

agreed that Whitefield had caused disturbances and praised him for it. Shurtleff rebuked the religious trend toward what he called Pelagianism, Arianism, and Deism, which he ridiculed as "free thinking."[7] Shurtleff looked upon Whitefield as a spokesman against low morals and declining theological purity. He wrote that Whitefield was not the cause of the disorders, but he was the one who exposed the theological errors of the people. Shurtleff believed that Whitefield "ought to be highly valued and regarded by us; it becomes us to be very thankful to him, but above all to give glory to God, that has raised up such an instrument, and made him the means of so much good to us."[8] While in Portsmouth, Whitefield took the time to cross the Piscataqua River and meet with Colonel William Pepperell and his wife in Kittery, Maine. In his *Journals*, Whitefield wrote:

> This day I went to visit General Pepperell and his Lady, who have always expressed great concern for me. At their desire I preached from the words out of Ecclesiastes: [blank space in the manuscript] And then returned to Portsmouth where I preached at their request also, another sermon to the Officers and Soldiers engaged in the Expedition[.] I spoke with much freedom, and have thought however some things have been not managed so well as some serious persons could have issue that good will come out of it to the people of God. I trust that the Lord will deal with others for their sake. A general fast was kept on Thursday, on which I preached twice. Under one sermon the Lord humbled the Hearers very much, and I trust he will send forth a prevailing spirit of repentance . . . But also give us Cape Breton. Lord, prepare us either for victory or defeat. But if it be thy will grant it may be a Garrison for Protestants and thy dear Children who will worship thee in spirit and in truth!

Colonel William Pepperell was a native of Kittery, Maine. He worked with his successful father in shipbuilding, trading, and warehousing businesses. He was an active member of the First Church in Kittery, under Rev. Samuel Moody. In addition to his mercantile activities, Pepperell served various terms in Colonial Massachusetts politics. As a merchant and a militia soldier, he served as the commander of the colonial forces preparing to attack the French fortress on Cape Breton Island. As the British and the French were at war, this French citadel was the location from which French ships raided the British colonies in New England.

Whitefield was asked to use his influence in the raising of men for the above-named expedition. Pepperell sought Whitefield's support for the endeavor. At first, Whitefield refused, but after Pepperell and

---

6   William Shurtleff, *A Letter to Those of His Brethren in the Ministry who refuse to Admit the Rev. Mr. George Whitefield into Their Pulpits*, (Boston, MA: Kneeland & Green Printers, 1745).
7   Ibid., p. 4.
8   Ibid., p. 9.

A painting of Sir William Pepperell of Kittery, Maine. Source: https://www.wikitree.com/wiki/Browne-2317.

other urged him to reconsider, Whitefield endorsed the expedition, and as the above quote states, he preached to the officers and soldiers going on the trip. The Rev. Samuel Moody of York, Maine, a staunch Whitefield ally, served as chaplain for the expedition. "Whitefield finally assented to the idea that the expedition was an effort in the cause of God and agreed to support it. He suggested as motto, *Nil Desperandum, Christo Duce* and the words were affixed to the flag."[9]

An example of Whitefield's ongoing influence upon the colonial militia deployed to Cape Breton Island is found in the diary of Massachusetts Militia chaplain Rev. Joseph Emerson of Pepperell. Emerson was a twenty-one-year-old chaplain who was deeply moved by Whitefield and the Great Awakening. Chaplain Emerson was deployed on a colonial ship for five months on board the frigate *Molineux* off Cape Breton Island. In 1745, Emerson wrote in his *Diary*:

> Friday March 22. Read a sermon or two in Mr. Whitefield's sermons preached in Scotland.
>
> Saturday March 23. Read two sermons in Mr. Whitefield but little opportunity for study on board. We live a rolling, tumbling life.
>
> Monday March 25. I read three sermons of Mr. Whitefield's . . .[10]

But not all the Colonial troops appreciated Whitefield's influence. A few days later, upon his second opportunity to preach to the militia soldiers, Whitefield wrote in his *Journals* that he "preached once more to the Soldiers who are now at Portsmouth ready to embark." Apparently while he was addressing the troops, the following incident occurred. "As I went along, one of the Captains, having a gun in his hand, wished that it was loaded for he would then in a few minutes send me either to heaven or hell. Blessed be God, all that go are not of such spirit. Lord pity and convert all that are."[11]

Whitefield received a cordial but not enthusiastic reception in Portsmouth. Before traveling into rural New Hampshire and then into southern Maine, he made one final preaching circuit around the churches in Portsmouth. He wrote in his *Journals*:

> I received the Holy Sacrament at the Church of England Congregation, where I have attended once or twice before. Everything was managed with decency and as much order as I have seen anywhere in America. Preached afterwards, and to large congregations, in the two meeting houses, as also once on Monday Evening, for the Rev'd Mr. Shurtleff.

The Church of England congregation in Portsmouth was Saint John's Church. With a wooden building constructed in 1732, this congregation grew as more and more English immigrants came to Portsmouth.

---

9 Arnold Dallimore, *George Whitefield: The Life and Times of the Great Evangelist of the Eighteenth Century Revival*, (Carlisle, PA: Banner of Truth Trust, 1980), vol. II, p. 202. The Latin motto for the expedition can be translated as "Christ Leads, Never Despair," or "If Christ be Captain, no fear of Defeat."

10 Rev. Joseph Emerson, *Diary Kept at the Siege of Louisburg, March 15-August 14, 1745*, (Cambridge, England: University Press, 1910), 10.

11 George Whitefield, *Journals*, p. 553.

Originally named Queen's Chapel after the wife of King George II, Queen Caroline, a visitor today to St. John's Church can see several items that were present when Whitefield visited the church in 1745, namely the pulpit Bible, the Book of Common Prayer, some of the original box pews, and the church bell, which was a prize of war from the 1745 Louisburg campaign. Rev. Arthur Brown was the rector from 1736 to 1773,[12] who is buried under the western entrance of the building.

When the awakening first reached Portsmouth around 1740, the Anglican Arthur Brown was unsure how to respond. In his personal correspondence, dated December 10, 1741, Brown mentioned George Whitefield and Jonathan Edwards, and that there was "an extraordinary work on foot in the Land." As a proper Church of England minister, Brown thought the revival was all "disorder and confusion," yet initially declined to pass "a definitive judgment" on the movement. While Brown was happy to welcome a surge of new members to his church as a result of the awakening, he wrote of "difficulties" and "adversaries" to his ministry in Portsmouth. He stated that he had to be always careful about what he said, "without giving offence to some of my own parish who seem to be wavering" towards Whitefield and the revival.[13]

An undated painting of Rev. Arthur Brown, Portsmouth, New Hampshire.

Source: https://www.wikitree.com/wiki/Browne-2317.

By the time of Whitefield's return visit in early March 1745, Rev. Arthur Brown had determined to openly oppose Whitefield. Whitefield mentioned above that he had visited this church before, but the exact date is unknown. It is interesting to note that, while he attended the Sunday service of the Church of England, and received communion, Whitefield was not allowed to speak or to assist in the celebration of communion with Brown.

Whitefield did not participate in public worship in the Episcopal Church in Portsmouth. Instead, he wrote above that he spoke "in the two meeting houses," a reference to the North Parish Church and the South Parish Church. Interest in Whitefield and his message was so pronounced in Portsmouth, that Rev. William Shurtleff of the South Church sponsored a Monday evening preaching event. Clearly most of Portsmouth supported or at least was fascinated by Whitefield. A letter was written by Whitefield from Portsmouth, dated March 12, 1745. In this one paragraph letter he spoke about sending correspondence to England and Scotland, and he stated, "America is pleasanter and pleasanter every day . . . The door of preaching opens wider and wider. O my dear friend, I could tell thee what would rejoice thy heart, wast thou here."[14]

An eyewitness of Whitefield's 1745 ministry in Portsmouth was a local magistrate named Daniel Pierce. A Harvard graduate in 1728, Pierce held various civic positions in Portsmouth and was a leading citizen of the community. In his journal, Pierce wrote succinctly, "Feb. 25, 1740. The Rev. Mr. Whitefield came to town and preached for Mr. Shurtleff, and the next day for Mr. Fitch."[15] The "Mr. Fitch" was Rev. Jabez Fitch of the North Church, who served in Portsmouth from 1724 to his death in 1746. In

---

12 *St. John's Church, Portsmouth, New Hampshire—Historical Guide*, (Portsmouth, NH: Published by St. John's Church, revised October 12, 2011).
13 "Letter from Rev. Arthur Brown," *The New England Historical and Genealogical Register*, (Boston, MA: Thomas Prince, Printer, 1852), vol. vi, pp. 264-265.
14 George Whitefield, *Works of George Whitefield*, p. 79.
15 Charles W. Brewster, *Rambles about Portsmouth: Sketches of Persons, Localities, and Incidents of Two Centuries*, (Portsmouth, NH: C.W. Brewster & Son, Printers, 1859), vol. I, p. 357.

An old photograph of the Rev. Jabez Fitch home in Portsmouth, NH.

Source: *"Walking Portsmouth,"* http://walkportsmouth.blogspot.com/2011/06/fitch-house.html.

1725, the church built a new parsonage for the Fitch family, and the home is still standing today in Portsmouth. Whitefield enjoyed the hospitality of the Fitch family in this home.

After completing several days of ministry in Portsmouth, Whitefield began a preaching tour at nearby towns in New Hampshire and Maine. He wrote in his *Journals*:

Went five miles out of town to Newington on Tuesday, and preached twice for the Rev'd Mr. Adams, twice on Wednesday for the Rev'd Mr. Blunt on the Island, and once at General Pepperell's, and twice for the Rev. Mr. Rogers of Kittery on Thursday, twice for the Rev'd Mr. Pike of Dover on Fryday. Once for the Rev'd Mr. Wise at Berwick.

This list of locations and ministers is interesting. In Newington, New Hampshire, Whitefield was welcomed by Rev. Joseph Adams of the Newington Town Church. A Harvard graduate in 1710, Adams taught school in Newington before he was ordained as their minister in 1715. He served the church until his death in 1783.[16] The meeting house was built in 1712 and is in remarkably good condition today. Here is one of the few meeting houses in New England still standing in which George Whitefield preached. The parsonage of Rev. Adams is still standing, in beautiful condition, a few hundred feet from the church building. Outside the church building is the original large granite bolder used to help women get on and off horses, before carriages became fashionable. The plaque outside the building states that the Newington Congregational Church is believed to be the oldest congregational church in continuous use in the nation.

The Newington, New Hampshire Congregational Church and meeting house was constructed in 1712 and is still used by an active church congregation. Photograph by Ken Lawson.

Back to Whitefield's *Journals* entry mentioned above. Rev. John Blunt ministered on what Whitefield called "the Island," a reference to the town of New Castle, which was an island community in the Piscataqua River connected to New Hampshire by ferry and later by two bridges. Blunt was a 1727 graduate of Harvard College, who served the church in New castle for about ten years. "He was honored in his parish, and continued his ministry with them until

---

16 Henry Whittemore, *History of the Adams Family, with Biographical Sketches . . .*, (New York: McDonald & Company Publishers, 1893), p. 9.

The parsonage of Rev. Joseph Adams in Newington is in very good condition. Built in 1717, George Whitefield refreshed himself here in the spring of 1745. If you look carefully to the left of the parsonage you can see the church meeting house. Photograph by Ken Lawson.

his death, which occurred in 1748, when he was forty-two years old."[17] Whitefield then wrote that he preached once "at General Pepperell's." This is a reference to Kittery, Maine resident Colonel William Pepperell, a member of the First Church in Kittery. Whitefield probably preached outdoors at the Pepperell home. Next is mentioned "Rev. Mr. Rogers of Kittery." This refers to Rev. John Rogers, who descended from a long line of Puritan descent from Ipswich, Massachusetts and from England. Whitefield then mentions that he preached twice for "the Rev'd Mr. Pike of Dover." This was James Pike of the Congregational Church in Somersworth, now Rollinsford, New Hampshire. Pike was a 1725 Harvard graduate who was ordained in Somersworth in 1739, serving there until his death in the church parsonage in 1792. An anecdote related to Pike and Whitefield has survived. Speaking of Rev. James Pike of Somersworth,

> His parish was very large, extending throughout what is Somersworth and Rollinsford, and it was his custom yearly to visit every home in the whole town, of whatever denomination or belief . . . He was the common scrivener for the whole parish; when they wanted any legal papers drawn they called on him to write them . . . When Whitefield came to this country in 1744 [actually March 1745] he was the guest of Mr. Pike for several days and preached in the meeting house one Sunday.[18]

A final minister Whitefield named from his brief preaching tour outside Portsmouth was Rev. Jeremiah Wise of Berwick, Maine. Berwick is located just across the Piscataqua River from New Hampshire. A Harvard graduate, Wise was related to the Wise family of Ipswich, Massachusetts, a family prominent in the 1692 Salem Witch Trials. Jeremiah Wise ministered in Berwick from 1707 to his death in January 1756, and was known as "a man eminent for his learning and piety."[19] Summarizing his preaching tour through these small New Hampshire towns, Whitefield wrote, "All seemingly hearty friends to and great sharers in the late blessed work of God. Their accounts of it were very entertaining. Every time the Lord was with us, but he seemed to keep the good wine until last, for on Saturday, many of God's people were filled exceedingly." Further, without identifying his specific location, Whitefield wrote, "On Fryday I preached, but the meeting house not being large enough to contain the Congregation, (Many ministers were present) the weather still continued to be uncommonly moderate. Few ever knew so mild a winter in New England before."[20]

Whitefield was fully convinced that his itinerant preaching style—traveling along a circuit and then returning to preach again in the same community—was an effective way to spread the gospel. Therefore, we find him again at Kittery and Portsmouth, reaping what he had sown earlier. He wrote in his *Journals,*

---

17 Sarah L. Bailey, *Historical Sketches of Andover . . . Massachusetts,* (Boston, MA: Houghton, Mifflin & Company, 1880), p. 440.
18 John Scales, *History of Strafford County, New Hampshire and Representative Citizens,* (Chicago, IL: Richmond-Arnold Publishing, 1914), p. 220.
19 W. Woodford Clayton, *History of York County, Maine: with Illustrations and Biographical Sketches,* (Philadelphia, PA: Everts & Peck Printing, 1880), p. 318.
20 George Whitefield, *Journals,* p. 552.

I preached twice last Lord's Day for Rev'd Mr. Rogers of Kittery, returned to Portsmouth on Monday Evening and preached once on Tuesday to a very large Auditory for the Rev'd Mr. Allen of [blank space in original] and came back and preached once more to the soldiers who are ready to embark.

The above-named Mr. Rogers is the familiar Rev. John Rogers, a Congregational minister in Kittery. The "Rev'd Mr. Allen" was William Allen of the Congregational Church in Greenland, New Hampshire. This was a rural farming community west of Portsmouth. Allen served this church from 1707 to 1760. The church building was located on a small hill. On the side of the hill is still standing a building that was a tavern and inn. Greenland Historical Society records state that Whitefield stayed in this inn, and later ministers considered it somewhat of a sensation to visit the inn in respect for Whitefield's memory. This former inn is now a private home.

In Kittery, Whitefield preached one last time for the soldiers departing for the Cape Breton expedition. Then he re-crossed the Piscataqua River by ferry and travelled a short journey inland to Exeter, New Hampshire. Waiting for Whitefield in Exeter was one of the most contentious meetings of all his New England tours.

This former inn was built around 1690. It is a few hundred feet down the hill from the Greenland Congregational Church. George Whitefield stayed here in 1745 and again in 1754. Photograph by Ken Lawson.

Previously, Whitefield had preached in the Exeter area in October 1740, and in November 1744. Exeter, New Hampshire was founded by dissidents from Massachusetts Bay Colony in 1638. The original boundary for Exeter was much larger than today, as over time the town was divided into five additional townships. The Exeter River was the lifeblood of the community, providing fresh water, abundant fish, and a water route to the ocean. In the mid-1700s, Exeter was a growing and successful colonial community, its residents working in lumbering, hunting, fishing, various trades, and farming. Whitefield had a firm antagonist in Exeter named Rev. John Odlin of the First Parish Church.

Called to the First Church in Exeter in 1706, John Odlin was a Harvard graduate in 1702. When he arrived in Exeter he was twenty-four years old, and he would serve this community until his death in 1754. The first decades of his ministry were unremarkable, as the minister and the town equally supported each other. In 1730-1731 a new meeting house was constructed, measuring sixty feet by forty-five feet with two galleries. The building had boxed pews and a raised high box pulpit with a sounding board. The steeple and bell were added in 1739. Town records show that, as the community grew, the minister received incremental pay raises.[21] During the Great Awakening of the early 1740s, Odlin sensed the influence of Whitefield in his church, but resisted the revival movement. A majority of the members of the First Church supported their minister in resistance to Whitefield, but a vocal minority pleaded with Odlin to allow Whitefield to preach in the First Church. Odlin and his like were of the group that "set their faces like a flint against his [Whitefield's] methods."[22]

---

21 Charles H. Bell, *History of the Town of Exeter, New Hampshire*, (Exeter, NH: The Quarter-Millennial Year, 1888), p. 180.
22 Ibid., p. 185.

There were other issues within the First Church of Exeter. As Rev. John Odlin got older and more eccentric and opinionated, he desired that his son Woodbridge Odlin be hired as his associate minister. The younger Odlin was like-minded with his father against Whitefield and the awakening. In 1743, the town voted to approve the hiring of Woodbridge Odlin to assist his father, but a vocal minority rejected the idea and formed an independent church society. For the next eleven years the First Church, and what would be called after 1755 the Second Church of Exeter, exchanged accusations and legal proceedings which disrupted the town. The town voted in 1744 not to release the separated group from paying the obligatory church tax to the First Church. "It was during that year [1744] that the Rev. John Odlin, learning that the Rev. George Whitefield was coming to Exeter, with the intention of preaching there, met him on the border of the town, and solemnly adjured him not to trespass upon his parochial charge."[23] But now in 1745, Whitefield was back in Exeter, and the contentions against him were severe and public.

Whitefield preached in the Exeter area in the fall of 1740 and again in the fall of 1744, but Rev. John Odlin had refused to allow Whitefield access to the First Church pulpit. Now the itinerant preacher was back. In March 1745, after leaving Portsmouth, Whitefield headed to Exeter. His *Journals* narrate his hostile reception.

> On Wednesday morning . . . I went to Exeter, where there has been much of the power of God, and, what is uncommon as far as I can hear, it has prevailed chiefly among the rich. Many of them . . . have been separated by Council and formed into a church. But I did not go to them as a separate body, but to preach to all in general.
>
> That my conduct might be as justified as might be, I called upon the Rev'd Mr. Odling [Odlin] the senior minister, and took with me a most unexceptional man to introduce me. He went in and desired Mr. Odling to speak with me privately, I being come to ask his leave to preach in his pulpit. He declined it and as soon as He came into his parlor, which was about filled with people, after a kind of salutation, He began with me and asked me whether I thought it for the Glory of God to preach in his Parish since it was so divided.
>
> I answered, "Yes, for if there had been faults on both sides, preaching the love of God and the meekness of the Lord Jesus must necessarily sweeten both." I also told him that I had heard there was a great division in his parish lately about settling one of his Sons, nay that his being settled had at least increased the separation, and yet I supposed He thought it for the Glory of God to have him settled.
>
> "Yes," says he, "but then," says He, "many that were against his son now were once more forward in inviting him."
>
> I replied, by way of argumentum ad hominem, that my conduct in coming to preach at Exeter was then after that account yet more justifiable, for he himself about 4 years ago had sent me an invitation to preach in Exeter by his Son who then set by him.
>
> Soon after this, his son, (who I suppose was his father's Colleague), took me up and asked me what right I had to preach in that Parish, since the people had entered into a Covenant.

---

23 Ibid., p. 186.

> I answered, that there was nothing to the purpose unless the people had entered into a Covenant when they chose him never to hear anyone besides himself. I also further told him that the people had a right to private judgment and that he could not, upon Protestant principles, deny the liberty of hearing for themselves. That he was welcome to preach and if He judged proper warn his people against me, but after he had done that, he had done all that He could do as a Christian Protestant Minister.
>
> He further told me that my practice was contrary to that of the Apostle. "For," says he, "when Paul came into the Synagogue of the Jews, did Paul stand up and speak of his own accord? No, he waited till the ruler of the Synagogue made a motion, and said, Bretheren if you have any word of Exhortation to the people say on."
>
> I replied, "I thought that was quite foreign to the point in hand, unless I was to come into his father's meeting house and stand up and preach without his leave. I rather thought it countenanced my proceedings, for Paul did preach, and the Rulers of the Synagogue disliked his preaching, and was Paul therefore silent? No, He separated the Bretheren and disputed for a whole Year in the school of one Tyrannus.
>
> "What," replied he, "will you countenance separations?"
>
> "Nay, sir, you brought the quotation."
>
> "But," says he, "that is not in the same chapter. If you please to examine you will find it so as I say."

How many hours this heated discussion carried on is not revealed. What we do see is that Whitefield had animated and determined opposition from Rev. John Odlin and his son, Rev. Woodbridge Odlin, in Exeter, New Hampshire. Whitefield had intended to privately ask John Odlin's permission to preach in his pulpit, but Odlin met Whitefield in "his parlor, which was about filled with people." Up to this point in the debate, only the two Odlin ministers were speaking against Whitefield. But as the argument continues, we read that other ministers in the parlor spoke up to rebuke the traveling evangelist. Both Whitefield and Odlin were testy, to the point of physical threats. Whitefield's *Journals* continued his narration related to the confrontation in John Odlin's parlor.

> Several other things passed pro and con till at last I freely told him that if he thought proper I would challenge him to dispute upon the point all the afternoon, publickly in the Meeting house, before the whole congregation and that I had authority to preach wherever souls were willing to hear, from the text, "whilst you have opportunity, do good to all men," and from that general Commission, "Go into all the world and preach the Gospel to every Creature," for as we pleaded in prayer the latter part of the promise, "Lo I am with you always, even unto the end of the world," the former part no doubt must be applicable to this as well as the Apostolick age.
>
> But this would not satisfy, neither did young Mr. Odling seem inclined to go into the meeting house, but debate the matter there. That I refused, and whilst we were talking further, and they were charging me with making confusion, in came Rev'd Mr. W_g and the Rev'd Mr. Y_r who was overheard to say, "Let us go and take him bodily."

Mr. W__r spoke very loud and told me what confusion I had occasioned at Topsfield. "At Topsfield," I said, "Pray what confusion did I make there?" I was called to preach by a vote of the Church and the Minister."

"But," said he, "Mr. Emerson was in a passion, and said he would lose his blood."

"Sir," I replied, "am I answerable for what Mr. Emerson said?" Or will you speak against his being in a passion, when you are in such a ferment yourself?"

"It is time," says he, "for us all to be in a ferment," or something to that purpose.

"But Sir," said I, "are you minister of Topsfield, or are you minister of this Parish? Is it not time enough for me to talk with you when I come into your Parish? I came here only to speak with Mr. Odling.

"No," replied he, "this is not my Parish, but by Mr. Odling's leave I will speak."

I told him He might if He pleased, but that I was going to preach and should not stay to hear him.

He told me I should hear him.

I replied, I would not, and so bowed and was going out, but he followed me and spoke many things very loudly, and just as I was going out He called me back and said to Mr. Odling, "Read the letter, read the letter."

I said, "What letter?" and said, "if it was a private letter, I desired I might have it privately, and if it was a publick letter, since they intended to read it before the company, they had as good let me have it from the press in a publick manner."

Upon this I took my leave and in about a quarter of an hour, after, one of Mr. Odling's sons brought me the following letter, which after having been told that it had not been read, I received.

It is interesting to speculate what letter was shown Whitefield at this time. It is doubtful that it was the Harvard *Testimony* against Whitefield, as that was written on December 28, 1744 and was already well in circulation by the time of his confrontation in Exeter in March 1745. More than likely, the aforementioned letter was the February 25, 1745 *Declaration* of the faculty of Yale College. This fourteen-page *Declaration of the Rector and Tutors of Yale College* had reached Exeter, New Hampshire by this time, and was considered a legitimate and articulate statement against Whitefield and his methods. The same accusations against Whitefield appear here as in various other pamphlets written against his preaching and ministry. The Yale Declaration speaks against Whitefield's itinerancy, his accusatory language, his mismanagement of finances for the orphans in Georgia, and his disrespect of parish boundaries. Added to these charges is the absurd remark that Whitefield intended to replace selected clergymen from New England with a supply of ministers from his orphan house.[24] Whitefield's *Journals* continued:

---

24 Richard Owen Robert, *Whitefield in Print: A Bibliographic Record of Works By, For, and Against George Whitefield*, (Wheaton, IL: Richard Owen Roberts Publishers, 1988), p. 708.

> Upon reading it I could not help pitying the gentlemen, that they should hold me in a party for above an hour, and then send me word they would hold no interview with me. Surely, thought I, this wisdom and way of behavior cometh not from above. This is never the way to keep a tottering ark from falling.
>
> Lord take it into thy hands, or it will be given over into the hands of the Philistines the Common Enemies of us all.
>
> After this I preached twice in the New Meeting House, it being a very snowy day, to very crowded assemblies, and spoke of the things which make for peace. The God of Peace and love was with us, and we had great reason to say, it is good for us to have been here.

Admittedly, in this dialogue we are only able to see Whitefield's side of the contention in Exeter. Clearly there were entrenched differences. Certainly, Whitefield's behavior and conversation with the ministers in Exeter was defensive and forthright. He believed that he had a call from God, and a biblical obligation, to preach to the masses, regardless of human obstacles or what he considered petty opposition. On the contrary, the ministers assembled against Whitefield in Exeter were sincerely concerned for the welfare of their communities and the orderliness of society. They genuinely lamented the disorders and emotionalism that sometimes accompanied Whitefield's preaching, seeing such excesses as disruptive and ungodly. The two sides were irreconcilable. One historian noted, "Mr. Odlin was unequivocally opposed to the work of Whitefield."[25] In response to this stalemate, Whitefield continued his itinerant ministry. He wrote above, "After this I preached twice in the New Meeting House, it being a very snowy day, to very crowded assemblies." This new meeting house was constructed by the separated group out from Rev. Odlin's First Church in Exeter. Their first permanent minister was Rev. Daniel Rogers of Ipswich, a Harvard tutor, who was ordained at the Second Church in Exeter in 1748.[26]

Another view of Whitefield preaching in Exeter in March 1745, was written by a resident of Exeter and sent for publication to the *Boston-Evening Post*. This unflattering portrayal of Whitefield presented him as obnoxious, disrespectful, and arrogant. The article begins, "Exeter, March 13, 1745. This Day the Rev. Mr. Whitefield preached Twice in this Town, at the House erected by the Separatists of this place." The main accusations against Whitefield preaching in Exeter were that "the Rev'd Pastors of said Town were never applied to, nor advised upon the Affair." That meant the ministers required their permission for Whitefield to preach in the town, but he never received their approval. Another accusation against Whitefield was that he "waited upon the Rev'd Pastors, suddenly, without any previous Notice given them of his being in Town." This meant the clergy of Exeter required Whitefield to make an appointment to see them, a prerequisite that Whitefield did not follow. The final main objection stated against Whitefield in Exeter was that there were "weighty objections . . . against him preaching" in Exeter, which Whitefield publicly ignored.[27] The underlying theme of this article is that the Separatist movement in Exeter, wholly endorsing the awakening under Rev. Daniel Rogers, was frowned upon by the established clergy.

After a tumultuous visit in Exeter, Whitefield resumed his itinerant ministry in the neighboring communities. His *Journals* records numerous names of ministers and their locations, but any attempt at identifying exact dates is difficult. We know he was in this area in March 1745, and preached through southeastern New Hampshire and into southern Maine. He had previously ministered in these areas in 1740 and again in 1744. Whitefield's *Journals* stated, "Preached twice to very large assemblies at Durham, for the

---

25 *The First Church in Exeter, New Hampshire: 1638-1888*, (Exeter, NH: Printed for the Parish, 1898), p. 66.
26 Ibid., p. 77.
27 *The Boston Evening-Post*, March 25, 1745, p. 2.

Rev'd Mr. Gillman, a holy man of God, remarkable for being an example of putting on the meekness and gentleness of Christ."[28] Based on the activities related to the awakening in Durham, it can be understood why Rev. John Odlin in nearby Exeter had reservations about Whitefield and the revival.

The above-mentioned Rev. Gillman was Nicholas Gillman of the First Church Congregational, in Durham, New Hampshire. He was born in 1708, graduated Harvard at age sixteen in 1724, and began his ministry in Kingston, New Hampshire in 1727. He was ordained to serve the church at Durham in 1742. "His health was not good and he preached only six years in Durham."[29] Gillman was an example of a New Light minister who endorsed some of the more extravagant behaviors associated with the awakening. To Gillman, outward signs of distress, and conviction in a preaching meeting, were legitimate signs of internal struggles for conversion. Rev. Samuel Chandler of Gloucester, Massachusetts visited Durham in 1746. Chandler wrote in his diary that he observed a preaching event in Durham at which members of the congregation had unusual physical responses to the preaching. Some contorted their bodies, others appeared to have convulsions or seizures. Chandler wrote, "some were falling down, others were jumping up, catching hold of one another, extending their arms, clapping their hands, groaning, talking."[30] Chandler opposed these outbursts but Gillman supported them, and a cordial ministerial argument developed between these two New Light ministers. With such emotional outbursts in Durham, it is no wonder that the staid and stoic Rev. John Odlin, in nearby Exeter, was so opposed to the revival movement. Gillman died in Durham after a short ministry in 1748. On his gravestone it was written:

> Here lyes the remains of the Rev'd Nicholas Gilman, who was pastor of the Church at Durham . . . He was endow'd with many amiable & useful Accomplishments. His manners were grave, easy and pleasant. He was exemplary in extensive Charity and Benevolence, eminent in Piety, Self-Denial & victory over ye world. A fervent, sound, persuasive Preacher, abounding in the work of the Lord.[31]

An account of preaching in rural New Hampshire, probably in March 1745, comes from the community of Derry-Londonderry. Rev. William Davidson, an Irishman educated in Scotland, came to the area in 1739 and was ordained to the ministry. He served this community for over fifty years in a steady but unremarkable manner. Davidson was no supporter of Whitefield and the awakening. "He is described as having been peculiarly mild and amiable in his disposition, and sincerely devoted to the interests of his people, by whom he was greatly beloved. He was not an exact theologian, nor a very effective preacher."[32] Davidson did not endorse Whitefield and opposed his coming to Londonderry. Speaking of William Davidson,

> It was during his ministry that the "great awakening" occurred in New England. At this time, the celebrated Whitefield preached in Londonderry, and the West Parish in the town, to a very considerable degree, participated in the general awakening of the churches. But Mr. Davidson, who was pastor of the East Parish, gave the new movement no countenance whatever. In this he was sustained by his people, and consequently his church remained unblessed. Subsequently, the discipline of the church was so much neglected, that there was scarcely any distinction between the church and the world.[33]

---

28 George Whitefield, *Journals*, p. 556.
29 Alexander W. Gillman, *Searches into the History of the Gillman or Gilman Family* . . . , (London, England: Elliott Stock Printer, 1895), p. 241.
30 Everett S. Stackpole and Winthrop S. Meserve, *History of the Town of Durham, New Hampshire* . . . , (Durham, NH: Published by the Town, 1913), p. 192.
31 Alexander W. Gillman, *Searches into the History of the Gillman or Gilman Family* . . . , p. 241.
32 Robert F. Lawrence, *The New Hampshire Churches, Comprising the Histories of the Congregational and Presbyterian Churches in the State* . . . , (Claremont, NH: Claremont Manufacturing Company, 1866), p. 41.
33 Ibid.

The above quote mentions the West Parish in Londonderry, New Hampshire as endorsing Whitefield's preaching and his itinerant ministry. The minister of the West Parish in Londonderry was Rev. David MacGregor. Ordained as a Presbyterian in 1737, MacGregor served here until his death in 1777. He was the first minister of the West Parish, and was an outspoken supporter of Whitefield and the revival. Londonderry was torn apart by the Great Awakening, as Rev. Davidson opposed the movement, while Rev. MacGregor endorsed the awakening. One report stated, "During this season of religious attention, the celebrated Whitefield visited the town, and preached to a very large collection of people in the open field, the meeting-house not being sufficiently large to accommodate the multitude assembled."[34]

As Whitefield travelled and preached in rural New Hampshire, he ministered to a hearty, pioneer people determined to survive the hardships of colonial life. In the mid-1700s, New Hampshire was inhabited by Europeans only along the coast and various inland communities a few hours carriage or horse ride from Portsmouth. The vast majority of New Hampshire was uninhabited, or sparsely populated by Indians. The colonial governor was Bennington Wentworth. In the late 1740s, Wentworth began issuing land grants to encourage the creation of new towns. Many New Hampshire men made a living by lumbering, as saw mills developed to build ships and other materials for the British Empire. Whitefield wrote in his *Journals*,

> Preached yesterday twice with much divine power to large Congregations for the Rev. Mr. Cushing at _[blank space] and today once for the Rev'd Mr. Main of Rochester outermost settlement in the province of New Hampshire, where they fetch masts for the King of Great Briton. They lie most exposed to the Indians, and are obliged here and adjacent provinces to build garrisons for their defense.

The above named "Rev'd Mr. Cushing" was Rev. James Cushing of the First Church Congregational in Plaistow, New Hampshire. Cushing was the first minister in Plaistow, which was originally the Second Church or the North Parish Church in Haverhill, Massachusetts. Once the boundary between New Hampshire and Massachusetts was established, Plaistow became a new town just north of Haverhill. Cushing was a Harvard graduate in 1725, and was ordained at the church in 1730. From all accounts, Cushing was a steady, compassionate, and balanced minister, deeply appreciated by his rural parish. One account stated, "Rev. James Cushing was a solid and fervent preacher, in conduct upright, prudent and steady, and recommended the amiable religion of his Master, by meekness and patience, condescension and candor, a tender sympathy with his flock, and a studious endeavor to maintain and promote the things of peace."[35] Whitefield wrote above that he preached for Cushing "twice with much divine power." Cushing skillfully guided his congregation through steady growth as a result of the Great Awakening, without controversy or extremes. Speaking of Rev. James Cushing of Plaistow,

> Nothing appears to have occurred, during his ministry, which continued about thirty-three years, that disturbed the harmony of the Church, or the comfort of the pastor. There was not, perhaps, what may be termed a revival of religion, yet a good number were added to the church—one hundred and sixty-four in all—one hundred and fifteen by profession, and forty-nine by letter.[36]

Another minister named in Whitefield's *Journals* entry above was "Rev'd Mr. Main of Rochester." This was Rev. Amos Main of the First Congregational Church in Rochester, New Hampshire. Born in York,

---

34   Edward L. Parker, *The History of Londonderry, Comprising the Towns of Derry and Londonderry, New Hampshire*, (Boston, MA: Perkins & Whipple Publishers, 1851), p. 150.
35   James S. Cushing, *The Genealogy of the Cushing Family ... who Came to America in 1638*, (Montreal, Canada: Perrault Printing, 1905), p. 60.
36   George W, Chase, *The History of Haverhill, Massachusetts: from its First Settlement, in 1640, to the Year 1860*, (Haverhill, MA: Published by the Author, 1861), p. 563.

Maine in 1708, and a Harvard graduate in 1729, Amos Main was a pioneer in the town of Rochester, serving as the town's first minister from 1737 to his death in 1760. Because of Indian threats, "The Rev. Amos Main occupied a garrison house near the top of Rochester Hill."[37] Main was a multi-talented and respected member of the community.

> One well known settler was the Rev. Amos Main, a greatly honored and beloved minister from 1731 until his death in 1760. In addition to his church responsibilities, he served as doctor, lawyer, and advised for the area and often travelled long distances away from Rochester. Although he carried his gun as well as his Bible, the Indians had so much regard for his character, he was never attacked.[38]

Amos Main was skilled in many areas. The First Congregational Church in Rochester still maintains their respect for the patriarch of their church, stating, "He was a man of many talents . . . He had served the church and town for 23 years. Pastor Amos Main was the first moderator, physician, and barrister, as well as the first pastor of Rochester."[39] In the mid-1700s, the Congregational Church was the only established church in town, although Quakers were present that met in homes. Main was a firm New Light, and fully supportive of Whitefield and the awakening. Whitefield wrote above that he "Preached . . . once for the Rev'd Mr. Main of Rochester." Main had the reputation that "it was evidently his one great object to lead sinners to repentance."[40] Over the years, Whitefield travelled in and around Rochester, and he always had an ally in Amos Main. Whether preaching in the Congregational meeting house, or outside on a hilltop beside the parsonage, Whitefield found success in Rochester. Speaking of Whitefield, "It is believed that he came to Rochester on his many travels throughout New England and preached from a rock on Rochester Hill across the street from the Rev. Joseph Haven's home."[41] In appreciation for Amos Main's ministry, in 1896 the town of Rochester erected a bronze statue dedicated to him on a granite base. Located downtown at the intersection of North Main Street and South Main Street, the inscription for the statue states, "This monument is erected to perpetuate the memory of Reverend Amos Main the first settled minister of the

A photograph of the Rev. Amos Main statue in downtown Rochester, New Hampshire.

Source: www.flickr.com.

---

37 Franklin McDuffee, *History of the Town of Rochester, New Hampshire, from 1722 to 1890*, (Manchester, NH: John B. Clarke Company, 1892), vol. I, p. 20.
38 "Rochester History," www.rochesternh.org/pages/HistoryofRochester.org.
39 "First Church Congregational, Rochester, NH—History," www.first-ucc.net/history.php.
40 Franklin McDuffee, *History of the Town of Rochester, New Hampshire, vol. I*, p. 85.
41 www.rochesterhistoricalnh.org/2014/07/30/rochester-first-churches. Rev. Joseph Haven was a later and famous minister in Rochester.

First Congregational Church of the Province of Rochester, from May 9, 1737 to April 5, 1760, when he died aged fifty-one years."

Whitefield continued his itinerant preaching tour in southeastern New Hampshire and southern Maine. Traveling on horseback, or sometimes in a horse-drawn carriage on dirt roads, Whitefield's health appeared to be vigorous. The March weather in New England agreed with him. Whitefield's *Journals* continued:

> Preached yesterday twice for the Rev'd Mr. Pike, and this morning once for the Rev'd Mr. Wise, of Berwick. All three Golden seasons whenever Jesus was pleased to light up the light of his countenance upon many souls. The mentioning of the sudden death of a man lately crushed to death in an instant by the rolling of a great Log over his body, was blessed, I believe, to put many in mind of and set to them upon preparing for the latter end.

Whitefield noted that he preached twice "for the Rev'd Mr. Pike." This was a reference to Rev. James Pike of the Congregational Church in Somersworth, New Hampshire. Pike was born in Newbury, Massachusetts in 1703, graduated from Harvard in 1725, and was ordained in the Dover community of Somersworth in 1730. He served this parish until his death in 1792.[42] Somersworth was a farming community located at a point on the Salmon River where the current ran swiftly, an ideal location for grist mills and saw mills. Lumber was sent down the river to shipyards in Kittery, Maine and Portsmouth, New Hampshire. James Pike was the first minister in Somersworth. He began to preach in the northeast part of Dover (now Somersworth) in 1727, and was ordained at the Congregational Church in 1730. "Mr. Pike, in his sentiments, was a Calvinist. He was a faithful servant of Christ; and lived in harmony with his people during his ministry."[43] The rural Somersworth community paid Pike with an annual salary, supplemented by land and firewood. "He was a great preacher and a good manager in parish affairs. He had no quarrel with his people."[44] It is noteworthy that, in the midst of ecclesiastical turmoil as a result of the Great Awakening, no controversies existed in Somersworth. Pike was a balanced and fair-minded New Light who gently guided his congregation through the disturbances of that era. His home was built as a garrison, where townsfolk slept at times out of fear of the Indians. During his 1744-1745 travels in New Hampshire, Whitefield was always welcomed in Somersworth by Pike. One account stated, "Rev. George Whitefield was a guest of the Rev. James Pike and was warmly welcomed."[45] Whitefield resided with Pike on several brief occasions as he passed back and forth on his preaching circuits.

In the above *Journals* entry from mid-March 1745, Whitefield wrote, "Preached . . . this morning once for the Rev'd Mr. Wise, of Berwick." Rev. Jeremiah Wise was called to the Congregational Church in Berwick in 1706. He was ordained there in 1707, and served in the riverside community of Berwick, Maine until his death in 1756. He was the son of the Congregational patriarch of Ipswich, Massachusetts, the Puritan Rev. John Wise.[46] In 1706, a new meeting house was constructed in Berwick for the popular Jeremiah Wise. The town was incorporated in 1713, and the first schoolhouse in Berwick was built in 1719. Berwick was once much larger than it is today, as rising population created several villages that later became separate towns. While vulnerable to Indian raids, Berwick was known for lumbering, fishing, farming, and diverse maritime and small commercial trades. As minister of the First Parish Church, Wise was known

---

42 William B. Sprague, *Annals of the American Pulpit* . . . , (New York: Robert Carter & Brothers Printers, 1859), vol. I, p. 189.
43 Jacob B. Moore, *Collections, Historical, and Miscellaneous; and Monthly Literary Journal*, (Concord, NH: J.B. Moore Publisher, 18123), vol. II, p. 148.
44 John Scales, *History of Stratford County, New Hampshire*, p. 219.
45 Alfred Catalfo, *The History of the Town of Rollingsford, New Hampshire, 1623-1973*, (Rollingsford, NH: New Hampshire Printers, 1973), p. 81.
46 Henry M. Dexter, editor, *The Congregational Quarterly*, (Boston, MA: Congregational Building, Chauncey Street, 1803), vol. v (October 1863), p. 342.

as "a man eminent for his learning and piety."[47] Speaking of Jeremiah Wise, "He was a doctrinal preacher, and an excellent and exemplary man. People in his day went to meeting to hear the gospel preached, not to be amused with the flowers of fancy and the figures of eloquence."[48] Whitefield had an evangelical and Calvinist friend in Pastor Jeremiah Wise in Berwick.

Having thoroughly crisscrossed southeastern New Hampshire on his 1744 and 1745 preaching circuits, in March 1745 Whitefield struck out for new territory. Previously he had received invitations to preach in rural, coastal Maine. Now, as spring appeared in northeastern New England, with his health robust, Whitefield commenced a new preaching circuit to the most northern and eastern European settlements in the American Colonies.

---

47   W. Woodford Clayton, *History of York County, Maine . . .*, (Philadelphia, PA: Everts & Peck Printers, 1880), p. 318.
48   William D. Williamson, "Sketches of the Lives of Early Maine Ministers," *Proceedings of the Maine Historical Society*, (Portland, ME: Published by the Society, 1893), second series, vol. iv, p. 321.

CHAPTER 18

WHITEFIELD'S MINISTRY IN EASTERN MAINE

LATE MARCH 1745

WHITEFIELD WAS A RELENTLESS ITINERANT. As a traveling evangelist he displayed at times almost unbounded energy. At other times he was serious ill, almost deathly sick. As he headed into rural southeastern Maine, he was thirty-one years old, still a relatively young man. But the demands upon his body, from his relentless itinerant preaching ministry, often slowed him down. During the early spring of 1745, Whitefield and his entourage travelled north and east along the Maine coastline, destined for Yarmouth. He wrote about his initial travels to rural Maine in his *Journals*. From Berwick, Maine, he wrote,

> Set out last Monday, very weak in body, and after many discouragements in my mind, upon a new Circuit, Eastward, where I was under an engagement to go if ever I came again to New England. The ground being just about to be broken up and the frost not gone out of it rendered riding dangerous. But being apprehensive that, taken altogether, this would be the most convenient season, and Messers. Pike, Rogers, and Wise, with several other Friends being willing to accompany me, we went on in the strength of Jesus Christ, and found everything far beyond expectation. By Saturday Evening we got as far as North Yarmouth, about a hundred and thirty miles East from Boston.[1]

This is the last entry in Whitefield's *Journals*, and it is insightful. First, he mentioned that he was physically and emotionally drained. Then he noted that he was beginning a new circuit, to an area he had not visited before, rural eastern Maine. He mentioned that the weather was still cold and slippery from frost, ice and snow. Whitefield named three ministers that travelled with him, at least part of the way to Yarmouth, Maine. They were Rev. James Pike of Somersworth, New Hampshire; Rev. John Rogers of Kittery, Maine; and Rev. Jeremiah Wise from Berwick, Maine. During the previous days Whitefield had preached, rested, and dined with these men who now accompanied him on horseback northeast along the Maine coastline. Whitefield casually noted above that several friends also travelled with this ministerial parade. This was no accident, as the roads could be treacherous, opponents to Whitefield could be belligerent, and the threat of an Indian raid was real but remote. If Whitefield's chronology is correct, he stated that they departed Berwick on a Monday and arrived at North Yarmouth on Saturday. That means he and his companions travelled about twenty miles per day for six days, nonstop. That was vigorous riding.

Now that Whitefield's *Journals* ends, we are forced to look to his personal correspondence for insights into his travels in eastern Maine. Unfortunately, none of that correspondence, if it ever existed, has survived. Therefore, local town histories, newspaper reports, and various diaries and other accounts will help at least

---

1   George Whitefield, *Journals of George Whitefield*, (1756: reprinted by Banner of Truth Trust, Carlisle, PA: 1985), pp. 557-558.

outline Whitefield's travels. "It is to be regretted that none of the biographers of Mr. Whitefield have noticed the event of his visit to North Yarmouth, interesting as it is to the inhabitants of that town."[2] In his last *Journals* entry, Whitefield mentioned that he had been invited to rural eastern Maine and that he had arrived at North Yarmouth. A local historical account gives some impressions on Whitefield's reception in eastern Maine.

> In 1740, during Whitefield's first visit to New England, he came to York, Maine to visit the venerable and devout Father Moody. Again, in 1744, he landed in York . . . From York he went to Boston, and other places in Mass., but in the early spring of 1745, he turned Eastward and entered the district of Maine. He came as far as Dunstan (now Scarborough Corner) intending to go farther; but there learning that some of Rev. Mr. Smith's people were opposed to his coming to Falmouth, he resolved to proceed no further. When this became known to the clergymen in the vicinity of Falmouth, Rev. Nicholas Loring, of No. Yarmouth, and Rev. Benjamin Allen of Cape Elizabeth, mounted their horses and rode to Dunstan, to persuade Mr. Whitefield to carry out his previous intention. And they succeeded. Mr. Whitefield came on with them, stopped in Falmouth and preached in Mr. Smith's pulpit, Saturday afternoon, and then rode to No. Yarmouth.
>
> On Sunday, March 24, Mr. Whitefield preached in Mr. Loring's pulpit, in the "Old Meeting House below the ledge"—much to the delight of the people. The next day he returned to Falmouth and preached again there, and thence went on westwards, never again extending his preaching tours so far into the District of Maine.
>
> It seems some religious interest attended Mr. Whitefield's labors in No. Yarmouth. More than the usual average united with the church there, during that year, though not so many as in some years of Mr. Loring's ministry.
>
> This narrative also shows the evangelical positions of Revs. Loring and Allen, who interested themselves so much to secure his visit. They, and all the congregational pastors in Maine, were in sympathy with Mr. Whitefield's success, though they disapproved of some measures that he had pursued, but which afterwards abandoned.[3]

It is worthwhile to note, while Whitefield received no ministerial opposition in Maine, individual churches were in turmoil over whether to support the revival. Key individuals within local churches opposed their pastors related to Whitefield. The measures that Whitefield had previously used, which the Maine clergy did not approve, were his denunciation of many clergymen as unregenerate, and his critique of the venerable Harvard and Yale Colleges. The three ministers mentioned in the above quote—Rev. Thomas Smith, Rev. Nicholas Loring, and Rev. Benjamin Allen—warrant further attention. Smith and Loring were Harvard graduates, while Allen graduated from Yale. All three men were born in various maritime towns in Massachusetts. They were all ordained Congregational ministers, who supplemented their income by teaching children in the meeting house in a day school. And all three men signed the 1743 *Testimony* of pastors, which met in Boston in the summer of 1743, in support of Whitefield and the revival.[4]

---

2   Amasa Loring, "Rev. George Whitefield," *Old Times: A Magazine Devoted to the Preservation and Publication . . . of North Yarmouth, Maine,* (vol.7, no.1, (January 1883), pp. 824-825.

3   Augustus Corliss, *Old Times: North Yarmouth, Maine,* (Somersworth, NH: New Hampshire Publications Company, 1977), pp. 825-826.

4   *The Testimony and Advice of an Assembly of Pastors of Churches in New England, at a Meeting in Boston, July 7, 1743, occasioned by the Late Happy Revival or Religion in the Land,* (Boston, MA: 1743).

Born in Boston in 1702, Thomas Smith graduated from Harvard College at age eighteen in 1720. He taught school and began preaching in 1722 or 1723 in Bellingham, Massachusetts. In 1725 he came to Falmouth, Maine, which was the furthermost English settlement in New England. Upon his ordination in Falmouth in 1726, he was the first and only ordained minister in the region. Smith ministered to poor settlers scattered in various maritime and inland villages. This was an extremely remote region, with the nearest large city, Portsmouth, about sixty miles, or three days travel away by land, and perhaps three or a few days travel by sea on a coastal trading vessel. Smith and his parishioners faced threats from famine, severe winter weather, and Indians. He was greatly admired in the community as a preacher and as a physician, as professional medical care was non-existent in early Falmouth. Smith was described as "rigidly Calvinistic," serving a rural ministry in which four hundred and fifty-nine people were added to the church roles during his long tenure. The largest annual church memberships came in the early-to-mid 1740s, "during the Whitefield excitement."[5] Smith died in Falmouth in 1795.

Rev. Nicholas Loring was born in Hull, Massachusetts in 1711, graduated from Harvard in 1732, and began preaching in North Yarmouth, Maine in 1736. The community was designated North Yarmouth to differentiate it from Yarmouth, Massachusetts south of Boston. The church met at "the old meeting house below the ledge" in an area susceptible to Indian raids. Indeed, in 1748 there was an Indian attack in North Yarmouth outside the meeting house, at which one of Loring's parishioners was killed. Loring, never in robust health, helped chase the attackers and was greatly admired by the townsfolk.[6] The First Church in North Yarmouth grew under his tenure. "A good degree of success attended his ministry. One hundred and fifty-eight members were received into the church, and the congregation steadily increased."[7] Of Loring it was stated, "He was faithful in administering discipline, kind and affectionate in spirit, and dwelt in great harmony with his people through his whole ministry of twenty-seven years, dying July 21, 1763, aged 52 years."[8] Loring was a New Light Calvinist. "Of his Christian experience and theological soundness, there is no room for doubts . . . His answer to their call, breathed forth a spirit of true spiritual life. The stand he took regarding the Great Awakening, and his eagerness to introduce Rev. George Whitefield to his people . . . are indicative of his decided position in that day."[9]

A sketch of Rev. Thomas Smith. Source: Journal of the Rev. Thomas Smith.

Rev. Benjamin Allen arrived in the Cape Elizabeth community of Falmouth, Maine in 1734. The church was established in 1733, and Allen was their first minister. Falmouth was then much larger that it is now, the original town being divided over the years into several townships. In anticipation of having their own minister, the community built a new meeting house for Allen in 1734, called the Second Parish Church of Christ in Falmouth. The building featured hand-hewn white oak timbers, two tiers of windows, galleries on three sides, and square box pews, and was the central structure in the village.[10] Their relations

---

5 Thomas Smith, *Journal of the Rev. Thomas Smith*, (Portland, ME: Joseph E. Bailey Printer, 1849), p. 13.
6 *Old Times in North Yarmouth, Maine*, vol. 6. No. 3 (July 1882), pp. 878-879.
7 Ibid., p. 879.
8 Ibid.
9 Ibid., pp. 878-879.
10 "First Congregational Church-history," http://fccucc.org/about/history. There were "great crowds" and there was "great opposition" experienced within the Maine churches at that time. See William Willis, *The History of Portland, from 1632 to 1864 . . .*, (Portland, ME: Bailey & Noyes Printers, 1865), p. 393.

with the First Church in Falmouth, under Rev. Thomas Smith, were excellent. Benjamin Allen was born in Tisbury, on the Massachusetts island of Martha's Vineyard. He was a Yale College graduate in 1708. He served as a minister in Bridgewater, Massachusetts from 1718 to 1728. Allen came to the Falmouth area in 1734, serving here until his death. He and his church folks were of a Presbyterian bent, as the community was settled by immigrants of the Scotch-Irish background.[11] Allen was an open supporter of the revival and defended Whitefield, allowing the itinerant preacher frequent access to his pulpit at the Second Church of Christ in Falmouth.

Whitefield's ministry in far eastern Maine has been mostly overlooked by his biographers. In 1900, J.P. Gledstone wrote a biography of Whitefield in which he had to concede that little detailed information was available about his itinerant travels in northern New England. Gledstone wrote, "The stay among his New England friends was more prolonged than usual. Upon the renewal of his journeys his course is not easily traced."[12] In Arnold Dallimore's two volume 1980 biography of Whitefield, he summarized the 1744-1745 ministry of Whitefield in New England in general terms, as follows: "Whitefield's stay in New England lasted nine months. During that time, in labours that saw him repeatedly taking the Gospel throughout its territory, he accomplished much of the purpose that had brought him there."[13]

In 1740, Whitefield spoke in York, but did not travel farther east into rural Maine. Nevertheless, his influence over the next few years permeated throughout these remote northeastern regions. When New England ministers met in Boston in July 1743 to discuss Whitefield and the awakening, several ministers from rural Maine were present or later signed their endorsement of the *Testimony*.[14] In 1744, Whitefield returned to America, arriving in York, Maine, causing celebration and concern throughout Maine churches. Churches and ministers debated whether they could support Whitefield, but theoretical debates became real when the itinerant preacher arrived in eastern Maine in March 1745. Clergy and congregations were forced to choose sides in the Whitefield controversy. Whitefield experienced great crowds as he preached in rural Maine. Some came to hear out of curiosity, others came from boredom, while many were deeply moved by his preaching and were outward supporters of the awakening. "And notwithstanding great opposition, the crowds which flocked to hear him were as large in proportion to the population as in other parts of the country."[15] But much of the antagonism, the rivalries, and the rapid influx of new members into churches had passed. By 1745, the revival wave had crested and past over remote eastern Maine. For example, in the First Church Congregational, under Rev. Thomas Smith in Falmouth, there were forty-eight admissions to the church in 1742, but only two new members after Whitefield's visit in 1745.[16]

It is fortunate that the diary of Rev. Thomas Smith of Falmouth has survived. Five years before the Whitefield visit of 1745, Smith addressed the Whitefield phenomena to his congregation. On October 5, 1740 Smith wrote, "I preached extempore A.M. about Mr. Whitefield." Smith supported the Great Awakening, even though he had not yet met Whitefield. Almost fifteen months later, on January 2, 1742 Smith was in the Portsmouth, New Hampshire area (Piscataqua) where he saw the results of the Great Awakening, recording, "I have been to observe and affect myself with the great work of God's grace." A few weeks later, Smith wrote

---

11 William Willis, *The History of Portland, from 1632 to 1864* . . . , (Portland. ME: Bailey & Noyes Printers, 1865), p. 383.
12 J.P. Gledstone, *George Whitefield: Supreme among Preachers*, (1900: reprinted by Ambassador Productions, Belfast, Ireland: 1998), p. 235.
13 Arnol Dallimore, *George Whitefield: The Life and Times of the Great Evangelist of the Eighteenth Century Revival*, (Carlisle, PA: Banner of Truth Trust, 1980), vol. II, p. 203.
14 *The Testimony and Advice of an Assembly of Pastors of Churches in New England* . . . The Maine ministers who signed the 1743 Testimony were Thomas Smith of Falmouth; Benjamin Allen of Falmouth, William Thompson of Scarborough, Samuel Jefferds of Wells, Nicholas Loring of North Yarmouth, John Hovey of Arundel, Moses Morrill of Biddeford, Samuel Moody of York, Samuel Chandler of York, and John Rogers of Kittery.
15 William Willis, *The History of Portland, from 1632 to 1864* . . . , p. 393.
16 Ibid., pp. 395-396.

of the revival in his hometown of Falmouth, Maine, stating on January 31 that he observed "The blessedest Sabbath Falmouth ever saw."[17]

With the spread of revival in eastern Maine came critics of the awakening. On January 23, 1743 Rev. Smith recorded in his *Journal*, "I have been in a poor, distracted frame, this and the preceding Sabbaths; lost all courage and ready to give up." Dissention and disunity in the church caused Pastor Smith great heartache. This ecclesiastical turmoil lasted a few years, creating havoc in tiny, coastal Falmouth. On October 31, 1744, Smith wrote that select leaders in the church "are like to be in a flame on account of Mr. Whitefield coming; the leading men violently opposing."[18]

Thomas Smith was careful to note his interactions with George Whitefield in the late winter/early spring of 1745. Excerpts are as follows.[19]

> January 24. Great and prevailing clamors every where against Mr. Whitefield.
>
> February 13. Minister's meeting related to Mr. Whitefield . . . had much uneasiness.
>
> March 19. We hear that Mr. Whitefield who was today at Biddeford, has got to Dunton.
>
> March 20. Mr. Whitefield having preached at Dunton [Dunstan] yesterday, and to day went back to Biddeford, but Mr. Loring and Mr. Allen sent letters with messengers, which brought him back.
>
> March 21. Mr. Whitefield preached A.M. at Biddeford, and returned to Scarborough and preached P.M. for Mr. Thompson.
>
> March 22. Mr. Whitefield preached A.M. for Mr. Thompson, and P.M. for Mr. Allen. I was over at Presumpscot; Messrs. Whitefield, Wise, and Rogers lodged at my house.
>
> March 23. Mr. Whitefield preached in my pulpit, A.M. Multitudes flocking from Purpoodock and elsewhere.
>
> March 24. Sunday. Mr. Wise preached to my people. Mr. Whitefield preached at North Yarmouth all day.
>
> March 25. We came home with eighteen persons who dined with me. Mr. Whitefield preached here P.M. to a great congregation.
>
> March 26. I heard Mr. Whitefield A.M. at Mr. Allen's and P.M. at Mr. Thompsons.

In his *Journal*, Thomas Smith of Falmouth, Maine records a sigh of relief, that those who opposed Whitefield and the revival were not in town when the itinerant preacher arrived. He wrote, "The wonderful providence of God is to be observed with respect to Mr. Whitefield, that Messrs. Loring and Thompson should come just as they did, and that Mr. Whitefield should come as he did, when . . . others were all gone out of town, so that there was no uneasiness; but all went well, and general reception. Thanks to God."[20]

---

17   Thomas Smith, *Journal of Rev. Thomas Smith*, pp. 95, 102.
18   Ibid., pp. 104, 114, 116.
19   Ibid., pp. 116-119.
20   Thomas Smith, *Journal of Rev. Thomas Smith*, p. 119.

A few days later, one of the anti-revival men in the Falmouth church returned. Smith wrote in his *Journal*, "April 2. Mr. Waite returned so that the parish is in a buzz about Mr. Whitefield."

Using the *Journal* of Rev. Thomas Smith of Falmouth, we can trace Whitefield's activities and his preaching schedule in rural eastern Maine. Whitefield departed the Kittery and Berwick, Maine area in mid-March 1745, arriving at Biddeford a few days later. This northeast route was a well-travelled, winding, one-lane dirt coastal road with stops in small towns along the way into remote Maine. Numerous small ferries transported people over the tidal rivers and estuaries. On March 19, Smith wrote that Whitefield was in Biddeford and Dunstan. Biddeford, Maine was incorporated as a town in 1653. The key to the community was the Saco River, which facilitated transportation for the lumbering industry, provided abundant fresh water, and the fishing was excellent. Small family saw mills and grist mills were powered by brooks that led into the Saco River. There were small groups of Quakers and a few Episcopalians in the area, but the minister in Biddeford that greeted Whitefield was Rev. Moses Merrill.

Born in Salisbury, Massachusetts in 1719 in a sea captain's home, Moses Merrill was a Harvard College graduate in 1737, earning a master's degree in 1740. He settled in Biddeford in 1742. Shortly thereafter he married. He and his wife had thirteen children, and the family was a pillar in the community. Merrill maintained a day school for his own children and others in Biddeford, as he served as the pastor of the First Church in Biddeford from 1743 until his death in 1778. He served two-thirds of his time in Biddeford and one-third of his time in Pepperellboro, now Saco, at the First Church of Christ in Saco, Maine.[21] A thoroughgoing evangelical, Merrill led his congregation in Biddeford to introduce the hymnal by Isaac Watts into worship services. He signed the 1743 *Testimony* in support of Whitefield and "He was an enjoyed and evangelical preacher" who openly supported and defended Whitefield against his many critics.[22] Thomas Smith's *Journal*, quoted above, states that Whitefield preached for Moses Merrill in and around Biddeford from March 19 to 21, 1745. One historian stated,

> About the time of Mr. Morrill's settlement [1742], there was a great religious excitement throughout New England, occasioned by the preaching of the celebrated Whitefield, many clergymen favoring, and others opposing, the somewhat irregular effects produced by it. Mr. Morrill was of the former class. Whitefield came into this quarter towards the close of 1744; we heard of him in Biddeford early the following year. In March [1745], he preached several times for Mr. Morrill, and the neighboring towns.[23]

Returning to the Rev. Thomas Smith *Journal*, on March 19 and 20, 1745 Smith wrote that Whitefield was in Dunton, Maine. This village was a tiny community within the larger town of Scarborough. Dunton [Dunstan] no longer exists, having been absorbed by Scarborough. Although Smith does not mention him by name, the minister in Dunton in 1745 was Rev. Richard Elvins.

Born in Salem, Massachusetts about 1710, Richard Elvins was employed in Salem in his family's baking business. When Whitefield came to Salem in 1740, the thirty-year-old Elvins was converted and called into the ministry. Being too old for formal divinity studies according to the custom of the day, Elvins worked in the family business by day and began an intense self-study program in preparation for ordination. "He possessed a sound mind, evangelical sentiments, and preaching talents . . . he betook himself to a course of reading and theological study . . . and, in less than four years, he was licensed to preach."[24] One account stated,

---

21 "Second Congregational Church," www.secondcongbiddeford.org/history.
22 William D. Williamson, "Sketches of the Lives of Early Maine Ministers," *Maine Historical Society*, (Portland, ME: Maine Historical Society, 1894), second series, vol. v, p. 212.
23 George Folsom, *History of Saco and Biddeford; with Notices of other Early Settlements . . .* , (Saco, ME: Alex C. Putnam Printer, 1830), p. 237.
24 William D. Williamson, "Sketches of the Lives of Early Maine Ministers," p. 323.

"Nov. 7 [1744]. Richard Elvins is ordained over Second Church in Scarborough. He had been a baker by trade . . . He became pious through the preaching of Mr. Whitefield. He possessed good understanding and was a useful minister."[25] Shortly after arriving in the Dunstan village of Scarborough, Elvins married the widow of the former pastor, and resided in the village until his death in 1776. As did his mentor George Whitefield, Richard Elvins "did not preach from notes but extempore, being gifted in speech."[26] As the first minister of the Second Church in Scarborough, Dunstan village, Elvins began his ministry in a tumultuous period of theological divisions. Yet Elvins had a clear, steady theological position. He supported the awakening and he publically endorsed Whitefield, allowing the itinerant to preach in his small meeting house in Dunstan with great affect.

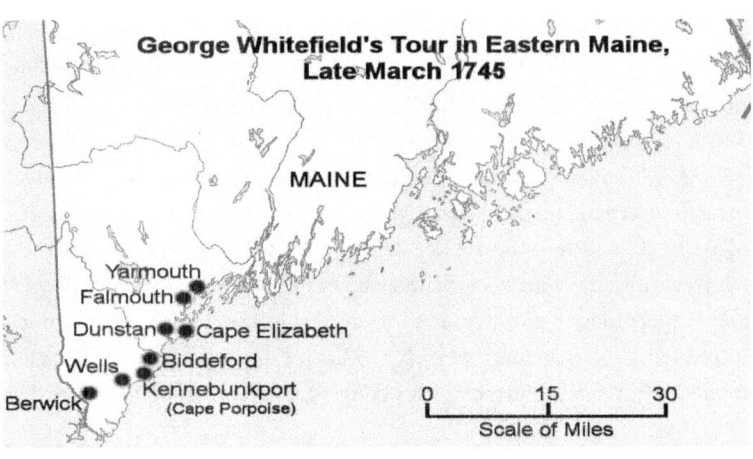

The next clergyman mentioned in Smith's *Journal* who supported Whitefield was Rev. William Tompson of Scarborough. Smith wrote that Whitefield preached for Tompson in Scarborough in the morning of March 22, and in the afternoon or evening on March 26, 1745. Scarborough is located just north of Biddeford. The first Europeans came to this area in 1630, but due to constant Indian attacks and other hardships, the community did not grow quickly, and was permanently resettled in 1714. The region was known for its expansive tidal salt marsh which produced salt hay for agriculture and exposed massive and productive clam beds at low tide. Fish abounded in the three fingers of the Monesuch River. British and New England settlers in Scarborough were active in exporting lumber, fish, and cattle. Small saw mills and grist mills were active, as was a fledgling shipbuilding industry. The First Church (Congregational) was founded in 1728, with Rev. William Tompson as minister.

William Tompson was born in Marshfield, Massachusetts in 1697. A Harvard College graduate in 1718, he settled in Scarborough in 1728, and served this rural maritime community until his death in 1759. In 1732, the town voted to build William and Anna Tompson a parsonage, where they could live and raise their sheep, cows, and chickens. They had a Negro hired hand to assist with the chores on their small farm. Tompson preached to villagers on both sides of the great marsh, at Black Point on the eastern side, and at Dunton, until Dunton called Rev. Richard Elvins to be their dedicated minister. Of Tompson it was stated, "His soul was baptized with the spirit of the gospel; a peacemaker, a sound minister, and a most excellent man."[27] Tompson signed the 1743 *Testimony* in support of Whitefield and the awakening. When Whitefield arrived in Scarborough, Maine, Tompson was forty-eight years old, with a wife and three young adult children. "He was held in high esteem by his townsmen," and upon his death in 1759 he was "sincerely lamented by the whole community."[28] The Tompson home appears to have been a place of domestic tranquility. The

---

25   Joseph B. Felt, *Annals of Salem*, (Salem, MA: W & S.B. Ives Printer, 1849), p. 427.
26   Leonard B. Chapman, *Monograph on the Southgate Family of Scarborough*, Maine . . . , (Portland, ME: Hubbard W. Bryant, Publisher, 1907), p. 5.
27   William D. Williamson, "Sketches of the Lives of Early Maine Ministers," *Maine Historical Society*, (Portland, ME: Maine Historical Society, 1893), vol. iv, p. 327.
28   Gideon T. Ridlon, *Saco Valley Settlements and Families; Historical, Biographical* . . . , (Portland, ME: Published by the Author, 1895), vol. II, p. 1175.

three children, two sons and a daughter, were all well-educated. The boys became prominent in legal and ministerial vocations. "Mr. Tompson built his house a short distance above the new church, and there he and his wife Anna reared their children . . . The Reverend Tompson invited the Reverend Whitefield and Parson Smith to stay with him and his wife. Mrs. Tompson was happiest when serving others."[29]

As Whitefield travelled along rural, coastal Maine, he had traveling companions. As he began his preaching circuit to far eastern Maine, he wrote that Revs. James Pike of Somersworth, Jeremiah Wise of Berwick, and John Rogers of Kittery, all of Maine, travelled with him. In the above referenced *Journal* by Rev. Thomas Smith of Falmouth, Smith wrote on March 22, 1745 that "Messrs. Whitefield, Wise, and Rogers lodged at my house." As a local guide, Smith also accompanied Whitefield and his entourage, introducing the traveling evangelist to his local ministerial friends. There were also occasions where Smith invited Whitefield to preach to his congregation in Falmouth. In his *Journal*, Smith noted,

> March 23. Mr. Whitefield preached in my pulpit, A.M. Multitudes flocking from Purpoodock and elsewhere.

> March 25. We came home with eighteen persons who dined with me. Mr. Whitefield preached here P.M. to a great congregation.[30]

The blistering cold and driving winds, so common in coastal Maine in March, did not prevent Whitefield from traveling and preaching regularly. In a community where people literally could freeze to death in winter, or starve to death throughout the long winter months, Whitefield preached and travelled relentlessly. There were no good roads such as he enjoyed around Portsmouth and Boston. Instead, people traveled on narrow, winding paths just wide enough for a horse and wagon or sled. The cold, snow, and ice were constant traveling hazards. A narrative of Whitefield's winter travels in New Hampshire and Maine appeared in the *Boston Gazette*, dated April 2, 1745. This narrative lists Whitefield's ministerial supporters in Maine. Those already mentioned above are Reverends Smith, Loring, Allen, Thompson, Elvin (Elvins) and Morrel (Merrill). Two ministers not already named are Reverends Hovey and Jeffries (Jefferds). The newspaper narrative stated that Whitefield preached, "once for the Rev. Mr. Hovey of Cape-Porpus, and twice for the Rev. Mr. Jeffries of Wells."[31] These two men deserve further study.

John Hovey was born in Cambridge, Massachusetts and graduated from Harvard College in 1725. He arrived in 1740 to the community of Cape-Porpus, now Cape Porpoise, which is today a part of Kennebunkport. This was a poor, maritime community. People subsisted from fishing, lumbering, and whatever farming they could scrape up out of the rocky soil. Hovey was ordained here as the Congregational minister in 1741.[32] Hovey declined a professorship at Harvard to become a frontier missionary in Maine. Being the most educated person in the community, Hovey wrote all the legal and contractual documents for the town.

Hovey served here until his dismissal in 1768, and his tenure was somewhat disruptive. The community was in a constant state of unsettledness, as the threats from Indians, the depreciation of money, the high mortality rate of fishermen, and the constant migration of people in-and-out of the community made life as the parish minister difficult. Added to this was the Whitefield controversies. For several years the New Light verses Old Light conflicts in other parts of New England did not reach Cape Porpus. But in 1745, Whitefield appeared in town. Hovey allowed Whitefield to preach from the pulpit of the Congregational Church. The tranquility Hovey enjoyed in Cape Porpus soon passed. Theological differences appeared among the people

---

29 Dorothy S. Libbey, *Scarborough becomes a Town*, (Scarborough, ME: B. Wheelright Company, 1955), p. 56.
30 Thomas Smith, *Journal of Rev. Thomas Smith*, p. 119.
31 *Boston Gazette*, April 2, 1745, p. 3.
32 Charles Bradbury, *History of Kennebunkport, from its First Discovery*, (Kennebunkport, ME: James K. Remich, Printer, 1837), p. 141.

of this small community. Masked as disputes over the minister's salary, or over the distance folks had to walk to church services, the community fragmented theologically. Some people were quite happy to have the famous Whitefield preach in the tiny Congregational meeting house, but others objected. Years of tension between Hovey and his community resulted in his dismissal or resignation as minister in 1768.[33]

Another minister not previously mentioned, for whom Whitefield preached in coastal Wells, Maine, was Rev. Samuel Jefferds. Founded in 1622, Wells was settled by people from New Hampshire, Massachusetts, and Great Britain. This oceanfront community made its living from the sea, as men worked in the fisheries, in trade, and in shipping. Others worked in lumbering and farming. Only a few miles from the sea, the land supported fields for orchards and pastures for livestock. The tidal mudflats produced abundant clams. Several small rivers powered family businesses such as saw mills and grist mills. Born in Salem, Massachusetts in 1702, Samuel Jefferds graduated Harvard College in 1722 and began at the Congregational Church in Wells in 1725. At that time, Wells was a frontier community still fearful of French privateers at sea and Indian raids from land. One source stated, "Mr. Jefferds, the settled minister, was very popular."[34] He was described as one "endowed with but ordinary intellectual powers" and "appears to have been a very acceptable minister, quietly pursuing his pastoral duties."[35] In March 1745, Samuel Jefferds met George Whitefield in Wells and asked the itinerant evangelist to preach to his working-class congregation. There was not great tumult in Wells over the Great Awakening or the visit of the esteemed Whitefield, as most in the area endorsed the revival. What did alarm Jefferds and his congregation were the poor copycats, the bombastic, untrained, and belligerent traveling preachers that taught the Bible poorly and harangued the clergy and the people.[36]

Jefferds supported the awakening and sought to spread the revival in his community, with mixed results. One account remarked, "Mr. Jefferds sustained the revival, though with much misgiving as to the danger in which the order of the gospel was involved. It does not seem to have reached Wells. The excitement died away without any additions to the church."[37] Another source stated that while there was no surge in church attendance, the congregation under Jefferds was known as an evangelically-minded group. Specifically, "Rev. Samuel Jefferds, a graduate of Harvard in 1722, and a spiritual teacher, who in the course of his professional labors and untiring zeal, through a period of twenty-six years, had the high satisfaction of witnessing the repeated effusion of divine influences, upon the people of his charge."[38]

Whitefield's most northern excursion into rural Maine was a success. Far from the tens-of-thousands that heard him preach in Boston, or the several thousand that heard him preach in Portsmouth, here in coastal Maine his congregations were in the dozens or perhaps the low hundreds. There was no local news publications, as the first newspaper in Maine was the *Falmouth Gazette* in 1785. In contrast to the urban crowds that listened to Whitefield speak in larger cities, these rural Maine residents attended religious services in working clothes, or in the best clothing they owned, which was not much.

The exact date in late March or early April 1745, when Whitefield departed Maine and re-entered New Hampshire, is unclear. The *Boston Gazette*, dated April 2, 1745, stated that Whitefield arrived in Boston a few days earlier. The next chapter will trace Whitefield's steps south from Maine into New Hampshire and Massachusetts.

---

33 *Collections and Proceedings of the Maine Historical Society*, (Portland, ME: Published by the Society), vol. iv, p. 423.
34 Edward E. Bourne, *A History of Wells and Kennebunkport from the Earliest Settlement to the Year 1820*, (Portland, ME: B. Thurston Company, 1875), p. 347.
35 Ibid., pp. 359, 361.
36 Ibid., p. 363.
37 Ibid., p. 364.
38 William D. Williamson, *The History of the State of Maine . . .* , (Hallowell, ME: Glazier, Masters, and Company, 1832), vol. II, p. 80.p.

CHAPTER 19

WHITEFIELD'S TOUR IN NEW HAMPSHIRE, NORTHERN MASSACHUSETTS, AND BOSTON

SPRING 1745

WHITEFIELD DEPARTED MAINE SOMETIME IN late March 1745. For the next several weeks it becomes difficult to exactly trace his steps. After ministering in rural coastal Maine, he headed south into the farmlands of inland New Hampshire. In the mid-1740s, this was the frontier. There was limited population in these pioneer settlements. There were no local newspapers. His preaching appointments were in agricultural communities, in open fields, in barns, or in the small wooden meeting houses that dotted the rural northern New England communities. Many settlers lived virtually hand-to-mouth, scraping out an existence and building communities out of the wilderness. Some anecdotal accounts of Whitefield's ministry in New Hampshire in the spring of 1745 have survived.

Londonderry, New Hampshire was carved out of the wilderness by devout Scots-Irish settlers in 1718. Many of these pioneers arrived in the New World because of religious persecution, their strict Presbyterianism ridiculed by the prevailing Roman Catholicism in Ireland. Londonderry was chartered in 1722. The farmlands were excellent, and the fishing thrived from three brooks that ran into the nearby Merrimack River. The first Presbyterian Church in America was founded in 1723 in Londonderry, New Hampshire. In the 1730s, as more-and-more settlers arrived, the Presbyterian Church thrived, and was the focal point of the community. Their custom was to celebrate communion twice per year. These occasions were three-day events, with extra preaching sessions and prayer meetings to prepare the people for receiving the sacrament of communion. In 1734, there were seven hundred participants approved for communion, coming from within Londonderry and numerous surrounding communities.[1]

In 1739, Londonderry created a second Presbyterian Church, to accommodate the increased population and to minimize travel for the congregants. Whitefield did not preach in Londonderry during his 1740 New England tour. But his influence in the area was clearly felt in Londonderry. One of the ministers in Londonderry, a Presbyterian named Rev. David McGregor (also MacGregor), became a firm Whitefield advocate.[2] As an illustration, in November 1741, McGregor was a guest speaker at the very pro-Whitefield Brattle Street Church in Boston. In his sermon titled, "The Spirits of the Present Day Tried," McGregor

---

1 Edward E. Parker, *The History of Londonderry, Comprising the Towns of Londonderry and Derry, New Hampshire*, (Boston, MA: Perkins & Whipple Publishers, 1851), p. 142.
2 David McGregor (1710-1777) was the son of the founding minister in Londonderry, Rev. James McGregor, who died in 1729. Due to the ministerial tensions in Londonderry, in 1745 Rev. David McGregor changed his presbytery to the newly formed Boston presbytery, while remaining at the church in Londonderry. McGregor took ministerial students into his home, and openly associated with other New Lights in New England. See Alexander Blaikie, *A History of Presbyterianism in New England . . .*, (Boston, MA: Alexander Moore, Publisher), 1881, p. 133. Frederick W. Loetsher, "Presbyterianism in Colonial New England," *Journal of the Presbyterian Historical Society, Vol. XI*, No. 3-4 (September/October 1921), pp. 102-106.

advocated for the ministry of George Whitefield, calling him "an eminent follower of Christ," and one who experienced "prodigious fatigue of body and mind" in his itinerant travels. McGregor stated that Whitefield's evangelistic appeals were "very consistent with modesty and truth," and that Whitefield was "a messenger of God." After speaking of the societal changes from the awakening, such as less swearing, drunkenness, and covetousness, McGregor also noticed the increase in Bible reading, the peacefulness of the people, and the improvement in prayer. McGregor wrote of Whitefield's opponents as "under the malignant influence of such a woeful prejudice, as to imagine that these and many other desirable effects are the work of the Devil? It is my hope, and shall be my prayer that God will remove your prejudices."[3]

When George Whitefield arrived in Londonderry in the spring of 1745, he was greeted by the town's two ministers, Rev. William Davidson of the older East Parish Church, and Rev. David McGregor of the newer West Parish Church. Whitefield first preached in Londonderry in early March 1745, on his roving itinerant tour, with remarkable results. A few weeks later he was back in the Londonderry area, now surrounded by controversy.

A photograph of the Rev. David MacGregor's home, the parsonage for the Congregational Church of the West Parish, Londonderry, NH. This house was built c.1735 and was torn down in 2006. Photograph by William Gorman.

Both Davidson and McGregor earned a theological education and were properly ordained Presbyterian clergy. But they were quite different men theologically. While Davidson and McGregor both claimed to adhere to traditional Protestant doctrines from the Reformation, Davidson was more open-minded theologically. He was a stickler for formality and ceremony, while somewhat of a freethinker in his doctrine. In contrast, McGregor of the West Parish Church was considered a better preacher and more evangelical that Davidson.[4] McGregor visited Boston in the early 1740s to see for himself the results of the Great Awakening. He was impressed, and he determined to seek a religious revival in Londonderry. In contrast, Davidson at the East Parish Church was not interested in the revival movement coming to Londonderry. Tension between the two ministers in Londonderry was inevitable. Speaking of the Great Awakening:

> During this period, the Rev. David MacGregor visited Boston and some other places favored with the divine manifestations, and having witnessed most striking displays of divine grace, in the hopeful conversion of multitudes, he returned to his people greatly enlivened and deeply impressed with the subject of a revival among his own charge. He accordingly delivered a series of very impressive discourses from Ephesians 5:14, "Awake! Thou that sleepest, and arise from the dead, and Christ will give thee light." The word, thus solemnly and pungently preached, was blessed as the means of awakening many of his people to a deep conviction of their guilt

---

3   William M. Gorman, editor, *The Works of Rev. David McGregor (MacGregore)*, 1710-1770, (Westminster, MD: Heritage Books, 2009), pp. 20-21.
4   Edward E. Parker, *The History of Londonderry*, p. 148.

and danger, and led to their hopeful conversion to God. Meetings for religious conference and prayer were frequent. The work extended to all classes, embracing more particularly the young, and a happy edition was made to the church. But while one flock in the town was, like Gideon's fleece, thus watered with the dews of heaven, the other remained dry. Mr. Davidson and his church stood aloof from all participation in the work, and rather deprecated its approach. During this season of religious attention, the celebrated Whitefield visited the town, and preached to a very large collection of people in the open field, the meeting-house not being sufficiently large to accommodate the multitude assembled . . . Unhappily, Mr. Davidson dissented from such evangelical views, opposed the religious movements of the day, and, as the consequence, shared not in the refreshing influences which descended copiously upon sister churches and congregations.[5]

Speaking of Rev. David McGregor of Londonderry, "His ministry was eminently evangelistic. He preached and labored for the salvation of his people. Sympathizing with the great evangelist, George Whitefield, he invited him to his pulpit; and his own fervid preaching and prayers were rewarded with revivals of religion."[6]

Londonderry was deeply divided by Whitefield and the awakening. For decades, Sunday morning tensions in the town existed, as rival Presbyterian congregants passed each other's meeting house to attend divine services in the East Parish or West Parish churches.[7] When Whitefield preached in Londonderry in 1745, members of both rival churches attended, as well as those few irreligious in the community. Londonderry was one of many New England towns deeply divided over Whitefield's methods and preaching.[8]

Another anecdotal account of Whitefield's influence, in New Hampshire in the spring of 1745, comes from the town of Nashua. Originally part of the Massachusetts town of Dunstable, Nashua became an independent town and part of New Hampshire in 1741, and was incorporated in 1746. Located at the confluence of the Nashua River and the larger Merrimack River, the community of Dunstable-Nashua was slow to develop and prosper. In the 1740s, Whitefield's teachings and methodology deeply divided Nashua. Shortly after Whitefield left the area in 1745, the First Congregational Church in Nashua called Rev. Samuel Bird in 1746 to be their new minister. Bird was an avowed follower of Whitefield and was happily identified as a New Light. The Whitefield phenomena in New Hampshire caused a surge in attendance at the Congregational Church, but not all the townsfolk in Nashua were happy. A new meeting house was constructed, but many in Nashua were not willing to pay the additional taxes necessary to support a New Light meeting house and minister.[9] One Nashua historian stated:

> There were many people in Dunstable [Nashua] that did not believe in Mr. Bird's preaching and who would not help to build him a church, so Jonathan Lovewell and a few other citizens built a church and paid for it themselves. This was called the Bird Meeting house. A few years later the people who did not believe in the "New Lights" were able to outvote the others and accordingly Mr. Bird was without a church and Jonathan Lovewell had a meeting house on his hands. Lovewell then bought the shares belonging to his friends and turned the meeting house into a dwelling . . . It is probably the only meeting house in the United States that was built directly for a follower of George Whitefield . . .[10]

---

5   Ibid., pp. 150-151
6   George F. Willey, *Willey's Book of Nutfield: A History* . . . , (Derry Depot, NH: George F. Willey Publisher, 1895), p. 139.
7   Edward E. Parker, *The History of Londonderry*, p. 148.
8   Harold W. Rose, *The Colonial Houses of Worship in America*, (New York: Hastings House Publishers, 1963), p. 248.
9   Edward E. Parker, *History of the City of Nashua, New Hampshire, from the Earliest Settlement of old Dunstable to the Year 1895* . . . , (Nashua, NH: Telegraph Publishing Company, 1897), p. 44.
10 James H. Fassett, *Early History of Nashua, New Hampshire* . . . , (Nashua, NH: Telegraph Publishing Company, 1915), p. 56.

Voted out of his own meeting house in 1751, Samuel Bird moved to New Haven, Connecticut where he continued as a Congregational minister. With Bird's departure the fledgling revival in Nashua abated, and the Congregational Church in Nashua had no settled minister until 1767.

One location where Whitefield was always welcomed was Newbury, Massachusetts. A senior minister in the Newbury community, that would later become Newburyport, was Rev. John Lowell. A Harvard graduate in 1721, Lowell initially was curious about Whitefield and allowed him to preach on October 4, 1740 in the meeting house. By the time Whitefield revisited Newbury in 1745, well over one hundred new members were added to Lowell's church as a result of the revival. "Mr. Lowell, usually most liberal, invited him to preach in the meeting house. The invitation was never repeated, although, owing to Whitefield's flaming eloquence one hundred and forty-three souls were added to the parish list of communicants."[11] It is significant to note that, even though there was a dramatic numerical increase in church members, an invitation from Lowell to Whitefield "was never repeated." Lowell served at the Newburyport church until 1767, meaning he had the chance to invite Whitefield back to preach numerous times, but he never did so. The Newburyport historian Minnie Atkinson speaks despairingly of Whitefield as a "zealot" and an "agitator." She wrote, "One famous zealot came to the village who was duly authorized to preach. This was the English evangelist, the Rev. George Whitefield. He was the foremost agitator in the so-called Great Awakening." She then mockingly states that Whitefield "preached in barns."[12] Lowell's non-support of Whitefield created a church split, the separate group eventually becoming the Old South Presbyterian Church, led by Whitefield's friend Rev. Jonathan Parsons.

Disturbing the awakening in northern Massachusetts was an eccentric man named Richard Woodberry from Rowley. In the summer of 1744, Woodberry, through his conversion, stated that he had achieved sinless perfection and physical immortality. He believed he had Christ-like powers to save or damn and travelled throughout the area in bombastic rants with "blasphemous and absurd speeches."[13]

As previously stated, it is impossible to trace George Whitefield's daily activities during his spring 1745, tour throughout rural northern New England. He no longer kept a journal and local newspapers did not yet exist. However, some reports have survived that give us glimpses into his ministry activities. We have already looked at several accounts of Whitefield's preaching and influence in New Hampshire. Some anecdotes also exist from his northern Massachusetts ministry in early 1745.

Whitefield visited Haverhill, Massachusetts in the spring of 1745. His first visit was in the fall of 1744, and he was not allowed to preach in the town. A few months later he returned, in early in 1745, to an antagonistic reception from the clergy.

Located on the Merrimack River, Haverhill was founded as a Puritan farming community in 1642, as energetic families cleared the forest and built their homes and farms. The community grew slowly. Mills for grist and saw mills were active industries. Farming, lumbering, the cattle industry, leather tanneries, and fishing were the common occupations. In the 1730s an epidemic swept through the growing community, killing over two hundred and fifty children. Shipbuilding connected this rural town to larger coastal communities. Congregationalism was the only established religion of the people.

When George Whitefield arrived in Haverhill in the 1740s, the three prominent ministers in Haverhill were all avowed Congregationalist. They were Rev. Edward Barnard of the First Parish; Rev. James Cushing of the North Parish; and Rev. Samuel Bachellor of the West Parish. All three men were Harvard trained ministers and all were, according to traditional Protestant Reformed Theology, of suspect orthodoxy. Rev. Barnard

---

11   Minnie Atkinson, *A History of the First Religious Society in Newburyport, Massachusetts*, (Newburyport, MA: News Publishing Company, 1933), p. 22.
12   Ibid.
13   Douglas L. Winiarski, *Darkness Falls on the Land of Light: Experiencing Religious Awakenings in Eighteenth-Century New England*. (Chapel Hill, NC: University of North Carolina Press, 2017), p. 311.

began his ministry at the First Church in 1743. He was identified as an "Arminian," meaning he did not accept historic Calvinism. He was described as a good speaker who "gradually departed from the Calvinistic system," and as a clergyman who did not insist on Trinitarianism.[14] Rev. Cushing of the North Parish served in Haverhill from about 1730 to his death in 1764. He was a stickler for formality and orderliness. In his congregation there was "no revival of religion," but rather there was "the most unruffled tranquility, peace and harmony, in his society."[15] Rev. Bachellor served the West Parish from its founding in 1734-35 to his dismissal for heresy in 1755. His accusations of heresy appear to have been based as much on doctrinal disputes as financial considerations.[16] These three ministers refused to allow Whitefield to preach from their pulpits in 1744 and again in 1745. The following account speaks of religion in Haverhill and Whitefield's visits to that town.

> Revivalism and revival preaching were discouraged. It is well known that when George Whitefield first came to New England [1740], there was a great difference of opinion as to the treatment which ought to be accorded to him. His wonderful eloquence was regarded by some as sensational and disorganizing. The conversions which occurred under his preaching they denounced as unreliable; they wanted nothing of the Great Awakening. There were many pulpits to which he was not admitted. Some clergymen welcomed him gladly and rejoiced in his wonderful work. Tradition tells us that Whitefield came twice to Haverhill . . . On the first occasion he did not preach in town at all, there being an indisposition to allowing him to preach in the meeting house. On the second visit he preached to a great congregation in the open air . . . The authorities of the town (so the story runs) sent him a warning to depart out of town. Instead of complying with their request, he read the letter at the close of his afternoon discourse, and observing, "Poor souls! They need another sermon," proceeded to give notice that he should preach at the same place at sunrise the next morning. He kept his word and addressed a large audience. The people who had been moved by Whitefield were not afraid of being called Separatists, or New Lights, or Anabaptists. Some of them happened to be among the most respected and wealthy people of the town.[17]

The pro-Whitefield folks from Haverhill could not convince their Congregational ministers, Barnard, Cushing, or Bachellor, to preach evangelistic messages or teach Calvinistic doctrines. For twenty years after Whitefield departed Haverhill in 1745, evangelical Calvinists laymen continued to meet within the Congregational churches, dissatisfied with their ministers. Then in 1765, the pro-revival people in Haverhill mostly departed their Congregational churches and helped form the first Baptist Church in Haverhill in 1765. The Baptist minister, Rev. Hezekiah Smith, was a firm advocate of Whitefield and the awakening.[18] The evangelical Congregationalists largely departed their Haverhill churches and were rebaptized by Smith to become what we would call today Reformed or Calvinistic Baptists, these townsfolk being composed of "prominent men in the town of Haverhill."[19]

It was probably in early April 1745, that Whitefield was in Haverhill. Although he preached many more times over the coming decades around the vicinity of Haverhill, there is no record of him ever again visiting this town. About fifteen miles from Haverhill is the town of Ipswich. Whitefield frequently visited Ipswich,

---

14 George W. Chase, *The History of Haverhill, Massachusetts, from its First Settlement in 1640, to the Year 1860*, (Haverhill, MA: Published by the Author, 1861), p. 553.
15 Ibid., p. 564.
16 Ibid., p. 567.
17 D. Hamilton Hurd, *History of Essex County, Massachusetts*, (Philadelphia, PA: J.W. Lewis & Company, 1888), vol. II, p. 1995.
18 Reuben A. Guild, *Chaplain Smith and the Baptists . . .* , (Philadelphia, PA: American Baptist Society, 1885), pp. 115, 138. John D. Broome, editor, *Life, Ministry, and Journals of Hezekiah Smith, 1737-1805*, (Springfield, MO: Particular Baptist Press, 2004), pp. 22, 29, 39, 41.
19 Henry C. Graves, *Historical Sketch of the Baptist Religious Society of Haverhill, Massachusetts . . .* , (Haverhill, MA: James A. Hale, Publisher, 1883), p. 7.

much to the delight of many townsfolk, and to the dislike of Rev. Theophilus Pickering. The following anecdote has survived.

> Whitefield during the year 1745 spent several days in Ipswich, Mass. The Rev. Mr. Pickering refused to admit him to his pulpit, giving his reasons for so doing in a published letter. Mr. Whitefield, in a reply he made to a pamphlet of the Bishop of London on the "Enthusiasm of the Methodists," had said that "all aught to be thankful for a pilot who will teach them to steer a safe and middle course." Mr. Pickering, in his reply to Mr. Whitefield's request for the use of his pulpit, quotes this expression and shrewdly inquires, "But what if the pilot should mistake the vane for the compass."[20]

Apparently in good health, Whitefield made his way south towards Boston. The *Boston Gazette* reported on April 9:

> On Tuesday last [April 6] the Rev. Mr. Whitefield came from the Eastward and preached in the evening for the Rev. Dr. Colman, on Wednesday at the Rev. Mr. Webb's meeting-house, and also on Thursday and Monday evening, at the Rev. Dr. Sewell's on Friday evening; on Wednesday, Friday, Saturday & Monday morning, he expounded at 6 o'clock at the Rev. Mr. Gee's and Mr. Webb's; and purposed to do so all this week.[21]

This is an interesting news report from which we can discern several things. We see that Whitefield was in good health. This is evident in that he preached twice a day in Boston for most days of the week. Also, we learn that interest in Whitefield's preaching was still high, as he preached twice per day, but not so high that he had to preach outside on the Boston Common, as he did in 1740. We also see that Whitefield had an ongoing core of senior ministers in Boston who openly endorsed his ministry and promoted revival. Reverends Colman, Webb, Sewell, and Gee were senior clergymen in Boston, men willing to endure the anti-Whitefield sentiment advocated by an outspoken few.

In church services at that time, parents and children sat or stood together. Whitefield often wept for the children of unbelieving parents, and many of the children responded. The following is an account of a child coming to faith from a Whitefield sermon in Boston:

> Mr. Whitefield preached in Boston to crowds of admiring hearers. But one of his most effective sermons, which was preached at Webb's chapel [Rev. John Webb, New North Church], was occasioned by the affecting remark of a dying boy who had heard him the day before. The boy had been taken sick immediately after the sermon, and had said, "I want to go to Mr. Whitefield's God," and then expired. This produced a profound impression upon Whitefield and touched the secret place of his thunder and his tears. He says, "It encouraged me to speak to little ones; but O! how were the old people affected when I said, "Little children, if your parents will not come to Christ, do you come and go to heaven without them!" After such a thrilling appeal, it is no matter of astonishment that "there were but few dry eyes." Few could have done this except a Whitefield! He well understood how to touch the tenderest cords that vibrate in a human bosom.[22]

An example of the anti-Whitefield mindset was evident in an advertisement in the April 18, 1745 edition of the *Boston News-Letter*. Here was an announcement for a new publication called, *Pride Humbled, or Mr.*

---

20 Joseph B. Wakeley, *Anecdotes of the Rev. George Whitefield, M.A.*, (London, 1772), pp. 140-141.
21 *Boston Gazette*, April 9, 1745, p. 3.
22 Joseph B. Wakeley, *Anecdotes of the Rev. George Whitefield*, pp. 333-334.

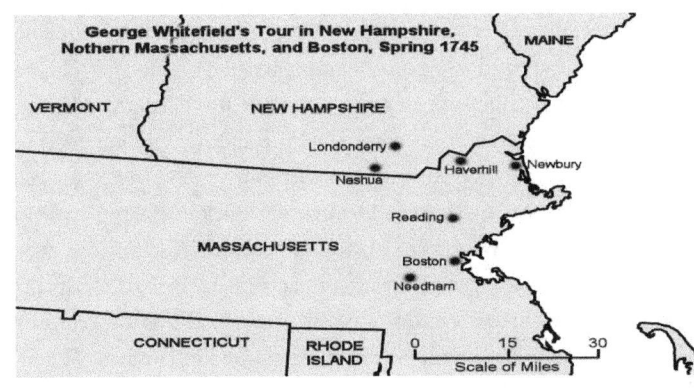

Hobby Chastised. Rev. William Hobby of Reading, Massachusetts was an articulate and outspoken supporter of Whitefield. Hobby was lambasted by many of his New England ministerial colleagues for his endorsement and defense of Whitefield's preaching and itinerant ministry. In the advertisement for this pamphlet critical of Hobby and Whitefield, the beleaguered Hobby is called "proud" and "deceived" among other things.[23] While Whitefield was in the area in 1745, Hobby wrote and published a carefully-worded, fifteen page pamphlet called, *A Vindication of the Reverend Mr. George Whitefield, against the Charges which Some have lately endeavored to fix upon Him: more Especially the Testimony of the Gentlemen at College.* As Whitefield preached in and around Boston, his allies rejoiced and his enemies plotted to undermine and silence his ministry. Nevertheless, he maintained a relentless preaching schedule in and around Boston. On April 23, 1745 it was reported:

> Last Tuesday the Rev. Mr. Whitefield preach'd for the Rev. Mr. Prince at the Rev. Dr. Colman's Meeting-House, and twice on Wednesday for the Rev. Mr. Townsend of Needham; on Thursday & Saturday Morning at six o'clock at the Rev. Mr. Webb's; on Lord's Day twice for the Rev. Mr. Hobby, and on Monday twice for the Rev. Mr. Putnam of Reading: This Morning he preach'd at 6 o'clock for the Rev. Mr. Webb at the Rev. Dr. Colman's. Congregations have been every where very large, and we hear that much of the divine Presence has accompanied the Word preached.[24]

This is an insightful summary of Whitefield's activities throughout much of April 1745. He continued to preach for his core supporters in significant Boston churches. He also travelled briefly to the outskirts of the Boston to preach for Rev. Jonathan Townsend at Needham, and to Reading, which was in the midst of theological controversy. In Reading, Whitefield preached for Rev. William Hobby at the First Church, and for Rev. Daniel Putnam of the Second Church in Reading (now North Reading). Daniel Putnam was a Harvard College graduate in 1717 who arrived in Reading in 1718, and was ordained at the Second Church (Congregational) in 1720. Putnam remained in this ministry until his death in 1759. Putman and William Hobby were allies in Reading, in support of the awakening and the itinerate ministry of Whitefield. Hobby was the more outgoing, articulate of the two men. It what may have been an attempt to reinforce the New Light leanings of Putnam, Whitefield preached for

The Rev. Daniel Putnam House is still standing in North Reading, Massachusetts. Built for Putnam in 1720, this was his home until his death in 1759. In this house Putnam entertained the traveling evangelist Rev. George Whitefield.

Source: North Reading Historical Society.

---

23   *Boston News-Letter,* April 18, 1745, p. 2.
24   *Boston Gazette,* April 23, 1745, p. 3.

Putnam in the northern settlement of Reading. In the almost forty-year tenure of Putnam in Reading, "During his ministry 194 persons were added to the church; he baptized 491 persons and married 11 couples."[25] These were not significant numbers for an evangelically-minded church during the period of the Great Awakening. Whitefield's preaching for Putnam, and sharing a meal with him at his parsonage in Reading, was intended to fortify the somewhat pensive Putnam during this period of antagonistic religious turmoil.

Whitefield had a strained relationship with the Baptists in Boston. Historically Puritan Boston had no sympathy for the Baptists. In the seventeenth century, the few Baptists in Boston met secretly. Technically, they were an illegal sect, as Massachusetts Colony law forbid speaking against infant baptism. In 1679, the Baptists in Boston met covertly in a small structure in the north of the city, that was also a tavern. This building was later expanded as the slowly growing Baptists were either persecuted, tolerated, or ignored in Boston.[26] There were two obvious reasons the Baptists in Boston and in New England did not support Whitefield. First, he was a Church of England minister, and the Church of England had historically been brutal to English Baptists. Second, Whitefield baptized infants, which was considered a grievous error by the Baptists.

While Whitefield traveled throughout the Boston area in the spring of 1745, the *Boston Evening Post* kept its readers fully aware of the anti-Whitefield literature available to the public. For example, in the newspaper's April 15, 1745 edition, the *Post* advertised three separate publications for sale that denounced Whitefield. The first was a reprint of *A Declaration of the Association of the County of New Haven in Connecticut convened at New Haven, Feb. 19, 1744, concerning the Rev. Mr. George Whitefield*. Another anti-Whitefield publication for sale was from Yale College, the famous pamphlet, *A Declaration of the Rector and Tutors of Yale College in New Haven, against the Rev. Mr. George Whitefield, his Principles and Designs*. Both of these denunciations of Whitefield related to southern Connecticut. A third advertisement against Whitefield printed in the April 15, 1745 edition of the *Boston Post* was from a rural ministerial fellowship in Massachusetts. It was titled, *Some Reasons given by the Western Association upon Merrimack River, Why they disapprove of the Rev. Mr. George Whitefield's preaching in the New England Churches*.[27]

In this Whitefield travelogue, we lose track of him for a few days. A glimpse of his whereabouts comes from the diarist Zaccheus Collins of Lynn, who wrote about his hay, his oxen, and tilling his soil, and then recorded on May 3, "George Whitefield preached on Lynn Town Common."[28] Departing the Boston area, Whitefield was heading south. We next learn of Whitefield in May 1745, in Rhode Island.

---

25 Lilly Eaton, *Genealogical History of the Town of Reading, Mass.*, (Boston, MA: Alfred Mudge & Son, 1874), p. 154.
26 Nathan Wood, *History of First Baptist Church, Boston, 1655-1899*, (Philadelphia, PA: American Baptist Society, 1899). Isaac Backus, *A History of New England, with Particular Reference to the Denomination of Christians Called Baptists*, (Newton, MA: Backus Historical Society, 1871).
27 *Boston Evening Post*, April 15, 1745, pp. 3-4.
28 Zaccheus Collins, *Diary of Zaccheus Collins of Lynn, 1726-1769*, (original manuscript at the Peabody Essex Museum, Phillips Library, Rowley, MA), vol. I, p. 314.

CHAPTER 20

WHITEFIELD IN RHODE ISLAND

MAY 1745

IN 1740, WHITEFIELD SUCCESSFULLY PREACHED to large crowds at Newport and Bristol, Rhode Island. However, a follow-up 1745 visit by Whitefield to Rhode Island is virtually unknown to his biographers. By the spring of 1745, Whitefield's *Journals* ceased, making his steps almost impossible to trace. At the same time, his personal correspondence was erratic. In Gilles, *Memoirs of George Whitefield*, written two years after Whitefield's death, there is a brief mention of his 1745 Rhode Island preaching tour. Gilles wrote, "As his bodily strength increased, and his health grew better, he began to move farther southward; and . . . he went through Connecticut, Plymouth, [and] Rhode Island, preaching to thousands, generally twice a day."[1] In Tyerman's exhaustive two-volume biography of Whitefield, he conceded that it is not possible to trace Whitefield's 1745 itinerancy in New England in detail. He wrote, "It is impossible, through want of materials, to trace the course of Whitefield during the next twelve months."[2] Dallimore did not mention Rhode Island when he wrote of Whitefield in New England in 1745; "Whitefield's stay in New England lasted nine months. During that time, in labors that saw him repeatedly taking the Gospel throughout its territory, he accomplished much of the purpose that had brought him there."[3] Even Benjamin Trumbull, in his standard work, *A Complete History of Connecticut, Civil and Ecclesiastical . . .* , could only quote Gilles as mentioned above, stating that Whitefield preached "through Connecticut, Plymouth, and Rhode Island," with no dates or details for this Rhode Island event.[4]

Nevertheless, we know that Whitefield did a brief preaching tour through Rhode Island, in May 1745. Newspaper reports, town histories, and other primary and secondary sources speak of this brief itinerant preaching ministry. One example is from the *Boston Gazette*, May 14, 1745, which reported, "We hear the Rev. Mr. Whitefield is got to Rhode Island, and has begun to preach there, having been at Providence and other places; but we have not yet been able to come to particulars, we must refer to our next text." Especially helpful is the testimony of a Providence, Rhode Island report, reprinted in the May 21, 1745, edition of the *Boston Gazette*. This account from Providence stated, "Yesterday was fortnight the Rev. Mr. Whitefield left Providence, after having preached Three times on the Lord's-Day, to large Congregations, & four Times before . . . " Then, after two days over the Rhode Island border into Massachusetts,

> On Wednesday he reached Rhode Island, where he was received most cordially by the Rev. Mr. Clapp and the Rev. Mr. Hillier, and preached four Times on the Week Days, and thrice

---

1 John Gilles, *Memoirs of George Whitefield*, (1772: reprinted by Hunt & Noyes, Middletown, CT: 1838), p. 106.
2 Luke Tyerman, *The Life of the Rev. George Whitefield*, (New York: Anson & Randolph & Company, 1877), vol. II, p. 152.
3 Arnold Dallimore, *George Whitefield: The Life and Times of the Great Evangelist of the Eighteenth Century Revival*, (Carlisle, PA: Banner of Truth Trust, 1980), vol. II, p. 203.
4 Benjamin Trumbull, *A Complete History of Connecticut, Civil and Ecclesiastical . . .* , (New Haven, CT: Published by Maltby and Co., 1818), p. 191.

on Lord's-Day to large Auditories; on Monday he preached twice for the Rev'd Mr. Billings of Little Compton, and on Tuesday twice at the new Meeting House at Tiverton; on Wednesday he preached again at Little Compton, & on Thursday after having preached at a Farmer's House along the Way, he came to Newport, on Rh. Island, and preached in the Evening to a large Auditory, and intended to continue there till after Lord's-Day, and then return by Way of Freetown this Week towards Boston.[5]

This newspaper account provides us a guide as to Whitefield's locations, dates, and sponsors on this brief Rhode Island preaching tour. The account states that "Yesterday was fortnight the Rev. Mr. Whitefield left Providence." That means fourteen days prior, Whitefield departed Providence. About his activities those days in Providence, the report states, "after having preached Three times on the Lord's-Day, to large Congregations, & four Times before." These seven preaching events in Providence we will now consider.

In 1745, Providence, Rhode Island was a thriving colonial town. Founded in 1636 by the prominent Baptist, Roger Williams, the town quickly became a place for outcasts from the established Colonial Congregational churches in Massachusetts and Connecticut. Baptists, Quakers, and Jews happily made Providence their home. When Providence was burned to the ground in 1676 during King Philip's War, the town rebuilt. This was a maritime community that slowly expanded its commercial, agricultural, and small industrial activities. Various languages were spoken on the streets of Providence, as ships frequented the port from other American colonies, Europe, and the West Indies.

By the time of Whitefield's visit in 1745, the population of Providence was approaching 4,000 residents. Almost one hundred years behind its neighbors in Massachusetts and Connecticut, the First Church Congregational in Providence was founded in 1720. The Second Congregational Church was established in 1743. Due to the revivals on the 1730s and early 1740s, the First Congregational Church had a contentious division. The first minister of the First Congregational Church was Rev. Josiah Cotton.

A Harvard College graduate in 1722, Josiah Cotton was ordained in 1728 at Providence. He served the Congregational Church in Providence from 1728 to 1747, after which he served churches in Massachusetts and New Hampshire. The Great Awakening deeply stirred Providence. The First Congregational Church generally supported the revival, and Cotton was mildly a New Light. An interesting summary stated that the First Church in Providence "was shaken to its foundations by this newly awakened zeal."[6] But overenthusiastic people in the church thought Cotton was not evangelical enough, that he did not overtly support the awakening to their liking. Parishioners soon railed against Cotton, making wild and absurd accusation against him,

A sketch of the 1723 meeting house of the First Church, Providence, Rhode Island. Rev. Josiah Cotton was the minister. This congregation was deeply divided when Whitefield came to town in May 1745. Source: https://firstunitarianprov.org /about-us/our-history/ history-first-unitarian.

---

5   *Boston Gazette*, May 21, 1745, p. 4.
6   Gertrude S. Kimball, *Providence in Colonial Times*, (Boston: Houghton Mifflin Company, 1912), pp. 195-196.

calling him an Anti-Christ. The church was roughly divided, and a new Congregational Church formed in Providence in 1743.

The Beneficent or Second Congregational Church in Providence called Rev. Joseph Snow to be their minister. The first parishioners were all discontented transfers from the First Congregational Church. By 1746, the Beneficent Church was meeting in downtown Providence and developed a building program for a new meeting house. Snow preached in homes, outside, and in other buildings until the new meeting house was completed in 1750. Snow stayed at the church until 1793.[7]

As mentioned above, the account from Providence, quoted in a May 21, 1745, Boston newspaper stated that, "Yesterday was fortnight the Rev. Mr. Whitefield left Providence, after having preached Three times on the Lord's-Day, to large Congregations, & four Times before . . . " The historic Baptist churches in Providence were not yet advocates of the revival, and they did not support Whitefield's 1745 visit. One source stated, "The Baptist congregations in Providence . . . rejected Whitefield and his enthusiastic presentation of the gospel."[8] Whitefield focused on the Congregationalists. It is not difficult to imagine the disruption his preaching caused to these two rival Congregational Churches. The First Congregational Church had a meeting house, built in 1723, while the Second or Beneficent Congregational Church met wherever it could. Since Whitefield visited in the nice May weather, most of their meetings were outdoors. The Beneficent Church was clearly "New Light" and was known as "the church of the common people."[9]

The tension in Providence in 1745 was rife, as the Baptists, Quakers, and First Congregational Church all opposed Whitefield, while curious members of these congregations joined the multitudes that went to hear Whitefield preach in the open air. Rev. Josiah Cotton of the First Congregational Church was unable to reconcile with his congregation and was bitterly degraded by the New Lights in town. In 1747, he departed the First Congregational Church in Providence, for ministries in Massachusetts and New Hampshire.

After his ministry in Providence, Whitefield's next preaching events in Rhode Island were in Newport. "On Wednesday he reached Rhode Island, where he was received most cordially by the Rev. Mr. Clap and the Rev. Mr. Hillier, and preached four Times on the Week Days, and thrice on Lord's-Day to large Auditories . . . "[10] Rev. Nathaniel Clapp was the minister of the First Church of Christ Congregational, in Newport. Previously, Clapp and Whitefield spent a few days together when Whitefield came to Newport the first time, in September 1740. Both men fully endorsed each other. However, Nathaniel Clapp was getting older, and the seventy-seven-year old clergyman would die a few months later, on October 30, 1745. Rev. Jonathan Hillier was the younger assistant to Clapp, but Hillier died between Whitefield's May visit and Clapp's October death. Clapp occasionally held religious services in a tavern in which the Rhode Island colonial government sometimes met. Whitefield likely refreshed himself here. The building is still standing today.

The elderly Nathaniel Clap was considered a throwback to the days of the Puritans, and he was greatly esteemed in Rhode Island. As a New Light, Clap lent credibility to the awakening in Newport. It is interesting to note that while Nathaniel Clapp welcomed Whitefield to Newport, his cousin the rector or president at Yale College, Thomas Clap, did not endorse Whitefield. Folks in the First Congregational Church affirmed that the doctrines of Whitefield and their minister, Nathaniel Clap, were the same.[11]

---

7   *Manual of the Union Congregational Church in Providence, RI*, (Printed by order of the church, 1894), p. 7.
8   Scott Bryant, *Benjamin Randall and the Awakening of the Freewill Baptists*, (Macon, GA: Mercer University Press, 2011), pp.50-51.
9   Edward Field, editor. *State of Rhode Island and Providence Plantations at the End of the Century*, (Boston, MA: The Mason Publishing Company, 1902), vol. ii, p. 136.
10 *Boston Gazette*, May 21, 1745, p. 4.
11 Charles E. Hammett, *A Sketch of the History of the Congregational Churches of Newport, Rhode Island, Compiled from the Records and Other Sources*, (Newport Historical Society, 1891), p. 95. The cousins Thomas and Nathaniel Clapp had variations in the spelling of their last name.

The Old State House is located near the Newport, RI waterfront. It was constructed in 1741 and was the meeting space for the Newport colonial legislature. The building looks much the same today as it did when George Whitefield was in Newport between 1740 to 1770. Photograph by Ken Lawson.

A clergyman against Whitefield in Newport was a Baptist minister, Rev. John Callender, Jr. of the United Baptist Church. Callender was born in Boston to Baptist parents, his father a shopkeeper. As a youth he was forced to worship in secret, as public Baptist meetings were not allowed in Puritan Boston. John graduated from Harvard college in 1726, was baptized the same year, and was licensed to preach in 1727 from the First Baptist Church in Boston. John Callender, Jr. was ordained in Newport at the United Baptist Church in 1731, serving there until his death in 1748.[12] When Whitefield arrived to preach in Newport in 1740, and again in 1745, he did not have the support of Rev. Callender and the Baptists. Callender did not support Whitefield because the itinerant evangelist was disruptive, he was ordained by the dreaded Church of England, and because Whitefield practiced and defended infant baptism.

Another minister in Newport who distanced himself from Whitefield was Rev. James Searing (1704-1755) of the Second Congregational Church. Searing served the church from 1731 to his death in 1755. When Whitefield was in Newport in 1745, he was not welcomed at this church. The official church records state, "1745 March 6th at the Society Meeting Thursday . . . that as much as the Reverend Mr. Geo. Whitefield is expected in town speedily and his preaching in many other places has caused great contentions and divisions in many churches; Voted that this meeting house be set against Whitefield and he is not allowed to preach in it."[13]

After Newport, Whitefield next preached in Little Compton, Rhode Island. The easiest way from Newport to Little Compton was by boat, crossing the mouth of the Sakonnet River, landing at the town of Sakonnet and then traveling north a couple of miles. Little Compton was founded in 1674 as a westernmost point of the Plymouth Colony. The town became part of Rhode Island Colony in 1746.[14] This was a maritime community without a large, deep harbor, so fishing was for subsistence only. Citizens had small farms, were multi-vocational, and raised animals for meat and dairy. There are numerous homes in Little Compton still standing that were present when Whitefield came to town in 1745. A Congregational Church meeting house

---

12 "Memoir of the Rev. John Callender, A.M.," *Collections of the Rhode Island Historical Society*, (Providence, RI, 1838), vol. IV, pp. 9-25.
13 *Second Congregational Church Records 1733-1834*, (Newport Historical Society, Vol. 5), p.13.
14 *The Two-Hundredth Anniversary of the Organization of the United Congregational Church, Little Compton, Rhode Island, September 7, 1904*, (Little Compton, RI: The United Congregational Society, 1906), p. 64.

was built in 1724, which lasted for over 100 years.¹⁵ The current meeting house dates to the 1830s, but has elements remaining from the 1724 meeting house in which Whitefield preached. There is a plaque in the current Congregational Church that commemorates the forty-four-year ministry of Rev. Richard Billings in Little Compton.

As the Congregational minister in remote Little Compton, Richard Billings welcomed George Whitefield. Billings was a Harvard graduate in 1698, and earned his Master of Arts degree from Harvard in 1701. He was ordained in 1704 and served in Little Compton for the rest of his life. He and his wife Sarah had seven children. He was a recent widower when Whitefield came to town in May 1745. For additional income, and as a service to the community, Billings also served as a justice of the peace, certifying deeds, marriages, and other legal documents. The Billings family was a pillar in the community. One source stated of Richard Billings, he was "a man of prominence and ability, much beloved, and exerted a strong influence over his charge. He had one idiosyncrasy, however; he firmly believed in cats as an article of diet, and fatted them for the purpose."¹⁶ Referring to Whitefield, "on Monday he preached twice for the Rev. Mr. Billings of Little Compton."¹⁷

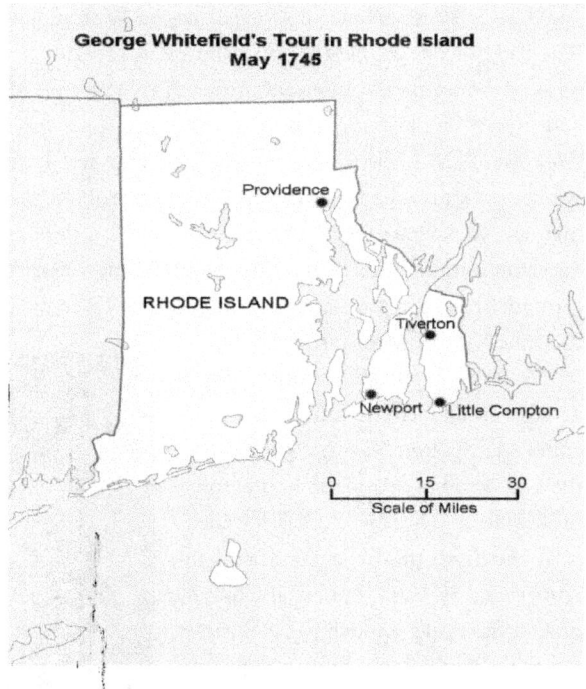

Whitefield's preaching in Little Compton reinforced the New Light theology of Billings. In the early-to-mid 1740s, the local Congregational Church received "a refreshing from the Lord," which resulted in numerous conversions, thirty-eight people added to the church membership, and dozens more began attending church services.¹⁸ The official history of the church states that seventy-five people were added to church membership in the wake of Whitefield's visit.¹⁹ The tiny community of Little Compton was hit with an awakening.

From Little Compton, Whitefield made a short trip north, about ten miles along a good road that overlooked the Sakonnet River, to Tiverton, Rhode Island. This small community was settled in 1694. Located in the southeast corner of Rhode Island, Tiverton was laid out and planned as a town with thirty buildings in 1710. The townsfolk worked in farming, ship building, fishing, and various other trades. Tiverton developed an industry related to fish oil that was prosperous. In speaking of Tiverton, "farming, and secondary occupations such as blacksmithing, tavern keeping, ship building, whaling, and running small saw and grist mills, prevailed throughout the eighteenth century."²⁰ The town was connected to the rest of Rhode Island by a ferry. "The growth of the southern part of the town resulted in the erection of a Congregational Church on Lake Road in 1747."²¹

---

15   *Historic and Architectural Resources of Little Compton, Rhode Island*, (Rhode Island Historical Preservation Commission, 1990), pp. 8-9.
16   "He Firmly Believed in Cats as an Article of Diet," http://www.vastpublicindifference.com/2011/02/he-firmly-believed-in-cats-as-article.html.
17   *Boston Gazette*, May 21, 1745, p. 4.
18   B.B. Edwards, compiler. *The American Quarterly Register*, vol. xi, (Boston, MA: Printed by Perkins & Martin, 1839), p. 264.
19   *The Two Hundredth Anniversary of the Organization of the United Congregational Church, Little Compton, Rhode Island, September 7, 1904*, (Little Compton, RI: 1904), p. 17.
20   *Historic and Architectural Resources of Tiverton, Rhode Island: A preliminary Report*, (Rhode Island Historical Preservation Commission, 1983), p. 1.
21   Ibid., p. 9.

The brief newspaper report that traced Whitefield's activities in Rhode Island stated that he preached "Tuesday twice at the new meeting-house in Tiverton."[22] It was in this partially constructed Congregational meeting house that Whitefield preached in Tiverton in 1745. The new meeting house was built not from controversy but because of population shifts. This was a daughter church from Billing's ministry in Little Compton. The Little Compton-Tiverton area was known as a community where "religion flourished."[23] Whitefield's preached in this partially constructed meeting house to a fledgling congregation with ten men as official members, although the total number of people who attended this historic meeting in Tiverton is unknown.[24] The minister of this new church in Tiverton was a Scotsman named Rev. Othniel Campbell. As minister of the only church in Tiverton with a meeting house, Campbell was often referred to as the "Town Minister."[25]

The Anglican Old Narragansett Church building, built in 1707, still stands today in Wickford, RI. George Whitefield was not invited to preach here when he toured Rhode Island in May 1745.

Source: www.stpaulswickford.org.

A Rhode Island minister who dreaded Whitefield's coming was Rev. James MacSparron (also McSparron) of the Old Narragansett Church, presently in Wickford. The church was founded as an Anglican missionary endeavor in 1706, called St. Paul's Episcopal Church, or Old St. Paul's Church. The Society for the Propagation of the Gospel in Foreign Parts, a Church of England missionary outreach, targeted this area for an Anglican church to be planted. The minister, James MacSparron, served here from 1721 to 1757. An articulate clergyman who adhered to the Church of England liturgies, MacSparron was no supporter of the awakening and was no endorser of George Whitefield.

MacSparron was well educated and was admired by the Church of England as a pioneer missionary in America, so much so that the University of Glasgow granted him the Doctor of Divinity degree in 1737. However, this Anglican congregation was never large. MacSparron had outreach programs to Blacks, Indians, and mixed-blood congregants, as well as White settlers in the area. In his long ministry at Wickford he only married one couple.[26] Even though MacSparron and Whitefield were both Anglican priests, no invitation was extended by MacSparron for Whitefield to preach. The Anglican meeting house at Wickford (Old Narraganset Church) was constructed in 1707, and still stands today with its box pews and organ built in 1680. On the next block of houses, connected by a stone path, is the current Saint Paul's Episcopal Church building, on which a commemorative plaque recognizing MacSparron is mounted. When George Whitefield passed through Rhode Island in 1745, Rev. MacSparron made the following notation: "May 20,

---

22 *Boston Gazette*, May 21, 1745, p. 4.
23 Thomas W. Bicknell, *The History of the State of Rhode Island and Providence Plantations*, (New York: The American Historical Society, 1920), vol. II, p. 593.
24 Ibid.
25 *A Patchwork History of Tiverton, Rhode Island*, (Tiverton, RI: Tiverton Historical Society, 1976), p. 22.
26 Robert A. Geake, *A History of the Narragansett Tribe of Rhode Island*, (Charleston, SC: History Press, 2011), p. 79. H. Newman Lawrence, *The Old Narragansett Church (St. Paul's) built A.D. 1707, a Constant Witness to Christ and His Church*, (Episcopal Diocese of Rhode Island, 1915), pp. 11-17.

1745. Mr. Whitefield has been one Sunday at Providence and two at Newport. Small numbers attend him now [compared to] some years ago. There is a change somewhere, in him or them."[27]

Whitefield began this brief May 1745, Rhode Island preaching circuit in Providence. He then preached in Newport, Little Compton, and Tiverton. Then he circled back to preach again at Little Compton and Newport. On his way from Little Compton to Newport, he "preached at a Farmer's House in the Way, he came to Newport on Rh. Island, and preached in the Evening to a large Auditory, and intended to continue there till after Lord's-Day . . . towards Boston."[28] Whitefield received opposition and support from ministers and their churches on this itinerant circuit in Rhode Island. Then he headed back to Boston by ship from Rhode Island, around Cape Cod, to again minister in the chief city in all New England.

An undated painting of Rev. James McSparron.

Source: https://www.geni.com/people/Rev-James-MacSparran /6000000021651532745

---

27 James MacSparron, *A Letter Book and Abstract of Out Services, 1743-1751*, (Boston, MA: Merrymount Press, 1899), p. 25.
28 *Boston Gazette*, May 21, 1745, p. 4

CHAPTER 21

WHITEFIELD IN AND AROUND BOSTON AND A PREACHING CIRCUIT TO THE NORTH AND WEST

JUNE AND JULY 1745

BOSTON, MASSACHUSETTS IN THE MID-1740S was a city deeply divided over religion. The huge outdoor revival meetings had passed into smaller but still crowded meetings within church buildings. The popular early morning lectures given by evangelical ministers, demanded by the people and initially well attended, had passed away. It appears that by 1745 the supporters of the awakening, and its opponents, had settled into a type of theological truce. Bostonians were weary of religious controversy. When Whitefield came to Boston in 1740, newspapers quickly thereafter printed his sermons and published editorials both for and against the itinerant preacher. A pamphlet war ensued between Whitefield's supporters and opponents. All things Whitefield were sensational. Yet by 1745, much of the heat of the dispute had passed. Boston remained deeply divided over Whitefield and the awakening, as the two sides settled into shepherding their congregations, teaching their parishioners, and protecting their own interests.

On May 2, 1745 George Whitefield wrote a letter while on board a ship ready to land at Charles-Town, next to Boston.[1] To expedite his vast correspondence, he delivered his previously written letters to the ship quartermaster and wrote a letter on board while the ship was in the harbor. This letter mentions that he had been in New England for the past six months. Whitefield wrote that he was deeply concerned by what he called Antinomianism in and around Boston. He remained in the city a few months longer.

Antinomianism comes from two Greek words, *anti,* meaning against or without; and *nomos,* meaning law. The word was transliterated from Greek to Latin, and became an English word about the time of the Protestant Reformation. The word literally means against or without law. The idea is that a Christian is free from moral or behavioral law because of God's grace. This Christian freedom could result in libertine behavior, since the Christian was positionally free from the guilt of the law. Such freedom could lead to irresponsible behavior and an apathetic or indifferent view of Christianity. Questionable activities could therefore be practiced or tolerated under the guise of spiritual freedom. Whitefield saw antinomianism as a perversion of the Christian faith, a theological misunderstanding, and a perversion of biblical teachings on holiness and separation from the world. "Antinomianism so stresses Christian freedom from the condemnation of the law that it underemphasizes the need of the believer to confess sins daily and to pursue sanctification earnestly."[2] Churches that practiced antinomianism became places of allegorical preaching and moralist teaching. Repentance from sin and accepting Jesus Christ as Lord and Savior were exchanged for outwardly

---

1   George Whitefield, *The Works of George Whitefield,* (1771: reprinted by Quinta Press, Shropshire, England: 2000), vol. II, pp. 79-80.
2   Sinclair B. Ferguson, David F. Wright, J.I. Packer, *New Dictionary of Theology,* (Downers Grove, IL: InterVarsity Press, 1988), p. 379

righteous living and religious devotion. Whitefield saw this as the heart of the gospel exchanged for a more open-minded expression of a weak, lifeless Christian faith.

One definition of antinomianism stated, "It is the unbiblical practice of living without regard to the righteousness of God, using God's grace as a license to sin, and trusting grace to cleanse of sin. In other words, since grace is infinite and we are saved by grace, then we can sin all we want and still be saved."[3] Antinomianism thus becomes subjective and experience based, not scripturally focused. Another definition stated, "Antinomianism describes a theological position in which the role of objective, external elements of Christianity (such as obedience to the moral law) are underemphasized and subjective, while internal elements of Christianity (such as the work of the Holy Spirit) are overemphasized."[4]

Whitefield saw the opponents of revival as antinomians, as those who sat within churches, claiming faith in Christ, but with no external evidence of faith. To him, they were trees without fruit, lifeless, indifferent, and irrelevant to the gospel. Whitefield saw them as unconverted moralists. "Moralism became so pervasive in Reformed churches in the eighteenth century that several strong reactions occurred . . . In America the Great Awakening led by the preaching of George Whitefield more successfully challenged the moralism of the churches."[5]

In his May 2, 1745 letter written from Charles-Town, Massachusetts, Whitefield addressed the antinomianism he saw in New England. He wrote, "Antinomianism, I find, begins to show its head and stalk abroad: May the glorious Redeemer cause it to hide its head again, and prevent His children's spirits being embittered against each other." This means Whitefield saw antinomianism, what he saw as the rejection of biblical doctrine, as the cause of the theological disputes and contentions among Christians. He did not see his evangelistic preaching, his itinerancy, or his emphasis on sin and repentance, as controversial, although not all Bostonians would agree. Whitefield continued, "Antinomianism seems only to be speculative; this is a great evil, but not so great as when it affects the practice, and leads the people of God unwarily into licentiousness."[6] Whitefield's criticism of the "speculative" aspect of antinomianism means he rejected their quest for subjective moral enlightenment to the neglect of distinct scriptural teachings. He saw this as leading to all kinds of immoral behavior.

Whitefield wrote his May 2, 1745 letter from Charles-Town at a time of significant civil and military unrest in New England. Colonial militias had formed under British leadership and were deployed to fight the French at Cape Breton Island, Nova Scotia, Canada. This was a troublesome time for Bostonians. Whitefield hoped that "the late outward troubles," meaning the civil and military unrest, would put to silence the antinomian leanings of many people. He wrote, "The late outward troubles I hope will do good, and put a stop to the many disputes and various sects which, like so many hydra's, always spring up when the Lord suffers [allows] false principles to abound." Then Whitefield continued in this letter, making personal remarks such as, "Blessed be His name, he continues to be very kind to us; we have been six months in these parts, and are now going northwards for the summer season." Writing from Charles-Town near Boston, Whitefield saw his months of New England ministry as blessed, and he prepared for a preaching circuit to the communities north of Boston. He experienced little public opposition. As a personal testimony, he wrote, "My temporal affairs begin to be settled; and I am blessed substantially to many souls. Jesus, I trust, has given me a more gospel-heart; and caused many of my professed most embittered enemies to be at peace with me."[7]

However, the *Boston Evening Post* was not at peace with George Whitefield. For several weeks in the spring and summer of 1745, the newspaper ran an advertisement for a pamphlet denouncing Whitefield. For example, on June 3, 1745 the *Post* advertisement stated, "This day is published, A Letter to the Rev. Mr.

---

3 "Antinomianism," *Dictionary of Theology*, https://carm.org/dictionary-antinomianism.
4 "Antinomian Controversy," *Concise Dictionary of Christianity in America*, (Downers Grove, IL: InterVarsity Press, 1995), p. 23.
5 Sinclair B. Ferguson, David F. Wright, J.I. Packer, *New Dictionary of Theology*, p. 379.
6 George Whitefield, *The Works of George Whitefield, vol. II*, p. 79.
7 George Whitefield, *The Works of George Whitefield, vol. II*, p. 80.

George Whitefield, an Itinerant preacher, within the Dominions of His Most Excellent Majesty George, III King of England . . . (Boston, April 30 1745) by Benjamin Prescott, A.M., Pastor of a Church of Christ in Salem . . . ." Prescott held a "clear-cut anti-Whitefield, anti-revival stance."[8] The *Boston Evening Post* was happy to promote Prescott's pamphlet to the detriment of Whitefield and the awakening.

In early June 1745, Whitefield departed Boston for another one of his many itinerant preaching tours. For almost two weeks he travelled and preached in places he had previously visited. He also preached at a few locations for the first time. Every stop on this itinerant evangelistic tour is not known, but the following June 1745, newspaper report from Boston deserves careful study.

> For about these twelve days last past the Rev. Mr. Whitefield has been out of Town, in which Time he has preach'd once on a Fast Day on the Account of the Cape Breton Expedition for the Rev. Mr. Emerson at Malden; four Times for the Rev. Mr. Hobby of Reading; five Times for the Rev. Mr. Mcgregre of Londonderry; twice for the Rev. Mr. Emmerson of Nisitiscet; once for the Rev. Mr. Hemmingway of Townshend; once at Groton Precinct at a new Meeting-House; once at Litchfield; once at Timberlane, once at Dunstable; twice for the Rev. Mr. Secomb of Harvard; once for the Rev. Mr. Bliss of Concord; and once at the Seat of Isaac Royal, Esq.—This Morning he return'd to Town, & intends, God willing, to preach at five this Evening at the Rev. Mr. Webb's, and to take his final Leave for this Season, one Day this Week.[9]

This is a valuable newspaper citation that gives many previously unknown details related to Whitefield's itinerant travels. Some of these ministers are longstanding Whitefield allies and their names have already been mentioned, such as Rev. Emerson at Malden and Rev. Hobby at Reading, both in Massachusetts; and the misspelt "Rev. Mr. Mcgregre" who was Rev. David MacGregor of the West Parish Church in Londonderry, New Hampshire. The above named Rev. Daniel Bliss at Concord, Massachusetts was an ongoing Whitefield ally, as was Rev. John Webb in Boston. But some new names of ministers and some new locations are also mentioned, such as Rev. Emmerson of Nisitiscet; Rev. Hemmingway of Townshend; a preaching event in Groton; preaching once each at Litchfield, Timberlane, and Dunstable; and preaching twice for the Rev. Secomb in the rural town of Harvard, Massachusetts. These activities warrant further attention.

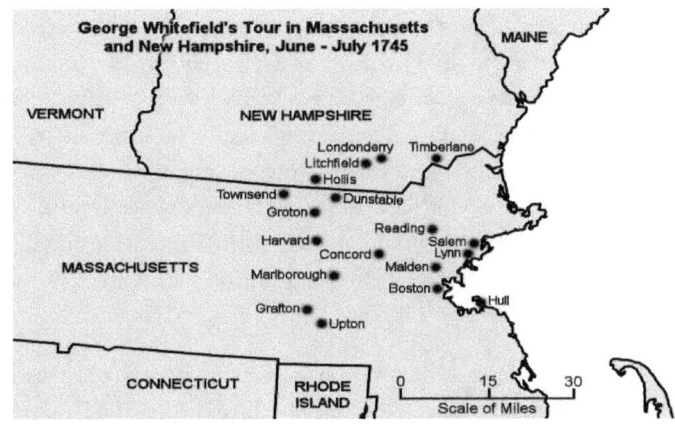

The *Boston Gazette* newspaper dated June 18, 1745 stated that Whitefield preached "twice for the Rev. Mr. Emmerson of Nisitiscet." Previously this community was part of Dunstable. After the 1741 realignment of the New Hampshire boundary with Massachusetts, Nisitiscet became Hollis, New Hampshire.[10] A town charter was granted Hollis in 1746. This densely forested area was cleared by the first settlers to make farmlands and pastures for livestock. Fresh water was abundant from the Nashua River and several ponds. When Whitefield arrived in Nisitiscet in 1745, the

---

8   Richard O. Roberts, *Whitefield in Print*, (Wheaton, IL: Richard O. Roberts, Publisher, 1988), p. 527.
9   *Boston Gazette*, June 18, 1745, p. 3.
10 Samuel A. Green, *The Natural History and the Topography of Groton, Massachusetts*, (Cambridge, MA: University Press, 1912), p. 156.

community had three or four dozen families with a small meeting house, a graveyard, and a town common.[11] The minister eagerly waiting to welcome Whitefield was Rev. Daniel Emerson.

Emerson was born in Reading, Massachusetts in 1716. After graduating Harvard College in 1739, he received private tutoring to prepare for vocational ministry. Emerson arrived in rural Nisitiscet about 1741, and was called in January 1743, to be the minister of this tiny pioneer community. He was ordained a few months later, in April, and served in Hollis until 1793. It was said that in his long service to his rural community, this country parson never had a dispute with the town or with his congregation.[12] Emerson was widely respected locally and throughout the region for his intellect, his piety, his generosity, and his appealing personality. "He taught school and fitted his students for college. He gave the land on which the meeting house was built. He was one of the ablest advocates of the New Light doctrine, and for many years was the leading and most influential minister in his section of the country."[13] Another source stated of Daniel Emerson, "The religious society in Hollis was well united in their popular and acceptable minister whose orthodoxy was without taint."[14]

George Whitefield had a friend and ally in Daniel Emerson. With the ridicule of many, Emerson publicly endorsed Whitefield and the Great Awakening when he signed the July 1743, *Testimony and Advice of a Number of Pastors*. Now Whitefield was in tiny Nisitiscet to say thank you to a fellow New Light, and to preach for Emerson. Details of that early June 1745, preaching event in Nisitiscet are missing. But a local historian made the following summary of Whitefield's effect in Nisitiscet: "Mr. Whitefield was an interesting character, and in this country he influenced the lives of thousands of persons; and the effect of his preaching in many families has been handed down from generation to generation even to the present day [1912]."[15]

In the *Boston Gazette* article of June 18, 1745, the above named "Rev. Hemmingway of Townshend" was Rev. Phineas Hemenway of Townsend, Massachusetts. Located about forty-five miles northwest of Boston, Townsend was first settled in 1676 and was founded in 1732. This was a remote farming and lumbering community. The community had no school until 1744, at which time the town voted to raise money for three one-room school houses. Hemenway was a Harvard graduate in 1730 who was installed as the minister of the First Church in Townsend in 1734. He oversaw the education of the children in town and served in Townsend until his death in 1760. Hemenway had not yet met Whitefield when he signed the 1743 *Testimony and Advice of the Late Venerable Assembly of Ministers*, which supported the awakening and endorsed the practices of Whitefield. Hemenway's family "took a firm stand in favor of the revival under Edwards and Whitefield," and his ministry in Townsend was known as an "evangelical work."[16] In June 1745, the itinerant Whitefield preached for Rev. Phineas Hemenway at the small First Congregational Church in Townsend. While the community was infatuated with Whitefield, not all supported his preaching style, his Church of England ordination, or his roving ministry. In a time of theological disruptions, the well-appreciated Hemenway maintained a balanced but unremarkable ministry.

> During Mr. Hemenway's pastorate which covered a period of some more than twenty-six years, the church increased in numbers from sixteen to seventy-nine . . . The church in Townsend, and its pastor, kept aloof from all these difficulties, which fact alone is sufficient to establish

---

11   Joan Tinklepaugh, "A Brief History of Hollis," www.hollishistoricalsociety.org/history-of-hollis-new-hampshire.html.
12   Samuel T. Worcester, *History of the Town of Hollis, New Hampshire, from its First Settlement to the Year 1879*, (Nashua, NH: Press of D.C. Moore, 1897), p. 53.
13   Ellery B. Crane, editor. *Historic Homes and Institutions and Genealogical and Personal Memoirs of Worcester County, Massachusetts*, (New York: The Lewis Publishing Company, 1907), vol. I, pp. 97-98.
14   Samuel T. Worcester, *History of the Town of Hollis, New Hampshire*, p. 75.
15   Samuel A. Green, *The Natural History and the Topography of Groton, Massachusetts*, p. 157.
16   Ithmar B. Sawtelle, *History of the Town of Townsend, Middlesex County, Massachusetts . . .* , 1676-1878, (Fitchburg, MA: Published by the Author, 1878), pp. 78, 80.

the wisdom of the conservative position taken by Mr. Hemenway . . . It appears that he was of exemplary character, social in his discourse with his people, adverse to all dogmatic controversies, both in and out of the pulpit, and determined only "to fight the good fight of faith."[17]

The next stop we know about on Whitefield's brief preaching circuit was Groton, Massachusetts. Located next to Townsend, Whitefield had an easy ride to this agrarian community. Welcoming him to Groton was Rev. Caleb Trowbridge, who was ordained in Groton in 1715. As a Harvard graduate in 1710, Townsend was the most educated member of his community. During his long tenure at the Congregational Church he assisted in the ongoing renovations of the meeting house. In the 1730s, a church bell was installed. By the time of Whitefield's visit in June 1745, the meeting house was newly restored and appeared to be a new building.[18] This explains the previously quoted newspaper article that stated Whitefield preached "once at Groton Precinct at a new Meeting-House."

An undated photograph of the Rev. Caleb Trowbridge house in Groton, originally built in 1725.

Source: https:// firstperiodnewengland.wordpress. com/towns-and-cities/ groton-massachusetts.

Shortly before Whitefield arrived in Groton, Trowbridge signed a document against Whitefield. Dated February 13, 1745, the pamphlet was called, *Some Reasons given by the Western Association Upon Merrimack River, Why they Disapprove of the Rev. Mr. George Whitefield's Preaching in the New England Churches*. Nine ministers signed this document, including Trowbridge of Groton. "The Rev. Caleb Trowbridge, who was ordained at Groton March 2, 1715, and remained there until the time of his death, on September 9, 1760, did not sympathize with Mr. Whitefield's views."[19]

The townsfolk of Groton were a rural people that mostly farmed. They also created many small family industries such as a soapstone quarry, a brick factory, and a pewter mill which produced various household items that were sold in Portsmouth, Boston, and other areas. The Congregational Church was the center of the town and Rev. Caleb Trowbridge was a leading citizen.[20] For whatever reason, Trowbridge allowed Whitefield to preach in his Congregational Church pulpit. One writer described Caleb Trowbridge, stating, "He was sober, discreet, laborious, devoted, and died [in 1760] highly esteemed and universally lamented."[21] There is no record of how Whitefield was received in Groton, but we do know that there was not a revival in the church in Groton under Trowbridge's pastorate.

The previously mentioned *Boston Gazette* newspaper article dated June 18, 1745, credited Whitefield with preaching at "Litchfield, Timberlane, and Dunstable." These will be looked at in order.

The rural farming community of Litchfield, New Hampshire was set off from Dunstable, Massachusetts upon the resolution of a boundary dispute in 1741. Litchfield was known for its lumber industries, its brick making, and for farming. The town was an important location for the ferry which crossed the Merrimack River, and was a stop for river trade. The historic churches in Litchfield were always small and poor.[22] The town

---

17 Ibid., pp. 83, 90.
18 Caleb Butler, *History of the Town of Groton . . .*, (Boston, MA: Press of T.R. Marvin, 1848), pp. 144-147.
19 Samuel A. Green, *The Natural History and the Topography of Groton*, Massachusetts, p. 156.
20 "Old Groton Meetinghouse," *First Parish Church of Groton, Massachusetts*, http://uugroton.org/nbu/public/misc/old-groton-meetinhouse.pdf.
21 *The Spirit of the Pilgrims for the Year 1832*, (Boston, MA: Published by Peirce and Parker, 1832), p. 66.
22 *History of Litchfield and an Account of its Centennial Celebration, 1895*, (Augusta, ME: Kennebec Journal Printers, 1897), p. 434.

voted to construct a meeting house in 1734, which was completed two years later. Rev. Joshua Tufts served the First Church in Litchfield from 1741 to 1744. A Harvard graduate in 1736, Tufts was from the Massachusetts Town of Newbury, which was a community supportive of the Great Awakening. It appears that Tufts was a New Light minister, although the Litchfield church records are missing from those years. When Tufts was dismissed from the church in 1744, the tiny congregation floundered. Attempts at combining the church with another congregation failed. For the next thirty years, Litchfield did not have a settled minister. That means that when George Whitefield preached in Litchfield in July 1745, he preached in a relatively new meeting house to a small group of New Light believers who did not have a minister. After 1744, "annual appropriations were made for the support of the gospel; but no settlement was effected until 1764, when the Rev. Samuel Cotton, of Newton, received a unanimous call."[23] Whitefield preached to a small group of rural folks in Litchfield. The next preaching stop for Whitefield that we know about was in Timberlane, New Hampshire.

The Timberlane community no longer exists. Once situated on fertile land between Haverhill, Massachusetts and Kingston, New Hampshire, the Timberlane settlement was first part of Haverhill, and was later absorbed by Hampstead in 1749. Those few dozen families that lived in Timberlane had quite a distance to travel on poor roads in all kinds of weather to attend church services. These services were conducted by Rev. James Cushing of the Haverhill North Parish Church, now called Plaistow, New Hampshire. From a very early date, the settlers in Timberlane sought to have church services locally. In good weather they made the trip to the North Parish to hear Cushing, but in foul weather they could not safely travel the eight or more miles to the North Precinct meeting house. In 1733, the folks at Timberlane made a petition to help alleviate their ministerial concerns:

> In the winter of 1733 a petition was sent to the church at the North Precinct [Rev. James Cushing], from twenty-five families who had moved to Timberlane, now Hampstead, "that by reason of the great distance of their dwellings from the meeting house they undergo many and great difficulties in attending the public worship of Almighty God," and asked permission to hold meetings by themselves in the winter season, in a log house probably patterned after the meeting houses of the early Puritans, with its thatched roof of hay or straw, and rough-hewn logs for pulpit and seats . . . They probably hired some neighboring minister to assist them in the service, or carried it on among themselves . . . [24]

Interestingly, this petition also asks for relief from financially supporting Cushing, who only occasionally traveled to Timberlane. It also does not address any theological issues. Apparently, the rural townsfolk were content with Cushing as a preacher, but the great distance they had to travel to church services precluded him having any real impact in the Timberlane community. In 1744, Cushing came out against Whitefield and the revival preachers that he thought caused more harm than good. Cushing signed a ministerial pamphlet, dated December 26, 1744, that renounced the awakening as having "great and grievous disorders."[25] But Cushing apparently had a change of heart. A few months later, Whitefield wrote in his *Journals*, February 1745, that he "Preached yesterday twice with much divine power to large Congregations for the Rev. Mr. Cushing" at Plaistow, New Hampshire.[26] Cushing endorsed or

---

23 *History of Litchfield, Hillsborough County, New Hampshire*, (Philadelphia, PA: J.W. Lewis & Company, 1885), www.nh.searchroots.com/documents/Hillsborough/History_Litchfield_NH.txt.
24 Harriette E. Noyes, *A Memorial to the Town of Hampstead, New Hampshire: Historic and Genealogical Sketches*, (Boston, MA: George B. Reed, Printer, 1899), vol. II, p. 14.
25 *A Letter from Two Neighboring Associations of Ministers in the Country, to the Associated Ministers of Boston and Charlestown, relating to the Admission of Mr. Whitefield into their Pulpits*, (Boston, 1744). See also Joseph Tracy, *The Great Awakening*, (1842: reprinted by Banner of Truth Trust, Carlisle, PA: 1989), p. 345.
26 George Whitefield, *George Whitefield's Journal*, (1756: reprinted by Banner of Truth Trust, Carlisle, PA: 1985), p. 556.

at least allowed Whitefield to preach at Timberlane. It must have been a remarkable experience to have the celebrated Whitefield preach to these farm folks at Timberlane. It is thoughtful to consider the internationally famous George Whitefield, who preached to tens-of-thousands in larger cities, was now routinely preaching outside in tiny, underprivileged communities such as rural Timberlane, to a small group of farmers.

The *Boston Gazette* newspaper article dated June 18, 1745, stated that George Whitefield preached "once at Dunstable," New Hampshire. He preached for his young ally, Rev. Samuel Bird in Dunstable. Dunstable was incorporated in 1673 as a huge, two hundred square miles community, before the boundary between Massachusetts and New Hampshire was settled. Throughout the 1700s, portions of Dunstable were selected to create new towns, always with controversy and disagreement. The Town of Dunstable was incorporated in 1746, while Rev. Josiah Swan was the Congregational minister. Swan was ordained in Dunstable in 1738. Soon thereafter the Great Awakening swept through the area, and Swan was not impressed. He feared the divisions that resulted from the preaching of largely untrained itinerants, and he opposed the excesses that sometimes accompanied the meetings of these New Light separatist groups. Swan opposed the revival and did not support the theology of Jonathan Edwards nor the evangelistic preaching of the itinerant George Whitefield. Swan was described as "a prudent, stirring, thrifty, but not over spiritual man."[27]

Josiah Swan had a contentious relationship with his church in Dunstable. The townspeople were generally unhappy with the government dividing of their community to create new towns. Some of the disagreements with Swan were "in consequence of a division of the town, by running the line between the provinces of New Hampshire and Massachusetts."[28] But specifically, many were discontented with the theology of Swan. Their dissatisfaction may have been enhanced by the fact that the increasingly smaller Dunstable community was still responsible to pay the minister's whole salary, a distinct burden imposed upon these rural people. However, the underlying dissatisfaction many had with Swan was his rejection of the revival. All of southern New Hampshire was influenced by Whitefield's visits in 1740 and in 1744-1745. Although there is no record of Whitefield visiting Dunstable before July 1745, "the people of the town were "invaded by an unusual religious excitement . . . The eloquence of Whitefield . . . affected the entire population of the State. So fascinated were the people that they forsook their ordinary occupations, laid aside their worldly schemes, and followed the wonderful preacher from place to place."[29]

In the summer of 1745, George Whitefield approached Dunstable. The First Church in Dunstable had divided over the awakening. Swan and the Old Lights retained the meeting house, while the New Lights, under the unordained Mr. Samuel Bird, held meetings in town. Speaking of Rev. Josiah Swan,

> "His lack of sympathy . . . with the New Light doctrines in general, estranged from him many of his pious hearers who had embraced the new faith. The differences in the church, the township controversies, and the religious excitement of the times, all combined to render Mr. Swan's position a difficult one . . . he was hardly equal to the exigencies of the hour; and failing to unite the opposing parties, he was dismissed."[30]

When Whitefield arrived in Dunstable in 1745, it was in direct support of the fledgling New Light group, in opposition to Josiah Swan, the settled minister of the town. Whitefield was welcomed to Dunstable by Samuel Bird.

---

27 Charles J. Fox, *History of the Old Township of Dunstable: Including Nashua, Nashville, Hollis, Hudson, Litchfield, and Merrimack, New Hampshire*, (Nashua, NH: Charles T. Gill, Publisher, 1846), p. 151.
28 "Churches and Ministers in New Hampshire," *Collections of the Massachusetts Historical Society*, (Boston, MA: Printed by Phelps and Farnam, 1823), vol. x, p. 55.
29 John W. Churchill, *History of the First Church in Dunstable-Nashua, New Hampshire*, (Boston, MA: The Fort Hill Press, 1918), p. 20.
30 Ibid., pp. 21-22.

Samuel Bird was born in Dorchester, Massachusetts in 1724. He attended Harvard College at the height of the Great Awakening in the early 1740s. While Harvard at first welcomed Whitefield, they shortly thereafter changed their position and publicly denounced the traveling evangelist. Bird was an outspoken advocate of Whitefield and the awakening, and was dismissed from Harvard before graduating for his lack of support for the college's anti-Whitefield position. Bird likely heard Whitefield preach at Harvard and in Boston in 1740 and again in 1744. "He was a student at Harvard College, and would have graduated in 1744, but for a criticism of the College authorities, dictated by religious enthusiasm."[31] We do not know how Samuel Bird came to settle in Dunstable. But we do know that he was welcomed by the New Light faction in the town, and that he served as the leader of this new group. When Whitefield preached for Bird in Dunstable in July 1745, the assembly was held outside, the meeting house being under the control of the Old Lights. After years of turmoil, Josiah Swan was dismissed from the pastorate of the First Church in Dunstable in 1746. Samuel Bird became their new minister, ordained in Dunstable in 1747. "Mr. Bird was a New Light, and his ordination was a triumph. His friends . . . stood by him, and by then the new meeting house . . . was erected."[32] Many in Dunstable were not happy with the ordination of Bird over the First Church, and a rival Old Light group formed. Bird stayed in Dunstable only a few years before accepting a ministry position in New Haven, Connecticut.

As referenced, the *Boston Gazette* of June 18, 1745, stated that Whitefield preached "twice for the Rev. Mr. Secomb of Harvard." This was Rev. John Seccomb (sometimes spelt Secombe or Seccombe) of the rural farming town of Harvard, Massachusetts. John Seccomb was born in Medford, Massachusetts in 1708 and graduated from Harvard College in 1728. In 1733 he settled in the farming town of Harvard, named after the founder of Harvard College, Rev. John Harvard. Seccomb was the first pastor of the original church in Harvard. The town had rich soil and was from the start a small but successful farming community. There was plenty of fresh water and fish in the Nashua River. This was a rural agricultural society.[33] The awakening came to Harvard in 1739, before the first visit of George Whitefield to New England in 1740. This movement lasted five years, 1739 to 1744, and "was neither excited nor assisted by Mr. Whitefield."[34] Most of the passions of the revival has subsided when Whitefield arrived in Harvard in July 1745.

Seccomb supported Whitefield in a region where many ministers did not endorse the itinerant evangelist. For example, after Whitefield first departed Massachusetts in 1740, ministers were forced to declare their position concerning the awakening in general and Whitefield in particular. A ministerial fellowship near Harvard, called the Marlborough Association, wrote and published a pamphlet in 1742 denouncing Whitefield and the revival. John Seccomb did not sign the document. His support of the revival caused division between himself and his local ministerial colleagues. "Although he and his congregation agreed in accepting the principles of the Great Awakening, his relations with ministerial associations were sometimes strained on this account."[35] While publicly endorsing Whitefield, and allowing the traveling evangelist to preach from his pulpit in Harvard, Seccomb did not support emotionalism or the raving sermons of bombastic itinerants who caused more harm than good.[36] When Whitefield preached in Harvard in the early summer of 1745, he was supporting a beleaguered pastor who was frequently ridiculed by his

---

31 "Rev. Samuel Bird," www.pa-roots.org/data/read.php?3620,820439. Mr. Bird was hardly the only student expelled from Harvard for his pro-Whitefield views. See George J. Gatgounis, "How Did Harvard College Respond to the Great Awakening," *The Christian Observer*, March 2, 2014, https://christianobserver.org/how-did-harvard-college-respond-to-the-great-awakening.
32 Charles J. Fox, *History of the Old Township of Dunstable*, p. 153.
33 Jeremiah Spofford, *A Gazetteer of Massachusetts: Containing a General View of the State*, (Newburyport, MA: Charles Whipple, Publisher, 1828), p. 210.
34 Henry S. Nourse, *History of the Town of Harvard, Massachusetts: 1732-1893*, (Harvard, MA: 1893), vol. I, p. 189.
35 "John Seccombe," *Dictionary of Canadian Biography*, http://www.biographi.ca/eu/bio/seccombe_john_4E.html.
36 Henry S. Nourse, *History of the Town of Harvard, Massachusetts*, p. 189.

peers for his support of revival. Later, Seccomb had several disputes with the townsfolk of Harvard, and the members of his congregation, over theology, finances, and alleged sexual misconduct. He lasted at Harvard until 1757, when he then not only left the town of Harvard in apparent disgust, but he also departed the American Colonies, settling in Nova Scotia, and changing the spelling of his name, adding an "e" to the end of his last name. John Seccomb (later Seccombe) was disgusted with ministerial life in Harvard and made a distinct separation from both the town and the entire American Colonies.[37]

Boston newspapers in the summer of 1745 were overwhelmed with political and military news from Canada and Great Britain, and with news from various colonial cities. These typically four-page newspapers were printed for mass production, with often a page or more of promotional advertisements with various products for sale. Whitefield's summer tour in and around Boston did not have the controversial aspects of his prior visits, and the Boston newspapers essentially ignored his travels and preaching for more temporal news. We do know that Whitefield had standing invitations to preach at some of Boston's largest churches, and he did so in the summer of 1745, to large crowds but not with sensational or controversial results. An individual who heard Whitefield preach in Boston in June 1745, was Rev. Thomas Smith of Falmouth, Maine. A Harvard educated Congregational minister and Whitefield supporter, Smith was in Boston on business and went to hear Whitefield preach. In the *Journal of Rev. Thomas Smith*, he wrote in the third person, stating, "June 22. [1745] Got home. While Mr. Smith was at Boston, he heard Mr. Whitefield twice."[38]

A sketch of downtown Boston, Massachusetts in the mid-eighteenth century. Prominent in the sketch is the Old State House, built in 1713, and the seat of the Massachusetts General Court until 1789. The building is now a museum and a National Historic Landmark.

Source: public domain image.

Having completed his preaching tour in the farmlands northwest of Boston, George Whitefield returned to cosmopolitan Boston. Boston had over 13,000 residents in 1730, and by 1750 the population had risen to 15,000 people.[39] In the mid-1700s, Philadelphia, New York, and Boston were the leading cities in North America. Boston Harbor was a crowded seaport, well-known to mariners and traders in Europe. Ships loaded in Boston with colonial goods regularly sailed for England, other American ports,

---

37 "John Seccombe," *Dictionary of Canadian Biography*. "History of St. Matthew's United Church, Nova Scotia," https://stmatts.ns.ca/about/history.
38 Thomas Smith, *Journal of Rev. Thomas Smith*, (Portland, ME: Joseph E. Bailey, Printer, 1849), p. 190.
39 "A Brief History of Early Boston," www.historyofmassachusetts.org/a-brief-history-of-early-boston. Robert Allison, *A Short History of Boston*, (Boston, MA: Commonwealth Editions, 2004). Anthony M. Sammarco, *Boston: A Historic Walking Tour*, (Charleston, SC: Arcadia Publishing, 2013).

and British Caribbean harbors. Vessels arriving in Boston brought sugar, rum, and servants-slaves from the Caribbean. Ships from England brought textiles and other manufactured niceties otherwise unavailable in Massachusetts. Immigrants frequented the taverns and boardinghouses of the city. Along the waterfront could be seen sailors, fishermen, and laborers, as well as the homeless and deranged.[40]

For some, money poured into Boston, and the city continued to grow. Visitors from sea or land arrived on a densely populated peninsula of land, hilly, with numerous church steeples adorning the skyline. Merchants who originally built their homes above their shops were often able to move out of the crowded waterfront area to build larger homes away from the noises and smells of the downtown. Many of these elegant brick or wooden clapboard homes are still standing today in various neighborhoods throughout the city. Merchants used their store windows to display for sale the latest European household items and clothing fashions. The economy was prosperous. Many skilled craftsmen supported Boston's maritime industries as shipbuilders, carpenters, barrel makers, metal workers, tanners, and a host of other activities. Throughout the city there were merchants, traders, furniture makers, printers, machinists, brick layers, butchers, cabinetmakers, and unskilled support activities.[41]

Many, but not all the wealthiest Bostonians, flocked to the Anglican Church, showing solidarity between their pragmatic British business connections and the Church of England. Yet even at King's Chapel, an Anglican congregation formed in Boston in 1686, an occasional rope maker, potter, sea captain, or baker could be seen at the same church service as a wealthy merchant, a civil official, a banker, or an attorney.[42] George Whitefield was not only unwelcome in such places, he was publicly denounced, as the Unitarian leanings of the congregation did not fit with Whitefield's Calvinist theology.[43]

Across the Atlantic, Great Britain took notice of the rise of Boston. The Massachusetts Bay Colony had grown into an equal trade partner and competitor with English ports and merchants. By the mid-1700s, England became dependent on Boston and other colonial cities for lumber, dried beef and fish, and various agricultural crops. Within a few decades, tensions between the colonists and Great Britain would erupt over trade restrictions, taxes, and the rights of colonists as British citizens.[44] But for now, in the summer of 1745, Whitefield preached in a cosmopolitan Boston community that was flourishing peacefully under the British flag.

One of Whitefield's favorite places to preach in Boston was at the New North Church, under Rev. John Webb. After preaching at several Boston churches in the summer of 1745, Whitefield prepared to depart the city for another preaching circuit. His last preaching appointment in the city before traveling was at the New North Church. A newspaper report stated, "Last Wednesday Evening the Reverend Mr. Whitefield preach'd an affectionate parting sermon here to a very large Assembly at Mr. Webb's."[45]

Rev. John Webb was born in Braintree, Massachusetts in 1687, and was therefore twenty-seven years older than George Whitefield. Webb was a Puritan minister in an era when Puritanism was being discarded or neglected in Boston. He graduated Harvard College in 1708, and served in a variety of teaching, chaplaincy, and pastoral ministries until he was ordained as the first minister of the New North Church in Boston in 1714. The formation of the New North Church out of the Old North Church was amicable, as population increases warranted a new meeting house in a new neighborhood. Most parishioners walked to church services, which could last from two-to-three hours. Then the folks went home for lunch and many returned for afternoon services. Between church services, lunch, and fellowship opportunities, attending the meeting house on the

---

40   Jennifer B. Gillis, *Life in Colonial Boston*, (Chicago, IL: Heinemann Library, 2003), p. 6. For a more detailed study see, William P. Marchione, *An Essential History of the Hub: Boston*, (Charleston, SC: The History Press, 2008).
41   Jennifer B. Gillis, *Life in Colonial Boston*, p. 10.
42   Patricia Bonomi, *Under the Cope of Heaven: Religion, Society, and Politics in Colonial America*, (New York: Oxford University Press, 2003), p. 93.
43   "A Brief History of King's Chapel," http://www.kings-chapel.org/history.html. For a thorough study, see James B. Bell and James E. Mooney, *The Records of Kings Chapel*, (Boston, MA: Colonial Society of Massachusetts, 2019).
44   For more details see, *The Metropolis of New England: Colonial Boston, 1630-1776*, (Boston, MA: Massachusetts Historical Society, 1976).
45   *Boston Gazette*, June 25, 1745, p. 3.

Sabbath could be an all-day event. As with most Boston churches, official church members at the New North Church were fined if they did not have a valid excuse for missing services. In the mid-1740s, this congregation was composed of many skilled and successful craftsmen in a growing Boston. Elders and deacons in the church were made up of brick masons, gold smiths, carpenters, shopkeepers, civic leaders, soldiers, metal smiths, and merchants. These talented men were appreciated for their diverse contributions to the community.[46]

In 1730, New North Church expanded its meeting house and improved their facility. They used the *Bay Psalm Book* until 1755, meaning that a verse from a biblical Psalm was read and then sung by the congregation. Then the leader would read the next verse, which was also sung by the assembly. Rev. John Webb ably served this growing church. Of Webb it was written:

> During more than thirty-five years [he] discharged the duties of that office with exemplary zeal, diligence and fidelity. He was a man or ardent, impulsive temper, of great energy, and of much decision of character. His labors, as a minister, were abundantly successful. He was a leading, efficient promoter of the Great Revival of 1740-3. No church in Boston shared more largely than his in the blessings of that glorious manifestation of Divine power and grace . . . He was a warm and active friend of . . . Whitefield . . . who visited Boston at that time, and whose labors were so greatly blessed in the Great Awakening.[47]

For membership, the New North Church required a public profession of faith in the new birth through Jesus Christ. To receive communion a member had to make a public testimony of faith and state that they accepted and obeyed the church covenant. As was common at that time, the church raised money to pay the minister, to care for the building, and to support various ministries through renting pews in the meeting house. The cost for pew rental depended on where you sat in the building. Men and women sat on separate sides and Blacks sat in the balcony.[48] The *Boston Gazette*, June 25, 1745, stated that Whitefield preached for Webb at the New North Church, "to a very large assembly." One of those in attendance when Whitefield preached at New North Church was the assistant minister, Rev. Andrew Eliot. Unknown to the parishioners, Eliot had some reservations about Whitefield.

Rev. Andrew Eliot joined the aging Rev. John Webb at the New North Church in 1741. He was a Harvard graduate in 1737 and was ordained at the church in 1742. While Webb was an outspoken advocate of Whitefield and the awakening, his assistant Eliot had reservations. There were passages in Whitefield's *Journals* that disturbed Eliot. He was also concerned with Whitefield's "enthusiasm," a derisive term for anyone who defied the Puritan norms of society by religious emotionalism. An enthusiast was a person who might claim private revelations from God or could claim to speak by divine inspiration. Often an enthusiast was evidenced by hysterical utterances or bodily gyrations. Such a religious leader would promote sectarian ideas and was seen as a direct threat to the religious and civil norms of that day.[49] Whitefield denied being an enthusiast, but some of his initial followers in New England did clearly evidence the traits of enthusiasm. This was a concern for almost all clergy in New England, New Lights and Old Lights. Whitefield was in the Boston area in the spring and summer of 1745 and preached often at New North Church. On April 15, 1745, Rev. Andrew Eliot wrote

---

46 Charles C. Wells, *New North Church: from Birth to Death in Early Boston*, (Oak Grove, IL: Chauncey Park Press, 2014), p. 11.
47 "Rev. John Webb," http://wc.rootsweb.ancestry.com. For more details the article on John Webb in William B. Sprague, *Annals of the American Pulpit: Trinitarian Congregational*, (New York: Robert Carter & Brothers, 1857), vol. I, p. 268.
48 Charles C. Wells, *New North Church: from Birth to Death in Early Boston*, p. 20-21, 53.
49 In the mid-1700s, the established New England clergy retained much of the stoicism of the founding Puritans. The culture promoted orderliness, predictability, and hierarchy. When Whitefield was charged with "emotionalism," he was being accused of sedition, rashness, and emotionalism. By breaking from the established protocols, Whitefield was accused of being licentious, subversiveness, and of having an over-heated imagination. See Jerome D. Mahaffey, *The Accidental Revolutionary: George Whitefield & the Creation of America*, (Waco, TX: Baylor University Press, 2011), pp. 31, 36, 56-58. Jessica M. Parr, *Inventing George Whitefield: Race, Revivalism, and the Making of a Religious Icon*, (Jackson, MS: University of Mississippi Press, 2015), 55, 59.

to Rev. Richard Salter of Mansfield, Connecticut, concerning Whitefield's preaching. Salter was firmly against the itinerant preacher, while Eliot mentions his reservations concerning Whitefield's preaching in Boston. A portion of this extended letter is as follows.

> As to Mr. Whitefield being the ringleader of those things of bad and dangerous tendencies which have prevailed among us, I am really at a loss what to say. In one sense he seems to be the accidental cause, as he was an instrument of stirring up a religious concern in the minds of great numbers, which concern the devil has unhappily improved to lead many astray, and give them a false and enthusiastic peace. But you'll say, has he not been the direct cause? Has not a vein of enthusiasm run through his writings, his preaching, and his conduct? I must needs say has been too much in all these which has appeared to me to border at least upon enthusiasm, and which I always thought had a very dangerous tendency, and I fear has had very unhappy effects. And I could heartily wish Mr. W. was more sensible of this, and was more disposed openly to acknowledge wherein he has mistaken nature for revelation, as I think he owns he may have done. I wish he could see light to own that he has done this in many instances, and would guard against the unhappy tendencies of many passages in his life and journals. I am persuaded that, in doing this, he would please God and serve religion . . . His best friends, I think, don't pretend to vindicate him wholly from the charge of enthusiasm, but I don't know that his greatest enemies have given him so severe an appellation as you do. The modest expression which the united ministers used in their Testimony against Mr. Davenport, suits me better,—that he is "tinctured with enthusiasm."
>
> I believe Mr. Whitefield does not pretend any extraordinary mission; if he does, he must produce better credentials than any he has yet, to induce me to receive him as one extraordinarily sent of God. I say nothing of his itinerancy, because I have great difficulties in my own mind about it; to mention would lead me beyond bounds. As to ministers inviting him I must be silent. I'll only say I have asked him but once. As to the state of religion among us, I am sorry that I must say that religion is at a low ebb. Christians are divided into parties, their spirits are roiled and disturbed; feuds and animosities are got to a prodigious height. Mr. W. is the grand subject of conversation. Both his friends and opposers discover too great warmth, and are much alienated from each other.[50]

We can clearly see from this insightful letter that ministers were deeply divided over Whitefield. The unwise and rash statements made by Whitefield in his youthful zeal were used against him when he returned to New England in 1744-1745. The mistakes by the youthful Whitefield were enhanced by some of his followers, leading to all kinds of "enthusiasm." Clearly this disturbed Rev. Andrew Eliot of the New North Church.

The June 25, 1745, edition of the *Boston Gazette* stated of Whitefield, "Friday he preached at Hull, Saturday at Cambridge; Lord's Day twice and yesterday once at Concord, with remarkable power."[51] Whitefield had preached several times before at Cambridge, and had resistance from Harvard College. Likewise, Whitefield had preached numerous times in Concord for his staunch ally, Rev. Daniel Bliss. But one location that we have not yet known about, where Whitefield preached in the summer of 1745, was Hull, Massachusetts.

The peninsula community of Hull was first settled in 1622. The town was built upon a series of rocks and sand bars that protrudes into Massachusetts Bay. Settlers filled in the land and had to continually reclaim land from the sea. Hull was well known for its expertise in the fisheries, as men harvested from the ocean flounder,

---

50   Charles C. Wells, *New North Church: from Birth to Death in Early Boston*, pp. 417-418.
51   *Boston Gazette*, June 25, 1745, p. 3.

mackerel, menhaden, shad, and in deeper waters cod, haddock, and occasionally halibut. It was easier to travel by water from Hull to Boston, as a series of packet boats transported fresh fish to the city and returned to Hull with various produce and commercial items. Hull was a working-class town dependent upon the sea. When George Whitefield visited Hull in 1745, the minister who welcomed him was Rev. Ezra Carpenter of the First Congregational Church.

Born in 1699, Ezra Carpenter was a 1720 graduate of Harvard College. He fully embraced the Puritan and Calvinistic heritage of his forefathers. Speaking of Carpenter, "He was ordained at Hull, Mass., November 24, 1725, and preached at that place twenty-one years . . . " He was known as "an able Divine, sound in ye faith, and a rational preacher of the Gospel—Respectable for his erudition—of manners easy, and polite in his conversation—pious and entertaining—A faithful Shepherd . . . "[52] When the Great Awakening swept through Massachusetts, Carpenter eventually supported the movement. His initial reluctance came from what he considered the flamboyant and obnoxious itinerant preachers who traveled around stirring up trouble. "He sympathized with the Whitefieldian revival but objected to the itinerating habits of Whitefield's followers."[53]

The maritime community of Hull was torn apart by theological disputes related to the awakening. Although Rev. Carpenter came out in favor of the movement, some thought he did not advocate enough for the revival. Others opposed the awakening and did not approve of Carpenter's pro-revival stance. It seems like almost no one was happy in the Hull Congregational Church. In 1743, a large group of New England clergymen endorsed the *Testimony* pamphlet in support of George Whitefield and the awakening. Carpenter signed the document, and it was widely printed. Also, in 1743 a council of pastors formed to mediate the dispute between the New Light Rev. Carpenter and some excited and opinionated members of the Hull church. Carpenter was exonerated. Yet by 1744, controversy about Carpenter still disrupted the Hull Congregational Church. The March 12, 1744 edition of the *Boston Evening Post* reported,

> The Town of Hull having for a long Time been disturbed by the preaching and exhorting of some rambling and turbulent Zealots, a Number of the People were so prejudiced against their Rev. and worthy Pastor [Ezra Carpenter], as to leave his Ministry, and exhibited Fifteen Articles of Charge against him relating to errors in doctrine.[54]

Apparently, some in the Hull Congregational Church did not appreciate Carpenter's sober and cautious acceptance of the revival. Others thought his preaching was not evangelistic enough. And some even questioned his orthodoxy. "The Rev. Ezra Carpenter, pastor of the church in Hull, was one of the signers of the "Testimony" of July, 1743; yet some of his people were dissatisfied, because, as they thought, he did not preach the doctrines of grace, and was an opposer to the revival."[55] When George Whitefield came to Hull in 1745, he came to support a friend in a disruptive church situation. Whitefield knew that Carpenter had put his reputation on the line when he signed the *Testimony* to support Whitefield and the awakening. Now the itinerant preacher came to Hull to support the beleaguered Carpenter. Those dissatisfied in Hull, who thought Carpenter was not evangelical enough, or questioned his commitment to the awakening, were silenced when the much-esteemed Whitefield preached from the Hull Congregational Church pulpit. Whitefield attempted to reconcile the congregation to their minister. Nevertheless, Carpenter was dismissed from the church in Hull in 1746.

As already noted, Whitefield frequently departed and returned to Boston on preaching circuits. Boston newspapers seemed to have tired of recording the everyday locations and ministries of the roving evangelist.

---

52 Benjamin Read, *The History of Swanzey, New Hampshire, from 1734 to 1890*, (Salem, MA: The Salem Press Publishing and Printing Company, 1892), p. 515.
53 Daniel Wadsworth, *Diary of Daniel Wadsworth, Seventh Pastor of the First Church of Christ in Hartford*, (Hartford, CT: The Press of the Case, Lockwood & Brainard Company, 1894), p. 116.
54 *Boston Evening Post*, March 12, 1744, p. 3.
55 Joseph Tracy, *The Great Awakening*, (1841: reprinted by Banner of Truth Trust, Carlisle, PA: 1989), p. 338.

After months of traveling in and out of the city, and speaking again and again at Boston's leading churches, local newspapers apparently lost interest. For example, in early July the *Boston Gazette* simply recorded that Whitefield had preached on the Boston Common the week before, with no notation of the size of the crowds of the texts of his sermons.[56] Other editions of the local newspapers did not carry any reports of his travels. What did appear in the Boston newspapers, in the spring and summer of 1745, were dozens of advertisements of pamphlets for sale either for or against George Whitefield. Also, there were occasionally letters printed in Boston newspapers, both supporting and denouncing Whitefield and the awakening.

A minister who observed Whitefield's ministry and influence in the first several months of 1745 was Rev. Ebenezer Parkman of Westborough, Massachusetts. Parkman was born in Boston to a working-class family. He attended Harvard College and graduated in 1721. He then taught school, studied for the ministry, and did substitute preaching. He was ordained as the first minister at the Congregational Church in Westborough, Massachusetts in 1724, serving there until his death in 1782. Westborough was located about thirty miles west from Boston. Rev. Parkman's extensive diary gives a fascinating glimpse into life in rural Colonial Massachusetts. His diary entries relate to local news, weather, crops, livestock, politics, and religious issues such as ordinations, theological debates, ministerial councils, and especially the concerns related to George Whitefield in New England. Throughout early to mid-1745, Parkman made numerous notations in his diary related to Whitefield. Summaries and excerpts are as follows:

This pen and ink drawing of Mr. Ebenezer Parkman is the only picture of him known to be in existence.

Source: "Parkman Genealogy," https://parkmangenealogy. wordpress.com/2009/11/14/rev-ebenezer-parkmans-grave-westboro-ma.

> January 8. Notations related to ministers meeting today at Southborough to make a public statement against George Whitefield.
>
> January 12. News reached him that Whitefield was preaching successfully in Boston.
>
> January 17. "The world full of Mr. Whitefield (as I hear) who is now preaching in Boston."
>
> January 22. Ministers were to meet at Marlborough against Whitefield, but Parkman wrote a letter stating that he would not attend.
>
> February 1. A resident of Westborough returned home from Boston with "several pamphlets against Mr. Whitefield. Parkman wrote that his area was "full" of such pamphlets. He wrote, "The world is much divided . . . God grant us wisdom, Grace, and Peace!"
>
> April 5. A notation that Parkman was in Boston and that George Whitefield was "preaching at Dr. Sewell's" meaning at the South Church in Boston.

---

56 *Boston Gazette*, July 2, 1745, p. 4.

April 6. Parkman heard Whitefield preach in Boston. He wrote, "Mr. Whitefield expounds every morning at Boston, as well as preaches very frequently as heretofore. The divisions on that occasion, I think, hotter than ever. The Lord have mercy on us for his great Name's sake."

April 15. "Indignation and Contempt cast upon Mr. William Hobby for his vindication of Mr. Whitefield."

May 15. Parkman met in Boston with Rev. Joseph Sewell, Rev. Joshua Gee, and Dr. Charles Chauncey. "Mr. Whitefield is subject, almost everywhere."

May 17. Parkman studied the Harvard Testimony against Whitefield. He visited Harvard College. He read pro-revival literature written by Rev. Gilbert Tennent.

May 31. While in Boston, Parkman noted that Rev. Peter Clark of Salem Village preached about the numerous errors of Whitefield, while George Whitefield and his wife Elizabeth were in the audience.

June 11. Parkman attended a ministerial meeting in Boston, where discussion was concerning "when a Testimony was drawn up against Mr. Whitefield, but which I strenuously denied and gave my reasons for my refusal of it."

June 26. After writing something in defense of Whitefield, he showed it to "Deacon Fry" as they rode together in a carriage.

June 28. "I saw Deacon Mirriam of Grafton going to Concord with a horse for Mr. Whitefield."

June 30. "Mr. Whitefield preaches at Grafton today and some number of my southern neighbors are gone to hear him."

July 1. "Mr. Whitefield, I hear, preaches at Grafton today, a.m., and at Upton p.m."

July 2. "Mr. Whitefield preached at Dr. Gotts and my wife heard him." Dr. Benjamin Gott was a prominent physician with a large home in Marlborough.

July 3. "Mr. Swift[57] of Acton his indecent vociferation concerning my not being present at . . . January 22 to bear my testimony against George Whitefield."

July 18. "Mr. Prentice and his wife went a while agoe along with Mr. Whitefield and his wife in their journey to Northampton and are not returned."

August 13. Parkman rode to a minister's meeting where the pastors disputed about Whitefield.[58]

---

57 Rev. John Swift served the Congregational Church in Acton from 1738 to his death in 1775.
58 Ebenezer Parkman, *The Diary of Ebenezer Parkman, 1745-1746*, (Worcester, MA: The American Antiquarian Society).

This detailed narrative by Rev. Parkman places Whitefield in some familiar places with familiar friends. We also notice that Whitefield was publicly denounced with his wife present by Rev. Peter Clark of the First Church in Salem Village (now Danvers). Why Whitefield attended a church service at this unwelcoming church is uncertain, as Clark had previously denounced Whitefield publicly and in print. Clark was adamant against the awakening and Whitefield. The Parkman narrative lists three new places where Whitefield preached—Grafton, Upton, and Marlborough. These will be looked at individually.

Grafton, Massachusetts, was purchased from local Indians in 1724. The town was officially established in 1735. The first minister in Grafton was Rev. Solomon Prentice, who was ordained to the church in 1731. The first Congregational meeting house was built in 1730 and stood for one hundred years, next to a schoolhouse and a burial ground.[59] This small, rural farming community was successful, as the mostly Puritan townsfolk lived simple lives.

The church in Grafton was greatly disrupted by the Great Awakening. Disputes with Rev. Prentice raged, some saying he was too much a revivalist, some stating that he was not evangelical enough, and others saying he should speak against the revival movement. Beginning in the late 1730s the church had various councils, disputations, attempts at dismissals, and a spirit of disunity plagued the congregation.[60] In the spring of 1744, Solomon Prentice wrote an eyewitness narrative of the awakening in his congregation and surrounding towns. His handwritten notes are on fragile paper, are side stitched, and are preserved at the Massachusetts Historical Society. Prentice wrote that many townsfolk were in deep conviction for their sins, and showed signs of repentance and conversion. He wrote of "a very discernable alteration in the manners and behavior of the young people," and that men who were "heads of families" were confessing their sins publicly. Some of the additional preaching meetings were so loud from the shouts of the people that he said he could not be easily heard. Prentice recorded that as he preached, many "cried out in distress" to Jesus to be saved. He stated, "There appears a very general concern in all ranks and ages of persons among us," and that "The people were greatly affected and awakened."[61]

When George Whitefield arrived in tiny Grafton in June 1745, the town went into a frenzy. Rev. Prentice signed the July 7, 1743 *Testimony and Advice of an Assembly of Pastors*, in support of Whitefield. Prentice happily endorsed Whitefield and was an outspoken advocate of the awakening. Not all in his church, or in the town, agreed. On June 30, 1745, Whitefield preached at Grafton. The results of his preaching were unremarkable. "Whitefield is said to have preached here one or more times, though not, as we can learn, with any very visible effect."[62] After the itinerate Whitefield departed Grafton, the opposers of Prentice and the revival gathered strength. Again, church councils and letters of reprimand were given to him by the Old Lights in his church. "Mr. Prentice was a great admirer of Whitefield, and became one of what were called "The New Lights;" His course was not approved by his society; and a controversy arose which led to his dismission, July 10, 1747."[63]

Upton, Massachusetts was incorporated in 1735 with land acquired from neighboring towns. Construction of the first church meeting house was completed in 1736. The first minister was Rev. Thomas Weld, who was ordained in Upton on January 4, 1738. During the controversial times of the Great Awakening, he had a tense relationship with his congregation. Weld supported Jonathan Edwards,

---

59 "History of Grafton," https://www.grafton-ma.gov/about-grafton/pages/history-grafton. The multi-generational Prentice family was well established in Grafton. See *Vital Records of Grafton, Massachusetts, to the End of the Year 1849*, (Worcester, MA: Franklin P. Rice Publisher, 1906), pp. 103-106.
60 Frederick C. Pierce, *History of Grafton, Worcester County, Massachusetts . . .* , (Worcester, MA: Published by the author, 1879), pp. 174-178.
61 Ross W. Beales Jr. editor, "Solomon Prentice's Narrative of the Great Awakening," *Proceedings of the Massachusetts Historical Society*, Vol. 83 (1971), pp. 130-147.
62 Frederick C. Pierce, *History of Grafton, Worcester County, Massachusetts, p. 174.*
63 Ibid., p. 170.

George Whitefield, and the revival movement. When Whitefield preached in Upton on July 1, 1745, Pastor Weld was elated but many of the townsfolk were not. He was officially dismissed from his pulpit in December 1744, but stayed on several more years as the pastor, as no suitable replacement could be found by the divided congregation.[64] In this tense atmosphere Whitefield preached, then moved on to his next appointment at nearby Marlborough.

Marlborough, Massachusetts was a pioneer Puritan town, founded in 1660 by settlers looking to farm. Located at a crossroads, the town slowly prospered. Numerous small taverns met the needs of travelers. Marlborough was huge, and was later divided up into several town as the population increased. By the early 1700s there were still homes in Marlborough that were fortified against Indian attacks. When George Whitefield came to town in July 1745, the Congregational minister was Rev. Aaron Smith. During theological disruptions from the revivals, Smith was ordained in Marlborough on June 11, 1740. From 1740-1760 he had a relatively calm ministry in Marlborough. As he got older, he was in poor health and the church folks sought another minister. "During this period, the 'Great Awakening,' or Whitefield movement, occurred; and while some churches were divided or disturbed, and others severed in twain, there was no particular commotion in this town."[65]

Related to Marlborough, the previously quoted journal of Rev. Ebenezer Parkman stated, "July 2. Mr. Whitefield preached at Dr. Gotts and my wife heard him." Dr. Benjamin Gott was a wealthy, popular physician who lived in Marlborough. Apparently, Whitefield preached outside at the large home of Dr. Gott, and not in the meeting house of Rev. Aaron Smith or Rev. Ebenezer Parkman in Marlborough. Not to be overlooked is that previously, in January 1745, an association of ministers met at Marlborough to denounce Whitefield and the revival.[66] Part of the proceedings from that meeting stated, "The devil himself, with all his cunning, could not take a more direct step to overthrow the churches of New England, hurt religion, and destroy the souls of men, than Whitefield had taken."[67]

Whitefield's travels in the summer of 1745 are hard to narrate chronologically. Apparently, he travelled from Marlborough on July 2 and arrived in Lynn late the next day. We have an interesting summer, 1745 account of George Whitefield in Lynn, northeast of Boston. Whitefield had already visited and preached several times in Lynn, namely in December 1744 and February 1745 for Rev. Edward Cheever of the Third Parish. Lynn is approximately fifteen miles northeast from Boston, along a good but winding coastal road. There was significant theological controversy in this port community, as the leading ministers in Lynn, Rev. Nathaniel Henchman of the First Church, and Rev. Edward Cheever of the Third Church, were in total disagreement about Whitefield and the awakening. Henchman was bombastic against Whitefield, while Cheever endorsed the traveling preacher. While much of Whitefield's summer 1745 ministry in the Boston area was not covered by Boston's newspapers, one article hostile to Whitefield did appear in the *Boston Evening Post*. In a letter from Lynn, dated July 3, 1745, the anonymous writer, probably Nathaniel Henchman or his surrogate, warned the people of Lynn that Whitefield was expected that day. The unnamed writer lambasts Whitefield as a deceiver, a deluder with reckless behavior. He does not want Lynn to "be misled or imposed upon and deluded" by Whitefield, who he calls "a person of your enthusiastic turn, and unjustifiable behavior."[68] This newspaper article tells us of the enduring antagonism between religious groups related to Whitefield and the revival. The next day a letter from Rev. Nathaniel Henchman was printed in the *Boston Gazette*.

---

64 Benjamin Wood, *A Centennial Address, Delivered at Upton, Mass., June 25, 1835*, (Boston: William Pierce, Publisher, 1835), p. 12.
65 Charles Hudson, *History of the Town of Marlborough, Middlesex County, Massachusetts . . .* , (Boston: T.R. Marvin & Son Publishers, 1862), p. 160.
66 *The Testimony of an Association of Ministers Convened at Marlborough, Jan. 22, 1744-45, Against the Rev. Mr. George Whitefield*, (Boston: T. Fleet, printer, 1745).
67 Richard O. Roberts, *Whitefield in Print*, p. 619.
68 *Boston Evening Post*, July 15, 1745, p. 1.

Lynn,

July 4 , 1745

Mr. Fleet,

Sir,

Yesterday morning the Rev. Mr. Whitefield came into my parish, attended by the Rev. Messieurs Hobby and Cheever, &c. and preached twice in the open field. As he was passing nigh my house, I delivered him a letter, of which I now send to you a copy, requesting you to publish it in your next paper, to prevent misrepresentations of its contents. Hereby you'll oblige, your very humble servant,

N. Henchman[69]

This brief note from Rev. Nathaniel Henchman reveals some of the tensions existing in the Boston area related to Whitefield's summer 1745, ministry. We notice that the traveling preacher had at least two companions with him, Rev. William Hobby of Reading, and Rev. Edward Cheever of Lynn. We also see that ministers opposed to Whitefield, like Henchman, were quite bold in their denunciations of Whitefield, confronting him personally and requesting that anti-Whitefield letters be published in local newspapers. It is interesting to note that the request by Henchman to print the anti-Whitefield letter in the *Boston Gazette* was not honored. Lynn was torn apart by the revival. Edward Cheever of the Third Church in Lynn (now in Saugus) endured several years of confrontations and accusations from Henchman, until Cheever in 1747 moved to a ministry in Eastham Massachusetts, where he died in 1794.[70]

---

69 *Boston Gazette*, July 2, 1745, p. 4.
70 Eugene D. Russell, "Harvard College and Lynn in Colonial Times," *The Registrar of the Lynn Historical Society,* (Lynn, MA: 1912), p. 88.

CHAPTER 22

WHITEFIELD'S MINISTRY IN WESTERN MASSACHUSETTS

EARLY JULY 1745

IT IS DIFFICULT TO TRACE the exact steps of Whitefield during his 1745 tour throughout New England. There are days or up to a week between events and locations that we know nothing about. However, there are many glimpses into his roving 1745 itinerate ministry that are revealing and fascinating.

One example of this is his summer 1745 preaching tour through western Massachusetts. We are not exactly sure by what westerly route Whitefield came to this area. We do know that on July 5, 1745 he was at Framingham, about fifteen miles west of Boston. From a religious diary kept by Mr. Ebenezer Goddard, of Framingham, we extract the following: "July ye 5, 1745, that dear servant of God, Mr. Whitefield, preached at Framingham. It is said he preached in a barn."[1] Why would the itinerant evangelist preach in a barn? Because the church in Framingham was temporarily without a minister. Rev. John Swift served the Congregational Church in Framingham for 45 year before he died on April 24, 1745. The church was divided over the revivals and it effected Swift's health. The next permanent minister in Framingham was Rev. Matthew Bridge, who was called by the church in December 1745 and ordained a few months later.[2] Whitefield arrived in Framingham after the death of Swift and before the installation of Bridge as the new pastor. The congregational church had divided leadership and decided to ban Whitefield from preaching in the meeting house. So, he preached in a barn in Framingham.

The key document that traces Whitefield's western Massachusetts preaching circuit is from a newspaper article originating in Boston, reprinted in Pennsylvania. The article is quoted in full as follows.

> On Friday July 12th the Rev. Mr. Whitefield preach'd for the Rev. Mr. White of Hardwicke twice, and once at Quabin, a new place, where there is no Minister, Saturday for the Rev. Mr. Abercrombie of Pelham, Lord's-Day for the Rev. Mr. Edwards of Northampton twice, on Monday and Tuesday once; on Wednesday for the Rev. Mr. Judd at Newhampton, where he was attended by many Friends with Muskets and Pistols on Account of the Indians, it being the outmost settlement: He kept the Thanksgiving at Northampton and preached at the Request of the Rev. Mr. Edwards, on Friday for the Rev. Mr. Williams of Hadley once, and in the Evening for the Rev. Mr. Parsons at the Swamp, on Saturday for the Rev. Mr. Billings at Cold Spring, on Lord's-Day for the Rev. Mr. Trowbridge, twice on Monday for the Rev. Mr. Harvey at Kensington, and went from thence to Long-Meadow.[3]

---

1   William Barry, *A History of Framingham, Massachusetts*, (Carlisle, MA: Applewood Books, 1847), p. 114.
2   Ibid., pp. 108-112.
3   *Pennsylvania Gazette* (Philadelphia, PA), August 15, 1745, p. 2. This article is a quote from a newspaper release from Boston dated August 5, 1745.

This detailed report provides many dates, names, and locations that enable us to trace the locations and activities of Whitefield on this July 1745, preaching circuit in western Massachusetts.

The first name and location reveals that, "On Friday July 12th the Rev. Mr. Whitefield preach'd for the Rev. Mr. White of Hardwicke twice . . . " Rev. David White was a Yale College graduate who came to Hardwick in 1736. As the Congregational Church's first settled minister, he was ordained in Hardwick in October 1736. He spent the rest of his life at this church, to his death in 1784. The early settlers of the town were successful, as lumbering, fishing, and farming prospered. Saw and grist mills were the first type of manufacturing, taking advantage of the free waterpower provided by numerous streams. The first meeting house was completed in 1738. It was a modest structure built as finances and donated labor allowed. A new meeting house was voted on in 1741, and was not completed until several years later, but was habitable.[4] It was in this unfinished Congregational meeting house that Whitefield preached, in the summer of 1745.

The minister in Hardwick, David White, was described as follows: "His talents were respectable, but by no means brilliant. His success in giving satisfaction to his people depended not so much on the energy of his mind, as on the meekness, simplicity, and purity of his heart. He lived in a troublesome period, both political and ecclesiastical . . . Rev. Mr. White . . . was eminently a man of peace."[5] White had some temporary ecclesiastical issues related to his deacons in 1748 and 1749, which caused minor and temporary disruptions. But his major controversy was related to the Great Awakening that swept through much of the Massachusetts Colony in the 1730s and early 1740s. Disruptions in western Massachusetts churches abounded, and Hardwick was not exempt. Speaking about Rev. White and the Congregational Church in Hardwick,

> Some churches were rent asunder. And this church did not entirely escape the ravages of the storm which swept through the land. A portion of its members withdrew, and were styled "New Lights," or more generally, "Separatists." They erected a meeting house, and established a regular meeting. Mr. White and his church manifested much forbearance, laboring with the dissatisfied, separating brethren, but never using the rod of excommunication. The effect of such measures was favorable. The separate party, as such, became extinct; some of its members removed from the town, and others were reconciled to the church; their meeting house was demolished, and Mr. White had the happiness to behold again a state of harmony and peace in his parish.[6]

Evidently, White's New Light position was the pattern for the Hardwick Congregational Church. The church granted him a significant pay raise in 1746, and he and the church experienced steady but not remarkable church growth for the next decades through the Revolutionary War period.[7]

Whitefield's preaching tour continued to the tiny town of Quabbin. "Rev. Mr. Whitefield preached . . . once at Quabbin, a new Place, where there is no minister . . . "[8] The fledgling town of Quabbin disappeared under water after the enormous Quabbin Reservoir was created in 1938. After preaching once at Quabbin, Whitefield then rode a few miles west to the farming town of Pelham. "Rev. Mr. Whitefield preached . . . Saturday for the Rev. Mr. Abercrombie of Pelham . . . "[9]

Pelham, Massachusetts Colony was settled by Scottish-Irish Presbyterians in 1738. These Scottish settlers came to America fleeing religious and civil persecution from Roman Catholics in Ireland. The location of the

---

4   Lucius R. Page, *History of Hardwick, Massachusetts, with a Genealogical Register*, (Boston, MA: Houghton, Mifflin & Company, 1883), pp. 178-181.
5   Ibid., pp. 192, 183.
6   Ibid., p. 193.
7   Ibid., p. 175.
8   *Pennsylvania Gazette*, August 15, 1745, p. 2.
9   Ibid.

town was selected because of its thick forests, rolling hills with fertile soil, and an abundance of fresh water from the Swift River and several smaller brooks. The Protestant and Calvinist beliefs of these settlers were unquestioned. The need for a Presbyterian minister in Pelham was paramount in the minds of the town leaders. At an August 6, 1740 town meeting, it was voted "to agree with a workman to rease [raise] a Meeting house and in Close [enclose] it and lay the under floor and hinge the Doors and mack [make] the windo [window] frames. They also "voted that the settling of a minister be a jorned [adjourned] for the present." Five men were to "be a comeety [committee] to proceed for the reasing [raising] of the Meeting house."[10]

In September 1741, the town of Pelham approached the Londonderry, New Hampshire Presbytery, seeking a ministerial candidate. Simultaneously, construction began on a Presbyterian meeting house, which would also serve as the Pelham town hall. At the May 11, 1742, Pelham town meeting, "voted that we intercede with Mr. Robert Abercrombie to be our Suplayer [supply, or temporary minister] as far as he can for this summer."[11] At the Pelham town meeting on November 8, 1743, it was voted that Abercrombie be settled as their permanent minister, and that his salary, the keeping of his horse, his firewood, and other arrangements be completed.[12] Most of the people of Pelham were satisfied with Abercrombie as their minister, though some resented that they now had to pay a ministerial tax to the town.

Rev. Robert Abercrombie of Ireland was a thirty-two-year-old Presbyterian minister surrounded by Congregationalists in western Massachusetts. He arrived in Boston in 1740, already a supporter of George Whitefield, as Whitefield's extensive itinerant ministries in the British Isles was well known. As a Presbyterian, Abercrombie preached for the Presbyterians in Boston and Worcester before learning of the new Presbyterian settlement in Pelham. Abercrombie had read of the Great Awakening in New England, and he was in full support. Any hesitancy New Light Congregationalists had towards Abercrombie were dissipated when Rev. Jonathan Edwards, and a committee of local Congregational ministers, ordained Abercrombie to the gospel ministry in Pelham on August 30, 1744, with Edwards preaching the ordination sermon.

> Rev. Robert Abercrombie . . . was a man in who the Scotch characteristics or resolute persistence and determination were very marked. He was . . . educated at the Edinburg University, where he had the reputation of being a profound scholar, familiar with Latin, Greek, Hebrew, and Syriac: and brought testimonials from the Presbytery of Edinburg and Kirkaleby, also recommendations from distinguished Scotch divines. A man of sound sense and ability, well equipped for his chosen profession: a strict disciplinarian, and possessed of a resolute purpose to demand rigid adherence to the doctrines and requirements of the Presbyterian Church of Scotland.[13]

It is interesting to consider the meeting of Whitefield and Abercrombie in Pelham, in the summer of 1745. Whitefield was an avid supporter of the revival in Scotland, and he began correspondence with leading Scott-Presbyterian ministers as early as 1739. In July 1741, Whitefield arrived in Scotland for a preaching tour, departing three months later in October. During this time, he developed a deep respect and admiration for Scottish Presbyterianism.[14] Whitefield did not actually visit Ireland and meet the Scott-Irish Presbyterians until 1751. But Whitefield knew of the stock from which Abercrombie came, and he supported the new minister when he preached for him in his newly completed meeting house in Pelham. The old meeting

---

10 C.O. Parmenter, *History of Pelham, Mass., from 1738 to 1898*, (Amherst, MA: Press of Carpenter & Morehouse, 1898), p. 38.
11 Ibid., p. 41.
12 Ibid., p. 45.
13 Ibid., p. 295.
14 Arnold Dallimore, *George Whitefield: The Life and Times of the Great Evangelist of the Eighteenth Century Revival*, (Carlisle, PA: Banner of Truth Trust, 1980), vol. II, pp. 88-98

house in Pelham, later the town hall, is now a museum sponsored by the town of Pelham. It is fascinating to walk in this historic building and see the enormous original hand-hewn beams that still hold up the building.

The *Philadelphia Gazette*, August 15, 1745, simply reported, "Rev. Mr. Whitefield preached . . . Saturday for the Rev. Mr. Abercrombie of Pelham." Imagine the scene—a Presbyterian minister, hosting a priest of the Church of England, in a community surrounded by Congregational Churches. Here two things came together as one, namely Calvinist theology, together with preaching that promoted the awakening. In Pelham, the interdenominational and evangelical aspect of the revival was apparent. Both during and after Whitefield preached in Pelham in 1745, there was no disruption, no controversy, and no church schism. "There is nothing upon the records to indicate that there was any trouble between pastor and people for the first two years of Mr. Abercrombie's pastorate."[15]

Whitefield's preaching tour took him next to Northampton, to Rev. Jonathan Edwards. This trip was an easy fifteen miles west from Pelham, the only obstacle being the ferry crossing of the Connecticut River. Since their first meeting in 1740, these two men had promoted revival in their own ways. For Whitefield, he was an incessant traveler, an itinerant evangelist who crossed the Atlantic Ocean to preach, and who travelled throughout England and Scotland promoting the awakening. In contrast, since their last meeting, Edwards had not travelled more than one hundred miles from Northampton. He was settled as a pastor, but would travel locally to preach, especially at ordination councils. While Whitefield wrote short pamphlets to defend his theological positions, Edwards wrote larger booklets defending his position on revival. Edwards also wrote longer, more detailed theological works, such as *Distinguishing Marks of the Work of the Spirit of God* (1741); *Some thoughts Concerning the Present Revival of Religion in New England* (1742); and *Treatise Concerning Religious Affections* (1743). Whitefield was an itinerant evangelist, while Edwards was a pastor, theologian, and local evangelist.

A photograph of the colonial meeting house in Pelham, Massachusetts. Constructed in 1743-1744, the building served as a location for religious services and town business. George Whitefield preached in this building in July 1745. Photograph by Ken Lawson.

---

15   C.O. Parmenter, *History of Pelham, Mass., from 1738 to 1898*, p. 300.

A newspaper report stated, "Rev. Mr. Whitefield preached . . . Lord's-Day for the Rev. Mr. Edwards of Northampton twice, on Monday and Tuesday once . . . "[16] Edwards was pleased to see that Whitefield had matured since their first meeting in 1740. The five-or-so years between their meetings had allowed Whitefield time to reconsider his often-bombastic accusations against clergymen as unconverted. Whitefield was now more prudent and was less inclined to rely upon "impulses," a term used to describe a direct, subjective leading from the Holy Spirit.[17] One account of Whitefield preaching for Edwards at Northampton, and then in neighboring towns, states:

> He visited the country again in 1745, and preached at Northampton June 15, and at Southampton June 17, and probably in other places. The leading men in Hatfield would not allow Whitefield to preach there, but many of the people came down to Northampton and Hadley to hear him. It has been said that when he preached in Hadley, his voice was heard in Hatfield.[18]

It is interesting to learn what Edwards thought of this second visit from Whitefield. In a letter addressed "To Friends in Scotland," dated mid-September 1745, Edwards wrote that "Mr. Whitefield's late visit to New England has been an occasion of the whole country's being in an uproar; but, I think, wholly without any fault of his, or at least, any fault committed by him." After describing the opposition to Whitefield from various clergy in New England, Edwards wrote, "They could find nothing against him; for in his last visit [three months prior] he conducted himself much more modestly, wisely, and inoffensively than before," meaning in 1740. Edwards continued defending Whitefield, saying, "All that he did was only to preach the pure doctrines of the gospel to the people, applying them with proper earnestness, carefully avoiding meddling with their controversies, behaving himself with admirable meekness . . . " Then Edwards describes what it was like to have George and Elizabeth Whitefield as houseguests for a few days.

A sketch of the home of Jonathan and Sarah Edwards. Here George Whitefield enjoyed the hospitality of the Edwards family in 1740 and in 1745. Source: Public domain image.

16 *Pennsylvania Gazette,* August 15, 1745, p. 2.
17 George M. Marsden, *Jonathan Edwards: A Life,* (New Haven, CT: Yale University Press, 2003), pp. 212-213.
18 Sylvester Judd, *History of Hadley . . . , Massachusetts,* (Springfield, MA: H.R. Hunting & Company, 1905), p. 330. The June dates in this quote should most likely be in July.

He with his lady was here at Northampton, almost a week in July last, and behaved himself so, that he endeared himself much to me; he appeared in a more desirable temper of mind and more solid and judicious in his thoughts, and prudence in his conduct, then when he was here before.[19]

Whitefield's next stop after Northampton was close by, nine miles away at Newhampton, now part of Southampton, Massachusetts. A newspaper report stated, "Rev. Mr. Whitefield preached . . . on Wednesday for the Rev. Mr. Judd at Newhampton, where he was attended by many Friends with Muskets and Pistols on account of the Indians, it being the outmost Settlement."[20] The town of Newhampton dates to 1730, when settlers from Northampton built and farmed on twenty-acre house lots, with additional farm land and forest land for wood. One house lot was reserved for a minister. This was a farming community that relied on visiting ministers to preach, baptize, and serve communion. In the first town meeting in 1741, town officials expressed the need to have a settled minister in Newhampton. The first full-time minister was Jonathan Judd.

Judd was a student at Yale College when he heard Whitefield preach there in 1740. He graduated from Yale in 1741, and after an interim time as the preacher at Newhampton, Judd was ordained at the church in June, 1743. Judd was a determined New Light and a firm supporter of the Great Awakening. One report stated, "The Rev. Jonathan Judd, the first minister, was ordained June 8, 1743. His house was palisaded, and provided with a watch-tower for security against the Indians."[21] Another account said of Judd of Newhampton:

> In February 1743 the Rev. Jonathan Judd of Suffield CT., a recent Yale graduate and the choice of the search committee, arrived in town. He was warmly received and called to be the first minister of the area which was by then called "New Hampton". On June 8th of that year, a Council of Churches met here for Rev. Judd's ordination, solemnized by prayer and the laying on of hands. The well known Rev. Jonathan Edwards of Northampton preached the sermon. A Confession of Faith and the church covenanting were adopted and signed by the original 32 members, and the church was incorporated. Rev. Judd remained here as our preacher for sixty years, until his death in 1803 . . . The first Meetinghouse, begun in 1737, was completed in 1752.[22]

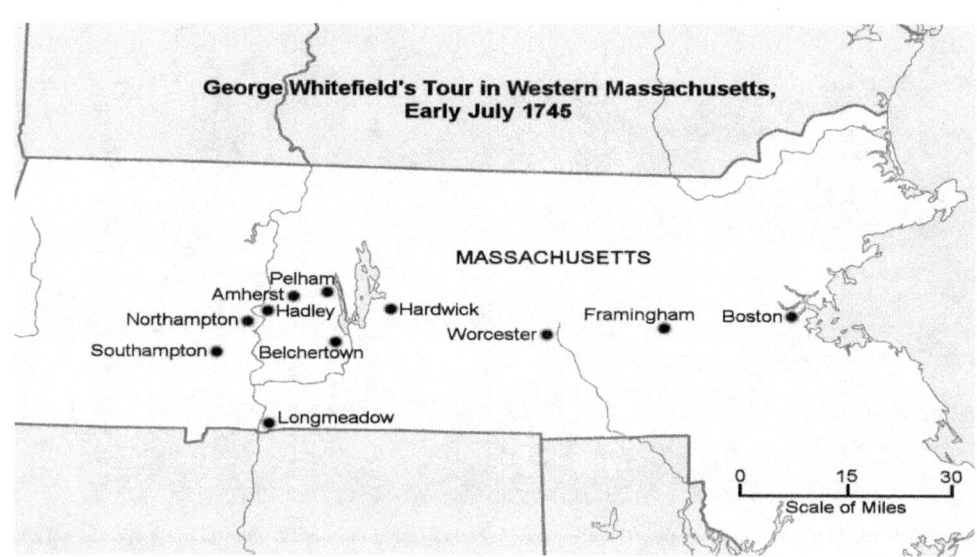

---

19 Jonathan Edwards, *Letters and Personal Writings of Rev. Jonathan Edwards*, (New Haven, CT: Yale University Press, 1998), vol. 16, pp. 175-179.
20 *Pennsylvania Gazette,* August 15, 1745, p. 2.
21 "Southampton, Massachusetts," http://capecodhistory.us/Mass1890/Southampton1890.htm.
22 "First Congregational Church of Southampton-History," http://www.shcong.org/about/history.

Rev. Jonathan Judd kept a diary. His diary entry for July 17, 1745 simply stated, "Mr. Whitefield preached here." There was no note on whether or not Whitefield and Judd dined together.[23] Whitefield spent only a few hours in Newhampton (now Southampton). He preached once for Jonathan Judd, on a Wednesday, in a military settling on account of threatening Indians. It would have been remarkable to listen to Judd, the Yale College student, speak to Whitefield about the latter's ministry on the Yale campus, and the influence he had on the younger Jonathan Judd. At the Center Cemetery in Southampton, the inscription on Judd's grave reads:

> To the memory of Rev. Jonathan Judd, the first minister of Christ in Southampton and of Mrs. Silence Judd, his amiable and worthy consort who died Oct. 25, 1783 in the 63rd year of her age. He saw his people of 30 families increase to nearly 1000 souls—was able, evangelical, and faithful in preaching, was eminent in piety, wisdom, meekness, benevolence, lived greatly respected and beloved, and after a ministry of more than 60 years rested from his labors July 28, 1803, in the 84th year of his age.[24]

The next day, a Thursday, Whitefield was back at Northampton with the Rev. Jonathan and Sarah Edwards family. A newspaper report stated, "Rev. Mr. Whitefield . . . kept the Thanksgiving at Northampton and preached at the request of the Rev. Mr. Edwards . . . ."[25] During the eighteenth century, thanksgiving events were times dedicated to prayer and attendance at religious services. Individual colonies commonly observed times of thanksgiving to God, typically proclaimed by the colonial governor. Locally, a town council could call for a day of thanksgiving for all the townsfolk to stop their routine activities and pause to give thanks to the Lord. Such thanksgiving events could be several times a year; they could be annual, or less frequent. We do not know the exact purpose of the thanksgiving event in Northampton in the summer of 1745, but we do know that Edwards asked Whitefield to preach that day in the Northampton Congregational Church.

It is interesting to contemplate the influence of the Jonathan and Sarah Edwards family on the newly married George Whitefield. In the summer of 1745, Jonathan and Sarah had ten children, the oldest seventeen years old, and the youngest, a son named Jonathan, was about three months old. Whitefield and his wife Elizabeth had only one child, who died young. In his 1740 visit to the Edwards' home, Whitefield wrote in his *Journals*, that he was duly impressed by the virtue of Sarah Edwards and the obedience and sensibleness of their young children.[26] Married in 1741, Whitefield's marriage to Elizabeth James has been the subject of some discussion. While no one claims that the George and Elizabeth Whitefield marriage was radiant and exceptional, to say that Whitefield had "a disappointing love life and a largely unhappy marriage" may be an overstatement.[27] Perhaps closer to the mark is that the Whitefield marriage was "acceptable," in that Elizabeth always supported her husband's itinerant ministries.[28] But clearly affectionate, romantic, exuberant love was not in this match.

From the Edwards' home in Northampton, Whitefield next visited the nearby town of Hadley. A newspaper report stated, "Rev. Mr. Whitefield preached . . . on Friday for the Rev. Mr. Williams of Hadley once . . . [29] In October 1740, Rev. Chester Williams of Hadley happily welcomed Whitefield

---

23 *Diary of Rev. Jonathan Judd*, courtesy of the First Congregational Church of Southampton, Massachusetts.
24 "Rev. Jonathan Judd," http://www.findagrave.com/cgi-bin/fg.cgi?page=gr&GRid=123688775.
25 *Pennsylvania Gazette*, August 15, 1745, p. 2.
26 George Whitefield, *Journals of George Whitefield*, (1747: reprinted by Banner of Truth Trust, Carlisle, PA, 1985), pp. 476-477.
27 Mark Galli, "Whitefield's Curious Love Life," http://www.christianitytoday.com/ch/1993/issue38/3833.html.
28 Doreen Moore, *Good Christians, Good Husbands? Leaving a Legacy in Marriage and Ministry*, (United Kingdom: Christian Focus Publishers, 2004). This book dedicates an entire chapter to the George and Elizabeth Whitefield marriage. In Arnold Dallimore, *George Whitefield: The Life and Times . . .* , he devotes a chapter to Whitefield's marriage, believing that their marriage was "a source of spiritual and cultural advancement for Elizabeth," and that George "looked on marriage as largely a help, he also considered it a hindrance," vol. II, pp. 111-112.
29 *Pennsylvania Gazette*, August 15, 1745, p. 2.

and allowed him to preach in the Congregational Church. This 1745 visit was no exception. Williams served in "a thriving rural hamlet" in which farming dominated the community. Hadley was reasonably prosperous, evident by the wealthy in town wearing European fashions and other luxuries of dress, and some carriages in Hadley became noticeably more elaborate and comfortable.[30] Chester Williams is perhaps best known as a supporter of the removal of Jonathan Edwards from his pulpit in Northampton. The issue was the inherent value of communion. Edwards taught that it was not a means of conversion.

Likenesses of Jonathan and Sarah Edwards, taken from portraits painted in their middle years.

Source: http://godswordtowomen.blogspot.com/2020/02/the-uncommon-romance-and-marriage-of.html:

Williams, who served as scribe of the ministerial council, did not agree, and Edwards was dismissed from the Congregational Church in Northampton in 1750. But in 1745 there was no controversy in Hadley. Whitefield preached to a large crowd outside. The minister in nearby Hatfield would not allow Whitefield to preach, so many from Hatfield travelled to Hadley to hear the famous itinerant preacher. One report stated that the church leaders in Hatfield did not welcome Whitefield, so many of the townsfolk went to nearby Hadley to see and hear him.[31]

After preaching in the morning at Hadley, Whitefield traveled and preached the same day for "Rev. Mr. Parsons at the Swamp."[32] Historic records refer to the Swamp by various names, such as the Great Swamp, the Lawrence Swamp, New Swamp, and other names. This area was originally part of Hadley, but became part of the town of Amherst in 1759.[33] The minister here was Rev. David Parsons II.

Parsons was born in 1711 or 1712, the son of a minister. He was a Harvard College graduate in 1729, and earned his master's degree there in 1732. He arrived in the Swamp, a neighborhood of Hadley, in 1735. He was the first minister of the community, and was ordained there at the official start of the Congregational Church in 1739. Construction began on the meeting house in 1741, and amazingly was not completed until 1753. He married Eunice about 1744, and the couple raised their children in the community. David Parsons resided here, in what after 1759 was called Amherst, until his death in 1781.

As stated above, Whitefield preached "in the Evening for the Rev. Mr. Parsons at the Swamp." Parsons was an intellectually gifted minister who dedicated his life to his community. He was described by a lifelong friend as:

> [A] man of strong intellectual powers, with a penetrating eye, giving token of that shrewd and judicial mind which made his counsel values; retaining his classical learning beyond

---

30 Alice M. Walker, *Historic Hadley: A Story of the Making of a Famous American Town,* (New York: The Grafton Press, 1906), p. 54.
31 Roberta B. Mouheb, *Yale Under God,* (Maitland, FL: Xulon Press, 2012), p. 57.
32 *Pennsylvania Gazette,* August 15, 1745, p. 2.
33 Edward W. Carpenter, et. al., *The History of the Town of Amherst, Massachusetts,* (Amherst, MA: Press of Carpenter & Morehouse, 1896), pp. 33, 468.

most men of his age, but with 'divinity' as his favorite study; a doctrinal preacher, reverent in manner, devout in temper and fervent in prayer. His sermons were scholarly and orthodox to a degree.[34]

The forty-two-year ministry of David Parsons in Amherst began in the tumultuous years of the Great Awakening. Parsons was an avid supporter of the revival. His church memberships surged in 1740 and 1741, and increased noticeably after Whitefield's visit in 1745. Yet there is no record of any division in Parson's church from the awakening. His calm and steady influence guided the church through theological controversies and surges in church membership. Indeed, the only significant issue that faced Parsons in these years was the mild controversy related to designated seating in church pews, as the place a person sat in the meeting house was typically representative of that person's standing in the community.[35] When George Whitefield came to town in 1745, he found a friend in David Parsons. In speaking of the "great religious awakening in which George Whitefield, the evangelist, took part," one writer spoke of the Swamp community, later part of Amherst, as follows:

An undated image of Rev. David Parsons, First Church, Amherst, Massachusetts. Source: An Historical Overview: The First Church of Christ in Amherst.

> There can be little question that this arousal of religious interest had a marked effect upon the membership of the new church, adding to its numbers and cementing them more closely in the bonds of Christian fellowship. Under the ministrations of David Parsons the church grew and prospered, with no serious church division among its members until his death, which occurred Jan. 1, 1781.[36]

Whitefield preached for Parsons in Hadley-Amherst in an unfinished building, "for though the parish voted in 1735 to build a 'meating-house,' the primitive structure covered with boards of spruce was not completed until 1752, though services were held in it before 1742."[37]

The official history of the church in the "Swamp," the First Church Congregational in Amherst, speaks favorably of the Whitefield visit to the area, and of the ministry of Rev. David Parsons. Speaking of the revival, "Of this refreshing the Amherst church enjoyed its share," with "thirty-five new members." The history of the church states that the awakening "deeply affected the moral and spiritual life of the community." A summary of the revival in the church stated, "It has of late pleased a kind and merciful God in a very wonderful manner to pour out his Spirit upon this people in awakening, convincing and convicting influences upon sinners and in refreshing and comforting influences upon saints."[38]

The next town Whitefield visited was southeast of Amherst, the tiny community of Cold Spring, now called Belchertown, Massachusetts. First settled in 1731, the town was named after a popular spring of cold water that served as the basis for settlement. This was a convenient place to stop for travelers in the surrounding wilderness. After the town had incorporated in 1761, it was named for Governor Jonathan

---

34   Ibid., p. 34.
35   Ibid., p. 38.
36   Ibid., p. 40.
37   "Massachusetts—American Local History Network," http://www.ma-roots.org/hampshirecounty/homes /strong. html.
38   *An Historical Review: One Hundred and Fiftieth Anniversary of the First Church of Christ in Amherst, Massachusetts,* (Amherst, MA: Amherst Record Press, 1890), p. 20.

Belcher, who first approved the settlement of Cold Spring. A newspaper report mentioned Whitefield's brief stop in Cold Spring; "Rev. Mr. Whitefield preached . . . on Saturday for the Rev. Mr. Billings at Cold Spring . . . "[39]

Rev. Edward Billings arrived at Cold Spring in 1739. A Harvard College graduate in 1731, he earned his Master of Arts degree there in 1734. Afterwards he did short-term missionary work before accepting the call to the pastorate at the new Congregational Church forming in Cold Spring. The town records are incomplete, and early church records are absent. We do know that Cold Spring was a tiny, rural farming community of about twenty families when Whitefield arrived in the summer of 1745.[40] A meeting house was constructed beginning in 1736, and the church formed in 1739. The town was so small and poor, that sustaining a minister by a tax was difficult. Some townsfolk had to pay the ministerial tax with firewood. Billings was perpetually underpaid. In 1741 he married, and Edward and Lucy Billings eventually had seven children, the first two in the home when Whitefield came to Cold Spring.

Billings was a supporter of Whitefield, but not a fanatic New Light. "Traditional history imputes to him unusual energy of character, ardent zeal and devotedness to the work in which he was engaged."[41] As Billings began his ministry at Cold Spring, there was "a prompt, persevering and ever wakeful vigilance to sustain the great truths of the Bible, in doctrine and duty, and to give them efficiency in life, was, in their view, the only condition on which blessings could be expected."[42]

There is no first-hand account of Whitefield's preaching and few hours stop in Cold Spring. We know he preached on a Saturday, probably in the unfinished Congregational meeting house, in July 1745. There was no known controversy from Whitefield's visit. Instead, the uncertainty in the church related to how to pay the pastor's salary as the town population fluctuated, and how to complete construction on the parsonage and the meeting house. The townsfolk were willing to help but were constrained by their poverty. Today, Cold Spring has disappeared into Belchertown.

In continuing his preaching route, Whitefield next preached nearby Cold Spring "on Lord's-Day for the Rev. Mr. Trowbridge . . . "[43] The "Rev. Trowbridge" is probably Rev. Caleb Trowbridge of Groton, Massachusetts. Next, "the Rev. Mr. Whitefield preached . . . twice on Monday for the Rev. Mr. Harvey at Kensington . . . "[44] This is a difficult person and location to identify. There never has been a town named Kensington in Massachusetts. There were significant people with the name Kensington in the Springfield community, but there is no recognizable connection between a Rev. Harvey and a location called Kensington. Perhaps the name Harvey was a first name, and the surname is lost. Wherever Kensington was, Whitefield preached there twice in one day. That community has not survived.

Whitefield's western Massachusetts tour ended at Longmeadow, Massachusetts. A newspaper article stated that he departed Kensington and "went from thence to Long-Meadow."[45] Settled in 1644, Longmeadow was a riverfront community with flat, rich farmlands along the Connecticut River, and rolling, forested hills nearby. Several streams teemed with fish. Located on the Connecticut border, the history of the town has always been tied to its larger neighbor in Springfield, Massachusetts. The first meeting house began to be built in 1714 and served the Congregational Church until 1767. The town grew slowly. When Whitefield preached here in July 1745, there were perhaps fifty families in Longmeadow. This was a frontier wilderness

---

39 *Pennsylvania Gazette,* August 15, 1745, p. 2.
40 "Historical Sketch of Belchertown, MA," http://history.rays-place.com/ma/hampshire/belchertown.htm.
41 Mark Doolittle, *Historical Sketch of the Congregational Church in Belchertown, Mass . . .* , (Northampton, MA: Published by Hopkins, Bridgman & Co., 1852), p. 30.
42 Ibid., p. 20.
43 *Pennsylvania Gazette,* August 15, 1745, p. 2.
44 Ibid.
45 Ibid.

town. It was known as the Third Parish of Springfield until 1783, when Longmeadow became an independent town.[46] The first minister in Long Meadow was Rev. Stephen Williams.

Stephen Williams was born in the frontier town of Deerfield. Massachusetts. in 1693. He was the son of a clergyman, and he received an excellent education at home. In 1704, when he was about nine years old, the town of Deerfield was raided by Indians, and the young Williams and many others were taken captive to Canada. This twenty-one-month experience as a captive of the Abenaki Indians gave him an expertise in Indian relations that served him well later in life. In 1713, Williams graduated from Harvard College. Shortly thereafter he was a candidate for the Congregational ministry at Long Meadow. He was officially called to the church in March 1715. Williams became active in missions to Indians and was involved in ordaining men who went to live with Indian tribes as Christian missionaries. A strict Calvinist, he adhered to the Westminster Confession and maintained a balanced, evangelical ministry in Long Meadow. Clearly Williams and Whitefield were of one mind. Williams served the Congregational Church in Long Meadow from 1714 as a candidate, to his death in 1782. His extended time at the church was interrupted three times, when he served as a chaplain for colonial forces in various Indian Wars. Even though Williams served in a small, remote parish, his diligence as a pastor, his reputation as an expert with Indians, and his patriotism was widely appreciated, so much so, that Dartmouth College granted him a Doctor of Divinity degree in 1773. His widely read journals made Stephen Williams somewhat of a celebrity in colonial America.

An undated portrait of Rev. Stephen Williams, of Longmeadow.

Source: www.memorialhall.mass.edu

When George Whitefield arrived in Long Meadow in July 1745, he met Stephen Williams again, for they had met in 1740. The town of Long Meadow was touched, but not overwhelmed, by the Great Awakening of the late 1730s and early 1740s. Williams supported the evangelical preaching that accompanied the revival, but he was opposed to the emotional extremes that sometimes accompanied the movement. He promoted a balanced awakening, supporting the revival but opposed to excesses. Williams and Whitefield were both Calvinists, and both actively opposed what was called at the time Arminianism, which really was the beginning of Unitarianism and Universalism in the Congregational Churches in New England.

Dr. Williams had always the reputation of being thoroughly Calvinistic in his religious views. "But it appears, from some of his letters . . . he was strongly conservative in the great Whitefieldian revival . . . he never seems to have yielded to undue excitement, but to have resisted what seemed to him of evil tendency, even though it was associated with much that he though worthy of being encouraged . . . [47]

Jonathan Edwards was fast becoming a leader among the western Massachusetts and Connecticut clergy. It is insightful to investigate what Edwards thought of Whitefield at this time. In correspondence with Rev. Thomas Clap, the rector or president of Yale College, Edwards wrote some telling remarks

---

46 "A Brief History of Longmeadow, Massachusetts," http://www.longmeadow.org. Thomas L. Higgins, *Longmeadow,* (Charleston, SC: Arcadia Publishing, 2018), pp. 13, 20-27.
47 William B. Sprague, *Annals of the American Pulpit: Trinitarian Congregational,* (New York: Robert Carter & Brothers Publishers, 1857), vol. I, pp. 285-286.

about Whitefield. Edwards' comments on Whitefield were first written in 1740, but were not released to the public until 1745. Edwards had twice entertained Whitefield in his home, and had heard the itinerant evangelist preach many times. Edwards was concerned that those who professed conversion in his church were genuinely born-again. Too often he had seen people profess faith in Christ, only later to fall away. Edwards did not want his congregation to appear to be converted, only later to denounce their faith. Edwards wrote to Clapp, "[A] people should look when they have heard the word preached, especially after they have heard it powerfully preached, after God has sent a messenger [Whitefield] with extraordinary fervency to deliver his message to them." Edwards wrote of Whitefield's "extraordinary earnestness" and "the loudness of his voice," and that he used "very plentiful arguments . . . set forth in a very earnest and forceable manner," and "the air of sincerity and fervency that is in the preacher, his positiveness, and the authority from which he seems to speak" enraptured Edwards' congregation in Northampton. Edwards also wrote that his congregation was "pleased with the adeptness of expression, and with the fervency, and liveliness, and beautiful gestures of the speaker."[48] The point of Edwards' writing was that his congregation trust in Christ alone and not the eloquence of any preacher.

Hindering Whitefield's reception in western Massachusetts were newspaper articles printed in Boston and distributed throughout the Massachusetts Colony. An example is an unsigned article from mid-July from *The Boston Evening Post*, which said of Whitefield:

> Upon your second coming to New England, it was given out (as we thought by you) that you would not preach in any pulpit without the settled Minister's content. But since you find yourself disbanded by many, you have betook yourself to the field . . . It is beyond Dispute, that you have sown the pernicious seed of separation, contention, and disorder among us . . . You have greatly impeded the success of the Gospel, and struck boldly, not only at the Peace and good order, but the very Being of these churches.[49]

Boston newspapers did not cover in detail Whitefield's 1745 travels in New England. Thus, our information on Whitefield's western Massachusetts preaching tour comes to an end. As best as we can tell, this was an 11-day preaching circuit in July 1745, by which Whitefield preached to large but not enormous crowds in rural parts of the Massachusetts Colony. Most of his listeners were farming folks. Some of his preaching events were in unfinished meeting houses, as the poverty of the community delayed construction. At one location, Whitefield preached while the men in the crowd carried weapons, out of fear of an Indian attack. While most of his preaching was endorsed by Congregational ministers, in Pelham his host was a Presbyterian clergyman. It must have been rewarding for Whitefield to meet young clergymen on this tour who he preached to while they were students at Yale College or Harvard College. Overall, Whitefield was in good health, and this was a largely successful preaching tour. At this point, in the summer of 1745, we briefly lose track of the ever-travelling Whitefield.

As Whitefield headed south, there is an account of his preaching in Windsor, Connecticut in 1745. Located just south of the Massachusetts border, Whitefield successfully preached in Windsor in the fall of 1740. Rev. Jonathan Marsh served the First Church in Windsor from 1707 to 1747. Now Whitefield was back. We know of his 1745 preaching in Windsor from the account of Daniel Marshall (1706-1784), who was present at Whitefield's preaching in 1745 and was converted. Marshall was a deacon in the First Church of Windsor, who, "at the age of thirty-eight, he heard Whitefield preach, caught his glowing

---

48   Extracts of the pamphlets exchanged between Thomas Clapp and Jonathan Edwards are found in Ava Chamberlain, "The Grand Sower of the Seed: Jonathan Edwards' Critique of George Whitefield," *The New England Quarterly*, vol. 70, No. 3 (September 1977), pp. 371-378.
49   *The Boston Evening Post*, July 15, 1745, p. 1.

spirit, and fully believed."⁵⁰ Another account states that Daniel Marshall heard George Whitefield preach in Windsor around 1745, and was converted.⁵¹ Marshall later was a successful Baptist preacher in the southern American Colonies.

We next read of Whitefield, several days later, in Rhode Island and Connecticut.

---

50   William Sprague, "Daniel Marshall," *Annals of the American Baptist Pulpit, (1860: reprinted by Solid Ground Christian Books, Birmingham, AL0, vol. I, p. 59.*
51   "Daniel Marshall," *New Georgia Encyclopedia,* www.georgiaencyclopedia.org/articles/arts-cultire/daniel-marshall-1706-1784. Thomas Ray, *Daniel and Abraham Marshall, Pioneer Baptist Evangelists to the South, (Springfield, IL: Regular Baptist Press, 2006).*

CHAPTER 23

WHITEFIELD'S TOUR FROM WESTERN RHODE ISLAND THROUGH CONNECTICUT

SUMMER 1745

THROUGHOUT WHITEFIELD'S 1744-1745 NEW ENGLAND tour, the New Lights and the Old Lights in New England became more entrenched. These two groups had chosen sides, and Whitefield's itinerate ministry forced people to take a stand one way or another. Now, instead of self-examination, the focus turned for many on examining others. Some of Whitefield's admirers took it upon themselves to imitate the itinerant evangelist, with often unfavorable results. New Light preaching, often from untrained and inexperienced men, became bombastic and accusatory towards Old Light ministers. This was a great concern, both to Old Light clergy and to New Light ministers, like Jonathan Edwards and most of the pastors in New England, who were typically educated, articulate, and balanced. Many fully embraced the revival, and fanaticism was opposed by both sides. In this tumultuous theological climate, the pen of Jonathan Edwards proved to be exceedingly helpful.[1]

Edwards was a prolific writer, a skilled communicator, and a detailed theologian. His most famous sermon, *Sinners in the hands of an Angry God*, was preached and published in 1741. In defense of the awakening, Edwards wrote in 1742, *Some Thoughts Concerning the Present Revival of Religion*, as an apologetic of the revival but not in support of emotional extremes. Located in Northampton, Massachusetts, near the border of the Connecticut Colony, Edwards' writings were quickly distributed throughout New England. Shortly before his 1745 visit to Connecticut, Whitefield visited Jonathan Edwards for the second time, in Northampton. These two like-minded ministers were determined to spread the message of revival and diminish extreme behavior and accusatory New Light preaching. But not all could easily forgive the excesses of the past. As Whitefield prepared to depart Rhode Island and enter Connecticut, he approached communities deeply divided over the awakening.

It is sometimes not possible to trace Whitefield's daily steps in New England. This may be because he was in a hurry and did not stop to preach at every location. He may have been sick or exhausted and did not write correspondence or linger. There are large gaps in his correspondence which means his locations are not evident. In the summer of 1745, we discover Whitefield in Westerly, Rhode Island.

Westerly is located at the southwest corner of Rhode Island along the Connecticut border. Oceanfront Westerly was known for its fisheries and shipbuilding. Whitefield had an ally in Westerly in Rev. Joseph Park of

---

1   Joseph Tracy, *The Great Awakening: A History of the Revival of Religion in the time of Edwards and Whitefield*, (Boston, MA: Published by Tappan & Dennet, 1842), pp. 213-214. There are many biographies of Jonathan Edwards. I recommend Iain H. Murray, *Jonathan Edwards: A New Biography*, (Carlisle, PA: Banner of Truth Trust, 1987); George M. Marsden, *Jonathan Edwards: A Life*, (New Haven, CT: Yale University Press, 2003); Owen Strachan and Douglas A. Sweeney, *The Essential Jonathan Edwards: An Introduction to the Life and Teachings of America's Greatest Theologian*, (Chicago, IL: Moody Press, 2018).

the First Presbyterian Church. A Harvard graduate in 1733, Park served in Westerly from 1733 to his death in 1793. During the period of the Great Awakening in 1740, Park was a supporter of the revivals and became "more evangelical."[2] Park had an extended but sometimes tumultuous relationship with the Presbyterians in Westerly, as his New Light teachings and endorsement of Whitefield, Jonathan Edwards, and the awakening in general was not always appreciated by his people.

When Whitefield preached in Westerly, Rhode Island in 1745, he preached to a community divided over the awakening. There were those who supported the revival movement and those that did not. Within the supporters of the awakening there were divisions. During the years 1742-1743, perhaps sixty Narragansett Indians experienced conversion and joined the Presbyterian church under Rev. Joseph Park. Some ethnic and cultural divisions arose, and the Indians formed their own prayer meetings led by the illiterate Narragansett Indian named Samuel Niles. Then Niles wanted to "exhort" in the Sunday morning church meetings. Rev. Park and the other church leaders did not like this idea, and Park reprimanded Niles and his supporters "for being noisy, by speaking and praying, in his meeting."[3] When Whitefield came to Westerly in the summer of 1745, all divisions within the church temporarily ceased. But in 1750, the Indians separated to form their own church.

An interesting anecdote of Whitefield and his wife Elizabeth shows the couple as entertained by an elder in the Presbyterian Church in Westerly, named Ezekiel Gavitt.

A photograph of the Rev. Joseph Park home, c. 1900. It was here in 1745 that Rev. Park and George Whitefield met before Whitefield preached in Westerly, RI.

Source: https://snippetbiographies.blogspot.com/2015/09/reverend-joseph-park-my-6th-great.html

> In this connection it may be mentioned that the renowned George Whitefield, on his way through New England, visited Westerly and stopped at the house of Ezekiel Gavitt. As his wife accompanied him, they brought with them some tea, a silver tankard, and cups. Mrs. Gavitt had never used the foreign luxury, and had no tea kettle. She, however, cleansed a common kettle, and so heated the water for the rare beverage. Mr. Whitefield halted at Paweatuck Bridge, where there were but two residences. He also visited the north portion of the town, now Hopkington. Crossing the state line, he preached in the home now owned by Mr. Peleg Clarke, senior, near Clarke's Mills. Here, in the waters of the Ashaway, he baptized Content Sanford, formerly of Newport, who married Mr. Thomas Langworthy. This was reported to have been the first instance of Baptism in that river. From all portions of this region the people flocked to hear the celebrated preacher.[4]

---

2 Frederic Denison, *Westerly, Rhode Island and its Witnesses: for Two Hundred and Fifty Years, 1626-1876*, (Providence, RI: J.A. & R.A. Reid Publishers, 1876), p. 67.
3 Thomas S. Kidd, *American Colonial History: Clashing Cultures and Faiths*, (New Haven, CT: Yale University Press, 2016), p. 206.
4 Ibid., p. 74.

Ezekiel Gavitt of Westerly, Rhode Island was an avowed New Light and stood firmly with Pastor Joseph Park through numerous disputes with the Presbyterian Church and the town of Westerly. The above quote states that Whitefield crossed "the state line" into Connecticut. This was to the town of Stonington. In Stonington, "he preached in the home now owned by Mr. Peleg Clarke, senior, near Clarke's Mills." This refers to the mariner and sea captain Peleg Clarke, originally from Newport, Rhode Island. Clarke's Mills was powered by the Ashaway River. Two individuals are mentioned in the town of Stonington, Connecticut, namely Content Stanford and Thomas Langworthy. Stanford was baptized by Whitefield, she being thirty-six years old. Her husband, Thomas Langworthy was a longtime resident of Stonington.

The Presbyterian Rev. Nathaniel Eells of Stonington was an ally of Whitefield. Eells was a 1728 Harvard College graduate who came to the church in Stonington and was ordained there in 1733. Several years after his arrival at the church, the sermons of Jonathan Edwards were distributed throughout Connecticut and a resurgence of interest in religion resulted. An awakening followed, and speaking of Eells, "he bent all his energies to the great work of salvation."[5] In the summer of 1745, Whitefield preached for Eels in Stonington.

> This revival of religion was continued for years, with the happiest results . . . Mr. Eells invited Mr. Whitefield to preach for him at the Centre Meeting-house. He accepted, came, and preached in the afternoon of July 19, [1745]. So great were the multitude to hear him that he left the meeting-house and spoke to the people from a platform erected under the shade of a large elm tree, near the church.[6]

Eells was well respected in Stonington. He preached at the Centre Meeting-House until 1762, after which he assumed more civil responsibilities throughout the town. "He pursued his labors with unremitting zeal and success."[7] Whitefield's July 19, 1745 meeting in Stonington helped Pastor Eells solidify his New Light leadership and preaching among these maritime townspeople.

As Whitefield preached along the Connecticut coastline on his way to New York, his itinerary was interrupted. His pattern of preaching once or twice a day and then briefly traveling to the next town was interrupted by an apparently urgent situation in New Haven. Instead of traveling in a straight line through southern Connecticut towards New York, he jumped ahead of his route, speedily traveling, probably by boat, from Stonington about sixty miles to New Haven. The several towns that Whitefield passed in this hasty trip he would return to visit in about a week. But for now, he rushed to Yale College and New Haven to confront a raging controversy.

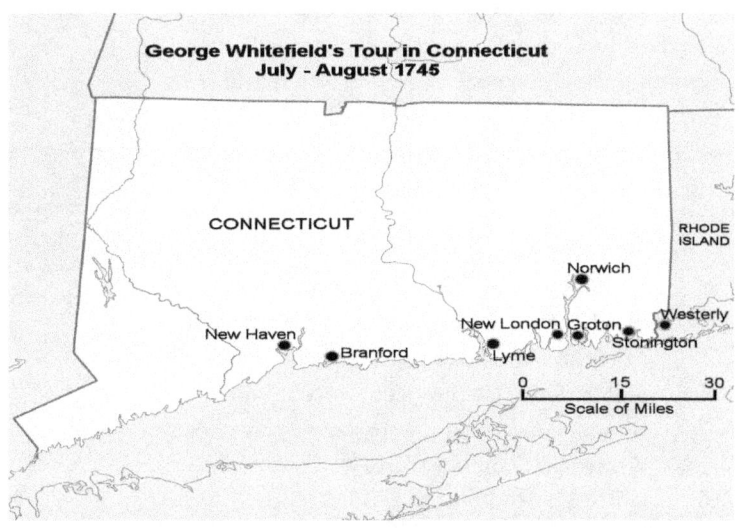

---

5   Richard A. Wheeler, *History of the First Congregational Church, Stonington, Connecticut, 1674-1874,* (Norwich, CT: T.H. Davis and Company, 1875), p. 95.
6   Ibid.
7   Richard A. Wheeler, *History of the Town of Stonington, Connecticut . . . ,* (New London, CT: Press of the Day Publishing Company, 1908), p. 362.

Five years earlier, Whitefield was welcomed in New Haven and invited to preach on the Yale campus in 1740. But followers of Whitefield, his imitators and admirers, showed little self-restraint in promoting the awakening. Under President Thomas Clapp, Yale went from a meticulously organized and structured college, to a school in which students skipped classes and departed the campus to hear revival preachers. In 1742, the Congregational Church in New Haven split between New Lights and Old Lights, and a rival Congregational Church was founded. Independent and unsponsored groups formed on campus to promote or oppose the revival. Students were expelled over their religious beliefs and their accusations against allegedly unconverted ministers. Clapp was gravely concerned that the structure, discipline, and authority of Yale, and his own leadership of the college, were being called into question. Disruptions shook the campus.[8]

The articulate Thomas Clapp took to his pen to oppose Whitefield's 1745 visit to New Haven. Although dozens of letters and pamphlets were written by Clapp to oppose the awakening, two will serve as examples. In 1745, Clapp wrote an eleven-page letter to Jonathan Edwards, intended to be published as a pamphlet. This letter, called *A Letter from the Rev. Mr. Clapp, Rector of Yale College in New Haven, to the Rev. Mr. Edwards of Northampton*, discusses and debates theology, civil procedures, and ecclesiastical proprieties, and descends to statements of personal animosity. Clearly, Clapp dreaded Whitefield's 1745 visit to New Haven. Also in 1745, Clapp wrote an eight-page letter, also intended for publication, denouncing both Edwards and Whitefield as extremists, disloyal to the Connecticut Colony and the established Congregational Church. This document, titled, *A Letter from the Rev. Mr. Thomas Clapp, Rector of Yale College at New Haven, to a friend in Boston*, seizes on some exaggerated statements made by Whitefield in the passion of his preaching.[9]

A portrait of Rev. Thomas Clapp from his time as rector (president) at Yale College.

Source: https://www.revolvy.com/page/Thomas-Clap.

Despite the overwhelming opposition to Whitefield in Connecticut, some Connecticut Colony ministers openly came out to support Whitefield. For example, the *Boston Gazette* published the following notice from a ministerial association in Connecticut, that welcomed Whitefield's pending visit:

> On Thursday next will be published, "Invitations to the Rev. Mr. Whitefield, from the Eastern Association of the County of Fairfield; with a letter from the Rev. Mr. Cook of Stratford, Connecticut, to a minister in Boston, concerning the former success of Mr. Whitefield's ministry there."[10]

When Whitefield arrived in New Haven in the summer of 1745, he understood that he was in a city of both friends and foes. Some of his friends were Rev. Jedediah Mills, a tutor at Yale College; and Rev. James Pierpont, a Congregational minister in New Haven and brother-in-law to Jonathan Edwards. The most vocal opponents of

---

8   Brooks M. Kelley, *Yale: A History*, (New Haven, CT: Yale University Press, 1999), p. 52. For an overview see Stephen Nissenbaum, *The Great Awakening at Yale College*, (Belmont, CA: Wadsworth Publishing, 1972).
9   Richard Owen Roberts, *Whitefield in Print: A Biographical Record of Works By, For, and Against George Whitefield*, (Wheaton, IL: Richard Owen Roberts Publishers, 1988), p. 75.
10 *Boston Gazette*, May 28, 1745, p. 4.

Whitefield in New Haven were Rev. Joseph Noyes, the First Congregational Church minister; and Rev. Thomas Clapp, Rector of Yale College. The religious climate in New Haven was tense. As one author stated:

> While matters were in this unsettled state, it became known that Whitefield was contemplating a second visit to America. He landed in October, 1744. In February, 1745, appeared the Declaration of the Rector and Tutors at Yale College in endorsement of the protest of the Harvard faculty against Whitefield and his conduct. But inspite of the increasing opposition, Whitefield . . . pressed on in the colonies in his ministry. He visited New Haven for a second time in 1745. Finding the college faculty hostile and Mr. Noyes unwilling to allow him access to the First Church, he spoke to thousands in the open air on the green from a platform beneath two great elms on the north side of the square. The unfriendly attitude of Mr. Clapp probably prevented many of the students from coming under the power of his words, and apparently no spiritual awakening attended his visit at this time.[11]

A very similar account speaks of opposition and acceptance of Whitefield's summer, 1745 visit to Yale College and New Haven:

> In the autumn of 1744, Whitefield visited New England a second time. Many ministers had by this time, become so much alarmed at the progress of the confusion that had ensued . . . that they looked upon his coming with dissatisfaction, fearing that it might cause a new outbreak of enthusiasm and disorder. The General Association of Connecticut, in June, 1745, hearing of his intention to pass this way, expressed their disapprobation, and advised that he be not invited to preach in any of the churches. Accordingly, when he passed through this place he was not invited as before, to preach in Mr. Noyes's pulpit. A great crowd, however, assembled from this and the neighboring towns to hear him; and he preached from a platform in the street,

A contemporary view of the New Haven Green, surrounded by Yale University, where Whitefield preached outside to Yale students and residents of New Haven and surrounding communities in 1745. Photograph by Ken Lawson.

---

11   James B. Reynolds, editor. *Two Centuries of Christian Activity at Yale*, (New York: G.P. Putnam's Sons, 1901), pp. 30-31.

before Mr. Pierpont's house, to a congregation on the green which neither of the meeting houses could have contained.¹²

Another account specifically mentioned the location and method by which Whitefield preached to thousands on the New Haven Green. Speaking of the large, shady elm trees under which Whitefield preached outside the Pierpont home, "Under their shade ... Whitefield stood on a platform, and lifted up that voice, the tones of which lingered so long in thousands of hearts."¹³ Another report spoke of the same incident in New Haven as follows:

> Sometime in the spring or summer of 1745, Whitefield passed through this place, and (in accordance with a recommendation from the General Association of the state, that he be not admitted to the churches,) being excluded from Mr. Noyes' pulpit, he preached from a platform in the street, in front of Mr. James Pierpont's house, to an immense congregation on the green.¹⁴

An undated likeness of Rev. James Pierpont of New Haven, CT. Source: https://www.geni.com/people/Rev-James-Pierpont /6000000002860715049

A farmer's wife from North Haven, Connecticut wrote about Whitefield's visit in 1745. Mrs. Hannah Heaton kept a forty-year *Diary* that revealed the everyday life of a typical eighteenth-century woman in Colonial Connecticut. Her life centered on family and the farm. Heaton was also a devout Christian, converted when Whitefield came to New Haven in 1740. Born in 1721 in Southampton, Long Island, New York, Heaton was married in 1743 by the Rev. Isaac Stiles, at the North Haven Congregational Church. She and her husband had four children, two that survived. Although there is no record of her ever attending school, her education as a child at home was more than adequate for her to function as a fully literate member of church and society. As a New Light, Heaton was not comfortable with Rev. Stiles. When Whitefield came to the area in 1745, he was not welcomed at the North Haven Congregational Church. Heaton began to attend a New Light congregation, which moved nearby to Wallingford in 1762. From her conversion in 1740, to her death in 1792, Heaton eagerly embraced the teachings of Whitefield and other New Light preachers.¹⁵

On "April 16, 1745," Hannah Heaton wrote a long letter to her extended family to explain her new faith. She conceded that the awakening had disrupted churches and divided homes, and she sought to make peace with her relatives. Heaton rather forthrightly described her dissatisfaction with "unconverted ministers," as she assumed Rev. Isaac Stiles to be. Her passion for her spiritual rebirth is evident throughout this letter. She pleaded with her family for their understanding about her beliefs, and she urged them to consider their own spiritual needs. At the end of this letter, she wrote in her *Diary*, "The August following after this letter was written my honored father went over to lime and was with mr Whitefield and he rit

---

12 Leonard Bacon, *Thirteen Historical Discourses, on the Completion of Two Hundred Years: From the Beginning of the First Church in New Haven*, (New Haven, CT: Durrie & Peck Publishers, 1839), p. 222.
13 Ibid., p. 177.
14 Samuel W.S. Dutton, *The History of North Church in New Haven ...* , (New Haven, CT: A.H. Maltry Publisher, 1842), p. 51.
15 Hannah Heaton, *The World of Hannah Heaton: The Diary of an Eighteenth Century New England Farm Woman*, edited by Barbara E. Lacey, (1793: reprinted by Northern Illinois University Press, 2003), pp. xi-xxiv.

to me thus blessed be god for it."[16] The *Diary* of Hannah Heaton is a remarkable 400-page document that records the joys and drudgery of a rural farm woman in eighteenth century Connecticut. Her eyewitness experiences with Whitefield, in 1740, here in 1745, and later in 1754, are noteworthy.

After an eventful visit in New Haven, Whitefield determined to backtrack and resume his itinerant preaching tour. He went to the next town to the east, to Branford, Connecticut. Whitefield had visited Branford in 1740 with notable success. This community of shipbuilders and maritime traders welcomed the itinerant evangelist again in the summer of 1745. The Congregational minister in Branford, Rev. Philemon Robbins, was an avowed New Light and pro-Whitefield clergyman. Speaking of Whitefield in Connecticut in 1745, "he found many towns and churches closed against him, among these most of those of the New Haven Colony. Branford Church, however, welcomed him, to the displeasure of the clergy in the neighborhood."[17] A year before Whitefield returned to Branford in 1745, "On August 18, 1744, the members of the church voted to request Mr. Whitefield to preach for them again. This brought about a new and hotter quarrel with the [ministerial] Consocation."[18] Rev. Philemon Robbins of the Congregational Church in Branford was an "open and pronounced friend" of Whitefield, and he "was made to suffer pains and penalties for his sympathy with Whitefield and his work."[19] Robbins welcomed the controversial traveling preacher to Branford in 1745.

We next discover Whitefield at Norwich, Connecticut. He preached here on August 1, 1745. Norwich was a major New England community, inland from the ocean but connected to the sea by the Thames River. Founded in 1658, historic Norwich can still be experienced by visiting the Norwichtown section of the city, where dozens of colonial era buildings still stand. Norwich was fortunate to have a deep anchorage at the Thames River, and at the same time be surrounded with productive farmlands. The community prospered as a trading center, with many foreign ships in port and numerous languages spoken on the streets of Norwich.

Norwich was torn apart by the Great Awakening of the early 1740s. In June 1743, twelve ministers from the counties of New London and Windham met in Norwich to express their support of the revival. Three ministers from Norwich signed the document: Rev. Benjamin Lord of the historic First Church; Rev. Daniel Kirtland of the Third Church; and Rev. Jabez Wight of the Fifth Church. These men endorsed the awakening in general terms, but were against emotional extremes, church divisions, and the denunciating vocabulary spoken by some itinerant revival preachers. The most prominent of these men related to Whitefield was Benjamin Lord.

A sketch of the parsonage of the First Congregational Church, Branford, Connecticut. Built in 1690, it was here that Rev. Philemon Robbins lived and hosted George Whitefield.

Source: http://www.firstcongregationalbranford.org/ history.html.

A Yale College graduate in 1714, Lord was ordained at the First Church Norwich in 1717. The early decades of his ministry in Norwich were unremarkable, until the awakening shook the community around 1740. Lord was torn between his congregation, which supported the revivals,

---

16 Ibid., p. 283.
17 J. Rupert Simonds, *A History of the First Church and Society of Branford, Connecticut, 1644-1919*, (New Haven, CT: Tuttle, Moorehouse & Taylor Printers, 1919), p. 84.
18 Ibid., p. 98.
19 "Thomas Robbins," *The New England Historical and Genealogical Register*, (October 1884), p. 366.

A painting of Rev. Benjamin Lord, First Church of Norwich, CT

Source: *Old Houses of the Ancient Town of Norwich*

and his duties as a member of the Corporation of Yale College, as Yale came out against Whitefield and the awakening. By 1743, Lord was agreeable to most aspects of the revival.[20] But when Yale published against Whitefield in 1745, Lord appears to have been swayed to the anti-Whitefield position.

While there were several doctrinal issues that divided Benjamin Lord from the revival movement in Norwich, one prominent concern was related to the admission of church members. The New Lights insisted that a conversion testimony be a prerequisite for church membership. But Lord and others agreed that the traditional method of church membership, that being a baptized person in good standing in the community could be a church member, should be retained. Lord believed that the Half-Way Covenant, in place for generations, was the accepted way to regulate church memberships, and he was unwilling to change.

In January 1745, a vote within the First Church supported Pastor Lord and the conventional method of church membership. The next month, a Separatist group from the First Church, not satisfied with Pastor Lord or the results of the church vote, began to meet in Norwich. In July 1745, a formal summons was given to the Separatist members to give a public account of their rebellion from the established order. These separated Christians asserted that they thought the First Church had become lax on admitting people to communion and to church membership, and they were dissatisfied with the preaching style of Benjamin Lord.[21] An individual separatist in Norwich, who distanced himself from Lord, was a prominent farmer named Mr. William Lathrop. A deeply religious man, Lathrop was a community leader in Norwich, "a useful and highly respected citizen." He and his spouse departed the First Church and joined the Separatist group. When he was summoned to appear before Lord to give an account, he remarked, among other things, that "the minister [was] denying the power of godliness," that Rev. Lord was "insisting on imprudencies and not speaking up for that which is good," and that Lord was "not praying for their [Separatist] meeting, and not giving thanks for . . . the preaching of Mr. Whitefield."[22]

Supporting Benjamin Lord at the First Church in Norwich was a June 1745 resolution by the General Association of Connecticut, a ministerial fellowship that advised the clergy to close their pulpits to Whitefield and to encourage their parishioners not to hear Whitefield preach in the open air. Determined to defend Whitefield and to spread New Light teachings was the minister of the fledgling Separatist group in Norwich, Rev. Jedediah Hide. Hide began preaching for the Separatist group in 1745 and was ordained by them in

---

20 Frances M. Caulkins, *History of Norwich, Connecticut: from its Possession by the Indians to the Year 1866*, (Hartford, CT: Lockwood & Brainard Press, 1873), p. 287.
21 Ibid., p. 320.
22 Mary E. Perkins, *Old Houses of the Ancient Town of Norwich, Connecticut, 1660-1800,* (Norwich, CT: Press of the Bulletin Company, 1895), p. 190.

October 1747. The group quickly constructed a meeting house and was a thorn in the side of Rev. Lord of the First Church. Hide stayed at the church until his dismissal in 1757, and the Separatist church dissolved in 1766.[23]

When Whitefield arrived in Norwich in early August 1745, the town was in religious turmoil. Whitefield intentionally chose to go inland to Norwich to support the new Separatist Church under Jedediah Hide. In some communities, Whitefield arrived, preached, and departed. In Norwich he lingered a few days to preach and strengthen the infant congregation and encourage their aspiring new minister. One report stated, "In the course of Whitefield's tour through New England, in the summer of 1745, he arrived at Norwich August 1st, and remained there several days."[24] Another account reported, "It was during the first four or five days of August 1745, that Whitefield was first in Norwich."[25] We do not know all the places in Norwich that Whitefield preached. Previously, he was endorsed by Rev. Daniel Kirtland of the Third Church and Rev. Jabez Wight of the Fifth Church. His previous endorsement by Rev. Benjamin Lord of the First Church had been revoked.

While in the Norwich area, it was said of Whitefield, "He held a great Indian meeting at Mohegan" in early August 1745.[26] The community of Mohegan, since absorbed by the town of Montville, was an Indian community of perhaps eight hundred or so people in the mid-1740s. Originally from the upper Hudson River Valley, they migrated to southern Connecticut and settled around the Thames River. During the incessant Indian Wars of the seventeenth and early eighteenth centuries in New England, the Mohegan people were allied with the English. Distinct attempts to evangelize the Mohegan Indians were made in Norwich after 1671, and reorganized in 1711 when mission stations for the Indians were established at Groton, Stonington, and Niantic, Connecticut. The most prominent Mohegan convert to Christianity was Rev. Samson Occum, who was moved by Great Awakening preachers in the early 1740s and was converted to Christ. In 1743, Occum began studying theology with Rev. Eleazer Wheelock, and from 1747 to 1749 he served as an assistant minister while a student under Rev. Solomon Williams in nearby New London.

The home in the center of this photograph on the Norwich Green was a tavern in the 1740s. It was common at that time for itinerant speakers like Whitefield to stay at this tavern and for speakers to set up platforms outside the building from which to address crowds on the Green. Photograph by Ken Lawson.

---

23   *Contributions to the Ecclesiastical History of Connecticut . . .*, (New Haven, CT: William Kingsley Publisher, 1861), p. 256.
24   Frances M. Caulkins, *History of New London, Connecticut . . .*, (New London, CT: Published by the Author, 1860), p. 459.
25   Frances M. Caulkins, *History of Norwich, Connecticut*, p. 321.
26   Ibid.

When Whitefield preached for the Mohegan people in the first days of August 1745, he ministered to a community in cultural transition from their historic Indian ways to the newer European ways. The Mohegan dressed as Europeans, spoke English, and listened to Christian ministers. Indian and English mixed freely in many coastal Connecticut towns. But not all the Mohegan professed Christianity, or they syncretized their native religion with Christian ideas. A former missionary to the Mohegan people, Rev. David Jewett was settled as the minister in the Montville community north of New London, Connecticut, in 1738.[27] It was with the permission of Jewett that Whitefield preached in the Mohegan community.

David Jewett was a Harvard-educated Congregationalist minister who was respected by Mohegans and the British settlers in Connecticut. An avowed New Light,

> Mr. Jewett was highly esteemed among his own people . . . he was a man of dignified deportment and very fervent in preaching. His animate manner and his energetic language made him very popular as a preacher. During his pastorate of about forty-five years, one hundred and thirty-six whites and twenty-one Indians received admission into the church.[28]

The Mohegan people were deeply moved by Whitefield's preaching on or around August 2-3, 1745, and they were eager to support the attempts of Jewett to combine the British and Indian church services into one New Light community. Whitefield's preaching for Jewett solidified his leadership in the North Parish Church and encouraged the integrated local worship of the Mohegan and English peoples in Mohegan-Montville.

About twelve miles east of New Haven, along a good coastal road is the town of Guilford, Connecticut. Whitefield traveled in ease along this road. A church was founded in Guilford in 1720, now called the North Guilford Congregational Church. The minister of the church in 1745 was Rev. Samuel Russell. He was a 1712 graduate of Yale College. Russell was described as "a faithful and worthy minister of the gospel," and that "the number admitted by him to the church is unknown."[29] Disturbing the peace for Rev. Russell in Guilford was a fledgling Church of England group that met in homes in the 1740s, who hosted traveling missionary Anglican priests that conducted religious services.[30] It is hard to determine the exact date that Whitefield preached in Guilford. An anecdote on his preaching, provided almost forty years later, called "the great meeting" in Guilford, stated:

> His text was, Anoint mine eyes with the eye-salve. After pointing out what was not the true eye-salve, he said "I will tell you what is the true eye-salve:—it is faith—it is grace—it is simplicity—it is virtue—it is virgin's water—Ah, Lord! Where can they be found? Perhaps not in this grand assembly."[31]

It is impossible to trace Whitefield's day-to-day route in Connecticut in 1745. There are accounts of him visiting the tempestuous town of Hebron. Hebron was in disarray from disputes over the location of the Congregational meeting house, and between Congregationalist and devotees to the Church of England. When a new meeting house was proposed in 1714, the town fractured into rival parties. The Congregational minister, Rev. John Bliss, served in Hebron from 1717 to 1734, when he denounced Congregationalism for allegiance to the Anglican Church. Legal proceedings were begun.[32] Bliss held Church of England lay

---

27   Henry A. Baker, *History of Montville, Connecticut . . . , 1640 to 1896*, (Hartford, CT: Press of the Case, Lockwood & Brainard Company, 1896), pp. 642, 651.
28   Ibid., p. 564.
29   Ralph D. Smith, *The History of Guilford, Connecticut: from its First Settlement in 1639*, (Albany, NY: J. Munsell, Printer, 1877), pp. 116-117.
30   William G. Andrews, *A History of Christ Episcopal Church in Guilford, Connecticut . . .* , (Guilford, CT: The Echo Press, 1895), pp. 34-48.
31   Samuel A. Peters, *A General History of Connecticut . . .* , (London, England: 1781), p. 210.
32   Gail D. Wojton, "St. Peter's Episcopal Church," www.stpetershebron.com/our-history/early-history-of-the-parish-1734-1976.

services in his home while the Congregationalists called Rev. Benjamin Pomeroy to be their minister in 1734. Rivalries, jealousies, and disputes over taxes, zoning, property management, and theology plagued the community through the 1740s.

When George Whitefield arrived in Hebron, Connecticut in the summer of 1745, he was met and endorsed by the Congregational minister Rev. Pomeroy. Located about thirteen miles southeast of Hartford, Hebron was known in colonial times for agriculture and the manufacturing of charcoal, bricks, textiles, lumber, paper, and other goods. The town was dominated by the Congregational Church, with a vocal and unsettled Anglican minority. Pomeroy was a Yale College graduate in 1733, and served in Hebron from 1734 to his death in 1784, his time at the church interrupted twice by Army chaplain duties in the French and Indian War, and in the Revolutionary War. As a dedicated New Light, Pomeroy was a friend of Eleazar Wheelock and the Indian School in nearby Lebanon, Connecticut. He was sometimes considered rash and impulsive. Pomeroy eagerly supported George Whitefield. A fair assessment of Benjamin Pomeroy stated:

> During the Great Awakening, he itinerated with James Davenport and often in places where he was not wanted by the ecclesiastical rulers. Consequently he found himself in considerable trouble with civil authorities. There appears to be evidence that he sometimes acted with less wisdom than he was capable and less charity than was Christian, but despite this, there is every reason to believe that he was also an instrument of considerable good, both at home and abroad.[33]

In the summer of 1745, George Whitefield preached for Benjamin Pomeroy in Hebron. No doubt this infuriated the Anglican Church of England members in Hebron, as Whitefield, who held ordination in the Church of England, preached to dissenters who doctrinally opposed the Anglican Church. Whitefield preached to an often disgruntled and litigious people in the town of Hebron, and he knew it. A former Connecticut governor, John S. Peters, noted of Hebron:

> They became eminent for their tactics in managing their suits and producing testimony to support their respective claims and their hard scrambles for the things that perish gave rise to a remark of the eccentric Mr. Whitefield in a sermon delivered in the town, "You Hebronians are more fond of the flesh than of the spirit and of earth than heaven."[34]

Another account of Whitefield preaching in Hebron in 1745 quoted the itinerant preacher as saying, "Hebron is the strong-hold of Satan; for its people mightily oppose the work of the Lord, being more fond of earth than of heaven."[35]

We next hear of Whitefield holding a series of preaching meetings in Groton, Connecticut. Groton was established in 1705, when the growing community separated from nearby New London. The first settlers in Groton were mostly farmers or ranchers with herds of cattle, pigs and sheep. The rocky soil quickly turned these settlers to the sea, and Groton became a thriving port community. The Thames and Mystic Rivers provided abundant fresh water and inland access for trade. The First Church in Groton dates to 1705. When Whitefield came to town in 1745, the minister at the church was Rev. John Owen, a Harvard graduate in 1723 who was ordained in Groton in 1727. A New Light, Owen served the First Church until 1753, teaching a conservative Calvinism and an evangelical theology. In 1743, he signed the controversial *Testimony* in support of Whitefield and the awakening. "Mr. Owen was distinguished for liberality of opinion towards those who differed from him in points of doctrine; advocating religious toleration to an extent that often

---

33   Richard Owen Roberts, *Whitefield in Print*, p. 524.
34   Frederic C. Bissell, *Hebron, Connecticut Bicentennial, August 23 to 25, 1908*, (Hebron, CT: 1910), p. 43.
35   Samuel A. Peters, *A General History of Connecticut . . .* , p. 140.

exposed him to the suspicions of his brethren and the rebukes of magistrates."[36] Whitefield preached for Owen at the First Church in Groton on August 8, 10, and 11, 1745.[37]

Groton was a large town, and it was difficult for many residents to travel to church in inclement weather, so the North Groton Congregational Church was formed in 1724. Their minister in 1745, when Whitefield preached in Groton, was Rev. Andrew Croswell. A Harvard College graduate in 1728, Croswell was ordained in Groton in 1736. "He was much in sympathy with Rev. George Whitefield . . . he espoused his cause and the result may have given rise to the animosity towards Mr. Croswell . . . [He was] an able preacher and a fluent writer; fond of argument, he dealt unsparingly with those who differed from him.[38] The official history of Groton states, "Mr. Croswell was orthodox and faithful, and, being of deep piety and an ardent natural temperament, he was ready for every good work . . . Being gifted with his pen as well as his tongue he wrote vigorously in defense of Whitefield . . . "[39] Another source spoke of Croswell and Whitefield as follows.

> No one was a more ardent revivalist than Andrew Croswell, pastor at Groton, Connecticut . . . At Groton, Croswell and his congregation experienced an awakening inspired by events in Northampton [under Rev. Jonathan Edwards]. During that time, he had a personal awakening and thereafter made the necessity of the new birth the centerpiece of his preaching. He became one of Whitefield's fiercest defenders when the itinerant came under attack by either Old Lights or Anglicans.[40]

Andrew Croswell's pro-revival writings were numerous.[41] Whitefield preached for Croswell at the North or Second Church in Groton on Saturday, August 10, 1745.

An eyewitness account has survived of Whitefield's preaching in Groton for John Owen at the First Church, and for Andrew Croswell at the Second Church. Mr. Joshua Hempstead of nearby New London saw and heard Whitefield preach several times in and around Groton. His diary is insightful.

> Thursday August 8. In the . . . afternoon I . . . stopped a while at Groton meeting house to hear Mr. Whitefield.

> Saturday August 10. In the foren [forenoon, or morning] Mr. Whitefield preached in ye meeting house to a grate assembly. Yesterday he preached in the North Parish here . . .

> Sunday August 11. Ye Rev'd Mr. George Whitefield preached again all day [i.e. morning and afternoon services] under ye oak tree in ye foren. Stood in his chair [his carriage seat] took it off his horse. Text from Rom. Chap 13 & first part of verse 14, put ye on the Lord Jesus Christ. Afternoon from Rev 3rd Chap-20th-ver. Behold I stand at the door and knock &c. a great assembly perhaps twice so many as could possibly sit in ye meeting house. Many from ye north parish, from Norwich, Groton, Stonington, Lyme East Society. An excellent preacher.

---

36 Frances M. Caulkins, *History of New London, Connecticut . . .* , p. 419.
37 Interestingly, a group of Baptists gathered in Groton, defying the Congregational autonomy. Encouraged by Whitefield's preaching, they formed a Baptist New Light congregation in Groton. See D. Hamilton Hurd, *History of New London County, Connecticut, with Biographical Sketches . . .* , (Philadelphia, PA: J.W. Lewis & Company Printers, 1882), p. 438.
38 Charles C. Whittier, *Genealogy of the Stimpson Family of Charlestown, Mass.*, (Boston, MA: David Clapp & Sons Press, 1907), p. 20.
39 Charles R. Stark, *Groton, Connecticut, 1705-1905*, (Stonington, CT: The Palmer Press, 1922), p. 197.
40 Frank Lambert, *Inventing the Great Awakening*, (Princeton, NJ: Princeton University Press, 1999), p. 245.
41 Rev. Andrew Croswell's pen was continually active during the Great Awakening and afterwards. His pamphlets were typically between ten to forty pages, too long for publication in newspapers. He supported traditional Calvinism and opposed the newer theological thinking of his day. Many of his writings are listed in Richard Owen Roberts, *Whitefield in Print*, pp. 193-194

Monday August 12. I went to East Lyme Society to hear Mr. Whitefield once more. He is gone to Lyme in order to go over to Long Island & so to New York & Georgia. His wife came thro New London near night to go to Lyme.⁴²

These diary notations speak of Whitefield preaching at the "Groton meetinghouse," which was where Rev. John Owen preached. The "North Parish" is also named, which was the location for Rev. Andrew Croswell's ministry. The "all day" Sunday services were held outside the First Church meeting house, due to the massive crowds. Particularly, the Sunday afternoon service on August 11 attracted multitudes from various local churches in different towns.

Across the wide Thames River from Groton is the town of New London. Although Whitefield's precise chronology in these communities is not exact, we have a good indication of where and when he preached in coastal southeastern Connecticut in early August 1745. One report noted that after Whitefield preached for the Indians at Mohegan north of New London, he spent time with Rev. David Jewett of the North Parish and then was in New London on or before August 8, 1745.⁴³ Another account stated about Whitefield, "He preached at the North Parish of New London August 9th, and in New London Town-plot, the 10th, taking for his text, 1 Peter ii.7, the first part of the verse. On Sunday, 11th, he preached twice in the open air, standing under an oak tree...."⁴⁴

In New London, Whitefield preached on August 10 and 11 to immense crowds. His ministry there was extremely challenging, as the New London community was deeply divided over excesses related to the awakening. Here all Whitefield's talents as a peacemaker and a reconciler would be severely challenged.

The First Church in New London was founded in 1652. This Puritan and maritime community became a central location for New England shipping and trade, and in 1710 the town was designated as the chief postal office for all the Connecticut Colony. In 1708 the Harvard-trained minister, Rev. Eliphalet Adams was ordained at the First Church, serving until his death in 1753. Due to a surge in church attendance as a result of the Great Awakening, the meeting house was enlarged in 1745 and 1746.⁴⁵ Before coming to the pastorate at First Church, Adams was a local missionary to the Mohegan Indians. An excellent linguist, he maintained a lifelong interest in the Mohegan people, and accepted Indian boys into his home to train for the ministry. He painstakingly labored with Rev. David Jewett in Mohegan missionary work "with no very eminent success."⁴⁶ When the Great Awakening reached New London after 1740, Adams was heartbroken by the excesses of some itinerant evangelists who bombastically denounced others and deeply divided the community. While a Calvinist and open to revival, Adams regretted the emotional extremes of the movement and was saddened by the thoughtlessness and impropriety of many. In March 1743, a fanatical excitement swept through New London, as normally responsible citizens apparently lost their senses and got caught up in a mob movement that resulted in a public bonfire to destroy objects of vanity such as superfluous books, gaudy jewelry, wigs, and immodest or fanciful clothing.⁴⁷

Rev. James Davenport was the instigator of this riotous behavior in New London. For two successive nights, a bonfire illuminated part of the city, with hundreds burning their vanities while praying, crying out, singing, and cheering. On the second night, Davenport got so excited that he took off his pants and threw them into the fire. His pants were quickly returned.⁴⁸

---

42 Joshua Hempstead, *Diary of Joshua Hempstead of New London, Connecticut*, (New London, CT: New London County Historical Society), vol. I, pp. 446-447.
43 Frances M. Caulkins, *History of Norwich, Connecticut*, p. 321.
44 Frances M. Caulkins, *History of New London, Connecticut . . .* , p. 459.
45 Ibid., p. 488.
46 John W. DeForest, *History of the Indians of Connecticut from the Earliest Known Period to 1850*, (Hartford, CT: W.J. Hamersley, Printer, 1853), p. 451.
47 Francis J. Bremer, editor, *Puritans and Puritanism in Europe and America: A Comprehensive Encyclopedia*, (Santa Barbara, CA: ABC-CLIO Publisher, 2016), p. 357.
48 "A Pants-Free Preacher Starts a Bonfire of the Vanities in New London," *New England Historical Society,* https://www.newenglandhistoricalsociety.com/a-pants-free-preacher-starts-a-bonfire-of-the-vanities-in-new-london.

Eliphalet Adams was heartbroken by the book-burning fiasco. He perceived his decades of ministry unravelling as irrational, extreme zeal overwhelmed Christian decency and propriety. Adams remained balanced. A splinter group separated from Adams and the First Church, led by Rev. Timothy Allen. On March 30, several local clergymen met with Adams in his home to console him from the abuse he personally received from the revival fanatics in New London. One of the ministers who came to New London was Rev. Jonathan Edwards of Northampton. A few years prior, Edward's writings and preaching helped initiate the awakening, but Edwards was no supporter of the excessive emotionalism and damage to property displayed in New London. He preached in the First Church for Adams on March 31, 1745, restating the biblical basis for revival, and exposing the zealots in New London as religious frauds. Religiously and socially, New London was in chaos.

An undated sketch of Rev. Eliphalet Adams, of the First Church, New London, CT

Source: https://www.revolvy.com/page/Eliphalet-Adams

The leader of the separatist group out of the First Church was a Yale graduate in 1736 named Timothy Allen. Allen was zealous for the awakening, an exuberant New Light, who was dismissed from his Connecticut Church in 1742 for his belligerence, unbalanced behavior, and fanatical and divisive teachings. Allen was dismissed from a Connecticut ministerial fellowship and arrived in New London in 1742, and quickly divided the community. He sought to start a ministerial school to train New Light preachers in New London for ministry throughout New England and elsewhere. Speaking of Rev. Timothy Allen:

> He preached in New London for some time. In the time of the Rev. George Whitefield, he was a zealous preacher, and a co-laborer with him in the great Reformation. He presided over a transient school, called the "Shepherd's Tent," in New London, for the purpose of educating men for the ministry in the separate churches.[49]

The Shepherd's Tent was a radical attempt to create a school for New Light ministers, with Timothy Allen as the superintendent. The school was intended to be "spontaneous" and "impulsive," not a divinity school with a detailed theological curriculum and precise study of biblical languages. Instead, students were trained to understand "impressions" from the Holy Spirit and encouraged to seek direct revelation from God.[50] The Connecticut legislature was not impressed.

> That thing called the Shepherd's Tent had been set up by Rev. Timothy Allen, at New London, to educate "gracious youths;" but the Connecticut Legislature, in 1743 made it penal for private or unknown persons to conduct such seminaries, and ordained that none should be admitted to the privileges of the ministry of the sanding order, without a diploma

---

49 Asa W. Allen, *Genealogy of the Allen and Witter Families: Among the Early Settlers of this Continent . . .* , (Salem, OR: Luther W. Smith, Printer, 1872), p. 109.

50 Robert W. Brockway, *A Wonderful Work of God: Puritanism and the Great Awakening*, (Cranbury, NJ: Associated University Presses, 2003), p. 134.

from Britain, Yale, or Harvard. The tent was shifted to the Narragansetts [Rhode Island] and soon given up.[51]

Allen was arrested but was released after the Shepherd's Tent was made an adjunct ministry of the Separatist Church in New London, allowing the school to continue. The ecstasy-focused school, deeply influenced by the inner-light theology of Quakerism, survived.[52] But after the March 1743 book-burning event in New London, the school lost students and moved. Allen eventually separated himself from the school, retracted his most excessive comments, and became a Presbyterian minister on Long Island, New York in 1748.[53] But catastrophic damage had been done to the churches in New London and to the revival movement in that disunified community.

George Whitefield had some culpability in the religious turmoil in New London. First, as a leader in the Great Awakening, Whitefield did not quickly denounce emotional extremes. Second, he initially did not correct itinerant revival preachers like Timothy Allen or James Davenport who incited crowds to the point of riotous behavior. Third, Whitefield rashly denounced the two ministerial schools in New England, Harvard and Yale, as intuitions of infidelity and unbelief. Although Whitefield later retracted some of his more defiant statements, and separated himself from emotional extremism in the awakening, the damage in New London had been done. Whitefield was partially to blame for the Shepherd's Tent debacle and the division in the First Church in New London. Now, in August 1745, Whitefield appeared for the first time in New London.

The crowds that greeted Whitefield in New London were immense. Some came out of curiosity, many were devout, others came for the show, while some came to agitate the controversy. It was critical for the continuance of the awakening in Connecticut for Whitefield to preach balanced gospel messages in New London, sermons that emphasized sound evangelical doctrine without tolerance for emotional extremes or divisive rhetoric. Whitefield had to separate himself from the fiasco of the Shepherd's Tent and Timothy Allen's extremism, while building bridges between offended and separated factions in the community. Whitefield willingly endorsed the ministries of Rev. David Jewett of the North Parish Church, and Rev. Eliphalet Adams of the First Parish Church. He preached on Friday, August 9, 1745, for Jewett, again on Saturday, August 10 for Adams, and for both ministers in the open air on Sunday, August 11, 1745, on the town common in New London. Whitefield was successful as a reconciler in New London. The emotional fanaticism passed. Adams stayed at the First Church until his death in 1753, while Jewett ministered at the North Parish Church to his death in 1783.

Whitefield may have stopped at Saybrook, Connecticut.[54] An account written about forty years after the fact spoke of an almost demented Whitefield calling down the wrath of God upon this coastal community.

> Time not having destroyed the walls of the fort at Saybrook, Mr. Whitefield, in 1740 [actually 1745] attempted to bring them down, as Joshua brought down those of Jericho, to convince the gaping multitude of his divine mission. He walked seven times around the fort with prayers and rams horns blowing—he called on the angel of Joshua to come and to do as he had done at the walls of Jericho; but the angel was deaf, or on a journey, or asleep; and therefore the walls

---

51 Richard Webster, *A History of the Presbyterian Church in America* . . . , (Philadelphia, PA: Joseph M. Wilson, Publisher, 1857), p. 258.
52 Clark Garrett, *Spirit Possession and Popular Religion: From the Camisards to the Shakers*, (Baltimore, MD: Johns Hopkins Press, 1987), p. 124.
53 Edwin Hatfield, *History of Elizabeth, New Jersey* . . . , (1868: reprinted by Applewood Books, n.d.), p. 575.
54 The Old Saybrook Historical Society has no record of this remarkable event. Correspondence from Dianne Hoyt, Old Saybrook Historical Society, December 5, 2019.

remained. Hereupon George cried aloud, "This town is accursed for not receiving the messenger of the Lord; therefore the angel is departed, and the walls shall stand as a monument of a sinful people." He shook off the dust of his feet against them, and departed, and went to Lyme.[55]

As Whitefield prepared to take a boat from New England, his last stop before departing was about fifteen miles west from New London along a good coastal road to Lyme, Connecticut. Lyme was settled in 1636 and became a town in 1667. Ideally located at the mouth of the Connecticut River as it empties into the ocean, Lyme has always been a maritime community. Situated between New Haven and New London, Lyme never grew as did its two larger neighbors. Located on the coastal road between these two larger cities, Lyme had local industries related to ship building, lumbering, fishing, and farming. Various trades supported the needs of the town, and a salt industry provided year-round work. By the mid-eighteenth century, Lyme had three noticeable classes of people—an unskilled labor class composed of dock workers, farmers, and common sea-hands; a middle class composed of ship builders, local merchants, sea captains, and skilled tradesmen; and an upper class comprised of ship owners, bankers, politicians, and lawyers. The host for Whitefield when he visited Lyme was Rev. Jonathan Parsons of the Congregational Church.

Born in West Springfield, Massachusetts, in 1705, Jonathan Parsons was an apprentice in a trade and studying at night, when he met Jonathan Edwards. Edwards encouraged the young Parsons to prepare for college at Yale for a general education. Parsons graduated Yale in 1729, interned at the Congregational Church in Lyme, Connecticut, and was called to be their minister in 1731. Parsons wrote of his time as a minister in the 1730s as a period when he had a passion for external appearances, dressing in expensive clothes with ruffles and jewelry. He embraced what was called an Arminian theology, with an emphasis on good works for salvation, rituals, and a minimization of the doctrine of eternal punishment in hell.[56] Parsons had a theological crisis in the late 1730s, and after a period of serious theological reflection, Parsons became a convinced New Light. When he heard Whitefield preach in New Haven in 1740, the two became lifelong friends. It is likely Whitefield stayed in the Parsons' home in 1740, although there is no record in Whitefield's *Journals* that he preached for Parsons at that time. In 1745, Whitefield was eagerly welcomed by Parsons to the pulpit of the Congregational Church in Lyme. One source stated that Whitefield was "often at Lyme, and the house of Mr. Parsons was always home."[57]

In the early 1740s, Jonathan Parsons was well known in Connecticut. His talents as a writer helped him spread his anti-Arminian message and his pro-revival beliefs. With his affirmed belief in Calvinism, Parsons was called a descendant of the Puritans in his theology. His avid support of Whitefield, and his preaching on the new birth for conversion, changed the social culture of Lyme.[58] Speaking of the revival in Lyme, Parsons wrote, "There was great opposition to the work, and several turned to be my enemies because I told them the truth, and raised many false reports of my doctrine."[59]

---

55 Samuel A. Peters, *A General History of Connecticut . . .* , (London, England: 1781), pp. 149-150. This account of an eccentric Whitefield in Saybrook is repeated in Clifton Johnson, *New England and its Neighbors*, (New York: MacMillian and Co., 1912), p. 142. This event probably never happened. First, Peters stated that Whitefield was in Lyme in 1740 but he was not in Lyme until 1745. Second, Peters was a Church of England minister who had some favorable things to say and write about Whitefield, so including this invented account may have been a way to placate his superiors in the Anglican Church who opposed Whitefield. Third, Peters gathered his information about four decades after the fact, at a time when the Whitefield excitement had not only passed, but was disdained. Also, Peters does not give his source for this bazaar incident. The account of Whitefield at Fort Saybrook was probably fabricated to make Whitefield look ridiculous to later generations.
56 Jonathan Greenleaf, "Memoir of the Rev. Jonathan Parsons, M.A.," *American Quarterly Register, vol. xiv,* (November, 1841), pp. 110-113.
57 Ibid. p. 111.
58 David E. Stannard, *The Puritan Way of Death: A Study in Religion, Culture, and Social Change*, (New York: Oxford University Press, 1977), pp. 141-142.
59 Jonathan Greenleaf, "Memoir of the Rev. Jonathan Parsons, M.A.," p. 114.

There is no record that Whitefield preached in Jonathan Parson's West Parish church, as his congregation was against it. But we do know that Whitefield preached in Lyme at the East Parish Church, for Pastor George Griswold. A Yale graduate in 1717, Griswold had a large family with numerous children at home when Whitefield came to town. For Jonathan Parsons, the revival controversy in Lyme became so divided between church and pastor that he requested that he be dismissed from the West Congregational Church, in October 1745. Whitefield knew of a new Presbyterian group forming in Newbury, (later Newburyport) Massachusetts, and recommended Jonathan Parsons to the fledgling church. Parsons became their first minister in March 1746.

Carolyn Wakeman, historian of the First Congregational Church in Lyme, wrote of Whitefield, "He indeed preached in Lyme's east parish, where Rev. Griswold strongly supported the Great Awakening, in August 1745. He spent that night at Solomon Miner's, near the rope ferry, and continued on with his wife the next day to New York."[60] We do not know how many nights

A portrait of Rev. Jonathan Parsons, from Origin and annals of "The Old South," First Presbyterian church and parish, in Newburyport, Mass., 1746-1896. This painting is now hanging in the Old South Presbyterian Church, Newburyport, Massachusetts.

Whitefield stayed in the Parsons' home or the Griswold's home, or how many times Whitefield preached in Lyme. But we do know that Whitefield's presence in Lyme greatly supported the revival movement in this waterfront community, leading to numerous conversions. Speaking of Jonathan Parsons in Lyme:

> He was a faithful and vigilant pastor; applying himself with great care to the wants of his people, both in public and in private. The success attending his ministry was great. During his residence in Lyme, he entertained charitable hopes that near two hundred persons were savingly converted . . .[61]

The previous *Diary* entry for Mr. Joshua Hempstead stated that Whitefield preached in East Lyme. Another account of this event, mentioning Jonathan Parsons, remarked,

> He invited the itinerant revivalist preacher George Whitefield to address his Old Lyme congregation during the height of the Great Awakening. On August 12, 1745, Whitefield gave an electrifying sermon standing atop a glacial erratic in Parson's backyard, a bolder hence known as the Whitefield Rock, and there irrevocably split the Congregational Church in two between the revivalist "New Lights" and the traditionalist "Old Lights."[62]

Joshua Hempstead wrote in his *Diary*, quoted above, that Whitefield "is gone to Lyme in order to go over to Long Island & so to New York & Georgia." Lyme was a significant port in Connecticut and was on

---

60   Correspondence from Carolyn Wakeman to Ken Lawson, November 19, 2019.
61   Ibid., p. 116.
62   Jim Lampos and Michaelle Pearson, *Remarkable Women of Old Lyme*, (Charleston, SC: The History Press, 2015), p. 14.

the coastal maritime trade route between New York and Newport, Rhode Island. Whitefield could easily catch a ride on a coastal schooner or other trading vessel on his way to New York. He departed Lyme on or around August 12, 1745. His next surviving letter is dated August 16, from Philadelphia. He would be back in New England in two years.

This photograph is of the Whitefield Rock in Lyme, Connecticut. The rock is atop a natural sloping field. The surrounding area is now developed. The original Congregational meeting house was about half a mile away. Photograph by Ken Lawson.

CHAPTER 24

WHITEFIELD'S LIFE AND MINISTRY

1745-1747

IN MID-AUGUST 1745, WHITEFIELD DEPARTED New England. His intention was to spend much of the winter at the Bethesda Orphanage in Georgia. This allowed him about four months to travel just over nine hundred miles, following the cooler weather preaching his way south. Whitefield was now in good health, his temporary health spasms subsiding. "Whitefield was now himself again, and began to move southward, hunting for souls."[1]

Whitefield departed Lyme, Connecticut and took a boat across the Long Island Sound to New York. Upon landing he noticed that "the seed sown had sprung up abundantly; and at the east end of Long Island I saw many instances."[2] He was pleased that the gospel seeds he had previously planted has prospered. As was his pattern, he preached in New York City, and on the way to Philadelphia he preached to a large group of Christian Indians in New Jersey. He was able to give testimony of the remarkable missions to Indians conducted by Rev. David Brainerd. Whitefield wrote, "A Blessed awakening had been begun and carried on among the Delaware Indians, by the instrumentality of David Brainerd . . . "[3] In New Jersey, Whitefield met with two like-minded revival preachers, the brothers William and Gilbert Tennent of the Presbyterian Church near Freehold, New Jersey in Manalapan Township. The Tennent brothers were itinerant preachers who encouraged the Great Awakening in several states, and who wrote and preached in defense of traditional Orthodoxy against many detractors.[4]

A recent photograph of the Old Tennent Presbyterian Church, Manalapan, New Jersey. Rev. William Tennent was the longtime pastor here. George Whitefield preached here to overflow crowds numerous times during his itinerant ministry.

Source: http://www.oldtennentchurch.org/Church_Location/churchhistory.html.

---

1 Robert Philip, *The Life and Times of George Whitefield*, (1837: reprinted by Banner of Truth Trust, Carlisle, PA: 2007), p. 324.
2 John Gilles, *Memoirs of George Whitefield*, (1772: reprinted by Pietan Publications, New Ipswich, New Hampshire, 1993), p. 106
3 Ibid.
4 Elias Boudinot, *Life of the Rev. William Tennent, formerly Pastor of the Presbyterian Church at Freehold, New Jersey . . .* , (1848; reprinted by Forgotten Books, 2015). Milton J. Coalter, *Gilbert Tennent, Son of Thunder: A Case Study of Colonial Pietism's Impact on the First Great Awakening in the Middle Colonies*, (New York: Greenwood Press, 1986).

After New Jersey, Whitefield wrote, "nothing remarkable happened during my way southward." But in Virginia he discovered that his printed sermons had had a distinct effect upon various groups of people who were awakened and gathered into groups to worship, "both white people and Negros, were converted to the Lord."[5] After a brief and uneventful trip through North Carolina, he wrote, "At Georgia, through the badness of the institution, and the Trustee's obstinacy in not altering it, my load of debt and care was greatly increased, and at times almost overwhelmed me." The financial responsibilities of the Bethesda Orphanage in Georgia were a lifelong concern for Whitefield. At the founding of the Orphanage in 1740, Whitefield had disputes with the Georgia trustees over construction costs, the hiring of staff, and the utilization of slaves for laborers.[6] These frustrations were ongoing. Through contributions collected from various locations and shipped to Bethesda, improvements were made to the property, more staff was hired, and the pressure of financial debt was temporarily abated.[7]

Whitefield spend much of the winter of 1745-1746 in Bethesda. Financial gifts came to the orphanage from throughout the New England Colonies and from Great Britain. He immersed himself in the immense undertaking of fortifying an orphanage for several dozen children, with more on the way, and purchasing nearby property and buildings needing renovation. Several hundred acres had to be prepared for the spring plantings while the academic training of the orphans was ongoing. Whitefield's efforts were successful, and he was able to leave the orphanage in capable hands as he began a new preaching circuit to the north.

For the next few months, it is difficult to trace Whitefield's steps exactly. Probably having departed Georgia by sea at Savannah, we next learn of Whitefield in the Middle Colonies. "Having found Bethesda prosperous, he started for Maryland, where he found thousands who had never heard of redeeming grace. This roused him anew."[8] Maryland was founded in 1634, and was notable for having been established with religious freedom for Roman Catholics. The Maryland Toleration Act, issued in 1649, was one of the first laws that explicitly defined tolerance of varieties of Christianity. After a series of violent acts between Roman Catholic Marylanders and nearby Puritans, the capital was moved in 1708 and renamed Annapolis, in honor of Queen Anne. In 1727 the newspaper *Maryland Gazette* began, and in 1729 the city of Baltimore was founded. The first Baptist Church in Maryland originated in 1742. The first Lutheran Church in Maryland dates to 1743, and the first Lutheran congregation was organized in Frederick in 1747. When Whitefield passed through Maryland in 1746, he wrote of the desperate heat, but joyfully stated, "Amazing love, Maryland is yielding converts to Jesus."[9]

From Maryland, Whitefield completed a series of preaching circuits in Maryland, Pennsylvania, and Virginia. On some of these evangelistic tours his wife Elizabeth was traveling with him. On August 26, 1746 from Philadelphia, Whitefield wrote,

> Favour is given to me in the sight of the rich and great, and the door for my usefulness opens wider and wider. I love to range in the American woods, and sometimes think I shall never return to England any more. I was never better in health, taken all together. My dear wife would send you a few lines, but she is weak by reason of a miscarriage about four days ago.[10]

---

5 John Gilles, *Memoirs of George Whitefield*, p. 107.
6 Edward J. Cashin, *Beloved Bethesda: A History of George Whitefield's Home for Boys, 1740-2000*, (Macon, GA: Mercer University Press, 2001), p. 22.
7 John Gilles, *Memoirs of George Whitefield*, p. 107.
8 Robert Philip, *The Life and Times of George Whitefield*, p. 328.
9 Ibid.
10 George Whitefield, *Works of George Whitefield*, (1771: reprinted by Quinta Press, Shropshire, England, 2000), vol. II, p. 83.

The full extent of Whitefield's travels in the backwoods of the rural Middle Colonies may never be known.[11] From Bohemia, Maryland, on the eastern side of Chesapeake Bay, Whitefield wrote on October 8, 1746, stating:

> I have been traveling and ranging in the woods, in the service of the best of Masters, who makes his work more pleasant to me every day. I trust that the time for favoring this and the neighboring southern provinces is come. Every where almost, the door is open for preaching; great numbers flock to hear, and the power of an ascended Saviour attends the word. It is surprising, how the Lord causes prejudices to subside, and makes my formerly most bitter enemies to be at peace with me.[12]

On the western side of Chesapeake Bay, Whitefield wrote from Annapolis, mentioning that his wife departed with a traveling companion to Bethesda, Georgia while he noted, "Lately I have been in seven counties in Maryland, and preached with abundant success."[13] On November 16, 1746 Whitefield was in Hanover County, Virginia, just south of the Maryland border. He wrote a letter to his friend Rev. Howell Harris in Wales, asking about the condition of the revival in the British Isles, mentioning that he hoped to preach in several counties in Virginia, and that "There is a sweet stirring among the dry bones."[14] This brief preaching tour in the Middle Colonies ended as Whitefield was back at the Bethesda Orphanage in Georgia for Christmas, 1746.

While Whitefield was in America, the revival work in Great Britain suffered. Divisions, rivalries, and factions formed between Whitefield's followers and those who followed John and Charles Wesley. Further, a spiritual renewal among the Moravians added a pietistic dimension to the revival.[15] After receiving a letter from a friend in London, Whitefield wrote back to him, stating, "Poor English friends! May Jesus heal their divisions."[16] These divisions were mostly a result of the ongoing contentions between Whitefield and John and Charles Wesley. As the awakening prevailed in 1741, so did the friction between Whitefield and the Wesleys. Both sides sought to coordinate and control various aspects of this new religious movement. Whitefield and John Wesley were both ordained by the Church of England, but they had different theological and practical emphases. Wesley was more Arminian[17] and Moravian, while Whitefield was a strict Calvinist. Yet both men pleaded with sinners for salvation with remarkable success. Wesley was more intellectual while Whitefield was more experiential. Both men were excellent organizers, but Whitefield eventually delegated the organization of the Calvinistic Methodists to others while he itinerated, while John Wesley maintained a firm control over his converts.

---

11   No detailed study of Whitefield in the middle or southern colonies has been written. For overviews of the awakening in these places see Charles H. Maxson, *The Great Awakening in the Middle Colonies,* (Chicago, IL: University of Chicago Press, 1920; Wesley M. Gewehr, *The Great Awakening in Virginia, 1740-1790,* (Durham, NC: Seaman Press, 1930).
12   George Whitefield, *Works of George Whitefield, vol. II, pp. 83-84.*
13   Ibid., p. 84.
14   Ibid., p. 86.
15   Pietism originated in Germany in the 1600s as a response to formal Lutheranism and their strict adherence to doctrinal statements. Instead, Pietists emphasized Christian love, sacrifice, experience, and service. Some Pietists emphasized mystic experiences and placed a focus on spiritual feelings. Pietism became a trans-denominational Christian movement and often led to separations within churches and denominations. Calvinists typically believed that Pietists were too subjective, too democratic, and too emotional. See Sinclair Ferguson, David F. Wright, J.I. Packer, *New Dictionary of Theology,* (Downers Grove, IL: InterVarsity Press, 1988), pp. 515-517.
16   George Whitefield, *Works of George Whitefield, vol. II,* p. 85.
17   "Arminianism" was a term loosely used by Calvinists against those who differed with their theology. It was used as a derogatory term often synonymous with faithlessness. This was not historic Wesleyan Arminianism. The Arminian beliefs of John Wesley originated from Jacobus Arminius (1559-1609). Arminius differed from other Protestant reformers like Luther and Calvin, as he saw humanity with more of a free will than Calvinism conceded. He also differed with the reformers in areas of eternal security for the Christian. See J.D. Douglas, *Who's Who in Christian History,* (Wheaton, IL: Tyndale House Publishers, 1992), pp.36-37

By the mid-1740s there was progress at reconciliation. The Wesleys and Whitefield simply did not agree on significant theological issues, such as original sin, predestination, unconditional election, irresistible grace, and the final perseverance or preservation of Believers. These differences were not based on any original thoughts from either side, but were longstanding differences that came forth from the Protestant Reformation. In a gesture at reconciliation, in February 1744 Whitefield collected and distributed a significant financial offering, designated for the followers of Wesley that were persecuted, beaten and robbed by hooligans. Later in 1744, John Wesley wrote that he no longer had a division with Whitefield, although there remained theological differences and pragmatic tensions. Ongoing were personality clashes, control issues, management of converts, rivalries over construction projects, and fund-raising concerns. Although John Wesley was more amiable to Whitefield in 1745, Charles Wesley remained distant from Whitefield until 1748. Therefore, while Whitefield travelled throughout the American Colonies from 1745 to 1747, his issues with the Wesley brothers were still very much on his mind.[18]

Sketches of Rev. John and Charles Wesley, mid-1700s.

Source: https://smecsundaymorningforum.org/2017/03/03/collect-john-and-charles-wesley-priests-1791-1788-mar-3.

During the Christmas holiday of 1746, Whitefield was at the Bethesda Orphanage catching up on his prolific correspondence and administrating affairs at the orphanage. Three letters have survived from this period. On December 24, 1746 Whitefield wrote from Bethesda to a friend in London who had previously responded to his preaching. Whitefield wrote,

> O that your eyes may be looking towards and waiting on the blessed Jesus: from him alone can come your salvation, he will be better to you than a thousand Whitefields.—I am afraid you are too desirous of having me with you; and indeed I long to see you and my other dear Christian friends, but America seems to be my scene of action for some time. The harvest is great in many places, and the laborers are very few. I am resolved in the strength of Jesus to range more and more; hunting for souls is a delightful work, and I am ashamed that I do no more.[19]

Also, on December 24 Whitefield wrote a brief letter to an unidentified friend in England, lamenting the divisions and strife that came upon his Tabernacle ministry in London while he was away. Whitefield

---

18   Arnold Dallimore, *George Whitefield: The Life and Times of the Great Evangelist of the Eighteenth Century Revival*, (Carlisle, PA: Banner of Truth Trust, 1980), vol. II, pp. 139-147. J.D. Walsh, "Wesley vs. Whitefield," *Christian History*, www.christianitytoday.com/ch/1993/issue38/3834.html. Tony Cooke, "Wesley vs. Whitefield: Brothers in Conflict," http://www.tonycooke.org/leadership-articles/wesley-whitefield. Kenneth E. Lawson, "Who Founded Methodism? Wesley's Dependence upon Whitefield in the Eighteenth Century English Revival," *Reformation and Revival*, (Summer 1995), pp. 39-50. For a detailed study see Ian J. Maddock, *Men of One Book: A Comparison of Two Methodist Preachers, John Wesley and George Whitefield*, (Cambridge, England: The Lutterworth Press, 2012).

19   George Whitefield, *Works of George Whitefield*, vol. II, pp. 86-87.

wrote of the confidence he maintained in God, saying "It is this promise that makes me now to rejoice in the midst of all the tribulations that has befallen my dear Tabernacle friends."[20] In a December 29, 1746 letter written from Bethesda, Whitefield wrote that he had received "a particular account how affairs stand in England" and that the ministry in England was in "a cloudy dark day." Whitefield encouraged his correspondent to endure "all future trials" and to "endure afflictions" in the ministry.[21]

Sometime after early January 1747, Whitefield began a preaching tour through the entire American Colonies. On January 23 he wrote a note from Charleston, South Carolina, in which he stated, "The Lord Jesus is pleased to give me great access to multitudes of souls, and I hope has withal given me as strong an inclination as ever, to go out and preach to them the unsearchable riches of his dying love . . . . In the beginning of March, I purpose, God willing, to set out for the northward again, and shall not lose any opportunity of writing, that offers in my way."[22] In a March 15, 1747 letter from Charleston, Whitefield was confident that the affairs at the Bethesda Orphanage were in good order, and he was ready to depart for northern places. On April 26 he wrote from Bohemia, Maryland, that he had just completed a five-week overland preaching trip from Charleston, and that he was soon to begin a three-week preaching circuit in rural Maryland. This was in full keeping with Whitefield's preach-and-return methodology, as he had preached through rural Maryland the summer before, and it was time for him to follow up. While traveling in the Middle Colonies, Whitefield heard that there were controversies and disputes in New England related to the awakening. He does not specifically say in which New England colony there were disruptions, or exactly what were the controversial issues. He wrote on May 6, 1747 from New-Town, Maryland:

> But what shall I say to dear New England's sorrowful circumstances? It pities me to hear that she is still lying in the dust. However, this has generally been the case: trying and distressing times have generally followed awakening and converting times. May Jesus second them with another alarm of his Holy Spirit, and then all will be well. Glad would I be to come and offer myself once more to do New England service; but I am afraid that many ministers and the heads of the people would not bear it.[23]

As Whitefield cryptically wrote, the "many ministers and the heads of the people" in New England who would not support him, probably referred, at least in part, to the presidents and faculty members of Harvard and Yale colleges. In the next several years this animosity against Whitefield would begin to subside, but for now, in the spring of 1747, the New England colleges still rejected Whitefield.

In early May 1747, Whitefield was in rural Pennsylvania. The rest of the month he itinerated in coastal Maryland, often traveling by boat to remote maritime comminutes on Chesapeake Bay and its numerous river inlets. On May 30, he reached one of his landmark destinations on his trip north, Philadelphia.

Whitefield had a longstanding, supportive relationship with Philadelphians. Whenever the itinerant preacher came to this cosmopolitan city, he typically settled in for weeks at a time.[24] Whitefield had a firm ally in Philadelphia, an entrepreneur, printer, and inventor named Benjamin Franklin. In the 1740s, Franklin was in his mid-thirties, with considerable influence in his city. Franklin first heard Whitefield preach in Philadelphia in the rain one evening in November 1739, and the two began a lifelong mutually beneficial friendship. Whitefield would provide Franklin copies of his sermons,

---

20 Ibid., p. 87.
21 Ibid., p. 88.
22 Ibid., p. 89.
23 Ibid., p. 93.
24 Nancy C. Ceperley, *Whitefield in Philadelphia: The Great Awakening of 1740*, (Columbus, GA: Brentwood Christian Press, 2014).

journals, and various correspondence for printing and distribution. Franklin would financially benefit from this arrangement.[25] Both men were public figures who understood the power of the printing press to influence the masses. Whitefield was certainly conscious of the value of promotion and advertisement for his preaching, and effectively used newspapers and other print media to his advantage.[26] On June 4, 1747 Whitefield wrote from Philadelphia that "Congregations were as large as ever. Next Monday sevennight I purpose, God willing, to set out for New York . . . I think to come by way of Long Island, and to return by Connecticut."[27]

The first surviving Whitefield letter from New York is dated June 28, 1747. In this note he stated, "I am as willing to hunt up souls as ever," but that he was recovering from "a great illness."[28] The next day he wrote that this northern excursion was improving his health, and that his strength was renewed, stating, "God has been pleased to bring my body to the very brink of the grave by convulsions, gravel, a nervous colic, and a violent fever. But as pain and afflictions abounded, consolations much more abounded, and my soul longed to take its flight in Jesus.[29] He continued, "From hence I purpose to go to Boston, and return by land so as to reach Charles-Town by November." That means his trip to the New England Colonies would be quick. This is verified in a letter he wrote from New York on July 4, 1747 stating, "I hope to be back in six weeks." In a letter the next day from New York, dated July 5, Whitefield wrote that there were "disputings among us" and that "I find fresh offenses must come" to "search and discover to us fresh corruptions, to try our faith."[30] This was Whitefield's last preserved letter before he arrived in New England, in Newport, Rhode Island. He came in good health, without his wife who he left behind as he anticipated a quick, aggressive tour throughout New England.

---

25 Peter C. Hoffer, *When Benjamin Franklin met the Reverend George Whitefield*, (Baltimore, MD: The Johns Hopkins University Press, 2011), pp. 1-3. Randy Petersen, *The Printer and the Preacher: Ben Franklin, George Whitefield and the Surprising Friendship that Invented America*, (Nashville, TN: Thomas Nelson Publishers, 2015).
26 Two books have recently been published that I believe overstate and exaggerate Whitefield's dependence of promotion and advertising, presenting him as a zealous marketer and publicist as well as an evangelist. Harry S. Stout, *The Divine Dramatist: George Whitefield and the Rise of Modern Evangelicalism*, (Grand Rapids, MI: Eerdman's Publishing, 1991). Frank Lambert, "Pedlar in Divinity"- *George Whitefield and the Transatlantic Revivals*, (Princeton, NJ: Princeton University Press, 1994).
27 George Whitefield, *Works of George Whitefield, vol. II*, p. 106.
28 Ibid., p. 109.
29 Ibid., p. 110.
30 Ibid., p. 113.

CHAPTER 25
WHITEFIELD'S MINISTRY IN NEW ENGLAND

SUMMER 1747

THE SUMMER, 1747 MINISTRY TRIP of Whitefield to New England is generally overlooked or unknown to his biographers. In a recent book by Jessica Parr, she writes of his itinerant ministry in New England in 1747 in five sentences, and stated, "The details of this voyage are scant, though it is clear that he continued to attract large crowds at his sermons."[1] John R. Andrews wrote, "During August, 1747, he again visited New England, leaving Mrs. Whitefield at Philadelphia," but with no ministry details.[2] E.A. Johnson, in his *George Whitefield: A Definitive Biography*, does not mention Whitefield in New England in 1747. Arnold Dallimore summarizes Whitefield's 1747 New England ministry in three sentences:

> Upon reaching New England, he found that, as he had expected, time had continued to heal the wounds there. Wiser practices were prevailing more and more, and prejudices were subsiding. He preached frequently, and after returning to Philadelphia, thus completing what he spoke of as an 'eleven hundred mile journey,' he stated that under his ministry in New England, 'The power that attended the Word seemed to be near the same as when the work began seven years ago.'[3]

This chapter will attempt to trace Whitefield's steps in New England in the summer of 1747.

The people of New England who received Whitefield on his third visit, in the summer of 1747, were in the midst of numerous cultural, military, and theological events. Culturally, the sensational composer George Frederick Handel was the rage of Europe and eastern American cities, since completing his *Messiah* in only eighteen days in 1741. Benjamin Franklin's *The General Magazine* provided news and cultural attractions to New England, complementing the two newspapers already existing in Boston. Humanist philosophers such as David Hume and George Berkeley were attaining a wide reading among secular aristocrats, and from the more liberal ministers in both Europe and New England. Further cultural events during this era came from industrial and scientific inventions, such as the development of cotton factories in England and advances in physics by English engineers in the Royal Society.

Militarily, New Englanders received news from Europe concerning feudal wars in central Europe between Prussian, Austrian, and Russian forces. Of more immediate concern to New Englanders was the state of war between France and England, in effect since 1744. After the colonists' victory over the French

---
1 Jessica M. Parr, *Inventing George Whitefield: Race, Revivalism, and the Making of a Religious Icon,* (Jackson, MS: University of Mississippi Press, 2015), p. 101.
2 John Richard Andrews, *George Whitefield: A Light Rising in Obscurity,* (London: 1879), p. 209.
3 Arnold Dallimore, *George Whitefield: The Life and Times of the Great Evangelist of the Eighteenth Century,* (Carlisle, PA: Banner of Truth Trust, 1980), vol. II, pp. 221-222.

in Louisburg in 1745, there followed an increasing inter-colonial political dimension previously unknown to colonial life. People became concerned, as never before, not only with local civic matters, but also with international wars which, in a few cases, influenced them directly and cost the lives of colonial men in military service. Whitefield's *Journals* and sermons were avidly read by these early colonial patriots.[4] The thirteen separate British Colonies in America began to see themselves more and more as an independent entity from the British king and the Church of England.[5]

Before Whitefield's third visit to New England, the theological climate was relatively stable. Yale College had received a new charter in 1745, while the College of New Jersey (later Princeton College) was founded in 1746. These two schools, in addition to Harvard College in Massachusetts Colony, prepared virtually all the candidates for ministry in the colonies in the mid-1700s. Every minister in New England would have access to a copy of Charles Chauncey's *Seasonable Thoughts on the State of Religion in New England* (1743) and Jonathan Edwards' *Treatise Concerning Religious Affections* (1746). Many clergymen would have copies of both documents, while many more would be impressed with Edwards' published sermon *Sinners in the Hands of an Angry God* (1741). Further, copies of Whitefield's *Journals,* and various editions of his sermons were constantly in demand by both friends and foes.

The deaths of several ministers during this period also affected the theological climate of New England. The death of William Tennent, Sr. of Pennsylvania in 1746 was certainly important news, as was, to a lesser extent, the death of the Dutch Reformed revivalist-pastor Theodore Frelinghuysen from New Jersey in 1748. Specifically in Boston, Whitefield's strong ally, Rev. Benjamin Colman of the Brattle Street Church, died in 1747.

A sample of Boston's newspapers helps to display the everyday issues and mood of New Englanders in the months preceding Whitefield's 1747 visit.

> To be sold at the lower end of Marblehead [Massachusetts], three dwelling houses with a barn and a garden to each of them; also a warehouse, wharf and fishing fences; with a lot of land of about five or six acres; also a lease and half for cows to summer in: all of which is convenient for fishermen or shoremen. Inquire of Jonas Dennis of said place.[6]

> We heard that last Tuesday as two men were returning with their grist from a mill, between Amaskeeg and Suncook [New Hampshire], they were fired upon by enemy Indians, supposed to be about 16, and one of them killed on the spot. The other escaped, very remarkably, for not withstanding that three bullets were shot through the brim of his hat, and ten through several parts of his coat, yet only two bullets just grazed the skin of his arm and side, and by running He escaped; the other man, named Starkee, was scalped by the enemy.[7]

> Yesterday arrived at Marblehead a vessel in 28 days from Lisbon, and brings advice, that a packet arrived there from England with an account, that Admirals Anson and Warren had taken and brought into England six French Men of War . . . and twelve transports, and the Admirals had left three Men of War in pursuit of the rest.[8]

---

4   "Those early chaplains were deeply studious men, reading such works as the sermons of George Whitefield." Parker C. Thompson, *From its European Antecedents to 1791: The United States Army Chaplaincy,* (Washington, DC: Department of the Army, 1978), p. 42.
5   Stephen Mansfield, *Forgotten Founding Father: The Heroic Legacy of George Whitefield,* (Nashville, TN: Highland Books, 2001). Jerome D. Mahaffey, *Preaching Politics: The Religious Rhetoric of George Whitefield and the Founding of a New Nation,* (Waco, TX: Baylor University Press, 2007).
6   *Boston Gazette,* March 17, 1747, p. 4.
7   *The Boston Weekly News Letter,* May 28, 1747, p. 2.
8   *Boston Gazette,* July 21, 1747, p. 3.

Whitefield was not immune to the rising political tensions of the day. In England, Whitefield and his followers were unfairly accused of disloyalty to the British crown. That charge was made because Whitefield, as a Church of England priest, preached in Methodist, Presbyterian, and other churches, giving the alleged appearance of disloyalty to the Church of England and the crown. The *Boston Gazette* ran the following defense of Whitefield:

> In yesterday's *Evening Post* I observed an extract from a late history of the Rebellion [controversy over the English crown] which I conclude was intended as a fling at the Rev. Dr. Whitefield. But does the printer imagine Mr. Whitefield in any way responsible for the political principles or behavior of those who admire and follow him as a preacher of religion? Can he suppose that his readers or any one man of sense will for this story be brought to think the worst of that gentleman? And yet unless that was his design, stupid as that was, what else can be conceived of? However, if Mr. Whitefield's loyalty must be judged from that of his followers, I doubt not his character will appear at least as fair as any of his opposers.[9]

In 1747, George Whitefield turned thirty-three years old. He had no way to know this, but his life was more than half over. His relentless itinerant schedule consumed his body. While he had episodes of ill health prior to 1747, the illness he had shortly before he returned to New England would be indicative of the health problems that would plague him the rest of his life. After spending Christmas in Bethesda, Georgia, Whitefield began a northern preaching tour. Numerous letters written by him survive, tracing his northward excursion through South Carolina, Maryland, Pennsylvania, and New York. In New York on June 9, 1747, Whitefield wrote that his "northern excursion" was going well, and that he did not know exactly when he would leave New York for New England.[10] In another letter written from New York with the same date, he said, "From hence I purpose to go to Boston."[11]

As Whitefield approached New England for the third time, many of the religious controversies of the past decade had died down. Churches that had divided over the awakening were now often reconciled or split amicably. The emotional extremes of the past were now over. With the decline of the excesses from revival came a return to normalcy in Colonial New England. In 1745, New Englanders won an important victory in King George's War when they captured Louisburg, Cape Breton Island, from the French. Whitefield's open support of the colonial forces, and his sermons and speeches of

A full-length portrait of George Whitefield, painted by Francis Kyte after 1743. Located at Westminster College, Cambridge University.

Source: www.bbc.co.uk/arts/yourpaintings/paintings/
owen-charles-whitehouse-ma-dd-student-professor-and-
presi204335

---

9   *Boston Gazette*, July 21, 1747, p.3. There was a newspaper rivalry in Boston related to Whitefield. *The Boston Gazette* published Whitefield's itinerary, letters of endorsement, and results of his preaching. *The Boston Weekly Newsletter* was run by Old Lights and did not so much as mention Whitefield's name between May and August 1747, while Whitefield was having remarkable local preaching success.
10 George Whitefield, *Works of George Whitefield, Letters*, (Great Britain: Quinta Press, 2000), vol. II, p. 109.
11 Ibid., p. 111.

thanksgiving for the American victory, did a lot to sooth tensions with his opponents. Politically, Massachusetts and Rhode Island were in discussions as to the exact location of their colonial borders. Pioneer settlements were started in western Massachusetts and throughout New Hampshire. Overall, New Englanders were more concerned about war with the French and their Indian allies than with theological debates.

It was no accident that Whitefield typically preached in the northern colonies in the summer, as the heat in the south severely weakened him. The cooler New England sea breezes refreshed his health. The psychological pressure of an inter-continental ministry, the burden of immense counseling by correspondence, the emotional trial from sometimes being geographically separated from his wife, and the physical stress caused by traveling on horseback or in a carriage in all kinds of weather weakened his already sensitive body. Added to these pressures was the financing and maintaining of the Bethesda Orphanage. Friends along his preaching circuits pleaded with him to take better care of his health, but Whitefield typically refused, sighting the urgency and obligation of his preaching ministry. Through much of June 1747, he was on a sick bed in New York suffering from exhaustion, fever, and convulsions.[12] Correspondents from Boston looked forward to his visit. Dallimore helps set the scene.

> But letters from Boston informed him that the time was ripe for him to return to New England. Accordingly, though very weak, he rose from his bed, forced himself into activity and set out on the long journey northward. Upon reaching New England, he found that, as he had expected, time had continued to heal the wounds in the work there. Wiser practices were prevailing more and more, and prejudices were subsiding. He preached frequently and after returning to Philadelphia, thus completing what he spoke of as 'an eleven hundred miles journey,' he stated that under his ministry in New England . . . , 'the power that attended the word seemed to be near the same as when the work began seven years ago.' Moreover, the cooler weather in the north had been beneficial . . . .[13]

It is this "eleven hundred miles journey" in New England in 1747 that will be the focus of this chapter.

On July 4, 1747, Whitefield wrote from New York that he would "to-morrow, God willing, intend posting away to Boston, and then I shall take a long, if not a final farewell of all my northward friends."[14] Clearly Boston was the center of operations for all Whitefield's New England visits. When Whitefield spoke about visiting his "northward friends," he meant his friends that were in Boston and Massachusetts, in Connecticut and Rhode Island, as well as in New Hampshire and what would later be called the State of Maine.

Whitefield would preach in Boston, spend a few weeks on a northward circuit, and return to the city. But the first stop we know about in New England, on his way to Boston, was in Newport, Rhode Island. There are glimpses of Whitefield's ministry in various towns that allow us to at least have a rough idea of where he travelled and preached. In the above quote, Dallimore sums up his several weeks New England ministry by saying, "He preached frequently . . . ." Tyerman says more, but only mentions nine towns by name describing Whitefield's 1747 New England tour.[15] Other Whitefield biographers make no mention of this New England preaching circuit, such as the book by Johnstone, which mistakenly dates Whitefield's time in America and can only summarily state, "In this manner Whitefield continued to labor in America . . . during which time he travelled over a great extent of country, and was subject to frequent attacks of illness."[16]

---

12 Arnold Dallimore, *George Whitefield, vol. II, p. 221.*
13 Ibid., vol. II, pp. 221-222.
14 George Whitefield, *Collected Works of George Whitefield, vol. II*, p. 112.
15 Luke Tyerman, *The Life of the Rev. George Whitefield*, (New York: Anson D.F. Randolf & Company, 1877), vol. II, pp. 174-175.
16 John Johnstone, *Sketches of the Life and Labors of the Rev. George Whitefield*, (Edinburg, Scotland: General Assembly of the Free Church of Scotland, 1759), p. 116.

While traveling through New England in the summer of 1747, Whitefield did not write any letters that have survived. He had long before ceased keeping a journal. However, after he departed New England, he wrote fourteen letters that we know of, which mentioned his just completed New England ministry. Interestingly, one of these letters speaks of where Whitefield was invited to preach, but he was unable to comply with the invitation. The letter is to Rev. Nathaniel Leonard, a Congregational minister in Plymouth, Massachusetts. Whitefield preached for Leonard to large crowds when he was last in that area, in December 1744. Whitefield was well received in Plymouth, and he made a friend in Nathaniel Leonard.

In the summer of 1747, Whitefield received an invitation to again preach for Leonard in Plymouth. His reply to that invitation is as follows:

To the Rev. Mr. L_____.

Bath-Town, North-Carolina, Oct. 11, 1747

Reverend and very dear Sir, It has given me much concern, that I could not comply with your kind invitation to Plymouth; but providence plainly pointed my course another way. God only knows what a cross it was to me, to leave dear New England too soon, I hope death will not be so bitter to me, as was parting from my friends. Glad shall I be to be thither again, before I see my native land. But future things belong to God. I would be just where he would have me, though it be in the uttermost parts of the earth . . . Be pleased to remember me in the kindest manner to dear Mr. F_____, and the whole circle of those reverend brethren, who dare confess Christ's work, and Christ's truths . . . .[17]

To navigate some sense of order for Whitefield's 1747 travels in New England, we shall look at his relevant surviving correspondence in chronological order. Then we will look at newspaper accounts that help trace his steps throughout New England. There is some inevitable repetition from the sources.

As previously mentioned, Whitefield wrote two letters dated August 20, 1747, from Newport, Rhode Island. These two letters speak of individual, local concerns and do not give any information of Whitefield's further travels. His next surviving letter is dated August 27, 1747, from New York to a Mr. D__. In this letter, Whitefield addresses mundane issues of finances and transportation, but then he writes, "My obligations to my glorious Jesus are increased by my late excursion to Charles-Town, Portsmouth, Boston, and other places in New England."[18] These named cities—Charles-Town, Portsmouth, and Boston, were very familiar locations for Whitefield.

Seven years earlier, on October 10, 1740 Whitefield first preached in Charlestown, Massachusetts. This town is the oldest neighborhood in Boston, first settled in 1624 and laid out as a town in 1629. This was a distinctly Puritan community, and original records from the earliest days have survived.[19] The ministers at the First Church Congregational in 1740 were Rev. Simon Bradstreet and Rev. Hull Abbott. They were reluctant to have Whitefield preach in their church, until Rev. William Cooper of the Brattle Street Church in Boston, vouched for Whitefield. Cooper actually escorted Whitefield to Charleston as a sign of support.[20]

---

17   George Whitefield, *The Works of George Whitefield, vol. II*, p. 136.
18   Ibid., p. 116.
19   For an overview see the booklet by Richard Frothingham, Jr. *The History of Charleston, Massachusetts*, (Charleston, MA: Charles P. Emmons, Printer, 1845).
20   George Whitefield, *George Whitefield's Journals*, (Carlisle, PA: Banner of Truth Trust, 1985), p. 471.

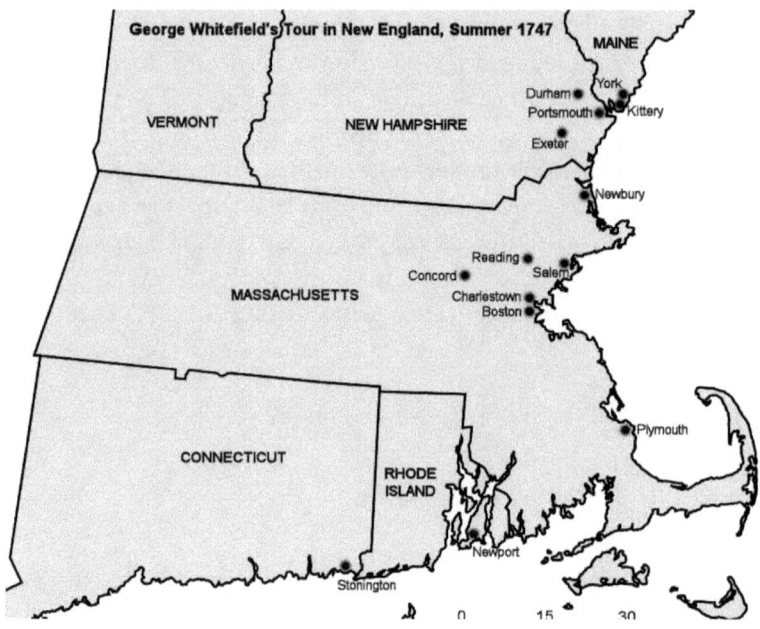

Whitefield's preaching in Charleston in 1740 resulted in about 80 people joining the church.[21] In 1741, Rev. Bradstreet died, replaced by Rev. Thomas Prentice. When Whitefield returned to the Boston area in late 1744 and early 1745, he preached in and around Boston for several weeks, but there is no specific reference to his preaching for Revs. Abbott and Prentice in Charleston. He may have, but the records are incomplete. However, in a letter dated August 27, 1747, quoted above, Whitefield stated that he had recently preached in "Charles-Town," Massachusetts.

When Whitefield came to Charlestown in the summer of 1747, he entered a thriving maritime community that was discussing public education, creating a school committee which came into being in 1748. He may have eaten, rested, or slept at the recently renovated Three Cranes Tavern, a popular stop for travelers through Charlestown. We do know that the First Congregational Church was working through some ministerial tensions between Abbott and Prentice. The issues were practical not theological, focused on such things as the preaching schedule, guidelines for pastoral visitations, the serving of communion, who would run the church business meetings, and the like.[22] Whatever their tensions, these clergymen worked together in Charlestown for over three decades. Abbott and Prentice were both Harvard graduates and both Calvinists. But they were not entirely sure of the lasting merits of the fanaticism that surrounded much of the awakening from several years prior. There is no record of the results of Whitefield's preaching in Charlestown in 1747.

Whitefield was cautious of the rising theological liberalism he sensed in places like Boston, but he was unaware of the growing Unitarian movement in the West Church Congregational. This church was founded in Boston in 1737 as an alternative to the conservative Calvinist churches in the city. Many wealthy merchants, businessmen, bankers, and others attended this church. Rev. Jonathan Mayhew was ordained at the West Church in 1747. Mayhew was so theologically liberal that it was difficult to get enough ministers to attend his ordination council. He was known as a skilled orator and a theological improvisor. "His religious views were independent and liberal . . . Mayhew's views on religion were more akin to that of the Unitarian traditions rather than to the Congregational fold in which he was a member."[23] Mayhew was not bashful in opposing the remnants of Puritanism in Boston. Boston began a new direction in 1747 with Mayhew's ordination. He was considered a leading citizen of the city and was esteemed by the rising anti-Puritanism in Boston.

---

21 William I. Budington, *The History of First Church Charleston* . . . , (Boston, MA: Charles Tappan Printer, 1845), p. 130.
22 Ibid., pp. 138-139.
23 "Jonathan Mayhew," www.totallyhistory.com/jonathan-mayhew. For a fuller study see J. Patrick Mullins, *Father of Liberty: Jonathan Mayhew and the Principles of the American Revolution*, (Lawrence, KS: University of Kansas Press, 2017).

In Boston, Whitefield had many close ministerial friends. These clergymen corresponded with Whitefield for years, and greatly encouraged his preaching and itinerant ministry. He received numerous invitations from these men, and in 1740, 1744-1745, and again in 1747, Whitefield preached in these churches for weeks at a time. Perhaps no city in the American Colonies had such helpful and eager ministerial support for Whitefield than Boston. The significant clergymen in Boston that openly endorsed Whitefield were Rev. Dr. Benjamin Colman and Rev. William Cooper of the Brattle Street Church; Rev. Dr. Joseph Sewell of the South Church; Rev. John Webb of the New North Church; Rev. Samuel Checkley of the New South Church; Rev. Joshua Gee of the Second Congregational Church; and Rev. Thomas Foxcroft of the First Congregational Church. Rev. Samuel Checkley of the New South Church was joined as a minister in Boston by his son, also named Samuel, who became a minister at the Old South Church in 1747.[24] Whitefield would preach for many of them in 1747. One place in Boston that Whitefield was not welcomed was at Christ Church Episcopal.

The second Episcopal Church in Boston, Christ Church was founded in 1722. Their first minister, Rev. Timothy Cutler, was called to be the rector in 1723. In the early 1730s, King George III sent various gifts to this church, such as silver communion items, which are still on display today. In 1740 a steeple was added to the church building, and in 1745 a special bell was cast in England and delivered for installation. English immigration to Boston created the need for a second Episcopal Church, and the Christ Church was growing. When Whitefield first came to Boston in 1740, Timothy Cutler was suspicious, hesitant, and then publicly opposed Whitefield and the awakening. Cutler was one who saw the revival "as reckless zeal and nothing more than an emotional binge."[25] On January 14, 1742, Cutler wrote a letter to the Bishop of London, calling the awakening in Boston "madness" promoted by zealots with "bitterness, fury & rage." He lamented the schisms and unstructured preaching meetings indoors or outdoors, asserting that "wickedness is justly feared to be the consequence of them."[26] When Whitefield returned to Boston in 1745, the Christ Church pulpit was closed to him. The same happened on this 1747 visit to Boston. Cutler was an intellectual who respected the pomp and ceremony of the Episcopal Church. He was an excellent linguist, logician, and rhetorician, "a man of extensive reading."[27] These were his characteristics in the ministry, "and it is the general testimony that a certain haughtiness of manner interfered seriously with his success."[28] Whitefield was not welcomed at Christ Church by Rev. Timothy Cutler.

An undated portrait of Rev. Timothy Cutler, Christ Episcopal Church, Boston.

Public domain image.

Whitefield's prior visits to Boston completely disrupted the ministerial culture of the city. Some clergy who were not converted now professed a conversion experience.

---

24 Chandler Robbins, *A History of the Second Church, or Old North, in Boston . . .*, (Boston, MA: Printed by John Wilson & Son, 1852), pp. 123-124.
25 Edwin S. Gaustad and Mark A. Noll, editors, *A Documentary History of Religion in America to 1877*, (Grand Rapids, MI: Eerdmans Publishing, 2003), p. 166.
26 Ibid., p. 168.
27 Franklin B. Dexter, *A Catalogue, with Descriptive Notices, of the Portraits, Busts, Etc., belonging to Yale University*, (New Haven: Yale University, 1892), p. 26
28 Ibid.

Others who already embraced the doctrine of conversion or regeneration, as practiced by the Puritan founding fathers, were affirmed in their faith. Many of the unconverted ministers resisted Whitefield and preached and wrote against him. A historian of the Great Awakening, Joseph Tracy, wrote, "At the time of Whitefield's third visit to America, from 1744 to 1748, there were not less than twenty ministers in the vicinity of Boston, who considered him as the means of their conversion."[29]

The next Whitefield letter that has survived is dated August, 27, 1747, from New York to a Mr. A__. Whitefield writes to express his "thanks for all past favors," and then stated, "I am of the same mind as when at Boston,—resolved to preach and work for Jesus, till I can preach and work no more."[30] This note simply tells us that Whitefield preached energetically in Boston, sometime in early August. But no details are provided. The next letter we know about from Whitefield is addressed to a Mr. W_, at Portsmouth, New Hampshire, dated August 27. Several weeks before, Whitefield was in Portsmouth and provided counsel to a man about to be married. He wrote, "You are shortly to enter into a new and untried state . . . marry in and for the Lord, or your life will be exceedingly uneasy and miserable."[31] This is solid premarital advice, but it gives us no details on Whitefield's public ministry in Portsmouth. A more insightful letter from Whitefield, to the itinerant minister Gilbert Tennent, is dated August 29, 1747 from New York.

> To the Rev. Mr. G_____T_____, New York, Aug. 29, 1747
>
> Rev. and very dear Sir,
>
> Not for want of love, but of leisure, has prevented my writing to you for some time past. Blessed be God, I can now send you good news from the Northward. My reception at Boston, and elsewhere in New England, was like unto the first. Arrows of conviction fled and stuck fast. Many, I hear, were wounded. Congregations were rather larger than ever, and opposers mouths were stopped . . . [32]

Compared to Whitefield's other visits to New England, relatively little is known of this 1747 tour. The reasons for this near-silence are several. First, international political concerns for New Englanders provided as much or more interest than the lingering work of revival. Second, Whitefield himself contributes to this lack of information on his 1747 trip to New England since he no longer kept a personal journal. Thirdly, while his preaching remained orthodox, he was less abrasive from his youthful zeal. He was simply less controversial than years before. Finally, the religious controversies of the 1740-1745 era had exhausted the sensitivities of the people. There was nothing new to be said. Old Lights and New Lights went about their separate ministries having little or nothing to do with each other. Further, Boston newspapers no longer covered Whitefield's agenda in detail.

Virtually no personal recollections have survived from individuals who heard Whitefield in 1747 in New England. Local historians have traditionally settled for second-hand accounts such as the following: "On his third visit to America, Whitefield came again to Newbury, and preached to a large congregation on July 29, 1747."[33] Contemporary newspapers provide an inconsistent narrative, with little elaboration, concerning this 1747 Boston visit. The *Boston Gazette* continued to be an ally of Whitefield during his popular 1747 visit in New England. But the *Boston Weekly Newsletter* was largely silent.

---

29   Joseph Tracy, *The Great Awakening*, (1842: reprinted by Banner of Truth Trust, Carlisle, PA: 1989), p. 393.
30   George Whitefield, *Works of George Whitefield, vol. II*, pp. 116-117.
31   Ibid., pp. 117-118.
32   Ibid.
33   John J. Currier, *Old Newbury: Historical and Biographical Sketches*, (Boston, MA: Damrell & Upman Printers, 1896), p. 527.

Boston Gazette, August 4, 1747, p. 3.

As in our Gazette of July 14, we informed our readers, that the representation of Mr. Whitefield's case [at New York] left some hope of his coming this way; for the gratification of his numerous friends, we would further inform:

That through the remarkable smiles of God on the advice of his physicians, his journey northward has been a means so far of restoring him, as to be come in a private manner to the seat of his friend Isaac Royal, Esq. at Charlestown on July 21, where on the next day several gentlemen of note from Boston went and paid him a friendly visit. Mr. Whitefield thought best to travel further still to the northward 'til he recovered a greater measure of strength, before he began to preach in public and, accordingly next morning, set out for Portsmouth, and that evening he began to preach in public there to a crowded audience, with as great acceptance as ever. Thence, he was invited to dine with Sir William [Pepperell] and his Lady at Kittery, who entertained him with their usual politeness and generosity.

Thence, he went and preached at York; the Reverend Moody and his people receiving him with the most hearty welcome. Thence, he returned to Portsmouth, where he preached again; and where there was no contention, but a perfect good humor, peace and quiet, all people treating him with gentleman-like civility, for which they are noted among the provinces. Thence, on Wednesday, July 29, he came and preached at Newbury; and would have come on to visit his many friends at Boston; but was so earnestly solicited to go back and preach in hopes of doing some good at Exeter and Durham, that he could not resist the opportunity. In a letter of his from Newbury, we learn that he would have told his friends the time of his coming to Boston, but that he desired to come as privately as possible.

Boston Gazette, August 18, 1747, p. 3.

In our Gazette on the 4th current, we informed that the Rev. Mr. Whitefield being at Newbury the Wednesday before, was in a manner certain of going back to Durham and Exeter; at which places we are informed he preached: then came back to Newbury, where on the Lord's day he preached again; Monday morning at Ipswich; and then returned to Mr. Royal's at Charlestown. Tuesday at one in the afternoon he came to Boston, upon which Dr. Colman desired him to preach his lecture that evening in his large church; and the people quickly filled it; the next evening at the New North; Tuesday afternoon at the Old North; Friday morning at the New North, Saturday at the Old North again: Lord's day he assisted in administering the Lord's Supper at the Presbyterian church in Bury Street; the next morning preached there; and in the afternoon at the new Baptist church; Tuesday morning at the New North, the assemblies crowded as usual: and Wednesday afternoon his farewell sermon on the hill by the North burying place; when the hill with its avenues were covered with people; and some thought there were twenty thousand.

Thursday morning he left this town; and at the desire of the condemned criminal preached in the square before the prison at Cambridge: Friday at Salem, Saturday at Reading; Lord's Day at Concord; Yesterday he set out for Rhode Island on his way to New York, etc.

He appears to be very feeble and in a declining state of health; and 'twas wonderful to all who were acquainted with him, to see and hear him preaching with his usual fervor and vivacity.

And his engagements in the South calling him away so soon, his many friends parted from him with peculiar reluctance, especially fearing they should see his face and hear his voice no more.

From New York on August 29, 1747, Whitefield wrote that his reception "at Boston, and elsewhere in New England," was similar to his first overwhelmingly successful preaching tour in New England in 1740. Perhaps he was exaggerating, but the recipient of this letter, Gilbert Tennent, was fully aware of the extent of the ongoing awakening in pockets in New England. For Whitefield to write that, "Congregations were rather larger than ever," is a remarkable statement, somewhat embellished, but nonetheless significant.[34] He saw his 1747 tour through New England as a remarkable success.

Whitefield's next surviving letter is dated August 29, 1747, also from New York. He wrote that when he left New England a few weeks prior, he was ill, but now his appetite had returned, and he was feeling better. He looked back upon his recent time in Portsmouth, New Hampshire, stating, "I hope those that were under concern at Portsmouth, find their convictions to abide. I pray GOD, they may have no rest, 'till they find rest in Jesus Christ! I salute them, and all the Redeemer's true followers . . . ."[35]

Whitefield had a welcome reception in Portsmouth in 1740 and in 1744-1745. In an October 1740, *Journals* entry, Whitefield wrote that Rev. William Shurtleff of the South Church, Portsmouth, welcomed him and the two happily supported each other.[36] Whitefield's preaching was well received. When Whitefield returned to Portsmouth in 1744-1745, he and Shurtleff again connected. But Shurtleff died in May 1747, Whitefield missing him by a few months. Another friend of Whitefield in Portsmouth was Rev. Jabez Fitch of the North Church. In his *Journals* dated November 22, 1744, Whitefield wrote of him and Fitch ministering together in Portsmouth. But Fitch died in November 1746. When Whitefield came to Portsmouth in 1747, he was welcomed by the new minister at North Church, Rev. Samuel Langdon, who had assisted Fitch at the church.

Samuel Langdon was a Harvard College graduate who was well respected by the people in Portsmouth from his chaplaincy duties with the 1745 expedition against the French at Louisburg, Nova Scotia. When he returned from the war, he was made the assistant minister at the North Church Congregational, where he served until 1774. His house is still standing in Portsmouth today. Langdon was an educator, scholar, theologian, and a supporter of Whitefield. He was granted the Doctor of Divinity degree from the University of Aberdeen in 1762.[37]

A 1907 photograph of the Rev. Samuel Langdon home in Portsmouth, New Hampshire. The house was newly constructed when Whitefield came to the area in 1747.

Source: Portsmouth Historical Society.

Returning to the Whitefield chronology in his letters; Whitefield continued moving

---

34 George Whitefield, *Works*, vol. II, pp. 117-118.
35 Ibid., p. 119.
36 George Whitefield, *Journals*, p. 467.
37 Joseph Foster, *The Soldier's Memorial, Portsmouth, N.H., 1893-1921*, (published by the Grand Army of the Republic, Portsmouth, NH, 1921), pp. 74-75.

south, preaching along the way, destined to see his Bethesda Orphanage in Georgia. The orphanage was a bold philanthropic adventure, but it also was a huge financial drain. Successfully organizing and administrating the orphanage was a high priority for Whitefield. Moving south from New York, his next preserved letter mentioning New England is dated September 9, 1747 from Philadelphia. In this large city Whitefield had many friends. Residing in Philadelphia for several days allowed him to preach regularly, and to catch up on his correspondence. Six of his letters, written September 9 to 11, 1747, reflect back on his recent preaching tour through New England. He wrote to an undetermined Mr. W_at Brattle Street Church in Boston, as follows.

> To Mr. W_____,
>
> Philadelphia, September 9, 1747.
>
> Very Dear Sir,
>
> Last night I heard of Dr. Colman's death. I bless God for granting him such an easy passage. Soon after the news reached me, I bowed my knee before the GOD and Father of our Lord Jesus Christ in behalf of your bereaved (and I could almost say desolate) church. O may the Lord of all Lords direct you in the choice of another, who may rule and feed you diligently with all his power. I shall be glad to hear what the great head of the church does for you . . . ."[38]

Dr. Benjamin Colman, and his ministry at Brattle Street Church, had a profound legacy in Boston. He began as the first minister of the church in 1699, serving there until his death in 1747. Whitefield preached for Colman in extended meetings over several days, both in 1740 and in 1744-1745. Now in 1747, their friendship was renewed only weeks before Colman's death. A skilled, multi-lingual minister, Colman displayed "zeal and prudence" related to Whitefield and the Great Awakening.[39] Colman rejoiced in the revival, while remaining balanced and occasionally critical of the extremes that sometimes accompanied the movement. Having earned his bachelor's degree and master's degree from Harvard, Colman was an exceptional writer who spread the awakening with his pen as well as his pulpit. He published over one hundred sermons, booklets, or larger works that were reprinted throughout the American Colonies and Great Britain. His amiable personality caused even his opponents to respect him.[40] In recognition of his international influence, the University of Glasgow in Scotland granted Colman the Doctor of Divinity degree in 1731. One historian stated,

> Dr. Colman was unquestionably one of the most attractive and popular preachers of his day. With a highly gifted and highly cultivated mind, he possessed a naturally ardent temperament, a most expressive and benignant countenance, and an uncommon solemnity and grace of manner, that never failed to rivet the attention of his audience. In his style of composition he was regarded as quite a model; and he is said to have contributed more than any other clergyman of that day to elevate at least the literary character of the New England pulpit.[41]

---

38 Ibid., pp. 121-122.
39 William B. Sprague, *Annals of the American Pulpit, Trinitarian Congregational*, (New York: Robert Carter & Brothers Printers, 1857), vol. I, p. 226.
40 Ebenezer Turell, *The Life and Character of the Reverend Benjamin Colman, D.D., late Pastor of a Church in Boston New England, who Deceased August 29th, 1747*, (Boston, MA: Printed by Rogers and Fowle, 1749), pp. 170-180.
41 William B. Sprague, *Annals of the American Pulpit, Trinitarian Congregational*, vol. I, p. 226.

Benjamin Colman was one of the leading New England ministers who supported the awakening. His endorsement of Whitefield in 1740, 1744-1745, and in 1747 led credibility to Whitefield throughout the New England Colonies. Coleman preached shortly before his death, and "spent the evening of his death in cheerful religious conversation."[42] Whitefield saw Colman only weeks before the popular Boston minister died, and wrote that he thanked God that Colman's death was "such an easy passage."[43]

In chronological order, the next surviving Whitefield letter related to his 1747 visit to New England is addressed to a Mr. and Mrs. F____, dated September 9, from Philadelphia. In this note Whitefield tantalizingly states, "I have lately been eleven hundred miles journey northward, and have found the Redeemer's strength magnified in my great weakness. The word ran and was glorified."[44] This reference to "northward" means New England. Another Whitefield letter, also dated September 9 from Philadelphia, to a Rev. Mr. H____, recorded, "When I received your letter, I was just returned from an eleven hundred miles journey northward, in which the rock of ages was pleased to let much of his glory pass before his dear people. I was enabled to preach about 30 times in New England, and am now coming forward towards you, and hope to see you in November . . . ."[45]

Whitefield wrote a letter to his friend and fellow itinerant evangelist, Gilbert Tennant, on September 10, 1747. The letter from Philadelphia contains several interesting views of Whitefield's recent ministry in New England.

To the Rev. Mr. T_____,

Philadelphia, Sept. 10, 1747

Reverend and very dear Sir, I suppose, ere this comes to hand, you will have heard how near I have been to my wished-for harbor, and how I have been obliged to put out to sea again. Blessed be GOD, since I must live, he does not permit me altogether to live in vain. The word ran and was glorified much in New England. The gathering of the people, and the power that attended the word seemed to be near the same as when the work begun seven years ago. I parted with my friends with great reluctance . . . [46]

This brief paragraph has several interesting aspects. Whitefield's statement, "The word ran and was glorified much in New England," is compelling, but gives no specific details of locations. When he mentioned that the power of his preaching was like "as when the work begun seven years ago," he made a remarkable statement. Seven years ago was 1740, in the midst of the unparalleled Great Awakening in New England, when Whitefield preached to thousands almost daily in meeting houses and in open fields. To compare his 1747 tour with his previous 1740 circuit through New England is an exaggeration. Whatever the case, Whitefield was greatly encouraged by his 1747 preaching tour through New England.

On September 11, 1747, Whitefield wrote a letter to Howell Harris in Wales, a region on the western side of the island of Great Britain. Harris and Whitefield were friends and co-workers in the Lord. They had travelled and preached together in Wales. After he was refused ordination by the Church of England for his theological views, Harris became the leader of the Welsh Calvinistic Methodist churches. Whitefield wrote to Harris from Philadelphia, as follows.

---

42 Richard Own Roberts, *Whitefield in Print: A Biographical Record of Works By, For, and Against Whitefield*, (Wheaton, IL: Richard Owen Roberts Publisher, 1988), p. 183.
43 George Whitefield, *The Works of George Whitefield, vol. II*, p.122.
44 Ibid.
45 Ibid., p. 123.
46 Ibid., p. 124.

To Mr. H_____H_____,

Philadelphia, Sept. 11, 1747

My very dear Brother, I wrote to you within these few months from this place, Boston and New York. My last letters were to inform you, that, GOD willing, some time next year I purpose to see England, if my outward affairs can be settled . . . We saw great things in New England. The flocking and power that attended the word, was like unto that seven years ago. Weak as I was, and have been, I was enabled to travel eleven hundred miles and preach daily . . . [47]

Here we some reoccurring themes in Whitefield's correspondence. He is happy to report, not a mediocre response, but "great things" from New England. And again, he compares his 1747 New England tour "like unto that seven years ago."

Whitefield's next surviving letter is addressed to Rev. John Wesley, a leader in the Methodist movement in Great Britain. Whitefield and Wesley had an on-gain-off-again friendship, which sometimes regressed to open theological disputes. In 1747, the two were cordial rivals with theological distinctions. In his September 11, 1747 letter to Wesley, Whitefield happily reports on his itinerant ministry in the American Colonies but is not hesitant to mention his disapproval of the alleged Wesleyan ideas of sinless perfection and universal atonement. In relation to his New England preaching tour, Whitefield summarized it to Wesley in once sentence; "I have been once more in New England. My entrance was as at the first, about seven years ago."[48] Then Whitefield moves on to other subjects and concludes his letter.

An old wood carved sketch of Whitefield preaching outside, later colored in.

*Source: https://www.wsj.com/articles/
book-review-george-whitefield-by-thomas-s-kidd-1423863426*

---

47 Ibid., p. 125.
48 Ibid., p. 127.

As previously stated, the exact locations and chronology of Whitefield's 1747 New England tour are unknown. However, in Tyerman's two-volume biography of Whitefield, he reveals several clues. First, we learn of a random Whitefield letter not gathered for the multi-volume *Collected Works of George Whitefield*. This correspondence places his arrival in Boston on July 20, 1747.[49] Next we discover a letter Whitefield wrote on August 9, 1747 to his friend Howell Harris in Wales, Great Britain. In this letter Whitefield reports, "I have been in New England nearly three weeks. The Lord is with me. Congregations are as great as ever. I could gladly stay in New England, but I must return to the southern provinces . . . "[50] Finally, Tyerman quotes from a periodical called the *New England Gazette*, by which we can trace Whitefield's activities with some detail;

> Mr. Whitefield came, on Tuesday evening, July 21, to the seat of his friend, Isaac Royal, Esq., at Charlestown; where, on the next day, several gentlemen of note from Boston paid him a friendly visit. On Thursday, the 23rd, he set out for Portsmouth, where he arrived on Friday, and, that evening, preached there, to a crowded audience, with as great acceptance as ever. Thence, he was invited to dine with Sir William Pepperell and his lady at Kittery, who entertained him with their usual great politeness and generosity. Thence, he went and preached at York; the Rev. Mr. Moody and his people received him with the most hearty welcome. Thence, he returned to Portsmouth, where he preached again, all the people treating him with gentleman-like civility. On July 29, he preached at Newbury, and would have come on to Boston, but was so earnestly solicited to go back and preach at Exeter and Durham, that he could not resist the importunity.[51]

While this list of locations does not include every place Whitefield visited in New England in 1747, it does show at least part of his preaching circuit. The locations mentioned here are Charlestown, Portsmouth, Kittery, York; again at Portsmouth, then Newbury, Exeter, and Durham. In this chapter we have already discussed Whitefield in Charlestown and Portsmouth. Now we will look at some other locations mentioned.

Kittery was a town now located in the southernmost part of what is now called the state of Maine. The senior minister in Kittery was Rev. John Newmarch, a Harvard graduate in 1690. In Whitefield's prior two visits to this area, in 1740 and in 1744-1745, he did not mention preaching in Kittery in his *Journals*. On these previous two visits Whitefield spent weeks in the Kittery area, namely across the Piscataqua River at Portsmouth, New Hampshire, and a few miles north of Kittery, at York, Maine. For whatever reason, Whitefield again did not preach for Newmarch in Kittery in July 1747.

The next town named in the *New England Gazette* article mentioned above is York, and the Rev. Mr. Samuel Moody. Moody began preaching in York in 1698, in a community that lived in daily fear of Indian attacks. Whitefield preached for Moody in York in 1740, and Moody stated that he thought 100 people in his congregation were newly converted.[52] At that visit Whitefield wrote that Moody was, "much impaired by old age."[53] In November 1744, Whitefield again preached for Moody at York, twice on a Sunday, where Whitefield was enthusiastically received. The above quote from the *New England Gazette* stated, "Thence, he went and preached at York; the Rev. Mr. Moody and his people received him with the most hearty welcome." Although Moody disdained the separations within churches that sometimes resulted from revivals, he remained a staunch Whitefield supporter. About three months after Moody and Whitefield met for the third time, in 1747, Samuel Moody was dead. He died at age seventy-one, on November 13, 1747.[54]

---

49 Luke Tyerman, *The Life of the Rev. George Whitefield*, vol. II, p. 174.
50 Ibid., p. 175.
51 Ibid. This quote is similar to the previously mentioned Whitefield account dated August 4, 1747, the *Boston Gazette*.
52 George Whitefield, *George Whitefield's Journals*, p. 467.
53 Ibid., p. 466
54 William B. Sprague, *Annals of the American Pulpit, Trinitarian Congregational*, vol. I, pp. 243-249.

After departing York, Whitefield took the ferry across the Piscataqua River to Portsmouth, New Hampshire. Having just departed Portsmouth a few days earlier, Whitefield continued his pattern of preaching and returning to an area, to water the gospel seeds previously planted. In Portsmouth, he again preached for Rev. Samuel Langdon. The *New England Gazette* article summarized, "Thence, he returned to Portsmouth, where he preached again, all the people treating him with gentleman-like civility." On July 29, Whitefield travelled twenty-two miles, crossed the Merrimack River by ferry, and preached at Newbury, Massachusetts, for his friend Rev. Jonathan Parsons.

Parsons had been at the new church in Newbury for about one year when Whitefield came to town. Parsons and Whitefield became friends when Whitefield came through southern Connecticut in 1740, where he and Parsons met. Again in 1745, the two were united in Connecticut, where Whitefield preached for Parsons outside at Lyme. Parsons began his ministry in Lyme, Connecticut in 1731, but by 1745, he and the church mutually separated. Whitefield introduced Parsons to a fledgling group of New Lights in Newbury, Massachusetts, who needed a pastor. Today known as Old South Presbyterian Church in Newburyport, the new Newbury congregation was greatly encouraged by Whitefield's 1747 visit. For the whole year before Whitefield arrived, there was controversy over Jonathan Parson's ordination. The Congregational Churches in

Under Rev. Samuel Moody, the First Church in York constructed a new meeting house in 1747. Major renovations were completed in 1882, but some of the original building remains. Whitefield preached here in the summer of 1747. Photograph by Ken Lawson.

the area were hesitant to ordain a minister to a Presbyterian Church, and the New England Presbytery, in Londonderry, New Hampshire, was not organized enough to sponsor a formal Presbyterian ordination council. The congregation, composed mostly of Scottish immigrants, requested a Presbyterian Calvinist minister. Therefore, the elders of the new church in Newbury ordained Parsons themselves.[55] For three decades Parson's faithfully served this congregation. Speaking of Jonathan Parsons in Newbury,

> The pastorate of Mr. Parsons spanned thirty years. He was peculiarly fitted for his place and work. Eminently scholarly and maintaining a correspondence with leading men of this and other lands, he was also a fervid revivalist and a man of affairs; choleric and passionate, he was ever swift to make amends; fond of fine clothes, ruffled shirt fronts and gold lace galore, he was also devotedly pious and wonderfully prevalent in prayer . . . his voice was under admirable control for majestic, persuasive or pathetic effects as occasion might require; as a whole a remarkable combination of contrasted characteristics.[56]

---

55 Horace C. Hovey, *Origin and Annals of "The Old South" Presbyterian Church and Parish in Newburyport, Mass., 1746-1896*, (Boston, MA: Damrell & Upham Printers, 1896), p. 29.
56 Ibid., pp. 34-35.

Had circumstances been the same as his first two visits to New England, Whitefield would have departed Newbury and preached his way south to Boston, typically stopping off along the way at Ipswich, Lynn, Reading, and Charleston. But pleas from area ministers temporarily diverted Whitefield from his intended southern route. Instead, he made a brief northwestern visit to Exeter and Durham, New Hampshire. The above quoted *New England Gazette* stated, "On July 29, he preached at Newbury, and would have come on to Boston, but was so earnestly solicited to go back and preach at Exeter and Durham, that he could not resist the importunity."

To preach in Exeter, Whitefield had to turn around, re-cross the Merrimack River, and proceed about ten miles towards Hampton. Then he took a westerly route several miles inland to Exeter.

In 1747, Exeter was a rural but prosperous town connected to the sea by the Exeter River which fed into the tidal Squamscott River. The main industries for Exeter centered on small mills and the timber industry. Exeter, New Hampshire was overwhelmed by the Great Awakening of the early 1740s. Whitefield did not preach in Exeter in 1740, but he did successfully preach at the nearby towns of Portsmouth and Hampton.[57] Rev. John Odlin of the First Congregational Church in Exeter did not support the revival. His congregation split in 1742, forming a Congregational Church in the Brentwood Parish part of Exeter. The separation was "an unceremonious departure" and was done with "bitter feelings,"[58] although a major reason for the separation was geography, not theology. At the same time, a theological dispute created the Second Congregational Church in Exeter, in 1744. This was clearly a division based on the Old Light beliefs of Odlin and the New Light beliefs of many in his parish. Rev. Daniel Rogers was ordained at the Second Congregational Church in 1744, serving there until his death in 1784. Rogers was a devoted friend of Whitefield. On report stated of Rogers, "He enjoyed the intimate acquaintance of Rev. Mr. Whitefield, and travelled with him through various parts of the country[side]."[59]

Whitefield visited Exeter, New Hampshire in February 1745. That was a tumultuous visit, which Whitefield recorded in four pages in his *Journals*. The First Congregational Church, under Rev. Odlin, opposed the awakening and he did not allow Whitefield to preach in the meeting house. Odlin had several ministers with him, all who publicly criticized Whitefield's methods, questioned his theology, and denied his legitimacy as an itinerant minister. Heated arguments arose, from which Whitefield excused himself. Whitefield then "preached twice in the new Meeting House," probably in the separatist church in the Brentwood neighborhood of Exeter.[60] No doubt this infuriated Odlin.

Two years later, Whitefield again appeared in Exeter, in July 1747. Tensions between the First Congregational Church and the new church in the Brentwood Parish of Exeter had not subsided. The new church insisted that it be released from having to pay the town tax to support Rev. Odlin, but civil officials did not agree. Therefore, the Congregational Church in Brentwood Parish had to pay for its separate worship with no compensation from the town, at the same time paying the town tax to support the First Church.[61] The new congregation in Brentwood supported the awakening and Whitefield. When Whitefield came to Exeter in 1747 the fledgling church did not have a settled minister. Instead, there was a rotation of six ministers that preached and were paid for their services.[62] Although the meeting house in Brentwood was framed in 1743, disputes within Exeter related to the Brentwood congregation lasted for years. When Whitefield preached in the Brentwood Parish of Exeter in 1747, it was in an unfinished meeting house. The

---

57 George Whitefield, *George Whitefield's Journals*, pp. 465-466.
58 Charles H. Bell, *History of the Town of Exeter, New Hampshire*, (Exeter, NH: 1888), p. 186.
59 "Dr. Daniel Rogers," http://freepages.genealogy.rootsweb.ancestry.com. William B. Sprague, *Annals of the American Pulpit, Trinitarian Congregational*, vol. I, p. 147.
60 George Whitefield, *George Whitefield's Journals*, p. 556.
61 Charles H. Bell, *History of the Town of Exeter, New Hampshire*, p. 186.
62 Benjamin A. Dean, Annals of the Brentwood, N.H. Congregational Church and parish, (Boston, MA: Press of T.W. Riley, 1889), pp. 9-11.

first permanent minister of the Congregational Church in Brentwood Parish of Exeter was Rev. Nathaniel Trask, who served from 1751 to his retirement in 1787.[63] Whitefield may also have preached for Rev. Daniel Rogers in the Second Congregational Church in Exeter.

The previously quoted *New England Gazette* stated that on July 29, 1747, Whitefield was on his way to Boston from Newbury, Massachusetts, but was detained by urgent please to come and preach in Exeter and Durham, New Hampshire. After preaching in Exeter, Whitefield travelled about twelve miles northeast on a good, strait road to Durham, where he was greeted by Rev. Nicholas Gilman. In March 1745, Whitefield preached twice for Gilman at the Congregational Church, after which Whitefield complemented Gilman for his example of holiness and meekness.[64] The two had a happy reunion in 1747. However, Gilman was in deteriorating health. Indeed, for all of his years in Durham, from 1742 to his death in 1748, Gilman was not robust. The Whitefield visit was the last significant event in Gilman's shortened life of thirty-eight years. A fervent New Light preacher, he died nine months after meeting Whitefield in Durham. His death was on April 13, 1748.[65] On Gilman's tombstone it was written,

> He was endow'd with many amiable & useful Accomplishments. His manners were grave, east and pleasant. He was exemplary in extensive Charity and Beneficence, eminent in Piety, Self Denial & Victory over ye World. A fervent, sound persuasive Preacher, abounding in the work of the Lord . . . .[66]

The religious climate in New England is evident in a diary entry from Rev. Ebenezer Parkman of Westborough. On June 17, 1747 Parkman attended a minister's meeting in Sudbury, Massachusetts. He observed that there was still tension between New Light and Old Light ministers. After the guest speaker preached, Parkman wrote of the sermon, "It seems indeed to have been compos'd in a Strain which many would term New Light, but there was not much ground, if any at all for anyone to make exception. But I saw plainly that it did not go down well with some gentlemen. I am heartily sorry that there are any Remains of the Bitter root among us. I returned to Marlborough home."[67]

From the Boston area in the summer of 1747, Whitefield proceeded to the middle and southern colonies. His next stop was in Rhode Island. Earlier, in 1740, Whitefield was a sensation in Rhode Island, and the Episcopal minister in Newport, Rev. James Honeyman, allowed Whitefield to preach in Trinity Episcopal Church. That was not repeated in Whitefield's 1745 and 1747 visits to Newport. Whitefield preached for Rev. Nathaniel Clapp at the First Church Congregational in Newport, both in 1740 and in 1745. But by Whitefield's 1747 visit, Clapp was deceased. And in his two previous visits to Newport, Whitefield did not preach in the Second Congregational Church.

When Whitefield arrived in Newport in the summer of 1747, there had been some changes in ministers. Rev. James Searing was still the minister of the Second Church Congregational, from 1731 to 1755. He did not welcome Whitefield in 1740 and in 1745, and there is no reason to believe that his mind had changed in 1747. After Nathaniel Clapp's death in late 1745, the new minister at the First Church Congregational was Rev. William Vinal (or Vinall). It was Rev. Vinal that welcomed Whitefield to Newport in 1747.

Whitefield wrote two letters from Newport in 1747. Unfortunately, these are short letters of one paragraph each. Both letters are addressed to unnamed individuals, both dated August 20, 1747. The first

---

63 Robert F. Lawrence, *The New Hampshire Churches: Comprising Histories of the Congregational and Presbyterian Churches in the State . . .*, (Claremont, NH: Claremont Manufacturing Company, 1856), p. 20.
64 George Whitefield, *George Whitefield's Journals*, p. 556.
65 Arthur Gilman, *The Gilman Family traced in the Line of Honorable John Gilman of Exeter*, (Albany, NY: Joel Munsel, Printer, 1869), pp. 55-64.
66 Alexander Gillman, *Searches into the History of the Gillman or Gilman Family . . .*, (London, UK: Elliott Stock, Printer, 1895), p. 241.
67 *Diary of Ebenezer Parkman*, transcribed by the Westborough Center for History and Culture, www.diary.ebenezerparkman.org.

letter relates to premarital advice for a woman. The second letter is also composed mostly of homey advice. But this letter also has a couple of sentences related to ministers who are not supporting their parishioners who experience a personal spiritual awakening.[68] Regrettably, no specific details of his preaching in Rhode Island were recorded.

Welcoming Whitefield to Newport was Rev. William Vinal of the First Church Congregational. Vinal was at the church less than two years when Whitefield came to town in 1747. A 1737 graduate of Yale College, Vinal was at the college during the Great Awakening, and was a committed New Light. Vinal served in Newport from 1745 to 1768. There was nothing remarkable or exceptional about his ministry in Newport. Apparently, the people liked him, and he was content to serve in the First Congregational Church for twenty-three years. There were no major controversies, revivals, or divisions in the church during his tenure.[69] The relative calm of his ministry should not be quickly dismissed, as the aftermath of the Great Awakening caused serious division and contentions in churches. At such a time, a steady, balanced ministry was necessary. One source succinctly stated the ordinariness of Vinal's time in Newport, by simply recording, "Rev. William Vinal was ordained pastor of the First Church Oct. 29, 1746, and was dismissed Sept. 21, 1768."[70]

An influential woman who attended the First Church Congregational in Newport was Mrs. Sarah Osborn. An indigent woman with an invalid husband, she was converted shortly after Whitefield's 1740 visit to Newport. To help pay bills, she began a school in Newport in 1744 that eventually had hundreds of students. Her evangelical witness in Newport was profound. With the full approval of her minister, Rev. William Vinal, Osborn led Bible study groups for women and children, and had a significant influence on the city. Evident throughout her numerous letters and journals is her exuberance for New Light doctrines. Several weeks before Whitefield arrived in 1747, she lamented her poor health that kept her away from three Sabbath meetings. She was devoted to pray for her minister and the church folks, and pleaded for the grace of God to be poured out in Newport.[71] When Whitefield came to Newport in 1747, Osborn had already prepared her children to pray for revival and to eagerly support the visiting evangelist.

The Church of England missionary Rev. James McSparran detested Whitefield. Serving at the Old Narragansett Church, or Saint Paul's Episcopal Church in Wickford, Rhode Island, McSparran dreaded Whitefield's frequent visits to the area. He believed the roving evangelist was a threat to the established order in New England, and that he was a disgrace to the Church of England. McSparran frequently wrote to the Bishop of London complaining about Whitefield. After Whitefield's 1747 preaching tour through New England, McSparran wrote to Rev. Thomas Sherlock, Bishop of London, reporting that his congregation had been spared from Whitefield's negative influence. He also reported to the Bishop that those who endorsed Whitefield on his 1747 tour were "Jesuit colonists," and that disorder followed Whitefield wherever he went.[72]

Whitefield departed Newport, Rhode Island by sea shortly after August 20, 1747. His next letter is dated from New York, August 27, 1747, in which he wrote that he had been "detained upon the water three or four days, and that he met his wife, Elizabeth, his "dear yoke-fellow" in New York.[73] Before reaching New York he stopped in the port of Stonington, Connecticut.

The last letter Whitefield wrote that we know about, that has mention of his 1747 preaching tour in New England, is dated October 11, 1747 from Bath-Town, North Carolina. In writing to an unidentified

---

68　George Whitefield, *Works of George Whitefield, vol. II*, pp. 115-116.
69　Charles E. Hammett, *A Contribution to the Bibliography and Literature of Newport, R.I.*, (Newport, RI: Published by the Author, 1887), p. 148.
70　B.B. Edwards and W. Cogswell, compilers. *The American Quarterly Register,* (Boston, MA: Printed by Perkins & Marvin, 1840), p. 267.
71　Samuel Hopkins, *Memoirs of the Life of Mrs. Sarah Osborn, who Died at Newport, Rhode Island on the Second day of August, 1796 . . .*, (Worcester, MA: Leonard Worcester Printer, 1799), pp. 100-101.
72　William Gibson and Thomas W. Smith, *George Whitefield: Tercentenary Essays*, (University of Wales Press, 2015), p. 28.
73　George Whitefield, *Works of George Whitefield, vol. II*, p. 116.

Mr. P_____, Whitefield gives spiritual advice and makes casual conversation. From rural North Carolina he wrote, "I am now proclaiming it [the gospel] in these uncultivated ungospelized parts." Then Whitefield remarked that he had been preaching previously throughout parts of North Carolina, Virginia, and Maryland. After more pastoral advice and homey comments, Whitefield closes this letter with an exclamation; "However, this I must say, New England friends are dearer to me than ever, and glad shall I be, if another sight of them before I die, be permitted to, very dear Sir, Yours most affectionately in Christ, G.W."[74] Whitefield's desire to revisit New England would happen seven years later, in 1754.

A mid-life sketch of George Whitefield in his wig and ministerial robe.

Source: https://lexloiz.wordpress.com/2009/11/07/ george-whitefield-visits-jonathan-edwards-part-3

---

74 George Whitefield, *Works of George Whitefield, vol. II*, p.137.

CHAPTER 26

A COMMUNITY IN TRANSITION

NEW ENGLAND IN THE 1750S

THE MID-EIGHTEENTH CENTURY WAS A period of tremendous change for the American Colonies. Bushman has captured this transition in his book on Colonial Connecticut, engagingly titled, *From Puritan to Yankee*. In this book he chronicles the decline of New England Puritanism and the rise of commercialism in Connecticut. Bushman skillfully traces the influences of immigration, secularism, and financial prosperity as detrimental to the faith of the Puritan founding fathers. Simultaneously, there grew an independence of colonial thought separate from Great Britain. An American consciousness developed that encouraged autonomy in religion, commerce, and government.[1]

The American Colonies in the mid-1700s were British in name and culture. Colonists happily showed allegiance to the British King George. They paid British taxes, obeyed British laws, submitted to British courts of law, served in colonial militias under the British military, and flew the British flag. The issues that plagued England quickly surfaced in the New World. Specifically in New England, there were ongoing military concerns, growing economic vitality, and tense ecclesiastical disruptions that transformed the region. An ongoing military conflict, known in America as the French and Indian War (1754-1763), began to raise a national moral consciousness among the various colonies. Economically, this period gave rise to international shipping, trading, and mercantile activities, creating a small but enormously wealthy class of citizens previously unknown in America. Salem, Massachusetts is a prime example.[2] Further, changes in religion continued to accelerate, establishing New Light evangelical orthodoxy as a legitimate pattern of thought, while non-orthodox theologies began to develop and prosper in New England.

The presence of French Roman Catholics in North America was a deep concern for the English Puritans and their descendants. The prolonged European wars between the English and French were transplanted to the New World colonies. The French presence along the Canadian coastline, only a day's sail from Boston, was a constant threat to New England merchants. These French outposts served as both privateer bases and trading stations, as well as homesteads for French Catholics. Military skirmishes and actual battles between the English and the French lasted through the early and middle 1700s.

Individual communities throughout New England were severely shaken by this prolonged military conflict with the French. Thousands of American colonists fought for the British. Newspapers from Boston, Massachusetts, and later Portsmouth, New Hampshire and Newport, Rhode Island, continually ran extensive front-page accounts of the military endeavors of local citizens in conflict with the French and Indians.

---

1   Richard L. Bushman, *From Puritan to Yankee: Character and the Social Order in Connecticut, 1690-1765,* (Cambridge, MA: Harvard University Press, 1967, 1980).
2   James D. Phillips, *Salem in the Eighteenth Century,* (Boston, MA: Houghton Mifflin Company, 1937).

An undated sketch of colonial Lynn, Massachusetts.

Source: https://www.peachridgeglass.com/2012/09/medicines-from-lynn-massachusetts

In 1748, the Treaty of Aix-la-Chapelle returned the Louisburg fortress and Cape Breton Island to the French. Many soldiers from New England fought in the 1750s to regain this area, as well as territories in other places from French forces. For example, Major Joseph Fry of Andover, Massachusetts was part of a spring 1755 expedition to Nova Scotia, as a commander under General Winslow. They were completely successful in subjecting the province of Nova Scotia (Acadia). A considerable number of privates in the expedition were from Andover. Other expeditions to Lake Champlain and Crown Point were less successful. Several Andover soldiers who died in military service are named in town records. Five deaths are named, two by sickness. "The sufferings undergone by the colonists in prosecuting these wars of the mother country were extreme, not only in their taxation and the generally unsettled condition of the country, which was in a perpetual commotion of military musterings, impressments, etc., and with the burden of many sick and disabled soldiers."[3]

In Ipswich, Massachusetts, a portion of which was known as Chebacco Parish, eighty men fought alongside the armies of the King of England against the French and Indians. Large numbers of Ipswich men took part in the assaults on Canada in the late 1750s, and a few more fought in sea battles in the West Indies against the French. For the American colonists, the great victory of the British Empire over the French was their victory, resulting in the almost total elimination of French sovereignty in America. In 1771, there were in Ipswich thirty-five veterans of this conflict, almost a quarter of the adult male population.[4]

The chaplains who served the colonists during this conflict were deeply affected by the Great Awakening of a decade before. Many ministers were generally united on Calvinistic theology and not overly concerned with polity. Hundreds of Congregational, Presbyterian, and other clergy united and fellowshipped together as military chaplains. These local church pastors who volunteered to fight against "The North American Babylon," were strongly influenced by George Whitefield. For example, during the 1755-1756 expedition to Crown Point in Nova Scotia, Rev. Samuel Chandler, a fervent New Light minister, was chaplain of his regiment. As a native of Andover, Massachusetts and later a pastor in York, Maine and Gloucester, Massachusetts, Chandler hosted Whitefield in his pulpit several times and wrote in defense of the New Light cause.

---

3   Sarah L. Bailey, *Historical Sketches of Andover, Massachusetts,* (Boston, MA: Houghton-Mifflin Company, 1880), pp. 244-245.
4   Christopher M. Jedry, *The World of John Cleveland of Ipswich*, (New York: W.W. Norton & Company, 1979), p. 124.

Perhaps the most obvious example of Whitefield's influence upon the colonial chaplains of the French and Indian War is Rev. John Cleveland of Ipswich (Chebacco). "It is said of Cleveland that he preached his whole parish into the army, then went himself."[5] Rev. Cleveland supported Whitefield since his college days at Yale, when the itinerant preacher spoke in New Haven. Cleveland served with Colonel Jonathan Bagley's regiment as chaplain, commissioned in March 1755. Their mission was part of a two-pronged attack into French Canada, under British General James Abercrombie. Colonial troops from Massachusetts and Connecticut joined the British regulars in this expedition.

Cleveland recorded how he and other New Light colonists were shocked at the carnal behavior of the British troops. There were uneasy relations between the provincials and the British regulars from the beginning. New England Puritan sensibilities were shocked by the low morals of the British Army troops. Cleveland later wrote to his wife that "Profane swearing seems to be the naturalized language of the regulars," he praying that God would remove wickedness from the camp "that stemmed mostly from the regulars' propensities for gaming, robbery, theft, whoring, bad-company-keeping, etc."[6]

A private recollection from an individual soldier from northern New England helps to display the experience of war against the French and Indians in the mid-eighteenth century.

A History of the Most Remarkable Things in My Life

> I, Jonathan Burnham the fourth, was born at Chebacco June the 9th, 1738, where I saw many remarkable things . . . The Lord sent two brothers, Mr. John and Ebenezer Cleveland, and the people built a house and settled John Cleveland, whose labors were greatly blessed for in one year ninety persons were taken into his church and many more wonderful things happened . . .

> When I was but fifteen years old, I went to live at Ipswich town, with Mr. Samuel Ross, to learn a blacksmith's trade, and was bound to him, . . . a good old man that built his house upon a rock and brought his family up in the nurture and admonition of the Lord, where I lived until I was nineteen years of age, and then I bought my time and enlisted in the service of King George the second, and slung my pack and marched to Fort Edward, where I slept sweetly, and the next day I slung my pack and followed my Colonel 7 miles to Brook Fort, half way to Lake George, where my Colonel was ordered to halt and keep that fort, and guard the teams to Lake George that sold provision to General Abercrombie's army. Early one morning the Indians gave us battle and killed 26 of our brave men, and scalped them, and ran into the woods to Canada, and sold their scalps for a guinea and a scalp to the French who were worse than the Indians themselves, as it was said; then General Abercrombie ordered my Colonel to lead on his men to Lake George, and he crossed the Lake on a Thursday and landed, and Friday marched his army to take Ticonderoga Fort, where he was beat and did retreat to his old encampment with weed on his hat dragging the ground! With the loss of more than nineteen hundred men; where I carried 'till my time was out, this was the year of '58, and then I was honorably dismissed and returned back to my good old master in Ipswich, who was glad to see me alive . . . [7]

---

5   Roy L. Honeywell, *Chaplains in the United States Army,* (Washington, DC: Department of the Army, 1985), p. 33.
6   Christopher M. Jedry, *The World of John Cleveland of Ipswich,* pp. 126-127. John Cleveland's letter to his wife is dated August 22, 1759.
7   Jonathan Burnham, *The Autobiography of Col. Jonathan Burnham of Salisbury, Massachusetts,* (Portsmouth, NH: S. Whidden, Printer, 1814), vol. I, pp. 4-5.

The prolonged conflict with France was the dominant issue in the mid-1700s in Colonial America. Virtually every community in New England experienced a fatality from this endeavor, while almost every town had numerous veterans from these wars. In reference to the effect of the war on Colonial Andover, Massachusetts,

> The war seems, therefore, the principal event of the time. Physicians, clergymen, all classes were brought into connection with the military affairs . . . .Some women of the time scarcely knew what it was to pass a year without anxious suspense for the fate of husband or son, brother or lover, in the war. [8]

The two sides of the Great Awakening, New Light revivalists and Old Light traditionalists found a common enemy in French Roman Catholicism. It is not that the Old and New Lights joined sides, but they had a mutual enemy. Old and New Light ministers did not suddenly exchange Sunday morning pulpits as friends to denounce the French, but they were generally cordial and united at civic assembles in unanimity against the French threat.[9]

While the news of war occupied the minds of New Englanders, subtle changes in economic stability began to develop. For example, both before and during the war with France, there developed a prosperous economic environment for much of maritime New England. This provided a dimension of life previously unknown in these communities. While some of the landlocked towns benefitted little from a growing economy, coastal cities experienced a sharp rise in business and financial resources in the 1750s.

Wenham, Massachusetts was a landlocked farming community that experienced a stagnation in its economy in the 1750s. Its population failed to grow, and its economy remained unchanged. The farmers of Wenham coped as best they could with diminishing resources, striving toward economic stability. In contrast to Wenham, the adjoining port city of Beverly experienced growth during that same period. Beverly, as Wenham's southern neighbor, participated in building a more maritime and commercially oriented economy. Beverly's merchants, traders, fishermen and farmers were able to adapt and expand their economic structure, adjusting well to population growth, migration, and a commercial world that reached across the Atlantic.[10]

The neighboring towns of Wenham and Beverly pose an interesting study of New England economics in the mid-1700s. Despite the location of each town in eastern Massachusetts, Wenham's farmers experienced the extremes of depopulation while Beverly's farmers, artisans, and mariners expanded their resources. Many out-migrants, whether they were matured sons or repeating migrants, successfully relocated in other New England farm towns or in seaports like Boston or Salem. But others were not successful, and in villages and seaports like Beverly and Wenham, a class of the migrant poor began to emerge. While some of these transients moved out of menial work as servants, others remained as seasonal agricultural laborers, never able to become the independent yeomen who was the American ideal. Below these laborers were those trapped in a cycle of poverty, dependent on poor relief and the charity of their neighbors.[11]

The Ipswich-Chebacco community in northeastern Massachusetts had the advantage of being both a coastal port and a farming community. In the mid-1700s, three-fourths of Chebacco's farmers lived on estates large enough to provide a comfortable existence. By the late 1760s, their investment in sheep was abundant and prosperous, twice the national average.[12] There was a small fleet of locally owned maritime vessels under twenty tons. Other major commercial enterprises were three sawmills, a gristmill, a tannery, a

---

8   Sarah L. Bailey, *Historical Sketches of Andover, Massachusetts*, pp. 281-282.
9   Harry S. Stout, *The New England Soul: Preaching and Religious Culture in Colonial New England*, (New York: Oxford University Press, 1986), pp. 238-240.
10 Douglas L. Jones, *Villages and Seaports: Migration and Society in Eighteenth Century Massachusetts*, (Boston, MA: University of New England Press, 1981), p. 27.
11 Ibid., p. 54.
12 Christopher M. Jedry, *The World of John Cleveland of Ipswich*, pp. 58-68.

brewery, and a tavern. The Ipswich-Chebacco village was an ideal colonial town, with a lifestyle of simple, hardworking prosperity reminiscent of similar communities back in England.

> The communities north of Boston experienced an interdependence based on a mutually beneficial economic relationship.

> Market towns like Salem and Beverly serviced the needs of the smaller, outlying farming towns, while the farming towns produced grain, cattle, wood, and hay for sale in the market towns. But the seaport towns also depended on the farming towns for a wide range of goods and produce. The people of Beverly, for example, sought to improve one of the roads between Wenham and Topsfield because "great numbers of the Inhabitants of Beverly have Great Dependence Upon Topsfield [and] the town above it for Provision, firewood, Bark and faggot for the fish Stages [and] are liable to Suffer in the winter Season Especially for want of firewood."[13]

The economic changes in New England were alluded to by the noted diarist from Salem, William Bentley. Bentley recollected that the city leaders in Salem debated "whether or not to warn strangers out of town in order to save the town from the charges of the poor." Bentley also noted the economic prosperity of Salem in the large number of wealthy merchants who had settled in the city. He recorded, "It is found, in fact, that the greater part of the whole property is in the hands of persons not town-born, and in the best streets, a majority of the freeholders are newcomers."[14] Salem served as a trading port since its settlement in the 1630s. Other nearby towns, such as Beverly, Marblehead, Newburyport, and Portsmouth, New Hampshire grew slowly as the economic climate matured.

Some routine examples of everyday life in northern New England help describe the cultural changes and events of the time:

> March 10, 1751-52, a committee was chosen to inspect all vessels that come into the Merrimack River "to see whether there are any cases of smallpox on board;" and the same committee was instructed to give immediate notice to the selectmen if they found any person sick with smallpox in any dwelling house within the limits of the town.[15]

> November 18, 1755, a few minutes past 4 o'clock A.M., another earthquake was experienced, more violent in its motions, and of a longer duration than any previously felt in this quarter of the globe. Its greatest violence in this town was felt in the neighborhood of Colon Street, where several chimneys were thrown down. Stone walls were also prostrated, and "the pewter shaken from the shelves in other parts of the town. Both in Beverly and Salem, a change in the quality of water was noticed. Water which had previously been soft and suitable for washing, became hard and unfit for that purpose.[16]

In her book on the history of Andover, Sarah Bailey contrasts the original settlers of the mid-1600s to those who lived in Andover in the mid-1700s. She wrote that the early period was of necessity a time of simplicity. Few families had wealth, very few had luxuries and elegances. But a hundred years had made great changes. In 1651, the representative to the General Court from Andover, dying, left an inventory of household

---

13 Douglas L. Jones, *Villages and Seaports*, p. 2. Quoted from a petition by John Herrick of Beverly, Massachusetts, July 1754.
14 William Bentley, *The Diary of William Bentley*, (Salem, MA: Essex Institute, 1907), vol. II, p. 188.
15 John J. Currier, *History of Newburyport, Massachusetts 1635-1902*, (Boston, MA: Dawcell and Upham Printers, 1902), p. 224.
16 Edwin M. Stone, *History of Beverly, Civil and Ecclesiastical*, (Boston, MA: J. Munroe and Company, 1843), p. 38.

goods in which not a piece of silver was named, and of which everything was humble in the extreme. Bailey then compares the simplicity of the original settlers to the material prosperity of those from equal social status from the mid-eighteenth century. She noted that in the Andover valuations and inventories of 1751-1771 are mentioned silver plates, chaises, and African and Caribbean slaves. Typical Andover homeowners had heirlooms of silver and mahogany, expensive decorative tapestries, family portraits, and handcrafted wardrobes and other furniture which showed wealth and refinement. Like many New England towns, Andover had reached a level of comfort and culture previously indulged only by persons of higher social rank.[17]

Economic prosperity in New England is well illustrated by the rise of New Haven, Connecticut. Founded in 1638 by Puritans, New Haven was a well-planned community with organized development centered on the meeting house. Because of its ocean port, New Haven quickly became a thriving center for trade between Europe, Africa, and the Caribbean. Beautiful homes adorned New Haven in the late seventeenth and eighteenth century. A merchant class prospered, as did various trades related to shipping, agriculture, shipbuilding, whaling, and other maritime activities. Numerous languages were spoken in this prosperous port city. The beautiful New Haven Green, with its comfortable colonial homes, was the rival of any town common in England.[18] Many of these homes still stand today.

Yale College came to New Haven in 1716. As the community grew, Puritanism was in decline. New Haven was the co-capital of Connecticut from 1701 to 1873, bringing numerous non-Puritan civil leaders, businessmen, and others to the city. The physical prosperity of New Haven was parallel to the decline in Puritanism. In the 1750s, New Haven had noticeably changed. Church services in the meeting houses became times for worship, but also to transact business and spread gossip. Attendance at religious events was expected, but the devotion of the congregation was divided between ecclesiastic and secular concerns. Puritan doctrines of original sin, repentance, and salvation became unfashionable, replaced by inspirational and devotional sermons with poetry, elegant grammar, and logic. Social sins grew in frequency and acceptance or at least toleration.[19]

In addition to military endeavors and a changing socioeconomic environment, there were numerous ecclesiastical issues in the mid-eighteenth century that helped shape American Christianity. New England continued to change, with religious issues often in the forefront of public debate. The Great Awakening changed everything.

Opponents to the awakening believed that the New Lights were intent on destroying the customs of a settled ministry. From the founding of New England in the early-to-mid 1700s, each congregation called its own pastor, who then ministered, often for the rest of his life, in that local parish. A preacher entered the pulpit of another congregation only by special invitation or arrangement. When the awakening erupted, New Light clergy and others who were not ordained, were frequently asked to speak in neighboring churches. Problems emerged when Whitefield and those who emulated him went from place to place preaching or exhorting with or without an invitation.

There were sporadic incidents of church upheavals. For example, in 1743 Nathaniel Wardell was a member of the Old South Church in Boston. His ministers, Joseph Sewell and Thomas Prince, were somewhat advocates of the awakening. In zealous statements he believed his ministers were working for Satan and were not supportive enough of the revival. Wardell then assumed pastoral duties by baptizing people. His pastors sought to bring Wardell to his senses but failed. He was forbidden to take communion in the Old South Church and was considered undesirable by the New Light churches in Boston. Wardell was placed under church discipline for five years; at which time he became a Seventh Day Baptist. Finally, in the summer of

---

17 Sarah L. Bailey, *Historical Sketches of Andover, Massachusetts*, p. 283.
18 J.L. Rockey, *History of New Haven County, Connecticut*, (New York: W.W. Preston & Company, 1892), pp. 97-143.
19 Edward E. Atwater, *History of the Colony of New Haven ... Connecticut*, (New Haven, CT: Printed for the Author, 1881), pp. 258-260.

1748, the disruptive and unbalanced Nathaniel Wardell was officially and publicly excommunicated from the Old South Church.[20]

Some of the divisions and separations caused by the awakening lasted into the 1750s. Tension still existed between Old Light and New Light congregations, though not nearly as much as in the early 1740s. One Old Light individual (unnamed) printed a rebuke of New Light preachers and divisions within local congregations. The following remarks were printed in Boston in 1748 and widely circulated:

> But then I would hope there are very few, if any of us, that would join with our brethren in drawing this conclusion . . . that therefore the Lord calls us to come out of the sanctuary, and have us separated from the church, leave the institutions of His house, and tarry at home, or meet in a private, separate way, with one or two that pretend to have more than ordinary of the spiritual presence of Christ with them. I say, I cannot persuade myself to believe that there are any of us that have as yet got to that height of wildness and infatuation, as to come to such a conclusion as this.[21]

The unknown author then restates his criticism of divisions within the churches with the following remarks: "But what, I pray, is all this to their purpose, who would justify themselves in separating from churches and ministers, because they have grown, as they say, dead and formal? . . . Will the Scripture justify such separation?"[22]

Another example of ecclesiastical tensions in the 1750s was in Ashford, Connecticut. The First Church in Ashford was started in 1718, and the meeting house was completed in 1723. At the time of the Great Awakening in the early 1740s, the minister at the church was Rev. James Hale. "It was evidently a hard struggle for existence with the First Church of Ashford. There were discordant elements in the population, and a factor of ignorance laid obstacles in the way . . . but with all the means used and efforts made the work was backward."[23] During the peak years of the awakening, Rev. Hale was older and ill, and the church did not have a revival. But church members went to neighboring churches to hear itinerant revival preachers, and many became New Lights. Rev. John Bass was installed as the new minister in Ashford in 1743. After a few years, many in the church became dissatisfied with the theology and ministry of Rev. Bass. By 1750, Bass had a revolt in his church. A movement in the church opposed their minister, even to the point of refusing to take the communion from him. Congregants accused Rev. Bass of being a weak Calvinist, particularly related to original sin, to his ignoring the need for the new birth, and to his belief in annihilationism compared to eternal suffering for the lost. Initially, Bass professed these doctrines as a traditional Calvinist, but over time his theology broadened, and many in his congregation did not like it. Several church meetings were held, and ministerial councils were called. Bass was dismissed from the church in 1751. He then wrote a pamphlet explaining that he indeed recanted his former beliefs in Calvinism, and that he did no longer believe in original sin, election, predestination, or an eternal suffering in hell.[24] The town of Ashford was torn apart by this ongoing scandal. After several years of bickering about a new minister, Rev. Timothy Allen, a New Light, was called by the Ashford church in 1757.

In the 1750s, the churches in New Hampshire continued to reach towards a population often disinterested in their ministries. The founders of New Hampshire were not inspired by religion. Unlike their Massachusetts neighbors, Puritanism was not relevant. New Hampshire settlers were motivated by business and financial concerns, not religious ideals.

---

20 *Boston Weekly Post Boy*, March 28, 1743, p. 1. *Boston Evening Post*, February 14, 1743, p. 1.
21 Anonymous, *A Caveat Against Unreasonable and Unscriptural Separations,* (Boston, MA: Queen Street, 1748), pp. 5,7.
22 Ibid., p. 7.
23 Dennis Partridge, "Church History of Ashford, Connecticut," *Connecticut Genealogy,* https://connecticut genealogy.com/windham/church_history_of_ashford.htm.
24 John Bass, *A True Narrative of an Unhappy Contention in the Church at Ashford,* (Boston, MA: 1751), pp. 3-11.

> The energetic proprietors of New Hampshire . . . were not moved to plant colonies in the wilderness to extend the area of freedom or promote the interests of religion, but to aggrandize their houses and increase their private fortunes . . . The men they hired to fell the trees, till the soil, fish, hunt and mine, in the new world, were not exiles for conscience's sake, but from love of gain. No provision was made by masters or servants for the preaching of the gospel.[25]

The first ministers to New Hampshire villages were Harvard-trained Congregational clergy, coming as missionary pastors starting new congregations. By the 1750s New Hampshire had some Quaker meeting houses, and several Presbyterian churches, but the vast majority of ministers were still Congregationalists. In 1750, the Congregational pastors of New Hampshire regularly corresponded with their dissenting clergy brethren in England, both sides in strong sympathy with each other. At the 1754 annual meeting of Congregational ministers in New Hampshire, their priority was to address "carelessness in religion" in their communities and in their congregations.[26] As New Hampshire grew in population, the ministers were unable to keep pace. At the 1758 annual meeting of New Hampshire Congregational pastors, Governor Benning Wentworth was asked to grant a charter for a college to train ministers, which eventually became Dartmouth College in 1768.

The effects of the 1740 Great Awakening had significant local effects in the 1750s. For example, Eunice Andrews of Ipswich Hamlet (now Hamilton), Massachusetts Colony was a teenager when Whitefield came to town in 1740. In 1747 she married and began attending a separatist meeting in the nearby Chebacco parish under Rev. John Cleveland. For several years she was under deep conviction, desiring to be right with God but confused and uncertain. She eventually embraced her newfound faith and interviewed with Rev. Cleveland for church membership. Based on her statement of faith, she was approved for church membership and placed her mark in the church record book on September 16, 1750.[27]

While some congregations were still experiencing tension and division because of the awakening, other churches began to thrive under the leadership of New Light ministers. One example of an assembly that grew from the awakening, and continued in peace to promote New Light theology, was the First Church in tiny Byfield, near Newbury and Ipswich, Massachusetts. Rev. Moses Parsons, pastor of the First Church from 1744 to 1783, wholeheartedly supported the New Light cause for forty years.

> In 1752, . . . Mr. Parsons appears to have become a warm admirer of Mr. Whitefield; his diary shows that he welcomed the great evangelist to his house and pulpit, took great pains to hear him elsewhere, was his fellow guest at other tables, and was a bearer at his funeral . . . Mr. Parsons' growing appreciation of Mr. Whitefield showed his candor and his love of the saving truth of the Gospel.[28]

A quick survey of several congregations in New England helps to describe the religious climate in the mid-eighteenth century. In Massachusetts, South Parish Church in Andover, under Rev. Samuel Phillips continued to prosper in a town with an increasing population. Rev. John Cleveland's leadership of the Chebacco Parish in Ipswich was solidified after 1747 when his Old Light nemesis, Rev. Theophilus Pickering, became sick and died at age forty-seven.[29] The ministry of Rev. John Barnard of North Parish in Andover

---

25 Edwin D. Sanborn, *Churches of New Hampshire: An Historical Discourse . . .* , (Bristol, NH: R.W. Musgrove, Printer, 1876), p. 7.
26 Ibid., p. 12.
27 For a full treatment of these times in Chebacco, see Anne S. Brown, "Visions of Community in Eighteenth Century Essex County: Chebacco Parish and the Great Awakening." *Essex Institute Historical Collections*, CXXV (1989), pp. 239-262.
28 John L. Ewell, *The Story of Byfield, a New England Parish*, (Boston, MA: George E. Littleton Printer, 1904), p. 107.
29 David T. Kimball, *Sketch of the Ecclesiastical History of Ipswich . . .* , (Haverhill, MA: Printed at the Gazette and Patriot Office, 1823), pp. 28-32.

(now North Andover) was relatively uneventful, as his Old Light theology, and sympathy with Arminianism, caused suspicion among the old Puritans in the community. In contrast, Rev. Jonathan Parsons of Old South Church in Newburyport was known as an active New Light since the early 1740s. Whitefield preached for Parsons numerous times, and the two men were devoted friends. Parson's ministry was so successful, that in 1756 his congregation built an enormous meeting house, one of the largest in New England.[30] In Rhode Island, the Quakers built a meeting house in Saylesville in 1704, and as a result of the Great Awakening, expanded their building with an adjoining two story structure in 1745. In Newport, Trinity Episcopal Church experienced growth in opposition to the awakening, so that their 1726 building had to be expanded in 1764. The Baptist Church in Providence built a meeting house in 1736, and while no revival took place in the church, growth was apparent in that a larger church building was constructed in 1775. In Connecticut, the First Congregational Church in Haddam, in the 1750s, did not experience any remarkable growth or events. Two ministers served the church in that decade: Rev. Joshua Elderkin (1749-1753) and Rev. Eleazer May (1756-1803). The church experienced slow growth while the town expanded. May encouraged revival and sought an awakening in his congregation and parish. A new meeting house was constructed in 1770-1771. May conducted "a fearless and faithful ministry" in a community in which he was deeply respected.[31]

An example of the remnants of puritanism in New England in the 1750s is found in the successful Boston merchant, Ebenezer Storer (1729-1807). Storer was from a prosperous mercantile family. He graduated from Harvard College in 1747 and earned an additional degree in 1750. Storer was a deacon at the Brattle Street Church and was of Boston's upper society. His *Diary* shows him to be an intensely spiritually-minded man of prayer and religious reflection. Many notations in his *Diary* concern the health and welfare of others, as well as his biblical ruminations. Storer read the Puritans regularly and often quoted from the hymns of Isaac Watts. He wrote, "I look unto Jesus by an eye of faith who suffered on the cross to shed his precious blood to reconcile lost sinners to God, may I be convinced, that there is no other name whereby I can be saved, but the name of the Lord Jesus." In an age of rising speculation regarding the Bible, Storer asserted, "I have owned my baptismal covenant & have solemnly given myself to God, having taken God as my Father, the Son of God for my Savior, the Holy Ghost for my sanctifier."[32]

By 1750, those New England communities that experienced a revival were either seeking to maintain the awakening, or remembering the movement as having passed. For those cities and towns that did not experience an awakening in the 1740s, there was no sign of another soon to come. One community that did not experience a large awakening was Salem, Massachusetts. The following account presents an interesting and unique explanation of why the awakening passed by this prosperous city:

> We may well ask why the movement made so little impression in Salem. The mass of people here were as much affected by Whitefield's preaching as were those in other places, but the leaders of the community were aloof. Their aloofness, no matter how they may have explained it, was probably due in part to the vivid memory of the witchcraft delusion and its horrible results. Men still in active life during the decade from 1740 to 1750 would remember Judge Sewall's recantation and apology and the shame that attended the recovery from the madness of those terrible days. The community had experienced a purgation of those emotions on which the fear of the supernatural rests. This is not the whole explanation. Salem men were beginning in those days the sea ventures which were to have so glorious a future. They

---

30   Horace C. Hovey, editor, *Origins and Annals of the "Old South" First Presbyterian Church and Parish, in Newburyport, Mass., 1746-1896*, (Boston, MA: Darwell & Upham Printers, 1896), pp. 30-35.
31   *The Two Hundredth Anniversary of the First Congregational Church of Haddam, Connecticut*, (Haddam, CT: 1902), p. 18.
32   "Diary of Ebenezer Storer, 1749-1764," *Congregational Library and Archives*, https://www.congregationallibrary.org/nehh/series2/StorerEbenezer, p. 19.

were not helplessly exposed to destructive forces beyond their control. They had achieved the emotional stability which comes from successful activity and a hopeful future.[33]

An influential minister on the north shore of Boston, who became known as a defender of orthodoxy and a reconciler of divided parties, was Rev. John Chipman. Pastor Chipman, a Harvard graduate in 1711, pastored the Second Church in Beverly from its inception in 1716 until his death in 1775.

> His influence abroad was commensurate with that exerted at home. He was frequently called to assist in ordinations, and in the settlement of difficulties that arose in the neighboring churches. His virtues, though of the sterner sort, were not the less real. In 1746, with Mr. Wigglesworth of Ipswich, he published a controversial pamphlet directed against Rev. William Balch of Bradford, who was accused of propagating Arminian tenets . . . the joint production of Messrs. Wigglesworth and Chipman is a pamphlet of forty-four pages. It is written in a temperate spirit, and dedicated to the ministers and Churches of our Lord Jesus Christ in New England. Mr. Batch's reply occupies ninety-two pages, and displays perspicuity and independence.[34]

John Chipman's reputation as an orthodox pastor and defender of New Light theology, extended throughout New England. Communities as far away as Leominster, then little more than a frontier village in the central Massachusetts Colony, asked his assistance in ecclesiastical disturbances. For example:

> July 23, 1757, letters signed Oliver Carter & Co. in behalf of about eighteen or nineteen brethren of the church in Leominster, Mass., were received and complied with, requesting the Pastor (Rev. John Chipman, Second Parish, Beverly) with delegates, to assist at a council convened for the purpose of examining a complaint against their pastor Rev. John Rogers. The letter set forth that he had denied the doctrine of original sin and had "rendered himself suspected of unsoundness, even in some of the fundamental doctrines of Christianity; most particularly of the Deity of the Lord Jesus Christ."[35]

Pastor Chipman's frequent requests to serve as a moderator of church disputes reveals a larger problem that had been developing since Whitefield's first visit to New England in 1740. In reaction to Whitefield, there appeared the developing influence of subjectivism in theology. There was a growing prejudice against doctrinal conformity and creedal affirmations by those who remained silent or openly opposed to the awakening. The subjective "moral consciousness" of humanity was replacing what others saw as the objective authority of God's Word.

An undated image of Rev. John Chipman, Second Church (Congregational), Beverly, Massachusetts.

Source: www.findagrave.com

---

33 Thomas H. Billings, "The Great Awakening," *Historical Collections of the Essex Institute*, (Salem, MA: Essex Institute, 1929), vol. 65, p. 104.
34 Edwin M. Stone, *History of Beverly, Civil and Ecclesiastical*, pp. 272-273.
35 Ibid., p. 268.

Prominence was given by many to the humanity of Jesus over the deity of Jesus. In contrast, Chipman remained a Calvinist and an evangelical. In the midst of this doctrinal uncertainty in New England, there arose by the 1750s a great theologian of international acclaim as a New Light defender of orthodoxy.

Rev. Jonathan Edwards first became recognized in 1734, when, as a thirty-one-year old country pastor in Northampton, Massachusetts, his congregation experienced a period of prolonged revival. During a series of sermons on the theme of justification by faith, hundreds of individuals in dozens of towns in the Northampton area experienced an awakening. In 1737, when Edwards published *Faithful Narrative of the Surprising Work of God . . . ,* his name was known throughout churches in the English-speaking world.[36]

After the awakening spread throughout the American Colonies, in 1743 Edwards published a major thesis entitled, *Some Thoughts Concerning the Present Revival of Religion in New England,* which theologically defended the movement as both biblical in nature and desirable for all the churches.[37] With Edwards' pen defending revival, and Whitefield's relentless travels in support of the awakening, Boston and other parts of New England had established pockets of orthodoxy that survived well past the mid-eighteenth century.

Edwards attempted to help resolve the numerous church disruptions of his day when he published in 1748, *An Humble Attempt to Promote Explicit Agreement and Visible Union Among God's People in Extraordinary Prayer.* Edwards' thesis was signed by five of the most prominent pastors Boston: Joseph Sewell and Thomas Prince of South Church in Boston, John Webb, pastor of the New North Church in Boston, Thomas Foxcroft of the First Church in Boston, and Joshua Gee, pastor of the Second Church in Boston. The influence of Edwards in New England is evident by the demand for his pamphlets to be republished, his sermons printed in newspapers, and his many invitations to speak at ministerial ordinations. For example, Edwards gave the ordination sermon of Job Strong of Portsmouth, New Hampshire in 1750. This ordination sermon by Edwards, called *Christ the Example of Ministers*, challenged those in attendance to follow the Lord Jesus in several ways: (1) His virtues; (2.) His seeking of souls; (3.) His prayers for souls of men; (4.) His diligence in His work; (5.) His suffering for salvation of souls; (6.) And his zeal mixed with gentleness and condescension.[38]

Defenders of orthodoxy in northern New England, such as the Rev. John Chipman of Beverly and the Rev. John Cleveland of Chebacco, received immeasurable assistance from the pen of Jonathan Edwards. In 1757, when *The Great Christian Doctrine of Original Sin Defended* was published, it was in an era when Unitarianism and Universalism were developing, which, among other beliefs, denied original sin. Edwards wrote the following remarks:

> I look on the doctrine [of original sin] as of great importance; which everybody will doubtless own it is, if it be true. For if the case be such indeed, that all mankind are by nature in a state of total ruin, both with respect to the moral evil of which they are the subjects; and the afflictive evil to which they are exposed, the one is the consequence and punishment of the other; then, doubtless, the great salvation by Christ stands in direct relation to this ruin, as the remedy to the disease; and the whole Gospel, or doctrine of salvation, must suppose it; and all real belief, or true notion of that Gospel, must be built upon it.[39]

---

36 Jonathan Edwards, *A Faithful Narrative of the Surprising Work of God in the Conversion of many hundred Souls in Northampton, and the Neighboring Towns and Villages of New Hampshire . . . ,* (Boston: 1738). This 140-page document is an eyewitness account of the awakening and its results.

37 Ibid., *Some Thoughts Concerning the Present Revival of Religion in New England, and the way in Which it ought to be Acknowledged and Promoted . . . ,* (Boston: 1743). This 228-page document assesses both the positive and negative aspects of the Great Awakening, seeing the movement as largely past.

38 Jonathan Edwards, *A Sermon Preached in Portsmouth at the Ordination of Job Strong, June 28, 1749,* (Boston, MA: 1750).

39 Jonathan Edwards, *The Great Christian Doctrine of Original Sin Defended: Evidence of its Truth Produced, and Arguments of the Contrary Answered,* (Stockbridge, MA: 1757). *The Collected Works of Jonathan Edwards,* (Carlisle, PA: Banner of Truth Trust, 1974), vol. I, p. 145.

New England in the 1750s was a community amid change. Ongoing inter-colonial warfare with the French and Indians created much grief and stress for New England families. Economically, the region experienced areas of tremendous growth and prosperity. Other areas stagnated. In the affairs of religion, much of the sensational aspect of the awakening waned, and the churches settled into the work of consolidating numerical and spiritual gains. Orthodox pastors acted as shepherds to their flocks and as defenders against the wolves of spreading unorthodox theologies and ideas, mainly from Europe.[40] Rhode Island prospered in the 1750s, as the population grew from 32,733 people in 1748, to 40,414 people in 1755. Ongoing boundary disputes with Massachusetts were settled in 1757. The city of Newport, Rhode Island thrived from merchant trade and other maritime activities. This prosperous community constructed a library in 1750 and began a newspaper for its cosmopolitan population in 1758.

The 1750s were a time of spiritual transitions. Rev. Isaac Backus (1724-1806) was born and raised in Norwich, Connecticut. He was raised in a community with an active New Light presence. Eventually, Backus became a Baptist minister. He was generally supportive of Whitefield and the awakening, but he later developed reservations about Whitefield's practice of infant baptism. In the 1740s, Backus knew a ten-year-old boy who was deeply convicted by Whitefield's preaching. In the 1750s, the young man was still struggling with issues of Christian faith and trust. As an adult, the boy told Isaac Backus the following story. "I was then convinced that neither myself, nor those who spoke with so much spite and malice [against Whitefield] were the children of God . . . They called them deluded, possessed with the devil, Highflyers, and New Lights . . . And from that time until I was twenty six years old, the Spirit of God was striving with me, by awakening my conscience, convincing me of sin, and that I must be born again." He stated that he "went on sinning and repenting,"

The Rev. John Cleveland house in Essex, Massachusetts. The home was originally built in 1713 and has been remodeled over the years.

Source: https://historicipswich.org/2016/10/18/historic-houses-of-essex-ma

---

40   "A large part of the stimulus towards such ideas came from the writings of thinkers across the Atlantic who had trod the same path from Calvinism to liberal theology somewhat earlier. But it is no less manifest that the development of some of the Puritan churches in America, especially some of those that most opposed the revival movement, had been leading them independently to results similar to those reached . . . in England." Williston Walker, *The History of Congregationalism in the United States,* (New York: The Christian Literature Company, 1894), p. 279.

drawing close to God then pulling away, until he was finally converted.[41] This man looked back upon his boyhood and teenage years in the 1750s as a time of deep spiritual turmoil and unrest.

By the 1750s, it is difficult to quantify the results of the 1740s awakening in New England. Churches were invigorated, lives were changed, standards of social behavior were elevated, and the faith of the founding Puritans was restated among their descendants of the fourth and fifth generations. Undoubtedly, in certain parishes, church memberships increased.[42]There were underlying aspects, too, which deserve mentioning. The numerical gains within orthodox churches happened at crucial times. The threats of unorthodox religious ideas, with their theological speculations was beginning to develop. Also, immigration increased the number of secular people who had no Puritan heritage and had no interest in Calvinism. And the Unitarian /Universalism movements began to gain respect and momentum among the aristocracy in coastal cities and at Harvard and Yale colleges. Amid this community of social, civic, and ecclesiastical change, George Whitefield made his fourth visit to New England in 1754.

---

41 Isaac Backus, *A History of New England, with Particular Reference to the Denomination of Christians Called Baptists*, (Newton, MA: Published by the Backus Historical Society, 1871), p. 324.

42 The periodical, *The Christian History* was a Boston based publication published annually in the 1740s. This periodical contained accounts of hundreds of individual awakenings and community revivals. The 1743 edition had 416 pages. See *The Christian History Accounts of the Revival and Propagation of Religion in Great Britain and America for the Year 1743*, (Boston, MA: Kneeland and Green Printers, 1744). This is the best source for accounts of the Awakening. Other first-person accounts of revival in colonial churches are found in Joseph Tracy, *The Great Awakening: A History of the Revival of Religion in the Time of Edwards & Whitefield*, (1842: reprinted by Banner of Truth Trust, Carlisle, PA: 1989). Richard L. Bushman, *The Great Awakening: Documents on the Revival of Religion, 1740-1745*, (Chapel Hill, NC: University of North Carolina Press, 1989). Thomas S. Kidd, *The Great Awakening: A Brief History with Documents*, (New York: Bedford/St. Martin's Press, 2007).

A sketch of George Whitefield preaching outside. Here the evangelist is showing his age.

Source: http://www.thearda.com/timeline/persons/person_94.asp.

CHAPTER 27

WHITEFIELD'S TOUR IN EASTERN NEW ENGLAND

FALL 1754

WHITEFIELD'S 1754 TOUR THROUGH NEW England has been largely overlooked or understated by his biographers. Tyerman covers this tour in two-plus pages with no attempt at a detailed chronology.[1] Gillies covers this entire preaching tour in three paragraphs.[2] Andrews accounts this preaching circuit in three pages, and stated that the forty-year-old Whitefield was in good health though wearing down.[3] Philip covers this tour in two pages,[4] while Dallimore wrote of this 1754 New England evangelistic tour in less than one page.[5] A reason for the lack of information on Whitefield's activities in New England in 1754 is that local newspapers no longer carried sensational articles about revivals. The controversy of the Great Awakening of the early 1740s had passed. As far as the newspapers in Boston were concerned, the phenomenon of Whitefield was over.[6] Further, in 1754 in New England, only Boston has newspapers, as the first newspaper in Connecticut began in 1755; the first newspaper in New Hampshire began in 1756; and the first newspaper in Rhode Island started printing in 1758. However, this chapter will look in detail at this successful several weeks preaching circuit through New England.

After departing New England in 1747, Whitefield preached, traveled, and exhorted through most of the British Isles. In addition to revisiting many of his old acquaintances throughout England, Whitefield traveled to Ireland, where his ministry was quite successful, and to Scotland, where crowds estimated at twenty thousand heard him preach in the open fields.[7] An eight-week stay on the island of Bermuda strengthened him for these numerous labors. Early in 1754, however, Whitefield prepared to take another trip to America. Whitefield landed in South Carolina on May 26, 1754.

Due to crossing the Atlantic, it had been eleven weeks since Whitefield last preached. He was now well rested and in better health than he had known for several years. He settled upon his administrative duties at the Bethesda Orphanage. He reviewed the school's finances, he coordinated construction projects, he insured that the Black slaves were treated with compassion, and he ministered to the orphans and the staff.8 Upon completing his duties at the Bethesda orphanage in Georgia, he traveled on an evangelistic tour through the northern colonies.

---

1 Luke Tyerman, *The Life of the Rev. George Whitefield*, (New York: Anson D.F. Randolph & Company, 1877), vol. II, pp. 335-337.
2 John Gilles, *Memoirs of George Whitefield*, (1838: reprinted by Pietan Publications, New Ipswich, NH, 1993), pp. 162-163.
3 John R. Andrews, *George Whitefield, A Light Rising in Obscurity*, (1879: reprinted by Elibron Classics, London, England, 2005), pp. 294-296.
4 Robert Philip, *The Life and Times of George Whitefield*, (1837: reprinted by Banner of Truth Trust, Carlisle, PA: 2007), pp. 443-44.
5 Arnold Dallimore, *George Whitefield: The Life and Times of the Great Evangelist of the Eighteenth Century Revival*, (Carlisle, PA: Banner of Truth Trust, 1980), vol. II, p. 371.
6 Lisa Smith, *The First Great Awakening in Colonial Newspapers: A Shifting Story*, (New York: Lexington Books, 2013), p. 7.
7 Arnold Dallimore, *George Whitefield*, vol. II, p. 360.
8 Edward J. Cashin, *Beloved Bethesda: A History of George Whitefield's Home for Boys, 1740-2000*, (Macon, GA: Mercer University Press, 2001), pp. 74-76.

In Philadelphia, Whitefield preached at the Academy and helped organize its functions, as the parent organization to the University of Pennsylvania. While in New Jersey, the officials at the College of New Jersey at Princeton asked him to speak at their September 1754 commencement, at which time the school conferred on Whitefield an honorary Master of Arts degree. Harvard and Yale may have still opposed Whitefield, but the new and prestigious college at Princeton endorsed the itinerant preacher.

In anticipation of an upcoming visit from Whitefield, Boston newspapers kept the public informed of the evangelist's movements toward Boston. Excitement grew, and ministers wrote letters and planned to have Whitefield speak in their churches. Other clergymen dreaded or ignored Whitefield's pending arrival.

Boston Gazette, August 27, 1754

[Philadelphia] Since the Rev. Mr. George Whitefield arrived here, he has preached almost every evening in the new Presbyterian church, and always to very crowded and polite audiences. We hear he intends to set out for Boston on Tuesday next, and designs to preach in the Philadelphia area at Neshaminey at four that afternoon; at Newtown on Wednesday, at ten in the morning, and at Newton at four in the afternoon.

Boston Gazette, September 3, 1754

[Philadelphia] On Monday evening last, a vast number of people assembled in the Academy yard, to hear the Rev. George Whitefield preach his farewell sermon; but it being likely to rain, he was obliged to deliver it in the new Presbyterian church, by which, is supposed, one half of those met were obliged to return to their homes without hearing him; the church being quite crowded, and vast numbers all around it: And next morning he set out for Boston.

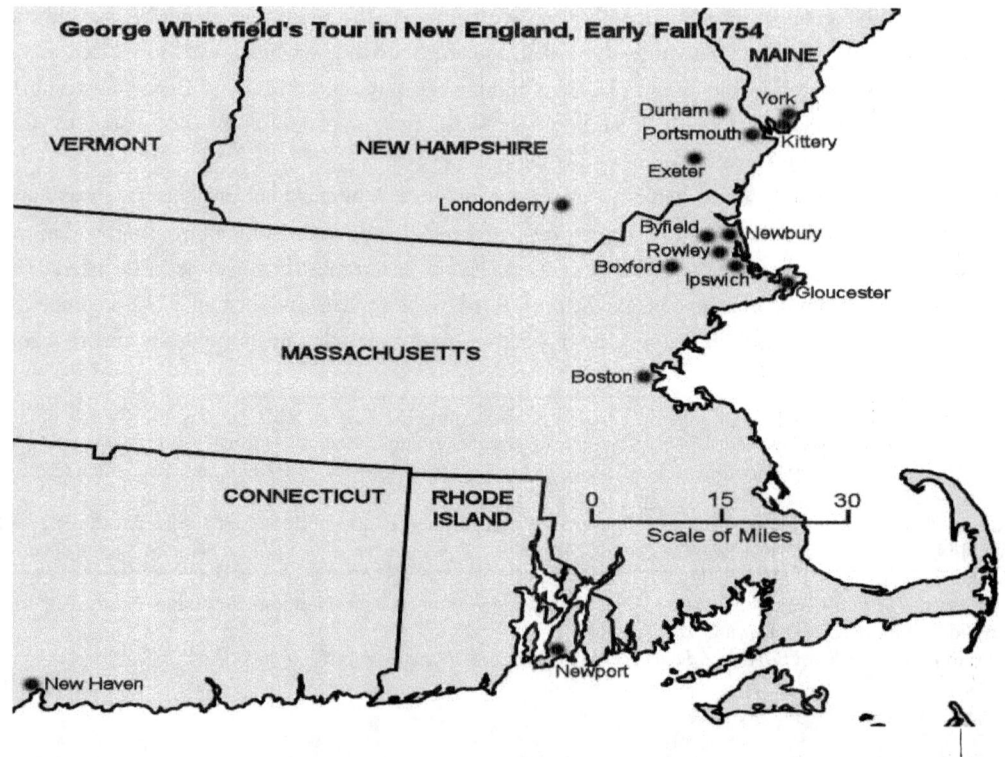

Boston Gazette, September 10, 1754

[New York] Saturday last the Rev. George Whitefield arrived here from Philadelphia; and yesterday morning at seven o'clock he preached to a moderate audience in the Presbyterian meeting in this city. In the evening of the same day, at five o'clock, he preached before a very crowded audience of near 2,000 persons, in the same place, on the latter part of the 12th verse of the IV Chapter of Amos. In his application to which, we are told, he was extremely pathetic [sympathetic] with regard to the Disturbances, not only on the frontiers of this province, but likewise on those of our neighbors.

It is interesting to observe the newspaper coverage Whitefield received from Boston printers. *The Boston Gazette* showed the same support for Whitefield as it did on the 1740 tour, his visits in 1744-1745, and his brief tour in 1747. *The Boston Gazette* considered Whitefield's ministry worthwhile news to be published. *The Boston Weekly Newsletter* continued its refusal to promote Whitefield or report his preaching success. In the fall of 1754, when *The Boston Gazette* printed weekly articles tracing Whitefield's steps in New England, *The Boston Weekly Newsletter* was silent. Their only mention of Whitefield's anticipated visit was a paid editorial column on the advertisements page in the September 26, 1754 edition. After speaking of some anticipated opposition to Whitefield's soon visit, the author concluded: "It is hoped, therefore, that a kind Providence will nevertheless send him to us, and may he come in the fullness of the gospel of peace."[9]

By the end of September 1754, Whitefield had definitive plans to visit New England. On September 27 he wrote from Newark, New Jersey, stating that "Affection, intense affection cried aloud, Away to New England, to dear New England directly." He was looking forward to "a large range in New England," meaning an extended preaching tour ranging throughout various areas. The new president of the College of New Jersey at Princeton, Rev. Aaron Burr, would initially accompany Whitefield on his travels.[10] On September 30, Whitefield wrote from Elizabethtown, New Jersey, "Tomorrow, God willing, I shall set out with the worthy President for New England."[11] The "worthy President" was Aaron Burr of Princeton. Whitefield and his traveling party arrived in Newport, Rhode Island in early October 1754.

The wife of Aaron Burr was Esther Edwards Burr, the third child of Rev. Jonathan Edwards and his wife Sarah. Beginning in October 1754, Esther Burr began keeping a journal. In this journal she has several references to George Whitefield. She wrote favorably of Whitefield preaching in Princeton in late September or early October, lamenting that she could not attend, probably due to her being a new mother. On November 14, 1754, Esther Burr defended Whitefield against a detractor, calling the criticisms of Whitefield "abominable" and "ridiculous."[12] On December 12, she wrote that she heard Whitefield was in New Haven, Connecticut, and she remarked, "I hope he will come to Newark once more. O that my heart might be prepared to receive good by him!" In June 1755, Esther Edwards had a social engagement with several people, one of whom was a well-mannered and delightful married woman who was formerly one of Whitefield's orphans from Georgia. In August 1755, she asked a friend in Boston to "send my love to Mr. Whitefield. I wish you would every time you wrote or as often as you think proper."[13] Esther Edwards Burr first met Whitefield when she was an eight-year-old girl in her parent's home and church in Northampton, Massachusetts in 1740. Like her parents, she appreciated and supported Whitefield and his itinerant traveling ministry.

During the mid-1700s Newport, Rhode Island rivaled Boston, New York, and Philadelphia as a major trade and cultural center. It also developed as a resort location, attracting vacationers from the Carolinas and

---

9 *Boston Weekly Newsletter*, September 26, 1754, p. 2.
10 George Whitefield, *Works of George Whitefield,* (1771: reprinted by Quinta Press, Shropshire, England, 2000), vol. III, pp. 103-104.
11 Ibid., vol. III, p. 104.
12 Carol Karlsen and Laurie Crumpacker, editors, *The Journal of Esther Edwards Burr, 1754-1757,* (New Haven CT: Yale University Press, 1984), p. 64.
13 Ibid., p. 144.

Caribbean seeking to escape the heat and humidity of summers there.[14] Since Whitefield was previously in Newport in 1747, the city had continued to grow. In 1749 a new lighthouse was built, facilitating maritime and commercial adventures. In 1750 a volunteer fire company was formed, and construction on the Redwood Library was completed. In 1752, the Marine Society was created as a type of academic and commercial think-tank to discuss and promote advances in maritime science and commerce. In 1754 there was talk about beginning to construct a synagogue in Newport, a project that came to fruition in 1763. In 1748 the population of Newport was 32,773, but by 1755 the population had expanded to 40,414. The colonial capital of Rhode Island still rotated between Newport and four other towns, until 1762, when Providence was designated the capital. The city prospered, as wealthy merchants, ship owners, industries related to the whaling industry, and others settled in Newport and built large homes, many which are still standing today. One source stated,

> The foundation for Newport's prosperity is through the establishment of the Atlantic triangle trade. The merchants of Newport became wealthy, importing molasses from the West Indies and distilling it into rum, which they exchanged in Africa for Negros, who in turn were exchanged in Barbados for more molasses—and so the vicious triangle ran. Great profits came to Newport's merchants and ship captains . . . .[15]

About the time of Whitefield's visit in early October 1754, foreign trade in Newport was equal to any city in Colonial America. Likely Whitefield refreshed himself at the White Horse Tavern, Newport's famous inn, which got its current name in 1730. There were small Quaker meeting houses in Newport, but the largest churches in Newport were the Trinity Episcopal Church; the First Congregational Church; and the Second Congregational Church. When Whitefield came to town in 1754, he was only welcomed to the First Congregational Church. Rev. William Vinall served at the First Congregational Church in Newport from 1745 to 1768.

Previously, when Whitefield came to Newport in 1747, Vinall happily greeted him. Active in Newport, civil records show that Vinall performed dozens of weddings. He was also known to have students live with him, ministerial students or otherwise, as he prepared them for college and freely shared his library. In 1754, Vinall hosted Whitefield for at least five preaching events over three days. Departing Newport about October 6, Whitefield and his traveling companion, Rev. Aaron Burr, President of Princeton College, travelled towards Boston. After ministry in Boston for about a week, Whitefield wrote two letters reflecting back on his recent visit to

A photograph of the White Horse Tavern, Newport, RI. Parts of the original building date to 1652. George Whitefield refreshed himself many times at this tavern. Photograph by Ken Lawson.

---

14 "Newport—History," http://www.city-data.com/us-cities/The-Northeast/Newport-History.html. Kenneth Walsh, *The Economic History of Newport: From the Colonial Era to Beyond the War of 1812*, (Bloomington, IN: AuthorHouse Publishers, 2014).
15 Richard V. Simpson, *Historic Tales of Colonial Rhode Island* . . . , (Charleston, SC: The History Press, 2012), p. 14.

Rhode Island. On October 14, 1754, Whitefield wrote to a Mr. V_____ from Boston, looking back upon his recent visit to Rhode Island, saying, "Surely my coming here was of God. At Rhode Island I preached five times. People convened immediately, and flocked to hear more eagerly than ever . . . ."[16] Another letter Whitefield wrote on October 14, to a Dr. S_____, stated, "At Rhode-Island and this place, souls fly to the gospel like doves to the windows. A divine power hath hitherto accompanied the word, and opposition seems to fall daily . . . ."[17]

Reports from Whitefield's ministry in Rhode Island travelled fast in New England. For example, the Baptist minister in Middleborough, Massachusetts, Rev. Isaac Backus heard a report from someone in town who recently saw and heard Whitefield in Newport. Backus recorded, "October 8 [1754] . . . Zachariah Paddleford told me this evening that he was in Newport last week and Mr. Whitefield came from Philadelphia and he heard him preach powerfully just after he came in on Friday evening from those Words To know the love of Christ which passeth Knowledge."[18]

The educator Mrs. Sarah Osborn was present in Newport in 1754 when Whitefield preached in her First Congregational Church. A deeply spiritual woman, Osborn rejoiced when Whitefield came to town. She was a leader in a growing evangelical community in Newport, a group that met regularly for prayer and Bible study. While her husband Henry Osborn was an under-employed tailor with health issues, Sarah Osborn displayed a radiant Christian testimony which drew people to her for spiritual advice.[19] Having taught school in Newport since 1744, the city was full of her admiring graduates who as adults respected her influence on their lives. Now the children of her prior students were becoming her students. This influential woman, converted after Whitefield visited Newport in 1740, was a staunch ally of revival and happily supported Whitefield when he came to Newport in 1754.

Whitefield arrived back in Boston on October 9, 1754 and stayed in the city for one week, "preaching with great success."[20] During this week in Boston, Whitefield wrote three letters that have survived. The first, dated October 13, stated that he was unable to write sooner due to traveling, sickness, and preaching, and that "They [his illnesses] leave me at Boston, where as well as in other places, the word hath run and been glorified, and people rather more eager to hear than ever."[21] The next letter Whitefield wrote was dated October 14, from Boston. In this one paragraph note he wrote, "People convened immediately, and flocked to hear more eagerly than ever." He elaborated:

> Thousands waited for, and thousands attended on the word preached. At the Old North, at seven in the morning, we generally have three thousand hearers, and many cannot come in. Convictions I hear to fasten, and many souls are comforted. Doctor S_____ hath engaged me once to preach his lecture. The polite, I hear, are taken, and opposition falls. What art thou, O mountain? Before our great Zerubbabel thou shalt become a plain. I preach at the Old and New North. Mr. P_____ and Dr. S_____ continue to pray for me.[22]

This paragraph warrants further attention. Whitefield notes that his preaching was heard not by hundreds but by thousands. Interest in his ministry was so high that huge crowds gathered early in the morning before the workday began. The above mentioned "Dr. S_____" refers to the evangelically-minded

---

16 George Whitefield, *Works, vol. III*, p. 106.
17 Ibid., p. 107.
18 William G. McLoughlin, editor, *The Diary of Isaac Backus*, (Providence, RI: Brown University Press, 1979), vol. I, p. 350.
19 Samuel Hopkins, *Memoirs of the Life of Mrs. Sarah Obsorn, who Died at Newport, Rhode Island on the Second day of August, 1796 . . .* , (Worcester, MA: Leonard Worcester Printer, 1799), pp. 70-71.
20 John Gilles, *Memoirs of George Whitefield*, p. 162.
21 George Whitefield, *Works, vol. III*, p. 105.
22 Ibid., vol. III, p. 106.

Rev. Joseph Sewell of the South Church, a longtime ally of Whitefield. The references to "mountain" and to "Zerubbabel" is an allusion to a biblical text in Zechariah 4:7, which prophetically describes the power of the word of God that will overwhelm the land of Israel. The "Old North" named twice above is the Old North Church, served in 1754 by Rev. Rev. Samuel Checkley, Jr. Also named is the New North Church. The previous minister there was Rev. Jonathan Webb, who died in 1750. His colleague since 1742, Rev. Andrew Elliot tolerated the New Light disposition of the New North Church. Elliot was a Harvard graduate in 1737, earning a second degree at Harvard in 1740. Elliot was deeply moved by Whitefield's preaching in Boston in 1740 and became an admirer. Elliot served the New North Church until his death in 1778.

A minister near Boston that dreaded Whitefield's arrival was Rev. John Browne of Cohasset. Located about fifteen miles southeast of Boston along Massachusetts Bay, this maritime community did not support the Great Awakening. Now called the First Parish Church of Cohasset, Browne's church was founded in 1721. A Harvard graduate in 1741, Browne came to the Cohasset congregation in 1746 and was ordained there in 1747. He was no Calvinist and did not endorse revivals. In June 1745, George Whitefield travelled near or through Cohasset to preach in Hull. Now in 1754, the itinerant Whitefield was back in the Boston area, and Browne was not pleased. John Browne of Cohasset was called "a minister of cheerful disposition and an outspoken defender of intellectual freedom."[23] Another source succinctly stated, "Rev. John Browne, of Cohasset . . . was a Unitarian."[24] Browne and the First Parish Church of Cohasset constructed a meeting house in 1747, which still stands today. Whitefield was not welcomed in this building.

Whitefield wrote another letter from Boston, dated October 14, 1754. He stated, "Souls fly to the gospel like doves to the windows. A divine power hath hitherto accompanied the word, and opposition seems to fall daily. Next week I purpose to go Eastward, and then I intend making as much haste as can be back to you."[25] The two important things from this note are that Whitefield received no visible opposition

A contemporary photograph of the First Parish Church (Unitarian), Cohasset, Massachusetts, built in 1747.

Source: www.panoramio.com

---

23 "First Church, Cohasset, Massachusetts, "http://www.firstparishcohasset.org/about/history." Jacob Flint, *Two Discourses Containing the History of the Church and Society in Cohasset . . .*, (Boston, MA: Munroe and Francis Publishers, 1822), pp. 15-18.
24 "Dr. Mayhew, the First Unitarian Preacher in America," *The Monthly Repository of Theology and General Literature*, (Paternoster-Row, Great Britain, 1821), vol. xvi, p. 333.
25 George Whitefield, *Works, vol. III, p. 107.*

to his preaching in Boston, as his enemies simply ignored him and stayed away. Second, he stated his intention to travel "Eastward," meaning he intended to begin a preaching circuit to the communities he often visited north and east of Boston. But before he departed Boston, he had an ongoing feud with Rev. Edward Holyoke, president of Harvard College in nearby Cambridge.

Holyoke was from a prominent Boston family. He graduated from Harvard in 1705, and earned his second degree there in 1708. He was a minister in Marblehead, Massachusetts until called to be the ninth president of Harvard College in 1736. He served the college until his death in 1769. Fourteen years earlier, when Whitefield first arrived in Boston in 1740, he antagonized Holyoke and the Harvard faculty with bombastic remarks against the spirituality of the college and the piety of the professors. A pamphlet war developed between Whitefield and Holyoke, with charges and accusations exchanged. In 1745, the last of the major pamphlets was written, a sixty-two-page diatribe against Whitefield by Professor Edward Wigglesworth of Harvard, with comments from President Holyoke.[26] When Whitefield arrived in the Boston area in the fall of 1754, he was not allowed to preach at Harvard, and Holyoke kept the students away from Whitefield's meetings.

Whitefield was a sensation in Boston. As in his previous visits in 1740, 1744-1745, and 1747, now in the fall of 1754 he was popular with the masses. Some of his previous ministerial allies in the city had died, and other old antagonists persisted. Dallimore briefly summarizes this Boston and New England visit as follows:

A painting of Rev. Edward Holyoke, ninth president of Harvard College, c. 1760s.

Source: www.harvard.edu/history/presidents/holyoke

> Upon leaving the New Jersey area, Whitefield moved toward New England. He especially delighted in being able to preach in territory he had never seen before. This was true of Rhode Island and he reported that people flocked to hear.
>
> Of course, Boston was a particular joy to him. Hundreds of people lined the streets awaiting his arrival and on several successive days they packed the Old North Church—even at seven o'clock in the morning. On one occasion the crowd was so dense he could not get in through the door and had to be put in through a window.
>
> During October, finding his health somewhat improved, Whitefield resumed his practice of traveling by horseback, and preached two or three times a day. In this re-invigoration his zeal knew few bounds. He journeyed, preaching as he went, northward almost to the borders of Canada—at least to the Northern settlements of the American colonies. Then he turned southward, starting the journey that was to take him back to Georgia, traveling all the way by land.[27]

Various newspaper accounts record items of interest from Whitefield's 1754 visit to Boston. Although *The Boston Weekly Newsletter* refused to publish news related to Whitefield's coming visit, they were compelled to briefly mention his activities while he ministered in Boston.

---

26 Edward Wigglesworth, *A Letter to the Reverend Mr. George Whitefield, by way of Reply to his Answer to the College Testimony against him* . . . , (Boston, MA: T. Fleet Printer, 1745).

27 Arnold Dallimore, *George Whitefield, vol. II*, p. 371.

Boston Weekly Newsletter, October 10, 1754, p. 2.

"Yesterday the Rev'd Mr. Whitefield came to town; and in the afternoon preached at the Old North Church to numerous auditory."

Boston Weekly Newsletter, October 17, 1754, p. 2.

"The Rev'd Mr. Whitefield intends to set out this afternoon for the Eastward, having preached every day since he arrived, excepting the last Sabbath, some days twice, and yesterday three times."

The Boston Gazette again placed itself in support of Whitefield, printing numerous brief articles in support of his preaching, and publishing articles in defense of his ministry. The following is a portion of an extended article which defended Whitefield before his critics:

The Boston Gazette, October 22, 1754, p. 3.

To the Gentleman who favored us with his Friend's Letter in Yesterday's Evening Post.—And was that all your Friend had to object against Mr. Whitefield?

You'll say it was enough . . . But was it worth your while to be at the expense of printing it? Has it not been printed enough already? No- Mr. Whitefield has not recanted—But honestly, Sir, Was it for the sake of offering Conviction to that Gentleman, and bringing him and his followers to a better Temper of mind, that you printed this notable epistle? Or did you not rather do it to raise feuds and animosities among the People? If so, the Attempt will, I hope, be in vain. Have you not heard that we are determin'd not to contend with one another? You should have wrote your friend in the country, that the people in Boston are disposed to be at Peace among themselves, and to treat each other as friends, however different their sentiments may be of Men and Things.

He need not have offer'd his little spark of contention, for in all Likelihood it will have no Purpose. Love, Gentleness, Condescension, there is reason to hope will prevail against the Designs of those who delight in Discord, and are never so much at peace with themselves, as when all is noise and confusion around them. Let me just hint to you, that if your Friend will be easy in the Country there will be no Danger of ill consequence of Whitefield's preaching in Boston.

After a week of ministry in Boston, Whitefield set off for a local preaching tour. He departed Boston for areas to the northeast on October 17, 1754. There are numerous reports and personal recollections about Whitefield from these local communities. Some accounts are generalizations, as the following indicates:

His letters to friends in England during his fourth visit to America state that he held two services in Newbury Monday, October 21, 1754, and a third service Tuesday morning, October 22, and also state that he has made arrangements to preach there the following Sunday, October 27.[28]

Details of Whitefield's visit to Newbury (later Newburyport) are abundant. For example, an anecdote from perhaps the 1754 visit stated:

---

28 John J. Currier, *Old Newbury: Historical and Biographical Sketches,* (Boston, MA: Damrell & Upman Printers, 1896), p. 527.

During one of Whitefield's visits to Newburyport, he attended a meeting in West Parish, accompanied by a daughter of Deacon Noyes, and dined with "Aunt Jenny Hazen" who lived on East Street, nearly opposite John Hazen's . . . Her fame as a theologian was widespread. Mr. Whitefield had heard of her, and at this time he came to hear from her. After a pleasant interview with her and the neighbors, he departed, leaving in the memories of those present this incident of dining with Whitefield as the most noted event of their lives.[29]

Whitefield's arrival in Newbury in 1754 marked the fourth time he ministered to this community. He preached in Newbury over a dozen times in his first three visits. The congregation that most welcomed him to Newbury in 1754 was the Old South Presbyterian Church, to which Whitefield had a long and personal relationship. He first preached in Newbury in September 1740. Through these meetings the community experienced a broad and serious awakening. Though unwelcome elsewhere in town, he found one pulpit open to him—that of Third Parish Church on Market Square. But now, in 1754, the whole city came to hear Whitefield. In Newbury, Rev. James Lowell of Third Parish Church was an initial supporter of Whitefield and the awakening. Yet, as public opinion changed in New England, Lowell put distance between himself and the New Lights of his parish. After a protracted struggle in which he refused to call a meeting to hear the complaints of the disenfranchised New Lights, a group of the latter withdrew.[30] Meanwhile, another group, this one from First Parish Church, had been frustrated by their pastors, the Revs. Christopher Tappan and his assistant John Tucker, who each refused to endorse the awakening. The New Light families from Third Parish Church and First Parish Church merged in 1743, as the following account details: "Thirty men with their families withdrew from First Church . . . And thirty-eight from the Third Church; and after a while they built a plain but ample chapel that was finished February 15, 1743, and served as our sanctuary for 13 years."[31] This group became the Old South Presbyterian Church which eagerly welcomed Whitefield to Newbury in 1754.

Whitefield's attachment to this church in Newbury was strong and affectionate. He recalled a prior visit to them in 1745. At one of his meetings, in front of the meeting house (presumably the crowd was too large to get into the building), someone hurled a stone over the heads of the listeners aimed at Whitefield. It nearly struck the Bible from his hand as he stood preaching at the side of the street. Characteristically turning the attack to good use, he responded, "I have a warrant from God to preach." Holding up the Bible, he continued, "His Seal is in my hand, and I stand in the King's highway."[32] The combined New Lights of Third Parish and First Parish thrived under the leadership of the Rev. Jonathan Parsons, whom Whitefield recommended to be their pastor. By the time of his 1754 visit to this newly formed church, they were in the midst of a building program, completed in 1756, in which their chapel increased its seating capacity to hold up to two thousand people. This structure is still used as a church building today.

> Here in this congregation Whitefield found a home when he was in New England. He preached repeatedly in the church. He did so [in 1754] in the partially completed 1756 church building. According to Dr. Vermilye, one old lady who lived to be 95 is reported to have said, "Didn't we have good times when we used to sit on the benches, no pews yet, and Mr. Whitefield preached." The large, austere interior that could originally hold 2,000 worshipers was thought to have been built that way because of the preaching here of Whitefield . . . overflow crowds made it necessary.[33]

---

29 Duane H. Hurd, *History of Essex County, Massachusetts*, (Philadelphia, PA: J.W. Lewis & Company, 1888), vol. I, p. 826.
30 Graydon McClellan, *Rev. George Whitefield*, (Newburyport, MA: Printed by the Old South Presbyterian Church, 1976), pp. 10-11.
31 Ibid.
32 Ibid., p. 9.
33 Ibid.

Another minister north of Boston with recollections of Whitefield was Rev. Moses Parsons of Byfield. He was born a few miles to the northeast of Byfield, in Gloucester in 1716, graduated from Harvard in 1736, and served the Byfield Parish from 1744 until his death in 1783. From before his ordination in June 1744, Parsons was an established New Light. Of the five ministers who participated in his ordination, each one signed the 1743 ministerial statement in support of the awakening and publicly endorsed the ministry of Whitefield.[34]

Moses Parsons led his New Light congregation in an unpretentious manner. In March 1745, less than a year after his ordination, a member of his parish complained, "I don't remember, sir, that you ever so much as gave thanks for such an unspeakable favor to the world as Mr. Whitefield."[35] The scenario continued,

> Mr. Parsons said in reply to Mr. Plumer's complaint, that he had justified Mr. Whitefield wherein he was unjustly blamed, as well as mentioned public charges against him of "imprudency or irregularity." He added, "I look on Mr. Whitefield as a good man and a faithful minister and as one has improved as an instrument to do much good." . . .
>
> Mr. Parsons appears to have become a warm admirer of Mr. Whitefield. His diary shows that he welcomed the great evangelist to his house and pulpit, took great pains to hear him elsewhere, was his fellow guest at the table, and was a bearer at his funeral.[36]

Pastor Moses Parsons of Byfield wrote in his journal on October 28, 1754:

> Monday Mr. Whitefield came, and preached from Luke 19:14 (But his citizens hated him, and sent a message after him, saying, we will not have this man to reign over us), dined here. Preached at Rowley p.m. Psalms 51:11 (Cast me not away from thy presence and take not thy Holy Spirit from me), then went to Ipswich and preached at 4 o'clock, but I did not hear him there.[37]

The previous divisions and controversies surrounding Whitefield's visits to the north shore of Boston were largely absent in this his fourth tour in the area. The town of Boxford is a good example of a community that had healed from the wounds of the awakening by the time of Whitefield's 1754 visit. Speaking of Whitefield,

> He preached considerably in our neighborhood, mostly in the open air, and wherever the people could be got together to be addressed. Mr. Whitefield urged a more earnest devotion to the work of God and the leading of a higher life—closer communion with the Father. In consequence of his teaching, many lay-preachers sprang up, who boldly proclaimed the truth, and their right, under the immediate command and influence of the Holy Spirit, to preach. These "New Lights" as they were called, rose up in many of these towns in this vicinity and throughout New England generally. In Boxford, the Second Church was disaffected by the "new doctrine" and some of their members, one of whom was John Woster, one of the deacons of the church, being persuaded of the correctness of the doctrines, embracing them, and lay-preaching was carried out in some of the houses, Deacon Woster's being one of them. The church records mention two of these itinerant preachers—Joseph Adams and Francis Woster—one, if not both, being residents of Boxford. This was in the summer of 1744. The church expounded upon the matter, and, believing the doctrines taught to be contrary and dangerous to the platform of the church

---

34 *The Boston Gazette,* July 10, 1744, p. 3, lists the five ministerial sponsors at the ordination of Moses Parsons as Revs. John Warren of Wenham, Samuel Wigglesworth of Ipswich, John White and Richard Jacques of Cape Ann, and Jedediah Jewett of Rowley. All these men were supporters of Whitefield and the Great Awakening.
35 John L. Ewell, *The Story of Byfield, a New England Parish,* (Boston, MA: George W. Littleton Publisher, 1904), p. 106.
36 Ibid., p. 107.
37 John J. Currier, *History of Beverly, Civil and Ecclesiastical,* (Boston, MA: J. Monroe and Company, 1843), p. 527.

which was then common throughout New England, they came to the conclusion that these members had committed a sin worthy of excommunication; and because they would not recant, their opinions in regard to itinerant preaching, they were suspended from communion. One of them said his wife was sick on her bed, therefore not being able to attend services in the meeting house, and he thought it no more right that he should have preaching in his house, where his wife could hear. The church was kept in an uproarious state for about four years, when its members were restored to the fellowship of the church.[38]

Mary Cleveland, wife of Rev. John Cleveland of the Chebacco (Ipswich) Parish, had fond recollections of Whitefield's visit in her home in 1754. Her journal has random entries, several years apart. Her recorded comments reveal the most important events of her life.[39]

September 5, 1742

Mr. Wigglesworth preached the funeral sermon on the death of my father from Romans the 14th chapter and 8th verse, and whether we die, we die unto the Lord.

January 6, 1750

I had a son born whose name is John. The Lord make him a beloved disciple continually to lean on the bosom of the Lord.

October 17, 1751.

The Lord . . . made me the living mother of another son . . . his name is Parker. Trust the Lord will enable me to give (the child) to Him (God) in baptism. 0 that I myself and all that I call mine, may be for God and for nothing (else) and may I never forget the goodness of God to me and mine.

October 28, 1754

The Rev. Mr. Whitefield came to our house and preached the next morning in Mr. Cleveland's meeting house and went to (the common) and preached two times and came and lodged with us that night. I think it is a great honor to have his company.

The diary of the Rev. Samuel Chandler of Gloucester is insightful towards the everyday events in a New England pastor's life in 1754, as well as in tracing the preaching route of Whitefield in northern New England.[40]

Jan 22—Exceedingly cold and windy. I went to Mr. White's and Deacon Stacy's; many perished with the cold.

Feb. 7—Went to Andover; found my mother sick, but the fever abated.

Feb. 13—My mother died at 9 3/4 o'clock.

---

38 Sidney Perley, *The History of Boxford, Essex County, Massachusetts*, (Published by the Author, 1880), pp. 178-179.
39 "Journal of Mary Cleveland," *John Cleveland Papers*, (Salem, MA: Essex Institute Historical Folders).
40 John J. Babson, "Diary of Rev. Samuel Chandler," *Notes and Additions to the History of Gloucester, (Salem, MA: 1891), pp. 33-35.*

Feb. 24—I preached all day; in the evening married Joseph Smith and Sarah Brown; visited Samuel Ingersall, sick of the palsy and senseless.

Apr. 9—I set out with Deacon Warner for York; lodged at my brother's at Newbury.

Apr. 12—Dined at Mr. Rogers', Kittery; Went through Scotland; lodged at Mr. Lyman's; saw many of the people of my former charge, also expressed much gladness to see me.

Apr. 18—Got to Ipswich to lecture; Mr. Foxcroft preached; got home at 8 o'clock.

May 2—I preached at Eastern Point, at John Gardner's; dined at Captain Sargent's with Mr. White; rode over in Captain Sargent's chaise; my horse.

May 26—I preached all day . . .

June 11—Was called in the morning to John Sargent's; prayed with him; he died soon after.

Aug. 24—General Training; the field officers came down with the troops; the five companies formed into one battalion.

Oct. 29—Mr. Whitefield came here, preached twice, Rev. 1:5-6, and went out of town.

Nov. 1—I attended the funeral of Mr. John Goodridge.

Nov. 21—It being training day, I preached Deut. 14:21; a sort of artillery sermon.

Dec. 13—I made about thirty pounds of candles; the wicks made before; finished by noon.

Dec. 20—Very cold; held the wedding at Mr. Woodward's.

Dec. 25—Preached at Mr. Gardner's.

In 1754, George Whitefield wrote numerous letters of personal correspondence that display his appreciation and respect for the New England people. Although only five known letters have survived from his 1754 visit to northern New England, they are rich in illustrations of the success of the gospel. Three of these letters are from Boston, in which he noted the large crowds and the eagerness of the people to listen. He noted that thousands attended his preaching, with no visible opposition, and that he sensed a special power when speaking.[41] Having thoroughly preached a familiar circuit in communities northeast of Boston, he ventured into New Hampshire.

---

41 George Whitefield, *Works, vol. III*, pp. 105-107.

CHAPTER 28

WHITEFIELD'S TOUR IN NEW HAMPSHIRE AND MAINE

OCTOBER 1754

IN 1754, THE NEW HAMPSHIRE Colony was concerned over rising civil tensions with the Province of New York over the New Hampshire Grants. Beginning in 1749, the Provincial Governor of New Hampshire, Benning Wentworth, issued enormous land grants on land west of the Connecticut River, in modern Vermont. These lands were also claimed by the Province of New York. Complicating matters was the fact that French troops with their Indian allies were roaming through these land grants, committing atrocities against New Hampshire settlers. In coastal New Hampshire in the 1750s, there was virtually no Indian presence, as disease and White migration forced the native Indians north and west towards Canada. Portsmouth was thriving from its prosperous maritime industries, as ships from throughout the Atlantic and Caribbean traded and refurbished in its harbor. Farmers in the countryside brought goods to sell in Portsmouth and traded or purchased supplies in the city.

Whitefield was very familiar with coastal New Hampshire and the nearby inland agrarian communities. He visited these areas in 1740, 1744-1745, and in 1747, and he had established friends and dedicated opponents. About October 22, 1754, Whitefield departed Massachusetts and arrived in Portsmouth, New Hampshire. On October 24 Whitefield wrote of his travels north of Boston,

> "What have I seen? Dagon falling everywhere before the Ark; enemies silenced, or made to own the finger of God; and the friends of Jesus triumphing in His glorious conquest . . . In the country a like scene opens; I am enabled to preach always twice, and sometimes thrice a day. Thousands flock to hear, and Jesus manifests forth His glory. I know you will rejoice, and join in crying Grace! Grace! I am now come to the end of my northward line, and in a day or two purpose to turn back, in order to preach all the way to Georgia."[1]

In Portsmouth, Whitefield's ally, Rev. Samuel Langdon of the North Church was still at the church, serving until his death in 1774. Rev. William Shurtleff of the South Church had passed away in 1747. The new minister at the South Church was Rev. Samuel Haven, who was ordained at the church in May 1752, serving there until his death in 1806.[2] Haven was a Harvard graduate in 1749. While a teenage student at Harvard

---

1   George Whitefield, *Works of George Whitefield* (1771, reprinted by Quinta Press, Shropshire, England, 2000), vol. III, pp. 107-108. The reference to Dagon falling before the ark of the Lord is a biblical reference to the triumph of the Israelites over the Philistines in I Samuel 5:1-5. The comment about the finger of God is a biblical allusion to Daniel chapter five, where the judgment of the Lord is declared upon unbelieving royalty in Babylon.
2   Caleb S. Gurney, *Portsmouth, Historic and Picturesque . . .* , (Portsmouth, NH: Published by the Author, 1902), p. 142.

he heard Whitefield preach in 1745 and was converted.³ He taught school for a few years and in evenings and on school vacations studied for the ministry. Later in life, Haven would be known as a distinguished American clergyman, identified as a patriot, scientist, and philanthropist with a national reputation. But for now, when Whitefield arrived in Portsmouth in 1754, Haven was a new twenty-seven-year old minister in an established church that had been committed to Whitefield and revivals since 1740. Much later in life, Samuel Haven would become a Unitarian.⁴ In 1754, however, Haven embraced the Calvinistic theology and evangelistic preaching of Whitefield.

Whitefield was in New Hampshire only a few days, then he went to Maine. In a letter dated October 25, 1754 he wrote, "Still the Lord of all lords stoops to accompany my feeble labors with his divine presence . . . Yesterday I preached at York and Kittery: at both places the Redeemer manifested forth his glory."⁵ York and Kittery were across the Piscataqua River from Portsmouth, in the area now called Maine. Like New Hampshire, Maine was under constant strain from French and Indian hostilities upon the inland settlements. In addition, coastal Maine was always suspicious of French maritime deprecations upon the fisheries and commerce.

In York, Whitefield's friend Rev. Samuel Moody died in 1747, replaced by Rev. Isaac Lyman. When Whitefield arrived in York, the deceased Moody lay buried a few hundred feet from the meeting house. A Yale College graduate in 1747, Isaac Lyman began preaching at the First Church in York in 1747 and was ordained there in 1749. He arrived as the church was constructing a new meeting house.⁶ Unlike his flamboyant and extroverted predecessor Rev. Samuel Moody, Isaac Lyman was known to be reserved, thoughtful, and sedate. He was not a natural, outspoken leader, but rather a balanced, discerning, and plain Christian minister. His preaching was doctrinal, organized, and logical, easy to understand, and unemotional. He was a man of prayer who longed for and experienced revivals during his long tenure at the First

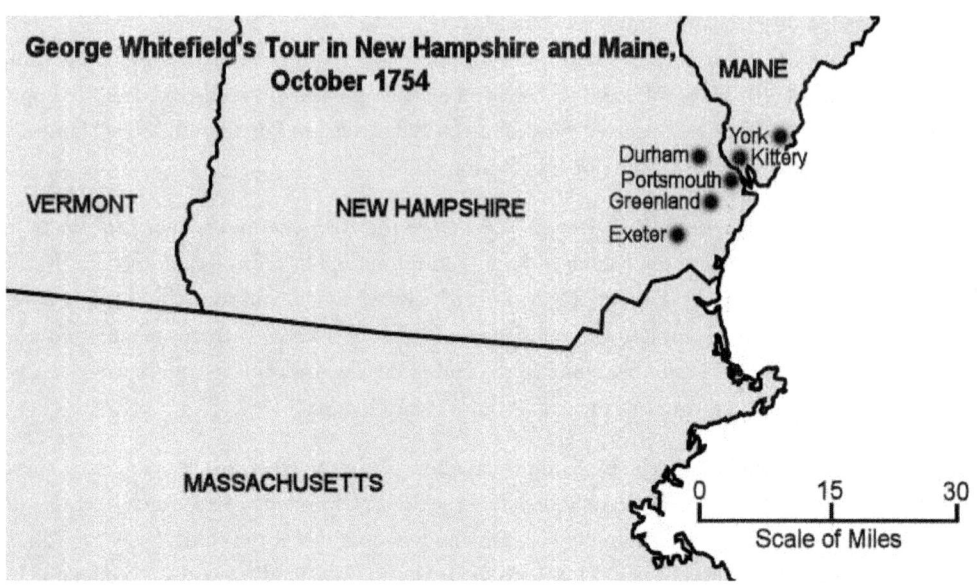

---

3   "Rev. Samuel Haven Fathered Seventeen," http://www.seacoastnh.com/famous-people/link-free-or-die/rev-samuel-haven-fathered-17/. For an overview, see Lawrence W. Craig, *A History of the South Church and Parish (Unitarian) and Universalist Church . . . in Portsmouth, New Hampshire*, (Portsmouth, NH: 1966).
4   Kathleen L.H. McInerney, *The True Story of the Haven Sisters*, (Printed by the Author, 2009), p. 5.
5   George Whitefield, *Works, vol. III, p. 108.*
6   W. Woodford Clayton, *History of York County, Maine: with Illustrations and Biographical Sketches . . .*, (Philadelphia, PA: Everts & Peck Printers, 1880), p. 228.

Church in York. He died in York in 1810.[7] Lyman may have heard Whitefield preach when the itinerant came through New England in 1745, when Lyman was a student at Yale College in Connecticut. Whitefield preached for Lyman on Wednesday, October 23, 1754 in York.

Also, on October 23 in nearby Kittery, Whitefield preached for Rev. Benjamin Stevens of the First Congregational Church. The road from York to Kittery is a windy, coastal road with numerous bridges over the tidal rivers and saltwater marshes. Whitefield had been around Kittery several times over the years. The previous minister at the First Church in Kittery, Rev. John Newmarch, was unable to continue his ministry after 1751, due to old age. Under Newmarch there was no revival in Kittery.[8]

Rev. Benjamin Stevens, a Harvard graduate in 1740, must have heard Whitefield in Boston in 1740. After graduation, Stevens remained at Harvard as a tutor, earning another degree in 1743. The son of a minister, Stevens preached in and around Boston until 1750, when he was called to assist the ill Rev. Newmarch in Kittery. Over the years, Newmarch did not welcome Whitefield but Stevens did allow the evangelist to preach in 1754 at the First Church in Kittery. Cool ocean breezes kept the meeting house comfortable in the summer, but cold winter winds off the bay made it very cold in the building. Speaking of Benjamin Stevens, "He was ordained and assumed the pastorate in 1751. He served in a more peaceful time in the parish—no disputes about other churches, no need to build new buildings, and the congregation was large, wealthy, and influential."[9] Stevens entertained Whitefield in the parsonage, a few hundred feet from the meeting house. Under Stevens' long tenure at the church the ministry did not thrive. Population shifts, the decline of the port due to the Revolutionary War, and new rival churches in the area all contributed to the stagnation of the First Church Congregational in Kittery.[10]

Built in 1730, the First Congregational Church of Kittery Point, Maine it is the oldest church building in continuous use in the state of Maine. The building maintains several original features, including the original 1730 pulpit, and the original two-aisle design common in early New England meetinghouses. George Whitefield preached here on October 23, 1754. Photograph by Ken Lawson.

---

7   *Collections and Proceedings of the Maine Historical Society,* (Portland, ME: Published by the Society, 1894), second series, vol. V, pp. 433-434.
8   Rodney L. Peterson, *The Contentious Triangle: Church, State, and University,* (Kirksville, MO: Truman State University Press, 1999), p. 297.
9   "First Congregational Church—Our History," http://www.kitterypointucc.org/church-history.html.
10 Everett S. Stackpole, *Old Kittery and her Families,* (Lewiston, ME: Press of Lewiston Journal Company, 1903), pp. 191-192.

In the quoted letter from Whitefield dated October 25, 1754 from Portsmouth, New Hampshire he noted that, "I am now going to Greenland, and Durham, and to-morrow shall preach at Exeter."[11] These three towns and their ministers will be looked at in order.

The Congregational Church in Greenland, New Hampshire was served by Rev. William Allen. In 1745, Whitefield preached in Greenland for Allen. Writing in his *Journals,* Whitefield noted that he preached on a Tuesday in March 1745, "to a very large Auditory for the Rev'd. Mr. Allen" at an unspecific location in southeastern New Hampshire near Portsmouth. Greenland was originally part of Portsmouth, becoming a separate parish in 1706. This farming and maritime community experienced slow growth in the eighteenth century. William Allen was their first minister. Born in Boston in 1676 and graduated from Harvard College in 1703, Allen began ministry in Greenland in 1707. He served this community until his death in 1760. The church was formed so that settlers would not have to travel too far to Portsmouth for church services.[12] Allen welcomed Whitefield in 1745 and again in 1754. Allen was a New Light evangelical but was not as confrontive as some of his revivalist brethren. Under his leadership "The Greenland Church was obviously healthy and growing rapidly."[13] Allen was called "a faithful pastor" who "worked tirelessly to lay the groundwork for a lasting church. During his lifetime here he baptized 1,092 and welcomed 293 new members into the congregation."[14] Whitefield preached for Allen in Greenland on October 26, 1754.

As a result of Whitefield's preaching in Greenland, the growing congregation committed to a building fund and petitioned the town to construct a new meeting house. While plans for the new church building were under way during Whitefield's visit in 1754, the building was completed in 1756. Although the building was constructed by Whitefield supporters, there is no record of him ever preaching in this building in his later visits to New England. Not that the congregation or Rev. Allen would not have him, but his itinerant travels in later visits did not take him to Greenland.

Whitefield was always eagerly welcomed in Greenland. When he visited the town, he stayed at the tavern or inn a few hundred feet down the hill from the church building. For hundreds of years the visits of Whitefield in Greenland were locally remembered and restated. For example, in *The Herald* newspaper, December 10, 1946, a former pastor of the church reminisced about his enjoyable time in Greenland. One of his reminiscences was, "I am thinking of the tavern where Whitefield, the firebrand of God, rested his glorious

The beautiful 1756 Congregational meeting house in Greenland, New Hampshire. Photograph by Ken Lawson.

---

11 George Whitefield, *Works, vol. III*, p. 108.
12 *Collections Historical and Miscellaneous, New Hampshire Historical Society,* (Concord, NH: J.B. Moore Publisher, October 1823), vol. II, p. 289.
13 Paul Hughes, "Some Episodes in Greenland's Church History," *Annual Reports of the Town of Greenland, New Hampshire 2004,* (Greenland, NH: Published by the Town, 2004), p. 5.
14 Frances Dion, *Upon this Rock: A History of the Community Congregational Church, Greenland, New Hampshire,* (Portsmouth, NH: Strawberry Bank Print Shop, 1956), pp. 4-5.

head and where the devout have made an appropriate home in the atmosphere of a shrine, still hypnotized by a vision of heaven."[15]

In Durham, New Hampshire, Whitefield's friend Rev. Nicholas Gilman died in 1748. In 1754, the new minister at the First Congregational Church in rural Durham was Rev. John Adams. Born in Boston in 1718 the son of a merchant, Adams graduated from Harvard College in 1745, amidst the contentious Whitefield controversy at the school. John Adams was the nephew of a previous minister at the First Congregational Church in Durham, Rev. Hugh Adams, who served the church from 1718 to his retirement in 1739. John arrived in Durham in 1748 and remained until he took a church position in Maine in 1778. Of John Adams it was stated, "He had a lively imagination, was a writer of ability, and at times, it is said, was very eloquent."[16] When John Adams arrived in Durham there were forty members of the Congregational Church. His first years in Durham were contentious, as older members of the congregation and the town did not like the fact that

The former tavern in Greenland, New Hampshire is now a private home. The building is a few hundred feet downhill from the meetinghouse. Here Whitefield rested on his visit in 1754. Photograph by Ken Lawson.

he was related to the previous minister they disliked. But John won over the people in the church and the town, serving for thirty years in Durham in a successful but not remarkable ministry.[17] Whitefield's preaching for Adams in 1754 solidified the revivalist tendencies of Adams in the minds of his congregation, with support from most and animosity from others.

About twelve miles south from Durham is the town of Exeter. Whitefield preached here on October 26, 1754. Previously, in March 1745, Whitefield had a contentious debate with Rev. John Odlin of the First Church. Odlin defiantly and publicly opposed Whitefield, preaching against him, writing pamphlets critical of him, gathering other ministers to oppose him, and event confronting him face-to-face demanding that he not preach in Exeter. As Whitefield's supporters in the First Church separated from Odlin and formed a new church, Odlin was furious. In 1747, Whitefield again visited Exeter and preached for the separated group that was still without a completed meeting house or a settled minister. But now in 1754, the separated group in the Brentwood Parish of Exeter had a meeting house and a minister, Rev. Nathaniel Trask, who served the church from 1751 to 1787. In addition, Whitefield had a friend in Rev. Daniel Rogers of the Second Church in Exeter. We do not know of if Whitefield preached in Exeter for both Trask and Rogers. But we do know Whitefield preached for Rev. Daniel Rogers on October 26, 1754.

---

15 Paul C. Hughes, Anna Hughes, Paul F. Hughes, *A Pleasant Abiding Place: A History of Greenland, New Hampshire*, (Greenland Historical Society, 2018), pp. 2078-2079.
16 D. Hamilton Hurd, *History of Rockingham and Strafford Counties, New Hampshire, with Biographical Sketches*, (Philadelphia, PA: J.W. Lewis & Company, 1882), p. 618.
17 Jacob B. Moore, *Collections, Topographical, Historical, and Biographical..*, (Concord, NH: J.B. Moore Publisher, 1823), vol. II, pp. 364-365.

Rogers was the minister of the Second Church in Exeter from 1755 to his death in 1785. Born in Ipswich, Massachusetts into a prominent family, he graduated Harvard College in 1725. He arrived in Exeter as a mature man in mid-life, eager to serve as pastor to a group of New Light separatists. "The relations between him and his people were always pacific."[18] Rogers arrived in Exeter sometime in the early 1750s, and was officially installed as the minister of the Second Church in 1755. When Whitefield came to Exeter in October 1754, he was happily greeted by Daniel Rogers. "He was a warm friend and admirer of the Rev. George Whitefield to whom he attributed his own conversion, and had that eloquent divine twice to preach to his Exeter Charge, first on the twenty-sixth of October, 1754, and again on the twenty-ninth of September, 1770, when Whitefield delivered his last discourse the day before his death."[19]

Rev. John Odlin of the First Church in Exeter was seventy-three years old in 1754 when Whitefield arrived, still serving as pastor emeritus while his son Woodbridge Odlin ministered at the church. Perhaps Whitefield's presence in Exeter contributed to the failing health of Odlin. John Odlin died in Exeter in November 1754, eleven years after his son became his ministerial colleague.[20] Woodbridge Odlin retained his father's anti-Whitefield beliefs.

Another minister in southern New Hampshire who did not welcome George Whitefield was Rev. Henry True of the Hampstead Congregational Church. Whitefield had a long history with this congregation. He preached in Hampstead on October 3, 1740, with tremendous results. Whitefield wrote in his *Journals*, "After dinner, I hastened to Hampstead, and preached to several thousands of people with a great deal of life and power."[21] Whitefield was again in this area, in the fall of 1744 and again in early 1745, encouraging the Great Awakening. To organize the revival in Hampstead, a group of New Lights paid for and constructed a new meeting house. A series of preachers ministered to the congregation until 1752, when the church settled Rev. Henry True to be their new minister. True was a 1750 graduate of Harvard College, and stayed at the Hampstead church until his death in 1782. The origins of this congregation traced themselves back to Whitefield's preaching in Hampstead in 1740, and his return visits in 1744 and 1745. But when Whitefield came again to the area on a preaching tour in 1754, he was not welcomed by the minister

A contemporary photograph of the colonial meeting house in Hampstead, New Hampshire. The structure was built by followers of George Whitefield in 1745. However, when Whitefield preached in the area in 1754, he was not welcomed here.

Source: www.colonialmeetinghouses.com/mh_hampstead.shtml

---

18 Charles H. Bell, *History of the Town of Exeter, New Hampshire*, (Exeter, NH: The Quarter-Millennial Year, 1888), p. 196.
19 Ibid.
20 *The New England Historical and Genealogical Register*, (Boston, MA: Samuel G. Drake Publisher, 1847), vol. I., p. 154.
21 George Whitefield, *Journals of George Whitefield*, (1756: reprinted by Banner of Truth Trust, Carlisle, PA: 1985), p. 467.

Henry True. True did not support the revival and he disliked itinerant preachers, and the finances and memberships of the church suffered. In a veiled reference to George Whitefield, a history of Hampstead spoke of the church and Henry True, stating, "Other ministers came into the place, and by their zealous and loud speaking, produced great commotion, but no revival among the people . . . it reduced his salary and the number of his hearers . . . "[22] The 1745 meeting house, which traces its origins to Whitefield and the awakening, is still standing today in Hampstead.

By the mid-1750s, ministers in New England were firmly established in either Old Light anti-revivalism or New Light evangelicalism. Through their persistence and solidarity, Old Light ministers survived the upheavals of the awakening and continued to preach and publish against Whitefield. Or they simply ignored him. Those ministers who supported the awakening did so cautiously, for Old Light faculty from Harvard College and Yale College stood ready to speak out against religious improprieties in New England.

Many Old Light clergymen were unsuccessful in persuading the masses to ignore Whitefield's 1754 tour through New England. Those who attempted to regulate revivalism or restrict Whitefield had little success in distracting the affection of others who clamored to hear Whitefield preach. After Whitefield preached in Cambridge, Massachusetts in 1754, Professor Wigglesworth of Harvard College followed Whitefield's visit with two lectures on *The Ordinary and Extra-ordinary Ministers of the Church*, in which the same anti-revival and anti-itinerancy arguments published in 1744 against Whitefield were repeated. Further, the charge of "bad intentions" brought by the faculty of Yale College, were endorsed by Harvard.[23] However, the 1754 effects of such anti-Whitefield jargon by these two ministerial schools in New England, upon average New Englanders, was minimal. Having successfully itinerated throughout New Hampshire and southern Maine, Whitefield returned to Massachusetts.

---

22 Isaac W. Smith, *History of Hampstead, New Hampshire, for One Hundred Years*, (Haverhill, MA: 1884), p. 26.
23 Joseph Tracy, *The Great Awakening: A History of the Revival of Religion in the Times of Edwards and Whitefield*, (Boston, MA: Tappan & Dennet Printers, 1842), pp. 366-367.

CHAPTER 29

WHITEFIELD'S PREACHING IN BOSTON AND WESTERN COMMUNITIES

OCTOBER-NOVEMBER 1754

WHITEFIELD WAS ILL. BURSTS OF energy were followed by times of disability. Pockets of opposition still confronted Whitefield, but for the most part controversies were minimal. "Altogether a better reception was given him by the country than he had received fourteen years before, and that . . . was gratifying enough. His weakness still clung to him, that is, his weakness of the flesh, and from this time he may be considered a confirmed invalid who refused to be invalidated; but his strength of heart was not at all diminished . . . ."[1]

Whitefield's travelogue continues. His letters help us trace his steps from New Hampshire back to Boston. Writing from Portsmouth on October 25, 1754, he looked ahead, stating, "The Sabbath is to be kept at Newbury. Monday I am to preach thrice—at Rowley, Byfield, and Ipswich; Tuesday at Cape Ann, and Wednesday night or Thursday morning at Boston . . . though I want another week in these parts."[2]

On Sunday October 27, 1754, Whitefield preached in Newbury, Massachusetts. He did not say how many times he preached on Sunday for his friend Rev. Jonathan Parsons at what would later be called the Old South Presbyterian Church in Newburyport. The week prior he preached there four times. In his typical preaching circuit fashion, Whitefield preached, departed, and returned shortly thereafter to follow up on his previous visit. Newbury was a community deeply divided from ministerial feuds, parish disputes, and theological controversy. Whitefield's preaching encouraged and strengthened his revivalist friends and further alienated his enemies.

Traveling from Newbury on well-packed dirt and gravel rural country roads, Whitefield preached three times on Monday October 28, at three nearby country churches. First, in Rowley, Whitefield was hosted by Rev. Jedediah Jewett. Although Whitefield travelled around Rowley in 1747, the last time Whitefield preached for Jewett was in February or early March 1745. Now, nine years later in 1754, Whitefield again ministered for Jewett in the Second Church of Rowley (now Georgetown), Massachusetts. Originally, Rowley was much larger than it is now, initially encompassing areas that are now known as the towns of Bradford, Boxford, and Georgetown. This was a rural farming community that sold or traded its produce in Gloucester, Salem, or Boston. Jewett was a firm advocate of the Great Awakening and continued to promote revivals in his church until his death in 1789. "In 1747," two years after Whitefield's last visit, "during the ministry of Mr. Jewett, the parish voted to build a new meeting house. Sixty feet by forty-two, with a steeple and spire; this house was

---

1 J.P. Gledstone, *George Whitefield: Supreme Among Preachers,* (1900: reprinted by Emerald House, Greenville, SC, 1998), p. 294
2 George Whitefield, *George Whitefield's Works,* (1771: reprinted by Quinta Press, Shropshire, England, 2000), vol. III, pp. 108-109.

completed in 1749, about fifty years after the erection of the last."[3] Jewett was an evangelical Calvinist well respected by his community in which he served for sixty years.

> Mr. Jewett was evidently a faithful parish minister. During his services here there were added to the church two hundred and nineteen . . . He was a skillful, fervent preacher of the doctrine of God's grace to lost men, through Jesus Christ; preached it as a doctrine according to godliness, so as to teach them, who had believed in God, to maintain good works. He also took heed to himself; was so pious, charitable, prudent, and patient, as to be an example to the flock.[4]

Later that same day, a few miles away Whitefield was sponsored by Rev. Moses Parsons of the First Church in Byfield. Parsons defended Whitefield to his critics and welcomed the evangelist to his pulpit. Byfield was a farming community with abundant fresh water and fish from the Parker River. In 1754, Byfield was in a dispute with Newbury over parish boundaries, causing a minor disruption in the community. The First Congregational Church under Moses Parsons experienced slow but steady growth in the 1750s, to the point that by 1766 a larger meeting house was necessary.[5] The third location Whitefield preached that day was in Ipswich, for Rev. John Cleveland of Ipswich Chebacco Parish, where he preached twice. This must have been an exhausting day. Then we find Whitefield the next day several miles to the east, on the maritime peninsula called Cape Ann.

In Gloucester on Cape Ann, on Tuesday, October 29 Whitefield preached two times. Rev. Samuel Chandler of the First Church in Gloucester supported Whitefield. Chandler was raised about thirty-five miles away in Andover, Massachusetts. He graduated Harvard College in 1735, and taught school and served as a minister in York, Maine from 1742 to his coming to Gloucester in 1750. Gloucester was fast becoming an important maritime community. Its connections to Great Britain through the fisheries brought money and European influences into this port city. Some Gloucester leaders became intrigued by what would later be called Universalism.[6] This influence was detected early in Gloucester by Chandler, which was what he considered to be religious infidelity from the authority of the Bible. Having the Calvinistic Whitefield in Gloucester in 1754 was a public statement by Chandler that he would not tolerate the faithless theological speculations from some in his community. The ministry of Samuel Chandler at the First Church Congregational in Gloucester was steady, conservative, and unremarkable. He was a diligent and orthodox pastor, and somewhat understated. Speaking of Chandler,

> He was a gentleman of clear apprehension, solid judgment, firm, and of a thoughtful, inquisitive temper of mind. These, sanctified and improved, fitted him for the high and honorable office he sustained, and which he discharged with fidelity. As a preacher, he delivered the truth as it is in Jesus; showing in his doctrines uncorruptness, gravity, and sound speech, that could not be condemned . . . He was blessed with a great degree of wisdom and prudence . . . The welfare of his people and of the church of God lay near his heart.[7]

Samuel Chandler of Gloucester wrote succinctly in his journal, "Oct. 29—Mr. Whitefield came here, preached twice, Rev. 1:5-6, and went out of town."[8]

---

3 Thomas Gage and James Bradford, *The History of Rowley: Anciently Including Bradford, Boxford, and Georgetown*, (Boston, MA: Ferdinand Andrews Printer, 1840), p. 24.
4 Ibid., p. 23.
5 John L. Ewell, *The Story of Byfield: A New England Parish*, pp. 107-109.
6 David Robinson, *The Unitarians and the Universalists*, (Westport, CT: Greenwood Press, 1985), p. 297.
7 John J. Babson, *History of the Town of Gloucester, Cape Ann: Including the Town of Rockport*, (Gloucester, MA: Published by Proctor Brothers, 1860), p. 329.
8 John J. Babson, "Diary of Rev. Samuel Chandler," *History of the Town of Gloucester*, p. 35.

According to a letter Whitefield wrote on October 25, 1754 from Portsmouth, New Hampshire, he planned to preach in Gloucester-Cape Ann on Tuesday, October 29, and then Wednesday night or Thursday morning arrive in Boston, completing his preaching circuit north and east of the city. The below quote is an example of how *The Boston Gazette* kept its New England readers informed of Whitefield's activities upon his return to Boston:

> *The Boston Gazette,* November 5, 1754, p. 3.
> On Thursday last in the forenoon the Rev. Mr. Whitefield returned to Boston from the North; at four in the afternoon preached at the South Church; Friday morning at seven at the Old North Church; at four in the afternoon at the South Church; Saturday at seven at the New North; at eleven at Charlestown; Lord's day twice at Concord; Monday at eleven in the forenoon in Charlestown; at four in the afternoon at the South Church; and at seven this morning at the South Church again.

This newspaper article helps trace Whitefield's relentless preaching schedule in and around Boston. In Boston, the South Church was served by Rev. Joseph Sewall, an evangelical preacher and longtime supporter of Whitefield. During the rising Unitarian movement in Boston in the nineteenth century, the Old South Church resisted Unitarianism and remain Trinitarian.[9] This later changed. Sewall served the church until his death in 1769, laying a foundation for Protestant orthodoxy that endured well beyond his lifetime. In the first few days of November 1754, Whitefield preached for Sewall at three weekday afternoon lectures and one early morning lecture, both designed to allow workers to attend the meetings.

In Boston, Whitefield also preached at the Old North Church and the New North Church. The Old North Church was served by Rev. Samuel Checkley, Jr. who ministered there from 1747 to 1768. He was a son of the minister of the same name at the New South Church in Boston. The younger Checkley was known as an eloquent speaker and an evangelical Calvinist with an "uncommon felicity in the devotional service of public worship."[10] The Old North Church under Checkley was one of the foremost churches in New England.[11]

A sketch of the Old South Church in Boston, in the early 1770s.

Source: "Heritage History," http://www.oldsouth.org/about/history

The New North Church was deeply affected by the Great Awakening under Rev. John Webb, who died in 1750. Before his death the church called a colleague for the elderly Webb, namely Rev. Andrew Elliott. Serving at New North Church from 1742 to his death in 1778, Elliott overlapped with Webb several years. Elliott was

---

9   "Heritage History," http://www.oldsouth.org/about/history. For a contemporary perspective, see *Old South Church in Boston: A Concise Theological, Historical & Whimsical Encyclopedia,* (Boston, MA: Published by Old South Church, 2020).
10 Chandler Robbins, *A History of the Second Church, or Old North, in Boston . . . ,* (Boston, MA: Printed by John Wilson & Son, 1852), p. 124.
11 Ibid., p. 123.

apprehensive about the excesses and divisions caused by the awakening in general and Whitefield in particular. A Harvard graduate in 1737, Elliott earned a second degree in 1740, at the beginnings of the religious turmoil on Harvard's campus.

In 1745, Andrew Elliott wrote that he was hesitant to endorse Whitefield due to the controversies and rivalries in the churches. Elliott criticized remarks in Whitefield's *Journals,* and asserted that Whitefield was too emotionally driven by his "experimental religion." Elliott was also unsure about the validity of itinerant preaching, and he simply was not comfortable with many aspects of Whitefield's ministry.[12] However, by 1754, many things had changed. Much of the divisiveness of the awakening had subsided. Whitefield's preaching remained Calvinistic and evangelical, but he refrained from attacking ministers and churches by name. A relative calm settled upon Boston's churches, as those who endorsed Whitefield and those who resisted him mutually got along. Elliott was persuaded to allow Whitefield to preach in the New North Church at seven o'clock on Saturday morning, November 2, 1754.

A fascinating eyewitness account of Whitefield preaching in Boston is recorded by an unidentified correspondent to Mr. Robert Treat Paine. Mr. Paine was born in Boston in 1731, the son of a minister who became a merchant. A Harvard College graduate in 1749, Paine was a merchant and a whaler before beginning law school in 1755. Later, Robert Paine would become famous as a lawyer in Taunton Massachusetts, a signer of the Declaration of Independence, and a supreme court judge. But in 1754 he was a businessman in maritime commerce when he received the following letter about Whitefield from an anonymous friend in Boston. The somewhat rambling letter is recorded Saturday at two o'clock, on October 12, 1754.

> Dreadful Tired, No not tired neither, Flustered I believe it is. Been to Meeting to hear Mr. Whitefield at Docr. Sewalls, a very full house but not Crowded, as beautiful an Assembly as Ever I was in. I have Enjoyed a perfect Tranquility ever since he came, and determined not to go till I could feel quite Easy & calm that I might be able to Judge for myself amidst a confusion of Prejudices. Thus Serene, I attended to a discourse From Jude 25th verse, Keep yourselves in the love of God.
>
> He began with a Harangue on Modern Atheism, Compared it with the Days of the Apostles & shewed us why these Epistles were written to the infant Churches. Described Jude, Compared him to Barnabas & called him a son of thunder, &c. Then recollecting himself that he was in Boston, Preaching to so Polite an Audience resolved to address them as reasonable Creatures & inform their Judgments before he attempted to rouse their passions. Therefore proposed to Explain what this Love of God was & 2nd Why we were Exhorted to keep it in our hearts & 3rd to apply this Exhortation to several Sorts of persons as those who had had this Love shed abroad in their hearts but had departed from their Love Entangled by the World. To those who had received abundant Testimony, but made no proper returns not having applied for the Grace of God but trusting to the Benevolence of their own hearts & Priding themselves in Efficacy of their Philosophy, &c. &c. &c. Thus much method gave me great hope that the Preacher had grown older. But it was a Sham; he ran directly into Story telling & then I found he was grown old for he told us a Dear Good man one favored of the Lord, who met with Severe trials about 3 years ago (But is Now Glorified) wrote to his friend in the time of his

---

12   William B. Sprague, *Annals of the American Pulpit—Trinitarian Congregational,* (New York: Robert Carter & Brothers Publishers, 1866), vol. I, pp. 417-418.

Trial, (I knew the man very well and his friend to whom he wrote Shewd, me the Passage) that his Trial was very sore but Gods Love was very sweet and Twenty more as roundabout as this.[13]

Nearby to Boston in Charlestown, Whitefield preached at the First Church for Rev. Hull Abbott and Rev. Thomas Prentice. Whitefield spoke at this church in 1740 and again in 1747 with remarkable success. By 1754, the First Church in Charlestown was known as an orthodox, Calvinistic church, in contrast with some other churches in the Boston area. Revs. Abbott and Hull addressed the laxity in doctrine common in that time and preached the need for repentance and individual salvation through Jesus Christ. After the initial Great Awakening shook the church in 1740 under Whitefield's preaching, their church history stated, "Little or nothing occurred to diversify our religious history till the [American] Revolution" [in 1775].[14] After the death of Hull Abbott in 1774, he was described as "an orthodox and able minister, and maintained a respectable standing among the clergy of his day . . . characterized by sound doctrine and ministerial faithfulness."[15] Whitefield preached in Charlestown for Hull and Abbott on Saturday morning, November 2, at eleven o'clock, and again on Monday, November 4 at the same time.

Rev. John Ballantine of Westfield, Massachusetts kept an extensive diary in which he made copious notes about pastoral visits, town news, funerals, family events, marriages, and other homey events. Around the time of Whitefield's 1754 New England visit, he wrote of local men who dug up Indian graves and turned in the decapitated heads for a bounty or reward, and he wrote of "a man [who] stood in pillory for making counterfeit money." It would have been helpful if Ballantine wrote more about Whitefield's 1754 visit to New England, for all he wrote on October 3, 1754 was "Mr. Whitefield in Boston."[16]

The *Journal of Rev. Israel Loring* of Sudbury is insightful. Sudbury is about fifteen miles west of Boston. Loring graduated from Harvard in 1701 and with a second degree in 1704, and was ordained in Sudbury in 1706, serving there until his death in 1772. He was a strict and serious Calvinist, and "he did not like the ways of Mr. Whitefield, the evangelist, and the excitement attendant upon his revivals."[17] As the first minister of the Congregational Church in Sudbury, Loring kept a detailed record of his activities and the events that surrounded his world. In October 1754, this unpublished, hand-written journal narrates events such as days of prayer, individuals on church discipline, baptisms, his falling at home at night when his candle extinguished, Bible texts preached on Sundays, accounts of his grandchildren, admissions to church membership, and much more. On October 31, 1754 Loring recorded,

> 31 October [1754]. Thrice has Rev. Whitefield visited New England. The first visit that he made was on Sept 18, 1740 when he came to Boston. The second was the year 1744 arriving at Boston from Portsmouth on Nov 26. The third was this year 1754. [He] came to Boston from Rhode Island with President Burr Oct 9. Preaching in numbers of towns tho vastly less the second time than the first. May the glorious head of the church [Jesus Christ] take care of his churches in this land and over rule all things to his glory and their good.[18]

The Baptist minister Rev. Isaac Backus was an eyewitness of Whitefield's preaching in Boston in 1754. Born in 1724 near Norwich, Connecticut, Backus was influenced by the works of Jonathan Edwards, George Whitefield, and Eleazer Wheelock, and was conveted as a teenager in 1741. He was

---

13 "From an Unidentified Correspondent," *Robert Treat Paine Papers*, vol. I, Massachusetts Historical Society, https://www.masshist.org/publications/rtpp/index.php/view/RTP1d196.
14 William I. Budington, *The History of First Church, Charlestown . . .* , (Boston, MA: Charles Tappan Printer, 1845), p. 137
15 Ibid., p. 136
16 John Ballantine, *Diary of Rev. John Ballantine*, (Worcester, MA: American Antiquarian Society, transcribed 1886), n.p.
17 Alfred S. Hudson, *The History of Hudson, Massachusetts, 1638-1889*, (Sudbury, MA: 1889), p. 355.
18 Israel Loring, *Journal of Israel Loring*, Unpublished Journal, Connecticut Historical Society Special Collections. In this journal entry Rev. Loring omitted Whitefield's 1747 visit to New England.

part of the New Light Congregational Church in Norwich, and was ordained in 1748. He became a Baptist in 1751 and served at the Middleborough Baptist Church in Massachusetts until his death in 1806. Backus would later be an outspoken patriot in the American Revolution, but in the 1750s he was the pastor of a small Baptist church and was deeply interested in revivals. Backus wrote of hearing Whitefield in Boston.

> 31 October-1 November [1754]. Set away early and got to Boston a little after noon; and heard Mr. Whitefield preach from Luke 19:14 in a clear manner . . . Next morning . . . went into Boston early to hear Mr. Whd. [Whitefield] and I and sundry others afterwards went in and heard him at 11 o'clock from Exod. 2:1-10. And he gave many ingenious observations and reflections from the words.

> Saturday Nov. 2. Got up this morning at 5 o'clock: went to the New North meeting house before 6: found the house crowded full of people which seemed wonderful to me to see such numbers of Boston gentery crowding the meeting house before Darkness was all dispelled. They sang, then Mr. Whitefield came in and had done his prayer before sunrise and he preached on 1 John 2:1. In the latter part of his discourse it seemed to me that I never see Christ appear more evidently to plead with Souls thro' any instrument in my Life. My heart was much affected, and loathed it's self for past Stupidity and folly and longed for greator strength ever to live for God. O! my leaness, my leaness! Great is the Lord's goodness in sending this his dear servant into these parts once more to Warn the Righteous and the Wicked: Astonishing is the assistance he has to preach so constantly 2 or 3 Sermons in a day. I came out of town about 10 o'clock and got home at night.[19]

About twelve miles northwest of Boston is Concord, where Rev. Daniel Bliss served the First Parish Congregational Church. Bliss was a Yale College graduate who served in Concord from 1738 to his death in 1764. Whitefield met Bliss in 1740, and in December 1744 he mentioned that he had had a welcome reception from Bliss in Concord. Whitefield also preached for Bliss on Sunday, August 21, 1747. Whenever Whitefield was on a preaching circuit in the Boston area, he visited Daniel Bliss in Concord. Now in 1754, Whitefield preached at the First Church in Concord twice on a Sunday morning, November 3, 1754.

Rev. Nathan Fiske graduated from Harvard College in 1754 and quickly began his ministry at the Third Church (Congregational) in Brookfield, Massachusetts. He was ordained at the church in 1756. In his writings, Fiske makes note of such things as squirrel hunting, teaching school, visiting Harvard College, weather observations, and drinking tea with

A later in life sketch of Rev. Isaac Backus, minister of the Baptist Church in Middleborough, Massachusetts.

Source: https://landmarkevents.org/
the-death-of-rev-isaac-backus-1806.

---

19 William G. McLoughlin, editor, *The Diary of Isaac Backus*, (Providence, RI: Brown University Press, 1979), vol. I, pp. 352-353.

friends. On November 12, 1754 he made a very brief reference to Whitefield, writing, "Waited on Mr. Geo. Whit."[20] Whether the two met or not is not known.

The Boston Weekly Newsletter refrained from reporting Whitefield's preaching agenda or successes until the following brief article, printed on page four of the November 7, 1754 edition.

> The Rev. Mr. Whitefield, purposing to leave this town to-day, preached a farewell sermon at the Old South Meeting House early in the morning to a vast assembly, several hundred people were in the house before three o'clock.

As Whitefield preached his way out of Boston, heading south towards Georgia, *The Boston Gazette* reported the following farewell activities:

> *The Boston Gazette,* November 26, 1754. p. 3.
> We are informed that the Rev. Mr. George Whitefield, upon earnest invitation, preached Friday forenoon, November 8 at Cambridge Old Precinct; and afternoon at Medford; Lord's Day at Concord twice; Monday the 11th at Framingham . . . the congregations generally crowded with people flocking around about and much affected.

Departing Boston, Whitefield crossed the Charles River on a ferry and preached at what *The Boston Gazette* called "Cambridge Old Precinct." Whitefield was not welcomed at the First Church in Cambridge, as Rev. Nathaniel Appleton had made it clear in 1745, that he was no advocate of Whitefield and he disdained revivals. Further, Whitefield was not welcomed at Harvard College in Cambridge, as the President, Rev. Edward Holyoke, had previously written, preached, and gathered others to oppose Whitefield. The expression "Cambridge Old District" used by Whitefield may refer to "Little Cambridge," now the town of Brighton, Massachusetts. Many wealthy Boston merchants lived there.[21] This community was originally part of Cambridge, but distance, and the difficulties in crossing the Charles River to attend church services, gave the community a separate identity. A religious society was formed in 1737, and a meeting house was built in 1744, but there was no settled minister. This community of about fifty families petitioned the Massachusetts General Court in 1747, 1748, and 1749 to be recognized as a separate entity, but they were denied. By the mid-1750s the community had regular year-round preaching from a variety of ministers. They again requested recognition from Massachusetts in 1758, but were again denied. Finally, in 1779, the community was authorized as a

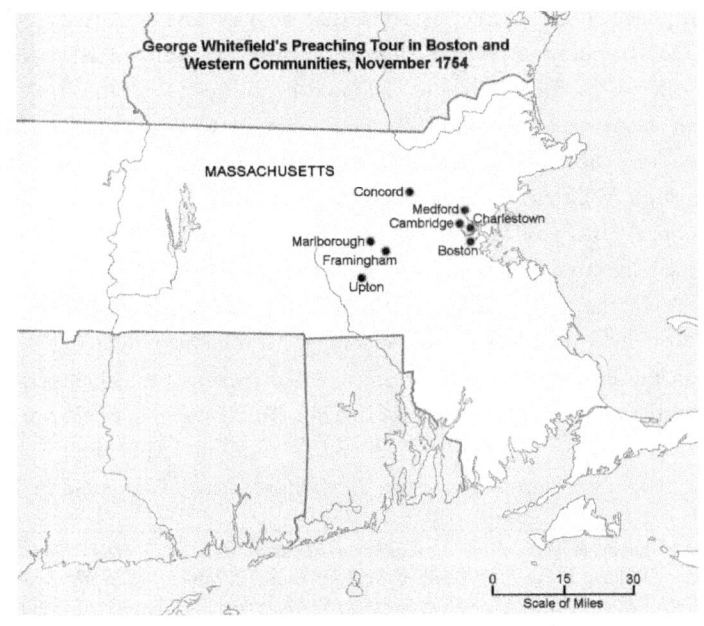

---

20 Nathan Fiske, *Rev. Nathan Fiske Papers, 1750-1799,* (Worcester, MA: American Antiquarian Society), box 1 (1754), n.p.
21 "First Congregational Church and Society in Brighton," http://oasis.lib.harvard.edu/oasis/deliver/~div00011. "Our History," *Brighton United Church of Christ,* https://brightonucc.org/about-us/our-history.

separate precinct of Cambridge with a designated minister.[22] When Whitefield was in the area in November 1754, there was a meeting house but no regular minister for the people.

The Harvard faculty was happy to see Whitefield depart. Two other Boston ministers that were pleased when Whitefield left the city was Rev. Andrew Elliott of the New North Church, and Rev. Timothy Cutler of the Christ Church Episcopal. Elliott tolerated Whitefield while he served as an assistant minister at New North Church under Rev. John Webb, but after Webb died in 1750, Elliott was more open about his suspicions of Whitefield. Elliott blamed Whitefield for the ecclesiastical divisions in Boston, and he did not allow the traveling preacher to speak in 1754 at the New North Church.[23] Likewise, Rev. Timothy Cutler of Christ Church Episcopal was a stickler for high church formalities, and was an outspoken advocate for the rituals and liturgies of the Church of England. Cutler saw Whitefield, a fellow Anglican priest, as a fanatic, a troublemaker, a false teacher. Cutler was "inflexible in his principles" and was "ever zealous" in the defense of Church of England doctrines and practices.[24]

Departing Cambridge on November 8, Whitefield travelled about ten miles north to Medford. This was new and hostile territory for the itinerant evangelist. Whitefield had preached in communities around Medford since 1740, but was never invited to the First Church Congregational. The minister at the First Church in Medford was Rev. Ebenezer Turell, a graduate of Harvard College in 1721. He then studied theology with a New Light minister in Boston, Rev. Benjamin Colman. Turell served at the Medford church from 1724 to his death in 1778. The church built a new meeting house in 1724 and constructed a larger building with three balconies in 1770. Numerically and physically, the Medford Congregational Church grew under Turell's leadership. "He served for 54 years, during which time he baptized 1,037 people, married 220 couples and admitted 323 communicants to the church."[25] Turell was known as a collector of fine silver and elaborate furniture. He donated an exquisite hand-carved chair to Harvard College which became the official president's chair.[26] Turell was completely against Whitefield and opposed the revivals of his day. The official history of Medford states, "Mr. Turell greatly disliked the religious methods and manners of Mr. Whitefield."[27]

In the 1740s Ebenezer Turell wrote pamphlets against Whitefield and his itinerant preaching, his subjective reliance on the moving of the Holy Spirit, his divisiveness and belligerent language, and Whitefield's insistence on the new birth for salvation. In 1745, Turell was one of several ministers that met in Cambridge to sign a declaration against Whitefield and to unite in closing their pulpits to Whitefield's ministry. Apparently, a fledgling group was meeting in Medford that did not support Rev. Turell and his denunciations of the

Rev. Ebenezer Turell of Medford, Massachusetts was an outspoken opponent of Whitefield.

Source: findagrave.com

---

22 Lucius R. Paige, *History of Cambridge, Massachusetts . . . 1630-1877*, (Boston, MA: H.O. Houghton & Company, 1877), p. 5.
23 William B. Sprague, *Annals of the American Pulpit, Trinitarian Congregational,* vol. I, pp. 417-418.
24 Robert G. Ingram, *Religion, Reform and Modernity in the Eighteenth Century . . .* , (Woodbridge, Great Britain: The Boydell Press, 2007), p. 19.
25 M.L. Clarke, "A Brief History of the First Parish Church in Medford, Massachusetts," http://www.uumedford.org/history.html. For an overview see Dee Morris, *Medford: A Brief History,* (Charleston, SC: The History Press, 2009).
26 Francis H. Bigelow, *Historic Silver of the Colonies and its Makers,* (New York: The Macmillan Company, 1917), P. 402.
27 Charles Brooks, *History of the Town of Medford, Middlesex County, Massachusetts . . .* , (Boston, MA: James M. Usher, Publisher, 1855), p. 236.

revival. This new group did not have a meeting house or a designated leader, and they eventually did not form a separate church. But in 1754, these few Medford citizens, unhappy with Turell's ministry, asked Whitefield to come and preach to them, and the itinerant preacher responded. Whitefield preached, probably in a home or in the open air, in Medford on Friday, November 8, 1754, obviously infuriating Turell. Speaking of Ebenezer Turell, "He was one of the many ministers opposed to Rev. George Whitefield. On the death of the latter, he delivered a sermon concerning him from the text, "Verily every man, at his best estate, is altogether vanity."[28]

Previously, Whitefield preached in Concord twice on Sunday, November 3, for Rev. Daniel Bliss. After a week of local itinerant preaching, he returned to Concord and preached again on a Sunday, November 10, 1754, for Bliss at the First Parish Congregational Church. It is significant that Whitefield preached two Sundays in a row at Concord, when he had numerous invitations to preach at various churches in the community.

According to the November 26, 1754 edition of *The Boston Gazette*, on Monday, November 11, George Whitefield preached in Framingham, Massachusetts. Located twenty-one miles west of Boston, Framingham was a farming community that supplied Boston with agricultural produce, dairy products, lumber, and meat. The first settlers in that area were unsuccessful, but in 1698 definite progress was made to settle and farm the area. The First Church of Christ was founded in 1701, the first school building was constructed in 1716, and the town common was designed in 1735. In 1745 the church voted to become Congregational, but it did not pass.[29] In July 1745, Whitefield came to Framingham and preached in a barn.[30] In 1746 Rev. Matthew Bridge came to the First Church in Framingham, serving until his death in 1775.

A Harvard College graduate in 1741, at the beginning of the anti-Whitefield fervor at the college, Bridge was not a supporter of Whitefield. His tenure in Framingham was not without disruptions. Speaking of Matthew Bridge in Framingham,

> His pastorate was by no means one of continued happiness with social fellowship on his part. A considerable number of his church members did not believe that he was "sound in the faith," and it was urged that he did not accept the "Five Points of Calvinism," generally accepted by the Congregational churches as essential features of true Christianity, and his relations to the methods of the "Great Awakening," as the revival preaching started by Edwards and Whitefield was called, displeased a large number. Very many withdrew from the church, feeling spiritually distressed, and organized in 1747, a new Congregational Church.[31]

When Matthew Bridge came to Framingham in 1746, many objected to his anti-revival stance. Gossip and dissention prevailed within the church and throughout the town. In 1747, those opposed to Bridge formally called a council and chose themselves a minister, Rev. Solomon Reed. Born in 1718, Solomon Reed was a Harvard graduate in 1739. He was ordained over the Second Church and Society in Framingham in January 1747. Reed supported Whitefield and the awakening. Of Reed it was stated:

---

28 Oliver A. Roberts, *History of the Militia Company of Massachusetts, now called the Ancient and Honorable Artillery Company of Massachusetts, 1637-1888,* (Boston, MA: Alfred Mudge & Son Printers, 1897), vol. II, p. 738.
29 "History of the Plymouth Church," http://www.plymouthchurchframingham.org/whoweare/history. Problems in the church in Framingham stemmed from Whitefield's visit on July 5, 1745. Separatists formed the Second Congregational Church under Rev. Solomon Reed in 1747. Reed remained in Framingham until 1757, and the church dissolved in 1759. See J.H. Temple, *History of Framingham, Massachusetts . . . , 1640-1880,* (printed by the Town of Framingham, 1887), pp. 211-213.
30 William Barry, *A History of Framingham, Massachusetts . . . ,* (Carlisle, MA: Applewood Books, 1847), pp. 114.
31 William D. Bridge, *Genealogy of the John Bridge Family in America, 1632-1924,* (Cambridge, MA: The Murray Printing Company, 1924), p. 78.

He appears to have been held in much consideration by the people in this place, among whom he was settled . . . to the great satisfaction of the society. A descendant wrote that 'he was esteemed an able, pure, zealous, devout preacher of the Orthodox order, was highly respected and esteemed by his society, and lived a quiet and peaceable life.'[32]

In the 1750s, Framingham was a disturbed and divided town. Growth created new financial issues for the community, such as the need in 1750 to construct four new school houses around the town. After 1750, the community was happy to have a resident physician, Dr. Ebenezer Hemenway. During the first few months of 1754, dozens of citizens died of a disease that swept through this rural town. Creating both civil and ecclesiastical tension in Framingham was the fact that the Second Church was still required to pay a tax to support the minister of the First Church, as attempts to alleviate this tax burden were unsuccessful in 1752 and beyond. Revs. William Bridge and Solomon Reed did not get along. Bridge was an Old Light, establishment minister, while Reed was a New Light revival preacher. In this disrupted community, Whitefield made a deliberate visit in 1754, to support Reed and his new congregation.

On November 26, 1754, *The Boston Gazette* reported on Whitefield, "Monday the 11th at Framingham . . . the congregations generally crowded with people flocking around about and much affected." No doubt the crown that heard Whitefield preach in Framingham was composed mostly of parishioners from Reed's Second Church, with others covertly coming to listen from Bridge's First Church, much to the distress of Pastor Bridge. Reed was described as "a zealous New Light preacher" and as "a disciple of Whitefield." Reed brought three young men from his congregation to Harvard to enroll them as ministerial students, but they were rejected on the grounds of their pro-revival, New Light doctrines.[33] Reed stayed in Framingham until 1756, after which he took a church in Middleboro, Massachusetts to his death in 1785. After Reed departed Framingham, the two rival churches began talks of reconciliation. Bridge was able to mend relations with most of Reed's congregation.

> The Rev. Matthew Bridge possessed such genuineness of character, of social, moral and religious standing, that this opposition to him was finally overcome, though the new church had secured a minister possessing qualities of mind and heart of most excellent character. After a consideration of separation for thirteen years, the new organization disbanded, many returning to the mother church.[34]

Although the disruptions caused by Whitefield's 1754 New England tour were minimal compared to his 1740 and 1744-1745 visits to the area, there were still those who publicly opposed the itinerant preacher. A defense of Whitefield's ministry was printed and presented on page three of *The Boston Gazette,* November 19, 1754.

> To the Publisher of *The Boston Gazette:*
>
> Whereas the Evening Post of last week has published, that the Rev. Mr. Whitefield preached in the market place of Cambridge without the invitation or consent of the minister; as lately also as Charlestown, that he entered the pulpit there;
>
> This is to inform the public that we are well assured, that no minister wither in New England, or any minister or Bishop or Arch-Bishop of Old, pretends to claim any power over any market place or common land in any town or parish. That the meeting houses in New England are

---

32   William Barry, *A History of Framingham, Massachusetts,* pp. 117-118.
33   *The American Biblical Repository . . . ,* (New York: George A. Peters Publisher, 1842), p. 196.
34   William D. Bridge, *Genealogy of the John Bridge Family in America,* p. 78.

built entirely at the expense of the people for their use and shelter from the weather . . . . The generality of the people in both those parishes by their Select-men invited and desired the Rev. Mr. Whitefield to preach in their respective parishes; that the ministers of them were too knowing, wise, good and just, to interfere with the rights of their people, or hinder them from improving, their rights in desiring and attending Mr. Whitefield's preaching.

On November 11, 1754, after preaching for Rev. Solomon Reed in Framingham, Whitefield preached nearby about fifteen miles southwest at tiny Upton, Massachusetts. Founded in 1731 from dividing up neighboring towns, Upton was an agricultural village with a few hundred folks in the 1750s. Farmers in this area initially travelled many miles to attend church services. The First Congregational Church in Upton was founded from a desire for residents to have a place of worship closer to their homes and farms. In December 1745 they voted to build a new meeting house, which was completed in 1736.[35] The terrain was mostly flat, ideal for farming after the woods were cleared. The West River provided abundant fresh water. Virtually every family in Upton maintained a small farm along with some other trade or vocation. The shoe industry was popular, as cattle were bought and sold for meat and leather, the leather used for shoes that were transported for sale to Boston. In the 1750s local Baptists began meeting in Upton. The Congregational minister who welcomed Whitefield to Upton was Rev. Elijah Fish.

A Harvard graduate in 1750, Fish came to Upton right out of college and was ordained at the Congregational Church in Upton later in 1750 or early 1751. Elijah Fish was known as a "staunch Calvinist" who frequently sat on church councils in Massachusetts and New Hampshire to oppose the rising Arminian trend, what would later be called Unitarianism.[36] Fish served in rural Upton for forty-four years, seeing several revivals, until his death in 1795. His successor in the ministry at Upton, Rev. Benjamin Wood, wrote of Fish, "After entering the work of the ministry, he made a point of explaining the gospel, and of giving his hearers a clear, connected, and extensive view of the great scheme of redemption. He shunned not to declare the whole council of God."[37] Wood wrote of the relationship of Elijah Fish and George Whitefield, as follows:

> I look back to the days of my much beloved predecessor, and I find revival after revival of religion took place under his ministration. Here the word spoken by him, and by others, was carried to the conscience and to the heart with a divine power. At one time within these hallowed walls did the voice of Whitefield fall, in demonstration of the Spirit, on the ears of breathless hearers. During the ministry of Mr. Fish, 110 were admitted into the church, and 464 were baptized.[38]

An eyewitness and tentative supporter of Whitefield's travels in these regions west of Boston was Rev. Ebenezer Parkman of Westborough. In September 1740, Parkman heard Whitefield preach and met him in Boston. Parkman was a thoughtful, non-confrontative New Light minister on the border of the wild frontier of western Massachusetts. Indians roamed freely in his community. In October 1740, Parkman's wife heard Whitefield preach at Marlborough, about twelve miles northeast from their home in Westborough. Rev. Parkman assisted Whitefield with his lodging. Parkman was a mild supporter of Whitefield who had to

---

35 "Church History, The United Church of Upton," http://www.unitedparishupton.org/about/church-history.html. Donald B. Johnson, *Upton's Heritage: The History of a Massachusetts Town,* (Published by the Town of Upton, 1984).
36 Charles A. Bemis, *History of the Town of Marlborough, Cheshire County, New Hampshire,* (Boston, MA: Press of George H. Ellis, 1881), p. 113.
37 Benjamin Wood, *A Centennial Address, Delivered at Upton, Mass., June 25, 1835,* (Boston, MA: Published by William Peirce, 1835), pp. 13-14.
38 Ibid., p. 20.

constantly defend his pro-revival positions against his ministerial neighbors in and around Westborough, Marlborough, and Upton. In *The Diary of Ebenezer Parkman*, the following notations were made.[39]

> October 11, 1754. Hear that Mr. Whitefield is at Boston.
>
> November 12, 1754. Mr. Whitefield preaches at Upton. I sent him a letter on three heads—the last of them requesting he would go to poor Smithfield.
>
> November 15, 1754. Mr. Warrin told me he delivered my letter into Mr. Whitefield's hands, and that he saw him read it.
>
> November 20, 1754. He had "a discourse about Mr. Whitefield, and my conduct with regard to him.

In later November 1754, Whitefield completed his preaching circuit in communities west of Boston and returned to the city. In Boston he briefly rested, answered his correspondence, and prepared for another itinerant preaching tour towards southern New England.

---

[39] Ebenezer Parkman, *The Diary of Ebenezer Parkman, 1754-1755*, edited by Francis G. Walett, (Worcester, MA: American Antiquarian Society).

CHAPTER 30

WHITEFIELD'S MINISTRY IN SOUTHERN MASSACHUSETTS, RHODE ISLAND, AND CONNECTICUT

NOVEMBER–DECEMBER 1754

DESPITE HARVARD COLLEGE AND YALE College publicly denouncing Whitefield, he maintained his relentless New England itinerant preaching schedule. Simultaneously, much of the attention of the British Colonists in America was centered on rising political and military tensions between Great Britain and France. Previously, the two sides had fought what history calls King George's War, 1744 to 1748, with inconclusive results. After a brief respite, tensions again grew between these two European powers and their colonies in North America. Antagonism grew over land claims and trade concerns, with both the British and the French seeking to win the favor of Indian tribes. Throughout 1753, skirmishes plagued the frontier of the British Colonies. By May 1754, there was an undeclared war, which became official in 1756. Militia units from the British colonies in New England would be called to fight to protect British interests in what Americans called the French and Indian War, which lasted from 1756 to 1763. It was in this time of rising civil unrest and military tension that Whitefield continued his Fall, 1754 preaching tour through New England.

In typical Whitefield fashion, the relentless itinerant retraced much his route from Boston south towards New York. Along the way he would travel through southern Massachusetts, Rhode Island, and Connecticut. One author lamented that there is little information about this southern New England circuit back to New York. As Robert Philip stated, "Little, I regret to say, is to be found in either his memoranda or letters to illustrate this ride, except proofs that many of his hearers must have ridden forty or fifty miles, in order to reach the line of his itinerancy."[1] While this lack of information for this Whitefield travelogue is generally true, there are glimpses of Whitefield's ministry as he departed Boston towards southern New England and New York in the late fall-early winter of 1754.

SOUTHERN MASSACHUSETTS

Whitefield's first biographer, John Gilles wrote that Whitefield departed Boston on November 7, 1754, at "four o'clock in the morning," taking "affectionate leave" from the group that gathered to say farewell.[2] An eyewitness at this early morning farewell was Mr. Joseph Gilman, a clerk-merchant in Boston. Gilman wrote,

> I do not improve the kind opportunity Providence had Indulged me with the hearing of Mr. Whitefield. I am sure you have not any reason to think so. I inform you that I rose at 4 in the

---

1 Robert Philip, *The Life and Times of George Whitefield*, (1837: republished by Banner of Truth Trust, 2007), p. 444.
2 John Gilles, *Memoirs of George Whitefield*, (1772: reprinted by Hunt & Noyes, Middletown, CT: 1838), p.163.

morning to hear him, and the morning he preached his farewell sermon I rose at half after twelve at Midnight for fear of oversleeping myself, and before 4 in the morning was at the South Church and waited for his coming. The meeting was exceedingly full and full of singing when I got there. I missed no opportunity to hear him.[3]

The next record we have of Whitefield's travels south from Boston is in Plymouth, Massachusetts. The minister of the First Congregational Church in Plymouth was Rev. Nathaniel Leonard, who served there from 1724 to 1760. Whitefield last preached for Leonard in Plymouth in December 1744. This church has maintained excellent records. Leonard was the scribe maintaining the Plymouth church records when Whitefield came to town in November 1754. Whitefield preached four times over three days in Plymouth. Leonard recorded:

1754

Nov. 16. There came hither again the Rev'd Mr. George Whitefield & Preached in the Evening it being Saturday 1 sermon.

17—The next Day being Lord's Day [Whitefield preached] three sermons

18—& the next Day viz Monday Morning [Whitefield preached] 1 sermon I waited upon him to Middleboro where he preached again on 3rd Day. May God make him more & more a great Blessing in his Generation & long Preserve his Life & usefulness to these & other Churches.[4]

Leonard mentioned that he escorted Whitefield from Plymouth to Middleboro, when he wrote, "I waited upon him to Middleboro where he preached again on 3rd Day." The ride from Plymouth was about 15 miles through flat terrain, an easy ride for an experienced rider like Whitefield. Leonard accompanied Whitefield because the minister in Marlboro, Rev. Sylvanus Conant, was new to Middleboro and had not yet invited Whitefield to preach in his pulpit.

Sylvanus Conant served the First Congregational Church in Middleboro from 1745 to his death in 1777. A 1740 Harvard College graduate, Conant came to a town deeply divided by the Great Awakening. During the 1740s, the First Church had many controversies and disruptive church meetings. Conant was a New Light and a supporter of Whitefield, but he was balanced, steady, and unemotional. A year after he started at the church, a large section of his congregation left and created a rival New Light church in town. This rival congregation was more zealous and passionate than thoughtful, and quickly turned on itself with internal disputes and division. The rival church built a new meeting house, but they dissolved in 1748 and most rejoined Conant at the First Church. It must have given Conant some satisfaction when he moved the First Church into the new meeting house constructed by his rivals. The older meeting house, built in 1690, was disassembled and used to build a new parsonage for Conant in 1755.[5] Whitefield coming to Middleboro was a moment of healing and unity for the congregation. No doubt Sylvanus Conant was thrilled that his formerly divided church, of which both sides supported Whitefield, could now be reunited and hear the famous itinerant preach in town for the first time.

---

3 Arthur Gillman, *The Gilman Family, traced in the line of Honorable John Gilman, of Exeter, NH* . . . , (Albany, NY: Joel Munsell, Printer 1869), p. 83. The last name of this family is variously spelt as Gillman or Gilman.
4 "Plymouth Church Records," *Publications of the Colonial Society of Massachusetts, vol. xxii, Collections,* (Boston, MA: Published by the Society, 1920), p. 301.
5 Thomas Weston, *History of the Town of Middleboro, Massachusetts,* (Boston, MA: Houghton, Mifflin and Company, 1906), pp. 311, 447-449.

Middleboro was a town which centered on the First Congregational Church. Townsfolk worked in various small industries made possible by the Nemasket River, which powered numerous mills and provided trout and herring and abundant fresh water. Various animals came to the river to drink, making hunting game easy. Conant's work at the church was difficult, and his congregation did not experience a revival under his ministry. Conant was described as follows:

> He was a strong man, he was a sound man whom many loved, his disposition was fortunate, for it was full of disposition for others . . . He found ways of doing good wherever he went . . . such glad interest for others beamed forth in his eyes that he seemed to have forgotten himself for others' welfare and their interests became his own.[6]

On November 19, 1754 Whitefield preached in Middleboro. The official history of the First Church in Middleboro states:

> When Mr. Whitefield preached among us, he met Mr. Conant near the meeting-house not long after his ordination and asked him how the work prospered on his hands; Mr. Conant was desponding and said, "Who is sufficient for these things?" On entering the pulpit, Mr. Whitefield announced his text, "I am this day weak, though crowned king," and preached with great power.[7]

Whitefield preached to an overflow crowd in the new meeting house for the First Church in Middleboro. The meeting space had galleries or balconies on three sides. Wooden pews with five-foot high backrests were rented by those who could afford them, the pews closest to the pulpit were reserved for the most distinguished people in town. Other uncomfortable pews with no backrest were available for the poorer folks. There was no heat in the meeting house, so in colder weather people bundled up. Some had coal heated foot-stoves to keep their feet and legs warm. Typically, people brought their lunches and ate and visited between the morning and afternoon services. Speaking of this church, "This was one of the churches where the great Whitefield preached during his visit to America. The church was then so crowded that his only way of reaching the pulpit was by a ladder to the window in the rear."[8]

Whitefield went from Middleboro west about ten miles to Taunton. There he met his long-time ally Rev. Josiah Crocker. Whitefield and Crocker spent time together in early January 1745 in Taunton, with Whitefield preaching in Crocker's pulpit with great success. Now in November 1754, the following Whitefield-Crocker anecdote may apply.

> The Taunton minister was a great friend of Whitefield . . . Mr. Whitefield preached in his pulpit, and . . . many were displeased with him for this. The people in Taunton, as elsewhere, were divided concerning what were called "new measures." But Mr. Crocker entered into them most heartily, and would be called at the present time a revival preacher. He was often invited to preach in neighboring towns, and persons came from a long distance, even as far as Plymouth, to listen to his sermons. The story is told of a woman who quieted her baby, weary from a long march, by shouting, "Crocker's Ahead."[9]

Rev. Isaac Backus heard Whitefield preach both in Middleboro, for Rev. Sylvanus Conant, and in Taunton for Rev. Josiah Crocker. Backus was the Baptist minister in Middleboro, and he and Conant were friendly, and both were New Lights. Backus wrote in his *Diary*:

---

6   Ibid., p. 315.
7   *First Church in Middleboro, Mass . . . A Historical Account . . .*, (Boston, MA: Published by the Church, 1854), p. 39.
8   Thomas Weston, *History of the Town of Middleboro, Massachusetts*, p.453.
9   D. Hamilton Hurd, *History of Bristol County, Massachusetts*, (Philadelphia, PA: J.W. Lewis & Company, 1883), vol. II, p. 788.

18-19 November [1754]. Went with my wife and heard Mr. Whitefield preach in the afternoon at Mr. Conant's meeting house on 2 Saml. 3:39 and laid open in a glorious manner how every Saint is Anointed King;—and yet that they have much weakness notwithstanding. A blessed Sermon it was to my Soul and tho' it was rainy coming home yet the benefit received did much overbalance that.

Next morning I went and heard him preach 2 Sermons at taunton, and tho' he delivered gospel truths, yet 'twas not with that power as yesterday. The wind bloweth When, as well as Where it listeth.[10]

RHODE ISLAND

In the mid-1750s, Rhode Island had solidified its determination to remain a free-thinking people. Numerous expressions of religious devotion prospered. Groups as diverse as Quakers, Baptists, Congregationalists, Jews, and Anglicans had growing congregations throughout the Rhode Island Colony. With the exception of the Anglican churches, most Rhode Islanders understood the validity of an individual relationship with God outside a formal hierarchy. For them, unity was based on similar experiences. Loyalty to a specific denomination often became strained by individual expressions of faith. The impulses of religious revivals came and went throughout Rhode Island. By the time of Whitefield's visit in the fall of 1754, most citizens were more concerned about the developing French and Indian War than were concerned about religious issues.[11]

On November 21, 1754 Rev. Ebenezer Parkman of Marlborough wrote, "Mr. Whitefield preaches at Upton. I sent him a letter on three heads—the last of them requesting he would go to poor Smithfield."[12]

Parkman requested that Whitefield visit "poor Smithfield." This is a reference to Smithfield, Rhode Island, about thirty miles south of Parkman's home in Westborough, Massachusetts. Parkman pitied the undeveloped, backward village of Smithfield because it did not have a settled minister and it had not experienced any revivals. Originally settled in 1631 as a farming community, Smithfield became a separate entity from Providence in 1731. There was a good, strait road into Massachusetts from Smithfield, but the town itself had little to offer. Religiously, the town was indifferent, with some Quakers and Baptists in the area. Subsistence farming kept the poor town going. The rivers that traversed through Smithfield powered several small family owned saw and grist mills. There was good timber, abundant fresh water, and steady work in the lime quarries, but the small town remained backward. When a stagecoach came through town, the community stopped to stare. A small Baptist group built a meeting house in 1701, and the Quakers constructed a meeting house in 1719, which was enlarged in 1755.[13]

Rev. Ebenezer Parkman of Westborough saw "poor Smithfield" as a spiritually destitute area, an agrarian community in need of the gospel. That is why he suggested to Whitefield that the evangelist visit the community. One account stated, "The first churches and schools were built in Smithfield during the 1700s. Early in the century, a small meeting house was erected on the road to Woonsocket . . . The structure was rebuilt several times, but the church never attracted a large congregation." Because there was no settled minister or school teacher, "Education was carried on in private homes for the most part,

---

10 William G. McLoughlin, editor, *The Diary of Isaac Backus,* (Providence, RI: Brown University Press, 1979), vol. I, p. 355.
11 William McLoughlin, *Rhode Island: A History*, (New York: W.W. Norton & Company, 1978), pp. 76, 80.
12 Ebenezer Parkman, *The Diary of Ebenezer Parkman, 1754-1755,* (Worcester, MA: The American Antiquarian Society).
13 Thomas Steere, *History of the Town of Smithfield, from its Organization in 1731, to its Division, in 1871,* (Providence, RI: E.L. Freedman Printer, 1881), p. 139.

but several school houses were erected in the eighteenth century."[14] Since the early records of Smithfield are nonexistent, we have no way of knowing whether or not Whitefield went to tiny Smithfield, a town of less than five hundred residents to preach. But we do know that he planned on going to Rhode Island in November 1754.

Whitefield travelled through Rhode Island a few weeks earlier, in early October 1754. Now he returned to water gospel seeds he had previously planted. Unfortunately, there are gaps in Whitefield's surviving correspondence. Tracing his exact movements is often difficult if not impossible. Assuming Whitefield visited Smithfield on or around November 13, we then lose track of the traveling preacher until we read of a letter he wrote on November 22 from someplace in Rhode Island. In this note he spoke of his travels throughout New England, saying:

> What you have heard is more than true. A more effectual door I never saw opened, than lately in Boston, and indeed in every place where I have been in New England; not a hundredth part can be told you. With great difficulty I am got to this place, where people, as I am informed, are athirst to hear the word of God. I shall therefore stay, God willing, till Monday, and then set forward to Connecticut in my way to New York . . .[15]

This paragraph has several points to consider. First, Whitefield is pleased that large crowds still attend his preaching in New England. Indeed, this is significant since this is his fourth New England tour, and the masses of people still flocked to his preaching. Second, he stated, "With great difficulty I am got to this place," which may be a reference to his poor health, or to the slow pace of travel. Third, the reference to "this place," is only identified as Rhode Island, as a place where people were "athirst to hear the word of God." Fourth, as a result of the eager reception he received in Rhode Island, he decided to prolong his stay a few extra days before he will "set forward to Connecticut in my way to New York."

After preaching on Sunday, November 24 in Rhode Island, Whitefield wrote the next day:

> This shows you where I am at present, going towards Georgia from Boston, where my reception hath been far superior to that fourteen years ago. In that and other places in New England, I have been enabled to preach near a hundred times since the beginning of October, and thanks be to God, we scarce had so much as one dry meeting.[16]

Previously, Whitefield visited Rhode Island in 1740, 1745, 1747, and several weeks earlier in 1754. On his first visit in September 1740 he preached in Newport three times and once in Bristol. In May 1745, Whitefield was in Newport. In August 1747, he preached only in Newport. In 1754, the Newport Congregational ministers were Rev. William Vinal of the First Congregational, and Rev. James Searing of the Second Congregational. Vinal supported Whitefield but Searing did not.

These few days of ministry in the Rhode Island Colony in November 1754 are overlooked by Whitefield's main biographers. An exception is an older biography by John Richard Andrews, who broadly stated, "Another month was spent in Rhode Island, Boston, and neighborhood, carrying the glad tidings of the gospel of peace to the multitude . . . At length, late in November, after fulfilling all his engagements, he proceeded south on his way to Georgia . . . [17] This is a generalization and does not provide us any details of Whitefield's late November 1754 ministry in Rhode Island, a ministry he wrote of in his November 22 letter as a place where people were "athirst to hear the word of God."

---

14 *Historic and Architectural Resources of Smithfield, Rhode Island*, (Rhode Island Historical Preservation Commission, 1992), p. 6.
15 George Whitefield, *Works of George Whitefield*, (1771: reprinted by Quinta Press, Shropshire, England, 2000), vol. III, p. 109.
16 Ibid., p. 110
17 John Richard Andrews, *George Whitefield*, (1879: reprinted by Elibron Classics, London, UK: 2005), p. 296.

CONNECTICUT

The erratic correspondence of Whitefield places him in Connecticut in late November 1754. He wrote a letter from Rhode Island dated November 22. His next letter was dated November 25, also from somewhere in Rhode Island. In the November 22 letter, Whitefield stated that, "I shall therefore stay, God willing, till Monday, and then set out to Connecticut in my way to New York."[18] Since the November 22 letter says he will depart for Connecticut on the next Monday, and the November 25 letter still has him in Rhode Island, that means Whitefield departed Rhode Island and entered Connecticut on or after November 26, 1754. There are various details about Whitefield's 1754 visit to Connecticut. One account remarked about the religious upheavals of the 1740s, and how capable Connecticut clergymen were able to encourage and sustain the awakening for decades in isolated areas throughout the colony. These ministers labored both within and outside their parishes to correct excesses and to promote revival. By the time of Whitefield's second visit to Connecticut, the larger momentum of the 1740s awakening had passed. This account states of his 1754 visit, "Whitefield made one rapid tour across the state from Springfield [Massachusetts] by Hartford and New Haven to New York."[19] One stop on this "rapid tour" across Connecticut in 1754 was in Norwich.

The thriving city of Norwich was an inland port, connected to the ocean by the deep and wide Thames River. Rev. Benjamin Lord was the senior minister, having arrived in Norwich in 1717. A Yale College graduate in 1715, "Mr. Lord merited the praise accorded to him, of being a Repairer of breaches and a Restorer of paths to dwell in. For twenty-seven years after his settlement, the pastor, the church and congregation acted harmoniously together, like brethren in unity."[20] But after the "twenty-seven years after his settlement," in 1744, Norwich was torn apart by excesses related to the Great Awakening. The community fragmented, and five rival and antagonistic churches were formed in the late 1740s and early 1750s. This was the community Whitefield visited briefly in 1754. One report stated:

> In 1748, it was voted to build a fourth church, which was not, however, begun until 1753. In 1752 . . . the frame of the fourth meeting house was built, the bell hung, and the clock set in its place, but a sufficient sum not having been raised to complete it, it remained in an unfinished state for several years. It was not completed until 1770. It is said that the Rev. Mr. Whitefield preached in this church, while in its unfinished condition, [1754] and fifteen years after, when he again came to Norwich, [1770] it was still unaltered. He publicly reproved the congregation for their neglect, and efforts were made to complete the work.[21]

In this Congregational Church community, Church of England sympathizers (Episcopalians) began meeting informally in Norwich in 1738. An Episcopal Church was formed here in 1747 in the Bean Hill community. In 1758 they officially organized as a church. George Whitefield was ordained by the Church of England, and might naturally have been welcome at this fledgling Episcopal Church on his 1754 visit. But he was not. The group met in what is now called the Edwin Gookin House in Norwich.[22] Apparently, Whitefield's message and his itinerant methodology was not acceptable to this group.

Another place we know Whitefield preached in Connecticut in 1754 was in Hartford. By the time of his 1754 Connecticut visit, Hartford was a major Connecticut city and shared duties as the colonial capital. The

---

18 George Whitefield, *Works,* Vol. III, *p. 109.*
19 William L. Kingsley, *Contributions to the Ecclesiastical History of Connecticut,* (New Haven, CT: William L. Kingsley, Publisher, 1861), p. 199.
20 Frances M. Caulkins, *History of Norwich, Connecticut . . . ,* (Hartford, CT: Press of Case, Lockwood & Brainard, 1873), p. 288.
21 Mary E. Perkins, *Old Houses of the Ancient Town of Norwich, 1660-1800,* (Norwich, CT: Press of the Bulletin Company, 1895), p. 353.
22 "Parish History," Christ Episcopal Church, Norwich, CT, www.cecnorwich.org/parish-history.html.

The Edmund Gookin House was built in 1724. It was the location for the first Church of England religious services in Norwich, Connecticut. In 1754, George Whitefield was not welcomed here to address this fledgling group. Photograph by Ken Lawson.

colonial legislative building was a wooden, seventy-foot long rectangular structure, two stories high with plenty of windows for fresh air and light. Hartford was a key location for mail, educational, governmental, and commercial activities. The community abounded with inns and taverns for transient political officials, merchants, farmers, and mariners. The riverfront thrived in warmer weather, as traders, soldiers, and travelers hovered around the warehouses, shops, and storefronts. Puritanism was fading as Hartford developed into a progressive and eclectic community. Two competing Congregational churches engaged the religious life of the people. A wealthy merchant and political class emerged in Hartford, with a taste for European luxuries. Young people were educated either at local schoolhouses, or under tutoring from a minister, or in a Free School (later called a Grammar School or a Latin School) in Hartford. Trade goods were bought and sold along the Connecticut River, connecting Hartford to the rest of the world. A rise in crime created the need for a new prison in 1753.[23]

On December 2, 1754 Whitefield preached in the newly constructed Second Congregational Church in Hartford. This meeting house was slow to be built, as the proper location for the building was contested. The structure was built downtown, and was sixty-six-feet long, forty-six-feet wide, with a sixteen-feet tall bell tower. The pulpit was on the west side. Final construction of the meeting house was not complete until early January, but the arrival of Whitefield in Hartford in late December was an event to be celebrated. Whitefield preached the first sermon in the almost completed church building. In speaking of the Second Congregational Church meeting house nearing completion, "It was occupied by the congregation January 5, 1755, but on December 2nd, Rev. George Whitefield preached in it the first sermon."[24] At this building dedication, the minister of the Second Congregational Church of Christ in Hartford was Rev. Elnathan Whitman.

The Second Congregational Church in Hartford dates to 1670. Elnathan Whitman served there as pastor from 1732 to 1777. A historical summary of the church stated of Whitman, "he was a preacher in the

---

23 William DeLoss Love, *The Colonial History of Hartford*, (Hartford, CT: Centinel Press, 1974), pp. 221-307.
24 Ibid., p. 212.

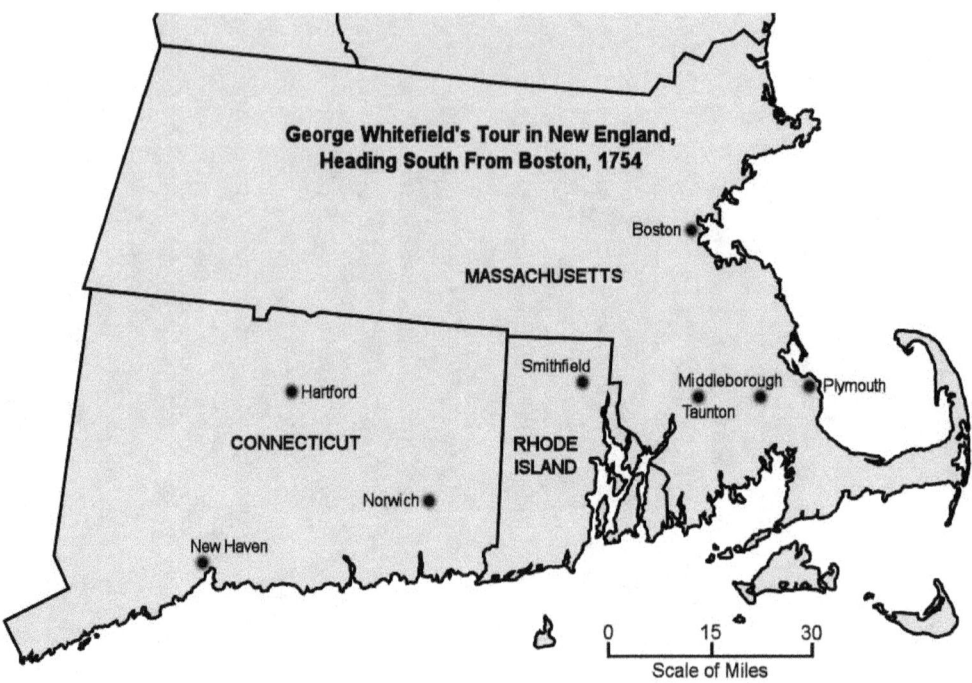

Great Awakening, that period of tremendous religious revival, and who saw our second meeting house built in 1754."[25] Whitman supported Whitefield when he came through the Hartford area in October 1740. As a 1726 Yale graduate, and a tutor at Yale College, Whitman was an established minister and a significant figure in Hartford. He stood for the historic Puritan values in an increasingly diverse and secular community. While church division and ecclesiastical controversy ripped through mid-eighteenth-century Connecticut, Whitman was a steady, reasonable voice for balanced revival. An extended account from the official history of the Second Congregational Church in Hartford mentions the disruptions from the awakening, the ministry of Whitefield, and the balanced approach taken by their New Light minister, Elnathan Whitman.

> If the Old Light in Connecticut had, at first, welcomed instead of opposing the great awakening which roused the churches from their empty covenant-ownings and drowsy and dreadful formalities, long before Whitefield came among them; if they had owned and made a place for emotion and enthusiasm and lay-preaching in religion; if their disposition, as well as their understanding, had not been in obstinate errors to the whole spiritual movement, the gracious work might have been guided and controlled in more orderly ways. If, when Whitefield first came through this colony, [in 1740] stirring the popular heart and conscience by his fervid eloquence, they had been content to overlook some things in so eminent an apostle, and had stood together with . . . Whitman . . . and others in furthering and guiding the work to which he gave such tremendous impulse, fanaticism would have had slight footing, enthusiasm would not have mounted to giddiness, errors and disorders might have been few and evanescent, and the "glorious work of God" would have been far more extensive and beneficent than it was.[26]

---

25 "The History of Your Congregation," *History of Second Congregational Church, Hartford, Connecticut*, http://www.southchurchhartford.org/ourhistory/history/default.html.
26 Edwin P. Parker, *History of the Second Congregational Church in Hartford,* pp. 118-119.

In his first Connecticut visit in 1740, Whitefield did not preach in Hartford, although he does mention that he passed through Hartford on October 22. At that time, he preached to large crowds at adjoining towns to Hartford, namely Windsor to the north and Wethersfield to the south. Now, in 1754, Whitefield stopped to preach in Hartford for his longtime supporter, Rev. Elnathan Whitman of the Second or South Congregational Church. An eyewitness to this event was Hartford resident Thomas Seymour, who recorded the following account in his memorandum book.

> Be it remembered.—The new meeting-house built in the South (Congregational) Society, in the town of Hartford, was begun in the fore part of the year of our Lord, 1752, was three years in building, and finished about the later end of the year 1754. And the Rev. and Pious George Whitefield (providentially here) preached the first sermon that was ever preached in it, and this was on Monday, the 2nd day of December, Anno Dom., 1754—a good omen for a new meeting-house.[27]

There are very few specifics related to Whitefield's 1754 tour through Connecticut. However, the towns of "Hartford and New Haven" are specifically mentioned as places Whitefield preached in his 1754 visit.[28] Hartford was already addressed above. Now his ministry in New Haven will be examined.

The last time Whitefield was in New Haven, in the spring of 1745, he was publicly opposed by Rev. Thomas Clapp of Yale College. But much had changed in New Haven between 1745 and 1754. As the rector or president of Yale College, Thomas Clapp was a conservative, orthodox Calvinist. Clapp was in full keeping with the Puritan founding fathers of Connecticut. He graduated from Harvard College in 1722, and served as a Congregational minister in Connecticut before his election to be the rector of Yale. Clap was known to be blunt, difficult, and confrontative. The trustees at Yale believed that Clapp's sternness would help hinder the fledgling Arminianism at Yale. He served as president of Yale from 1740 to 1766, a period that was known for both controversies and the growth of the college.[29]

Initially, Clapp simply could not accept itinerant preachers like Whitefield upsetting the order and discipline of Yale College. A few years before Whitefield's 1754 visit to New Haven, Thomas Clapp was embroiled in controversies. For example, in 1746, Clapp expelled students from Yale for their role in establishing a new, separate Congregational Church in New Haven. In 1747, Yale held a lottery, a scandalous act for historic Puritans, in order to raised money for a new building on the Yale campus. The beginning of Episcopal Church services in 1752 disrupted the traditional Puritan idealism of New Haven, so much so, that Clapp feared potential students would no longer study at Yale but would choose to study instead at Princeton or Harvard. It appears that Thomas Clapp was neither an Old Light nor a New Light. His theology was distinctly New Light, but he sided with the Old Lights in opposition to the disorderliness resulting from roving itinerant preachers. In 1755, Clapp appointed a New Light, Rev. Naphtali Daggett, as Yale's first professor of divinity. Unable to get along with both the Congregational and Episcopal clergy in New Haven, Clapp founded the Yale Campus Church in 1757.[30]

Amid this religious confusion and contention in New Haven, Whitefield arrived in 1754. One account succinctly stated, "1754. Dec. 3-5. Whitefield's . . . visit to Yale."[31] As rector or president of Yale College, Thomas Clapp changed his mind about opposing Whitefield. There are several reasons for this dramatic

---

27 Ibid., p. 119.
28 William L. Kingsley, *Contributions to the Ecclesiastical History of Connecticut,* p. 199.
29 William B. Sprague, *Annals of the American Pulpit: Trinitarian Congregational,* (New York: Robert Carter & Brothers, Publishers, 1857), vol. I., pp. 343-349.
30 Roberta B. Mouheb, *Yale Under God: Roots and Fruits,* (Maitland, FL Xulon Press, 2012), pp.56-57
31 James B. Reynolds, editor. *Two Centuries of Christian Activity at Yale,* (New York: G.P. Putnam's Sons, 1901), vol. 70, p. 311.

change, as Clapp previously led the charge against Whitefield in both preaching and publishing against the itinerant evangelist.

Clapp changed his view on Whitefield because, first, he realized that he needed Whitefield's support. The student body of Yale clamored to hear Whitefield, and to oppose the students while the theological climate of the college was already delicate, would have been suicidal for Clapp. Second, Clapp now endorsed Whitefield because the intense fervor and disruptions of the awakening had subsided. The Old Lights and the New Lights were in two distinct and recognizable camps, and Clapp and Whitefield were basically in the same New Light camp. Third, the Yale students that Clapp had expelled for supporting revival meetings and itinerant preaching, such as John Cleveland and his brother Ebenezer, had become successful, orthodox Congregational ministers. This reflected poorly on Clapp. Fourth, Clapp had the time to thoroughly study the prior claims of Whitefield, that many clergymen in New England were unconverted ministers. In the 1740s, this greatly offended Thomas Clapp. But by Whitefield's 1754 visit to Yale, Clapp understood that Whitefield was mostly correct, as the Old Lights from the 1740s became in many cases Arminians, Episcopalians, Unitarians, Universalists, or Deists.[32] This greatly disturbed the strict Calvinism of Clapp.

Whitefield's early December, 1754 ministry in New Haven was opposed by Rev. Joseph Noyes of the First Congregational Church. Noyes was, like Thomas Clapp, an opinionated and difficult man. Noyes was the minister at the church from 1716 to 1761. As a confirmed Old Light clergyman, Noyes resisted the awakening in New Haven, and in particular opposed Whitefield. Church records from the First Congregational Church in New Haven make this apparent. While New Light churches experienced significant growth in members from revivals, Noyes' church did not. For example, in 1739 and 1740, before the impact of Whitefield was felt in New Haven, the First Church averaged about twelve new members annually. After Whitefield departed New Haven, church memberships for 1741 spiked at twenty-eight new members, the largest annual spike in the old church records. This was a temporary manifestation of anti-Whitefield sentiment in New Haven. After that initial surge, church memberships plummeted. From 1742 to 1754, new church memberships averaged just over four people annually.

When Whitefield arrived in New Haven in 1754, the pulpit of the First Congregational Church was closed to him. Significantly, new church memberships for the church in 1755, 1756, and 1757, in the aftermath of Noyes rejecting Whitefield, were zero, two, and three respectively.[33] When we realize that new church members were gained both from children being born and baptized, and from adults making a commitment to the church, we see that the First Congregational Church in New Haven greatly stagnated from its refusal to embrace the revival and from their rejection of Whitefield.

However, another church in New Haven eagerly welcomed Whitefield in 1754. In 1742, in the aftermath of Whitefield's 1740 tour through Connecticut, a separatist group withdrew from Rev. Joseph Noyes and the First Congregational Church in New Haven. These forty-three separatists were confirmed New Lights. They eagerly supported Whitefield. This independent church was not able to call a pastor until Rev. Samuel Bird arrived in 1751. The church was named the White Haven Society, which, after several mergers and name changes in the nineteenth century, today is known as the First Church of Christ in New Haven.

Samuel Bird served this church, the White Haven Society, from 1751 to his dismissal from poor health, in 1768. Bird was a Harvard College student set to graduate in 1744, but his New Light ideas were not welcomed on the campus. He was denied graduation due to his criticism of school authorities, and for his

---

32 William W. Sweet, *Religion in Colonial America,* (New York: Charles Scribner's Sons, 1942), pp. 312-313. Williston Walker, *A History of the Congregational Churches in the United States,* (New York: Charles Scribner's Sons, 1916), pp. 267-279. Sydney E. Ahlstrom, *A Religious History of the American People,* (New Haven, CT:Yale University Press, 1972), pp. 349-353, 356-359, 388-397.

33 Franklin B. Dexter, *Historical Catalogue of the Members of the First Church of Christ in New Haven, Connecticut (Center Church), 1639-1914,* (New Haven, CT: 1914), pp. 80-91.

"religious enthusiasm." He served churches in Massachusetts and New Hampshire before installed as pastor at the church at New Haven in 1751.[34] Details about the founding of the church, and the calling of Bird as the first minister, are as follows:

> The occasion of the establishment of this church was the difficulties which grew out of the religious excitement in the time of Whitefield, or, to write more accurately, out of the sad degeneracy in religious doctrine and feeling which had been long increasing in New England. In May, 1742, forty-three persons, who had become dissatisfied with the preaching of Rev. Joseph Noyes, pastor of the First Church in New Haven, were formed into a distinct church. This step drew down upon them the indignation of the "Old Lights," and the persecuting hand of the legislature. Many and sharp were the trials which the seceded underwent. It was not until October, 1751, that their first pastor, Rev. Samuel Bird, was installed. In the year 1758, the legislature effected an amicable division of the Society, designating Mr. Noyes' adherents as the "First Society," and Mr. Bird's as the "White Haven Society." Mr. Bird was dismissed in 1768, on account of ill health.[35]

At Yale College, the student body in the early 1750s was spiritually stagnant. The controversies of the previous decade had created a religious numbness or indifference. An apathetic attitude prevailed on campus. One account of the student body at Yale stated:

> Little changed in the student's spiritual lives in the following years until 1753, when Rector Clapp did an about-face. During the years following the expulsion of the Cleveland brothers, a complete revolution had gradually taken place in his religious views and in his attitude toward New Light preaching. He had studied the matter thoroughly, had doubtless observed the faithful work of the New Light clergyman in the Separatist Church in New Haven, and had become convinced of his sincerity. When George Whitefield returned to New Haven for the third time in December 1754 it is recorded that in the evening he made a visit to the Yale president, who "treated him much like a gentleman."[36]

When Whitefield visited Yale College at New Haven, one author stated that the date was "December 1754" but the exact date is unclear,[37] although an early December 1754 date fits well with Whitefield's chronology.

Previously, Whitefield had had a tumultuous relationship with Yale College. In late October 1740, he was welcomed to Yale by the college president, Rev. Thomas Clapp. Whitefield preached to thousands in New Haven, both on the Yale campus and in the town. Initially, all appeared well. But later, Whitefield wrote some unflattering things about the college, and the students, zealous to follow Whitefield's example, began itinerant preaching to the detriment of their studies. Soon disorders abounded on the Yale campus. In February 1745, Yale printed an influential fourteen-page pamphlet against Whitefield and the disorders of the awakening. This critique of Whitefield greatly strengthened his opponents, so much so, that in his extensive 1744-1745 travels in New England, Whitefield did not preach at Yale College, but did preach outside to a huge crowd in New Haven. In his 1747 New England tour, Whitefield bypassed New Haven. But in early December 1754, Whitefield again returned to New Haven and Yale.

Between Whitefield's 1745 and 1754 visits to New Haven, much had changed. A new ministerial school in Princeton, New Jersey began as a direct rival to Yale. President Thomas Clapp appears to have had a genuine

---

34 "Bird, Rev. Samuel," *Obituary Records Online*, http://pa-roots.org/data/read/php?3620,820439.
35 Samuel H. Riddel, *The American Quarterly Register*, (Boston, MA: Press of T.R. Marvin, 1843), vol. xv, pp. 198-199.
36 Roberta B. Mouheb, *Yale Under God*, p. 57.
37 Ibid.

change of mind related to Whitefield and the awakening. And the student population at Yale was growing from young men converted in revivals, who sought New Light teaching and formal ministerial training.

As a direct result of the need for educated New Light ministers, the College of New Jersey (later Princeton College) was founded in 1746. For the first fifty years of the school, the students and faculty were centered on Nassau Hall, a large and beautiful stone building still very much used by Princeton University today. Men converted in the awakening sought ministerial training, but since Harvard and Yale came out against Whitefield, Princeton would be the new training center for New Light clergymen. Princeton had very respectable Presbyterian leaders as faculty, drawing Presbyterian and Congregational students from throughout many of the thirteen colonies. The rise of Princeton certainly gave President Thomas Clapp at Yale some concern. Because of his anti-revival stance, Clapp stood to lose potential students to Princeton. Certainly, this was a concern, but Clapp was more than pragmatic. He appears to have had a genuinely change of mind regarding Whitefield and the awakening.[38]

The influx of students at Yale in the late 1740s and early 1750s was a result of young men converted and called into the gospel ministry as a result of the Great Awakening. Clapp sought to accommodate these students by instituting gradual changes in the administration and theology of the college.

In 1745 he created a new college charter, approved by the trustees that granted him as president more autonomy and allowed him the power to make administrative changes at Yale independent of the Connecticut courts.[39] Then he began planning and raising funds for the construction of a new, larger building to better house the college, plans that saw the building completed in 1752. In 1746 Clapp sought to create a new position at Yale dedicated to teaching orthodox Christian doctrine, a professorship of divinity. The first professor of divinity, Rev. Naphtali Daggett, was a New Light minister.[40] In 1753, Clapp and the fellows of the college passed some very conservative resolutions reinforcing their commitment to the veracity of the Bible, restating their allegiance to the Westminster Confession, and the need to endorse these beliefs by all those teaching at Yale College.[41] Naphtali Daggett was a key person in this process. Also in 1753, Clapp created a chapel on the Yale campus to encourage New Light preachers. Clearly, Thomas Clapp and the leadership at Yale evaluated the growing theological drift at Yale and had sought to restate traditional Protestant orthodoxy.

It was becoming apparent that many Old Light ministers who opposed Whitefield and the revival did so for pragmatic as well as theological reasons. Whitefield's insistence on the authority of the Bible and the need for the new birth for salvation did not resonate well with the newer, liberal thinking sweeping through parts of New England. Clapp was not impressed with this abandonment of historic orthodoxy. Therefore in 1754, when Whitefield arrived in New Haven, he was welcomed by Thomas Clapp at Yale.

The late November-early December 1754 meeting between Clapp and Whitefield at Yale must have been initially awkward. Clapp was an intellectual, a renowned scholar and the president of a very successful college. Clapp was fifty-one years old when he met Whitefield in their face-to-face reconciliation meeting. Whitefield was a forty-year-old itinerant preacher, not in the best of health, gaining weight and seemingly wearing out. Yale College was prospering, and the antagonist Whitefield was now an ally, perhaps even a friend to Clapp. The antagonism which resulted from disputes and rivalries of the Great Awakening of the 1740s had passed. President Clapp had a favorable attitude toward Whitefield and the two apparently reconciled their differences.[42]

---

38   "Thomas Clapp," *Concise Dictionary of Christianity in America*, (Downers Grove, IL: InterVarsity Press, 1995), p. 85.
39   James L. Kingsley, *A Sketch of the History of Yale College in Connecticut*, (Boston, MA: Printed by Perkins, Marvin & Co., 1835), p. 12.
40   James B. Reynolds, Samuel H. Fisher, Henry B. Wright, *Two Centuries of Christian Activity at Yale*, pp. 32-33.
41   James L. Kingsley, *A Sketch of the History of Yale College in Connecticut*, pp. 13-15.
42   James B. Reynolds, Samuel H. Fisher, Henry B. Wright, *Two Centuries of Christian Activity at Yale*, p. 31.

A contemporary photograph of Connecticut Hall, on the campus of Yale University. The building was constructed 1750-1752 and was visited by Whitefield on his 1754 tour to New Haven. This is the only colonial era structure still standing on the Yale campus. Photograph by Ken Lawson.

A farm woman in North Haven observed Whitefield's 1754 visit to nearby New Haven. Mrs. Hannah Heaton was a typical eighteenth-century woman in Connecticut. Her life centered on her family and the farm. What made her distinct was her active evangelical faith. While not supported in her faith by her husband and sons, she nevertheless was an outspoken New Light. She had separated from the North Haven Congregational Church and joined a separatist or New Light group. She was in New Haven when Whitefield came in 1740 and in 1745, and she happily anticipated the itinerant evangelist when he arrived again in 1754. In her *Diary*, Heaton eagerly expected Whitefield's next visit. A few days before he arrived, she dreamed that he came to New Haven to speak directly to her. Two days before he arrived, copies Whitefield's sermons were distributed throughout the town. When passages from his sermons were read to her, she interpreted that as the fulfillment of her dream. Heaton wrote that not all in New Haven were pleased that Whitefield was coming to town. Apparently, some opposed him, some supported him, and most ignored him.[43]

In early December 1754, Whitefield departed New Haven on his way to New York. He was in Connecticut for about one week. This was a rapid trip, and only three preaching locations are known in the Connecticut Colony—Norwich, Hartford, and New Haven. As previously stated, Whitefield's correspondence at this time was erratic. A newspaper notice stated that Whitefield arrived in Philadelphia on December 18.[44] On December 27, 1754, Whitefield wrote a letter from Bohemia, Maryland. In this letter he summarized his previous month's ministry in the northern colonies. He wrote,

> I have just now taken leave of the northern provinces, [New England, New York, New Jersey, and Pennsylvania] where I have been traveling and preaching for near these five months. I suppose in all, I may have rode near two thousand miles, and preached about two hundred and thirty times; but to how many thousands of souls cannot be well told. Oh what days of the Son of Man have I seen! God be merciful to me an ungrateful sinner! I am now forty years of age,

---

43 Hannah Heaton, *The World of Hannah Heaton*, Barbara E. Lacey, editor. (1793: reprinted by Northern Illinois Press, 2003), p. 68.
44 *New York Mercury (New York City)*, December 23, 1754, p. 3.

and would business permit, would gladly spend the day in retirement and deep humiliation before that Jesus for whom I have done so little, notwithstanding he hath done and suffered so much for me. Well! To-morrow, O blessed Jesus, through thy divine assistance, will I begin, and travel for thee again.[45]

---

45 George Whitefield, *The Works of George Whitefield: Letters 1753-1770*, p. 111.

CHAPTER 31
WHITEFIELD'S LIFE AND MINISTRY

1754-1763

AFTER LEAVING NEW ENGLAND IN December 1754, Whitefield headed south, destined for Georgia. He preached in Maryland through December, Virginia in January, spending the remainder of the winter in Bethesda, Georgia. On March 3, Whitefield wrote from Charleston, South Carolina, expecting a ship soon that would take him to England. At that time, he wrote of the return of his illness and his physical limitations. A few weeks later he was still waiting for his trans-Atlantic passage, writing on March 17 about his beloved Bethesda orphans and his expectation that a ship would depart for England in the coming week.[1] On March 27, 1755, Whitefield brought his visit to America to a close and set sail for England.

The years between Whitefield's fifth and sixth visits to America found him pastoring enormous congregations and continuing his itinerant ministry. He frequently left his unofficial home-base in London to evangelize throughout England, Ireland, and Scotland. During these years he experienced the most severe and ongoing persecution in his career. Violent opposition caused important changes that effected the rest of his days and contributed significantly to his already weak health and eventually his early death.[2]

In the 1750s-1760s, the people Whitefield ministered to, throughout the British Isles, were a people at war with France. They were eager to speculate over the latest philosophical and academic subjects, and were developing a taste for culture that had little to do with the English Puritanism of a hundred years earlier. British soldiers and sailors fought the French around the world, in such places as Canada, the Mediterranean, the West Indies, the American Colonies, and even in the South Pacific. This worldwide hostility did not cease until the signing of the Peace of Paris in 1763.

Much of Great Britain paid close attention to the King's attempt to develop a British Colony in India. News of one hundred and twenty British soldiers being jailed and later dying in India in 1756, labeled the area "The Black Hole of Calcutta." Others with more philosophical interests could study Jonathan Edward's work on *Careful and Strict Inquiry into the Modern Prevailing Notions of Freedom of Will* (1756) or his *Christian Doctrine of Original Sin Defended* (1758). Those with more liberal tendencies could read works by the German Immanuel Kant, who rose to prominence after 1755, or the Frenchman Voltaire, who wrote a *Treatise on Tolerance* in 1763, and compiled a *Philosophical Dictionary* in 1764.

While Mozart toured Europe as a six-year-old musical prodigy, and major advances were made in atmospheric science, astronomy, and human anatomy, Whitefield continued to preach the same simple message

---

1 George Whitefield, *Works of George Whitefield*, (1771: reprinted by Quinta Press, Shropshire, England, 2000), vol. III, pp. 116-117.
2 Arnold Dallimore, *George Whitefield: The Life and Times of the Great Evangelist of the Eighteenth Century Revival*, (Carlisle, PA: Banner of Truth Trust, 1980), vol. II, p. 383. Whitefield received various death threats and was assaulted on several occasions. For details, see E.A. Johnston, *George Whitefield: A Definitive Biography*, (United Kingdom: Stoke-on-Trent, 2008), Vol. II, pp. 302, 307-308, 314-315, 321-323.

of years past: the total depravity of the human heart, man's helplessness to save himself, and the absolute necessity of the new birth to receive forgiveness of sins. Much of the British Isles were opposed, sometimes violently, to Whitefield's old-fashioned gospel message.

The Long Acre Chapel, at the edge of London's theater district, was the site of much resistance to Whitefield's ministry. Opponents of his message and methods went to great lengths to hinder his ministry, as he explained in correspondence to the Bishop of London:

> Indeed, my Lord, it is more than noise. It deserves no milder name than premeditated rioting. Drummers, soldiers, and many of the baser sort, have been lured by subscription . . . A copper furnace, bells, drums, clappers, marrow bones and cleavers and such like instruments of reformation, have been provided for and made use of by them, from the moment I have begun preaching to the end of my sermon.
>
> By these horrid noises, many women have been almost frightened to death, and mobbers encouraged thereby to come and riot at the chapel door during the time of divine service, and then insult and abuse me and the congregation after it hath been over.
>
> Not content with this, the chapel windows, while I have been preaching, have repeatedly been broken by large stones of almost a pound weight (some now lying by me) which though leveled at, providentially missed me, but at the same time wounded some of my hearers . . .[3]

Dublin, Ireland, was the scene of a vicious mob attack, by which Whitefield was nearly murdered in broad daylight. After three weeks of ministry to the largely Roman Catholic citizens of Dublin, the following incident occurred:

> Dublin, July 9, 1757
> You have heard of my being in Ireland and of my preaching daily to large and very affected auditories . . . All being over, I thought to return home the way I came; but to my great surprise, access was denied, so that I had to go near half a mile from one end of the green to the other, through hundreds and hundreds of Papists and others.
>
> Finding me unattended, (for a soldier and four Methodist preachers who came with me, had forsook me and fled) I was left to their mercy; but their mercy, as you may easily guess, was perfect cruelty.
>
> Vollies of hard stones came from all quarters, and every step I took a fresh stone struck, and made me reel backwards and forwards, till I was almost breathless, and all over a gore of blood . . . .
>
> But providentially, a minister's house lay next door to the green; with great difficulty I staggered to the door, which was kindly opened to, and shut upon, me . . . .
>
> For a while I continued speechless, panting for and expecting every breath to be my last . . . At length a carpenter, one of the friends that came in, offered me his wig and coat, that I might go off in disguise. I accepted of and put them on, but was soon ashamed of not trusting my Master . . .

---

3   George Whitefield, *Works of George Whitefield*, vol. III, pp 168-169.

I determined to go out . . . immediately deliverance came. A Methodist preacher, with two friends, brought a coach; I leaped into it, and rid in Gospel triumph through the oaths, curses and imprecations of whole streets of Papists unhurt, though threatened every step of the ground.[4]

These examples of physical persecution against Whitefield severely affected his health and limited his ability to travel. Yet demands for his sermons, journals, and speaking requests by correspondence continued to increase. He faced the problem of how to reach an ever-expanding audience, many of whom were strangers who he could not personally meet. To fund and promote his religious enterprises, Whitefield developed a reliable system of contacts through which he circulated information on the success of local revivals, solicited funds for various philanthropic adventures, and encouraged others in the practice of revival preaching.[5]

The opposition Whitefield experienced by some could not overshadow his popularity with others. Thousands met at all times of the day to hear him preach in London. In 1756, he had constructed a second meeting house in London, the Tottenham Court Chapel, which became the largest non-Conformist church in the world at that time.[6] The building was enlarged in 1759. Mrs. Elizabeth Whitefield was buried there. When George Whitefield died in America in 1770, his funeral service was preached by John Wesley at this location.

Whitefield's use of the printed page was revolutionary. He sought and found ways to spread news of revivals throughout the English-speaking world. Though often in poor health and occasionally the object of violent attacks, he was able to continue to spread both his message and his influence. Revivalists in America and the British Isles swapped accounts of awakenings to provide encouragement and hope for further successes. Improvements in shipping enabled communication to become more reliable, and allowed news of a particular revival to spread across the Atlantic in a few weeks. As one author stated:

> Ministers used trans-Atlantic contacts for the discussion of theological questions, the nature of piety, and the practice of revivalism . . . [A] real significance of the mid-eighteenth-century revivals was . . . their combination of traditional Puritan practices with fresh evangelical techniques and attitudes.[7]

Whitefield used the ever-expanding print trade in both England and America to his advantage. While printers and booksellers were looking to make money, Whitefield's concern was for disseminating the gospel beyond the reach of his voice. Not only did he continually supervise the publication of his sermons, Whitefield also published evangelical literature other than his own. For example, in 1755 he published *The Believer's Knowledge of a Living Redeemer* by one of his itinerant associates, Thomas Adams. He also republished a sermon by the old Puritan John Foxe, called *A Sermon of Christ Crucified*. Further, in 1755 Whitefield edited as well as published a revival handbook, called *A Communion Mornings Companion*, for use at the celebration of the Lord's Supper.[8]

With the avid support of Benjamin Franklin in Philadelphia, Whitefield and his associates developed a successful method of promoting revival through published testimonials, endorsements, and advertisements for the latest collections of sermons.[9] Further, religious debates were recorded in newspapers rather than confined to ministers' meetings. Whitefield was able, through personal visits and the use of the printed

---

4   Ibid., pp. 207-209.
5   Frank Lambert, *"Pedlar in Divinity"- George Whitefield and the Trans-Atlantic Revivals, 1737-1770*, (Princeton, NJ: Princeton University Press, 1994).
6   Michael A.G. Haykin, *George Whitefield*, (Grand Rapids, MI: EP Books, 2014), 46
7   Susan O'Brien, "A Trans-Atlantic Community of Saints: The Great Awakening and the First Evangelical Network," *The American Historical Review*, (October 1986), pp. 813-815.
8   Frank Lambert, "Pedlar in Divinity," p. 89.
9   Peter C. Hoffer, *When Ben Franklin Met the Reverend Whitefield: Enlightenment, Revival, and the Power of the Printed Word*, (Baltimore, MD: Johns Hopkins University Press, 2011). Randy Petersen, *The Printer and the Preacher: Ben Franklin, George Whitefield, and the Surprising Friendship that Invented America*, (Nashville, TN: Thomas Nelson Publisher, 2015).

page, to construct and hold together a transatlantic revival network which lasted through all his adult life. With his vigorous use of the press, Whitefield helped to create a new public sphere of religion that extended throughout the American Colonies and beyond. By 1760, Whitefield managed a network of book distributors and publishers, by which he coordinated and promoted revival on both sides of the Atlantic.

Through Whitefield's extensive preaching and publishing ventures, it became abundantly clear that spreading and promoting revival was his primary emphasis. By the 1760s, even his harshest critics no longer accused him of attempting to exalt himself or dominate an evangelical empire. Rather, in the process of promoting revival, Whitefield increasingly deferred his own place of seniority to John Wesley.

A well published theological debate between Whitefield and Wesley was prominent in the 1740s. By the late 1750s, however, both parties agreed to disagree and remained at peace for the sake of the ongoing revival movements. After the 1750s, "As opportunity permitted, Whitefield rendered to Wesley's societies and congregations throughout the Kingdom, an amount of valuable service, the results of which cannot now be rightly estimated."[10] Indeed, without Whitefield's leadership, advice, and cooperative spirit, John Wesley's life and ministry may not have had the prominence that his reputation now enjoys. Wesley's dependence on Whitefield lasted for decades.[11] Whitefield tried to convince evangelicals to concentrate on the gospel truths that all major Protestant denominations agreed with, and to exercise tolerance in areas of disagreement. Only through Whitefield's tireless labors were his own Calvinistic followers able to live in peace with Wesley's Arminian ideals. Charles Wesley, writing in October 1756, declared:

> I rejoiced to hear of the great good Mr. Whitefield has done in our Societies. He preached everywhere as universally as my brother. He warned them everywhere against apostasy, and strongly insisted on the need for holiness after justification . . . He beat down the separating spirit, highly commended the prayers and services of our church, charged our people to meet their bands and classes constantly, and never to leave the Methodists . . . In a word: he did his utmost to strengthen our hands, and deserves the thanks of all the churches, for his abundant labor of love.[12]

Whitefield's followers were not always as gracious to Wesley as he was himself. Both Whitefield and his Calvinist disciples knew Wesley was a follower, "certainly a compulsive borrower of other people's ideas," and that "Wesley was only the coordinator and cannibalizer of a wide range of renewal groups under local leaders."[13] Yet Whitefield remained a supporter of Wesley, receiving criticism from all sides. Knowing that his followers disliked Wesley, Whitefield told his friends of his own funeral arrangements in the following manner:

> I have prepared a vault in this (Tottenham Court Road) chapel, where I intend to be buried, and Messrs. John and Charles Wesley shall also be buried there. We will all be together. You will not let them enter your chapel while they are alive. They can do no harm to you when they are dead.[14]

Whitefield's name recognition in London, around 1760, was sensational. The entire city knew of his preaching throughout the British Isles. Those who rejected Whitefield's message, however, were also outspoken in their criticism. On one hand, Whitefield became the joke of the populace, often ridiculed in comic theater productions and victimized by an arrogant burlesque of his character. On the other hand, Whitefield preached in private homes of nobility, and was appreciated by much of the English aristocracy.

---

10 Luke Tyerman, *The Life and Times of the Rev. George Whitefield*, (New York: Anson D.F. Randolph & Company, 1877), vol. II, p. 246.
11 For a detailed study see Kenneth E. Lawson, "Who Founded Methodism? Wesley's Dependence upon Whitefield in the Eighteenth Century English Revival," *Reformation and Revival*, (Summer 1995), pp. 37-55.
12 Arnold Dallimore, *George Whitefield*, vol. II, p. 352.
13 Henry O. Rack, "Religious Societies and the Origins of Methodism," *Journal of Ecclesiastical History*, (October 1987), p. 584.
14 Arnold Dallimore, *George Whitefield*, vol. II, p. 387.

In 1761 the Countess of Huntington built a chapel for Whitefield in London, which she paid for by selling some of her jewels.[15]

Politically, in 1760 Great Britain transitioned from King George II to King George III. The devastating Seven Years War, from 1756 to 1763 caused at least 20,000 British deaths and greatly increased the national debt. At age twenty-two, the new King George III oversaw the expansion of English rule in India and the extension of British commerce around the world. In 1761, the Bridgewater Canal was dug between the coal mines of Worsley and the textile industrial center of Manchester, the first canal constructed not following a natural waterway. History has labeled King George III a good man, perhaps overwhelmed by the numerous disruptions of his era. Under his rule it was said that the sun never set on the British Empire. As with his predecessor, King George III was unaffected by the Whitefield and Wesley evangelicalism that had spread in England.

Through most of 1761 and 1762, Whitefield's already unstable health failed him. For twelve months he was nearly an invalid, confined to bed or to his personal quarters, and he rarely preached. As he convalesced, Whitefield longed to return to the Bethesda orphanage and tour the American Colonies once again with the gospel message.

In 1763, the Seven Years' War, known in America as the French and Indian War, came to an end, making ocean passage safer. Temporarily enjoying better health, Whitefield seized this opportunity, preaching a farewell sermon to his London congregation in February 1763. After a brief preaching tour through Scotland, Whitefield set sail to America that summer.

---

15   Helen C. Knight, *Lady Huntington and Her Friends; or The Revival of the Work of God in the Days of Wesley, Whitefield . . . and others in the Last Century*, (New York: American Tract Society, 1853), p. 314.

A portrait of George Whitefield, painted in 1760 by Robert White. Collection of Mansfield College, University of Oxford.

Source: www.bbc.co.uk/arts/yourpaintings/paintings/ reverend-george-whitefield-17141770-ma-222616

CHAPTER 32

WHITEFIELD'S TOUR IN SOUTHERN NEW ENGLAND

EARLY 1764

AS WITH MOST OF WHITEFIELD'S other New England tours, his 1764 travels through New England have been neglected by his biographers. Nigel Scotland covers these productive months of ministry in five sentences.[1] Arnold Dallimore covers the same period in a few paragraphs,[2] as does E. A. Johnston.[3] James P. Gledstone overlooks Whitefield's entire 1764 New England ministry, stating that these ministry months were merely "a long delay in the north of the colonies."[4]

As the year 1764 began, Whitefield knew this was the year he would turn fifty years old. For three decades he had abused his body, traveling and preaching in all kinds of weather. His physical constitution was never robust, but at times he appeared healthy and spry. Other times he was laid out in a bed for days or weeks at a time.

In the mid-eighteenth century, the American Colonies were changing. Slavery was becoming an entrenched institution in southern colonies, so much so that Georgia had to outlaw aspects of slavery in 1749. By the 1750s, a Philadelphia inventor and political speculator named Benjamin Franklin was becoming an inter-colonial household name. The French and Indian War lasted from 1754 to 1763, which proved to be a great drain on many of the colonies. In 1754 the Albany Congress met in New York to discuss a unified plan for defense against the French and Indians, the first trans-colonial attempt at a unified government. At the end of the French and Indian War, the colonies rejoiced as King George III addressed the expanded boundaries of Great Britain's possessions in America, now including all of Canada and all lands from the thirteen American Colonies to the Mississippi River. While Whitefield was in New England in 1764, the widely unpopular Sugar Act was passed by the British parliament, to raise revenues from the American colonists as a result of debt from the French and Indian War. Three months later, after Whitefield departed New England, the Currency Act became law, meaning the colonies could no longer print their own money, making dependence on Great Britain even stronger.

It had been twenty-four years since Whitefield first preached in New England in 1740. Many who heard him preach in that earlier time had passed away. An entire generation of New Englanders had been born since the Great Awakening of the early 1740s. Shortly before Whitefield arrived in southern New England in 1764, Connecticut began its first newspaper, the *Connecticut Gazette* out of New Haven. In 1764, Hartford began printing a newspaper, the *Connecticut Courant*. In Rhode Island, the border dispute with Massachusetts was resolved in 1757, with Rhode Island gaining territory. In 1762 Newport had a newspaper, the *Mercury*.

---

1 Nigel Scotland, *George Whitefield: The First Transatlantic Revivalist*, (Oxford, England: Lion Hudson Limited, 2019), p. 187.
2 Arnold Dallimore, *George Whitefield: The Life and Times of the Great Evangelist of the Eighteenth-Century Revival*, (Carlisle, PA: Banner of Truth Trust, 1980), vol. II, pp. 432-433.
3 E. A. Johnston, *George Whitefield: A Definitive Biography*, (Stoke-on-Trent, England, 2008), vol. II, pp. 179-180.
4 James P. Gledstone, *George Whitefield: Supreme Among Preachers*, (Greenville, SC: Ambassador International, 1998), p. 321.

On December 2, 1763 a new synagogue was dedicated in Newport. In 1764, Brown University was founded in Providence, Rhode Island.

Whitefield approached southern New England from New York City. Various news reports speculated as to his travel schedule. On January 2, 1764, the *Boston Gazette* wrote that Whitefield was in New York, and that, "The Rev. Mr. Whitefield, we hear, was to take passage in the Newport Pacquet-boat the first week in January, for Rhode Island, in his way hither."[5] The so-called "Newport Pacquet-boat" refers to one of the numerous small wooden boats, typically with two sails, that were designed for coastal and inland river trading and shipping. These packet boats delivered the mail, passengers, and other small items on short trips along the coast. Whitefield took a "Paquet-boat" from New York City along the Connecticut coast. Another newspaper updated Whitefield's itinerary, predicting, "The Rev'd Mr. Whitefield was to leave New-York last Tuesday, for Newport," that date being January 17, 1764.[6]

CONNECTICUT

Connecticut newspapers paid little attention to Whitefield's coming. In 1763, as Whitefield headed towards New England from the south, there was hardly any mention of his soon coming. On August 12, 1763 the *New London Summary* mentioned in a sentence that Whitefield arrived from Scotland to Virginia. A month later the same newspaper reported on September 16, that Whitefield departed Virginia for Philadelphia.[7] On December 9, 1763 the *New London Gazette* reported that Whitefield was on his way from Philadelphia to New York. The next account of Whitefield in the *New London Gazette* was on March 2, 1764. Remarkably, for the days Whitefield was in New London preaching to large crowds, the local newspapers did not report on these events. Perhaps the newspaper editors in New London did not support the Whitefield excitement. The *New London Gazette* did print when Whitefield was out of New England and back in New York.[8]

After departing New York, we can generally trace Whitefield's route. He wrote an insightful letter from Boston dated March 3, 1764. In this letter he looked back upon his previous several weeks of ministry since departing New York. Specifically, in tracing his route through New England, Whitefield names the cities of New London and Norwich, Connecticut. He wrote, "To Mr. R___ K___n, Boston, March 3, 1764 . . . Since leaving that place [New York] a sweet influence has attended the word at . . . New-London, Norwich, and Providence on the main land . . . ."[9] Thus we have three stops along the coast from the Newport packet boat tracing Whitefield's route to Boston, namely New London and Norwich, Connecticut; and Providence, Rhode Island.

In early February 1764, Whitefield made a stop from his packet boat in New London, Connecticut. He had been here before, in early August 1745 when he preached in the First Church of Christ Congregational for Rev. Eliphalet Adams, and in the North Parish (Second Congregational) Church for Rev. David Jewett. Adams died in 1753, replaced in 1757 by Rev. Mather Byles. Jewett was still in New London until his death in 1783. Whitefield would have noticed the changes in the city, as a recognizable wealthy class emerged from the wildly successful maritime industries related to whaling, commerce, light manufacturing, and fishing. The city was connected by water to the West Indies and to Europe. Numerous languages were spoken on the streets of New London. While Whitefield may have preached for both Jewett and Byles in New London, we have two accounts of Whitefield preaching for Rev. Byles in the First Church Congregational in New London.

---

5   *Boston Gazette* (Boston, MA), January 2, 1764, p. 4.
6   *Boston Post-Boy* (Boston, MA), January 23, 1764, p. 3.
7   *New London Summary* (New London, CT), August 12, 1763, p. 1, and September 16, 1754, p. 3.
8   *New London Gazette,* June 29, 1764, p. 3.
9   George Whitefield, *The Works of George Whitefield: Letters 1753-1770,* (1771: reprinted, Shropshire, England: Quinta Press, 2000), vol. III, p. 305

One record of Whitefield preaching in New London in 1764 comes from the *History of New London, Connecticut*, which recorded, "Mr. Whitefield again visited New London in 1763 [1764]. He crossed the sound from Long Island, Monday, Feb. 5th, and preached on Wednesday evening, in the Congregational meeting-house, from Phil. 1.21. The next day he proceeded to Boston."[10] Another report of this preaching event, from Boston, stated, "We hear that the Rev. Mr. Whitefield preached to a crowded audience, at the Rev. Mr. Byles' meeting at New London, last Wednesday, and was to set out from thence the next day, on his way to this place."[11] But Whitefield still had numerous stops to make before he arrived in Boston. One of those stops was in Norwich, Connecticut.

Norwich was easily reached by the packet boat that travelled up the Thames River from the coast at New London. As quoted above, on March 3, 1764, Whitefield wrote from Boston that he had recently completed a ministry visit to "New-London, Norwich, and Providence," where "a sweet influence has attended the word . . . ." Whitefield had been in Norwich in 1745 and again in 1754. The community grew, but growth was hindered by the 1754-1763 French and Indian War. However, after 1760, the town began to expand. Shipbuilding and its support activities comprised a major industry, supporting the rise of Norwich as an international port of call. Located on a major overland stage route connecting to New York, Boston, Providence, and Hartford, the Norwich community thrived.

There were about 6,000 people in Norwich in 1764. Whitefield's prior host, Rev. Benjamin Lord, was still ministering in Norwich. This town was deeply divided by the awakening decades prior, and was still feeling the effects in 1764 of religious turmoil. For example, in 1762 a group separated from a group that separated from the First Church Congregational in 1744. This new group met in the Bean Hill section of Norwich, but quickly displayed theological confusion. The minister, named Reynolds, converted from Congregational to Baptist, and was publicly re-baptized. The church never grew, became Unitarian, and folded.[12] Besides Whitefield's remark that he preached in Norwich in 1764, there is a brief eyewitness report of that event by Rev. Jacob Eliot.

A Harvard graduate in 1720, Jacob Eliot of the Congregational Church in Lebanon, Connecticut sought to help reconcile the ecclesiastical disputes in nearby Norwich. Eliot was ordained in 1729 as the first minister of the Goshen Congregational Church in Lebanon.[13] Eliot had heard Whitefield preach several times over the years and was in full support of the itinerant evangelist. Eliot was part of a Connecticut ministerial fellowship that publicly endorsed Whitefield. While opposing excesses of the awakening, Eliot supported the revival. The disruptions in the churches in Norwich caused Eliot to act as a peacemaker. He visited and preached at Norwich, about twelve miles from Lebanon, seeking to promote revival and calm the passions of the people. One time that Eliot was scheduled to preach at Norwich was in early February 1745. However, Eliot turned the pulpit in Norwich over to George Whitefield. In his *Diary*, Eliot recorded simply, "Feb. 7, 1764. Reverend Mr. Whitefield preached at Norwich for me."[14]

In February 1764, Rev. Isaac Backus of Middleboro, Massachusetts was in Norwich, Connecticut and heard Whitefield preach. Backus had heard Whitefield ten years earlier in 1754 and was impressed. Backus wrote in his *Diary* as follows:

---

10 Frances M. Caulkins, *History of New London, Connecticut . . .*, (New London, CT: H.D. Utley, Publisher, 1895), p. 460.
11 *Boston Evening Post*, February 13, 1764, p. 3.
12 Frances M. Caulkins, *History of Norwich, Connecticut . . .*, (Hartford, CT: Press of case, Lockwood & Brainard, 1878), p. 322.
13 Speaking of Rev. Jacob Eliot, "With great acceptance and success, he sustained the pastoral office among this people. During his ministry about 350 persons were added to the church. Rev. Mr. Eliot's death occurred April 22, 1766 in the 66th year of his age and the 37th of his ministry." *History of the Goshen Church in Lebanon, Connecticut*, http://goshenchurch.com/about/history.
14 Jacob Eliot, "Diary of Rev. Jacob Eliot," *The Historical Magazine . . . Concerning the Antiquities, History, and Biography of America*, (Morrisania, NY: January, 1869), p. 35.

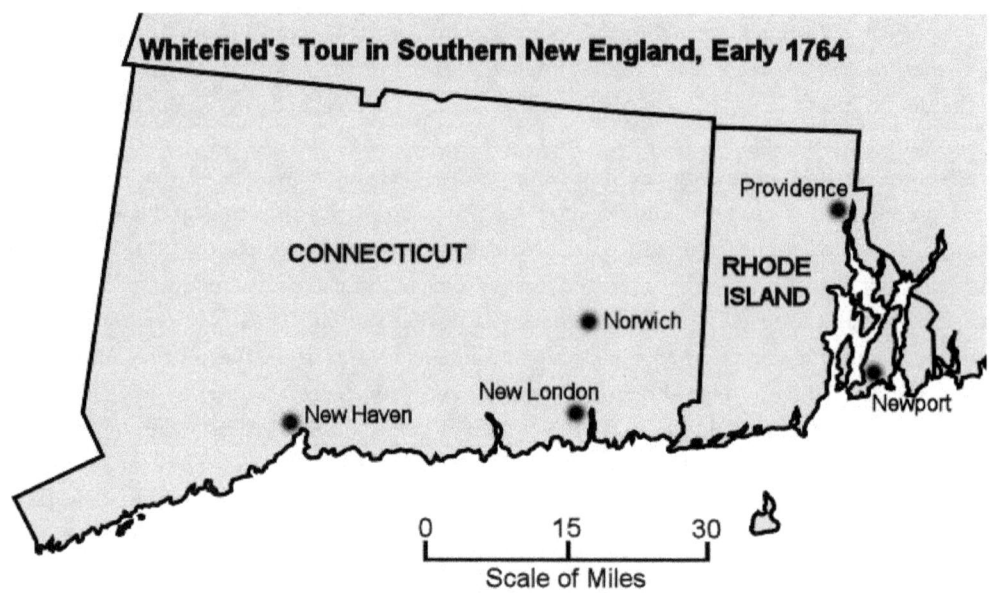

Friday Feb. 10. [1764] The Rev. Mr. Whitefield . . . came over to New London the beginning of this week where he preached once, and arrived in Norwich today. I had the favor of seeing and conversing with him at Col. [Hezekiah?] Huntington's near night. His temper and conversation appeared exceedingly heavenly. In the evening I heard Mr. Samson Occum preach, an Indian man that Mr. Wheelock of Lebanon educated, who has been ordained to go and preach among the heathen. He came now with Mr. Whitefield from New York.[15]

While on this early 1764 preaching tour through Connecticut, Whitefield preached at Yale College in New Haven. Whitefield had a long and tumultuous relationship with Yale. He first preached at Yale in the fall of 1740, with enormous crowds both on campus and at nearby churches, with the support of Yale president Rev. Thomas Clapp. After Whitefield departed, overzealous imitators of Whitefield caused divisions and disruptions. Revolts within the student body erupted, as students thought the faculty did not fully embrace the awakening. When Whitefield returned to New Haven in 1744, he was not welcomed to preach at the College, so he preached in the open air to thousands, publicly defying Yale. The Yale College president and faculty wrote publicly against Whitefield and the revival in February 1745. When Whitefield returned to New Haven in 1754, President Clapp was polite and more accepting to the traveling evangelist. Clapp was apparently rethinking his resistance to the New Light movement, as many of the New Light preachers he knew in Connecticut and elsewhere were serving in balanced, active, orthodox ministries.

In 1755, Clapp appointed a New Light minister, Rev. Naphtali Daggett, to be the minister of the new college chapel and a professor of Divinity. Much had changed at Yale since the first awakening in the 1740s, from acceptance, to rejection, and then back to acceptance of the revival.[16]

In early 1764, Whitefield was welcomed to Yale College by the college chaplain and divinity professor, Rev. Naphtali Daggett. Born in 1727 in Attleboro, Massachusetts, Daggett was raised in a town visited several times by Whitefield in the 1740s. A graduate of Yale in 1748, Daggett served as a Presbyterian

---

15 William G. McLoughlin, editor, *The Diary of Isaac Backus*, (Providence, RI: Brown University Press, 1979), vol. I, pp. 550-551. Although Isaac Backus had heard Whitefield preach a few times before over the years, this was their first in-person meeting. Rev. Samson Occum was a graduate of Rev. Eleazer Wheelock's Indian school in Lebanon, Connecticut.
16 James B. Reynolds, et. al., *Two Centuries of Christian Activity at Yale*, (New York: G.P. Putnam's Sons, 1901), pp. 35-36.

minister in Long Island, New York, before returning to Yale College in 1755. In 1766, when Thomas Clapp retired, Daggett became the interim president of Yale until 1777. Whitefield had an ally in Daggett at Yale.

An interesting anecdote from Whitefield's visit to Yale in 1764 comes from Dr. George P. Fisher, who was later a professor of church history at Yale Divinity School. Fisher recorded the local account of Whitefield preaching on campus. After the defeat of the French in the French and Indian War in 1763, rivalries existed on the Yale campus between English and French students. Sometimes bitter antagonisms developed. For example, in early 1764 some youthful and unwise English students made some inappropriate public displays against the French, which disturbed the French students on campus. Determined on revenge, the French students covertly gained admission to the kitchen where the student's food was prepared, and poisoned food that was placed on the English student's tables. Many English students got desperately ill, but immediate medical aid avoided a catastrophe, and there were no fatalities. Whitefield preached at Yale shortly after this food poisoning incident, and used it as a vivid sermon illustration and dire warning of death and judgment upon the unsuspecting. Thomas Clapp and Naphtali Daggett endorsed Whitefield preaching to the students. The student body was deeply stirred by Whitefield's message, his oratory skills, and his compassion, and "a considerable number were brought to repentance."[17] One student who was converted by Whitefield's sermon at Yale in 1764 was Isaac Lewis.

Rev. Naphtali Daggett of Yale College.
Source: Public domain image.

Born around 1745, Isaac Lewis was a student at Yale when the juvenile pranks between English and French students occurred. He was on campus during the poisoning incident, and he was present in the Yale College chapel when George Whitefield preached to the faculty and the student body in February 1764. Lewis graduated from Yale in 1765, and began preaching in Wilton, Connecticut in 1768. In 1786 he settled as a minister in Greenwich, Connecticut, resigning that pastorate in 1818 due to a disability. In 1818 he was chosen as a fellow of Yale College. Rev. Isaac Lewis died at home in Greenwich at nearly one hundred years old in 1840. Lewis was quite vocal about his conversion experience after listening to Whitefield preach at Yale in 1764. He retold the story many times of how he became a Christian while a young man under the influence of the famous George Whitefield. Decades later, while preparing for his funeral, Lewis insisted that the funeral sermon be based on the biblical text that Whitefield used at Yale College some sixty-six years earlier, the text preached that led to his conversion.[18]

The reconciliation of Whitefield to Yale College was a significant event. Hundreds of New England clergy looked to Yale for leadership. The support Whitefield received from Yale in 1764 must have been a significant event in his life. A Yale historian noted,

> Whitefield was invited to speak in the College chapel. He accepted and preached with great power from the text, For other foundation can no man lay than that is laid, which is Christ Jesus . . . After he had taken leave of the students, such was the impression he had made on their minds, that they requested the President [Thomas Clapp] to go after him to entreat him

---

17 George P. Fisher, *Discourse Commemorative of the History of the Church of Christ in Yale College . . .*, Preached in the College Chapel November 22, 1857, (New Haven, CT: T.J. Stafford, Printer, 1857), p. 31.
18 William T. Lewis, *Genealogy of the Lewis Family in America . . .*, (Louisville, KY: Courier-Journal Job Printing, 1893), pp. 97-98.

for another quarter hour's exhortation. He complied with the request and the effect was what he [Whitefield] called the crown of the expedition.[19]

A sketch of the president's home at Yale, where Thomas Clapp and George Whitefield reconciled.

Source: Public domain image.

During his extensive 1764 preaching tour throughout New England, Whitefield considered his acceptance at Yale "the crown of the expedition." Many who were once his outspoken enemies were now his avowed friends, including President Thomas Clapp of Yale.

> The last picture we have of these two [Clapp and Whitefield] is indeed a pleasant one—the venerable president acting as the representative of the student body, standing by the chaise in which the famous preacher was seated about to depart and earnestly pleading for even "one more quarter hour's exhortation" from the very man whose preaching had been characterized in 1745 as "a scheme to vilify and subvert our colleges." After years of misunderstanding, faculty and students found through the Christian earnestness and sincerity of the Great Evangelist a common meeting ground and a means of lasting reconciliation.[20]

An exact day-by-day account of Whitefield's travels in Connecticut in early 1764 is unknown. However, we do know of a few locations Whitefield visited from the letters of his friend Rev. Eleazar Wheelock. Wheelock served the Congregational Church in Lebanon, Connecticut, where he also founded a missionary school for Indians. On April 15, 1764 Wheelock wrote a letter to Whitefield from Lebanon discussing missionary activities to the Indians. In that letter he made the comment, "When we parted at Norwich," meaning Wheelock and Whitefield were recently together in that Connecticut town. Wheelock also stated that Whitefield was destined for Rhode Island.[21] In that same letter, Wheelock told Whitefield that after

---

19 James B. Reynolds, et. al., *Two Centuries of Christian Activity at Yale*, p. 35.
20 Ibid., p. 36.
21 David McClure and Elijah Parish, *Memoirs of the Rev. Eleazar Wheelock, Founder and President of Dartmouth College . . .*, (Newburyport, MA: Edward Little Printer, 1811), p. 244.

his recent preaching in nearby East Hampton there was "surprising progress of the work of God, at East Hampton, since you were there."[22]

The minister in East Hampton, when Whitefield arrived in 1764, was Rev. John Norton. The Congregational Church in East Hampton was organized in 1748, and their meeting house was built in 1755 with square pews and galleries on three sides of the meeting area. This congregation was originally called the Third Church of Chatham. Rev. Norton arrived in East Hampton in 1748 to his death in 1778 of smallpox. Norton was a 1737 graduate of Yale College, at a time when the awakenings were very much on people's minds. When Whitefield came to town, Norton and his wife Eunice had nine children, with perhaps six or so children still living at home. Although a fire years ago destroyed early church and town records, we know that Rev. Norton was known as a strict observer of the sabbath, and that "he was well versed in the doctrinal views of the church of his time," and he "compared well" with the average preachers of his day.[23] Shortly after Whitefield departed East Hampton, Wheelock wrote that "scores [were] converted in a few days."[24]

George Whitefield had a supportive, long-term relationship with Eleazar Wheelock. The two were together in Connecticut off-and-on in the early spring of 1764. For example, Whitefield encouraged Wheelock to write to William Legge, the Earl of Dartmouth in England, to seek support of Wheelock's fledgling Indian missionary school in Lebanon. Whitefield and Wheelock met face-to-face to discuss this, which resulted in Wheelock writing to Lord Dartmouth on March 1, 1764, with an endorsement from Whitefield.[25] Something similar happened between Whitefield, Wheelock, and Selina, Countess of Huntington. On March 7, 1764, Wheelock wrote to Lady Huntington in England, explaining the work of Indian missions in Connecticut and seeking her financial support. Interestingly, Wheelock had seen Whitefield several days earlier in Lebanon and wrote this account of the itinerant preacher.

> The Rev. Mr. Whitefield (by whose motion and encouragement I have assumed this boldness) has lately travelled through New England, and preached as his broken state of health would allow, to as good acceptance as ever he did. He is now at Boston, and designs to return back to the southern governments, and from thence to England.[26]

A Connecticut community that invited Whitefield to preach was Canterbury. Located in eastern Connecticut along the Quinebaug River near the Rhode Island border, Canterbury was known for small family owned mills and farms. The Congregational Church in Canterbury was stirred by the Great Awakening of 1740, but was distracted by a moral scandal between the minister and a female congregant. In 1744, Rev. James Cogswell became the new minister and led the church through various schisms related to revival preaching and itinerant preachers. Cogswell opposed separatism, a separate church was formed, and the ecclesiastical life of Canterbury was unsettled.

In 1764, George Whitefield traveled through Connecticut. Cogswell wrote that Whitefield, "rode in his chariot with a gentleman, had a waiter to attend on him, and Sampson Occum, ye Indian preacher, who rode on one of the horses, there being three to ye chariot."[27] Cogswell was pressured by his congregation to invite Whitefield to preach. He resisted, then relented and invited the itinerant Whitefield to preach in the Congregational meeting house. "Mr. Cogswell, after much hesitation about

---

22 Ibid.
23 *One Hundred and Fiftieth Anniversary 1748-1898 of the Congregational Church of East Hampton* (Chatham,) Conn., November 30, 1898, (published by the church, 1898), p. 45.
24 David McClure and Elijah Parish, *Memoirs of the Rev. Eleazar Wheelock,* p. 244.
25 Baxter Perry Smith, *History of Dartmouth College,* (Boston, MA: Riverside Press, 1878), p. 25.
26 David McClure and Elijah Parish, *Memoirs of the Rev. Eleazar Wheelock*, p. 241.
27 "CT Genealogy," https://connecticutgenealogy.com/windham/canterbury_connecticut_church_history.html.

the propriety of such a step, decided to ask him to preach, but Mr. Whitefield declined doing so. The visit of Whitefield, which occurred in 1764, was an event which excited great attention from the people."[28] Whitefield declined preaching invitations for two basic reasons. He was either too ill to comply, or he had a prior engagement.

Continuing Whitefield's travelogue, a newspaper posting dated February 13 from Newport, Rhode Island stated, "The Rev. Mr. George Whitefield left New-London last Thursday, and intended to proceed directly to Boston."[29] One stop along the way to Boston was in Providence, Rhode Island Colony. On March 3, 1764, Whitefield wrote from Boston that he had recently completed a ministry visit to "New-London, Norwich, and Providence," where "a sweet influence has attended the word . . . "[30] Other Connecticut towns he visited he did not include in this brief summary.

RHODE ISLAND

In his previous travels, Whitefield had made many trips in and around Providence, Rhode Island. He preached there for Rev. Joseph Snow in 1745 at the Beneficent or Second Congregational Church, endorsing Snow's separation from the First Church in starting a New Light congregation. Whitefield was in the area, in Newport, in 1747 and again in 1754, but there is no surviving record of him preaching in Providence at those times. But in 1764, Whitefield preached on two occasions in Providence, once on his way to Boston in February, and again in June, as he travelled from Boston towards New York City.

On his prior 1745 visit to Providence, Whitefield was in the thick of the Great Awakening controversy. The Baptists, Quakers, and the First Church Congregational all opposed Whitefield. But now, in 1764 the controversy had abated. Each group became civil towards each other, and Providence prospered as a thriving maritime and trading center. Unfortunately, in 1758 the two-story wooden town meeting house burned to the ground. In 1759 an elegant new state house was erected on North Main Street, a two-story wooden Victorian-style structure with an elaborate tower. In 1760 the population in Providence was about 4,000 people. In 1764, the College in the English Colony of Rhode Island and Providence Plantations was established in Providence, later renamed Brown University. A class of prominent merchants built large homes, many which still are standing today. In the 1760s, as tensions with Great Britain increased, the Episcopal Church in Providence was generally disliked and unpopular.[31]

Rev. Joseph Snow of the Second Church (Congregational) had an extended and successful ministry in Providence. He served at the church from 1745 to his death in 1803. He and Whitefield were clearly like-minded. His decades of ministry, guiding a congregation through theological disruptions, two wars, and innumerable social and cultural changes as America prospered, all speak well of his character and skill as a minister. One account stated,

> Mr. Snow must have been a rare man to have such influence over a body of people who were zealous for the faith, and who had separated from the mother church in times of great excitement . . . But after the separation was completed the new church went on with apparent harmony and steady growth . . . Mr. Snow had much of the ardor of youth, and the intense zeal of those who belonged to what was called the "New Light" party, he certainly had also a great deal of modesty and self-control.[32]

---

28 Ibid.
29 *Newport Mercury* (Newport, RI), February 13, 1764, p. 3.
30 George Whitefield, *The Works of George Whitefield*, vol. III, p. 305.
31 Thomas M. Clark, *An Historical Discourse, Delivered at St. John's Church, Providence, R.I . . .* , (Hartford, CT: The Church Press, pp. 15-16.
32 James Gardiner Vose, *Sketches of Congregationalism in Rhode Island . . .* , (New York: Silver, Burdett & Company, 1894), pp. 89-90.

Joseph Snow was not a formally trained minister. His occupations as a youth were a lumberman, a sawmill worker, but especially a carpenter. Through his ordination process he came to believe in the doctrines of Calvinism, something which he and Whitefield had in common. Though a rugged outdoorsman, his love for the Bible drew him close to the more educated and articulate Whitefield. "Mr. Snow was not a liberally educated man. He was a man of one book, and that the Bible. Yet he was not unacquainted with works of theology . . . he preached with unabated zeal for fifty-seven years."[33] Snow was able to minister successfully in Providence, a city that was influential, expanding, wealthy, and educationally progressive. Snow "earnestly sought to win souls to Jesus Christ that they might be saved, and his beloved master glorified."[34]

In 1764, as Whitefield travelled towards Boston from New York, he was eagerly welcomed by Snow in Providence. A local newspaper, *The Providence Gazette*, reported on February 18, 1764,

> Wednesday last the Reverend Mr. George Whitefield came to Town from the westward, and met with a polite reception;—on Friday morning he preached a sermon to about two thousand people, at the Rev. Mr. Snow's church, from John v.25, Verily verily I say unto you, the Hour is coming, and now is, when the Dead shall hear the Voice of the Son of God; and they that hear shall live.—In the afternoon of the same day he set out for Boston.[35]

Further, "In Mr. Snow's church . . . itinerant preachers still roused attention. Whitefield . . . preached in Providence. The church was enlarged, and yet with growing years a spirit of caution prevailed."[36] This February, 1764 preaching event by Whitefield was followed up by him preaching again for Snow a few months later, resulting in dozens of additions to the church membership role. Whitefield then travelled south along a good road to Newport.

Rev. Isaac Backus of Middleboro, Massachusetts was doing itinerant preaching, and was in Providence and heard Whitefield preach for Rev. Joseph Snow. Backus wrote in his *Diary*,

> 15-16 February [1764] . . . Next day I came to Providence, found that Mr. Whitefield who left Norwich on Monday arrived here last night.

> Friday Feb. 17. Heard him [Whitefield] preach at 11 o'clock at Mr. Snow's meeting house to about as many people as he did at Norwich, and to as good purpose on John 5:25. After meeting I set off and reached my house in the evening: found my family well. This has been as remarkable a journey as I ever traveled. I had proposed to go sooner, but was prevented by the weather and so was brought to this juncture when I was to see and hear so many of Christ's servants from a distance and especially him [Whitefield] who has done so much for his divine master and has attained so great a likeness to him: what I saw and heard in and from him gave my soul a very great spring heavenward, as well as the wonderful revival of religion in my native place. Wonderful indeed are all God's dealings.[37]

In the mid-eighteenth century, Newport, Rhode Island was one of the most important cities in Colonial America. The city was well planned, growing continually. Wealth poured into Newport from various maritime activities such as whaling, local shipping, and international commerce. The Newport waterfront teemed with activity. The community sought to improve its growing education, cultural,

---

33 Ibid., pp. 90-91.
34 Ibid., p. 92.
35 *The Providence Gazette*, (Providence, RI), February 18, 1764, p. 3.
36 James Gardiner Vose, *Sketches of Congregationalism in Rhode Island . . .*, p. 96.
37 William G. McLoughlin, editor, *The Diary of Isaac Backus*, vol. I, pp. 552-554.

and social standing. In walking the streets of Newport in 1764, one could easily imagine being in an established and successful European port city. Whitefield understood the significance of the gospel being fully established and continually supported in Newport. This is evident from the fact that in every New England visit Whitefield completed, he visited Newport. Previously, he had been in Newport in 1740, 1745, 1747, and 1754. Now in 1764 he returned to briefly stop in town on his way to Boston. Whitefield had two objectives in visiting Newport—to preach the gospel, and to encourage the work of revival from past years.

As already mentioned, on January 2, 1764, the *Boston Gazette* wrote that Whitefield was in New York, and that he "was to take passage in the Newport Pacquet-boat the first week in January, for Rhode Island . . . " Another previously quoted newspaper report updated Whitefield's itinerary, stating in mid-January 1764, "The Rev'd Mr. Whitefield was to leave New-York last Tuesday, for Newport." After leaving New York and making several stops in coastal Connecticut and at Providence, Rhode Island, Whitefield's boat arrived in Newport in February 1764.

In 1763, several months before Whitefield arrived in Newport in 1764, the elaborate Touro Synagogue was completed, built for the thriving Jewish community in recognition of the original Portuguese and Spanish Jews who came to Newport in 1658. This synagogue is still active today. In 1763, the port of Newport handled 51,210 tons of cargo, comparable to any port in the New World.[38] After Whitefield departed, the passage of the Sugar Act in April, 1764 was violently opposed in Newport, as the city made large sums of money from producing rum from sugar-based molasses. To enforce the tax, Great Britain sent several ships to the American Colonies, including the *HMS St. John* to Newport. In July, allegedly, crew members from the *HMS St. John* stole goods from Newport warehouses. In response, a group of Rhode Islanders, an unofficial militia, manned Fort George on Goat Island in Newport harbor and fired cannon shots against the *HMS St. John*. The shots were one of the first open acts of rebellion against British law in the British American Colonies. The canons were fired under orders from local officials, but an all-out battle was avoided, as the Rhode Islanders dispersed before another British ship arrived on the scene.

The Old Brick Market, built in 1760, was the center of maritime commerce in Newport. Here the captain of George Whitefield's boat had to register the ship's arrival in port in January 1764. The building is now a museum. Photograph by Ken Lawson.

---

38 Kenneth Walsh, *The Economic History of Newport, Rhode Island*, (Bloomington, IN: AuthorHouse Publishers, 2014), p. 174.

Whitefield's friend, Rev. William Vinal, was still the minister at the First Congregational Church in Newport. At the Second Congregational Church, Whitefield's antagonist, Rev. James Searing, was replaced by Rev. Ezra Stiles. Stiles is a fascinating character in American theological and educational history. He was a brilliant linguist, a keen theologian, and an avid correspondent to leading figures in Europe and the American Colonies. Interestingly, the relationship between Ezra Stiles and Whitefield was supportive but never intimate.

Ezra Stiles was a student at Yale College when the school openly published against Whitefield. He graduated in 1746, and was a tutor at Yale in 1754 when the college changed its position and endorsed Whitefield. As a student, Stiles probably heard Whitefield preach. In 1755, Stiles became the minister at the Second Congregational Church in Newport, Rhode Island. Up to this point in his life, his exposure to Whitefield had been inconsistent. The college he graduated from, and later worked at as a tutor, opposed, and then supported Whitefield. Then, the church he began serving in 1755, the Second Congregational in Newport, had openly resisted Whitefield. Now, in 1764, Whitefield came again to Newport. There is no surviving account of Stiles and Whitefield meeting in Newport. Had such a meeting happened, the detailed diaries of Stiles would certainly have mentioned it. What is insightful is what Stiles wrote about Whitefield long after the itinerant departed.

An undated painting of Rev. Ezra Stiles.

Source: http://www.riheritagehalloffame.com/ inductees_detail.cfm?iid=391

Ezra Stiles was a leading intellectual in America. He studied the classics in Greek, he was fluent in Latin, and he had a keen interest in ancient languages. He was a prolific writer and travelled widely as a speaker and preacher. Stiles was a Calvinist who rejected the growing deism of his day. A biographer of Stiles stated that as the son of a New Haven minister, he was raised to love the Puritans. He was a bibliophile who actively supported the library and athenaeum in Newport.[39] After Whitefield came to Newport in 1764, Stiles used his remarkable intellect to study the man. There is no record of Whitefield preaching for Stiles at the Second Congregational Church in 1764. Yet Stiles saw the positive influence Whitefield had had in Newport on his past visits, how the First Congregational Church under Rev. Vinal had supported Whitefield and prospered without religious fanaticism.

One factor that drew Ezra Stiles towards Whitefield was the glowing reputation the evangelist had among the common citizens of Newport. While Stiles was the minister of the Second Congregational Church, an influential woman in the First Congregational Church had a profound influence upon all of Newport. Mrs. Sarah Osborn began teaching school in Newport in 1744. Osborn was a 1740 Whitefield convert and a vocal advocate of revivals. Unknown dozens or more of the members of Stiles' church were educated by this devout Christian schoolteacher. Children in Stiles' Sabbath School were educated during the week at Osborn's day school. By the 1760s, she was the unofficial leader of a widespread revival in Newport that influenced both the First and Second Congregational Churches.[40] A

---

39 For a full treatment of his life, see Edmund S. Morgan, *The Gentle Puritan: A Life of Ezra Stiles, 1727-1795*, (New York: W.W. Norton & Company, 1962).

40 Samuel Hopkins, *Memoirs of the Life of Mrs. Sarah Osborn, who Died at Newport, Rhode Island on the Second day of August, 1796 . . .*, (Worcester, MA: Leonard Worcester Printer, 1799), pp. 70-71.

dedicated journalist, Osborn wrote of hundreds that came to her home every week, men and women of all ages, ethnicities, and financial status, to pray, encourage, and support one another in New Light teachings. Her unqualified support of Whitefield helped pave the way for the itinerant's 1764 visit to Newport.

After Whitefield departed Newport in 1764, Ezra Stiles began to reassess his prior negative impressions of Whitefield. In 1767, Stiles wrote of Whitefield and his followers, "During all ye years I have been so employed, I have been reviled & traduced as an enemy of Christ . . . by all or most of the followers of Mr. Whitefield; tho I always believed & said I believed yet he was a sincere good man, but weak & often mistaken."[41] In 1768, Stiles was critical of Whitefield's loose management of the orphan house in Georgia, its poor financial records, and the lack of long-term direction for that ministry. Stiles accused Whitefield of being one who "loves church power," yet also spoke of "a real regard I have for Mr. Whitefield, not withstanding his mistakes and blunders."[42] It is interesting to note that when Whitefield came to Newport six years later, in 1770, he was allowed to preach in the Second Congregational Church under Rev. Ezra Stiles. This congregation had voted against Whitefield preaching there in 1745 but had since changed their minds about him. The people of Second Congregational were "very desirous of hearing him" in 1770, and Stiles complied.[43]

Whitefield arrived in Newport sometime in February 1764. We do not know exactly the date he arrived or how long he stayed. But we do have a record of when he reached his destination, Boston. The *Boston Evening-Post* reported on February 20, 1764, "Last Saturday evening [February 18] the Rev. Mr. WHITEFIELD arrived in Town from the Southward." Currently there is no record of where Whitefield stopped from Newport on his way to Boston. If he were in an urgent hurry, he could have taken a carriage and been there in two or three days. If he went by ship it may have taken days longer.

---

41   Ezra Stiles, *Extracts from the Itineraries and other Miscellanies of Ezra Stiles, D.D. 1755-1794*, (New Haven, CT:Yale University Press, 1916), p. 432.
42   Ibid., p. 600.
43   Ezra Stiles, *The Literary Diary of Ezra Stiles*, (New York: Charles Scribner's Sons, 1901), vol. I, p. 61.

CHAPTER 33

WHITEFIELD'S TOUR IN EASTERN AND SOUTHERN NEW ENGLAND

1764

IN THE 1760S, MUCH OF life in rural New England had not changed in a hundred years. Typically, women still worked from morning past nighttime in domestic chores such as gardening, caring for children, creating butter and cheese, making homespun clothing, housework, laundry, canning of foods, cooking, and general supervision of domestic life. Rural men lived much as those a century before. They farmed, hunted, cared for livestock, managed horses, cut wood, and traded with others for goods or services. Many New Englanders who lived in larger cities like Portsmouth, New Hampshire, Salem and Boston, Massachusetts, Newport, Rhode Island, and New Haven, Connecticut lived in relative luxury compared to their rural contemporaries.[1]

The *Boston Gazette* kept its readers well informed of Whitefield's coming visit. As in previous visits, the *Boston Weekly Newsletter* was silent concerning Whitefield's approach to Boston. Here are some excerpts from the *Boston Gazette* heralding Whitefield's preaching journey:

December 19, 1763
[New York] The Rev. Mr. Whitefield preached twice since last: and at one of his sermons (the Sunday before last), £130 was collected for the benefit of the poor of the Presbyterian Congregation in this city.

January 2, 1764
[Boston] The Rev. Mr. Whitefield, we hear, was to take passage in the Newport Pacquet-boat the first week in January, for Rhode Island in his way hither.

January 16, 1764
[New York] Last Friday in the afternoon, the Rev. Mr. Whitefield visited the Seal of this city; and preached on those words from St. Matthew, Chapter XXV 38, 39, 40, "When we saw thee a stranger, and took thee in? Or naked and clothed thee? And the King shall say unto

---

1   There are many good books on everyday life in Colonial New England. See Francis J. Bremer, *The Puritan Experiment: New England Society from Bradford to Edwards*, (Hanover, NH: University Press of New England, 1995). Allegra Di Bonaventura, *For Adam's Sake: A Family Saga in Colonial New England*, (New York: W.W. Norton & Company, 2013). Richard L. Bushman, *From Puritan to Yankee: Character and Social Order in Connecticut, 1690-1765*, (Cambridge, MA: Harvard University Press, 1998). Jere R. Daniell, *Colonial New Hampshire: A History*, (Hanover, NH: University of New England Press, 2015). Thomas S. Kidd, *American Colonial History: Clashing Cultures and Faiths*, (New Haven, CT: Yale University Press, 2016).

them, Verily I say unto you, in as much as ye have done it unto one of these, my brethren, ye have done it unto me." That truly reverent man delivered an excellent discourse on a subject, which self-seeking must have made very affecting to his hearers, who were greatly edified by the salutary advice he gave to them. Then the good man, being informed that no provision was made for the support of debtors, he generously gave, out of his purse, enough to purchase ten cords of wood for the use of the poorest prisoners, and promised to make a collection for their relief, and for discharging a few, who are confined for small debts, which are not the consequence of either extravagance or idleness—what a pity, that such a godlike man's constitution is almost worn out by apostolic labors.

February 6, 1764
[New York] January 23. The Rev. Mr. Whitefield left this city on Tuesday last, and went over to Long Island, intending for Boston. He has spent seven weeks with us, preaching twice a week, to more general acceptance than ever; and been treated with great respect by many of the gentlemen and merchants of this place . . . in his last sermon he took a very affectionate leave of the people of this city, who were extremely affected by it, and expressed great concern at his departure. May God restore this great and good man (in whom the gentleman, the Christian and the accomplished orator shine forth with such peculiar luster) to a perfect state of health, and continue him long a blessing to the world and the Church of Christ.

The above-quoted letter dated February 6, 1764 helps us understand why an exact chronology of Whitefield's travels is difficult. He was sick, resting often, and was preaching only "twice a week." The silence of *The Boston Weekly Newsletter* was finally broken when, after months of ignoring the coming Whitefield, the following announcement was made:

February 16, 1764
The Rev. Mr. Whitefield preached last Wednesday at New London—today he set out for this place, and is expected in a day or two.

A member of the New Brick Church, and later a member of the Second (Old North) Church in Boston, John Tudor saw Whitefield enter Boston in 1764. Tudor kept a diary with random entries. As a merchant and maritime insurance man, Tudor made various diary notes related to the weather, politics, tensions with the French and later the British, and numerous notes on the maritime industries. On February 18, 1764, John Tudor wrote, "This afternoon Mr. Whitefield arrived in Boston from the Southward. Preach'd at Dr. Sewell's . . . to a large and Crowded assembly."[2]

Upon arriving in Boston in mid-February 1764, Whitefield received a hearty welcome, both from his old acquaintances and from the general public. It had been twenty-four years since the initial Great Awakening had shaken the city, and evidence of genuine conversions and persevering faith was abundant. Many old friends welcomed the aging revival preacher to the city.

> Whitefield's body showed the ravages of time. In place of the buoyant, youthful-looking Whitefield, audiences encountered a much older and more corpulent Whitefield—the figure who is in fact featured in most of his portraits. He moved and breathed with difficulty, and could not sustain the bursts of passion that had formerly marked his ministry.

---

2   John Tudor, *Deacon Tudor's Diary . . . A Record of More or Less Important Events in Boston, from 1732 to 1793, by an Eyewitness*, (Boston, MA: Press of Wallace Spooner, 1896), pp. 15-16.

But still the crowds flocked. They came partly from respect, partly from curiosity, and partly just to hear an American legend. Absence did little to dim the American memory of their great evangelical friend or lessen their appreciation. Wherever Whitefield traveled, word-of-mouth reports spread the news of his arrival. Listeners who were too young personally to remember the earlier Whitefield heard stories from those who had been there. Sales of Whitefield's Journals increased as Americans reminded themselves of the fearless institution baiter who could draw thousands at the mention of his name.[3]

Boston had a special welcome for Whitefield. Four years earlier, in 1760, Boston had a devastating fire in which several hundred homes were destroyed. By 1761, Whitefield had collected a huge contribution from his London congregations for the victims of the fire. Now Boston had the opportunity to publicly thank the evangelist for his benevolence.

> Boston, February 20. [1764] Monday last, at a very general meeting of the freeholders and other inhabitants of this town, it was voted unanimously that the thanks of the town be given to the Rev. Mr. George Whitefield, for his charitable care and pains in collecting a considerable sum of money in Great Britain, for the benefit of the distressed sufferers by the great fire in Boston, 1760. And a respectable committee was appointed to wait on Mr. Whitefield to inform him of the vote, and to present him with a copy thereof: which committee waited on him accordingly, and received the following answer: -
>
> GENTLEMEN,—This vote of thanks for so small an instance of my goodwill to Boston, as it was entirely unexpected, quite surprises me. Often I have been much concerned that I could do more upon such a distressing occasion. That the Redeemer may ever preserve this town from such like melancholy events, and sanctify the present afflictive circumstances to the spiritual welfare of all its inhabitants, in the hearty prayer of, Gentlemen, Your ready servant in our Common Lord,
>
> GEORGE WHITEFIELD.[4]

The Boston newspapers carried random announcements that Whitefield had returned. Although Whitefield's presence in Boston was again well-received, the attention of the public was often on other matters. Newspapers throughout 1763 and 1764 concentrated on two despairing themes to New Englanders: an increase in Indian hostilities on remote New England villages, and a dreadful smallpox epidemic in Boston. Even so, the following announcements of Whitefield's arrival were made:

> *The Boston Gazette,* February 20, 1764
>
> The same evening (Saturday last) the Rev. Mr. Whitefield arrived in Town from New London.
>
> *Boston Newsletter,* February 23, 1764
>
> The Rev. Mr. Whitefield arrived in town from the Southward, last Saturday afternoon, and on Tuesday forenoon he preached to a large audience in the Old South Meeting-house.

---

3   Harry S. Stout, *The Divine Dramatist: George Whitefield and the Rise of Modern Evangelicalism,* (Grand Rapids, MI: Eerdman's Publishing, 1991), p. 250.

4   *The New Hampshire Gazette,* March 2, 1764, p. 2.

Certainly, Boston had changed since Whitefield's first visit in 1740. Over twenty four years, the colonial seaport had become an international center of commerce. Population had dramatically increased, as the city took on the look of a cosmopolitan European city. Port cities were especially full of merchants, immigrants, transients and seamen, with a small but exceptionally wealthy class of citizens controlling commerce. The British flag flew proudly over the city. Charles Chauncey of Boston's First Church was still active, while

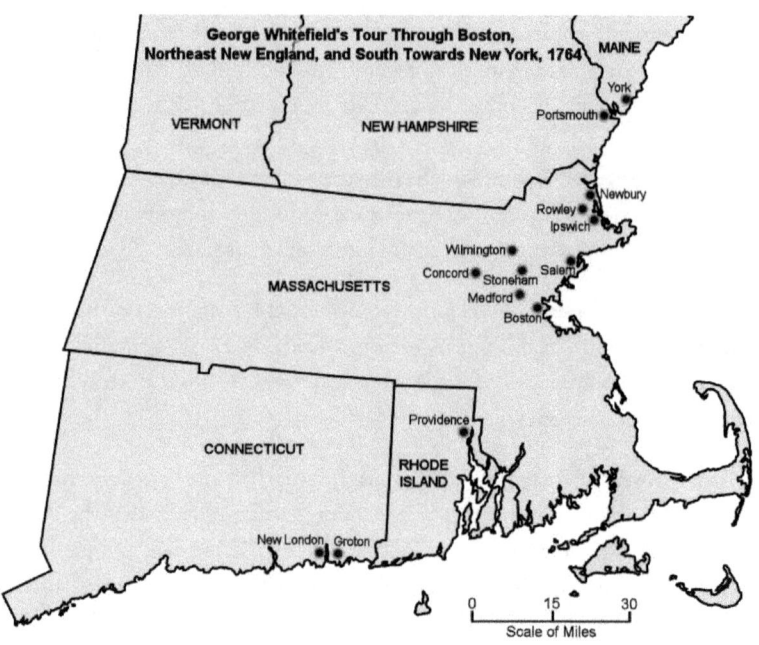

Jonathan Edwards from Stockbridge and later Princeton had died in 1758. Indeed, a whole new generation received Whitefield in Boston, as some ministers in the area were young children at the onset of the 1740s Great Awakening. A newspaper report stated, "Last Tuesday afternoon the Reverend Mr. Whitefield preached to a large audience at the Old South Meeting House in this Town . . . And on Saturday he preached again at the same place from Jude verse 21, Keep yourselves in the Love of God."[5] Whitefield recorded his welcome in Boston as follows:

> Boston, March 3, 1764
>
> At Boston I have been received with the usual warmth of affection. Twice have we seen the Redeemer's stately steps in the great Congregation. But as the smallpox is likely to take on a universal spread through the town, I purpose making my country tour and then turn to Boston in my way to the Southward. Invitations come so thick and fast from every quarter that I know not what to do. I cannot boast of acquiring much additional bodily strength, any otherwise as the cool season of the year helps to keep me up. Twice a week is as often as I can with comfort ascend my throne.[6]

Rev. Samuel Cooper of the Brattle Street Church in Boston was an avowed Whitefield supporter. Over the years, Cooper maintained his fidelity to the New Light cause, and was able to build cooperation with local Old Light clergy. Cooper appears to have been a peacemaker, as he shared meals, exchanged pulpits, and celebrated communion services with both New Light and Old Light ministers. Cooper's diary had the following notes related to Whitefield:

> 1764.
>
> March 1. Preached Thursday lecture. Mr. Whitefield present.
>
> May 20. Preached at home all day. Mr. Whitefield present P.M.[7]

---

5   *New Hampshire Gazette*, March 2, 1764, quoting from a Boston report dated February 27, 1765.
6   George Whitefield, *Works of George Whitefield*, (1771: reprinted by Quinta Press, Shropshire, England, 2000), vol. III, p. 310.
7   "Notes from the Rev. Samuel Cooper's Inter-Leaved Almanacs of 1764 and 1769," *The New England Historical and*

Newspapers in Boston were oddly silent about Whitefield's preaching. During his stay in Boston, he experienced a temporary improvement in his health. He desired to begin an extensive journey revisiting friends in northern New England, then to continue northward into Canada. After departing Boston, we read about Whitefield and his first stop outside the city: "Saturday last the Rev. Mr. WHITEFIELD set out from hence on his way for Portsmouth, and preached Yesterday at the Rev. Turell's Meeting-House in Medford to a large audience."[8] His preaching stop in Medford, several miles northwest from Boston, was for Rev. Ebenezer Turell of the First Church.

Born in Boston in 1702, Ebenezer Turell graduated from Harvard in 1721. He served as the Congregational minister in Medford from 1724 to 1778. In early March 1764, Whitefield preached for Turell "to a large audience." Apparently Turell's ministry was well appreciated in Medford. Four years after Whitefield departed, the church voted to build a new meeting house, sixty feet by forty feet, with pews on the floor and in the balcony.[9]

Notwithstanding his occasional illness, Whitefield continued preaching and, as usual, experienced great success. From Concord, fifteen miles northwest of Boston, Whitefield wrote on March 10, 1764,

> I can only preach twice or thrice a week with comfort. And yet a wider door than ever is opened all along the continent. A beginning is made in Boston. But as the small pox is spreading there, I purpose preaching for a while in adjacent places. With what success, you may know hereafter.[10]

Whitefield had a longtime ally in Concord. Rev. Daniel Bliss, a Yale College graduate in 1732, served at the First Church (Congregational) in Concord from 1738 to his death in May 1764. Over the years, Bliss and Whitefield had endured the ridicule of their Old Light opponents. Both men were vilified by their adversaries. Whitefield peached for Bliss in Concord numerous times over the decades since the Great Awakening in 1740. "He was a personal friend of the great Whitefield and like him was bold, zealous, impassioned and enthusiastic in his preaching. He was one of the most distinguished of the clergy, who in his day were denominated New Lights by their opponents, and was several times before a council on account of difficulties in doctrinal points."[11] When Whitefield and Bliss met in March 1764, in Concord, they met for the last time. Two months later, Bliss was dead at age forty-nine. "His last and most powerful sermon was delivered March 11, 1764 in the presence of George Whitefield and made such an impression on his mind that Mr. Whitefield remarked: If I had studied my whole life, I could not have produced such a sermon."[12] More details of this event are provide by Lemuel Shattuck, in his *History of Concord*.

> Mr. Whitefield visited Concord again, March 10, 1764. The next day being Sabbath, Mr. Bliss at the special request of Mr. Whitefield, preached in the morning and Mr. Whitefield in the afternoon. This was one of Mr. Bliss's most powerful efforts . . . But it was the last time Mr. Bliss ever appeared in the pulpit. He was soon after taken sick with a consumption in which he languished till his death . . . During the ministry of Mr. Bliss, 290 persons were admitted to the church in full communion, 328 owned the covenant and 1,424 were baptized.[13]

Genealogical Register, (Boston, MA: Published by the Society, 1901), vol. 55, pp. 145-146.
8   *Boston Post-Boy,* March 5, 1764, p. 3.
9   "A Quiet Country Town: 18th Century Medford," *Medford Historical Society,* 2016).
10 George Whitefield, *Works of George Whitefield,* vol. III, p. 310.
11 John W. Jordon and James Hadder, *Genealogical and Personal History of Fayette and Greene Counties, Pennsylvania,* (New York: Lewis Historical Publishing Company, 1912), vol. II, p. 469.
12 "Daniel Bliss," www.findagrave.com, p. 2.
13 Lemuel Shattuck, *History of Concord, Middlesex County, Massachusetts . . . ,* (Acton, MA: Russell, Odiorne, and Company, 1835), p. 181.

The almost twenty-five-year friendship between Daniel Bliss and George Whitefield lasted through the best and the worst of the awakenings.

> In 1741, the celebrated Whitefield preached here, in the open air, to a great congregation. Mr. [Daniel] Bliss heard that great orator with delight, and by his earnest sympathy with him, in his opinion and practice, gave offense to him and a part of his people. Party and mutual councils were called, but no grave charge was made good against him . . . The Council admonished Mr. Bliss of some improprieties of expression, but bore witness of his purity and fidelity in the office. In 1764, Whitefield preached again at Concord, on Sunday afternoon, Mr. Bliss preached in the morning and the congregation thought it was the better of the two sermons. It was also his last.[14]

After writing on March 10 from Concord, Whitefield preached through the country towns and maritime cities of northern New England. On March 2, 1764, the *New Hampshire Gazette* helped welcome Whitefield to New Hampshire by printing a favorable account of his financial contribution to victims of an epidemic in Boston. His next preserved correspondence is from Portsmouth:

> March 23, 1764
> At present, my way is clear to go on preaching till I can journey southward. The enclosed will inform you what hath been done by one sermon in Providence, formerly a most ungodly place, forty miles south of Boston. At Newbury, which I left yesterday, is a stir indeed. On Lord's Day I shall begin here.

> March 30, 1764
> You will know from others, what cheer the Redeemer gives us in America. Good cheer, Mrs. M_____, good cheer. He rains down righteousness; he rains down bread from heaven on the congregations. This supports (and at times overcomes) my tottering tabernacle.[15]

Rev. Thomas Smith of Falmouth, Maine, wrote in his journal on April 4, 1764, "Mr. Whitefield I hear is at York."[16] York, Maine was only a few miles northeast from Portsmouth, New Hampshire. Whitefield had two pastoral allies in York, Rev. Isaac Lyman of the First Church; and Rev. Samuel Lankton of the Second Church. In 1749, Lyman replaced the popular Rev. Samuel Moody at the First Church, who died in 1747. As a youth born in Northampton in 1725, Isaac Lyman had Rev. Jonathan Edwards for his pastor. Lyman, a Yale College graduate in 1747, was a student at the college when Whitefield was denounced by the Yale president and faculty in 1745, and he may have heard Whitefield preach outdoors in New Haven at that time. Isaac Lyman served in York from 1749 to his death in 1810. Another Whitefield ally in York was Rev. Samuel Lankton of the Second Church. Known as an evangelical and pious minister, Lankton settled at the church in 1754, and served in York for over forty years. Many of his parishioners were Scottish immigrants and Calvinists who would have happily welcomed George Whitefield.[17]

While preaching in New Hampshire and Maine, some ministers watched Whitefield and dreaded his coming to their towns. One was Rev. Samuel Williams of the Congregational Church in Bradford, Massachusetts. A descendant of the original Puritans who settled Massachusetts, Williams practiced "religious

---

14 Josephine L. Swayne, editor, *The Story of Concord,* (Boston, MA: E.F. Worchester Press, 1906), p. 35.
15 Ibid.
16 Thomas Smith, *Journal of the Rev. Thomas Smith,* (Portland, ME: Joseph S. Bailey, Printer, 1849), p. 198.
17 William D. Williamson, *The History of the State of Maine from its First Discovery, A.D. 1602 to the Separation, A.D. 1820 . . . ,* (Hallowell, ME: Glazier, Masters, & Smith, 1839), vol. II, p. 279.

rationalism" and was called by his biographer "a citizen of the Age of Reason."[18] A Harvard College graduate in 1761, Williams sat under the college tutelage of Rev. Nathaniel Appleton. The loathing Appleton had towards Whitefield influenced his students. "Appleton was tolerant of nearly everyone except George Whitefield and other itinerant revivalists."[19] Samuel Williams was a minister in Bradford from 1764 to 1779, after which he became a professor at Harvard. Upon his arrival in Bradford in 1764, the New Light evangelically-minded members of his church departed for the Congregational Church in nearby Rowley, or assisted in founding the First Baptist Church across the Merrimack River in Haverhill. Williams had open antipathy towards Jonathan Edwards and George Whitefield, and recoiled at their Calvinistic insistence on the depravity of mankind.[20] Williams was passionate about science and especially cosmology. He was relieved that Whitefield's illness prevented the itinerant from visiting Bradford.

A sketch of Rev. Samuel Williams, about the time he opposed George Whitefield in 1764.
Source: todayinscience.com.

Another minister north of Boston that dreaded the arrival of George Whitefield was Rev. Jacob Bailey, an Episcopal minister in rural Dresden, Maine. Whitefield had travelled into rural Maine in the early spring of 1745, and Bailey did not look forward to his return visit. Bailey was born in Rowley, Massachusetts in 1731 and grew up in a rural community that fully embraced the Great Awakening. As a youth he heard Whitefield preach in Rowley, but the evangelist "failed to stir his enthusiasm."[21] Bailey rejected the revival movement and did not accept the Puritan influences of his minister, Rev. Jedediah Jewett.[22] Bailey believed the town of Rowley to be "a place remarkable for ignorance, narrowness of mind, bigotry."[23] He was prepared for college by Jewett and graduated from Harvard in 1755, at a time when Whitefield was not welcomed on campus.

While a student at Harvard, Bailey heard Whitefield preach in Boston at a public execution in 1754.[24] After graduation, Bailey taught school for a few years in Kingston and Hampton, New Hampshire. Then he taught school in Gloucester, Massachusetts in 1758, and was ordained as a Congregational minister. Thereafter, Bailey studied for ordination in the Church of England, an unpopular endeavor in Colonial New England. He departed Gloucester for England, where he heard Whitefield preach outside to thousands. Bailey was amused by what he believed to be the carnival atmosphere of outside evangelical preaching.[25] He was ordained as an Anglican priest and returned to New England in March 1760.

Jacob Bailey's first assignment as an Episcopal priest was at Frankfort, now called Dresden, Maine. Frankfort was a new, planned community with the founders of the town requesting an Episcopal Church. Bailey was a frontier missionary for the Church of England. His ministry was among a hardscrabble and gritty people that sought to carve a town out of the Maine wilderness. They experienced harsh weather,

---

18 Robert Rothschild, *Two Brides for Apollo: The Life of Samuel Williams, 1743-1817*, (Bloomington, IN: iUniverse Press, 2009), pp. xxiv, xxix.
19 Ibid., p. 16.
20 Ibid., p. xxix.
21 James S. Leamon, *The Rev. Jacob Bailey, Maine Loyalist: For God, King, Country, and Self*, (Amherst, MA: University of Massachusetts Press, 2012), p. 20
22 Ibid., p. 13.
23 Ibid., p. 12.
24 Ibid., p. 20.
25 Ibid., p. 4.

poor roads, limited contact with the outside world, wild animals, infestations of mosquitoes, and occasional confrontations with Indians. Bailey opposed Puritanism and its Calvinistic doctrines.[26]

We get some insight as to what Jacob Bailey thought of George Whitefield from an interaction between Bailey and a longstanding Whitefield supporter, Rev. Jonathan Parsons of Newbury, Massachusetts. In August 1754, while Bailey was still a student at Harvard, he was home in the Rowley area. Whitefield was soon to return to that area on an itinerant preaching tour. As Rowley was near Newbury, Bailey went to church services at Parson's meeting house on August 11, 1754. Jonathan Parsons and Jedediah Jewett were friends and both were concerned about Jacob Bailey's Harvard education and his anti-revival learnings. Bailey and Parsons spent that Sunday together, sharing meals, conversation, and attending two church services at what is now called the Old South Presbyterian Church in Newburyport. The college student Bailey was not supportive of Whitefield's pending visit and told the minister Parson so. Bailey said, "I had some discourse with Mr. Parsons upon diverse subjects, but most especially concerning those rambling preachers, that have dispersed themselves over these parts of the country, to the great disturbance of both ministers and people."[27] Ten years later, with Bailey now a newly ordained Episcopal priest in Rural Maine, Whitefield approached. Whitefield planned to itinerate into rural Maine, but his health forced him to reconsider. Bailey breathed a sigh of relief that the premier of "those rambling preachers" was not coming to Frankfort, Maine after all.

When Whitefield arrived in Newburyport, he was greeted by his long-time friend Rev. Jonathan Parsons. This was the first time Whitefield had seen the new church building for what would be later called the Old South Presbyterian Church. The facilities were beautiful. The exterior of the building today looks very much like it did when Whitefield first saw it in 1764.

Under Rev. Jonathan Parsons, this meeting house was constructed in 1756 in what is today downtown Newburyport, Massachusetts. The inside has been altered and updated but many original features remain. The outside is virtually the same as the original. Photograph by Ken Lawson.

Throughout Whitefield's 1764 tour in New England, opposition was minimal. Denominational rivalries of the past were no longer antagonistic. Tensions between New Lights and Old Lights had faded away, overwhelmed by the political uncertainties of the day and the routines of life. A March 15, 1764 Boston newspaper account stated, "Friday last the Rev. Mr. WHITEFIELD preached at Charleston; and yesterday at Medford. He has been desired to postpone his preaching in this Town for some Time, as there might be danger of spreading the Small-Pox, by such crowds of People attending his lectures."[28] Whitefield then headed north. For example, an account of Whitefield in

---

26 Charles E. Allen, *Rev. Jacob Bailey: His Character and Works*, (Lincoln County Historical Society, 1895), p. 12.
27 William S. Bartlett, *The Frontier Missionary: A Memoir of the Life of the Rev. Jacob Bailey*, (New York: Stanford and Swords Publishing, 1853), pp. 28-29.
28 *The Pennsylvania Gazette*, March 15, 1764, p. 2.

Portsmouth, New Hampshire dated March 30, 1764, reveals his welcome by various denominations and civil leaders, and the large crowds drawn to his preaching.

> Portsmouth, (New Hampshire) March 30.
>
> Last Saturday Morning the Reverend Mr. WHITEFIELD preached to a crowded Auditory in the Rev. Mr. Haven's Meeting-House, and on Tuesday in the Rev. Dr. Langdon's—He had at a moderate computation five thousand hearers—He preaches again Tomorrow at the same place, at ten o'clock—The different Denominations of Christians, unite in attending his lectures.
>
> The next Morning after Mr. WHITEFIELD came to Town, he was waited upon by the Selectmen, and a Number of other Gentlemen, to welcome him to this Place.[29]

This report narrates Whitefield's overwhelming acceptance in Portsmouth from March 23 to 27, 1764, and shows that the aging and sometimes sickly evangelist could gather energy to occasionally preach to thousands indoors or in the open air. In Portsmouth, Whitefield suffered an illness which confined him to bed for many days. A London newspaper reported this incident weeks later, on May 12, 1764:

> We are informed by the latest letters from the Rev. Mr. Whitefield that his intentions were to have visited Nova Scotia, Cape Breton, Quebec, Montreal and from thence Southward to all the British back settlements, 'til he came to Georgia; but his health being greatly impaired, his intentions were altered.[30]

The account of Ruth Blay in Portsmouth deserves note. As a schoolteacher and seamstress, Ruth Blay (1737-1768) was executed for "private burial and concealment of a bastard child."[31] Ruth was raised in southern New Hampshire during the Great Awakening and its aftermath. The Blay family, like their neighbors, were influenced by the many visits of George Whitefield through the area. Ruth and her family are all listed as church members and appear to be typical citizens of that day. Southern New Hampshire was experiencing increased frustrations with policies from Great Britain. At age thirty one, the unmarried Ruth Blay was pregnant. She concealed her pregnancy, and delivered the child in secret. Apparently, the child was born dead. The ashamed Ruth discarded the corpse in a barn. The dead child was found, Ruth was put on trial and convicted, and she was publicly hung by the neck until dead. She was buried in an unmarked grave. The saga of Ruth Blay reveals life in the Portsmouth area in the mid-1760s. It was a time of religious conviction, rising secularism, and political uncertainty.

South of Portsmouth, across the Merrimack River, is Newburyport. An anecdote from Whitefield's 1764 visit to Newburyport has survived. The account is of a worrisome mother and her pre-teenage daughter's love of dancing.

> The mother of a young lady at Newburyport having told Whitefield that her daughter was fond of dancing, he gave her a reproving look which she never afterwards forgot, and his reply pierced her conscience. Whitefield, with a peculiar tone, said, "My dear young friend, do you not know that every step you dance is on the brink of hell?" That young lady became Mrs.

---

29 Quoted in the *Boston Post-Boy*, April 2, 1764, p. 3.
30 Arnold Dallimore, *George Whitefield: The Life and Times of the Great Evangelist of the Eighteenth Century Revival*, (Carlisle, PA: Banner of Truth Trust, 1980), vol. II, p. 433.
31 Carolyn Marvin, *Hanging Ruth Blay: An Eighteenth Century New Hampshire Tragedy*, (Charleston, SC: The History Press, 2010), p. 84.

Pearson, who died in 1852, the oldest person in the parish, having arrived at the advanced age of ninety-eight. She was the last survivor in that place of those who had the great privilege of listening to the magic eloquence of Whitefield.[32]

Whitefield arrived back in Boston on April 10, after about five weeks of preaching up and down northern New England. Again, he visited Salem, Ipswich, Rowley, Newburyport, and other small towns. An anecdote from this period relates to Rev. Isaac Morrill of Wilmington, Massachusetts. From 1741 to his death in 1793, Morrill served at the Church of Christ (Congregational) in Wilmington. Located about fifteen miles northwest of Boston, colonial Wilmington was a small farming community. Isaac Morrill was not a supporter of the awakening, he did not endorse the Calvinism of the Puritan founding fathers, and he openly opposed George Whitefield. Wilmington town history states:

> Rev. Whitefield was traveling through the colonies, preaching a new style of religion . . . Rev. Morrill not only refused to allow him the use of the pulpit of the Church of Christ, but also took to horseback and visited every family in town, forbidding them from attending Rev. Whitefield's service. Rev. Whitefield did preach in Wilmington, beneath an elm tree that stood near Middlesex Avenue in North Wilmington. A picture of that elm is to be seen on the town seal. It is possible that some Wilmington people didn't listen to him, but tradition says it was "only Indians."[33]

Isaac Morrill is renowned in Wilmington as a founding father of the town. He served as a military chaplain and was an outspoken advocate for independence from Great Britain. In May 1780, Morrill sat on a committee to endorse the Constitutional Convention in Cambridge, Massachusetts. He was a respected religious and civil leader, and a pillar of the Wilmington community.[34] "Isaac Morrill may be listed as being among the greatest men ever to have lived in Wilmington."[35] He was not, however, a supporter of George Whitefield, as the following account reveals:

> Rev. Mr. Morrill of Wilmington, was a decided Arminian, and a bitter opponent of Whitefield. It is said that Whitefield once sent an appointment for preaching on the common by the meeting-house in Wilmington, when Father Morrill mounted his horse, and rode to every house in town to forbid attendance, thus carrying the notice to every family, and securing for Mr. Whitefield an overwhelming congregation.[36]

The Rev. Isaac Morrill house in Wilmington, Massachusetts. Photograph taken c. 1910.

Source: http://homenewshere.com/ wilmington_town_ crier/news/article_23c17540-da53-11e0-a633- 001cc4c03286.html

---

32 Joseph B. Wakeley, *Anecdotes of the Rev. George Whitefield*, (London: 1772), pp. 341-342.
33 Larz Neilson, "The Fighting Parson," *Wilmington Town Crier*, October 19, 1983.
34 Annie Morrill Smith, *Morrill Kindred in America . . .* , (New York: The Lyons Genealogical Company, 1864), p. 62.
35 Larz Neilson, "The Fighting Parson," p. 1.
36 *Contributions to the Ecclesiastical History of Essex County, Massachusetts*, (Boston, MA: Congregational Board of Publication, 1865), p. 19.

In an interesting twist of fate, Isaac Morrill is mostly forgotten in Wilmington, while everyday, tens-of-thousands of Wilmington residents live and work under the town seal, which depicts the Whitefield Elm, under which the itinerant evangelist preached in 1764.

Unfortunately, no correspondence from Whitefield has survived from his spring 1764, itinerant travels in northeastern Massachusetts. As he travelled southward towards Boston, Whitefield was not welcomed in Salem by Rev. Thomas Barnard. As a member of the Puritan Barnard family that helped found the Massachusetts Bay Colony, Thomas Barnard was born in Newbury, Massachusetts to Puritan parents. He was a man of high intellect but was not a gifted public speaker. Doctrinally, he was called an Arminian, meaning he did not accept the Calvinistic beliefs of his Puritan forefathers. While his hometown of Newbury was consumed with the Great Awakening, Barnard was not a supporter of the movement. "He left Newbury on account of opposition from the friends of Whitefield; studied and practiced law after his dismissing; but afterwards returned to the ministry and was settled at Salem, September 18, 1755."[37] Barnard had not seen or heard Whitefield since the itinerant travelled through Massachusetts in 1754, and he dreaded his return. Barnard was academic, quiet, and disposed to intellectual pursuits in the comfort of his study. He saw Whitefield as an agitator, a bombastic troublemaker who unsettled the orderliness of society. Barnard was relieved when Whitefield travelled in the area and no religious disruptions occurred in Salem in 1764. The same could not be said for nearby Rowley.

Rev. Jedediah Jewett of Rowley was an outspoken New Light who welcomed Whitefield and supported the revival. Whenever Whitefield was in the area, he had an eager reception and an open pulpit in Rowley. The Congregational Church under Jewett had periods of revival off-and-on over the years. In 1764, because of Whitefield's visit, a period of revival swept over parts of the town, and attendance at the church increased. One historical account from Rowley stated that the period of revival after Whitefield's visit lasted through 1764 and into 1765, with "several dozens" added to the Congregational Church membership.[38] From Rowley, Whitefield headed south about twenty miles to Boston.

As Whitefield approached Boston, Boston newspapers announced his imminent return to the city. For example, the *Boston Weekly Newsletter*, dated April 19, 1764, stated, "Tuesday last the Rev. Mr. Whitefield came to town from the eastward: his ill state of health has not yet permitted him to preach." Whitefield's correspondence, written in Boston after returning from a preaching tour to the northeast, reveals some of the successes of his recent travels.

> April 20, 1764
>
> How I do long to see you! I have been at my *ne plus ultra* northward, and am now more free and capable settling my affairs southward.
>
> At present, by my late excursions I am brought low; but rest and care may brace me up again for some little further service for our glorious Emmanuel. A most blessed influence hath attended the Word in various places, and many have been made to cry out, "What shall we do to be saved?" O for such a cry at the Southward!

---

37 *The First Centenary of the North Church and Society in Salem, Massachusetts*, (Salem, MA: Printed for the Society, 1873), p. 171.
38 Thomas Gage and James Bradford, *The History of Rowley: Anciently Including Bradford, Boxford, and Georgetown*, (Boston, MA: Ferdinand Andrews, Printer, 1840), p. 23.

A recent photograph of part of the Rowley town common. Here Whitefield preached to multitudes. The home of Rev. Jedediah Jewett is on the far right. Photograph by Ken Lawson.

April 23, 1764

I find I can do but little for him, and by a late return of my disorder; was in danger of doing less. But, in his name, I am recovered and yesterday got upon my throne once again. Words cannot express the eagerness of the people to hear. I was meditating an escape to the Southward last week; but Boston people sent a gospel hue and cry after me, and really brought me back. Lord Jesus, let it be for Thy glory, and for Thy people's good![39]

Whitefield continued to preach in the Boston area for a few more weeks. *The Boston Gazette,* April 30, 1764, reported, "Tuesday last the Rev. Mr. Whitefield preached at the Old North; and Saturday at the Old South meeting house, to very crowded auditories. He is to preach next Wednesday at the New North." Some of the ministers and throngs of people begged Whitefield for a 6 a.m. lecture, to hear the Scriptures expounded before the workday began. He was willing to accommodate, stating, "People here beg earnestly for a six o'clock morning lecture. I hope to get strength to satisfy them."[40] Further, Whitefield stated:

Friends have ever constrained me to stay here, for fear of running into summer's heat. Hitherto I find the benefit of it. Whatever it is owing to, through mercy, I am now much better in health than I was this time twelvemonth, and can now preach thrice a week to very large auditories without hurt. Every day I hear of some brought under concern, and, I trust when I remove, a blessing will be left behind. This is the will of grace. To the glorious giver, purchaser and applier of it, be all the glory.[41]

In the spring and early summer of 1764, George Whitefield preached in Boston as often as his health allowed. Several times a week he preached in familiar meeting houses, supported by his clergy friends and their congregations. For the several newspapers in Boston, Whitefield preaching almost daily was no longer

---

39 Ibid., pp. 310-312.
40 Arnold Dallimore, *George Whitefield: The Life and Times,* p. 311. Letter dated May 19, 1764.
41 Luke Tyerman, *The Life of the Rev. George Whitefield,* vol. II, p. 476. *George Whitefield, Works,* vol. III, p. 311.

news. For all of May 1764, Whitefield preached in Boston as his health allowed, but the city newspapers were silent concerning his day-to-day activities. This silence was broken in the June 7, 1764 edition of the *Boston News-Letter*, which stated, "The Rev. Mr. GEORGE WHITEFIELD having preached his Farewell Sermon on Tuesday last, at the Old South, intends setting out this day, or To-morrow, for the Southward."[42] An extended notice of Whitefield departing Boston was printed a few days later by the *Boston Post-Boy*.

> Last Tuesday morning the Rev. Mr. Whitefield preached his farewell Sermon at the Rev. Dr. Sewall's Meeting-House.—He has resided about nine Weeks in this Town, and preached as often as the state of his Health would permit, to large, crowded, and attentive Auditories.—He has met with great Acceptance among all denominations of Judicious Christians, and we trust Religious Impressions which will never be erased, are form'd among the Minds of many, by his awakening, instructive and edifying discourses.[43]

Unfortunately for Whitefield, Boston newspapers focused on whether his public preaching should be canceled because of the small pox epidemic. Extended debates in print attempted to determine if the common health of the city was endangered by these large public events. One account stated:

> His excellency the governor and some of the honorable of his majesty's counsellors from a generous concern for the safety of the town of Boston, having been pleased to take into consideration, the tendency of Mr. Whitefield's lectures, to collect a great concourse of people of all ranks from this metropolis, were of opinion; that the continuance of those lectures would be a means of spreading the small pox, and therefore that it would be best for Mr. W. to suspend his labors for some time—and two of the honorable gentlemen were desired to acquaint Mr. Whitefield of this appreciation and opinion . . . The Selectmen upon application to them were of the opinion that there was no danger from his preaching, and had refused to desire him to desist: Finally, after mature deliberation, Mr. W. Judg'd it best and his duty to preach on the Saturday following, and to notify another lecture, though this had been omitted (canceled), tis presumed from a due regard to the opinion of his excellency and their honors.[44]

Whitefield the evangelist had great compassion for New Englanders. He admired their Puritan heritage and was encouraged by the many ministers and laymen from the area who enthusiastically supported his work. In the 1740s, he had been overwhelmed by their response at the beginning of the Great Awakening. As he continued to preach his distinctly Bible-based evangelical message, Whitefield longed to see theological orthodoxy stabilized in New England.

> He believed in man's ruin by sin; in the certain interminable woe that awaited the impenitent; in the mercy of God through Jesus Christ, and the free hope of salvation through faith in the cross. Such were his views, and under this conviction he looked upon his audiences. He saw but one hope set before them, and with his whole soul moved and melted by the love of Christ on one hand, and the love of souls on the other, he pressed every hearer, with all the energy of a dying man speaking to dying men, to accept the great salvation.[45]

---

42   *Boston News-Letter,* June 7, 1764, p. 3.
43   *Boston Post-Boy,* June 11, 1764, p. 3.
44   *The Boston Gazette,* March 5, 1764, p. 2.
45   J.B. Wakeley, *The Prince of Pulpit Orators: A Portraiture of Rev. George Whitefield,* (New York: Carleton & Lanahan Publishers, 1871), pp. 36-37.

The diary of Rev. Samuel Cooper shows the everyday concerns and typical events of 1764, and briefly notes Whitefield's activities. Cooper was a graduate of Harvard College who succeeded his father, Rev. William Cooper, as minister of the Brattle Street Church in Boston. Samuel Cooper served there from 1745 until his death in 1783. Cooper wrote the following remarks in his 1764 *Journal*.[46]

An undated painting of Rev. Samuel Cooper, Brattle Street Church, Boston.

Source: https://www.masshist.org/database/ viewer.php?item_id=3462&mode=large&img_ step=1&&pid=38&noalt=1&br=1

Feb. 19   I preached at Kingston P.M. Mr. Dana candidate for me A.M. Dr. Chauncy P.M.

Feb. 26   Exchanged [preaching] Mr. Checkley . . . at home P.M. Baptized Sam; son of Sam and Lucy Rotch.

Mar. 1   Preached Thursday lecture. Mr. Whitefield present.

Mar. 11   Preached all day. Baptised John Pimm of Richard and Sarah Green.

Apr. 8   Exchanged [preaching] Mr. Checkley A.M. At home P.M.

Apr. 12   Public fast.

May 6   Preached at home and administered Lord's Supper.

May 20   Preached at home all day. Mr. Whitefield present P.M.

May 30   Married Jacob Wemdell to Marsha Oliver.

Another Boston diarist, Mr. John Boyle, captured Whitefield's 1764 visit in his writings. Boyle was a printer and bookseller in Boston. He painted a well-rounded picture of the events surrounding the evangelist's tour.[47]

Feb. 12   Died after a short illness in the 46 years of her age, Mrs. Sarah Savage, Consort to Mr. Samuel Phillips Savage.

---

46   "Notes from the Rev. Samuel Cooper's Interleaved Almanacs of 1764 and 1769," *The New England Historical and Genealogical Register,* (Boston, MA: 1901), vol. 55, pp. 145-146.

47   "Boyle's Journal of Occurrences in Boston," *The New England Historical and Genealogical Register,* (Boston, MA: 1930), vol. 84, pp. 164-165.

Feb. 18   Arrived in town from New York, that eminent servant of Jesus Christ, Mr. George Whitefield.

Feb. 26   Many persons in town have lately been visited with the smallpox, some whom have died.

Mar. 3   Rev'd. Mr. Whitefield set out for Portsmouth. He has preached twice a week since he came to town.

Mar. 5   The small pox is now 10 families of the town.

Apr. 1   Arrived in 6 weeks from London, Capt. Calef . . . Dr. Samuel Marshall [came] with passengers.

Apr. 18   Arrived in town from Portsmouth Rev'd. Geo. Whitefield, who had been preaching in the Eastward.

May 7   An act of Parliament is now pending for levying certain Army Duties in the American Colonies.

May 9   Died of the small pox in the 32 year of her age, Mrs. Deborah Torrey, Consort of Mr. Samuel Torrey, merchant.

June 5   Mr. Whitefield preached his farewell sermon at the Rev'd Dr. Sewall's meeting-house. He had resided about nine weeks in this town, and preached as often as the ill state of his health would permit, to large, crowded, and attentive auditories.

While in the Boston area in the early spring of 1764, Whitefield learned of the death of his friend Rev. Daniel Bliss of Danvers. The Bliss obituary, printed in Boston newspapers a week later, revealed his undisputed character and spirituality.

Supplement to *The Boston Gazette*

(Concord) May 17, 1764.

On the 11th instant died here, the Rev. Mr. Daniel Bliss, late pastor of the Church of Christ in this place, in the 50th year of his age . . . .He early became a preacher; and after a proper time of probation in this town, had the oversight of a flock of Christ committed to him by his solemn ordination. He continued laboring in the Word and doctrine among his people until his last sickness and death; and being possessed by a great degree of zeal for the interest of Christ's kingdom and the good of souls, he exerted it in his ministerial labors. He was a fervent preacher and maintainer of the Doctrines of Grace, and was to a good degree a faithful steward of the mysteries of Godliness; and an instrument in the hand of God, of greatly enlarging and building up the Church of Christ in Concord . . . .

As a young boy, Timothy Farrar heard Whitefield preach in Concord, Massachusetts and was converted. After advanced schooling, he became both a county judge and a state superior court judge in New Hampshire. His extended obituary notice reveals his genuine conversion and the integrity of his religious convictions.

> The religious character of Judge Farrar deserves special notice. It commenced in early life. At the age of thirteen, he listened to a sermon from Whitefield, preached at Concord, his native town. He had taken a seat in the gallery directly in front of the speaker, that he might have the best opportunity to observe his manner, and obtain a correct impression of the man. But as the preacher uttered his message, curiosity soon gave place to the conviction of the sacred importance of the truths uttered. He was deeply impressed. That sermon was never forgotten. The conviction of its truths was practical and permanent—and although he did not for several years make a public profession of religion, yet he dated the dawn of his Christian life from that sermon. His theology was of the Puritan school, and his life was in correspondence, and partook largely of the Puritan element. His religion was the religion of principle, and had its application to his whole life—yet not of mere principle; his heart and warm affections were in it. He enjoyed religion, and especially in the later part of his life.[48]

The 1764 tour of Boston and northern New England found Whitefield in fragile health, well-received by the people, and in his usual activities of itinerant preaching and personal letter writing. Whitefield, though physically weak, did his best to maintain and encourage religious revival. These efforts appeared to be successful upon his departure from Boston in the summer of 1764. A summary of his recent ministries was in *The Boston Gazette*, June 11, 1764.

> The Rev. Mr. Whitefield preached his farewell sermon last Wednesday, at the Old South Meeting-house, and the day following he set out on his journey to the Southward. The notice he gave of his departure was sudden; and it was the more affecting to his friends, as there is but little reason to expect he will ever have another opportunity of making another visit here. His lectures have been attended by persons of figure and rank, as well as others; and of the opinion of those of his hearers who are allowed to be the best judge, they have been adapted to promote the common cause of Christianity. His auditories have been continually numerous, attentive and very affected: which affords reason to believe that his preaching has been greatly successful: He has been assiduous in his labors among us, notwithstanding his bodily infirmities: and as he still appears to be influenced, in his general design, by a benevolent disposition towards mankind, it would be hardly doing justice to the town, not to add, that during his short residence in it, the inhabitants have shown him particular marks of their affection and esteem.

On June 1, 1764, Whitefield was in Boston waiting for maritime transportation to begin his southward travels. While waiting for a boat he could still preach in the city. In a letter he penned on that date, he described his New England ministry as overwhelmingly successful. He wrote that "friends constrained him to stay" and that, "I am in much better health . . . and can now preach thrice a week to very large auditories without hurt. Every day I hear of some brought under concern; and I trust, whenever I remove, a blessing will be left behind." He also stated, "In about a fortnight [two weeks or less], God willing, I purpose to set forward. It will be hard parting. But heaven will make amends for all."[49] Several days later he was still awaiting transportation, for his June 1 letter has an appendix dated June 7, which stated, "Parting here hath been heart breaking: I

---

48 *The New England Historical and Genealogical Register*, (Boston, MA: 1849), vol. 3, p. 291.
49 George Whitefield, *Works of George Whitefield*, (1772; reprinted by Quinta Press, Shropshire, England, 2000), vol. III, p. 311.

cannot stand it. I must away for the southward."[50] Whitefield wrote that he was awaiting "a packet," meaning a maritime vessel that made various stops in ports to deliver mail, to deliver and receive supplies, and to transport travelers. He had often found an ocean trip restorative to his fragile health. In early June 1764, a Rhode Island businessman named Samuel Tillinghast was in Boston and made the following diary notation on June 10: "Windy weather. Mr. Whitefield held M'g [meeting] at Newton. Very warm."[51] Mr. Tillinghast was a Baptist shopkeeper and merchant in Providence and Warwick, Rhode Island. He referenced Whitefield speaking in Newton, Massachusetts. This was at the First Church Congregational, where Whitefield preached with great effect in 1740. The previous minister who welcomed Whitefield, Rev. John Cotton, died in 1757. The new minister at the church was Rev. Jonas Meriam, who served the church from 1758 to 1780.

There is no way to know how many stops the coastal packet made on the journey from Boston to New York, or how long the vessel stayed in each port. We do have, however, a June 1764, account of Whitefield preaching in southern Connecticut, on his way to New York. In Groton, Connecticut, Whitefield had a friend in Rev. Jonathan Barber. Whitefield and Barber met in 1740, when the roving evangelist first preached through southern Connecticut. They became devoted friends, so much so that Whitefield persuaded Barber to become the administrator at the Bethesda Orphanage in Georgia. After many years of service at the orphanage, Barber eventually became the pastor of the First or South Society (Congregational Church) in Groton in 1758. In 1764, when Whitefield travelled through Groton, he and Barber had a memorable reunion. One account stated,

> In the same year [1764], he [George Whitefield] returned from Boston by way of Providence. He travelled in his chariot, and stopped in Groton at the house of Mr. Barber, where he was received as a welcome and much honored guest.
>
> Notice had been given of his coming, and at ten o'clock next morning he preached, standing on a scaffolding that had been extended for the purpose, on a level with the second story of Mr. Barber's house, and upon which he stepped from the chamber window. All the area around was thronged with the audience. Many people had left home the day before, or had travelled all night to be upon the spot. At the conclusion of his discourse, he entered his chariot and went on his way, a multitude of people accompanying him on horses, or following on foot to Groton ferry, four miles. After crossing the ferry he was received by a similar crowd on the town [New London] wharf. He remained in town but an hour, and then proceeded on his journey to the south . . . .[52]

Whitefield was moving in haste. This account helps fill in a large gap in Whitefield's chronology. We read here that he departed Boston, stopped in Providence, preached at Groton, and travelled to New London to await transportation to New York. Tragedy awaited. The July 14, 1764 edition of *The Providence Gazette* stated, "Tuesday last the Rev. Mr. Whitefield set out for the southward; but the day following his servant having drunk some cider, and the weather being very warm, went into the water at Mr. Watson's ferry, to cool himself, and was soon after found drowned in not more than 2 feet of water."[53]

The next preserved letter Whitefield wrote is dated June 25, 1764, from New York. Reflecting on his recent New England preaching tour, Whitefield wrote, "The New England campaign is over, and I am thus far on my way to Georgia." He elaborated on his Boston ministry with a reference to a Mr. Smith, who showed hospitality to the itinerant preacher while he was in the city. Whitefield stated, "Mr. Smith, my

---

50 Ibid., p. 312.
51 Cherry F. Bamberg, editor, *The Diary of Capt. Samuel Tillinghast of Warwick, Rhode Island, 1757-1766*, (Rhode Island Historical Society, 2000), p. 329.
52 Frances M. Caulkins, *History of New London, Connecticut . . .* , (New London, CT: H.D. Utley, Printer, 1895), p. 460.
53 *The Providence Gazette*, July 14, 1764, p. 3.

faithful host, writes thus: "Your departure [from Boston] hence never before so deeply wounded us, and the most of this people; and they are injudicious enough to propose sending a book full of names to call you back. Your enemies are few, and even they seem to be at peace with you."[54]

Perhaps the greatest result of Whitefield's 1764 tour through New England was that he was now reconciled with Harvard College. The February 20, 1764 public letter from President Edward Holyoke and the college trustees praised Whitefield for his Christian character and benevolence. The feud had passed.

The following poem served as a farewell to Whitefield from Boston. It appeared in a highly unlikely place—the *Boston Weekly Newsletter,* on June 7, 1764.

> To the Rev. Mr. Whitefield, on his Departure:
>
> And must thou go? Farewell thou sacred Guide! God speed thy labors, God thy Strength support so great the Harvest, and the Field so wide.
>
> So from the Labors, and the Day so wicked, Go thou Man of God! Still, still display,
>
> All the rich Treasures of the heavenly Tongue, We owe thee much, and much our hearts would pay,
>
> Take all we can—a Blessing and a Song: We bless thy Zeal, and yet would urge thee Stay,
>
> Admire thy Haste, thy Presence yet implore, Babes of thy Prayer—supporting our tottering way,
>
> One parting Blessing and we wisht no more: Go run collect Manna far and wide,
>
> Thy Master's Kingdom thro' these Realms extended, Ten Thousand Converts rising at thy Side,
>
> Late, very late to God may'st thou ascend: On life's last Verge with Joy may'st thou survey,
>
> A numerous Harvest to thy Labors given, wrap'd in that Prospect. Then put off thy clay
>
> And crown the Transport with joys of Heaven.
>
> Amen.

---

54 George Whitefield, *Works of George Whitefield*, p. 312.

CHAPTER 34

NEW ENGLAND IN TRANSITION AND TURMOIL

1764-1770

THE NEW ENGLANDERS WHITEFIELD FIRST visited in 1740 bore little resemblance to those he preached to in 1764 and 1770. Almost thirty years of growth and prosperity had created a trans-Atlantic economic giant in Boston. Newport, Rhode Island was a major Colonial American port city. Smaller cities such as Groton and New London, Connecticut were booming, as were Salem, Massachusetts and Portsmouth, New Hampshire. In many areas, prosperity abounded, and material wealth was significant for many. In addition to financial changes, New Englanders were experiencing new directions and emphases in theology. By the mid-1760s, New England was no longer considered a land of Puritan orthodoxy.[1] Adding more confusion to this cultural turmoil, New Englanders sensed an increased militancy against Great Britain. Indeed, blood would be shed between British and New England colonists between Whitefield's 1764 and 1770 visits to the region.

Peaceful rolling hills, crooked roads, and isolated village hamlets were scattered along coastal New England in 1740. By the 1760s there developed larger towns, better roads, commercial centers, urban row houses, and factory buildings. The Merrimack and Ipswich rivers in Massachusetts supplied an endless amount of fish to the fishing industry, while deep-sea fishing in Rhode Island and other places provided an excellent catch. The lumber industry in many inland communities, such as Norwich, Connecticut was also experiencing growth and profit. Enormous amounts of lumber were timbered and delivered to coastal ports, to be either cut and milled, or sold in-the-rough and shipped overseas. New England ships loaded with fish, lumber, and other goods traded with European merchants for manufactured goods or slaves from Africa. New Haven and New London, Connecticut were prosperous port cities. Profits from fishing and trading created an elite mercantile class. In Massachusetts, port cities like Boston, Salem, Marblehead, and Newburyport became affluent. These port cities, in return, controlled local economic, cultural, and political life.[2]

There was significant development and success in merchant trading in New England. These merchants, who displayed a passion for entrepreneurial success, often led outwardly secular lifestyles. For example, William Gray, born in Lynn, Massachusetts in 1750, was raised in a home involved in the shoe manufacturing industry. By age twenty-eight he owned his own thriving business, he became active in the shipping trade, and he eventually became a state senator and the first bank president in Salem in 1792. In his memoirs there is little or no mention of religion or God, and no mention of Whitefield's frequent visits to the area. Mr. Gray was an extremely wealthy,

---

1   Richard L. Bushman, *From Puritan to Yankee: Character and Social Order in Connecticut, 1690-1765*, (Cambridge, MA: Harvard University Press, 1908).
2   Ronald N. Tagney, *A Country in Revolution: Essex County at the Dawning of Independence*, (Manchester, MA: Cricket Press, 1976), p. 11.

non-religious man who exerted considerable influence in the community.³ This was the face of the emerging New England.

Other examples of a new prosperous class of citizens were Richard Derby and Benjamin Pickman of Salem. Mr. Derby, the son of a sea captain, developed a sailing and trade business which became a huge enterprise with the West Indies and European markets. Derby then obtained interests in ship-building, real estate, and local politics, making him one of the most influential men in New England.⁴ Benjamin Pickman was already the son of a wealthy Salem fishing family when he expanded the family business into the Caribbean, providing salted and dried fish for slaves, while selling cod, lumber, barrels, grain, livestock, and other goods to European markets. Further, he imported large amounts of sugar, molasses, cotton, and indigo into New England.⁵ Neither Mr. Derby nor Mr. Pickman, in their extensive diaries or journals, express much religious faith or spiritual conviction.

In contrast to the pragmatic and business emphasis in the lives of Richard Derby and Benjamin Pickman of Salem, Massachusetts is the life of Benjamin Lyon (1729-1769) of Woodstock, Connecticut. Benjamin was married to a local woman, Mary May, in 1752 in the Woodstock Congregational Church. They are both buried in the East Woodstock Cemetery. The couple had thirteen children, not all survived to adulthood. In contrast to urban Salem, Woodstock was a rural farming community. Benjamin was a captain in the local Connecticut militia. His vocation is unknown. What is apparent in the life of Benjamin Lyon was his devout evangelical faith. He was actively involved in the life of the Woodstock Congregational Church, which was served by Rev. Abel Stiles from 1737 to his death in 1783.⁶

As a Yale College graduate in 1733 and in 1736, Rev. Stiles brought his pro-revival views to remote Woodstock. Benjamin Lyon was fully supportive of the awakening. His diary, written in neat handwriting and carefully dated, was bound with string, and is owned by the Connecticut Historical Society. In his diary, Lyons begins the year 1764 by lamenting his sins but rejoicing in Jesus as his savior, writing, "I pray that Jesus Christ may be magnified in me." Lyon recorded his frequent reading of Puritan books. He rejoiced in

A sketch depicting part of Salem, Massachusetts about 1765.

Source: *Salem in the Eighteenth Century.*

---

3   Edward Gray, *William Gray of Salem, Merchant*, (Boston, MA: Houghton Mifflin Company, 1914).
4   James D. Phillips, *The Life and Times of Richard Derby, Merchant of Salem, Massachusetts, 1712-1783*, (Cambridge, MA: Riverside Press, 1929).
5   Benjamin Pickman, *The Diary and Letters of Benjamin Pickman of Salem, Massachusetts, 1740-1819*, (Newport, RI: 1929).
6   Clarence W. Bowen, *Woodstock: An Historical Sketch*, (New York: G.P. Putnam's Sons, 1886), pp. 39-42.

"grace to stand complete in Him," and he recorded, "Blessed Jesus thou art my hope, my strength, my righteousness, my portion of happiness for evermore." Lyon frequently prayed for revival in the churches of New England. On January 30, 1764, he wrote, "Blessed Jesus, thou art my refuge, my hope, my righteousness, my Lord & Savior, my all, my portion forever."[7]

By the 1760s, cultural and economic self-sufficiency was becoming apparent in many New England communities. The homes of merchants, politicians, sea captains, and successful farmers began to display a grace and elegance previously seen only in the homes of the super wealthy in New England. Primitive carpentry became more artistic and refined, elegant brass fixtures replaced common pewter, and paintings by well-known artists hung in the finer homes. Church meeting houses lost their box-like appearance and functional simplicity, as Georgian towers, chandeliers, and elegant woodwork graced the interiors. Expensive carriages driven by servants transported the wealthy, while European clothing trends and styles sold quickly in coastal markets and in successful inland communities.

The financial prosperity of much of New England helped contribute to ever-increasing educational opportunities for a portion of society. Alstrom explains: "By 1763, secondary schools had made Americans residing in the older, more settled regions the most literate people in the world, while New England possessed an educational system that was probably excelled nowhere."[8] Wealthy New Englanders invested in local preparatory schools, sent their children to colleges, and continued to expand opportunities for the next generations. Harvard (founded 1636), Yale (founded 1701), Brown (founded 1764), and Dartmouth (founded 1769) provided the wealthy population of New England with educational opportunities and investment potential previously unknown in America.

Amidst the changing economic climate in New England, new movements in theology were taking shape. What was called the colonist's "Arminianism" was actually a movement away from the strict Calvinism of the Puritans and their Westminster Confession. Indeed, such tendencies became apparent because of Whitefield's first visit in 1740. Because of Harvard's social presence and intellectual orientation toward Europe, a certain European cosmopolitanism developed in the larger New England cities. Sophistication, secular values, and social refinement were the obsession of some who would not tolerate the Puritan theological concepts of human depravity and original sin. There was "an impressive merchant aristocracy that preferred a religious stance looking out on wide contemporary horizons rather than back to old Puritan ideals."[9]

Salem, Massachusetts is an example of a community that never fully embraced the awakening, nor fully endorsed Whitefield. By the 1760s, this prosperous port community was sending trading vessels around the world. There developed an elite class of fabulously wealthy bankers, ship owners, investors, merchants, and others. Many of the mansions of these millionaires are still standing on Chestnut Street and other places in Salem. Worldly pursuits dominated the community. A courthouse conducted the king's business and brought lawyers and others to Salem to live and work. The latest European fashions were on full display, while the working class had steady employment. The word "Yankee" initially meant those New Englanders with Puritan roots, but in the later eighteenth century the word soon came to mean all New Englanders. As James D. Phillips wrote of Salem, "The Yankee people were by then no means the pure English race culled from the Puritan stock."[10]

There was at least one voice in Salem resisting the transition from Puritan to Yankee. Rev. James Diman (1707-1788) was ordained at the Second or East Church in Salem in 1737, and spent over five decades at the church. A Harvard graduate in 1730, Diman was from Long Island, New York. George Whitefield preached in Salem in 1740, and traveled around the city many times over the years. Whitefield made no note of Diman in his *Journals*. The Second Congregational Church, under Rev. James Diman, was Puritan in beliefs and practices at a time when

---

7   *Diary of Benjamin Lyon, 1729-1769*, (original manuscript, Connecticut Historical Society).
8   Sydney E. Ahlstrom, *A Religious History of the American People*, (New Haven, CT: Yale University Press, 1972), p. 346.
9   Ibid., p. 389.
10 James D. Phillips, *Salem in the Eighteenth Century*, (Boston, MA: Houghton Mifflin Company, 1937), p. 177.

Puritanism was almost unknown in eclectic Salem. He was known as a "conservative" amidst the liberalizing culture of Salem in the mid-eighteenth century. "The Reverend James Diman, of the East Church . . . was a man of grave and awe-inspiring mien, a stern Puritan of the old school who greatly disapproved of the liberalism" of his day.[11] The gaieties and merriment of secular Salem had no appeal to him, and he was sometimes excluded from social functions.

Ministerial associations in New England had no binding legal power, and were incapable of stopping the descent into liberalism. There was no synod system among the congregational ministers by which they could hinder the propagation of liberal views or refuse to ordain "Arminian," better labeled moderate Calvinists leaning towards Unitarianism. In the context of increased independence and prosperity, and an unstructured ministerial hierarchy, it is hardly surprising that religious views that comforted the wealthy and conformed to their progressive lifestyles were prominent. By the end of the 1700s, more than three fourths of the one hundred oldest churches in eastern Massachusetts had abandoned their orthodox Puritan heritage for Unitarianism, Universalisms, or both.[12]

A 1760s portrait of Rev. James Diman of Salem, Massachusetts.

Source: Museum of Fine Arts, Houston, Texas.

Beverly, Massachusetts serves as a case study of ongoing religious turmoil felt by the awakening of decades past. The First Church in Beverly was founded in 1667. Because of shifting population, the Second Church in Beverly was started in 1713. Over the decades, as Whitefield travelled throughout the area, Rev. Joseph Champney of the First Church never supported Whitefield or the awakening, while Rev. John Chipman of the Second Church was an ongoing and outspoken Whitefield supporter. The official history of the First Church in Beverly states,

> Whitefield delivered sermons in several Essex County churches and certainly increased religious passions among their members . . . Rev. Champney was not impressed by Whitefield, and never invited him to come to Beverly, nor is there any record of any member of the Beverly Parish requesting his appearance . . . with the ordination of Rev. Champney [in 1729], the last official signs of the Puritan experiment vanished.[13]

Dr. Nathaniel Ames of Dedham, Massachusetts saw the religious controversies of his days as petulant and irrelevant, even idiotic. As a physician and author, he was widely known and reasonably wealthy. He was of the upper society in Dedham, and hobnobbed with the elite of Boston. Ames was of a Unitarian persuasion, and wrote that he saw no difference if "a person worshipped Jehovah or Jupiter." In his *Almanac for 1765*, Ames wrote against those "who under the pretense of religion" travel up and down "sowing sedition" and "railing disputes about holy trifles, destroying that universal charity that ought to warm the breath of every Christian towards every class of men . . . "[14]

The awakening had whet New England's appetite for alternative styles of religious expression. Those who sought enthusiastic revival preaching turned to Separatist meetings or Baptist preaching when available. Most Quakers remained Quakers. Those of an Old Light viewpoint often joined the more genteel Anglicans

---

11   James D. Phillips, *Salem in the Eighteenth Century*, p. 265
12   Sydney E. Ahlstrom, *A Religious History of the American People*, p. 390.
13   Charles E. Wainwright, *Tales from the Attic: A Celebration of the First 350 Years of the First Parish and Church in Beverly Massachusetts*, (Beverly, MA: Published by the First Church, Beverly, MA: 2017), pp. 25-26.
14   Nathaniel Ames, *Almanac for 1765*, (Boston, MA: R&S Draper, Printers, 1765), np. Original at the American Antiquarian Society, Worcester, MA.

to escape the revival's confusion, while some Congregationalists stayed in their ancestral churches, indifferent to the tumultuous changes around them in the theological world.[15]

An example of a New Light congregation that resisted the widening theological views of the day was the Chebacco parish in Ipswich (now Essex) Massachusetts. A few months after George Whitefield travelled through the area in 1764, Lucy Andrews gave her testimony to the Chebacco church. She was a married woman with small children at home. Her account is like accounts of spiritual awakening from the peak of the revival in the 1740s. Mrs. Andrews stated,

> I was awakened to a Sight of my lost condition, that I had been a Sinner all my days and done nothing but sin . . . I saw that every Sin deserved damnation, and that I was cut off. And then I had a view of Christ's Loveliness and of his wonderful condescending love in coming down to dye [die] for sinners. And my burden carried off . . . And I found Comfort in my soul and had such a sense of Christ's love and loveliness, that I could part with all for him . . . I find my mind is changed, that my heart is towards God and in religion, whereas it was before wholly in and after the world. I desire more Grace, and the Prayers of God's people for me that I may be made to press forward in the Christian life.[16]

By the mid-1700s, Natural Philosophy—that is, a system of thinking based on natural revelation and human reasoning and calculation—challenged and eventually superseded the Puritan ideals of New England's founders. Even Whitefield's prior four enormously successful evangelical tours through New England could not alter the course of this movement. A new vocabulary began to dominate polite conversations, with thoughts of nature, reason, and natural law being the most popular. Initially, any separation between the world of biblical revelation and the world of natural science had not been considered. Yet, as thinkers like John Locke and the more radical Thomas Paine became popular, words such as depravity, atonement, propitiation, divine satisfaction, and election were exchanged for the philosophical speculations of English, French, and German theologians and thinkers. Abstraction replaced orthodoxy and natural reason overtook biblical revelation throughout much of elite New England.[17]

Over time, the New Lights matured out of revivalism and rested upon their Edwardsian or Puritan foundation, while Charles Chauncey of Boston's First Church and Jonathan Mayhew of Boston's West Church were the primary spokesmen for the new rationalistic thinking. These men guided Protestant liberalism on its aggressive course, which eventually led to victory.[18] Orthodox ministers warned their people of danger when flawed human reason was placed above or alongside biblical revelation, believing that such a compromised form of Christianity was simply Deism.

> The "deist" believed in an impersonal God who, once he had created the universe, left it alone. Doubting the divinity of Christ, he was skeptical of the Bible as divine revelation: Christianity offered man an excellent set of ethics but little more. The American deist was a milder man than his French counterpart; he privately depreciated organized religion, but publicly supported it.[19]

Many congregations paid little or no attention to the turbulent theological changes sweeping across New England. For example, in Beverly, Massachusetts the First Church was apparently more interested in updating

---

15 James W. Schmotter, "Clerical Professionalism and the Great Awakening," *American Quarterly*, (Summer 1979), p. 167.
16 "Relation of Lucy Andrews, November 11, 1764." *John Cleveland Papers*, Essex Institute, box 1.
17 Martin E. Marty, *Pilgrims in Their Own Land: 500 Years of Religion in America*, (New York: Penguin Books, 1984), pp. 154–162. Williston Walker, *A History of the Congregational Churches in the United States*, (New York: Charles Scribner's Sons, 1916), pp. 267–274.
18 Charles E. Smith, *Yankees and God*, (New York: Hermitage House, 1954), p. 259.
19 David Hawke, *The Colonial Experience*, (New York: MacMillan Publishing, 1985), p. 436.

their congregational singing than in defining theological orthodoxy. By a vote in 1764, the deacons were authorized to select singers and seats were appropriated to their use, "that the spirit of singing Psalms might be revived, and that part of worship conducted with more regularity." This arrangement continued until 1774, when a choir was regularly installed in "the front seats of the parish, to pitch the tune and take the lead in singing."[20] Church records reflect nothing of the theological upheaval of the day, as the congregation slowly drifted into liberalism and away from its Puritan roots.

An undated image of Rev. Samuel Phillips, South Parish in Andover, Mass.

Source: https://en.wikipedia.org/wiki/Samuel_Phillips_(reverend)

Another church which paid little attention to the theological controversies of that day was the South Parish Church in Andover, Massachusetts. Rev. Samuel Phillips, first pastor of the South Parish, graduated from Harvard in 1708, was ordained in 1711, and served in Andover for sixty years until his death in 1771. During the Great Awakening he was a distant observer. Of the numerous New England testimonies both for and against Whitefield, the name of Samuel Phillips is not recorded. His fellow minister in Andover, Rev. John Barnard of North Parish signed the 1743 *Testimony* against Whitefield, but Phillips did not.[21] A second petition of anti-revival ministers was signed in 1745, originating from a ministerial association meeting on January 1. Again, Phillips of Andover did not endorse the proceedings. He was distant and unattached to the controversies. On the other extreme, the July 1743 ministerial meeting of pro-revival clergy in New England circulated a petition signed by almost one hundred ministers. Although several of Samuel Phillips' friends, with whom he exchanged pulpits, signed the petition supporting Whitefield and the revival, his own name is absent. Phillips stayed between both positions and appeared unmoved by the theological climate of his day. This neutrality lasted until his death in 1771.

The emotionalism and divisiveness of the Great Awakening caused New England pastors to think critically about practical issues of church discipline, evangelism, church membership, and soteriological issues related to who is a Christian and how a person is saved. It was more than an Old Light against New Light controversy, and both sides had articulate spokesmen that denounced the excesses of the awakening.[22]

The revival movement received tremendous support through President Thomas Clap of Yale College. Clap initially supported Whitefield in 1740, then quickly changed his mind to oppose the itinerant preacher. As time passed, Clap again came out in support of Whitefield. By the 1760s, Yale and its graduates were assuming a role in the American evangelical movement that they would not relinquish for over a century."[23]

Much New Light attention and support in the 1760s in New England centered on the work of the Rev. Eleazer Wheelock of Connecticut. In 1754, Wheelock began an Indian mission school to train Native Americans in the foundations of the Christian gospel before sending them back as ministers to their native people. By 1769, his school received an invitation from New Hampshire to transfer there and establish a college. This institution, later called Dartmouth College, sent Indian and Caucasian New Light ministers throughout New England and into the westward expanding colonial settlements, as well as to the Native American tribes in the northeast.

Before Whitefield's final visit to New England in 1770, the Calvinistic orthodoxy of the revival had fragmented. Various influential scholars either built upon ideas of Jonathan Edwards or downplayed some of his most difficult points. Whitefield's broad evangelical Calvinism would not have noticed the subtle nuances of theological emphasis in Edwards' followers. Two prominent students of Edwards were Joseph Bellamy and

---

20   Edwin M. Stone, *History of Beverly, Civil and Ecclesiastical*, (Boston, MA: J. Monroe & Company, 1843), p. 255.
21   Sarah L. Bailey, *Historical Sketches of Andover . . . , Massachusetts*, (Boston, MA: Houghton, Mifflin and Company, 1880), p. 434.
22   Williston Walker, *A History of the Congregational Churches in the United States*, (New York: Charles Scribner's Sons, 1916), pp. 266-267.
23   Sydney Ahlstrom, *A Religious History of the American People*, p. 290.

Samuel Hopkins. Bellamy defended at length Edwards' belief that church membership should be reserved for only the converted, while Hopkins departed from his mentor's views on sin and atonement into a less rigorous but still professedly Calvinist theology. Further, Bellamy defended his adapted Calvinism against Unitarianism.[24] Three branches of Protestant Theology emerged in New England; the traditional Calvinists, the moderate Calvinists, and those Unitarians and Universalists that renounced Calvinism.

At Yale in 1740, Whitefield preached with great success to the affected student body. One student present was Samuel Hopkins, who remembered, "The assemblies were crowded and remarkably attentive, and people appeared generally to approve, and their conversation turned chiefly toward him and his preaching." Hopkins attended Whitefield's public lectures and the private meetings he held with the undergraduates, "and highly approved of him."[25] But not all members of Yale approved of Whitefield, and Hopkins found himself defending the evangelist in the discussions following his departure.

Hopkins and Bellamy remained Calvinists yet embraced moderate ideas that seemed to contradict some of the sharper points of historic Westminster Calvinism. For example, Bellamy apparently embraced the concept of universal atonement as compared to Edwards' particular or limited atonement. Yet Edwards wrote a supportive preface to Bellamy's book *True Religion Delineated*, which proposed the idea of universal atonement. Hopkins also expanded on Edwards' concept of Christ's atonement, asserting that Jesus died for all (not merely the elect), including Negros and Indians, as well as white people, while still insisting on the new birth as a prerequisite for salvation.[26]

Previously, in 1746 the College of New Jersey (later Princeton College) was founded as a New Light revival Presbyterian school for training ministers. In 1764 the College of Rhode Island was founded in Warren, Rhode Island. The school moved to Providence in 1770 and changed its name in 1804 to what we call today Brown University. As a sign of the open-mindedness of Rhode Islanders, and the weakening Puritanism in New England, the college was not primarily a ministerial school, and accepted students from all religious denominations. The Philadelphia Association of Baptist Churches sent a delegate to establish the college, and in working with local like-minded Congregational and other ministers in Rhode Island, the school was a success.

Political leaders in England developed more dependence on the American Colonies to finance the British debt after the defeat of the French in the Seven Years' War. English colonization efforts, from India to the Caribbean, created an enormous financial drain on the British Parliament. The Molasses Act of 1733, which regulated the distribution and sale of molasses from the West Indies, had been largely ignored until 1760, when it was enforced to the letter. For New Englanders who had a strong taste for rum and molasses candy, this decree was not welcomed. Complaints by Bostonians and others increased in 1764, when the Revenue Act restricted colonial trade in such commonly used goods as hides, lumber, and other products. New England mariners and merchants, from New London, Connecticut to Portsmouth, New Hampshire and all places in-between, were furious. Tensions built further when the British Navy began to aid the customs service by enforcing American colonial trade regulations, with British warships and armed sloops patrolling colonial ports looking for smugglers.

The Stamp Act of 1765 proved to be intolerable for the British colonies in America. Essentially, the Stamp Act required a predetermined fee for all legal transactions, to be paid upon issue of requested documents. This required no duty officers, as any document without the new official stamp was rejected by the courts. Riots

---

[24] Joseph A. Conforti, "Joseph Bellamy and the New Divinity Movement," *The New England Historical and Genealogical Register*, (1983), vol. 137, pp. 126-138. Joseph A. Conforti, *Samuel Hopkins and the New Divinity Movement* . . . , (Grand Rapids, MI: Christian University Press, 1981). For an overview of these theological changes, see Douglas A. Sweeney and Allen C. Guelzo, *The New England Theology: From Jonathan Edwards to Edwards Amasa Park*, (Eugene, OR: Wipf and Stock Publishers, 2006).

[25] Stephen West, *Sketches of the Life of the Late Rev. Samuel Hopkins*, (Hartford, CT: Hudson & Goodwin Printers, 1805), pp. 30-31.

[26] C. P. Smith, *Yankees and God*, pp. 265-266.

broke out in cities throughout the thirteen American Colonies. By November 1, when the stamps were to go on sale, none were available anywhere in America, for nearly every distributor had resigned his post.[27]

In Massachusetts, there had been plenty of trouble about the Stamp Act. Every bill of sale, every legal judgment, and every will-and-testament had to have a stamp on it, paid in cash. With so little hard money in the colony, this imposition would drain away valuable resources. At the Boston courthouse, Concord's representative met with assemblymen of other Massachusetts towns. They voted that a circular letter be dispatched inviting all the British colonies in North America to send delegates to New York for a Stamp Act Congress to oppose the tax.[28]

Beverly, Massachusetts acted in rejection of the Stamp Act. Beverly held a special town meeting on October 25, 1765, specifically to continue resistance of this unwelcome law. Records from this meeting say, in part:

> We can't without criminal ingratitude . . . nor without the highest injustice to ourselves and to our posterity, consent to yield obedience to any law whatsoever by its natural constitution of just construction deprives us of the liberty of "Trial by Juries" or our choosing meet [appropriate] persons to represent us in assessing or taxing our estates for his majesties service . . . and to what in you lies to prevent all unconstitutional draughts on the public treasury.[29]

On March 18, 1766, Parliament repealed the Stamp Act. But by 1767, the Revenue Act was in place, which imposed custom duties on items colonists had to import from England, such as glass, tea, silk, and paper. Again, large public protests ensued. The British government responded with a warship in May of 1768, to give a show of force to support recent unpopular laws. When the enormous fifty-eight-gun frigate *Romney* began to patrol Boston and other area harbors, and with an increasing number of British soldiers on land enforcing laws not welcomed by the colonists, a virtual state of war existed in some people's minds.

In the fall of 1768, Rev. John Cleveland of Chebacco Parish in Ipswich (Essex), Massachusetts wrote his first political essay for the newly founded *Essex Gazette* newspaper. His theme was in protest of increasing taxation without proper legal representation from the colonists.

> Is it not the birthright of Englishmen to be free? Can they be free if they are taxed, to raise a revenue, without their consent? . . . Is there here not a such thing belonging to Englishmen as property? Can one man dispose of the property of another without his consent and not be guilty of robbery?[30]

The first recorded protest against British taxation, which ended in a death, occurred a few miles out at sea, off the Massachusetts coast. In 1769, a British officer was killed while attempting to recruit Marblehead seamen for the British navy. This little-known account is recorded as follows.

> Bold, impetuous seamen were not easily satisfied with the merchant's printed protests and resolutions, when hardly a voyage escaped obnoxious harassment by the British, even to rummaging through a man's private sea chest. If another shove towards radicalism was needed, the incident early in 1769 proved it. Captain Thomas Powell's brigantine, Pitt Packet, was homeward bound from Europe when the British man-o-war, Rose, cruising around the bay, sent officers aboard Pitt Packet with the intention of impressing Marblehead seamen to serve in the British navy. The unarmed seamen defiantly shut themselves in the forepeak and after being shot at by a "limey" lieutenant, they

---

27 David Hawke, *The Colonial Experience*, p. 538.
28 Townsend Scudder, *Concord, an American Town*, (Boston, MA: Little, Brown & Company, 1947), pp. 69-70.
29 Thomas A. Askew and Jean M. Askew, *Beverly, Massachusetts and the American Revolution: One Town's Experience*, (Beverly, MA: American Revolution Bicentennial Committee, 1975), pp. 11-12.
30 Christopher M. Jedry, *The World of John Cleveland: Family and Community in Eighteenth Century New England*, (New York: W.W. Norton & Company, 1979), pp. 131-132.

used the only weapon at hand, a harpoon, to finish him off. Overwhelmed by Rose's crew, the Marbleheaders were carried away to prison in Boston . . . the Marbleheaders were acquitted on the excuse that the slain lieutenant had no specific orders to impress seamen. Even as they left the courthouse, there were British field guns across the street facing the court of justice doors.[31]

Antagonism between the British troops and Boston citizens increased during the fall and winter of 1769. Both children and adults ridiculed and publicly humiliated British soldiers. The number of British troops on hand in Boston, too few to enforce order but enough to promote resentment, gave Boston the appearance of a militarily occupied city. This tense situation erupted on March 5, 1770, when a mob assaulted a sentry on duty at the customhouse. Reinforcements were called, under the leadership of Captain Thomas Preston, who tried to reason with the taunting crowd. Amid chaos, someone yelled to fire, and five Boston citizens were killed and many more wounded. Newspaper accounts labeled this bloody event "The Boston Massacre." A Boston diarist recorded his impressions at this time.[32]

> March 3: A quarrel between some of the 29th Regiment of the Ropemakers—yesterday and today.

> March 5: This night be the 29th Regiment on duty. A quarrel between the soldiers & inhabitants. The bell rung. A great number assembled in King's Street. A party of the 29th under the command of Captain Preston fired on the people—they killed five, wounded several others, particularly Mr. Edward Payne in his right arm . . .

> March 6: Most all the town in uproar & confusion. The Governor and Council met . . .

> March 7: A military watch tonight

> March 8: I attended the funeral of the four unhappy people that were killed on Monday last. Such a concourse of people I Never saw before—I believe ten or twelve thousand. One corps with their relations followed the other & then the selectmen and inhabitants. A military watch again tonight.

A crowning achievement for Whitefield in the 1760s was his reconciliation with Harvard College. Whitefield and President Edward Holyoke were bitter antagonists, each writing and preaching against the other. But the generosity of Whitefield in supporting Bostonians after the catastrophic fire in 1760, and the benevolence of Whitefield after the Harvard library was destroyed by fire in 1764, seems to have won over Holyoke to Whitefield's side. Further, Holyoke acknowledged that the emotional extremes of the awakening in the 1740s had long since passed, and that legitimate, enduring, and balanced New Light ministers were successful throughout New England. On August 28, 1768, Harvard College officially thanked Whitefield for his raising of financial support for the school and his acquiring volumes of books for the college library. This was an immense compliment to Whitefield, and the pressure in New England of having Harvard against him was passed.[33]

The 1760s was a turbulent period in New England history. Historic Protestant doctrines were increasingly dismissed, explained away, or ignored. Life values had altered significantly from those of the founding Puritan

---

[31] Priscilla Lord, *The Spirit of '76 Lives Here: Marblehead*, (Random, PA: Chilton Books, 1972), p. 93.
[32] John Rowe, *Letters and Diaries of John Rowe, Boston Merchant, 1759-1762, 1764-1779*, (Boston, MA: W.B. Clarke Company, 1903), pp. 197-199.
[33] Arnold Dallimore, *George Whitefield: The Life and Times of the Great Evangelist of the Eighteenth Century Revival*, (Carlisle, PA: Banner of Truth Trust, 1980), vol. II, pp. 428-429.

fathers. A humble desire to live simply and apart from worldly temptation and extravagance, was replaced by a mercantile class that sought wealth and found it. The Puritan dream of a holy community slowly faded through affluence, immigration, and spiritual indifference. The desire of the forefathers, for a peaceful Kingdom of God on earth, was collapsing under the rising militant atmosphere and civil unrest of the day.

A sketch of George Whitefield from the 1760s.

Source: www.revival-library.org

CHAPTER 35

THE PROSPEROUS MINISTRY AND FAILING HEALTH OF GEORGE WHITEFIELD

1764–1770

WHITEFIELD DEPARTED NEW ENGLAND IN the summer of 1764. His health was erratic. His intention was to spend the cooler summer months in the northern colonies, and the mild winter months in the south. In early September he lingered in New York, preaching to large but not enormous crowds. Whitefield's correspondence helps trace his movements towards the Bethesda orphanage in Georgia. On June 25, 1764 he wrote from New York, "Hitherto the Lord hath helped me. The New England winter campaign is over, and I am thus on my way to Georgia."[1] His next surviving correspondence was dated August 8, 19, and 25, the latter stating that he was preaching out on Long Island, outside New York City. On September 21, Whitefield wrote from Philadelphia that he planned to winter in Georgia, and in the spring return to Great Britain. He was welcomed to the new College of New Jersey ministerial school at

A sketch of Whitefield ministering to the orphans at Bethesda, outside Savanna, Georgia, winter 1765-1766. Source: Mack M. Caldwell, George Whitefield: Preacher to Millions, p. 119.

---

1   George Whitefield, *Works of George Whitefield*, (1771: reprinted by Quinta Press, Shropshire, England, 2000), vol. III, p. 312.

Princeton, New Jersey, writing from "Nassau Hall," the main college building, on September 25. Princeton had granted Whitefield an honorary Master of Arts degree ten years earlier, in 1754.

We next read of Whitefield writing from Philadelphia on October 19; New Brunswick, North Carolina on November 22; Charles-Town, South Carolina on December 2; and Savannah, Georgia, near the Bethesda orphanage, on December 19, 1764. He had travelled over one thousand miles in six months, preaching along the way. There were accounts of large crowds at his preaching events, but no significant revivals were recorded.

Whitefield had a lot of work to do at the Bethesda Orphanage. There were bills to pay, buildings to be maintained, curriculums to be developed, and long-term planning to complete with the faculty and staff. In addition, Whitefield had the added responsibility at Bethesda to facilitate burdensome administrate requirements in order to create a college at the orphanage. As far back as 1739, Whitefield had aspired to create both an orphanage and a college at Bethesda. Now, almost three decades later, the orphanage was running and the college was close to a reality. There was land to acquire, a charter to obtain, finances to raise, and buildings to erect.[2] For the next few years Whitefield would pursue his dream of a college at Bethesda, a dream that would eventually be unanswered.

Why was the orphanage at Bethesda so special to Whitefield? There may be several reasons. First, looking into Whitefield's mind is the idea that he suffered a deprived childhood and wanted to therefore protect helpless orphans. Whitefield's father died when he was two years old, and although his mother remarried several years later, he understood what it was like to be a child in a difficult home situation. Second, Whitefield had a longing to be a parent which remained unfulfilled. George and Elizabeth Whitefield continually tried

An early sketch of the Bethesda Orphanage founded by George Whitefield.

Source: https://www.thegospelcoalition.org/blogs/ryan-reeves/ history-today-george-whitefield-founds-an-orphanage.

---

2   Arnold Dallimore, *George Whitefield: The Life and Times of the Great Evangelist of the Eighteenth Century Revival*. (Carlisle, PA: Banner of Truth Trust, 1980), vol. II, p. 435.

to be parents, with Elizabeth suffering numerous miscarriages. Their one child that survived childbirth died very young. A third reason Whitefield longed to create and sustain the Bethesda orphanage was that he simply loved children. He laughed with and celebrated with his orphans and the orphanage staff as his own family members, and he rested and relaxed in their company. At Bethesda there were no theology squabbles with the staff or the children. It was a refuge for the beleaguered evangelist.

A fourth reason Whitefield poured so much of himself into the orphanage was that in these young people he saw the future of the revival movement and the next generation of evangelical preachers. In order to maintain the momentum of the movement after his death, new young men and their families were needed to preach, teach, and serve as missionaries. Whitefield longed for his orphans to become ministers of the gospel.[3]

A fifth reason Whitefield founded the orphanage was to teach deprived children a skill or a trade so that they could be contributing members of society to help the Georgia Colony prosper.[4] The sixth reason Whitefield founded the Bethesda orphanage was that he did so in Christ-like compassion. As a Christian, Whitefield desired to follow the example of Jesus, to whom children flocked and from whom Jesus used many illustrations of the need for child-like faith for salvation. A seventh reason Whitefield created the orphanage was that there was a desperate need for such an institution. Mortality rates for adults were high; homeless children in urban areas was a disgrace; and some reprehensible settlers in Georgia, fleeing legal proceedings in England, arrived in the Georgia Colony to start a new life anonymously, abandoning their families and children in the New World.

Whitefield spent most of the winter of 1765-1766 at Bethesda. Dallimore stated, "Nevertheless, he remained at Bethesda through the winter months—December 1764 to February 1765. No place on earth was so dear to him and during these months he enjoyed its surroundings, gave oversight to its activities, and further considered his plans for the college. In this somewhat relaxed life he experienced a considerable improvement in health."[5] Being temporarily reinvigorated, Whitefield set aside his immediate plans to return to England and began a preaching tour. His inconsistent correspondence traces his steps to Charles-Town, South Carolina on March 15; to Wilmington, North Carolina on March 29; to outside Philadelphia on May 4; to his departure from New York to England on June 10, 1765.

Whitefield arrived at Plymouth, England on July 7, 1765. He was again in poor health. Tyerman stated, "Upon the whole, Whitefield's health was not improved by his visit to America. He had worked when others would have rested . . . he came back to England scarcely able to preach at all."[6] A few months later, John Wesley wrote of Whitefield as "an old man, fairly worn out in his master's service, though he has hardly seen fifty years."[7]

In the 1760s, Great Britain was a world power. After the end of the Seven Year's War in 1763, England focused on expanding its overseas territories. The British East India Company had trading centers as far away as Gibraltar, west Africa, India, Sumatra, He-On-Kong (later Hong Kong), numerous smaller Islands in the southern Pacific, and throughout North America. Exotic and luxurious items entered British ports as Englishmen sailed the world as traders, scientists, and military men. At home, King George III encouraged the Industrial Revolution, as textile and other factories rapidly developed in urban areas. In 1769, Captain James Cook departed on his first voyage to explore the Pacific, eventually circling the world. This scientific and exploratory journey also created new trading partners and reinvigorated numerous British overseas territorial

---

3 For a thorough study, see Edward J. Cashin, *Beloved Bethesda: A History of George Whitefield's Home for Boys, 1740-2000*, (Macon, GA: Mercer University Press, 2001).
4 Susan M. Miller, *George Whitefield: Clergyman and Scholar*, (Philadelphia: Chelsea House Publishers, 2001), p. 47.
5 Arnold Dallimore, *George Whitefield: Life and Times*, vol. II, pp. 435-436.
6 Luke Tyerman, *The Life and Times of the Rev. George Whitefield*, (New York: Anson D.F. Randolph & Company, 1877), vol. II, p. 487
7 Ibid., p. 490.

claims. The journals of Captain Cook were wildly popular in all classes of English society, and encouraged greater maritime explorations. In 1765, Parliament passed the Stamp Act to raise taxes in the American Colonies, which would prove disastrous. Religiously, the Wesleyans continued to form local religious societies while remaining attached to the Church of England. While Whitefield traveled and preached, Wesley preached, organized, and discipled. Tension existed between the teachings of Whitefield and Wesley on the new birth and justification by faith, in contrast to the formalism and liturgy of the established Church of England. In 1769, Richard Boardman and Joseph Pilmore, Wesley's first official Methodist missionaries, arrived in the American Colonies.

Though physically weak, Whitefield reestablished his relationship with his influential sponsor, the Countess of Huntington. Lady Selina Huntington, a devout evangelical Christian and endorser of revival preachers, founded numerous chapels throughout England at locations where the wealthy and the nobility vacationed. By her own example she attended chapel services preached by evangelical ministers, and she invited the wealthy and elite of British society to attend. Such aristocracy might never attend a public Methodist or dissenting meeting, but an invitation from Lady Huntington to attend a gospel meeting, in one of her private and often secluded chapels, was often hard to refuse. In October 1765, Whitefield preached at the opening services of such a chapel in the city of Bath, in southwest England about halfway between London and Essex. For the four years Whitefield would be in England, he was in frequent correspondence with the Countess of Huntington, often preaching in her numerous chapels.[8]

An issue Whitefield brought with him from colonial New England to England was the Indian school founded by Rev. Eleazar Wheelock in Connecticut. Whitefield devised the idea of an Indian Christian visiting England to promote the Indian missionary work. In 1766 the plan came to fruition when Rev. Samson Occum, an Indian from the Mohegan tribe, came to England and preached hundreds of times to tens-of-thousands of listeners. Accompanied by Rev. Nathaniel Whitaker of Salem, Massachusetts, Occum was a preaching sensation, raising large amounts of money for the Indian missionary school. Even the King of England gave generously to the cause. Whitefield happily endorsed Occum. They travelled together, and Whitefield wrote him letters of recommendation.[9] Thanks to Occum and Whitefield, the missionary school founded by Wheelock gained an influx of funds, allowing the school to move to New Hampshire to be closer to unevangelized Indians. Shortly thereafter the school was renamed after an influential British donor, Lord Dartmouth, eventually becoming Dartmouth College in Hanover, New Hampshire.

An ongoing irritant to Whitefield in England was his tense relationship to John and Charles Wesley and their followers. Since the time of the Great Awakening in 1740, Whitefield and the Wesley brothers were often at odds. The dominating personalities of these men created antagonistic episodes, on-again-and-off-again, for decades. Whitefield appears to have condescended to John Wesley in many ways, seeking to be a peacekeeper and to remain focused on his itinerant evangelistic ministry. Over the years, John and Charles Wesley also made initial gestures for reconciliation. But the followers of these men and their movements often were antagonistic. Whitefield's Calvinistic and non-denominational ministry leaders at times collided with Wesley's followers who held strict Methodist and Arminian beliefs. In the 1760s, some of Wesley's followers became carried away with Perfectionism teachings, to the point that they claimed holiness equal to angels, and that they were incapable of sinning. This caused a deep and emotional division among the Arminian Methodists, severely fragmenting Wesley's ministry. Remarkably, Wesley in part blamed Whitefield for these divisions. Instead, Whitefield spoke to the over-zealous leaders of the divisive Wesley group, being effective as a peacemaker. Unfathomably, John Wesley continued to be antagonistic

---

8 For an overview of her life, see Helen C. Knight, *Lady Huntington and her Friends*, (New York: American Tract Society, 1853).
9 The writings of Samson Occum contain dozens of benevolent references to Whitefield. See Samson Occum, *The Collected Writings of Samson Occum*, (New York: Oxford University Press, 2006), especially pp. 264-271.

to Whitefield, recognizing that Whitefield helped heal the breach while at the same time accusing him of creating the original division.[10] One cannot help but feel the frustration and interference experienced by Whitefield as he recently returned to England from his extended stay in the American Colonies, only to face ongoing controversies with the Wesleys.

Ever the restless itinerant preacher, Whitefield conducted a series of evangelistic tours through England, Wales, and Scotland. Though his health was delicate, in the spring of 1767 he began a two-month preaching tour. Tracing Whitefield's correspondence allows us to follow his steps. He wrote a letter from London on March 4, 1767 which discussed business matters. His next letters trace his route to Norwich on April 11; Rodborough on May 13; Gloucester, his hometown, on May 20, 21, and 25; Haverford-West in Wales on May 31 and June 1; back to Gloucester on June 10; and finally returning to London by July 21, 1767.[11] On this preaching circuit he spoke in all kinds of weather, within church buildings and outside in the fields. At some of these meetings thousands attended. He frequently reached a town exhausted from traveling. The weather was typically chilly and damp. Sleeping accommodations were humble. For three months Whitefield maintained this schedule, encouraged by the crowds that heard him preach, although no revival resulted. Whitefield called himself a "gospel rover" and truly such extended preaching trips showed this to be true.[12]

In the late 1760s, Whitefield was encouraged by various helpers that assisted him with his diverse ministries. Two able men, Mr. Scott and Mr. Joss, assumed many of Whitefield's responsibilities for the work in London, while Rev. Rowland Hill commenced a successful itinerant preaching ministry patterned after Whitefield. Further, in 1768 Whitefield benefited from the services of a ministerial aid, a type of personal assistant named Mr. Cornelius Winter. Converted under Whitefield's preaching in 1755, Winter was a poor boy who was excited and active in Whitefield's London ministries. He travelled with the evangelist, securing lodging, screening interviewers, providing transportation, and helping to meet Whitefield's personal needs. As Whitefield was frequently weak from traveling and exhausted from preaching, the assistance he received from these men was invaluable. Winter was the most valuable of these assistants, as he lived and travelled with Whitefield for the last years of the itinerant's life. A daily eyewitness of Whitefield's activities, Winter recorded:

> Perhaps Mr. Whitefield never preached greater sermons than at six in the morning, for at that hour he did preach winter and summer, on Mondays, Tuesdays, Wednesdays, and Thursdays . . . His style was now colloquial, with little use of motion; pertinent expositions, with subtitle remarks . . . Now ministers of every description found a peculiar treasure in relaxing their minds from the fatigues of study, and were highly entertained by his particularly excellent subjects, which were so suitable to the auditory, that I believe it was seldom disappointed.[13]

In the summer of 1768, Whitefield traveled north for a preaching circuit in Scotland. Over the decades, he had made over a dozen preaching trips to this area. Previously he had been well received in Scotland, and this trip was to be no exception. Mrs. Whitefield did not travel with her husband, as she was in diminished health and busy administrating his affairs in London.

Four letters have survived from Whitefield's summer 1768 preaching circuit in Scotland. All posted from Edinburgh, these letters speak of Whitefield's preaching successes and his failing health.

---

10   Arnold Dallimore, *George Whitefield, vol. II*, pp. 460-463.
11   George Whitefield, *Works of George Whitefield, vol. III*, pp. 344-350.
12   Mack W. Caldwell, *George Whitefield: Preacher to Millions*, (Anderson, IN: The Warner Press, 1929), p. 81
13   William Jay, compiler, *Memoirs of the Life and Character of the Late Cornelius Winter*, (Philadelphia, PA: B. Redman, Printer, 1823), pp. 26-27.

For example, on July 15 Whitefield wrote, "Thanks be to his great name, for ordering my steps this way . . . Twenty-seven year old friends and spiritual children, remember the days of old; they are seeking after their first love, and there seems to be a stirring among the dry bones. I cannot yet tell when I shall move." Writing on July 2, Whitefield stated, "My journey hither was certainly of God. Could I preach ten times a day, thousands and thousands would attend. I have been confined for a few days [from sickness] but on Monday or Tuesday next hope to mount my throne again." Whitefield then stated that he received generous contributions to Rev. Eleazar Wheelock's Indian mission school in Connecticut, and that "I am only in danger of being hugged to death. Friends of all ranks seem heartier and more friendly than ever." On July 4, Whitefield commented that sickness had slowed him down, and speaking of his body, he wrote, "the earthly house of this tabernacle pulls me down." He continued, "However, this is my comfort, the Redeemer still vouchsafes to smile upon my feeble efforts . . . In Edinburgh, I trust, the prospect is promising. The fields are white ready unto harvest. Who knows but some wheat may be gathered into the heavenly garner? Many of my old friends are safely housed."

In his last surviving letter written from Scotland on July 9, 1768, Whitefield wrote, "Everything goes on better and better here. But I am so worn down by preaching abroad, and by talking at home almost all the day long, that I have determined, God willing, to set off for London next Tuesday afternoon."[14] Summarizing this Scotland tour, "His arrival in Edinburgh, as it was the last visit which he was ever to pay to that capital, was also one of the most gratifying, and glad remembrances of former days seemed to mingle their delightful feelings with prospects of present usefulness."[15]

A short time after he returned from Scotland, Whitefield's wife died. George and Elizabeth Whitefield were married on November 14, 1741. Their almost twenty-seven years of marriage ended with her death at age sixty-five. Always placing his ministry before his wife, Whitefield was a demanding absentee husband. His wife appears to have been as much an administrative assistant as a wife, companion, and lover. Cornelius Winter, who lived with the Whitefields through the last days of Elizabeth's life, saw her husband as formal and stiff in the home.[16] Five days after her death, Whitefield preached her funeral sermon. Two days later he expressed his eagerness to be about the gospel ministry.[17]

An interesting side note to Whitefield's 1765-1769 ministry in England was his developing relationship with the American inventor, scholar, and diplomat Benjamin Franklin. They first met in Philadelphia in 1740 and remained friends. Years later, the two men overlapped in England, as Franklin in 1766 was representing the American Colonies in protests against the Stamp Act. As Franklin was criticized by both British and colonial leaders, Whitefield came to his defense. These two men, opposites in many ways, maintained a decades-long mutually beneficial friendship that lasted until Whitefield's death in 1770. Whitefield preached, Franklin published his sermons, and both sides benefited from the publicity. As Whitefield travelled throughout England preaching and promoting the Bethesda orphanage and proposed college, Franklin heartily endorsed these projects. Whitefield longed to see the intellectual skeptic Franklin converted to Christ but did not see this result.[18]

The boyhood account of John Knight deserves mentioning. He was a six-year-old boy in Gloucestershire, England when he heard Whitefield preach in 1769. As an elderly man in 1844, Mr. Knight recalled how Whitefield pled in tears for the salvation of souls. Knight stated, "My father held me up in his arms, and

---

14 George Whitefield, *Works of George Whitefield, vol. III*, pp. 370-372.
15 John Johnstone, *Sketches of the Life and Labors of the Rev. George Whitefield*, (London and Edinburgh, n.d.), pp. 225-226.
16 Arnold Dallimore, *George Whitefield, vol. II*, pp. 471-472.
17 Luke Tyerman, *The Life and Times of the Rev. George Whitefield, vol. II*, p. 555.
18 Peter C. Hoffer, *When Benjamin Franklin met the Reverend Whitefield*, (Baltimore, MD: The Johns Hopkins University Press, 2011), p. 120

though so young I well remember to have seen the tears run down the cheek of that Servant of God while preaching the love of his Master to dying sinners."[19]

The last sermons Whitefield preached in England were in late August and early September 1769. His health had been so broken that he was temporarily an invalid. When his health improved, he preached, then often collapsed and rested for days. While preaching, his usual logical train of thought was often interrupted by mumbling and self-serving comments about his abilities or reputation. Clearly his mind and his body were failing. Whitefield's last sermon preached in London was on Wednesday morning, August 30, 1769. In this text he wondered from clichés to ramblings about prior friendships, egotistically asserting his own accomplishments. Intermixed in the sermon were biblical references and various applications of scripture truths. His last sermons in England were preached at Gravesend, on September 3, 1769. At this event Whitefield's voice returned, and he stated:

> Sunday September 3. Preached this morning at the Methodist Tabernacle, from John xii.32. The congregation was not very large, but God gave me great freedom of speech. In the afternoon, I preached from the Market Place, from Genesis iii.13, to a much larger, but not more devout auditory. In the outskirts, some were a little noisy, but most were very attentive, and I was enabled to lift up my voice like a trumpet.[20]

What Whitefield did not state, or did not understand, was that his ill health was affecting the effectiveness of his preaching. After listing numerous belligerent, derogatory, and self-serving statements made by Whitefield in his last sermons in England, a careful Whitefield biographer was forced to admit:

> These *Whitefieldiana* might easily be multiplied, but sufficient have been given to show the familiar, and (as some will think) the objectionable style used by Whitefield at the close of his public ministry. His sermons now, as compared to those he published at the commencement of his career, were notably inferior . . . They were neither scriptural expositions nor doctrinal disquisitions; but free and easy talk, intermixed with anecdotes, personal reminiscences, and quaint quotations.[21]

The enfeebled Whitefield embarked for America on September 4, 1769, but finally departed England on September 25. After a long and tumultuous voyage of nine weeks, he arrived at Charleston, South Carolina on November 30. He had two traveling companions, Mr. Cornelius Winter, mentioned previously, and Mr. Richard Smith. Smith was a young man who was a constant daily companion to Whitefield and was present at Whitefield's death almost one year later. Whitefield preached successfully for ten days in Charleston, then departed in an open

Throughout much of his adult life, Whitefield was in unstable health.

George Whitefield in bed in poor health, a common occurrence in the 1760s. Sketch by Valerie Borgal.

---

19 Michael A.G. Haykin, *George Whitefield*, (Grand Rapids, MI: EP Books, 2014), p. 57.
20 Luke Tyerman, *The Life and Times of the Rev. George Whitefield*, vol. II, p. 568.
21 Ibid., pp. 567-568.

boat for Savanna, Georgia, safely arriving without incident on December 14. After ten days of ministry in Savannah, the recently widowed and childless Whitefield went to his beloved Bethesda Orphanage to celebrate Christmas and New Year's Day with his orphanage family. "Here he spent the winter months at Bethesda among the children whom he called his prizes. These whom he had supported and prayed for were now a blessing to him in ministering to his comfort in his closing days."[22]

But not all of Whitefield's winter activities were confined to the orphanage. His correspondence places him in Charleston, South Carolina from February 10 through March 4, 1770. In Charleston, he preached occasionally but was consumed with correspondence, as ships from England brought him numerous letters which needed to be promptly answered. His heath temporarily restored, he longed for a northern gospel preaching tour to the middle colonies, and perhaps to his beloved New England. But first, affairs at Bethesda needed attention. Throughout much of the month of April 1770, Whitefield was at the Bethesda orphanage coordinating long-term planning for the orphanage, ministering to the staff and children, and discussing building expansions. From Bethesda on April 21 he wrote, "Blessed be God, I was never better, at this season of the year, in bodily health; never more comfortable in my soul."[23]

Departing Savannah by boat on April 24, Whitefield arrived in Philadelphia on May 6, 1770. On May 9 he wrote from Philadelphia, "I was enabled to preach to a large auditory, and am to repeat the delightful task this evening. Pulpits, hearts, and affections, seem to be as open and enlarged towards me, as ever . . . As yet I have my old plan in view, to travel in these northern parts all summer, and return late in the fall to Georgia."[24] After a few months stay in Philadelphia, the largest city in the American Colonies, he wrote from New York on June 30, 1770: "I have been here just a week. Have been enabled to preach four times, and am to repeat the delightful task this evening. Congregations are rather larger than ever."[25] A month later, on July 29, 1770, Whitefield wrote from New York City of his just completed itinerant evangelistic tour in upstate New York and western New England. He wrote,

> Since my last, and during this month, I have been above a five hundred miles circuit, and have been enabled to preach and travel through the heat of the day. The congregations have been very large, attentive, and affected . . . O what a scene of usefulness is opening in various parts of this new world! All fresh work, where I have been. The divine influence hath been as at the first. Invitations crowd upon me both from ministers and people, and from many, many quarters.[26]

Whitefield's pioneer preaching tour in western New England, which he described above as "All fresh work," meant he had never been there before. This western New England trip will be the subject of the next chapter.

---

22   Mack W. Caldwell, *George Whitefield: Preacher to Millions*, p. 118.
23   George Whitefield, *Works of George Whitefield, vol. III*, p. 420.
24   Ibid., p. 422.
25   Ibid., p. 424.
26   Ibid., pp. 424-425.

CHAPTER 36

WHITEFIELD'S MINISTRY IN WESTERN NEW ENGLAND

JULY 1770

WHITEFIELD EMBARKED FOR AMERICA ON September 4, 1769 in good health, following a rewarding four-year ministry in England. While delayed a few weeks in England due to inclement weather, Whitefield continued his copious letter writing, maintaining communication between friends, promoting peace between different factions in the evangelical movement, and simply recording his everyday life experiences.

The ship carrying Whitefield and his two traveling attendants, Cornelius Winter and Richard Smith, arrived at Charlestown, South Carolina, on November 30, 1769. The next day he preached in the city, and remained in the area until December 10 when he set sail for Georgia, intending to visit his beloved Bethesda. Whitefield found the Bethesda property full of activity, with the orphanage possessing new buildings, and expansion projects just completed. Four years after his last visit to Georgia, Whitefield observed a newly flourishing Georgia Colony.

Whitefield's stay at Bethesda was brief. As one who longed to preach the gospel to the masses, he could not stay long to supervise at Bethesda. He had a director and full staff to oversee the work. Whitefield, upon inspecting the ministry at Bethesda, strongly desired "another Gospel range"—an evangelical tour through the colonies. His correspondence at this point shows his eagerness to again perform the work of an itinerant evangelist.

> Bethesda, January 11, 1770. Everything here exceeds my most sanguine expectations. I am almost tempted to say "it is good to be here." But all must give way to Gospel-ranging. Divine Employ!¹[1]

> January 15, 1770. The increase of this once so much despised colony is indescribable . . . All admire the goodness, strength and beauty of late improvements . . . my bodily health is much improved, and my soul is on the wing for another Gospel range.[2]

By April 1770, Whitefield had attended to the details of the orphanage, establishing Robert Wright as director of Bethesda, therefore readying himself for another lengthy "gospel range." Shortly after leaving Bethesda, he wrote of his intentions to head north to the densely populated areas of the colonies for his preaching ministry.

---

1   Luke Tyerman, *The Life of the Reverend George Whitefield*, (New York: Anson D.F. Randolph & Company, 1877), vol. II, pp. 573-574.
2   Arnold Dallimore, *The Life and Times of the Great Evangelist of the Eighteenth Century Revival*, (Carlisle, PA: Banner of Truth Trust, 1980), vol. II, pp. 490-491.

Savannah, April 24, 1770: Five in the morning, I am just going to the boat in order to embark for Philadelphia. Mr. Robert Wright is a quiet, ingenious creature; and his wife is an excellent mistress of the family. Such a set of helpers I have never met with. They will go on with the buildings at Bethesda, while I take my gospel range to the northward.[3]

Extracts from several of Whitefield's letters trace his preaching success and his northern route toward New England.

Philadelphia, May 9, 1770. This leaves me a two day inhabitant of Philadelphia. I embarked at Savannah in the Georgia Packet, on the twenty-fourth ultimo, and arrived here the sixth instant. The evening following, I was enabled to preach to a large auditory, and was to repeat the delightful task this evening. Pulpits, hearts, and affections seem to be as open and enlarged towards me as ever. Praise the Lord, O my soul. As yet I have my old plan in view; to travel these northern parts all summer and return in the late fall to Georgia.

Philadelphia, May 24, 1770: I have now been here near three weeks; and if about a week more, I purpose to set out for New York on my way to Boston. A wide and effectual door I trust, has been opened in this city. People of all ranks flock as much as ever: I preach twice on the Lord's Day, and three or four times a week besides, yet I am rather better than I have been for many years. This is the Lord's doing.

While ministering in the southern American colonies, Whitefield was often thinking of a return trip to New England. Clearly his reception there in 1764 was noteworthy, as old animosities, particularly from Harvard College and Yale College, were passed away. The thousands who heard Whitefield preach in meeting houses or in the open fields, were remarkable. Now it was time again, in 1770, to return.[4] His health was stronger. From Philadelphia on May 24, 1770, he wrote, "And in about a week more I purpose to set off for New York in my way to Boston."[5]

After ministering in New York City, Whitefield made a preaching tour to the north, a few hundred miles roundtrip along the Hudson River Valley and then into western New England. This was new territory for him. He preached heading north along the Hudson River, reached the Albany-Schenectady area, preached some more then turned around. He then headed twenty to thirty miles southeast into some of the western-most settlements of Massachusetts and Connecticut.[6] Another source stated, "He preached up the North River as far as Albany and Schenectady, preaching in all the towns and villages along the route, and returning preached at Great Barrington, Norfolk, Salisbury, and Sharon."[7]

In a letter dated July 29, 1770, Whitefield listed the named of places he preached in this circuit as follows; Albany, NY; Schenectady, NY; Great Barrington, MA; Norfolk, CT; Salisbury, CT; Sharon, CT; Smithfield, NY; Powkeepsy [Poughkeepsie], NY; Fishkill, NY; New Rumbert [unknown], New Windsor, NY; and Peckshill [Peekskill], NY.[8] Four places on the preaching circuit was in New England, namely Great Barrington, Massachusetts; and Salisbury, Norfolk, and Sharon, Connecticut.

---

3   John Gilles, *Memoirs of George Whitefield*, (1838: reprinted by Pietan Publications, New Ipswich, NH: 1993), p. 206.
4   Ibid., p. 422.
5   Ibid., p. 423.
6   Helen Evertson Smith, *Colonial Days and Ways*, (New York: The Century Company, 1900), p. 231.
7   Charles F. Sedgwick, *General History of the Town of Sharon, Litchfield County, Connecticut . . .* , (Amenia, NY: Charles Walsh, Printer and Publisher, 1877), p. 36.
8   George Whitefield, *The Works of George Whitefield: Letters 1753-1770*, pp. 424-425.

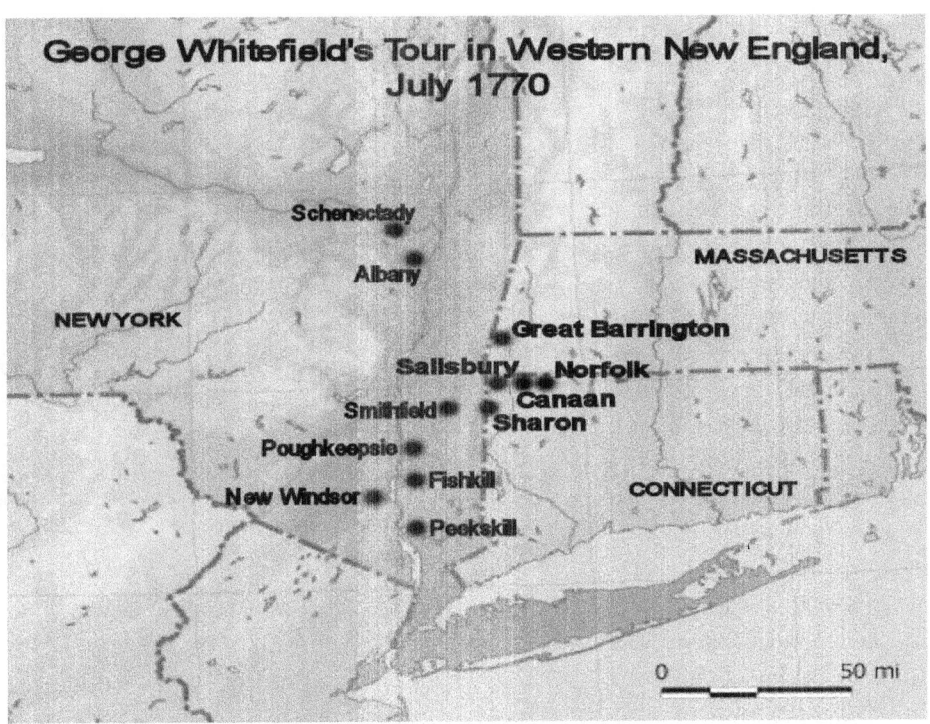

Whitefield's visits to these four New England towns, plus another town named Canaan, will now be examined further.

Great Barrington, Massachusetts was founded in 1724 on an Indian path that connected the Albany, New York area to Springfield, Massachusetts. The Congregational Church was formed in 1743, and its first pastor was the then unknown Rev. Samuel Hopkins. The meeting house was constructed in 1742 as a plain, wooden building, without any ecclesiastical decorations. The growing congregation used this building for sixty-nine years.[9] Hopkins was a local boy who grew up nearby, graduated from Yale College in 1741, and then studied theology as a ministerial intern with Jonathan Edwards in Northampton, Massachusetts. When Hopkins arrived as the first pastor of the North Parish Congregational Church in Sheffield (later Great Barrington), he came to a small town of only thirty families. In his twenty-six years of ministry at the Great Barrington church, Rev. Hopkins began to develop an inter-Colonial reputation as a skilled theologian and writer. Some of his theological views were opposed by the stricter Calvinists. Hopkins believed in an evangelical Calvinism, an evangelistic Protestant theology that differed from the more traditional and rigid Calvinism as practiced, for example, by the scholars at Princeton College. Hopkins remained orthodox in his theology but he did view various doctrines, such as total depravity and the extent of the atonement, in a broader way that other Calvinists. He and Jonathan Edwards remained lifelong friends. Over the course of his ministry in Great Barrington, Hopkins saw 116 people received into the church.[10]

Hopkins was dismissed from the church in 1769, as the town could not or would not continue to pay his salary. When Whitefield arrived in Great Barrington in the summer of 1770, the church was without a minister. Indeed, the church would be without a permanent minister until 1787. Whitefield was not in full agreement with all that Hopkins wrote and taught in modifying Calvinism, but he thought enough of Hopkins to preach to his former church folks, as they were as sheep without a shepherd. In a July 29, 1770 letter, Whitefield specifically named Great Barrington as a place at which he preached. But since this congregation

---

9 *Manual of the First Congregational Church of Great Barrington, Mass.*, (Cambridge, MA: Riverside Press, 1873), pp. 9-10.
10 Charles J. Taylor, *History of Great Barrington, Massachusetts*, (Great Barrington, MA: Clark W. Bryan & Co., Publishers, 1882), p. 385.

was without a minister, and the meeting house was infrequently used, no record of his preaching there remains. From Great Barrington Whitefield headed south into Connecticut.

In the early 1770s, Congregationalism dominated northwestern Connecticut, and was still the official denomination of the Connecticut Colony. Here were numerous smaller valley towns where attendance at the Congregational church was expected, and sabbath-keeping was strictly enforced. There were always a few "outsiders" in every town that did not respect the central place of the church in society, but most people lived by a moral and biblical code like the Puritans of a century before. The transformation from Puritanism to a broader Christianity was slower in rural northwestern Connecticut than in larger New England communities. Nevertheless, "In many communities church membership came to be regarded as a hereditary privilege, or a right to which decent people had a natural claim. Right belief and orderly conduct were often emphasized rather than experiential evidence of conversion or regeneration."[11] Whitefield would preach an awakening message to both church members and non-church members, as he saw all in need of the new birth.

A sketch of the Congregational meeting house in Great Barrington, where Whitefield preached in the summer of 1770.

Source: Howard J. Conn, *The Congregational Church of Great Barrington, 1743-1943.*

Located in extreme northwestern Connecticut, Salisbury was established in 1741. Before the English settled here, the Indians and the Dutch were present. Salisbury had a successful iron industry that was the lifeblood of the town, which produced various items such as hinges, nails, horseshoes, axes, plows, shovels, and various domestic hardware items. The only minister in Salisbury was Rev. Jonathan Lee, a Yale College graduate in 1742. The community had a small population spread over a wide geographic area. When Whitefield came to Salisbury in the summer of 1770, the town had a population of about 1,900 people. Rev. Lee served in Salisbury until his death in 1788.[12]

Lee must have heard Whitefield preach when he was a student, when the evangelist came through New Haven and preached at Yale in 1740. Lee came to Salisbury in the midst of the Great Awakening and its fallout in 1744. He married the step-daughter of Rev. Thomas Clapp, the rector of Yale, named Elizabeth Metcalf. Lee was committed to the awakening but saw little evidence of the movement in his own congregation in Salisbury. To help with his finances, and to benefit the community, Lee served as headmaster of a small school he created that met in the meeting house. This was a college preparatory program. Lee's most famous student at the school was Ethan Allen, who arrived in 1754 as a farm boy, who later became a colonial American patriot and Revolutionary War hero. Jonathan Lee was known as "a celebrated schoolmaster and popular New Light preacher."[13] His long tenure at the church and school was only interrupted once, when he volunteered in 1756 to serve as a chaplain to colonial troops in the French and Indian War. An account of Whitefield preaching for Rev. Jonathan Lee in Salisbury, Connecticut stated:

---

11   Arthur Goodenough, *The Clergy of Litchfield County [Connecticut]*, (Litchfield County University Club, 1909), p. 9.
12   Malcom D. Rudd, *An Historical Sketch of Salisbury, Connecticut*, (New York: 1899), pp. 10-11.
13   William S. Randall, *Ethan Allen: His Life and Times*, (New York: W.W. Norton & Company, 2011), p. 96.

Lee's church grew steadily but there is no record of revivals before the advent of George Whitefield in 1770 who preached in June to a great crowd gathered under the open sky on the Parade Ground in Salisbury Center. This was the last tour in America of this famous revivalist. He had gone up the Hudson on a preaching tour to Albany, and on his return preached at Great Barrington, Norfolk, Salisbury, and Sharon. Dr. Hamilton, an ear witness of the sermon, told Governor Smith of Sharon that when he was descending the hill (presumably by the Coffin wood) he distinctly heard Whitefield announce his text. What effect Whitefield had in Salisbury, if any, is unknown. There are only three admissions of church members in 1771 by profession, none in 1770.[14]

When Whitefield came to rural communities like Salisbury, much of the activity of the town and neighboring towns ceased, as hundreds or more listeners would come to hear the famous evangelist. Often the church meeting houses were not large enough to hold the crowds. This was the case in Salisbury. One report recalled:

> The meeting house in Salisbury, at that time, was small, and to accommodate the immense number of hearers which came together on the occasion, Mr. Whitefield preached in the open air. The meeting was holden on the public square near the meeting house. The late Dr. Hamilton informed Governor Smith that, on his way to this meeting, while descending the hill, nearly half a mile from the meeting, he heard the preacher distinctly announce his text, "Turn ye to the stronghold, ye prisoners of hope."[15]

As stated, in Salisbury Whitefield preached in the open air "on the public square near the meeting house." This meeting house is gone with a newer church building across the street. The "public square" was a

A sketch of the Congregational Church meeting house in Salisbury, CT. The structure was built in 1751. The building could not hold the people who came to hear Whitefield preach there in the summer of 1770. Source: Salisbury Historical Society.

---

14 Julia Pettee, *The Rev. Jonathan Lee and his Eighteenth Century Parish: the Early History of Salisbury, Connecticut*, (Salisbury, CT: The Salisbury Association, 1957), pp. 150-151.
15 Charles F. Sedgwick, *General History of the Town of Sharon*, p. 63.

parade field for the militia, but is now paved roads and several buildings. One original building still stands in Salisbury by the now gone public square. Built in 1746, the Old Bushnell Tavern is only a few hundred feet from its location in 1770 where Whitefield preached. The location of the Tavern was a type of sounding board used to accentuate the volume of Whitefield's outside preaching. This large structure is now a private home.

Another stop Whitefield made on this Hudson River Valley tour was in Norfolk, Connecticut. Located only a few miles from Salisbury, Norfolk was a small community surrounded by dense woods. First settled in 1744 and incorporated as a town in 1758, Norfolk had rocky soil and a hilly terrain which made large scale farming difficult. Numerous streams running near the community powered various small family mills. Never a thriving town, the people of Norfolk survived by farming, lumbering, and by working in small industries related to metallurgy. A meeting house for the Congregational Church and for government matters was under construction by 1759, but was not completed until January 1770, six months before Whitefield arrived in town.

A contemporary image of the 1746 Old Bushnell Inn. It was across the street from the Congregational church and the public square in 1770 when Whitefield preached outside in Salisbury. Today it is a few hundred feet from its original location. Photograph by Ken Lawson.

The minister in Norfolk that welcomed Whitefield to preach was Rev. Ammi R. Robins (or Robbins). A 1760 graduate of Yale College, Robins came to Norfolk in 1761. The son of a Congregational minister, Robins ministered in this rural community his entire adult life, often having to be paid by the townsfolk with produce, dairy products, meat, and other goods.[16] A biographical summary of Ammi Robins stated:

> Mr. Robins was fitted for college by his father and went first to Nassau Hall (now Princeton) . . . and was transferred to Yale that he might be nearer home . . . After graduation he taught school for a time at Plymouth, Mass.; studied theology with Dr. Joseph Bellamy, and was ordained at Norfolk, Oct. 28, 1761, within thirteen months after his graduation and at the

A sketch of Rev. Ammi R. Robins of Norfolk, CT. From The Clergy of Litchfield County by Arthur Goodenough.

---

16 Theron W. Crissey, *History of Norfolk, Litchfield County, Connecticut 1744-1900*, (Everett, MA: Massachusetts Publishing Company, 1900), pp. 14-15.

age of twenty-one. Here he continued for fifty-one years, till his death. The church was new, but under his ministry grew into one of the largest and most prosperous in the state. With his ministerial labors he connected those of a teacher and almost always had a number of students with him fitting for college.[17]

The above quote mentions that Ammi Robins taught school for a while in Plymouth, Massachusetts. Although he certainly knew the name of Whitefield as a student at Yale, he was not there when Whitefield came through in 1754. In his student days at Yale in the late 1750s, Robins observed the college beginning to change its antagonistic stance against Whitefield. In Plymouth, Whitefield had preached in years past, and Robins would have heard the name of Whitefield spoken with respect and admiration by members of the First Congregational Church in Plymouth. In July 1770, in rural Norfolk, Connecticut, the itinerant Whitefield found an ally in Robins. A popular preacher, Robins travelled through much of New England as a guest speaker in dozens of Congregational churches. His long tenure at the Congregational Church in Norfolk was briefly interrupted by his service as a colonial army chaplain in the American Revolution. Speaking of Rev. Ammi R. Robbins, "He had a naturally good constitution and vigorous health, a fine voice and a gift for extempore preaching. He believed in revivals, and some of great power attended his ministry. He preached about 6,500 sermons, and is said to have conducted worship in every town in the state but three . . . "[18]

The parsonage of Rev. Ammi R. Robbins in Norfolk, CT. This photograph was taken shortly before the home was demolished in 1884. In 1770, George Whitefield slept in this large, comfortable post-and-beam home. Source: Norfolk Historical Society.

A witness to Whitefield's preaching in Norfolk was an early settler of the town named Robert McEwen. He listened to the sermon and accepted it. He wrote in his diary, "July, ye 17, in yr. 1770. Heard ye famous Mr. Whitefield preach at Norfolk from John 5:25, which I hope was a word in season for me."[19] McEwen was converted and soon after joined the Norfolk Congregational Church. A further narrative of this preaching event in Norfolk is as follows:

> During George Whitefield's seventh and last visit to America, in 1769 and '70 he came into this neighborhood, and was listened to as always by attentive crowds, yet there was among Congregationalists a very strong objection to his labors as tending to many excesses; a feeling which now can scarcely be comprehended. Mr. Robbins did not share it, but received the great preacher to his house and entertained him. The room in which he slept, the north-east front chamber, became afterwards an object of interest to the clergy from its association with

---

17 Edward and George Dickerman, *Families of Dickerman Ancestry: Descendants of Thomas Dickerman, an Early Settler of Dorchester, Massachusetts,* (New haven, CT: The Tuttle, Morehouse & Taylor Press, 1897), p. 539.
18 Ibid., p. 540.
19 Theron W. Crissey, *History of Norfolk, Litchfield County, Connecticut,* p. 382.

him. He preached in a large barn, it is said, on the old Ives place, July 17, 1770, to a large and solemn audience.[20]

Congregational church membership rolls in 1770 in Norfolk do not show any significant increase in church members after Whitefield departed. Using ten years as a sample, the numbers of new church members annually from 1765 to 1775 are as follows.[21]

Year	# new members
1765	1
1766	10
1767	9
1768	14
1769	7
1770	8
1771	9
1772	7
1773	8
1774	8
1775	10

A prominent citizen of Great Barrington, Gamaliel Whiting was married to Anna (Gillett) Whiting. The couple had at least ten children that survived. Mr. Whiting kept a journal that has not survived but extracts from that journal are available. For example,

> It is pleasant to know, that we learn from the memorandums of Lieutenant Gamaliel Whiting . . . that the celebrated Rev. George Whitefield, on the occasion of his last visit to this country, and but a short time previous to his decease, preached here for several successive days. Mr. Whiting's memorandum is as follows: "1770, July 12, Mr. Whitefield preached at Great Barrington, from 2nd." From this place Mr. Whitefield went to Canaan, Norfolk, and Sharon, and Mr. Whiting records "Sunday July 15, went to Canaan and heard Mr. Whitefield."[22]

This journal or memorandum of Gamaliel Whiting speaks about Whitefield preaching in the towns of Great Barrington, Canaan, Norfolk, and Sharon. He omitted Salisbury, and he informs us that Whitefield preached in the town of Canaan and that he heard him preach there.

Canaan, Connecticut is located between Salisbury and Norfolk. The town of Canaan was incorporated in 1739. The primary industries in Canaan were related to mining and smelting iron. Many of the forests in Canaan were cleared to feed the furnaces that smelted the iron. A Congregational church was begun early on in Canaan. But by 1769, an increase in population caused an amicable division of the Congregational church into two separate churches.[23] The older church in southern Canaan was pastored by Rev. Daniel Farrand. He was ordained in Canaan in 1752 and served in the town to his death in 1803. Rev. Farrand attended Yale College but then transferred to Princeton, graduating in 1750. "In 1752, he was ordained pastor of the church of the South Parish of Canaan, commonly called South Canaan. Here he continued in the quiet

---

20 Ibid.
21 *Baptisms, Marriages, Burials, and List of Members Taken from the Church Records of the Rev. Ammi Ruhamah Robbins, First Minister of Norfolk, Connecticut, 1761-1813,* (Norfolk, CT: 1910), pp. 8-10.
22 Charles J. Taylor, *History of Great Barrington, Massachusetts,* p. 322.
23 Elizabeth Clark, "Canaan Falls Village Town History," *Town of Canaan, Connecticut,* https://www.canaanfallsvillage.org/history.

and faithful discharge of his duties until near the close of his life."[24] Farrand was described as "thoroughly Calvinistic," and was known as a wise, learned, and respected minister of unquestioned integrity. But he was not considered a skilled public speaker.[25]

The new Congregational church in the north part of Canaan was pastored by Rev. Asahel Hart. He was a graduate of Yale College in 1764. Rev. Hart was around twenty-six years old when he began preaching for the separated folks. In 1768 they built a new meeting house that was forty feet by fifty feet. Hart was ordained in March 1770 at the new North Congregational Church in Canaan. His ordination council had several Whitefield supporters, such as the nearby Rev. Jonathan Lee of Salisbury and the Rev. Ammi Robins of Norfolk. The young minister Asahel Hart was not a well man. He never married. He served at the new Congregational church in the north part of Canaan until his death in 1775, at around age 33.[26]

As previously noted, Gamaliel Whiting of nearby Great Barrington wrote, "Sunday July 15, went to Canaan and heard Mr. Whitefield." Who George Whitefield preached to that Sunday is not clear. He may have preached for Rev. Daniel Farrand at the older Congregational Church in south Canaan. Or he may have preached for the new Congregational Church under Rev. Asahel Hart in the northern part of Canaan. Or Whitefield may have preached outside to both congregations. The Canaan/Falls Village historian Midge Cortesi stated that "nothing remarkable resulted from Whitefield's visit to Canaan in July 1770."[27]

Another New England location we know about on Whitefield's brief western New England tour is Sharon, Connecticut Colony. Having previously preached in Norfolk and Salisbury, Whitefield rode south on this preaching circuit, ultimately heading to his starting point in New York City. Located about twenty-five miles southwest from Norfolk, the town of Sharon, Connecticut was incorporated in 1739. A community carved out of thick forests along the Housatonic River, Sharon boasted of rich farmlands and over a dozen lakes. The first Congregational Church meeting house was built in 1741, the second constructed in 1767. When Whitefield arrived in July 1770, the minister who welcomed him was Rev. Cotton Mather Smith.

A Yale College graduate in 1751, Smith was a descendant, from both his parents, of the original Puritans that settled New England. After Yale he spent time as a missionary to Indians with the famous Rev. Jonathan Edwards in Stockbridge, Massachusetts. Smith preached for at least a year in Sharon until his ordination there in 1755.[28] Cotton Mather Smith's long ministry in Sharon was described as follows.

> Mr. Smith was the minister in Sharon for more than fifty years, and during the whole of that period occupied a large space in public affairs. Probably no minister ever had, in a greater degree, the confidence and affection of his people. He was never spoken of by those who knew him, but with the most unqualified respect and veneration.[29]

The meeting house for the Congregational Church in Sharon was constructed amidst tension in the town. Those citizens who lived several miles away, over the mountain, thought it too far and dangerous to travel to church in foul weather. The location for the new building was debated, and a central location near the original meeting house and the town common was decided. When completed in 1767, the new meeting house was "the largest church in Litchfield County, [yet] scaffolds had to be built round it for the crowd that assembled to hear the English evangelist Whitefield in 1770."[30]

---

24 William B. Sprague, *Annals of the American Pulpit: Trinitarian Congregational*, (New York: 1866), vol. I, p. 490.
25 Ibid., p. 492.
26 *History of Litchfield, Connecticut*, (Philadelphia: J.W. Lewis & Company, 1881), p. 484.
27 Marge Cortesi interviewed by Ken Lawson, May 21, 2017.
28 Charles F. Sedgwick, *General History of the Town of Sharon*, pp. 55-56.
29 Ibid., p. 57.
30 Chard P. Smith, *Brief History of Sharon*, (July 1949: Courtesy of the Sharon Historical Society).

On June 18, 1770, George Whitefield preached inside the Congregational meeting house in Sharon to a large crowd gathered inside and nearby on the common. But not all in Sharon were pleased with Whitefield or his invitation to preach by Rev. Cotton M. Smith. A later minister in Sharon wrote,

> Whitefield was here in 1770, and it was the influence of the liberal consecration of Parson Smith that gave the great gospel Hercules a hearing in the church; for many were opposed—and he was expecting to speak in the orchard across the street. He was entertained by Parson Smith at his house as well as his pulpit, and the congregation to hear him was so large that scaffoldings were erected all around the meeting-house—that the crowds might listen through open windows.[31]

The town common or town green in Sharon is largely unchanged today from colonial days. This was a public area designed within the town settlement as open space for grazing, for recreation, for town assemblies, for militia practice, or for a quiet, central place within the often noisy and dirty colonial villages. When Whitefield preached within the Congregational church in Sharon, the windows were open so those on staging around the building, and those standing on the common, could listen to the sermon. There is today a memorial stone and plaque in Sharon that recalls Whitefield's visit to the town.

A new Congregational meeting house was constructed in Sharon in 1767 for Rev. Smith, completed the next year. This meeting house was one of the largest structures in the county, yet the congregations on Sundays typically filled the building.[32] The building was also full when meetings were called to protest increasing British interference in the colonist's lives. There was no way the crowd gathered that day to hear Whitefield could all fit inside. An extended account of Whitefield preaching in Sharon stated:

> On the 18th day of June, 1770, the Rev. George Whitefield, a celebrated itinerant minister of the Church of England, passed through the town on a preaching tour . . . There was considerable opposition to his being permitted to preach in

A memorial stone commemorates the location and event when George Whitefield preached in Sharon, CT. The plaque says, "Site of the 2nd House of Worship in Sharon. George Whitefield preached here June 18, 1770. Text, 'Marvel not that I saith unto thee, ye must be born again,' John 3:7. An immense congregation assembled." Notice the common space or town green. It is a long, narrow open space a thousand or more feet long. Photograph by Ken Lawson.

---

31 Gerald S. Lee, *About an Old New England Church*, (Sharon, CT: W.W. Knight & Company, 1891), pp. 19-20.
32 Charles F. Sedgwick, *General History of the Town of Sharon*, p. 62.

the meeting house, but the influence of Parson Smith prevailed, and the doors were opened. An arrangement had been made for him to preach in the orchard of Mr. Jonathan Gillet, directly opposite the meeting house . . . in case he should be refused admission to the usual place of worship. An immense congregation, from this and the neighboring towns, assembled on the occasion, and that all the hearers might be well accommodated with seats, extensive scaffolds were erected around the house. His text was the words of our Savior addressed to Nicodemus,—"Marvel not that I say unto you, ye must be born again." He discoursed upon the doctrine of the new birth with the most astonishing power and eloquence. The concluding words of the sermon were a quotation, with a little variation, from the last verse of the fourth chapter of Solomon's Songs: "Awake O north wind and come thou south, blow upon this garden, that the spices thereof may flow out. Let my Beloved come into this garden, and eat his pleasant fruits . . . ."[33]

When Whitefield was in Sharon in 1770, the common or town green was surrounded with homes, businesses, taverns, hardware stores, and the like. One of the few original buildings still standing on the Sharon common is this private home, built in 1739. It has been much altered but many of the original features of the house are still intact. Photograph by Ken Lawson.

Many of the folks of Sharon, Connecticut were moved by Whitefield's sermon. In Wakeley's book on Whitefield, he recorded that "The sermon was preached to an immense multitude with astonishing power and eloquence, and there was a moving and a melting time." Wakeley stated, "The sermon made a life-long impression on those who heard it. It was an era in the history of the place, and was talked of as a day of wonder till that generation had passed away." Wakeley continued, "So impressed were the people of Sharon with his great oratorical powers that it is no wonder they followed him into the adjoining towns for several successive days in order to hear him again and again."[34]

A story has survived about one of Whitefield's converts in Sharon, Connecticut. She was still faithful forty years later, living in a village near Sharon and "still retained the primitive fire he had then kindled." Around the year 1810 she still venerated the name of Whitefield, and spoke admiringly of his person and his eloquence. Those who spoke with her while she was in her nineties noted that she was fervent in prayer,

---

33 Ibid., p. 64.
34 Joseph B. Wakeley, *Anecdotes of the Rev. George Whitefield, M.A.*, (London, 1722), p. 358.

and that "She was the only convert of Whitefield's we ever saw, and she had more life and fire in her than some whole churches."[35]

Perhaps the most intriguing thing about Whitefield's visit to Sharon, Connecticut was that he almost died. A local source in Sharon stated, "Whitefield stayed with Parson Smith while in Sharon and was very ill during the night before he preached."[36] This was a huge understatement. Were it not for the efforts of Rev. Cotton Smith's wife Temperance, Whitefield would have died in Sharon. On June 17-18, 1770, the night and morning before He preached, Whitefield was incapacitated by chocking. Temperance Smith had some basic medical training. "She spent the entire night by his bedside . . . doing her utmost to enable the sufferer to get his health, under the violent attacks of asthma which, three months later, ended his career."[37] Using local oral histories and family written accounts, the Sharon Historical Society compiled the following extended narrative of Whitefield's ministry and illness in Sharon.

> The Rev. George Whitefield, minister of the Church of England . . . was traveling through this region on a preaching tour. He had spoken at Albany and Schenectady; and, crossing the River, had visited Great Barrington, Norfolk, and Salisbury. There had been some objection to his welcome in free churches, for he was regarded as distinctly of Tory sympathies and a representative of the crown of King George. But Pastor Cotton Mather Smith, the local pastor who was much beloved of his congregation and the townspeople, prevailed upon the opponents to listen to the good news of this messenger of God . . . The visitor [Whitefield] was invited after his engagement at Salisbury, where he addressed an immense assembly, to spend the night of the 17th of June at the parsonage of Parson Smith. . . .
>
> Whitefield suffered greatly from persistent attacks of asthma. Mrs. [Temperance] Smith, who was practiced in attendance on the afflicted, was called into service on this occasion . . . Family tradition and diaries relate the attention of Madam Smith to Mr. Whitefield. She used various kinds of treatment, but especially she burned dried stramonium leaves that he might inhale the smoke to the relief of the hard and heavy breathing. Almost the entire night she waited at his bedside; but before dawn he was able to gain a few hours of sleep. The spasmatic attacks subsided, he drank several cups of strong coffee; and then felt able to fulfill his duty in the pulpit. Just a few hours before it had seemed doubtful whether he would survive the night of agony; but as the time of his appearance drew near, he felt fit for the task and was enthusiastic in his gratitude to Madam Smith for her kind favor as a nurse.[38]

The children and other relatives of Rev. Cotton and Temperance Smith recalled their family matriarch in Sharon taking good medical care of Whitefield. They also wrote and spoke of Whitefield's preaching as "so powerful in his delivery of his message regarding the Second Birth, his voice soft as a flute and piercing as a fife, reaching with persuasive [persuasion] to hearers in the last row." The Smith family members were present and recalled, "He preached a lengthy sermon and showed no signs of weakness." They also stated that many of them remembered and retold his gospel message after the fact, especially his conclusion taken from the Song of Solomon.[39] Helen Evertson Smith was a descendant of Rev. Cotton and Temperance

---

35   Ibid., pp. 382-383.
36   Charles C. Tiffany, *History of Sharon, Connecticut,* (unpublished 1942: Courtesy of the Sharon Historical Society), p. 22.
37   Helen Evertson Smith, *Colonial Days and Ways*, p. 232.
38   Leonard Twynham, "An Important Marker in Sharon, Conn.," Courtesy of the Sharon Historical Society. The "Important Marker" in this article is the memorial stone and plaque dedicated to Whitefield in Sharon.
39   Ibid., p. 2.

Smith. In the early-to-mid-1800s, she was a small girl who heard many first and second person accounts of her older relatives who heard and watched Whitefield in Sharon in 1770. The account of his visit was passed to the Smith children, grandchildren, and beyond. What was emphasized most in these recollections was his eloquence as a speaker.[40]

As a result of Whitefield's preaching in Sharon, "Many of the inhabitants of Sharon followed him for several successive days, to hear the word of life from this devoted minister of the cross."[41] Heading south, he had preaching appointments in Amenia and Smithfield, New York. There were many residents of Sharon that travelled from place-to-place to hear Whitefield over several days.

Many parts of Litchfield County, Connecticut were moved by Whitefield's summer 1770 visit. Others were indifferent. The 1745 ban by the General Association of Connecticut clergy against Whitefield preaching in the Congregational churches in Connecticut had not been redacted.[42] Some clergy welcomed Whitefield and others did not. Some local confusion and excitement accompanied his 1770 visit, which then passed away.

Whitefield wrote a letter on July 29, 1770 from New York City, having just returned from his Hudson River preaching circuit in upstate New York and western New England. He summarized, "Last night I returned hither, and hope to set out for Boston in two or three days."[43]

---

40   Helen Evertson Smith, *Colonial Days and Ways*, pp. 231-232.
41   Joseph Belcher, *George Whitefield: A Biography with Special Reference to His Labors in America*, (New York: American Tract Society, 1857), p. 430.
42   Arthur Goodenough, *The Clergy of Litchfield County*, p. 12.
43   George Whitefield, *The Works of George Whitefield, vol. III*, p. 425.

CHAPTER 37

WHITEFIELD'S MINISTRY IN SOUTHERN NEW ENGLAND AND BOSTON

AUGUST 1770

IN THIS WHITEFIELD TRAVELOGUE, IT is impossible to trace the exact footsteps of Whitefield in New England daily. In the last chapter he was in western New England and upstate New York. We then discovered him in Connecticut, headed towards Rhode Island and Boston. On August 3, 1770, the *New London Gazette* reported, "Saturday night last the Rev. Mr. Whitefield arrived here from Albany."[1] That was the last 1770 mention of Whitefield's travels in Connecticut in that newspaper.

CONNECTICUT

An anecdote has survived from Whitefield in Connecticut in early August 1770. Rev. Solomon Williams served the Congregational Church in Lebanon, Connecticut from 1722 to his death in 1776. Solomon Williams had a daughter named Eunice who was about 13 years old in 1770. When an older woman, Eunice wrote about Whitefield's visit to Lebanon in 1770. She was an eyewitness to the events that unfolded as follows.

> The presence of George Whitefield had drawn many people from other districts to the Lebanon meeting house. When Whitefield's sermon from the text, "Take not thy Holy Spirit from me," was over, and the service concluded, Whitefield and Williams left the building. Many who had remained, however, reported an eye-witness, "became so perfectly frantic—jumping, dancing, singing and praying, that the scene seemed to form a sort of Bedlam. The outcome was as follows:
>
> Good Deacon Huntington—Dr. Williams' right hand man—having continued in the church, as a witness to what passed, went straight to his pastor to see if he could not do something to quell the disorder. Dr. Williams and Mr. Whitefield both hastened to the church; and, on entering, such was the noise and tumult on every side, that the presence of the two ministers was not immediately observed. They went forward to the Deacon's seat, and Mr. Whitefield, stamping his foot with great violence on the floor, exclaimed with a voice of thunder—"What means all this tumult and disorder?" Instantly there was silence through the house; but some of them quickly remarked that they were so much delighted to see and hear their spiritual father, and were so filled with the Spirit, that they could not forbear their demonstrations of joy. Whitefield replied to them with great mildness of manner—"My dear children, you are

---

1 *New London Gazette,* August 3, 1770, p. 3.

like little partridges, just hatched from the egg. You run about with egg shells covering your eyes, and you cannot see and know what you are doing"

The effect of this gentle expostulation was that the disorder entirely ceased, and they withdrew quietly to their several homes.[2]

Whitefield wrote a letter in late July 1770 from New York City, hoping to set out for Boston in a few days."[3] That means he planned to depart New York City sometime around August 1, 1770. After traveling quickly through Connecticut, he arrived in Newport, Rhode Island either on August 3 or 4, 1770.[4] Therefore, Whitefield took a hasty voyage in a boat from New York City to Newport, on Long Island Sound for a couple of days. We have no way of knowing why he went by the familiar town of New Haven and other coastal Connecticut towns in his direct trip from New York to Lebanon, Connecticut, then to Newport.

We can trace some of Whitefield's southern New England route through a narrative provided by a Whitefield biographer, Luke Tyerman. He wrote that Whitefield arrived in Newport on August 4 and stayed until August 8. He then went to Providence, staying there August 9 to 13. He then was in Attleboro on August 13 and Wrentham on August 14, both in Massachusetts. On August 15 he was in Boston.[5] On his way to Boston from New York, we can trace Whitefield's route at Newport and Providence, Rhode Island, and the towns of Attleboro and Wrentham.

RHODE ISLAND

In August 1770, Newport, Rhode Island was a hotbed of patriotic discontent against Great Britain. Whitefield entered a city furious at Great Britain for the Sugar Act tax of 1764, and the Stamp Act tax of 1765. Newporters saw these taxes, imposed upon them from across the ocean without their input or vote, as violations of their rights as British citizens. In 1765, citywide demonstrations occurred in March against the Stamp Act, and in June against the impressments of Newport men into the British Navy. In 1767, the British Parliament passed a series of laws called the Townsend Acts, designed to pay the salaries of civil officials loyal to the king; to enforce trade regulations against smuggling; and to raise tax revenues. Violence erupted in Newport in 1769, when a colonial vessel accused of smuggling was confiscated by the British and renamed the *HMS Liberty*. This vessel patrolled around Newport, and after a confrontation with Rhode Island colonists, was seized and burned in Newport Harbor. This was one of the first acts of violence against British rule in the America Colonies.

Whitefield's arrival in Rhode Island was anticipated by several New England newspapers. For example, the *Boston Post-Boy* of August 6, 1770 noted that Whitefield had departed New York "last Tuesday afternoon" and arrived at Newport on Friday August 3. The August 9, 1770 edition of the *Boston Post-Boy* stated, "The Rev. Mr. Whitefield arrived at Newport last week on his way to this town." The August 10, 1770 edition of *The Connecticut Journal and New Haven Post-Boy* posted an announcement dated August 6, stating that Whitefield had departed New York on his way to Newport, Rhode Island. Except for his stop in Lebanon, there is no surviving record that Whitefield stopped in Connecticut on his way from New York to Rhode Island. Records have not survived. He probably traveling along a coastal route by schooner delivering mail or supplies.

---

2   William B. Sprague, *Annals of the American Pulpit—Trinitarian Congregational*, (New York: Robert Carter & Brothers Printers, 1857), vol. I, pp. 324-325. Iain H. Murray, *Jonathan Edwards: A New Biography*, (Carlisle, PA: Banner of Truth Trust, 1981, reprinted 2000), pp. 218-219.
3   George Whitefield, *The Works of George Whitefield, vol. III,* p. 425.
4   Ezra Stiles, *The Literary Diary of Ezra Stiles, January 1769 to March 13, 1776*, (New York: Charles Scribner's Sons, 1901), vol. I, pp. 60 and 61. Stiles kept an exact diary, and recorded both on August 2 and August 4, that Whitefield had just arrived in Newport.
5   Luke Tyerman, *The Life of the Rev. George Whitefield*, (New York: Anson D.F. Randolph & Company, 1877), vol. II, p. 592.

In 1770 Newport, Rhode Island was one of the most significant cities in the American Colonies. Faithfully serving as a Newport minister in these difficult days was Rev. Ezra Stiles of the Second Congregational Church. Stiles arrived in Newport in 1755. An educated and articulate clergyman with a keen theological mind, Stiles was welcomed and successful in Newport. Stiles was fluent on the major political and ecclesiastical issues of his day, and frequently corresponded with colonial and European authorities. Previously, Whitefield came to Newport in 1764, but there is no record that he met Stiles, and he was not invited to preach at the Second Congregational Church. But by 1770, the objections Stiles had towards Whitefield, mainly from Whitefield's loose administrative style with money and the over-zealous nature of some Whitefield admirers, had ceased.

The Rev. Ezra Stiles house in Newport was built for him in 1756 as the minister of the Second Congregational Church. George Whitefield was a visitor here in 1770.
Source: https://www.cruisebe.com/ezra-stiles-house-newport-rhode-island

The following narrative of Whitefield in Newport is provided by the eyewitness account of Rev. Samuel Hopkins, who was a contemporary and friend of both Whitefield and Ezra Stiles. Hopkins had recently settled in Newport.

> It is pleasant to open the curtains of the past, and look upon our Newport minister, as, four months after his installation, he was enjoying a visit from Mr. Whitefield. Hopkins had listened with delight to Whitefield, thirty years before, at New Haven; and on the 3rd of August, 1770, welcomed him as a guest at the old Newport parsonage. At five o'clock, on the afternoon of August 4, Whitefield "preached to a very crowded audience at Mr. Hopkins's meeting-house," from Ps. li. 11: "Take not thy Holy Spirit from me." A young Jewess heard him, "and greatly admired his preaching the gospel of Christ." On the next morning, the Sabbath, he preached for Dr. Stiles, from Job xxii.21: "Acquaint now thyself with him, and be at peace." At six o'clock in the afternoon, he preached from I Cor. iii:11, in the fields adjoining Mr. Hopkins's meeting-house, to a thousand or fifteen-hundred hearers. While preaching, he stood on a table, which is still reverently preserved. On the 7th of August, he preached at five o'clock P.M., from Zech. ix.12, at Mr. Thurston's Baptist meeting-house, to an audience of thirteen-hundred within the walls, and four or five hundred without. After preaching, he dined at Major Otis's, with Mr. Hopkins, and Mr. Thurston, and Dr. Stiles. At six o'clock on the next morning, he preached, from Gen. i.2, to eleven-hundred hearers, in Mr. Hopkins's meeting-house. After service, he dined with Messrs. Hopkins, Thurston, Stiles, and Rusmeyer, the Moravian pastor in Newport, at the house of Mr. John Wanton, a Quaker. In the afternoon, he left for Providence, and before two months had passed away, he died in Newburyport.[6]

---

6   Samuel Hopkins, *The Works of Samuel Hopkins,* (Boston: Doctrinal Tract and Book Society, 1852), vol. I, p. 86. Think of the denominational make-up of this ministerial meeting. The denominations represented in fellowship here were Congregational, Baptist, Moravian, Anglican, and Quaker.

The old First Congregational Church building, as it now looks in Newport, RI. Photograph by Ken Lawson.

The "Mr. Hopkins's meeting-house" was the First Congregational Church building. This building is still standing in what if now a densely populated area of Newport, on Mill Street a few blocks from the harbor. The structure is clearly recognizable as a former church building, and is now divided up into housing units. The above mentioned "fields adjoining Mr. Hopkins's meeting-house" is Touro Park, a few hundred feet uphill from the church building. This was the same spot where Whitefield preached outside to a large crowd thirty years prior, in 1740.

Rev. Ezra Stiles was the other significant clergyman in Newport in 1770. It must have given Whitefield great satisfaction to be invited by Stiles to preach in the Second Congregational Church. The meeting house, constructed in 1735, is still standing in Newport, though it has been greatly altered over the years. The parsonage of Ezra Stiles is in Newport and is recognizable as the colonial home in which Stiles entertained Whitefield. Stiles made journal entries dated August 4 to 8, 1770, which described in some detail his interaction with Whitefield in Newport.

[August] 4. Yesterday the Rev. George Whitefield . . . arrived here from New York. At V o'clock this Afternoon he preached at Mr. Hopkins' Meeting-house on Ps. Li, II, *Take not thy holy Spirit from me.* In 1745 my Congregation passed a Vote against his preaching in our Meetinghouse. But my people being very desirous of hearing him, the committee met & agreed that notwithstanding that vote it is expedient, to ask him to preach for me tomorrow; accordingly I have asked him.

Ldsdy [Lord's Day] 5. A.M. Rev. Mr. Whitefield preached for me from Job, *Acquaint now thyself with God & be at peace.* P.M. I preached Jn. iii, 16,17. Mr. Whitefield [came to] dinner . . . at VI P.M. he preached on I Cor. Iii,ll, Other found, & c. in the fields adjoining Mr. Hopkins Meet [Meeting house] to a thousand or fifteen hundred people.

7. Evening lecture V P.M. at Mr. Thurston's Baptist meeting. Mr. Whitefield preached, Zech ix, 12 *Turn ye to the stronghold, ye prisoners of hope.* About one Thous. Persons below & three hundred in the galleries; 4 or 500 around abroad.

8. At VI o'clock this morning Mr. Whitefield preached on Gen. 1,2, *and the earth was without form, &c* to about eight hundred below & three hundred in Galleries of Mr. Hopkins' Meetinghouse, a few abroad. Dined with him . . . with the Rev Mess Hopkins, Thurston, Rusmeyer, and sundry Gentlemen . . . No minister except a Baptist ever before preached in Mr. Thurston's Baptist meeting . . . At III P.M. Mr. Whitefield departed hence for Providence.[7]

This lengthy quote from Ezra Stiles' diary will receive further attention from the three persons mentioned in the quote: Rev. Ezra Stiles, Rev. Samuel Hopkins, and Rev. Gardner Thurston.

Ezra Stiles mentions that his Second Congregational Church in Newport had previously voted to forbid Whitefield from preaching in their meeting house. That refusal was under the previous minister, Rev. James Searing, and applied to Whitefield's visits to Newport in 1745, 1747, 1754, and after Stiles arrived in 1755, to Whitefield's 1764 visit. However, after Ezra Stiles came to the church, a gradual change was noticeable in the congregation. The church folks were "very desirous to hear him" and voted, with Stiles approval, to make it so. Since this was a last-minute request, Whitefield only preached once for Stiles in the Second Congregational Church, on Sunday morning, August 5, 1770.

Rev. Samuel Hopkins is mentioned three times in the diary entries from Ezra Stiles. After arriving in Newport in April 1770, Hopkins ministered at the First Congregational Church until his death in 1803, interrupted only from the 1776 to 1780 British occupation of Newport. His predecessor at the church, Rev. William Vinal, was a firm Whitefield supporter. It was in this church pulpit that Whitefield preached in his several prior visits to Newport. Hopkins kept up the tradition of welcoming Whitefield to the church.

A likeness of Rev. Ezra Stiles, later in life.

Source: https://commons.wikimedia. org/wiki/File:Ezra_Stiles_by_ Reuben_Moulthrop.jpg

Samuel Hopkins is an interesting character in American church history. As a farm boy who loved books, he graduated from Yale College in 1741. He heard Whitefield preach at Yale while a student in 1740, and he heartily approved. After graduation, he studied in the home of Rev. Jonathan Edwards. Hopkins eagerly embraced the theology and philosophy of Edwards, and then went further in his theological speculations and philosophical suppositions. He possessed a keen mind but was not a particularly good public speaker. A famous Unitarian preacher of the next generation, Rev. William E. Channing, remarked, "He was the very ideal of bad delivery; such tones never came from any human voice within my hearing."[8] Hopkins struggled with his assurance of salvation, in a relentless pursuit of purity that left him frustrated. Some of his logical speculations related to the love of God, and whether a Christian could love God enough to be willing to be damned. On the other hand, his teachings on selfless love, without regard to rewards, caused his contemporaries to pause and do self-examination. His intellectual speculations and philosophical inquiries got him in trouble in many places. His evangelistic style of Calvinism laid some foundation for the Second Great Awakening which shook

---

7 Ezra Stiles, *The Literary Diary of Ezra Stiles*, pp. 61-62.
8 Dan Graves, "Samuel Hopkins' Unusual Theology," http://www.christianity.com/church/church-history/timeline/1801-1900/samuel-hopkins-unusual-theology-11630343.html. William Ellery Channing (1780-1842) was raised in a wealthy family in Newport. He grew up in the Second Congregational Church with Rev. Ezra Stiles, and later attended the First Congregational Church under Rev. Samuel Hopkins. Later he was ordained and became a famous Unitarian minister in Boston.

The Second Congregational Church building as it looks today. The building was constructed in 1735. George Whitefield preached for this congregation under Rev. Ezra Stiles in 1770. The parsonage for Rev. Stiles was across the street. The church structure is now divided into housing units. Photograph by Ken Lawson.

America in the early nineteenth century. Based on his writings, his entire theological system has been called Hopkinsian or the New Divinity.[9]

Hopkins was often in theological disputes or religious debates with others. He was a Calvinist and a New Light, but some of his ideas, compared to traditional Calvinism, bordered on unorthodoxy. That meant both the orthodox and the unorthodox criticized him. In opposition to a rigid Calvinism that emphasized election and predestination, Hopkins stressed the human responsibility to respond to the gospel message. Another area of dispute was the role of the Holy Spirit in salvation and in the Christian life. Some asserted that a direct revelation from the Spirit was possible, while others believed that the Spirit moved through the scriptures which revealed God to men. Theologians like Jonathan Edwards and Samuel Hopkins debated these and other issues with deists on one side and rigid Calvinists on the other side. An account of Hopkins in a theological discussion with Whitefield has been preserved from 1770. Hopkins had been recently installed as the minister of the First Congregational Church in Newport, when the following exchange was recorded.

Hopkins had listened with delight to Whitefield thirty years before, at New Haven; and on the 3rd of August, 1770, welcomed him as a guest at the old Newport parsonage. While Mr. Whitefield was at Newport, he was invited, with Mr. Hopkins and others, to breakfast with a religious family, about five miles from town. On their way, Mr. Whitefield said to Mr. Hopkins, "I am sorry that you New England ministers employ so much of your time in controversy. I wish you would devote your attention more immediately to the conversion of sinners." Mr. Hopkins replied, "I have not published so large a pamphlet in the way of dispute as yours against Mr. Wesley." A fit reply, to Which Mr. Whitefield rejoined, "O, the doctrine of Mr. Wesley was so contrary to the faith, and so dangerous, that a regard for the cause of Christ compelled me to attempt its refutation." "That same motive," said Mr. Hopkins, "may have influenced others. It certainly did influence me in what I have written." After a considerable pause, Mr. Whitefield said, "It is not surprising, and much to be regretted, that good Mr. Edwards should deny the witness of the Spirit?" Mr. Hopkins replied, "I did not know that he had. What do you understand, sir, by the witness of the Spirit?" Mr. Whitefield paused in apparent study for a definition. Mr. Hopkins said, "Do you mean by it an impression on the imagination, by some immediate communication from the Spirit, that your sins are forgiven, and that you are a child of God?" "No," said Mr. Whitefield, "that does not express my opinion." "Do you mean then," said Mr. Hopkins, "an influence of the Spirit of

---

[9] For a thorough study on this topic see Joseph A. Conforti, *Samuel Hopkins and the New Divinity Movement,* (Grand Rapids, MI: Eerdman's Publishing, 1981).

God, exciting such a love for God and Jesus Christ, such clear views of their character, as that the subject of it knows from experience and from Scripture, that he is a child of God and an heir of salvation?" "this," said Mr. Whitefield, "more accords with my views." "Yet this," said Mr. Hopkins, "is that witness of the Spirit for which Mr. Edwards pleads, in distinction from the former, which he represents as the species of enthusiasm.[10]

An undated painting of Rev. Samuel Hopkins.

Source: www.yaleslavery.org

According to Hopkins' diary entries for early August 1770, Whitefield preached for him on Saturday afternoon, August 4; Sunday evening August 5 at 6:00 PM outside the meeting house to upwards of 1,500 people; and Wednesday morning at 6:00 AM to about 1,000 people inside the First Congregational Church meeting house for Rev. Hopkins.[11] Another minister Whitefield preached for in Newport was the Baptist Rev. Gardner Thurston. Ezra Stiles wrote that Whitefield preached for Thurston on Tuesday evening, August 7, 1770 in the Baptist meeting house in Newport. Up to 1,800 people attended that meeting, both inside and outside the building.[12]

Gardner Thurston was born in Newport in 1721 and raised in the Second Baptist Church. He learned a trade and had deep evangelical tendencies even as a boy. At age twenty he made a public profession of faith and was baptized by his minister, Rev. Nicholas Eyers. Through active participation and the discipleship of Eyers, Thurston was called to preach and licensed by the church in 1748. Thurston served as an assistant to Eyers until 1759, when he was ordained as pastor of the Second Baptist Church. Thurston then served as minister of the church until his retirement in 1801, after which he died a year later. Thurston was educated for the ministry by Eyers and through his utilization of the excellent library in Newport. His attributes were described as follows:

> Mr. T. was endowed with an excellent disposition, and possessed a good natured constitution, with a quick and brilliant imagination. He was mild, religious, studious and amiable in his family; lively and engaging in all the social circles of real friendship; tender, melting, solemn and devotional among the sons and daughters of affliction; easy and graceful in all his public movements. His voice was strong and melodious, and his heart alive in the great and arduous work of the ministry of reconciliation.[13]

When Whitefield preached for Thurston in the Second Baptist Church in Newport, he addressed an evangelically minded congregation that thrived on revivals. A few years prior to his visit, the church had had some minor controversy related to singing in services—should the Psalms alone be sung, or could Psalms and hymns also be sung? The congregation decided, after about one year of meetings, upon the latter course.[14] An account of Whitefield preaching here was recorded in the diary of Rev. Ezra Stiles:

---

10   Samuel Hopkins, *The Works of Samuel Hopkins . . .* , vol. I, pp. 86-87.
11   Ezra Stiles, *The Literary Diary of Ezra Stiles*, pp. 61-62.
12   Ibid., p. 62.
13   William Rogers, "Memoirs of Rev. Gardner Thurston," *Evangelical Magazine and Religious Intelligencer,* (November 1810), p. 404.
14   J.O. Choules, *A Sermon Preached November 26, 1829, being the Day of Thanksgiving, containing a History of the Origin and Growth of the Second Baptist Church in Newport, R.I.,* (Providence, RI: H.H. Brown Printer, 1830), pp. 12-13.

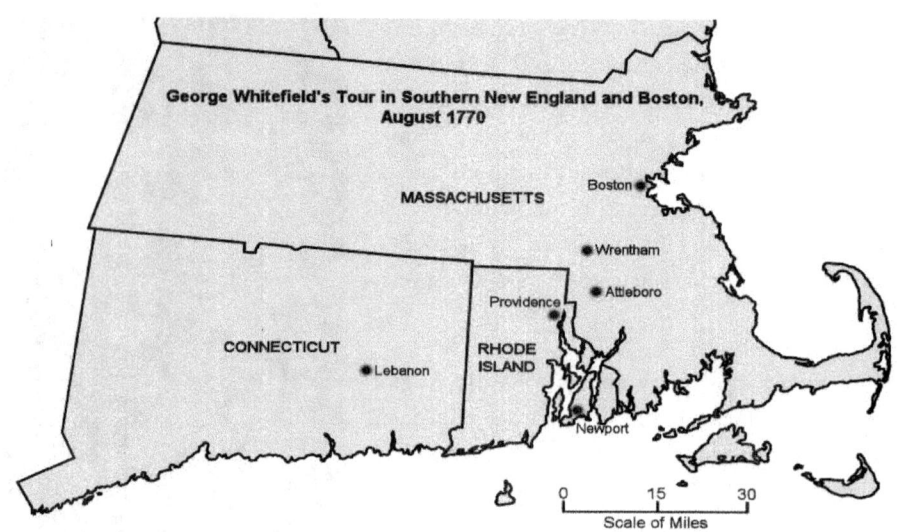

[August] 7. Evening lecture V P.M. at Mr. Thurston's Baptist meeting. Mr. Whitefield preached, Zech ix, 12 *Turn ye to the stronghold, ye prisoners of hope.* About one Thous. Persons below & three hundred in the galleries; 4 or 500 around abroad.[15]

This was a remarkable meeting. On a Tuesday evening, in and around a Baptist meeting house, Whitefield preached to perhaps 1,700 people in Newport. The next morning Whitefield preached for Samuel Hopkins, had a meal with Thurston and Hopkins and others, and departed Newport for Providence, Rhode Island. The novelty of Whitefield, a Church of England priest, preaching in a Baptist meeting house was not lost on Ezra Stiles. Even fellow New Lights in Newport, such as the Congregationalist Stiles and others, had not been invited to preach in this Baptist pulpit. Stiles wrote, "No minister except a Baptist ever before preached in Mr. Thurston's Baptist meeting . . . "[16] Happy to see Whitefield return to Newport in 1770 was the long-time schoolteacher, Mrs. Sarah Osborn. Having taught school in Newport for over twenty-five years, Osborn was a figurehead in the community, not only from her education of school children, but from her outspoken New Light beliefs. In the 1740s she was elected the head of a female religious society and served in this capacity for over half a century. She and her assistants educated many of the children of Newport, from 1744 until her eyesight gave out in 1774. Previous to Whitefield's 1770 visit, Osborn was a leader in a revival that influenced hundreds from all classes of society in Newport.[17] An active member of the First Church of Christ Congregational, under Rev. William Vinal, and after April 1770 under Rev. Samuel Hopkins, Sarah Osborn was one of many longtime Newport residents who remembered the previous visits of Whitefield with great satisfaction.

Newspapers in Colonial America were notoriously opinionated. They were sometimes inconsistent in publication and were often late in reporting current events. Sometimes the reporting of significant news had to be decreased so space could be made for newspaper advertisements. A summary of Whitefield's several-day ministry in Newport was provided by a Connecticut newspaper.

Newport, August 6 . . . Last Friday, arrived here, from New York, the Rev. Mr. Whitefield, who has preached once at the Rev. Mr. Hopkins's Meeting-House, once at the Rev. Dr.

---

15 Ezra Stiles, *The Literary Diary of Ezra Stiles,* pp. 61-62.
16 Ibid., p. 62.
17 Catherine A. Breckus, *Sarah Osborn's World: The Rise of Evangelical Christianity in Early America,* (New Haven: Yale University Press, 2013), p. 4.

Stiles's, and once in the fields, to very large Audiences, giving universal Satisfaction; and is to preach at the Rev. Mr. Thurston's Meeting-House tomorrow Evening at 5 o'clock, and the next day, we hear, will set out for Boston.[18]

It is difficult to determine the success of Whitefield's preaching ministry in Newport in 1770. He was welcomed by the leading Protestant ministers in the town. He preached to large audiences. But there was no revival, and no visible sign that his preaching led to remarkable results. The church folks of Newport were already well-taught in the gospel, with doctrinal preaching from their own ministers. The local newspaper, the *Newport Mercury*, summarized Whitefield's preaching in Newport in matter-of-fact conciseness, with no comments on the size of the crowds or the effectiveness of his ministry.

An undated sketch of Rev. Gardner Thurston, Baptist pastor in Newport, RI.

Source: http://www.rihs.org/ wp-content/ uploads/2017/04/ RHS_Journal-75-1_v5.pdf

Newport, August 13. Last Tuesday evening the Rev. Mr. Whitefield preached to a very numerous assembly, at the Rev. Mr. Thurston's Meeting-House; the next morning, at 6 o'clock, he preached at the Rev. Mr. Hopkins's, and in the afternoon set off, in one of the packets, for Providence, on his way to Boston.[19]

Whitefield's next stop on his way to Boston was in Providence, Rhode Island. His host was Rev. Joseph Snow of the Second Congregational or Beneficent Church. Whitefield preached for Snow twenty-five years earlier, in 1745, and again in 1764. When Whitefield arrived in Providence in August 1770, the town was holding public meetings related to increased tensions with Great Britain over taxes and restrictions on shipping. Simultaneously, the influential Quaker population was sponsoring public rallies to criticize Providence merchants who benefited from slavery in the southern colonies and the Caribbean islands.[20] Snow's ministry at the church was steady, balanced, and consistent. A year before Whitefield arrived in 1770, the church elected seven men to serve as deacons to assist with the physical affairs of the church. This congregation was said to have an "amicable and catholic spirit . . . manifested toward other evangelical Christians," and speaking specifically of Joseph Snow, "His doctrines were drawn from the Bible, which he studied on his knees . . . His voice and action in the pulpit showed him to be in earnest in his Master's cause."[21]

Providence was a community of businessmen, merchants, tradesmen, and mariners. In 1770 there was a growing military presence in the town, as the Colonial Rhode Island militia was increasingly visible and active in training and in resisting British encroachments on sea and land. An anecdote has survived of Whitefield's interaction with a Rhode Island militia general in Providence in 1770.

Near the close of his life Mr. Whitefield was the guest of a general at Providence, Rhode Island. His wife and three daughters, as well as himself were serious, but not decidedly

---

18   *The Connecticut Journal and New Haven Post-Boy*, August 10, 1770, p. 4.
19   *Newport Mercury*, August 13, 1770, p. 3.
20   Thomas W. Bicknell, *History of the State of Rhode Island and Providence Plantations*, (New York: The American Historical Society, Inc., 1920), pp. 509, 731.
21   Mark Tucker, *Centennial Sermon Preached before the Beneficent Congregational Church and Society in Providence, R.I., March 19, 1843*, (Providence, RI: Knowles & Vose Printers, 1845), pp. 26, 30.

religious. It was Whitefield's usual custom when stopping with a family to converse with each member on the subject of experimental religion. But in this instance he had departed from it. The last night that he was to spend in the house came, and he retired to bed but not to sleep. Something came to him in the night saying, "O man of God! If these people perish their blood shall be upon thy head." He listened, but the flesh said, "Do not speak to these people; they are so good and kind that you cannot say a harsh thing to them." He rose and prayed. The sweat ran down his brow like rain. He was in fear and anxiety. At last a happy thought struck him. He took his diamond ring from his finger and wrote upon one of the panes of glass in the window, "*One thing thou lackest.*" In the morning he went on his way. After he was gone the general, who had great veneration for Whitefield, went into his room, and the first thing that arrested his attention was the sentence on the window pane, "*One thing thou lackest.*" This was just the case with the general. He was amiable and courteous, but he lacked the principal thing. It was a word in season. It was like a nail fastened in a sure place by the Master of Assemblies. The Spirit of God blessed it to his soul and to the salvation of his house.[22]

Tyerman stated that Whitefield was in Providence, Rhode Island from August 9 to 12, 1770.[23] The Beneficent Church under Rev. Snow had three building additions by 1770, had a spire nearly 100 feet tall, and named Whitefield as one of the "eminent ministers" and "celebrated men" who preached in the meeting house.[24] A newspaper report from Providence stated, "On Tuesday last the Rev. Mr. Whitefield arrived here. The next day he preached at the Rev. Mr. Snow's Meeting-House, and on Thursday at the Rev. Mr. Rowland's, each time to crowded auditories."[25]

The mentioned "Rev. Mr. Rowland" was David S. Rowland of the First Congregational Society. Rowland was born in Connecticut and was a 1743 graduate of Yale College, at a time when controversies over the awakening and Whitefield at Yale were excited. The college denounced Whitefield, but many students, like Rowland, supported the itinerant preacher. In 1745, Rowland sought ordination but he was initially rejected, the ordination council insisting that he denounce Whitefield. The council required Rowland to "not countenance and encourage Mr. Whitefield by inviting him to preach or attending his administrations or on any other Itinerant Preachers, or any other of the errors, separations or disorders prevailing in ye country."[26] Another source recorded that Rowland refused to "repudiate the excesses of Whitefield and other revivalists," and his ordination was postponed.[27] Rowland refused to denounce Whitefield, and his ordination was delayed until another council with different ministers was formed in 1747. He was ordained at a church in Plainfield, Connecticut and then served in Providence, Rhode Island. His ministerial career was described as an "unquiet career," as he was in constant disputes with his Old Light contemporaries.[28] Rowland arrived in Providence in 1762 and resigned in 1774. "Here he ranked very high among the clergy of that day; and he was equally admired for his talents and beloved for his amiability of temper."[29] Speaking of David Rowland,

---

22 Joseph B. Wakeley, *Anecdotes of the Rev. George Whitefield, M.A.*, (1872; reprinted BiblioLife Reproductions), pp. 332-333.
23 Luke Tyerman, *The Life of George Whitefield*, vol. II, p. 592.
24 James G. Vose, *Commemorative Discourses Preached in the Beneficent Congregational Church*, (Providence, RI: Beneficent Congregational Church, 1869), p. 27.
25 *The Providence Gazette*, August 11, 1770, p. 3.
26 Daniel Wadsworth, *Diary of Rev. Daniel Wadsworth, Seventh Pastor of the First Church of Christ in Hartford, Connecticut*, (Hartford, CT: Press of the Case, Lockwood & Brainard Company, 1894), p. 131.
27 Henry R. Stiles, *The Histories and Genealogies of Ancient Windsor, Connecticut . . . 1635-1891*, (Hartford, CT: Press of the Case, Lockwood & Brainard Company, 1891), vol. I, p. 376.
28 Daniel Wadsworth, *Diary of Rev. Daniel Wadsworth*, p. 131.
29 Henry R. Stiles, *The History of Ancient Windsor, Connecticut . . .*, (New York: Charles B. Norton, Printer, 1859), p. 431.

His deep knowledge of the Scriptures and the humble fervor which he preached the Oracles of God were manifested in the consciousness of all who heard him. A natural sweetness of temper, improved by a pure Christian affection, made him dear to the people of God, and to a numerous thriving family.[30]

Obviously, Rowland was enamored with Whitefield. Having followed Whitefield's preaching career since he was an impressionable student at Yale, Rowland was thrilled to have the traveling Methodist evangelist, ordained by the Church of England, preach in his Congregational Church pulpit in Providence. From Providence, Rhode Island, Whitefield preached his way northeast towards Boston. The *Boston Gazette* reported, "Tuesday last the Rev.d Mr. Whitefield, arrived in Town, from Providence, having the day before preached at Attleborough, and that morning at Wrentham."[31]

SOUTHERN MASSACHUSETTS

It was a short carriage ride from Providence to Attleboro, Massachusetts. This was Whitefield's next stop towards Boston. Twenty-five years earlier, Whitefield held successful meetings in Attleboro for Rev. Habijah Weld, the Congregational minister. In 1745, Whitefield preached twice for Weld and the two clergymen shared a communion service, an unusual and controversial act. In 1770, Weld was still at the church and still active in ministry. No account has survived of Whitefield's August 13, 1770 stop in Attleboro and meeting with Habijah Weld. Weld served at the church until his death in 1782.

The next and last location where we know Whitefield preached on his way to Boston was at Wrentham, Massachusetts. The route Whitefield travelled—from Attleboro to Wrentham to Boston—was the same preaching route he took in 1745. Back then, the two ministers in Wrentham were Rev. Henry Messenger at the First Congregational Church, who died in 1750; and Rev. Elias Haven of the Second Congregational Church, who died in 1754. In his 1745 visit to Wrentham, both ministers openly supported Whitefield and eagerly embraced the awakening. But now two new ministers were in Wrentham when Whitefield arrived in August 1770.

In 1770, the minister at the First Congregational Church in Wrentham was Rev. Joseph Bean, who served the church from 1750 to his death in 1784. Bean was a New Light, evangelical minister who took a steady, balanced approach to his ministry. A biographical summary stated,

> He was ordained Dec. 5, 1750, and died Dec. 12, 1784, in the sixty-sixth year of his age, and thirty-fifth of his ministry. He was greatly beloved by his people, and to this day [1845] his memory is fondly cherished . . . While he was minister, there was no year in which there were not additions to the church. There was a steady ingathering, rather than any large addition at any one time.[32]

Bean appears to have maintained the evangelical position of his predecessor. Under Bean's tenure there was no large-scale awakening, as in the early 1740s, but the church was sympathetic to revival. Speaking of Rev. Bean, "He was a gentleman of unblemished reputation, and highly esteemed for his piety and virtue. He had the character of a plain, faithful, affectionate, and profitable preacher. He was of a feeble constitution, but lacked not in zeal, sparing no pains in promoting the good of his people."[33]

---

30 "Early Records of Windsor, Connecticut," *The New England Historical and Genealogical Register*, (Boston, MA: Samuel G. Drake, Publisher, 1851), 462.
31 *The Boston Gazette,* August 20, 1770, p. 2.
32 *Historical Sketch, Articles of Faith, and Covenants of the Original Congregational Church, in Wrentham, Mass.*, (Boston, MA: S.N. Dickinson & Co. Printers, 1845), pp. 5-6.
33 *The New England Historical and Genealogical Register . . . for the Year 1855*, (Boston, MA: Samuel G. Drake, Publisher, 1855), vol. ix, p. 59.

The other minister in Wrentham in 1770 was Rev. Nathaniel Emmons. He arrived at the Second Parish Congregational Church in Wrentham in 1769. A Yale graduate in 1769, he attended the college at a time when Whitefield was back in the good graces of the school. He spent his entire ministerial life in Franklin-Wrentham, retired in 1821, and was buried there in 1840. Emmons became famous (some would say infamous) from his theological speculations and philosophical wanderings. While he always remained a Calvinist, Emmons was of the Samuel Hopkins—New Divinity movement. But Emmons went beyond Hopkins in some theological theories, and came to some conclusions that startled his contemporaries. He was an avid supporter of revivals and developed a systematic theological scheme through which he trained a hundred or more ministers. Traditional Calvinists in New England, and at Nassau Hall in Princeton, condemned him, as did the deists and Unitarians.[34] But that was all later, for in 1770 in Wrentham, Emmons was a new, young minister in a smaller town that welcomed Whitefield.

An undated sketch of Rev. Nathaniel Emmons.

Source: www.pcahistory.org

Unfortunately, no records remain that speak of Whitefield preaching at the First and Second Congregational Churches in Wrentham in 1770. Clearly, Whitefield had allies in Rev. Joseph Bean and Rev. Nathaniel Emmons. Had a great stirring occurred in either church, it is likely that some record would have remained of that event. Instead, records are absent or silent. Whitefield's next stop that we know of was his destination at Boston, Massachusetts.

---

34 Samuel H. Cox, *Interviews: Memorable and Useful*, (New York: Harper & Brothers Publishers, 1855), pp. 147-151. In this text is a valuable almost 70-page interview with Rev. Nathaniel Emmons.

CHAPTER 38

THE FINAL VISIT TO NORTHERN NEW ENGLAND AND WHITEFIELD'S DEATH

1770

GEORGE WHITEFIELD WAS TIRED. HE had travelled too many miles, and his delicate constitution was worn out. He was close to working himself to death. His restlessness for souls was all-consuming. He simply had to preach, to teach, and to evangelize. "When Whitefield was compelled by weakness to preach only once a day on weekdays and three times on Sundays he said that he was on 'short allowance.' He was distressed at being able to preach so little. It was a common thing for him to spend forty hours a week in actual preaching."[1]

Boston and area newspapers kept the public informed of Whitefield's approach. These Massachusetts colonists now had several newspapers: *The Boston Gazette* and *Boston Weekly Newsletter* being longstanding newspapers, with the *Boston Post Boy, The Massachusetts Spy,* and *The Essex Gazette* now also in print. All these papers mentioned Whitefield's impending visit and his first activities after his arrival.

> The Old South Church (Third Church) of Boston eagerly anticipated another visit from Whitefield. Over his prior five visits beginning in 1740, he preached to a collected total of at least forty thousand people over dozens of preaching opportunities. The church record, dated the Lord's Day, August 5, 1770, shows how enthusiastic the leaders of Old South Church were in expectation of Whitefield's soon arrival:

> Voted—that Deacon Jeffries and Deacon Phillips . . . together with Col. Jackson be a committee to wait on the Rev. Mr. George Whitefield when he comes to town, which event is very soon expected, and make him the offer of the pulpit to preach in, whenever he shall think proper Lord's Day excepted.[2]

Whitefield's 1770 acceptance in Boston can be understood in several ways. First, since his initial visit to New England thirty years earlier, Whitefield had matured in his preaching language. While still speaking the same gospel truths, he did not resort to naming specific clergymen as unconverted. Second, Whitefield no longer kept a journal, which meant that his enemies did not have access to his unguarded personal thoughts and opinions. In the past, Whitefield unwisely allowed his *Journals* to be too quickly published, and he learned from that mistake. Further, over a thirty-year period, many of Whitefield's most vociferous opponents had died, and the next generation of New England ministers were not so belligerent towards the

---

1   Mark M. Caldwell, *George Whitefield: Preacher to Millions*, (Anderson, IN: The Warner Press, 1929), pp. 111-112.
2   Hamilton A. Hill, *A History of the Old South Church (Third Church)*, (Boston, MA: Riverdale Press, 1890), pp. 125-126.

roving evangelist. Also adding to Whitefield's acceptance by the New England Colonies was his patriotic support of the colonists during various wars with France, as he unabashedly endorsed the colonists in the 1745 expedition against the French at Cape Breton Island, and supported the colonial militiamen in the 1754-1763 French and Indian War.

Further, by the time of Whitefield's final visit to New England in 1770, the attention of the colonists was more focused on rising political tensions and dissatisfaction with Great Britain than on theological controversies. Whitefield had earned their trust. His benevolent activities included his support of Wheelock's Indian school in Connecticut (later Dartmouth College in New Hampshire); his generosity to the city of Boston after the dreadful fire of 1760; and his financial contributions to the citizens of Boston after a small pox epidemic hit the city in the early 1760s. After 1764, Whitefield was endorsed by Yale College and Harvard College. His unsolicited acts of charity won over the masses.[3]

In the summer of 1770, much of Boston welcomed Whitefield with open arms. With his health temporarily restored, he preached at least once a day in and around the city. The *Boston Post-Boy* recorded,

> Tuesday last the Rev. Mr. Whitefield, arrived in Town from Providence, having the day before preached at Attleborough, and that morning at Wrentham; Wednesday afternoon he preached at the Old North Meeting-House; Thursday afternoon at the Old South; Friday morning at the New Brick; and this morning at the Old South, to very crowded Auditories.—He is to preach again tomorrow morning at the New-North.[4]

These were all familiar and welcoming places for Whitefield to preach. Two stops where Whitefield preached not mentioned in this newspaper article were at Milton and Roxbury Plain.[5]

As Whitefield approached Boston from the south, he approached a city that had significantly changed since he first preached there thirty years prior. What was once a colonial port was now a major British city with international influence. Ships from Boston sailed the world, bringing great wealth to the city. European Enlightenment ideas, with the exulting of human reason, were in stark contrast to the ideas of the Puritan founding fathers and the preaching of Whitefield. Wealth bred materialism, corruption, and moral ambiguity. In mid-August 1770, Whitefield preached a sermon at the Old North meeting house in which he attacked Enlightenment thinking, with its theological liberalism, as a false religion. He asserted that such unbelievers were Deists, not Christians, and they approached God with a false religion, as did Cain in the Bible. In response to Whitefield, a Boston newspaper called *The Massachusetts Spy* printed an extended editorial article critical of Whitefield. The unnamed author of this article ridiculed Whitefield's assertion that blood was necessary for atonement. The author defended the bloodless sacrifice of Cain and diminished the need for the blood atonement of Christ on the cross as necessary for salvation.[6] Such an editorial would have been unwelcome in Puritan Boston in the 1740s. While Whitefield preached to crowded assemblies, there was no revival. Only a small percentage of Bostonians listened to him preach. Most people in Boston ignored Whitefield, as they were overwhelmed with the secular businesses of commerce and political instability with Great Britain.

With Harvard College no longer opposing Whitefield, there remained no authoritative voices against his Boston ministry. Old rivals such as Charles Chauncey had long since stopped printing and preaching against the New Lights, as Chauncey developed his own theological convictions toward Unitarianism and

---

3   Robert Philip, *The Life and Times of George Whitefield*, (1837: reprinted by Banner of Ruth Trust, Carlisle, PA: 2007), pp. 555, 560-61, 565-566. J. P. Gledstone, *George Whitefield: Supreme Among Preachers*, (1880?: reprinted by Emerald House, Greenville, SC: 1998), pp. 344-350. E.A. Johnston, *George Whitefield: A Definitive Biography*, (Stoke-on-Trent, Great Britain, 2008), vol. II, 513-517.
4   *Boston Post-Boy, August 20, 1770, p. 2.*
5   John Gilles, *Memoirs of George Whitefield*, (1838: reprinted by Pietan Publications, New Ipswich, New Hampshire, 1993), p. 259.
6   *The Massachusetts Spy*, August 18, 1770, p. 4.

Universalism. Yet Whitefield's movements in and around Boston were still newsworthy. For example, *The Massachusetts Spy* wrote, "Yesterday the Rev. Mr. George Whitefield, preached at Charlestown. And, this day at Cambridge. Tomorrow he is to preach at the Old South meeting-house in this town."[7] Whitefield preached nearly every day during this 1770 visit in eastern Massachusetts, as the following chart displays.[8]

August
13	Attleborough, MA
14	Wrentham, MA
15-18	Boston, MA
19	Malden, MA
20-25	Boston, MA
26	Medford, MA
27-28	Cambridge, MA
29-30	Boston, MA
31	Roxbury Plain, MA

September
1	Milton, MA
2	Roxbury, MA
3	Boston, MA
5	Salem, MA
6	Marblehead, MA
7	Salem, MA
8	Cape Ann, MA
9	Ipswich, MA
10-11	Newburyport, MA
12-13	Rowley, MA

From September 13-17th a severe cough and chest cold detained Whitefield from public ministry. When he recovered, he continued his September preaching schedule.

17-19	Boston, MA
20	Newton, MA

Gilles's chronology quoted above places Whitefield in Malden on August 19, 1770. The Congregational Church in Malden was then installing its new minister, the eighteen-year-old Rev. Peter Thatcher. Having graduated Harvard the year before, Thatcher was known as a skilled orator and devout Puritan. He was from a distinguished Colonial Massachusetts family. Whitefield heard the young, newly ordained Thatcher preach, and was impressed. Whitefield called Thatcher "the young Elijah," a reference to the skilled Old Testament preacher and prophet. Whitefield believed Thatcher to be the ablest preacher in the American Colonies. The Congregational Church in Malden had previously supported Whitefield for decades, under Rev. Joseph Emerson, and this would continue under Thatcher. Referencing Thatcher, "No young man preached to such crowded assemblies as he. Whitefield called him the young Elijah. He was a thorough Calvinist, and earnest for the Puritan faith."[9] Speaking of Peter Thatcher,

---

7   *The Massachusetts Spy*, August 28, 1770, p. 4.
8   John Gilles, *Memoirs of George Whitefield*, p. 259.
9   *The Register of the Malden Historical Society, 1910-1911*, (Lynn, MA: Frank S. Whitten, Printer, 1911), vol. I, p. 38.

A current photograph of the Rev. Jedediah Jewett house in Rowley, Massachusetts. Whitefield refreshed himself here many times between 1740-1770. Across the street from the house is the Rowley common where Whitefield preached outside to large crowds. Photograph by Ken Lawson.

Though plain of speech and manners, even to roughness, in his daily life, in the pulpit a melodious voice and fervent speech, joined with a rich glow of fancy, held the attention of the cultivated and won the applause of the multitude. Where he preached the house was crowded; and so marked were his abilities, even at the outset of his career, that the celebrated Whitefield, who could only have seen and heard him about the time of his ordination, referred to the singular furor of his prayers, called him "the Young Elijah," esteemed him as the ablest preacher in America, and looked upon him as one born for the defense of New England orthodoxy . . . Whitefield was in Boston and its vicinity in August and September [1770], and from what is known of his movements, he must have been in Malden prior to the ordination, or two or three days after.[10]

The Malden Historical Society stated of Thatcher, "September 19, 1770 ordained."[11] Rev. Peter Thatcher served in Malden from 1770 to 1784, after which he served at the Brattle Street Church in Boston from 1785 to 1802.

About September 10-11, 1770, Whitefield preached in Newburyport. A teenage girl in Newburyport named Sarah Noyes was eager to hear the itinerant preacher, as his name was spoken all over the area. She was forbidden to do so by her father, John Noyes, a deacon in the Third Church in Newbury. After being denied the use of the church building, Whitefield preached at a private home. When an old woman, Sarah related the following Whitefield account from her youth to her descendant Sarah Anna Emery.

> I have often heard my great aunt Sarah Noyes describe the sensation produced by the eloquent divine. My great grandfather, Deacon John Noyes, fully sympathized in the disapproval evidenced by his pastor [Rev. William Johnson], and he issued a strict edict forbidding any of his family attending what he termed "those disorderly assemblies." Aunt Sarah, then a girl in her teens, entertained, as was natural, a strong desire to see and hear one whose name was

---

10 Deloraine P. Corey, *The History of Malden, Massachusetts, 1633-1785*, (Malden, MA: Published by the Author, 1899), pp. 655-656.
11 *The Registry of the Malden Historical Society*, (Lynn, MA: Frank S. Whitten, Printer, 1918), vol. 5, p. 64.

on every tongue, and whose words and their effects were the chief topics of conversation on every side. At last, after much fear and trembling, she mustered courage to make a clandestine attempt to satisfy her curiosity. An evening meeting was to be held at a house in the vicinity, and she determined to brave her father's displeasure, if her absence was discovered, and go. It was a dark, cheerless night, when, with a throbbing heart, stealing down the stairs and noiselessly opening the door, she ran lightly down the gravel walk. Her hand was on the latch of the front gate, when a voice, in an authoritarian tone, exclaimed "Go back!" Startled, affrighted, she stopped, turned, and peered on all sides into the darkness.

No one was in sight. Through the uncurtained window she could see her father and the other members of her family seated around the bright wood fire. Concluding that, owing to the nervous timidity which this disobedience to paternal mandates had caused, imagination had conjured up this voice. With another long and searching look around, she opened the gate. "Go back!" reiterated the voice, even more decidedly than at first, just in her ear.

"What could it mean?" Again she stopped, waited, looked and listened. Nothing unusual could be seen, and not a sound could be heard save the wind sighing through the trees. Sarah Noyes was a resolute girl, not easily turned from any purpose she had deliberately formed, neither had she much belief in the supernatural. Thrusting back her fears, with a strong will she stilled her throbbing heart, and with a firm step, she again started forward. "Go back, go back," thundered the voice, in such a powerful and authoritarian tone, that, thrilling in every nerve, the astonished girl, completely subdued, hastily turned, and fled into the house. Though she lived to a great age, and could never be reckoned a credulous person, to the last hour of her life she firmly believed that this was a Divine interposition to keep her from evil.[12]

On September 10, The *Boston Gazette* reported, "Tuesday the Rev'd Mr. Whitefield set out for the Eastward."[13] The *Essex Gazette*, from Salem, reported in the September 11-18, 1770 edition, "Friday the Rev. Mr. Whitefield came to town. We hear he went no farther than Newbury, having been taken ill on the road; he is now much better and preached this morning at 8 o'clock, at the Rev. Dr. Elliot's. He preached to-morrow morning at 8 o'clock, at Old South."[14]

Whitefield's acceptance in Boston in 1770 was sensational. Although he began to show serious medical problems, Whitefield sought to fulfill the dozens of preaching invitations extended to him from all around New England. *The Boston Evening Post* published a letter to all the ministers in New England, thanking them for opening their pulpits and supporting the ministry of Whitefield. This front page article stated, in part,

The Boston Evening Post, September 17, 1770, p.1.

You can't but be pleased, to see such numbers, in consequence of your shining example, attending this zealous preacher [Whitefield], as it must naturally tend to make your own preaching afterwards more acceptable to them.

---

12 "George Whitefield—The Cross-Eyed Calvinist Bedevils the Conservative Colonists," *New England Historical Society,* http://www.newenglandhistoricalsociety.com/george-whitefield-cross-eyed-calvinist-bedevils-conservative-colonists/. For a fuller study of Newburyport at that time, see the book by Sarah Anna Emery, *Reminiscences of a Nonagenarian*, (Newburyport, MA: William H. Husse Printer, 1897).
13 *The Boston Gazette,* September 10, 1770, p. 2.
14 *Essex Gazette* (Salem, MA), September 11-18, 1770, p. 2

Several eyewitnesses to Whitefield's 1770 Massachusetts tour have recorded their impressions in personal diaries. For example, the Rev. Nathaniel Cutler, graduate of Yale College in 1765, a Boston schoolteacher and later a pastor in Ipswich, wrote of Whitefield in 1770 as follows.[15]

> August 14, Tuesday. Mr. Whitefield preached at Mr. Bean's meeting house in Wrentham: Mr. Balch, Mr. Dean, my wife and myself went up to hear. Large assembly. He began his exercise at 8 o'clock. His prayed half an hour. Sang 3rd psalm, old version. Text 11 chapter Luke, 13th verse: "If ye being evil know how to give good gifts to your children; how much more shall your heavenly Father give the Holy Spirit to them that ask Him." His text was handsomely opened; his subject turned principally upon the necessity of the assistance of the Divine Spirit in performing all our duties. He had not so much as the heads of his sermon written—even flighty and rambly—his audience not over-much affected. He had many good expressions, and many odd, and improper for the pulpit. Not at all pleased with him on the whole, as his discourse was not at all enlightening or instructive, but very broken, and interwoven with impertinent stories. His gestures were extravagant, though natural and easy. His sermon an hour and a half, and all the substance, I imagine, might have been delivered handsomely in ten minutes. After meeting, he had a coach at the meeting house door, stepped in, and rode to Mr. Man's, where he refreshed himself and set out immediately for Boston. He preached in his black gown. Came home after meeting. Rained considerably, which was much wanted, as it had been extremely dry.
>
> September 1, Saturday. Rode to Milton to hear Mr. Whitefield, the Lieutenant Governor present. Preached much better than at Wrentham. I liked his preaching well. Dined at Mr. Robins' with Father Balch, Mr. Taft, Mr. Weld, and Mr. Niles, a young candidate. Mr. Whitefield dined with the Governor.

Mr. Ashley Bowen, a seaman and dock worker in Marblehead, Massachusetts recorded Whitefield's presence in his personal journal.[16]

> [1770] September 5. This day employed in fixing sails for Captain Courtis. We hear that Mr. Whitefield preaches at Salem today.
>
> September 6. This day completed all the sails, viz. Two topsails and a course for Brig. General Wolfe. This day at 10 o'clock, Mr. Whitefield began to preach at Marblehead. After dinner I set out for Andover.

In the Rev. Moses Parsons' journal, he records the following brief remarks related to Whitefield's ministry in the area. Parsons served in the Byfield-Newbury, Massachusetts community. Rev. Parsons' notations cover only a few days, from the time Whitefield was present in the immediate vicinity, to his brief illness and subsequent rest after September 13, 1770.[17]

> September 10, Monday. Went to Portsmouth to hear Mr. Whitefield; dined at Mr. Little's with him.

---

15 William and Julia Cutler, *Life, Journals, and Correspondence of Rev. Manasseh Cutler*, (Cincinnati, OH: Robert Clarke & Company, 1888), vol. I, pp. 24-26.
16 Ashley Bowen, *The Journals of Ashley Bowen of Marblehead*, (Salem, MA: Peabody Museum, 1973), vol. II, p. 253.
17 John J. Currier, *History of Beverly, Civil and Ecclesiastical*, (Boston, MA: J. Monroe & Company, 1843), p. 527.

Tuesday, September 11. Went to conference at Amesbury. Mr. Prince preached. Mr. Whitefield preached at Newburyport.

September 12. Went to Rowley to hear Mr. Whitefield preach.

September 13. Cloudy, some rain. Went to Mr. Chandler's to hear Whitefield.

The above mentioned "Mr. Chandler" was the Harvard trained Rev. James Chandler of the Second Church in Rowley. Chandler was the founding pastor of the church and served in Rowley until his death in 1791. Chandler was well-respected and capable in many areas. He was an ecclesiastical and civil servant in his rural community, supplementing his church duties by his work in legal matters and his experiments in botany. As an oddity, Chandler kept a pet baboon. Serving side-by-side with Chandler in the Second Congregational Church was Mr. Asa Chaplin, who was a church elder for decades. Chandler and Chaplin were close friends and the pillars of the Second Church.[18] An anecdote has survived related to a conversation between Chandler and Chaplin on the arrival of Whitefield in 1770.

> Tradition says that Mr. Chandler was earnest in persuading Elder Asa Chaplin to attend a service in Georgetown [Rowley] where Whitefield was to preach, and that the elder objected, saying that he had no fault to find with his own minister. "But," said Mr. Chandler, with an emphatic gesture, "Mr. Whitefield does not preach as I do; he preaches with power.[19]

Perhaps the most extensive diarist who mentioned Whitefield's 1770 visit to New England, was John Rowe of Boston. Rowe was one of the foremost merchants in the city, owning houses and building lots downtown, pasturelands in the country, and extensive properties on the harbor docks. Rowe was an obvious supporter of Whitefield. His diaries normally were full of mercantile activities, reports of ships in port, political news and other secular notations. But while Whitefield preached through the Boston area, Rowe's diaries were almost entirely devoted to recording Whitefield-related events. It is as if daily life changed for Rowe when Whitefield was in town. Rowe outlines Whitefield's travels as follows.[20]

August 10. The Rev. Mr. Whitefield came to town this day . . .

August 16. Mr. Whitefield preached at the Old North yesterday first time—after dinner I went to Dr. Sewall's meeting-house & heard Mr. Whitefield preach from the 9th chapter of Zechariah & 12th verse, "Turn ye to the Strong. Hold Ye Prisoners, of Hope." I liked this discourse.

August 17. Mr. Whitefield preached at Dr. Elliot's this morning.

August 18. Mr. Whitefield preached this morning at Mr. Pemberton's.

---

18 "Personal Sketches of Early Inhabitants of Georgetown, Mass," *Essex Institute Historical Collections,* (Salem, MA: Essex Institute, 1905), vol. 41, p. 176.
19 D. Hamilton Hurd, *History of Essex County, Massachusetts,* (Philadelphia, PA: J.W. Lewis & Company, 1888), vol. I, p. 820.
20 John Rowe, *Letters and Diaries of John Rowe, Boston Merchant, 1759-1762, 1764-1779,* (Boston, MA: W.B. Clarke Company, 1903), p. 22.

August 20. Mr. Whitefield preached at New North, Dr. Elliot's.

August 21. Mr. Whitefield preached this morning at Dr. Sewall's. August 22. Mr. Whitefield preached at New North.

August 23. Mr. Whitefield preached again this morning at Dr. Sewall's.

August 24. In the forenoon I went to old Dr. Sewall's meeting & heard Mr. Whitefield preach from 22nd chapter of St. Matthew & II, 12 & 13 verses. This was in my opinion a clever discourse.

August 26. I have been married twenty-seven years yesterday.

August 28. Mr. Whitefield preached yesterday at Cambridge, this day at Charlestown.

August 29. Mr. Whitefield preached at Old South.

August 30. Mr. Whitefield preached at New North.

August 31. Mr. Whitefield preached at Jamaica Plain.

Sept. 1. Mr. Whitefield preached at Milton this day.

Sept. 2. Mr. Whitefield preached at Roxbury this day.

Sept. 3. Mr. Whitefield preached at Old South.

Sept 4. Mr. Whitefield set out for Portsmouth—I should have gone to Port Shirley with the proprietors, but was very busy.

John Rowe's journal continued with routine journal entries from September 5 to 28, displaying his mercantile activities. Whitefield was at that time preaching in the coastal communities of Boston's north shore. Most of these weeks for Mr. Rowe were consumed by meetings with other Boston merchants and with government leaders at Faneuil Hall, to discuss the tenuous political situation with Britain. Mr. Rowe records, "Sept 30. The Rev. Mr. Whitefield died suddenly this morning, much lamented."[21]

What the merchant John Rowe could not know was that the widow of Harvard president Edward Holyoke, was happy to hear Whitefield preach twice in the Boston area. Whitefield and Harvard College had a contentious relationship that was only reconciled shortly before President Holyoke's death in June 1769. After Holyoke's death, his widow, Mary (Vial) Holyoke, continued to support Whitefield, as did her husband shortly before he died. Mary Holyoke kept a diary, in which she mentions her seeking out Whitefield to hear him preach twice, and sharing refreshments with him in a casual evening meeting. She wrote:

---

21 Ibid., pp. 22-23.

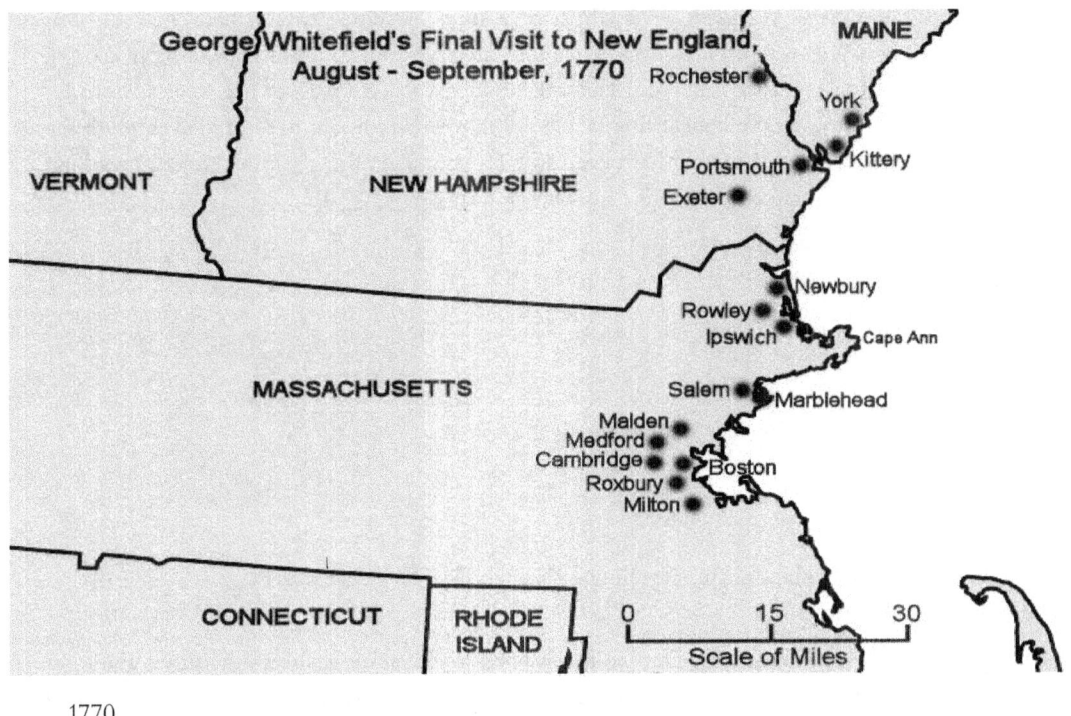

1770.

Sept. 5. Mr. Whitefield preached. I heard him. We drank tea and spent the evening at the fort.

Sept. 7. Went to hear Mr. Whitefield.[22]

Unfortunately, there remain only two letters written by Whitefield during his 1770 tour of northeastern New England. His extensive letter writing, which he had dutifully accomplished for the past few months, now dwindled. This can be accounted for by his rapidly declining health and his relentless daily preaching labors. Because of their significance as the last-known letters written by Whitefield, they shall be quoted in full.[23]

Boston, Sept. 17, 1770. Dear. Mr. W_____T,

I am afraid, as Mr. E_____n, mentioned your writing that your letter hath miscarried. But, blessed be God! I find all was well, only I want to know what things are wanted, that I might order them from Philadelphia, by Captain Souder. Fain want I to contrive to come by him, but people are so importunate for my stay in these parts, that I fear it will be impractical. Lord Jesus, direct my goings in Thy way! He will! He will! My God will supply all my wants, according to the riches of his grace in CHRIST JESUS. By a letter, received last night from Mr. W_____y, of July 5, I find that Mr. D_____n has arrived, Anderson failed, and that all orders would immediately be complied with. Two or three evenings ago, I was taken in the night with a violent lax, attended with wretching and shivering, so that I was obliged to return from Newbury, &c., &c; but through infinite mercy, I am revived, and tomorrow morning hope to begin again. Never was the word received with such eagerness than now.

---

22 "Diary of Mrs. Mary (Vial) Holyoke, 1760-1800," *The Holyoke Diaries, 1709-1856*, (Salem, MA: The Essex Institute, 1911), p. 74.
23 George Whitefield, *Works of George Whitefield*, (1771: reprinted by Quinta Press, Shropshire, England, 2000), vol. III, pp. 425-427.

All opposition seems as it were for a while to cease. I find God's time is best. The season is critical to outward circumstances. But when forts are given up, the LORD JESUS can appoint salvation for walls and for bulwarks; He hath promised to be a wall of fire 'round about his people. This comforts me concerning Bethesda, though we should have carried through the summer's heat so well; I hope it hath been so with you, and all my family. Hoping, ere long, to see you, I must hasten to subscribe myself, my dear Mr._____T.

Yours, &c., &c., &c.

G.W.

The following is the last-known letter Whitefield wrote:

To Mr. R_____k_____n,

Portsmouth, New Hampshire, September 23, 1770. My very dear friend,

Your letters, of May 2 and 22, came to hand. New York Packet is always the surest and most centrical medium of conveyance. Before I left Boston, of Friday afternoon, I left a large packet in the hands of a young man, who promised to deliver it to you safely. You and Mr. H_____, may peruse all, and communicate what you think proper. By this time I thought to be moving southward. But never was greater importunity used to detain me longer in these northern parts. Poor New England is much to be pitied; Boston people most of all. How falsely misrepresented! What a mercy, that our Christian charter cannot be dissolved! Blessed be God for an unchangeable Jesus! You will see, by the many invitations, what a door is opened for preaching His everlasting Gospel. I was so ill on Friday, that I could not preach, though thousands were waiting to hear. Well, the day of release will shortly come, but it also does not seem as yet; for by riding fifty miles, I am better, and hope to preach here to-morrow. I trust, that my blessed Master will accept of these poor efforts to serve Him. O for a warm heart; O to stand fast in the faith, to quit ourselves like me, and be strong! May this be the happy experience of you and yours! I suppose letters are gone for me, in Anderson, to Georgia. If spared so long, I expect to see it about Christmas. Still pray and praise. I am so poorly, and so engaged when able to preach, that this must apologize for not writing to more friends. It is quite impracticable. Hoping to see all dear friends about this time proposed, and earnestly desiring your prayers, I must hasten to subscribe myself, my dear, dear sir;

Less than the least of all,

G.W.

The farthest north Whitefield travelled on his 1770 visit to New England was to York, now in the state of Maine. This was his third visit to York, his prior visits being in 1740 and 1744. Whitefield's friend Rev. Samuel Moody's long tenure at the First Church ended at his death in 1747. The current minister was Rev. Isaac Lyman. Lyman was a student at Yale College when that institution took a firm stand against Whitefield.

Graduating from Yale in 1747 and assisting the elderly Moody until his death, Lyman was ordained at the Congregational Church in York in 1749. Isaac Lyman was born in 1724 and grew up in Hampton, Connecticut. He was reared in the culture of the Great Awakening of the mid-1730s in the Connecticut River Valley.[24] He must have heard Whitefield preach in or near his hometown in 1740. The influence of Jonathan Edwards in nearby Northampton was profound. The official history of First Church in York states, "Mr. Lyman maintained the high standard of Christian character and faithful service established by his predecessors, and at the close of his fruitful ministry [in 1810] was held in high honor by a united people, who regarded him with the veneration of a beloved father."[25]

Some interesting anecdotes from Whitefield's 1770 New England tour are now presented:

> In 1770, Rev. George Whitefield visited Newburyport and preached in the meeting-house in Federal Street September 10 and 11. The Bible that he used on these occasions has been carefully preserved and is still used on special occasions. After a brief visit to Portsmouth and Exeter, NH, he returned to Newburyport and died suddenly Sunday morning, September 30, at the residence of Rev. Jonathan Parsons of School Street.[26]

Rev. Nathaniel Whittaker of Salem, Massachusetts was an interesting man. A graduate of the Presbyterian sponsored College of New Jersey (later Princeton College) in 1752, Whittaker was trained for the ministry by some of the most intelligent, Calvinistic, New Light ministers in America. He preached successfully at an enclave of New Light beliefs at Norwich, Connecticut, where he served both as a church minister and as a missionary to local Indians.[27] Already acquainted with George Whitefield, the two met in England in 1766, when Whittaker was raising financial support for Wheelock's Indian School in Connecticut (later Dartmouth College in New Hampshire). In 1767, the University of St. Andrews granted Whittaker the Doctor of Divinity degree. He accepted a call to serve at the Third Church (Congregational) in Salem, Massachusetts in July 1769. It was in this capacity that Whitefield preached for Whittaker in Salem in September 1770.

An image of Rev. Nathaniel Whittaker painted while in England sometime about 1767. Public domain image.

> Doctor Whitaker (Pastor since 1769 of Salem's Third Church) was a man of great determination, or he could not have carried his church with him into the Presbyterian form of church government . . . From the time of the burning of the church (in the Salem fire of 1774) he never had a fixed salary, but depended upon the weekly collections. His idea of a new church building was something after the model of Whitefield's church in London, namely, a large square structure with a pyramidal roof and a dome and belfry. It was not decently

---

24 David Ramsay, "When Rev. Whitefield Came to York," Seacoastonline.com, December 14, 2016.
25 Frank L. Garfield, "Historical Sketch of the Church," *Manual for the First Congregational Church of York, Maine, January 1915*, http://www.fpyork.info/fpc/historicalsketchchurch3.html.
26 John J. Currier, *History of Beverly, Civil and Ecclesiastical*, p. 521.
27 *Proceedings of the Essex Institute, Vol. I, 1848-1856*, (Salem, MA: Printed for the Institute, 1856), p. 124.

finished for some years afterwards, but from it originated the name "tabernacle." The Rev. George Whitefield's visit to Salem in 1770 may have had its influence on this.[28]

Whitaker's ministry in Salem was surrounded by unsettledness. As far back as the 1740s, long before Whitaker arrived, Salem was torn apart by religious controversies. Churches split over theology, preferences for ministers, financial disputes, or for geographic convenience. Those who retained Puritan ideals were disappointed with the cosmopolitan worldliness of this bustling port city. Both New Light and Old Light Congregationalists looked with disdain at St. Peter's Episcopal Church, founded in Salem in 1733. The Great Awakening never shook Salem as it did Boston and other New England cities.[29] The previous two ministers at the Third Church in Salem were advocates of revival and New Light theology, but significant numbers of converts did not stream into the church. When Whittaker arrived, he was welcomed by a congregation of like faith. As the new minister, Whittaker attempted to transform the church polity from Congregational to Presbyterian, and was ultimately successful, to the frustration of many. Speaking of Whittaker in Salem, "He was one of the notabilities of the town, eminent by his talents and ability, troublesome as a disputant and controversialist. He preached here fifteen years, during which time he was almost constantly engaged in some war of words upon the topics then occupying the public mind."[30]

The topics most discussed by the people of Salem were the tense relationship with Great Britain; Calvinism verses Arminianism; trade and commerce; taxes; and small pox inoculations. Whittaker was described by one of his church deacons as, "a man of uncommon intellectual powers—of extensive erudition—orthodox in sentiment—a distinguished preacher—of dignified, commanding personal appearance; and especially of consummate skill and tact in accomplishing his own purposes."[31] Nathaniel Whittaker was one of the few men who befriended and publicly endorsed George Whitefield both in Great Britain and in America. Several miles from Salem, Whitefield preached in rural farming communities. An interesting account has survived relating to Whitefield's ministry in rural Rowley (later Georgetown). The specific incident relates to the dedication of a new meeting house for Rev. Samuel Chandler.

> A forenoon in September 1770, Mr. Whitefield dedicated the South meeting house in New Rowley, now Georgetown. The exact date of that important event is not known. It is judged that the day of the dedication at New Rowley, which Gage's *History of Rowley* says may have been 12, 13, or 22, Wednesday, Thursday or Saturday, would have been opportune for the great occasion at Linebrook. The church was nearly filled to repletion, and the multitude, some 2,000 to 3,000 persons, were obliged to occupy the open field. On the Ellsworth road, north side, 14 rods from the corner at the county road, is a large flat rock or ledge, with perpendicular front, that became the improvised pulpit of the reverend clergyman. It was beautifully situated to the open field and provided a fine opportunity for the stentorian voice and impressive eloquence. The ledge is known as Pulpit Rock.[32]

> Mr. Whitefield made a final visit to this parish, but a short time before his death, and while here preached what the people were pleased to call the dedication sermon. Had it been considered such at the time, with the fame of the speaker some record, either by the church or parish, would have been made of it, but as there is none, it appears as if it was a little questionable,

---

28 James D. Phillips, *Salem in the Eighteenth Century*, (Boston, MA: Houghton Mifflin Company, 1937), p. 343.
29 James D. Phillips, *Salem in the Eighteenth Century*, p. 165.
30 *Proceedings of the Essex Institute*, p. 123.
31 Ibid., p. 124.
32 *Historical Collections of the Essex Institute,* (Salem, MA: 1915), vol. 51, p. 242.

even then, to recognize Whitefield as exactly regular [Orthodox]. The text selected was I Kings 8:11, "The glory of the Lord hath filled the house of the Lord." The meeting house was unfinished . . . the hearers, however, were many, seated on the timber blocks and rough boards scattered through the edifice. It is said that the service was in the morning, and probably either on September 12 or 13, as he was in Rowley on both those days. A journey of many miles seems to have been at any time just a holiday jaunt for him.[33]

At Pulpit Rock, Whitefield preached outside to a huge crowd from a large granite boulder. Today the site is overgrown. A plaque marks the location of Whitefield's preaching outside to this farming community. One account designated that this was the spot "where the Rev. Whitefield preached to multitudes."[34] Another report remarked:

> Pulpit Rock was next door to the Church building in Rowley. Reverend George Whitefield, on one of the important Church celebrations, preached to more than 2000 persons at Pulpit Rock. The congregation was too large for the Church so the people sat outside and listened as Rev. Whitefield gave his sermon while standing on top on the huge rock. Pulpit Rock is still used today as a special meeting place for local churches. Pulpit Rock is a granite ledge about 20 feet high and set back about 50 yards north of Leslie Road.[35]

Whitefield's preaching at "Pulpit Rock" in Rowley-Georgetown has gained the notice of various local historians. For example, a Rowley historian noted that the new meeting house was fifty-five feet by forty feet and was framed in 1769 by a group of volunteer workers in one day. "This house was dedicated, September 1770, and the dedication sermon preached, by the eminent Rev. George Whitefield, of England, from I Kings 8:11, 'The Glory of the Lord hath filled the house of the Lord.'"[36] Another local historian spoke of Rev. James Leslie, from the nearby town of Topsfield (previously Linebrook), who was a friend of Rev. Samuel Chandler of Rowley. Apparently, Leslie attended the dedication sermon by Whitefield at Pulpit Rock for Chandler's church in Rowley: "Once, during Mr. Leslie's pastorate at Linebrook, the

A field preaching service in Georgetown, Massachusetts, 1764.

A drawing of George Whitefield preaching from Pulpit Rock, in the farming Georgetown-Rowley community, Massachusetts, to a large group in an open field. Sketch by Valerie Borgal.

---

33 Joseph Belcher, *George Whitefield: A Biography with Special Reference to His Labors in America*, (New York: American Tract Society, 1857), p. 433.
34 *Rowley Reconnaissance Report: Massachusetts Landscape Inventory Program*, (Massachusetts Department of Conservation and Recreation, 2005), p. 19.
35 "Historic Ipswich Massachusetts," http://historicipswich.org/ipswich-historical-commission/ipswich-cemetreries/leslie-road-burial-ground.
36 Thomas Gage, James Bradford, *The History of Rowley: Anciently Including Bradford, Boxford, and Georgetown, from the Year 1639 to the Present Time*, (Boston, MA: Ferdinand Andrews, Printer, 1840), p. 32.

Pulpit Rock, currently near the Rowley-Georgetown, Massachusetts line. Whitefield stood on the rock and preached here to a large crowd of rural folks in September 1770. Photograph by Ken Lawson.

distinguished pulpit orator and nation-wide evangelist, Rev. George Whitefield preached . . . from a large, flat rock . . . known as Pulpit Rock."[37]

After his return to the Boston area from his familiar northeastern preaching circuit, Whitefield preached at the First Congregational Church in Newton, near Boston. The minister was Rev. Jonas Meriam, who served the church from 1758 to 1780. Whitefield "preached in Newton before crowded and attentive audiences . . . on September 20, 1770."[38]

On September 25, Whitefield departed Boston, heading north along the coastal roads. Many in Portsmouth, New Hampshire eagerly anticipated his visit. While he was a few days away from the city, a Portsmouth newspaper recorded:

> We hear the Reverend Mr. GEORGE WHITEFIELD came as far as Newbury last week, and intended to have been in Town last Monday, several Gentlemen and Ladies having made Preparations for his Reception . . . a Gentleman took a single horse Chaise, and set out last Monday Noon in order to desire that Worthy Person to pay us a Visit as soon as possible, who will be gratefully received by Persons of all Denominations, as they have still an affectionate Sense of his former labors in this Place, and elsewhere. He is expected in Town this afternoon, or To-morrow Noon in the Coach.[39]

Whitefield was again physically indisposed. Yet, on September 23rd, 1770 he resumed preaching at Portsmouth, New Hampshire where he remained two days until the 25th. One account stated that the crowds were so large that Whitefield, ill and overweight, had to enter the church building through a window due to the size of the crowd inside the building.[40] He then continued north, preaching in Maine, at Kittery on September 26th, at York on the 27th, then back in New Hampshire at Portsmouth on the 28th, and the 29th in Exeter. That would be his last public sermon. A local newspaper report kept track of his daily activities:

---

37 M.V.B. Perley, "James Leslie of Topsfield, Mass," *The Historical Collections of the Topsfield Historical Society,* (Topsfield, MA: Published by the Society, 1915), vol. 20, p. 98.
38 Samuel F. Smith, *History of Newton, Massachusetts: Town and City, from its Earliest Settlement to the Present Time, 1630-1880,* (Boston, MA: American Logotype Company, 1880), 219.
39 *The New Hampshire Gazette,* September 21, 1770, p. 3.
40 Joseph B. Wakeley, *Anecdotes of the Rev. George Whitefield,* (London, 1772), p. 383.

Last Sunday Morning came to Town from Boston, the Reverend GEORGE WHITEFIELD, and in the Afternoon preached at the Rev. Dr. HAVEN'S Meeting House; Monday morning he preach'd again at the same Place to a very large and crowded Audience:—Tuesday morning a most numerous Assembly met at the Rev. Dr. LANGDON'S Meeting-House to hear him again, which is said will hold near six thousand people, and was well fill'd, even the Alley's, where he preach'd, to general Acceptance,—Wednesday he preached at the Reverend Mr. JOHN ROGER'S Meeting-House, in Kittery, and Yesterday at the Rev. Mr. LYMAN'S in York, to which place a Number of Ladies and Gentlemen from Town accompanied him.

THIS MORNING, at Ten o'clock the Rev. Mr. WHITEFIELD, will preach at the Rev. Dr. LANGDON'S Meeting-House in this Town.[41]

Four ministers are mentioned in this newspaper account. Rev. Dr. Haven was Joseph Haven of the First Congregational Church in Rochester, New Hampshire. Haven assumed ministerial responsibilities at the First Church in Rochester sometime after the death of their minister, Rev. Samuel Hill in 1764. Interestingly, Haven was not ordained by the church until 1776, and he served there until his death in 1825.[42] Rev. Dr. Langdon was Samuel Langdon of the North Church in Portsmouth, New Hampshire. Langdon supported Whitefield as far back as the 1740s. He was awarded the Doctor of Divinity degree from the University of Aberdeen, Scotland, in 1761. Langdon taught school in Portsmouth and ministered at his influential church until he was called to the presidency of Harvard College in 1774. Rev. Mr. John Rogers was from the First Congregational Church in Kittery, Maine, and was an avowed Whitefield supporter for decades. Rev. Mr. Isaac Lyman was from the First Church (Congregational) in York, Maine, and was likewise a long-standing Whitefield advocate.

A civil magistrate in Portsmouth named Daniel Pierce kept a journal of activities and news in his community. Interspersed with news about shipping, trade, and political unrest were brief notations made concerning Whitefield preaching in Portsmouth. Pierce recorded,

1770.

Sept 24. Mr. Whitefield preached yesterday in the afternoon, and this forenoon in Mr. Haven's meeting-house.

Sept 25. Mr. Whitefield preached this forenoon at Mr. Langdon's meeting-house to a full audience, from the 15th Luke and 2nd verse.[43]

A glimpse into Whitefield's highly successful preaching experiences in the Portsmouth, New Hampshire area is provided by the following published letter, dated September 28, 1770, just two days before Whitefield's death:

Last Sunday morning came to town, from Boston, the Rev. George Whitefield; and in the afternoon he preached at the Rev. Dr. Haven's meeting-house: Monday morning, he preached again at the same place, to a very large and crowded audience. Tuesday morning, a most numerous audience met at the Rev. Dr. Langdon's meeting house, which, it is said, will hold

---

41 *The New Hampshire Gazette* (Portsmouth, NH), September 28, 1770, p. 3.
42 "First Church Congregational, Rochester, New Hampshire," http://first-ucc.net/history.php.
43 Charles W. Brewster, *Rambles about Portsmouth: Sketches of Persons, Localities, and Incidents of Two Centuries,* (Portsmouth, NH: C.W. Brewster & Son Printer, 1859), vol. I., p. 357.

nearly 6,000 people, and was well-filled, even the aisles. In the evening, he preached at the Rev. John Rogers' meeting house in Kittery; and Yesterday, at the Rev. Lyman's, in York, to which place a number of ladies and gentlemen from town accompanied him. This morning (Friday) he will preach at the Rev. Dr. Langdon's meeting house here in this town.[44]

Similarly, a newspaper report dated October 5, 1770 looked back upon Whitefield's recent ministry in Portsmouth, stating that he "preached to a most numerous Congregation in Dr. LANGDON'S Meeting-House, there being at least six thousand Persons who attended:—He had preached to near an equal Number once before, in said Meeting-House, and twice in the Rev. Doctor HAVEN's the same week, with great fervor."[45] One man who heard Whitefield preach in Portsmouth at this time was a young man named Mr. Benjamin Randall.

Benjamin Randall was born in New Castle, New Hampshire in 1749. As a youth he was thoughtful of religious ideas but was uncommitted. As a teenager he went to sea, then was employed as a sail maker in Portsmouth. In 1770, at age twenty-one, Randall was in Portsmouth when George Whitefield arrived on September 23. He called Whitefield's arrival "distasteful to me," since Randall was opposed to the disruptions caused by the itinerant evangelist and his New Light doctrines. Randall stated that Whitefield's preaching was "all delusion and enthusiasm," and that he and other itinerants "preached only because they would not work." Randall wanted to have Whitefield "whipped out of town."[46]

An undated portrait of Rev. Samuel Haven, Second or South Congregational Church, Portsmouth, New Hampshire.

Source. Findagrave.com

Since many residents of Portsmouth went to hear Whitefield preach, Randall also participated "as a mere spectator" and was "disgustful" of the event. He wrote, "I was resolved that his preaching would have no effect on me," but he also wrote, "The power with which he spake was a torment to me."[47] Randall then mocked Whitefield and departed. The next day he again heard Whitefield preach in Portsmouth and was deeply convicted, writing later, "The last time I heard his blessed voice proclaim the glorious gospel was on the 28th of Sept.—Friday before the Sabbath on which he died. He spake from Mark xvi. 15,16. O, how wonderfully he spake as one having authority, and not as the scribes; but it still raised a dreadful spirit of opposition within me."[48] This was the last time Benjamin Randall heard Whitefield preach. Randall's journal narrates the subsequent events.

> The next Sabbath, September 30, 1770 . . . the minister of our town went to Portsmouth to preach at the great meeting house, and I went with him. At noon, as I went from the place of worship . . . a man came riding along, and as he rode, he cried, "Mr. Whitefield is dead. He died this morning at Newbury, about six o'clock." As soon as his voice reached my ears, an arrow from the quiver of the Almighty struck through my heart; and a mental voice sounded through my soul, louder than ever thunder sounded through my ears. The first thoughts that passed through my mind were, Whitefield is now in heaven, and I am in the road to hell. I

---

44 John Gilles, *Memoirs of George Whitefield*, p. 211.
45 *The New Hampshire Gazette,* October 5, 1770, p. 3.
46 John Buzzell, editor. *The Life of Elder Benjamin Randall*, (Limerick, ME: Published by Hobbs, Woodman & Company, 1827), p. 10.
47 Ibid., p. 11.
48 Ibid., p. 12.

shall never hear his voice any more. He was a man of God, and I have reviled him, and spoken reproachfully of him. He has taught me the way to heaven; but I regarded it not . . . I trembled. Every part of my body was affected, as well as my mind.[49]

For the next two weeks, Benjamin Randall wrote that he was in spiritual turmoil. He panicked over his destiny in perdition. When calmed, he thought about Whitefield's teachings on the necessity of the new birth, and then Randall despaired. He agonized until he dwelt on scripture and prayed to accept the grace of God through Jesus Christ, and was thereby converted.[50]

Although Whitefield was sickly, he had been sick before, and none in New England expected his imminent death. In the fall of 1770, he was fifty-six years old, and was worn out beyond his years. Daily he appeared to get weaker. An anecdote from Whitefield's time of illness in Portsmouth, shortly before his death, is from a Negro servant who pleaded to see him face-to-face.

One oft-told story captures the love of many blacks for the famous evangelist. When Whitefield once lay near death in a Portsmouth home, an old Negro woman begged to see him. Word of her request was carried to Whitefield who nodded that she should be brought to him. The aged woman entered his room and sat on the floor, praying and peering intently into his eyes. Finally, she whispered, "Master, you just go to heaven's gate. But Jesus Christ said, Get you down; you must not come here yet but go first, and call some more poor Negroes." Within hours, Whitefield was well.[51]

The last sermon Whitefield would ever preach was in Exeter, New Hampshire, on September 29, 1770. After a week of daily preaching in the Portsmouth-Kittery area, Whitefield turned south, revisiting acquaintances from earlier in the month, and ultimately heading for Bethesda, Georgia. By noon of that day he reached the town of Exeter, in which he had many allies and enemies over his several visits since 1740. He had not planned to preach, but was persuaded to do so, and preached from the text "Examine Yourselves, Whether Ye be of the Faith." He preached standing on a huge hogshead, a large barrel used in shipping. As he approached his platform, a bystander said:

> "Sir, you are more fit to go to the bed than to preach." To which Whitefield answered, "True, Sir," but turning aside, he clasped his hands together and looking up, spoke, "Lord Jesus, I am weary in Thy work, but not of Thy work. If I have not yet finished my course, let me go and speak for thee once more in the fields, seal Thy truth, and come home and die."[52]

A sketch of George Whitefield preaching his last sermon, on a hogshead in Exeter, New Hampshire, by Valerie Borgal.

---

49 Ibid., pp. 13-14.
50 Ibid., pp. 16-18.
51 Stephen Mansfield, *Forgotten Founding Father: The Heroic Legacy of George Whitefield*, (Nashville, TN: Highland Books, 2001), p. 233.
52 John Gilles, *Memoirs of George Whitefield*, p. 270.

A somewhat over-flattering eyewitness account of Whitefield's personality, preaching abilities, and his character was printed in *The New Hampshire Gazette*:

> It is now about thirty Years since he first arrived in Boston: and has several times taken a Tour along the Continent from Georgia to Old York in the Massachusetts [later the State of Maine].—He always appeared to be truly pious and very extraordinary Personage, both in his public Performances throughout Europe, and in his different visits in most parts of British America . . . and though he was much troubled with the Asthma, yet the Charms of his Rhetoric and Oratory, were surprising—He always appeared to speak from the Heart; and as to his Fervency and Zeal, perhaps unequalled by any since the Days of the Apostles.—With what Frequency and Cheerfulness did he ascend the Desk, the Language of his Actions being ever, "Wist ye not that I must be about my Father's Business."[53]

A man who was present for Whitefield's final sermon in Exeter, New Hampshire described the preacher and his message as follows:

> The subject was "Faith and Works." He rose up sluggishly and wearily, as if worn down and exhausted by his stupendous labors. His face seemed bloated, his voice was hoarse, his enunciation heavy. Sentence after sentence was thrown off in rough, disjointed portions, without much regard to point or beauty. At length his mind kindled, and his lion like voice roared to the extremities of his audience. He was speaking of the inefficiency of works to merit salvation, and suddenly cried out "Works! Works! A man gets to heaven by works! I would as soon think of climbing to the moon on a rope of sand!"[54]

Another gentleman present in Exeter, wrote of this September 29, 1770 preaching event.

Mr. Whitefield arose and stood erect, and his appearance alone was a powerful sermon. He remained several minutes unable to speak; and then said, "I will await the gracious assistance of God; for He will, I am certain, assist me once more to speak in his name." He then delivered, perhaps, one of his best sermons. "I go," he cried, "I go to rest prepared; my sun has arisen, and by aid from Heaven, has given light to many. It is now about to set for—no, it is to rise to the zenith of immortal glory. I have outlived many on earth, but they cannot outlive

This small roadside marker is at 74 Front Street, Exeter, New Hampshire. It is about 1,000 feet from the current location of the Congregational Church. This spot was in 1770 a more open area, large enough for a huge crowd to gather. The inscription on the marker reads, "GEORGE WHITEFIELD HERE PREACHED HIS LAST SERMON, SEPT. 28, 1770." Photograph by Ken Lawson.

---

53 *The New Hampshire Gazette*, October 5, 1770, p. 3.
54 Joseph Belcher, *George Whitefield*, p. 435.

me in heaven. O thought divine! I soon shall be in a world where time, age, pain and sorrow are unknown. My body fails, my spirit expands. How willingly would I live forever to preach Christ! But I die to be with Him."[55]

Whitefield had planned to preach indoors, but the crowd of six thousand forced him to preach outside.[56] Lucy Hidden Pearson heard Whitefield preach his final sermon in Exeter. Mrs. Pearson lived in the Byfield-Newbury area all her life, serving in the Old South Presbyterian Church until her death in 1852. As a young lady, she heard Mr. Whitefield preach his final sermon. Her story is as follows.

> Lucy Hidden Pearson, as a girl of sixteen years of age, had walked with her mother all the way from her home in Rowley to Exeter, N.H., to hear this great preacher, and she carried the memories of the event dearly in her mind until she died. When an old lady so feeble that she could not rise from her bed, she would tell of Whitefield and his remarkable power. So enthusiastic would she become that she would almost scream with excitement. What must have been the power of this man when this old lady retained so vividly the memories of his great revival of so many years before.[57]

Following his remarkable preaching effort in Exeter, New Hampshire, Whitefield was met by the Rev. Jonathan Parsons, Presbyterian minister at Newburyport. They journeyed together after dinner to Parsons' home, where they would spend the night. Parsons was the well-respected pastor of one of the largest congregations in New England. Upon their arrival, after crossing the Merrimack River, Whitefield was so exhausted he could not pull himself out of their boat without assistance. Word quickly spread throughout Newburyport that Whitefield was once again among them. A crowd formed around Parsons' home, eager to hear from Whitefield. This scene is amply described by Tyerman.

> While Whitefield partook of an early supper, the people assembled at the front part of the parsonage, and even crowded into its hall, impatient to hear a few words from the man they so greatly loved. "I am tired," said Whitefield, "and must go to bed." He took a candle and was hastening to his chamber. The sight of the people moved him; and, pausing on the staircase, he began to speak to them. He had preached his last sermon; this was to be his last exhortation. There he stood, the crowd gazing up at him with tearful eyes, as Elisha at the ascending prophet. His voice flowed on until the candle which he held in his hands burned away and went out in its socket. The next morning he was not, for God took him.[58]

One of Whitefield's traveling companions, Richard Smith, provides an invaluable account of the last hours of Whitefield's earthly life.

> On Saturday, September 29, 1770. Mr. Whitefield rode from Portsmouth to Exeter (fifteen miles), in the morning, and preached there to a very great multitude in the fields. It is remarkable that, before he went out to preach that day (which proved to be his last sermon) Mr. Clarkson, senior, observed him more uneasy than usual, said to him, "Sir, you are more fit to go to bed than to preach." . . . His last sermon was from 2 Corinthians Xiii. 5: "Examine yourselves, whether ye be in the faith; prove your own selves: know ye not your own selves, how that Jesus Christ is in you,

---

55 Arnold Dallimore, *George Whitefield: The Life and Times*, vol. II, p. 503.
56 "The Last Sermon of George Whitefield," *Exeter Historical Society*, www.exeterhistory.org.
57 *Historical Collections of the Essex Institute, vol. 62*, pp. 69-70.
58 Luke Tyerman, *The Life of the Rev. George Whitefield*, vol. II, p. 598.

except ye be reprobates?" He dined at Capt. Gilman's.[59] After dinner Whitefield and Mr. Parsons rode to Newburyport. I did not go there till two or three hours after them. I found them at supper. I asked Whitefield how he felt after his journey. He said, "he was tired, therefore he supped early and would go to bed." He ate a very little supper, talked but little, asked Mr. Parsons to discharge the table, perform family duty; and then retire upstairs. He said, "that he would sit and read till I came to him," which I did as soon as possible; and found him reading in the Bible, with Dr. Watt's psalm lying open before him. He asked me for some water gruel, took half his usual quantity; and, kneeling down by the bedside, closed the evening with prayer. After a little conversation, he went to rest, and slept till two in the morning, when he awoke me for a little cider, of which he drank about a wineglass full. I asked him how he felt, for he seemed to pant for breath. He told me, "His asthma was coming on; he must have two or three days' rest. Two or three days' riding without preaching, would set him up again." Soon afterward, he asked me to put the window up a little higher (though it was half up all night) "For," he said, "I cannot breathe, but I hope I shall be better by and by; a good pulpit sweat today may give me relief: I should be better after preaching." I said to him, I wished he would not preach so often. He replied, "I would rather wear out than rust out." I then told him, I was afraid he took cold preaching yesterday. He said, "he believed he had," and then sat up in bed, and prayed that God would be pleased to bless his preaching where he had been, and also to bless his preaching that day, that more souls may be brought to Christ; and pray for direction, whether he should winter at Boston, or hasten to the southward—prayed for a blessing on Bethesda college, and his dear family there; for the Tabernacle and Chapel congregations, and all connections on the other side of the water; then laid himself down to sleep again. This was nigh three o'clock. At about quarter past four he waked and said, "My asthma, my asthma is coming on; I wish I had not given out word to preach in Haverhill, on Monday;[60] I don't think I shall be able; but I shall see what to-day will bring forth. If I am not better tomorrow, I shall take two or three-day's ride!" He then desired me to warm him a little gruel: and, in breaking the firewood, I waked Mr. Parsons, who, thinking I knocked for him, rose and came in. He went to Whitefield's bedside and asked him how he felt, himself. He answered, "I am almost suffocated. I can scarce breathe; my asthma chokes me." I then was a bit surprised, to hear how quickly and with what difficulty he drew breath. He got out of bed, and went to the open window for air. This was

---

59   The Gilman family was well established in Exeter and southern New Hampshire. Captain Nehemiah Gilman and his wife Martha hosted the ailing Whitefield in Exeter. Nehemiah Gilman owned fifty acres of productive land and was active in the civil affairs of Exeter. In July 1771, Nehemiah and Martha Gilman professed faith in Jesus Christ and were baptized by the itinerant Baptist preacher, Rev. Hezekiah Smith of Haverhill, Massachusetts. See *The Journals of Hezekiah Smith, 1762-1805*, in John D. Broome, *Life, Ministry, and Journals of Hezekiah Smith, 1737-1805*, (Springfield, MO: Particular Baptist Press, 2004), p. 382

60   Whitefield's desire to visit Haverhill, Massachusetts was driven by his recent friendship and ongoing correspondence with the Baptist preacher, Rev. Hezekiah Smith (1737-1805). Smith was born in Long Island, New York. He graduated from Princeton College in 1762, at a time when Princeton was very much in support of Whitefield. Hezekiah Smith was a Baptist. He came to the Congregational Church, west parish, Haverhill, Massachusetts in 1764, and started a Baptist church in Haverhill in 1765. He remained here until his death in 1805. Following Whitefield's example, Smith did itinerant ministry for weeks or months at a time, and helped found dozens of Baptist churches in New England and elsewhere. Smith and Whitefield first met in 1762. Over the next seven years, their paths crossed, especially at the orphanage at Bethesda, Georgia, where Smith was doing itinerant preaching in Baptist churches. The older Whitefield was an example to the younger Smith, and Smith modeled his itinerant preaching on the Whitefield model. They spent a few days together at Bethesda in December 1769. Here the two made plans for Whitefield to preach for Smith at his Baptist Church in Haverhill, in October 1770. In August 1770, Whitefield was nearby in Massachusetts. Hezekiah Smith attempted to see Whitefield, but missed him. Smith wrote in his diary, "Aug. 28 (Tuesday) went as far as Bifield [Byfield] in order to see Mr. Whitefield but was disappointed." At that date Whitefield was around Cambridge and Boston. Whitefield did not preach for Smith in Haverhill in 1770, although it was on Whitefield's mind as he was close to death. See "The Journals of Hezekiah Smith, 1762-1805," in John D. Broome, *The Life, Ministry, and Journals of Hezekiah Smith*, pp. 18, 22, 41, 108-109, 210, 359, 369. Reuben A. Guild, *Chaplain Smith and the Baptists . . .*, (Philadelphia, PA: American Baptist Society, 1885), pp. 115, 138.

exactly at five o'clock. Soon afterward, he turned himself to me and said, "I am dying." His eyes were fixed, his upper lip drawing inward every time he drew breath; he went towards the window, and we offered him some warm wine with lavender drops, which he refused. I persuaded him to sit down on a chair, and have his cloak on; he consented with a sign, but could not speak. I then offered him the glass of warm wine. He took half of it, but it seemed as if it would have stopped his breath entirely. In a little time he brought up a considerable amount of phlegm and wind. I then began to have some small hopes. Mr. Parsons said he thought Mr. Whitefield breathed more freely than he did, and would recover. I said, "No sir, he is certainly dying."

I was continually employed in taking the phlegm out of his mouth with a handkerchief and bathing his temples with drops, rubbing his wrists &c., trying to give him relief, if possible, but all in vain; his hands and feet were as cold as clay. When the

A sketch of Whitefield's last public appearance, September 29, 1770, by Valerie Borgal.

doctor came in and saw him in the chair leaning upon my breast, he felt his pulse and said, "he is a dead man." Mr. Parsons said, "I do not believe it; you must do something." He said, "I cannot: he is now near his last breath." And indeed as it was; for he fetched but one gasp, and stretched out his feet, and breathed no more. This was exactly six o'clock. We continued rubbing his legs, hands and feet with warm cloths, and bathed him with spirits for some time, but all in vain. I then put him into a warm bed, the doctor standing by, and often raised him upright, putting spirits to his nose for an hour, till all hopes were gone. The people came in crowds to see him; I begged the doctor to shut the door.[61]

An eyewitness of the final public speech of Whitefield, on the steps within the Jonathan Parson home, was recalled by his then fifteen-year-old daughter Lydia. Lydia heard Whitefield preach, and entertained him in the Parson home as a child in 1764 and as a teenager in 1770. Lydia married Moses Greenleaf and moved to Maine. Years later, in rural Williamsburg, Maine, Lydia Parsons Greenleaf told an account of her being present in her parent's house when Whitefield died in Newburyport in 1770. She told the account to her minister, Rev. Joseph Underwood a year before her death in 1834. Underwood recorded:

> I remember preaching . . . in a new and commodious barn, belonging to Simon Greenleaf, Esq. His mother was a daughter of Rev. Jonathan Parsons, formerly of Newburyport, who, while we were at her son's house, entertained us with a deeply affecting account of the last day and night of the Rev. George Whitefield, who died at her father's house. She, then in her girlhood, was one of those who listened to the last public address he ever made, standing on the stairs, as he was retiring to his chamber to lay down his head upon the pillow of death that night.[62]

---

61 John Gilles, *Memoirs of George Whitefield*, pp. 211-213.
62 Silas McKeen, *A History of Bradford, Vermont: Containing Some Account of the Place of its First Settlement in 1765 . . .*, (Montpelier, VT: J.D. Clark & Sons, Publishers, 1875), p. 217.

News of Whitefield's unexpected death quickly spread throughout New England. In Portsmouth, New Hampshire the civil magistrate Daniel Pierce wrote in his journal, "Sept. 30. About noon Edmund Davis brought the shocking news that Mr. Whitefield died this morning at 6 o'clock at Newbury."[63] About one hundred miles away in Longmeadow, Massachusetts, Rev. Stephen Williams, a longstanding Whitefield admirer, wrote in his diary, "Oct. 5. I understand yet the Rev'd Mr. Whitefield is dead, yet he died at Newbury with an asthma—he has been abundant in his labors & I hope has done good—Ye Lord Sanctify this providence."[64] In the midst of various handwritten notations concerning sermon notes, home visits, births, baptisms, deaths, small pox concerns, and his own spiritual comments, the *Journal of Rev. Israel Loring* of Sudbury Massachusetts, about fifteen miles west of Boston, had this notation on the death of George Whitefield.

> Sept 30 [1770] Lord's Day morning departed this life the Rev. Mr. George Whitefield at Newbury-Port. Taken with asthma and [. . . ?] passed almost instantaneously [. . . ?] from the times he has visited New England. The first was on Sept [. . . ?] 1740 when he came to Boston. The second in the year 1744 arriving at Boston from Portsmouth on Nov [. . . ?] The third was in the year 1754 [he] came to Boston with professor Burr. The fourth and last was in the year 1770.[65]

In Boston, John Tudor, a deacon in the Second (Old South) Church in Boston, wrote in his diary:

> 1770. Sept 30. (Sabbath-day morning) About 6 o'clock, died very suddenly at Newbury of an asthmatic fit almost universally lamented, that excellent man of God the Rev. Mr. George Whitefield in the 56 year of his age. He had been on a visit to Portsmouth, at which place and at Kittery &York he had preach'd, the morning he died at Newbury, on his return to Boston, had not this sorrowful event taken place. His body as buried under Mr. Parson's Meeting-House at Newbury. Doc'r Eben Pemberton preached his funeral sermon at the Thursday Lecture Oct 11th, from 1 Peter 1st & 4th To an Inheritance Reserved for you in Heaven. The sermon was printed.[66]

The house where George Whitefield died in September, 1770 is still standing in Newburyport, Massachusetts. Photograph by Ken Lawson.

---

63   Charles W. Brewster, *Rambles about Portsmouth*, p. 357.
64   Stephen Williams, *Diary of Stephen Williams of Longmeadow, Massachusetts*, (Longmeadow, MA: Richard S. Storrs Library, 2011), p. 330.
65   Israel Loring, *Journal of Rev. Israel Loring,* (Unpublished Journal, Connecticut Historical Society Special Collections). Loring's journal entry omits the 1747 and the 1764 visits of Whitefield to New England.
66   John Tudor, *Deacon John Tudor's Diary . . . A Record of More or Less Important Events in Boston, from 1732 to 1793, by an Eye Witness*, (Boston, MA: Press of Wallace Spooner, 1896), p. 35.

CHAPTER 39

THE LEGACY OF WHITEFIELD IN NEW ENGLAND

THE LONGTIME HARVARD SCHOLAR PERRY Miller (1905-1963) was an expert on Colonial New England. Miller strongly disfavored Jonathan Edwards and George Whitefield. He firmly denounced revivals, he saw the awakenings of colonial times as from natural causes, he stated that Edwards "preached a distasteful and happily outmoded brand of hell-fire and brimstone," and he spoke of Whitefield as "a more repulsive individual never influenced history."[1] But not all have agreed with Miller's denunciations.

"It is likely that during his life, on both sides of the Atlantic, he was the most famous person after the king."[2] A recent biography of Whitefield stated, "By any standards Whitefield was one of the world's most remarkable and influential preachers."[3] Ronald Knox, while being critical of religious "enthusiasm," wrote of Whitefield, "Any man with a reasonable capacity for admiration must stand awestruck at the record of both his labors and success."[4]

The widely-known George Whitefield died in Newburyport, Massachusetts, on September 30, 1770. The poor health that had limited Whitefield's labors for many years had ended his earthly life. Shortly thereafter, the following poetic tribute to Whitefield was printed in the *New-Hampshire Gazette*.

I.

WHITEFIELD is gone! That Orator divine,
Whose Presence, Voice, and Gesture cou'ld command
Our close Attention—and our Thot's confine,
Whilst his wise Documents we did attend.

II.

With Plainness and with Energy of Speech,
The sacred Gospel-Truths He wou'd impart
T' attending Throngs—and ardently beseech,
That these might be impress'd on ev'ry Heart.

---

1   Perry Miller, *Jonathan Edwards*, (Lincoln, NE: University of Nebraska Press, 1949), pp. 133-134, 567.
2   William Gibson and Thomas W. Smith, *George Whitefield: Tercentenary Essays*, (University of Whales Press, 2015), p. 77.
3   Nigel Scotland, *George Whitefield" The First Transatlantic Revivalist*, (Oxford, England: Lion Hudson Limited, 2019), p. 270.
4   Ronald Knox, *Enthusiasm: A Chapter in the History of Religion*, (Oxford, England: Clarendon Press, 1950), p. 491.

III.

JESUS, the Object of his constant love,
Was the chief Subject which our WHITEFIELD Chose–
Hence to this Jesus, in yon' Realms above,
He's gladly gone—to take his sweet repose,

IV.

No more shall we his Countenance behold
As heretofore—his pleasant Voice no more
Shall captivate the Ears of young and old–
For He's now landed on the Heav'nly Shore.

V.

His Joys are full—while miserable we
Are left behind to mourn the heavy Loss,
Both to ourselves, and all AMERICA–
No Whitefield now with Tears to plead our Cause![5]

The immediate reaction of friends in the area was deep sadness and disappointment. About a week after Whitefield's death, news of his demise reached Rev. Stephen Williams, who was about one hundred twenty-five miles from Newburyport, in Longmeadow, Massachusetts. Whitefield preached for Williams in Longmeadow in October 1740, with good results. On October 6, 1770 Williams wrote in his *Diary*, "I understand yet the Rev. Mr. Whitefield is dead, yet he died at Newbury with an asthma—he has been abundant in his labors & I hope has done good—ye Lord sanctify this providence."[6] To many New Englanders, Whitefield had been a longtime friend, a co-defender of the faith, and an example of Christian love and benevolence. To others he was a nuisance, a relic of a distasteful Puritan past. He lay dead before their eyes, as thousands flocked to pay their final respects to the man who had been for so long their companion, or their antagonist, in the gospel of Jesus Christ.

The following eyewitness account of Whitefield's funeral, provided by his traveling companion Richard Smith, aptly describes events as they occurred. Next, we shall survey the enduring legacy of Whitefield among the people of New England, while concluding with passages from funeral sermons preached by local ministers from around Boston. Smith's narration follows.[7]

> The Rev. Mr. Parsons, at whose house my dear master died, sent for Captain Fetcomb, and Mr. Boardman, and others of his elders and deacons, and they took the whole of the burial upon themselves; prepared the vault, and sent and invited bearers. Many ministers, of all persuasions, came to the house of the Rev. Mr. Parsons, where several of them gave a very particular account of their first awakening under his ministry, several years ago, and also of many in their congregations, that to their knowledge, under God, owed their conversion wholly to his coming among them, often repeating the blessed season they had enjoyed under his

---

5   *New-Hampshire Gazette*, October 12, 1770, p. 3.
6   Stephen Williams, *Diary of Stephen Williams*, (transcribed and printed by the town of Longmeadow, MA), vol. 7, p. 290.
7   John Gilles, *Memoirs of Rev. George Whitefield*, (Middletown, CT: Hunt & Noyes Publishers, 1836), pp. 213-214.

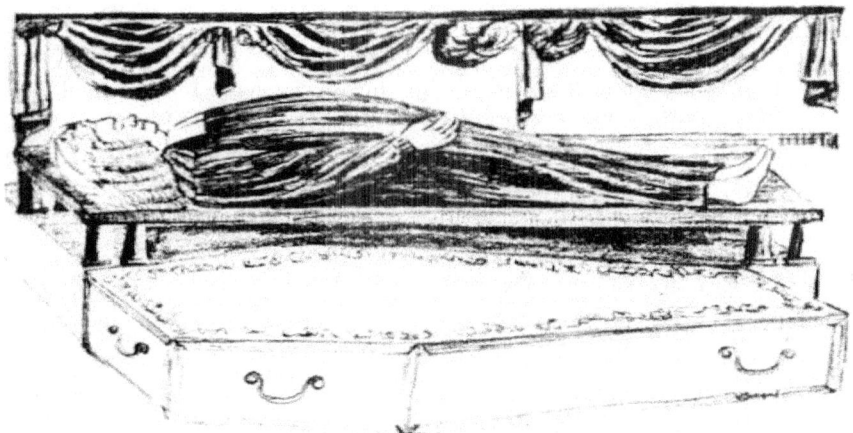

A sketch of Whitefield's corpse on display in the Old South Church, Newburyport, Massachusetts. Sketch by Valerie Borgal.

preaching: and all said, that his visit was attended by more power than any other; and that all opposition fell before him. Then one and another of them would pity and pray for his dear Tabernacle and chapel congregations, and it was truly affecting to hear them bemoan the calamity of America and England. Thus they continued for two hours conversing about his great usefulness, and praying that God would scatter his gifts and drop his mantle among them. When the corpse was placed at the foot of the pulpit, close to the vault, the Rev. Daniel Rogers made a very affecting prayer and openly confessed, that under God, he owed his conversion to that dear man of God, whose precious remains now lay before them. Then he cried out, O my father my father! Then stopped and wept, as though his heart would break, and the people weeping all through the place. Then he recovered and finished his prayer, and sat down and wept . . .

Some of the people weeping, some singing, and so on alternately. The Rev. Mr. Jewett preached a funeral discourse, and made an affectionate address to his brethren, to lay to heart the death of that useful man of God; begging that he and they might be upon their watchtower, and endeavor to follow the blessed example. The corpse was then put into the vault, and all concluded with a short prayer, and dismission of the people, who went weeping through the streets to their respective places of abode.[8]

Boston newspapers, and the newly formed *Essex Gazette* immediately printed announcements of Whitefield's death. This was big news, both for his supporters and his detractors. Soon, all the English-speaking world would read of the passing of the renowned itinerant evangelist.

The Boston Gazette, September 25-October 2, 1770, page 1.

Last evening we were informed by a melancholy messenger from Newburyport, that yesterday morning about VI o'clock, at that place, the Reverend and renowned GEORGE WHITEFIELD was, by a sudden mandate, summoned to the bosom of his Savior! He had been preaching in diverse parts of this province since his arrival from the southward, with his usual diligence and energy; was now from a tour to the Province of New Hampshire on

---

8   The three ministers named in this paragraph are Rev. Jonathan Parsons of Newburyport, MA; Rev. Daniel Rogers of Exeter, NH; and Jedediah Jewett of Rowley, MA.

his return to this town, but being seized with a violent fit of the asthma, was in very short space translated from the labors of this life, to the entertainments of a better . . . .He has, for a long course of years, astonished the world as a prodigy of eloquence and devotion! With what frequency and cheerfulness did he ascend the Desk, the language of his actions being ever "wist ye not that I should be about my Father's business;" With what divine pathos did he not plead with . . . the impenitent sinner to the practice of piety and virtue!

Filled with the Spirit of Grace, he spoke from the heart; and with a fervency of zeal, perhaps unequalled since the days of the Apostles . . . he was unrivaled in the command of an ever crowded and admiring auditory . . . It was to be wished, that the good impressions of his ministry may be long retained; and that the rising generation, like their pious ancestors, may catch a spark of that ethereal flame which burnt with such distinct luster, in the sentiments & practice of this faithful servant of the Most High God.

The Boston Evening Post, October 11, 1770, p. 1.

Yesterday morning at 6 o'clock died very suddenly at Newbury, of an asthmatic fit, almost universally regretted, that man of God the Rev. Mr. GEORGE WHITEFIELD, in the 56th year of his age; he had been on a visit to Portsmouth, at which place, and at Kittery and York, he preached every day last week; and was to have preached yesterday morning at Newbury, on his return hither, had not that sorrowful event taken place.

The News of Whitefield's death travelled quickly. The week following, Boston newspapers lamented the passing of this famous and controversial minister. Some admired him, others detested him, and many were simply indifferent. But the announcement of his death was profound. The following is an example.

The Boston Evening Post

October 18, 1770, page 1.

Early on Monday morning last a number of gentlemen set out from hence for Newburyport . . . his funeral was attended by a great concourse of people on Tuesday afternoon . . .

Mr. Whitefield always appeared to be a truly pious and very extraordinary personage . . . He kept up his zeal and popularity to the last discourse, which he delivered the day before his death to an audience of at least six thousand in the open air and tho' he was mutch troubled with the asthma, yet the charms of his rhetoric & auditory were surprising . . . [He] was unwilling to tarry here any longer than he could be serviceable to mankind. Such was the character of the person whose departure we lament.

At the close his earthly life, the legacy of George Whitefield extended throughout the English-speaking world. As his biographer Luke Tyerman explained:

George Whitefield was pre-eminently the outdoor preacher; the most popular evangelist of the age;—a roving revivalist,—who, with unequaled eloquence and power, spent above thirty years in testifying to enormous crowds, in Great Britain and America, the gospel of the grace of God. Practically, he belonged to no denomination of Christians, but was the friend of all. His labors, popularity and successes were marvelous, perhaps unparalleled. All churches in England, Wales, Scotland, and the British settlements in America, were permanently benefitted by his piety, his example, and the few great truths which he continually preached.⁹

★★★

There were lasting results from Whitefield's vast ministry. To understand this influence we will focus first on the New England colonies in general, and then on the north shore of Boston in particular.

Throughout New England, the number of individuals who were converted under Whitefield's preaching is known only to God. An exact number of persons regenerated from death to life cannot now be determined. Yet, some interesting conclusions may still be drawn. Whitefield had little opportunity in New England to ascertain how many people received eternal benefit from his labors. "When he saw hundreds or thousands at a time melted by his eloquence, he called it a 'gracious melting,' thanked God for the display of His power, hoped they would prove true converts, and hurried away to preach the gospel to other thousands."¹⁰

A 1769 sketch of Rev. George Whitefield.

Source: https://www.georgia encyclopedia.org/articles/ arts-culture/george-whitefield-1714-1770

Whitefield's work as a revival preacher, an awakener, can have no statistical calculation. Some perspective of his effectiveness as an evangelist may be understood by the size of the large crowds he attracted. Another way to consider his effectiveness is through new additions to church memberships. But as a revival preacher, being one who caused those who attended church regularly to revive or re-examine their faith, we find Whitefield to be immensely successful.

The churches of New England, since the Half-Way Covenant of a half-century prior, had regularly admitted to church membership people of outward moral and ethical worth, without them necessarily being regenerated. Thus, in hundreds of examples, God called people out of physical church buildings and into His spiritual and universal church, the true body of Christ, with Whitefield's preaching being the instrument used. Tracy explains the work of Whitefield as a revivalist, stirring up spiritual life amongst lethargic church members.

> The increase in the number of churches and church members is a very inadequate measure of the increase of piety. Great numbers of church members were converted. We must remember that the practice of admitting to communion all persons neither heretical nor scandalous, was generally in the Presbyterian Church, and prevailed extensively among the Congregational churches. In consequence, a large proportion of the communicants in both were unconverted persons. Of course, there was no census of the unconverted members . . . or of the conversions among them; nor would any of them be counted as additions to the churches. In some cases, the revival seems to have been almost wholly within the church, and to have resulted in the

---

9   Luke Tyerman, *The Life of the Rev. George Whitefield*, (New York: Anson D.F. Randolph & Company, 1877), vol. II, pp. iii-iv.
10 Joseph Tracy, *The Great Awakening*, (1842: reprinted by Banner of Truth Trust, Carlisle, PA: 1989), p. 389.

conversion of nearly all the members. A large addition ought to be made, on this score, to the estimated number of conversions.[11]

In addition to those unnamed thousands converted under Whitefield's New England ministry, there were numerous ministers who, while serving a congregation as an ordained clergyman, were yet unconverted. Again, an exact number of these men is not available. For example, at the time of Whitefield's 1744-1745 visit, there were not less than twenty ministers in the Boston area who considered him the means of their conversion.[12] This says nothing of the large number of converts who, after their conversion, devoted their lives to preparation for the gospel ministry. Schools such as Harvard, Yale, and Dartmouth in New England and Princeton in New Jersey, were flooded with young converts eager to study orthodox theology as introduced to them by Whitefield. This new generation of orthodox ministers served as a balance to the rising Unitarian- Universalist movements in the colonies.[13] Further, Whitefield had direct influence on ministerial education in New England through his support of the founding of what would later be Dartmouth College in New Hampshire and Brown University in Rhode Island.

Rev. Ezra Stiles of Newport, Rhode Island observed the preaching skills of Whitefield first-hand, and was impressed. However, after Whitefield's death, many copycats appeared seeking to mimic the famous evangelist. Stiles was not impressed. He wrote, "When Mr. Whitefield died in 1770 about a dozen or 20 set out to his successors & struggled for his Eminence, but proved dying & extinguished lights. None could ever equal him in that wherein he excelled & exceeded all men."[14]

It is easy to speculate and generalize as to the enduring legacy of Whitefield in America. While avoiding both extremism and oversimplification, some general remarks are appropriate. First, John Wesley and the Methodist movement in Britain and America were very dependent on Whitefield for success. It was Whitefield who taught Wesley the art of outdoor preaching. It was Whitefield who introduced Wesley to significant evangelical sponsors and leaders in England. Whitefield willingly allowed Wesley to organize and control the converts of the revival in Great Britain. In America, the growth of Methodism was built on a foundation laid by Whitefield. In 1769, John Wesley sent two men, Richard Boardman and Joseph Pillmore, to organize Whitefield's American converts into Methodist Societies. Whitefield welcomed them.

The lack of success that Wesley's Arminian Methodist ideas had in New England is a testimony to the Calvinistic legacy of Whitefield and historic Puritanism in New England. In 1771 shortly after Whitefield's death, Wesley commissioned Rev. Francis Asbury (1745-1816) as Methodism's first foreign missionary to America. Asbury's gospel message and personality made him popular and successful in most of America, but not in New England. While Asbury was a great admirer of Whitefield's oratory ability and field preaching, and even paid a respectful visit to Whitefield's Newburyport tomb in 1802, Asbury was no Puritan or Calvinist. Asbury was an Arminian in the Protestant Reformation use of that word. As a result, his success in New England was limited. In June 1802, Asbury preached in Marblehead, Massachusetts but was only able to attract "a room full of mostly women." Speaking of both Newburyport and Boston, Asbury complained, "Everything thrives but religion."[15] This lack of Wesleyan success in New England, while attributed partially to John Wesley's support of Great Britain in the Revolutionary War, was extensively due to the successful Calvinist legacy of Whitefield in New England.

---

11   Joseph Tracy, *The Great Awakening*, p. 391.
12   Ibid., p. 393.
13   George W. Cooke, *Unitarianism in America*, (Boston, MA: American Unitarian Association, 1910). Conrad Wright, *The Beginnings of Unitarianism in America*, (Boston, MA: Beacon Press, 1966). Ernest Cassara, *Universalism in America: A Documentary History of a Liberal Faith*, (Boston, MA: Beacon Press, 1971).
14   Ezra Stiles, *The Literary Diary of Ezra Stiles: January 1, 1769-March 13, 1776*, (New York: Charles Scribner's Sons, 1901), vol. III, p. 275.
15   Terry D. Bilhartz, editor, *Francis Asbury's America*, (Grand Rapids, MI: Zondervan Press, 1984), p. 39.

After his death, Whitefield's popularity in New England remained strong in the memories of those who knew him. Even those who had never met Whitefield understood his influence on the religious climate of the time. His non-denominational, evangelical preaching and writing allowed supporters of the awakening to unite, regardless of denominational distinctions. As one author remarked,

> After the Great Awakening highlighted the theology the sects had in common, an eminent Presbyterian could say that Baptists differed from his sect "only in the point of infant baptism," a Congregationalist could become president of the Presbyterian Princeton (i.e., Jonathan Edwards), and Quakers could join with others in humanitarian projects without feeling that they had soiled their consciences.[16]

The ongoing influence of Whitefield in New England is evident by the republication of his sermons after his death. For example, in 1797 there remained enough interest in Whitefield in Portsmouth, New Hampshire that ten of his sermons were printed and hard-bound, and sold in Portsmouth bookstores, then distributed throughout New England.[17] Further, the demand for Whitefield literature was so high in Salem, Massachusetts in 1801, that a local printer reproduced the 231-page *Memoirs of Rev. George Whitefield*, by John Gillies. Certainly, the legacy of Whitefield was passionately carried on, in places, by his New England followers after his death.

Whitefield's influence on the thoughts and ideas of the American colonists was significant. He taught them the value of independent thought apart from ecclesiastical control, and instructed his followers on the primary importance of an individual's relationship to God. The effect of this new thinking on religious liberty in Christ loosened the colonists from dependence on Great Britain in ecclesiastical matters. The independence from the mother country in religious affairs quickly transferred to political control, as tensions between the colonies and Britain soon intensified into the American Revolution.[18]

In the eighteenth century, English kings downplayed religious liberty in favor of a government-sponsored church to support a unified administration, with the king as sovereign. Congregational, Presbyterian, Baptist, and all other separatist or independent groups were often considered disloyal to England and in rebellion to God. The Church of England was dependent upon secular, political support in order to survive. The vast majority of colonists in New England were from independent ecclesiastical backgrounds. These autonomous English churches, whether Quaker, Congregational, or Presbyterian in polity, were under the general authority of the King of England, yet not supportive of the Church of England. There was no unity between the distinct independent denominations in America, until George Whitefield united them through his incessant travels in support of the Great Awakening.

As a Church of England priest, Whitefield was an enigma. He always supported his ordination vows as an Anglican priest, yet he also encouraged revivals in Congregational, Baptist, and Presbyterian churches in the American Colonies. He preached for various separatist clergymen, and celebrated communion in diverse independent churches. The colonial churches were the center of religious and social life in New England. As these churches developed an independent mindset away from the Church of England, they joined in an intercolonial movement of religious and political unity. Their rejection of an Anglican bishop in America was

---

16   David Hawke, *The Colonial Experience,* (New York: Macmillan Publishing Company, 1885), p. 419.
17   George Whitefield, *Ten Sermons Preached on Important Subjects,* (Portsmouth, NH: Pierce & Larkin Printers, 1797).
18   Bernard Bailyn, *The Ideological Origins of the American Revolution,* (Cambridge, MA: Harvard University Press, 1967). Alice M. Baldwin, *The New England Clergy and the American Revolution,* (Durham, NC: Duke University Press, 1928). Peter N. Carroll, editor, *Religion and the Coming of the American Revolution,* (Waltham, MA: Ginn & Company, 1970). Nathan Hatch, *The Sacred Cause of Liberty,* (New Haven, CT: Yale University Press, 1962). Stephen Mansfield, *Forgotten Founding Father: The Heroic Legacy of George Whitefield,* (Nashville, TN: Highland Books, 2001). Jerome D. Mahaffey, *Preaching Politics: The Religious Rhetoric of George Whitefield and the Founding of a New Nation,* (Waco, TX: Baylor University Press, 2007).

symptomatic of their disdain of the British king. Whitefield was the key unifier, the common denominator that linked religion, revival, and political independence.[19]

Whitefield's doctrine of Christian liberty was based on an individual's personal relationship with God through the atoning death of Jesus Christ. Any person could have full freedom and acceptance before a holy God because of personal saving faith in the propitiatory blood of Christ. Thus, the regenerated person had an entirely new way of life, a spiritual rebirth independent of any endorsing council or ecclesiastical influence. Church of England ministers in New England, and elsewhere, disagreed.

> Certain of Whitefield's teachings are of special significance . . . He believed that there were certain fundamental divine laws which a Christian subject must first obey and that he had the right to question and, if necessary, to break rules and laws that were contrary to these principles. He preached this freedom openly. When accused of breaking the church canons, he wrote to the Bishop of London, "Your Lordship knows full well that the canons and other church laws are good and obligatory when conformable to the laws of Christ and agreeable to the liberties of a free people; but when invented and compiled by men of little hearts and bigoted principles . . . to bind up the hands of a zealous few, they may be legally broken."[20]

An interesting study relates to Whitefield's influence on New England pastors who volunteered as Colonial Army chaplains in the Revolutionary War. It was completely consistent with New Light theology to apply liberty in Christ towards the pursuit of the Kingdom of God without outside interference, unjust taxation, or a corrupt Anglican hierarchy. While no study has been done relating Whitefield's influence upon colonial army chaplains, some helpful conclusions may still be drawn from the number of New Light chaplain volunteers from Boston's north shore. For example, Rev. Benjamin Balch of Danvers and Rev. William Emerson of Concord were both New Light ministers who encouraged revival, supported Whitefield, and served as chaplains to the Colonial Army in the American Revolution. Rev. Hezekiah Smith of Haverhill was also a respected and well-liked New Light pastor. Smith followed Whitefield's example of itinerant evangelism and was widely accepted by supporters of revival. Smith served as chaplain to the 4th Continental Infantry, served as a brigade chaplain, and occasionally as an aide-de-camp.[21] Rev. Samuel Spring of Boston, and later Newburyport, was a Princeton graduate in 1771 and a devotee of Whitefield, who served as a Colonial Army chaplain. One of the most influential pulpits in America, both for New Light doctrine and for patriotic rebellion, was the Old South Presbyterian Church in Newburyport. Rev. Jonathan Parsons was a longtime supporter of Whitefield, allowing New Light itinerant evangelists to preach frequently in his church, and publishing pamphlets in defense of the Great Awakening. It was in the home of Jonathan Parsons that Whitefield had died, and it was under Parsons' pulpit that Whitefield lay entombed. Before Colonel Benedict Arnold began his 1775 expedition into Quebec, his forces assembled at the Old South Church, as Whitefield's corpse lay beneath them. Whitefield's influence upon the colonial army soldiers was as follows:

> Assembling at Newburyport on Sept. 17, the soldiers listened to their chaplain, Rev. Samuel Spring, lead in a worship service. Chaplain Spring described the service in his own words: "On the Sabbath morning the officers and as many of the soldiers as could be crowded onto the floor of the house, were marched into the Presbyterian Church in Federal Street. They marched in with colors flying, and drums beating, and formed two lines, through which I

---

19 Stephen Mansfield, *Forgotten Founding Father*, pp. 110-113.
20 Alice M. Baldwin, *The New England Clergy and the American Revolution*, p. 57.
21 Parker C. Thompson, *The United States Army Chaplaincy: from its European Antecedents to 1791*, (Washington, DC: Department of the Army, 1978), pp. 249, 262, 267.

passed—they presenting arms and the drums rolling until I was seated in the pulpit. Then the soldiers stacked their arms all over the aisles, and I preached to the army and to the citizens, who crowded the galleries, from this text: "If thy spirit go not with us, carry us not up hence."

Following the service the unit officers visited George Whitefield's crypt, opened it, and finding his collar and wrist bands intact, cut them in pieces for treasured relics.[22]

A clear example of a New Light devotee of Whitefield, who was an ardent patriot and Colonial Army chaplain, was Rev. John Cleveland of Ipswich-Chebacco parish, Massachusetts. Cleveland was an enthusiastic supporter of Whitefield. From rural Chebacco, Cleveland wrote numerous articles and preached many sermons on Christian religious and civil liberty before serving as a chaplain in the War of Independence. In open letters published in the *Essex Gazette*, Cleveland asked, shortly after the battles of Lexington and Concord;

Is the time come, the fatal era commenced, for you to be deemed rebels, by the Parliament of Great Britain? Rebels! Wherein? Why, for asserting that the rights of men, the rights of an Englishman belong to us . . .

O my dear New England, hear thou the alarm of war! The call of Heaven is to arms! To arms! . . . Behold what all New England must expect to feel, if we don't cut off and make a final end of those British sons of violence, and of every base Tory among us . . .

We are, my brethren, in a good cause; and if God be for us, we need not fear what man can do . . . O thou righteous judge of all the earth, awake for our help. Amen and amen.[23]

John Cleveland witnessed men from his Chebacco (now Essex) New Light assembly enthusiastically enlist in the war for liberty. For political, financial, and religious reasons, volunteers were readily available. Under rising military pressure from Great Britain, Cleveland reminded his readers in the *Essex Gazette* of the right to fight in order to maintain the Puritan ideals of New England's founding fathers.

What shall we do to save ourselves from the distresses brought upon us by an untoward generation? I answer, be not cast down, O America! Be not discouraged, O Boston! . . . Let all ranks and orders of men reform from every immorality and vicious practice, and pray to the God of Heaven and Earth, the preserver of men . . . to break every weapon formed and forming against us,—to maintain our rights and privileges, civil and religious; and above all things, to make us a holy and truly virtuous people, and to preserve us pure from the growing pollutions in the world.[24]

In 1775, John Cleveland matched his actions to his words in defense of his New Light worldview. Previously, in the French and Indian War, he served as a chaplain. In the Revolutionary War, "He preached all the young men among his people into the army and then went himself, taking his four sons with him."[25] There are dozens of examples of New England clergymen who supported Whitefield and fought for independence from Great Britain. His influence upon colonists in the Revolutionary was profound.[26]

---

22 Ibid., p. 122.
23 John Cleveland, "To the Inhabitants of New England," *Essex Gazette*, April 18 and 25, 1775.
24 John Cleveland, *Essex Gazette*, May 31, 1774, p.1.
25 Christopher M. Jedrey, *The World of John Cleveland of Ipswich, Massachusetts*, (New York: W.W. Norton & Company, 1979), p. 135.
26 Cedric B. Cowing, *The Great Awakening and the American Revolution: Colonial Thought in the Eighteenth Century*, (Chicago, IL: Rand McNally & Company, 1971).

Whitefield's enduring legacy to America has taken many dimensions. Certainly, his interdenominational attitude encouraged unity between various separatist Protestant groups. Edwin S. Gaustad, a premier historian of the awakening in New England, wrote:

> The fact that Whitefield was still a priest of the Church of England . . . was a bountiful source of confusion and irritation to his Anglican brethren in New England. With mournful disgust, Commissary Roger Price observed that "to the Quaker he becomes a Quaker; to the Anabaptist an Anabaptist; to the Presbyterian and Independent, a Presbyterian and Independent . . . Whitefield did nothing to allay suspicions, for he never even suggested that the dissenters were in error.[27]

Indeed, the only New England ecclesiastical denominations that did not support Whitefield were the Quakers and the Church of England (Anglicans). The Quakers were mostly indifferent while the Anglicans were often hostile to Whitefield. The above-named Commissary, Roger Price, represented the official opposition of the Church of England against Whitefield. Price was positioned as the rector at King's Chapel in Boston, with additional duties over all the Anglican Churches in New England. As the representative of the Bishop of London, Price officially spoke the formal rejection of Whitefield by the Anglican Church in New England. This did not, however, prevent the various separatist denominations from flocking to Whitefield. For example, in July 1742, the revival preacher and Presbyterian, Rev. John Moorhead of Boston remarked, "I can't express the wonderful things which God is a doing, and is already Manifested among Indians, Negros, Papists, and Protestants of all denominations."[28]

Whitefield's influence on the Church of England in the New England colonies deserves recognition. As Congregational, Presbyterian, and Baptist churches debated the awakening and its subsequent results, many folks in various communities tired of these religious debates. There developed an attraction to the Church of England. After all, New Englanders were British citizens, and the Church of England was the established church of the British Empire. The groups that separated out of the Church of England – namely Baptists, Congregationalists, Quakers, and Presbyterians – were constantly bickering over theology, church polity, soteriology, and other significant issues. The lunatic fringe from the awakening resided within these separated church denominations. For many, the mother church, the Church of England, had great appeal. As so-called New Light preachers vehemently denounced others as tools of the devil, the sedate, predictable, and tolerant Church of England had great attraction to many. The disorderliness of the awakening and its subsequent often inflamed debates drew many to the orderly worship of the Anglican rituals of the Church of England. Stratford, Connecticut minister Rev. Samuel Johnson noted that in 1742 there were about two thousand Anglican Church of England members in Connecticut. Three decades later, he put the number of Church of England members at twenty-five thousand in New England, worshiping in seventy-four congregations. This fantastic Anglican church growth in New England is directly attributable to anti-Whitefield backlash against his message and his itinerant preaching, as well as a rejection of the excesses of the Great Awakening and its aftermath. New England towns such as Salem and Boston, Massachusetts, Portsmouth, New Hampshire, and many others saw significant church grown in their Anglican congregations.[29]

George Whitefield had a noticeable influence on ministerial education in New England. His acceptance by Harvard and Yale Colleges, then his rejection, then his ultimate acceptance by these schools effected ministerial training for generations. Whitefield was also significant in the founding of Dartmouth College,

---

27 Edwin S. Gaustad, *The Great Awakening in New England,* (Gloucester, MA: Peter Smith, Publisher, 1965), p. 119.
28 Ibid., p. 124.
29 Douglas L. Winiarski, *Darkness Falls on the Land of Light: Experiencing Religious Awakenings in Eighteenth-Century New England.* (Chapel Hill, NC: University of North Carolina Press, 2017), pp. 436, 449-452.

eventually located in New Hampshire. And the revival that Whitefield encouraged among the Baptists in Rhode Island compelled the founding in 1764 of what would eventually become Brown University in Providence. All four of these colleges in New England were directly influenced by Whitefield.[30]

While Puritanism as a political reality failed throughout all New England, the theological basis of Puritanism, namely Calvinism, still survived throughout much of New England in the mid-eighteenth century. The oratory genius of Whitefield attracted innumerable crowds, but his Calvinistic doctrines deeply divided the people. Articulate scholars such as Rev. Jonathan Edwards of Northampton, Massachusetts sought to intellectually defend Calvinism, while against these doctrines the so-called Arminians, better described as Unitarians, Arians, or Universalists, became emboldened in their anti-Whitefield and anti-Calvinist teachings. As Gaustad stated:

> Arianism, Unitarianism, and Universalism found advocates in Eastern Massachusetts. Within the lifetime of many of the principals of the Awakening the central issues of an evangelical Christianity—general or particular atonement, a human or divine Christ, reason or revelation, reform or regeneration, free or earned grace—were subject to severe testing.[31]

There was no longer the pretense of a unified colonial ministry in America. Free thinking, liberally-minded clergymen no longer sought to slowly soften the sharp points of Calvinism. Instead, the Calvinistic doctrines from the Protestant Reformation were attacked or dismissed by many emboldened New England clergy. Out of this theological turmoil developed what has been called the New England Theology. Developed by Whitefield supporters Joseph Bellamy and Samuel Hopkins, and others, the New England Theology was an evangelistic Calvinism that emphasized the sovereignty of God and the accountability of man to repent and accept Christ. In contract to strict Calvinism that taught a limited atonement only for the elect, the newer theology endorsed the idea of a universal atonement for all humanity, sufficient for all to be saved, efficient only to the elect. There would not have been a New England Theology if Whitefield had not been so successful as an evangelistic Calvinist in Colonial New England.[32]

An undated sketch of Rev. Benjamin Randall.

Public domain image

Whitefield might not have appreciated some who looked to him for inspiration. First, there was Benjamin Randall of New Castle, New Hampshire. Born in 1749 and raised in southeastern New Hampshire, Randall as a young man had several opportunities to hear Whitefield preach. Crediting Whitefield in 1770 for influencing his conversion, Randall at first joined the local Congregational Church. But he became dissatisfied with Calvinist theology and raised questions related to predestination and infant baptism, both

---

30 "How the Great Awakening Affected Society: Education, Missions, Humanitarianism, Women & the Gospel," *American Heritage Educational Foundation,* April 20, 2018, pp. 1-2. For a thorough study, see Douglas Sloan, *The Great Awakening and American Education,* (New York: Columbia University Press, 1973).

31 Edwin S. Gaustad, *The Great Awakening in New England,* p. 126.

32 Frank H. Foster, *A Genetic History of the New England Theology,* (Chicago, IL: The University of Chicago Press, 1907), pp. 41-56. Oliver D. Crisp and Douglas A. Sweeney, *After Jonathan Edwards: The Courses of New England Theology,* (New York: Oxford University Press, 2012), pp. 20, 44, 132, 172, 219.

An undated sketch of Rev. John Murray of Gloucester and Boston, MA. Public domain image.

of which Whitefield supported. After a brief period as a Calvinistic Baptist preacher, Randall embraced an anti-Calvinist soteriology and endorsed baptism by immersion only for those who professed faith in Jesus Christ. He was ordained in 1780 in New Durham, New Hampshire and is considered the founder of the Free Will Baptists in America. Randall got his evangelistic zeal but not his theology from George Whitefield. One source accurately stated, "The Free Will Baptist Churches have occasion to bless God for raising up and sending Whitefield out to preach; their founder's heart [Benjamin Randall] was given its peculiar fire, though not its peculiar doctrines, from the blessings of God upon his [Whitefield's] eloquence and love."[33] Whitefield would have thanked God for Randall's conversion, but would have disagreed with him on some major Bible doctrines.[34]

Another admirer of Whitefield who did not follow his Calvinist or Reformed doctrines was John Murray of England, later from New Jersey and Massachusetts. Born in England in 1741 into a strict Calvinist home, Murray joined a Whitefield congregation near London in 1760. Initially, Murray was a firm supporter of Whitefield and admired the itinerant preacher. He sought "to attach" himself to Whitefield; the two dined together, and Murray attended numerous events where Whitefield was preaching.[35] Murray wrote of his deep conviction after hearing Whitefield preach about hell and the desperate need of all men to come to the blood of Christ for atonement. These Calvinist doctrines both terrified and overwhelmed Murray. Seeking some theological consolation, Murray began to meet with some who "abhorred the very name of Whitefield."[36] After deep religious reflection, and detailed theological reading from a wide variety of sources, Murray denounced Whitefield and Calvinism. He was excommunicated from the Tabernacle Church in London in 1770, and came to the American Colonies to begin again. Murray served in New Jersey, and in 1774 he settled in Gloucester, Massachusetts as a Unitarian minister, then in Boston in 1793. For one who initially respected and admired Whitefield, Murray developed theological ideas opposite and antagonistic to Whitefield's theology. Murray did not believe in an inerrant Bible; he did not accept blood atonement in Jesus Christ; he rejected the doctrine of hell; and he did not support the doctrine of the new birth. This man, who

A pencil sketch of Ms. Jemima Wilkinson from David Hudson's "History of Jemima Wilkinson," 1821.

---

33 Robert F. Lawrence, *The New Hampshire Churches, Comprising the Histories of the Congregational and Presbyterian Churches in the State..*, (Claremont, NH: Claremont Manufacturing Company, 1866), p. 338.
34 Frederick L. Wiley, *Life and Influence of the Rev. Benjamin Randall, Founder of the Free Will Baptist Denomination,* (Philadelphia, PA: American Baptist Publication Society, 1915).
35 John Murray, *The Life of the Rev. John Murray, Preacher of Universal Salvation,* (Boston, MA: Universalist Publishing House, 1869), p. 111.
36 Ibid., 131-134.

was once a member of a Whitefield church in England, came to denounce the foundational teachings of Whitefield's life and ministry.

A woman who began as an admirer of Whitefield but became a religious eccentric, was the Quaker Jemima Wilkinson of Rhode Island. Born in 1752 into a devout Quaker home in Cumberland, Rhode Island, the outgoing and precocious Jemima Wilkinson rebelled as a young woman from her Quaker parents.[37] Physically attractive and intelligent, Wilkinson was in spiritual turmoil when she heard Whitefield preach in Rhode Island in 1770. She developed peculiar theological views as a prophetess and was the founder of a celibate, reclusive religious commune. A summary of her life stated:

> Rhode Island produced one new religious prophet in the Awakening . . . Her name was Jemima Wilkinson, and she was a Quaker who was caught up in the revival at a late stage when George Whitefield returned to the Colony in 1770. She was eighteen at that time, and when she began attending religious meetings outside the Quaker faith, she was disowned by the Society of Friends. In 1776 she became very ill and had a vision of heaven. Upon recovery, she was convinced that she had actually died and was then sent back to earth by God to convey a special message. An attractive, forceful, and eloquent speaker, she travelled throughout southern New England on horseback from 1776 to 1790, making many converts to her new sect, which she called the Universal Friends . . . But some of her followers believed she was the female incarnation of God . . . [She] encouraged celibacy. She also advocated pacifism (which was not popular after 1776) and predicted the imminent second coming of Christ. In 1790 she moved to western New York, where she founded a small community . . . She died there in 1819, without ever returning to Rhode Island. Her sect died with her.[38]

Needless to say, George Whitefield would be aghast at the teachings of his one-time admirer, Jemima Wilkinson.

During Whitefield's 1764 tour in Boston, an eleven-year-old servant girl named Phillis Wheatley heard him preach and was converted. She belonged to Mr. John Wheatley of Boston and was a household slave. Phillis was born in Africa, and sold into slavery at age seven or eight. The Wheatley family encouraged her to read, write, and pursue poetry. She was the first African American poetess to make money in poetry. She was granted her freedom in 1773. Her listening to Whitefield in 1764, and in 1770, changed her life. At Whitefield's death, at age seventeen Phillis penned a poetic eulogy to the itinerant Whitefield.[39]

A late eighteenth-century sketch of the poetess Phillis Wheatley. The wording around the sketch says, "Phillis Wheatley, Negro Servant to Mr. John Wheatley, of Boston.

Source: https://www.biography.com/writer/phillis-wheatley

ON THE DEATH OF REV. MR. GEORGE WHITEFIELD, 1770
by Phillis Wheatley
Hail, happy saint, on thine immortal throne,
To thee complaints of grievance are unknown;

---

37 David Hudson, *History of Jemima Wilkinson: a Preacheress of the Eighteenth Century*, (Geneva, NY: S.P. Hull, Printer, 1821), p. 14.
38 William McLoughlin, *Rhode Island: A History*, (New York: W.W. Norton & Company, 1978), pp. 79-80.
39 Phillis Wheatley, "On the Death of Rev. Mr. George Whitefield," https://allpoetry.com/On-the-Death-of-Rev.-Mr.-George-Whitefield,-1770.

We hear no more the music of thy tongue,
Thy wonted auditories cease to throng.
Thy sermons in unequall'd accents flow'd,
And ev'ry bosom with devotion glow'd;
Thou didst in strains of eloquence refin'd
Inflame the heart, and captivate the mind.
Unhappy we the setting sun deplore,

So glorious once, but ah! it shines no more.
Behold the prophet in his tow'ring flight!
He leaves the earth for heav'n's unmeasur'd height,
And worlds unknown receive him from our sight.
There Whitefield wings with rapid course his way,
And sails to Zion through vast seas of day.
Thy pray'rs, great saint, and thine incessant cries
Have pierc'd the bosom of thy native skies.
Thou moon hast seen, and all the stars of light,
How he has wrestled with his God by night.

He pray'd that grace in ev'ry heart might dwell,
He long'd to see America excell;
He charg'd its youth that ev'ry grace divine
Should with full lustre in their conduct shine;
That Saviour, which his soul did first receive,
The greatest gift that ev'n a God can give,
He freely offer'd to the num'rous throng,
That on his lips with list'ning pleasure hung.

"Take him, ye wretched, for your only good,
"Take him ye starving sinners, for your food;
"Ye thirsty, come to this life-giving stream,
"Ye preachers, take him for your joyful theme;
"Take him my dear Americans, he said,
"Be your complaints on his kind bosom laid:
"Take him, ye Africans, he longs for you,
"Impartial Saviour is his title due:
"Wash'd in the fountain of redeeming blood,
"You shall be sons, and kings, and priests to God.

Great Countess, we Americans revere
Thy name, and mingle in thy grief sincere;
New England deeply feels, the Orphans mourn,
Their more than father will no more return.

> But, though arrested by the hand of death,
> Whitefield no more exerts his lab'ring breath,
> Yet let us view him in th' eternal skies,
> Let ev'ry heart to this bright vision rise;
> While the tomb safe retains its sacred trust,
> Till life divine re-animates his dust.

Testimonies to the life and ministry of Whitefield were recorded by two of his New England friends. Rev. Nathaniel Whitaker (c.1710-1795) was the longtime pastor of the Third Church in Salem, Massachusetts, ministering to that assembly from 1769 to 1795. Whitaker preached a thirty-eight-page funeral sermon on the death of George Whitefield, which was quickly published in Salem and elsewhere.[40] In the sermon introduction to Lady Huntington, Whitaker states:

> Although your ladyship has been denied the mournful satisfaction of dropping a tear at his grave, which has been indulged to us, it is no small satisfaction to me and his mourning friends here . . .
>
> I will make no other apology for recalling to your minds this mournful event, but that I have in providence been prevented from appearing at this desk before this time, since the doleful tidings reached our ears, that the Reverend George Whitefield was no more.
>
> Among those who have been bright examples in fulfilling their work, perhaps there has not been, for ages, one who imitated the Lord with more exactness than the lately deceased, ever to be remembered and much-lamented Rev'd George Whitefield, whose death is the occasion for this discourse.
>
> I shall not attempt to draw the character of this eminent servant of Christ at full length: This would require a more able hand than is now employed . . . my text to be a brief summary of his character; He wrought the works of Him that sent him while it was day.
>
> As he was a scholar so he was the polite gentleman. Few perhaps ever exceeded him in true politeness. He well knew how to support his dignity, and yet was easy of access by all, and affable and courteous to the meanest. He would most gratefully acknowledge the smallest tokens of kindness and respect from the meanest of his fellow men, and express his satisfaction in opportunities to gratify them.
>
> As a public speaker and orator he was excelled by none, and was a pastor for all. He commanded the attention of his crowded auditories, and people of all persuasions and tempers, being charmed with the manner of his address, hung on his lips with eager attention. And he had the wit of winning the affections and pleasing the fancies of his hearers, while at the same time, by divine skill, he darted truth into their minds . . . .

---

40   Nathaniel Whitaker, *A Funeral Sermon, on the Death of the Reverend George Whitefield . . . Preached in Salem on Wednesday the 27th of October Following, by Nathaniel Whitaker, D.D. Pastor of a Church of Christ in Salem,* (Salem, MA: 1770).

> As a preacher he was full of power and energy. It was most commonly apparent that he preached in the demonstration of the Spirit and with power. He was concerned to inform the judgment, at which he had a happy talent, by familiar appeals to common sense and experience, and to the infallible oracles of divine truth . . . in this method of preaching he was equaled by none.
>
> But to crown all, he was an eminent Christian. Most people call themselves by this name, but few, alas, comparatively profess the thing. The first impressions on his heart, at his conversion, were powerful, and God gave him a large portion of His Spirit, and filled him with a fervent love to Christ and souls. This animated him in all his course, and made him feel the importance of doing his work while it was day.
>
> He was concerned to fill up his time with duty and diligence, and for the salvation of souls, that he spared no pains or labor; and even spent his life to fulfil his ministry and testify the gospel of the grace of God.
>
> Mr. Whitefield lived long enough to triumph over . . . reproaches, and to establish his character as an honest man, so as to stop the mouths of his very enemies, except such as will not attend to evident facts, and delight in defamation and calamity . . .
>
> And shall such a friend be forgotten? Love and gratitude forbid this, while thousands, in Europe and America, have monuments erected in their hearts, erected there by the word of truth which he preached, and by the Spirit of the living God which accompanied it, and has made them as his epistle, never to be erased through the annals of eternity.
>
> But I recall my thoughts from the tomb, the dark abode where the dust of our friend is departed—let us rather view and imitate this fervent servant of Christ who is done his work and gone to rest before us—he whom we loved has gone to Heaven.

Whitefield would have been pleased to know that his evangelical message resonated in New England long after his death. Many of his supporters continued his Calvinistic and evangelistic message. For example, shortly after Whitefield's death in 1770, there developed a missionary organization in New Hampshire committed to evangelizing both Indians and White settlers. Founded by Whitefield's converts in and around Portsmouth, the group was still active one hundred years after his death. As a result of the Great Awakening, some New Light churches prospered. Other churches were deeply divided and experienced contentious debates. Some churches were unaffected, while other congregations openly opposed Whitefield and the awakening. In southeast New Hampshire, the Piscataqua Missionary Society kept the message and the methods of Whitefield going into rural New Hampshire settlements. Elaborating on this idea,

> The state of things above alluded to, led to the foundation of the Piscataqua Missionary Society in the early part of the present century, an institution that has been of great service to all the interests of religion in that region. It is proper to remark, that in this portion of the State, a century later, the influence of Whitefield was great and good, and the efforts of the friends of truth, in sending missionaries, and the blessing of God upon the churches that were planted there, have done much to foster true piety among the people.[41]

---

41 Robert F. Lawrence, *The New Hampshire Churches,* p. 13.

Perhaps the longest lasting effect of Whitefield's ministry in New England came from two men who heard him preach, then became ministers in the southern American Colonies. These men were Shubal Stearns (1706-1771) and Daniel Marshall (1706-1784). Shubal Stearns was born in Boston in 1706, to parents with Puritan heritage. At age nine he moved with his parents to Tolland, a farming community in north-central Connecticut Colony. In the fall of 1740, and in the summer of 1745, Whitefield preached in the vicinity of Tolland. Shubal Stearns heard Whitefield preach and was converted.[42] A separate church was formed in Tolland, where Stearns was ordained in 1746. He developed Baptist views. Stearns departed Connecticut in 1754 to do itinerant preaching and church planting in Virginia and then famously in North Carolina. His church in North Carolina, the Sandy Creek Baptist Church, experienced numerous revivals, and allowed Stearns to travel widely in North Carolina, Virginia, and South Carolina as an itinerant preacher. Several dozen churches were started by Stearns and his troupe, and thousands professed a conversion experience. Shubal Stearns died in November 1771, in Randolph County, North Carolina.[43]

The other New Englander who heard Whitefield preach and became a successful minister in the southern colonies was Daniel Marshall. Born in 1706 in Windsor, Connecticut, Marshall was a farmer who was educated at home. Born to devout parents, he served for twenty years as a deacon in the First Church Congregational in Windsor. Marshall came under the influence of Whitefield's preaching in Windsor in 1745.[44] Marshall became a separatist Congregationalist, and began missionary work to Indians and then lay preaching in Connecticut, New York, and Pennsylvania. His second wife was Martha Stearns, the sister of the itinerant Baptist preacher Shubal Stearns. He expressed Baptist convictions in 1754. From 1754 to 1781, Daniel Marshall preached in Virginia, North Carolina, and South Carolina. Numerous churches were started under his influence, and thousands made professions of faith in Christ. In 1771, Marshall and his family and others moved to Columbia County, Georgia, where he started the influential Kiokee Baptist Church. From this church he trained dozens of preachers, promoted revival, and pastored a growing local congregation. Daniel Marshall died in Columbia County, Georgia in November 1784.[45]

A final tribute to Whitefield's New England legacy was recorded by the Rev. Jonathan Parsons of Newburyport, Massachusetts. Parsons was escorting Whitefield the day before his death, was his host the evening before he died, and was present as Whitefield passed to his Savior. Excerpts from his funeral sermon, preached to thousands with Whitefield's corpse placed below the pulpit, are as follows:[46]

"For me to live is Christ; to die is gain." Philippians 1:21

> Now, if it is the duty and privilege of believers to live so devoted to God in Christ, then it is a duty and privilege, by consequence, so to live, as to maintain the dear and full evidence of their great gain by death . . . Self-dedication to God in Christ, is an evidence of our fitness to die; and a sense of this dedication, is a plain evidence of meetness for the inheritance of the saints in light.

---

42 Bettie G. Bunce, *Shubal Stearns and Separate Baptist Beginnings in North Carolina*, (Bedford, VA: 1976).
43 "Shubal Stearns," *North Carolina History Project*, www.northcarolinahistory.org/encyclopedia/shubal-stearns-1706-1771/. William Cathcart, editor, "Shubal Stearns," *The Baptist Encyclopedia*, (Philadelphia: 1881), vol. III, p. 1098. John Sparks, *The Roots of Appalachian Christianity: the Life and Legacy of Shubal Stearns*, (University of Kentucky Press, 2001).
44 William Sprague, "Daniel Marshall," *Annals of the American Baptist Pulpit*, (1860: reprinted in 2005 by Solid Rock Christian Books, Birmingham, AL). vol. I, p. 59.
45 "Daniel Marshall," *New Georgia Encyclopedia*, www.newgeorgiaencyclopedia.org/articles/arts-culture/daniel-marshall-1706-1784.
46 Jonathan Parsons, *A Funeral-Sermon on the Death of Mr. George Whitefield*, (Portsmouth, NH: 1770).

I might have enlarged upon this divine subject, and have inferred many useful instructions; but instead of all other things, I shall turn my discourse to the very melancholy and affecting occasion, the sudden and surprising death of the Rev. Mr. GEORGE WHITEFIELD, who died by a fit of the asthma, at six o'clock this morning, in my chamber. In him, I believe, we have the whole of the text exemplified: he could say with our apostle, "For me to live is Christ; to die is gain."

Since my first acquaintance with him, which is about thirty years ago, I have highly esteemed him, as an excellent Christian, and an eminent minister of the Gospel. A heart so bent for Christ, with such a sprightly, active genius, could not admit of a stated fixed residence in one place, as the pastor of a particular congregation; and therefore, he chose to itinerate from place to place, and from one country to another; which indeed, was much better suited to his talents, than a fixed abode would have been—I have often considered him as an angel flying through the midst of heaven, with the everlasting gospel, to preach unto them that dwell on the earth; for he preached the uncorrupted word of God, and gave solemn warnings against all corruptions of the Gospel of Christ . . .

In many things, his example is worthy of imitation; and if in anything he exceeded, or came short, his integrity, zeal in God, and love to Christ and the gospel, rendered him, in extensive usefulness, more than equal to any of his brethren. In preaching here, and through most parts of America, he has been in labors more abundant, approving himself a minister of God, in much patience, in afflictions, in watchings, in fastings, by pureness, by the Holy Ghost, by love unfeigned; as sorrowful, yet always rejoicing; as having nothing, yet possessing all things. And God, that comforteth those that are cast down, has often comforted us by his coming; and not by his coming only, but by the consolation wherewith he was comforted in us, so that we could rejoice the more . . .

The last sermon that he preached, though under the disadvantage of a stage in the open air, was delivered with such clearness, pathos, and eloquence, as to please and surprise the surrounding thousands. And as he had been confirmed by the grace of God, many years before, and had been waiting and hoping for this last change, he then declared, that he hoped it was the last time he should ever preach. Doubtless, he then had such clear views of the blessedness of the open vision, and the complete fruition of God in Christ, that he felt the pleasures of heaven in his raptured soul, which made his countenance shine like the unclouded sun.

In an appendix to Jonathan Parsons' funeral sermon, he related the events that happened during the interment of Whitefield's corpse, as it was placed under the pulpit of the Old South Presbyterian Church in Newburyport.

Early on the morning after his death, Mr. Sherburne of Portsmouth sent Mr. Clarkston and Dr. Haven, with a message to Mr. Parsons, desiring that Whitefield's remains might be buried in his own new tomb, at his own expense; and in the evening several gentlemen from Boston, came to Mr. Parsons' desiring that the body might be carried there. But as Whitefield had repeatedly desired that he might be buried before Mr. Parsons' pulpit, if he died at Newburyport, Mr. Parsons thought himself obliged to deny both of their requests.

The following account of his interment is subjoined to this sermon, *viz*:

–October 2, 1770. At one o'clock all the bells in the town were tolled for an hour, and all vessels in the harbor gave their proper signals of mourning. At two o clock the bells tolled a second time. At three, the bells called to attend a funeral. The Rev. Dr. Haven of Portsmouth, The Rev. Messrs. Daniel Rogers of Exeter, Jedediah Jewet, and James Chandler, of Rowley, Moses Parsons, of Newbury, and Edward Bass of Newburyport, were pall bearers. The procession was from the Rev. Mr. Parsons' of Newburyport, where Whitefield died. Mr. Parsons and his family, together with many other respectable persons, followed the corpse in mourning. The procession reached only one mile, when the corpse was carried into the Presbyterian church, and placed on a bier in the broad aisle, over which the Rev. Mr. Rogers made a very suitable prayer in the presence of about six thousand persons, within the walls of the church, while many thousands were on the outside, not being able to find admittance . . .

After this the corpse being put into a new tomb before Mr. Parsons' pulpit, which the gentlemen of the congregation had prepared for that purpose, and before it was sealed, the Rev. Jewet gave the following exhortation: "He who was but a little while ago making a bright and beautiful figure, and acting a vigorous and useful part among the living, is now the proprietor of the grave. The residue of his day is cut off . . . But many of us have had an intimate friendship with, or an affectionate regard for the dear and pious Mr. Whitefield; and have as opportunity presented, attended on his ministrations with profit and delight; having hung on his lips, heard his sweet voice, and seen and felt something of the fervor of his spirit . . .

Is there nothing to relieve us, when our heart is almost overwhelmed within us, on occasion of the removal of this excellent servant of Christ, who was so dear to us in the bonds of love and grace? Yes. Precious in the sight of the Lord is the death of his saints.[47]

---

47   "An Exhortation at the Grave," Ibid., p. 28ff.

A booklet size woodcut drawing of George Whitefield giving testimony from beyond the grave. The idea was that as Whitefield had gone to the grave, all others will follow—so beware.

Source: Description of the Last Judgment, a poem by John Peck of Boston, 1771. https://blogs.princeton.edu/graphicarts/2011/05/description-of-the-last-judgeme.html

APPENDIX A

SIGNIFICANT NEW ENGLAND MINISTERS WHO PUBLICLY SUPPORTED GEORGE WHITEFIELD AND/OR THE AWAKENING

THE TESTIMONY AND ADVICE OF AN ASSEMBLY OF PASTORS OF CHURCHES IN NEW ENGLAND, AT A MEETING IN BOSTON, JULY 7, 1743, OCCASIONED BY THE LATE HAPPY REVIVAL OF RELIGION IN MANY PARTS OF THE LAND. (BOSTON, MA: 1743).

[The following ministers either signed the original document or pledged their agreement to the document shortly thereafter].

Samuel Moody of York, ME
Joseph Sewell of Boston, MA
Ames Cheever of Manchester, MA
William Hobby of Reading, MA
John Warren of Wenham, MA
Jedediah Jewett of Rowley, MA
John Moorhead of Boston, MA
James Chandler of Rowley, MA
John Seccomb of Harvard, MA
Amos Main of Rochester, NH
James Diman of Salem, MA
David Goddard of Leicester, MA
Daniel Bliss of Concord, MA
Elias Haven of Wrentham, MA
Samuel Chandler of York, ME
Joshua Tufts of Litchfield, NH
John Porter of Bridgewater, MA
Josiah Crocker of Taunton, MA
Francis Worcester of Sandwich, MA
Joseph Baxter of Medfield, MA
John Webb of Boston, MA
Joseph Adams of Newington, NH
John Chipman of Beverly, MA

John White of Gloucester, MA
Samuel Wigglesworth of Ipswich, MA
Thomas Prince of Boston, MA
James Pike of Summersworth, NH
Nathan Webb of Uxbridge, MA
John Emerson of Topsfield, MA
Solomon Prentice of Grafton, MA
Othniel Campbell of Plymouth, MA
Ward Cotton of Hampton, NH
John Cotton of Halifax, MA
Phineas Hemmingway of Townshend, MA
Samuel Bachellor of Haverhill, MA
Samuel Tobey of Berkley, MA
Thomas Balch of Dedham, MA
Samuel Hill of Marshfield, MA
Samuel Veazie of Duxborough, MA
Jonathan Ellis of Plymouth, MA
Daniel Emerson of Dunstable, MA
Benjamin Colman of Boston, MA
Nathaniel Eells of Scituate, MA
John Cotton of Newton, MA
James Allin of Brookline, MA
William Cooper of Boston, MA

Thomas Foxcroft of Boston, MA
Joseph Emerson of Malden, MA
James Bayley of Weymouth, MA
Thomas Smith of Falmouth, MA
Josiah Cotton of Providence, RI
Joseph Dorr of Mendon, MA
Benjamin Bass of Hanover, MA
Ezra Carpenter of Hull, MA
Ebenezer Parkman of Westborough, MA
Simon Bradstreet of Marblehead, MA
Andrew Eloit of Boston, MA
John Rogers of Ipswich, MA
Peter Thatcher of Middleborough, MA
Jonathan Russel of Barnstable, MA
William Thompson of Scarborough, ME
John Hovey of Arundel, ME
Moses Morrill of Biddeford, ME
Stephen Williams of Springfield, MA
Jonathan Edwards of Northampton, MA
John Woodbridge of Hadley, MA
Edward Billing of Coldspring, MA
Chester Williams of Hadley, MA
Oliver Peabody of Natick, MA
David Hall of Sutton, MA
John Wales of Raynham, MA
Nathaniel Appleton of Cambridge, MA
David McGregore of Londonderry, NH
Benjamin Lord of Norwich, CT
Solomon Williams of Lebanon, CT
Jabez Wright of Norwich, CT
Samuel Mosely of Windham, CT
Eleazer Wheelock of Lebanon, CT
David Jewett of New London, CT
Benjamin Ruggles of Middleborough, MA
John Graham of Woodbury, CT
Reuben Judd of Woodbury, CT
Hezekiah Gold of Stratford, CT
Ebenezer White of Danbury, CT

Joshua Gee of Boston, MA
Henry Messinger of Wrentham, MA
Nathaniel Leonard of Plymouth, MA
Nathaniel Rogers of Ipswich, MA
Habijah Weld of Attleborough, MA
Samuel Checkley of Boston, MA
Hull Abbot of Charlestown, MA
Ebenezer Turell of Medford, MA
Thomas Prentice of Charlestown, MA
John Fowle of Hingham, MA
Thaddeus MacCarthy of Kingston, MA
Jeremiah Wise of Berwick, ME
William Shurtleff of Portsmouth, NH
Benjamin Allen of Falmouth, ME
Samuel Jefferds of Wells, ME
Nicholas Loring of North Yarmouth, ME
John Rogers of Kittery, ME
Peter Raynolds of Enfield, CT
Samuel Allis of Somers, CT
David Parsons of Hadley, MA
Timothy Woodbridge of Hatfield, MA
Daniel Putnam of Reading, MA
John Tucke of Gosport, NH
Benjamin Bradstreet of Gloucester, MA
Ivory Hovey of Rochester, MA
Jonathan Parker of Plimpton, MA
Joseph Meachem of Coventry, CT
Hezekiah Lord of Preston, CT
Daniel Kirkland of Norwich, CT
John Owen of Groton, CT
Jonathan Parsons of Lyme, CT
Benjamin Pomroy of Hebron, CT
John Blunt of Newcastle, NH
Anthony Stoddard of Woodbury, CT
Joseph Bellamy of Woodbury, CT
Samuel Cook of Stratfield, CT
Jedediah Mills of Ripton, CT

APPENDIX B
SIGNIFICANT NEW ENGLAND MINISTERS WHO PUBLICLY DID NOT SUPPORT GEORGE WHITEFIELD AND/OR THE AWAKENING

THE TESTIMONY OF THE PASTORS OF THE CHURCHES IN THE PROVINCE OF MASSACHUSETTS BAY, IN NEW ENGLAND, AT THEIR ANNUAL CONVENTION IN BOSTON, MAY 25, 1743, AGAINST SEVERAL ERRORS IN DOCTRINE AND DISORDERS IN PRACTICE ... (BOSTON, MA: 1743).

[The following influential clergymen promoted this influential document after a majority of thirty eight ministers in attendance endorsed the document as a majority].

Nathaniel Eells of Scituate, MA[1]	Charles Chauncey of Boston, MA
Benjamin Prescott of Salem, MA	John Handcock of Braintree, MA
Nathaniel Appleton of Cambridge, MA	

A LETTER FROM TWO NEIGHBORING ASSOCIATIONS OF MINISTERS IN THE COUNTRY, TO THE ASSOCIATED MINISTERS OF BOSTON AND CHARLESTOWN, RELATING TO THE ADMISSION OF MR. WHITEFIELD INTO THEIR PULPITS. (BOSTON, MA: 1745).

[The following ministers north of Boston believed Whitefield practiced and spoke many errors and he was not welcomed in their churches].

Caleb Cushing of Salisbury, MA	Joseph Whipple of Hampton Falls, NH
John Lowell of Newbury, MA	Pain Wingate of Amesbury, MA
Jeremiah Fogg of Kensington, NH	Nathaniel Gookin of North Hampton, NH
Elisha Odlin of Amesbury, MA	Peter Coffin of Kingston, NH
William Parsons of South Hampton, NH	Samuel Webster of Salisbury, MA
John Barnard of Andover, MA	Joseph Parsons of Bradford, MA
William Balch of Bradford, MA	James Cushing of Haverhill, MA

---

1 Rev. Nathaniel Eells of Scituate, MA had previously signed *The Testimony and Advice of an Assembly of Pastors of Churches in New England*, at a Meeting in Boston, July 7, 1743, occasioned by the Late Happy Revival of Religion in Many Parts of the Land, (Boston, MA: 1743). He supported Whitefield. Apparently, his role at the May 25, 1743 meeting was only as a scribe. See Joseph Tracy, *The Great Awakening: A History of the Revival of Religion in the Time of Edwards & Whitefield*, (1842: reprinted by Banner of Truth Trust, Carlisle, PA, 1976), pp. 289-292, 358-359. Yet Eells did sign an anti-Whitefield resolution in January 1745.

Christopher Sergeant of Methuen, MA
John Cushing of Boxford, MA
Edward Barnard of Haverhill, MA

William Johnson of Newbury, MA
Thomas Barnard of Newbury, MA

RECORDS OF A MINISTERIAL ASSOCIATION WHICH MET AT BOSTON, JANUARY 1, 1745. (BOSTON, MA: 1745).

[The following ministers met to discuss Whitefield in New England. They wrote that there were "many weighty objections which lie against the said Mr. Whitefield with respect to his principles, expressions and conduct," and that "the churches of this land are endangered].[2]

John Handcock of Lexington, MA
John Cotton of Newton, MA
Warham Williams of Waltham, MA
Ebenezer Turell of Medford, MA
Samuel Cook of Cambridge, MA

William Williams of Weston, MA
Nathaniel Appleton of Cambridge, MA
Seth Storer of Watertown, MA
Nicholas Bowes of Bedford, MA

THE SENTIMENTS AND RESOLUTION OF AN ASSOCIATION OF MINISTERS, CONVENED AT WEYMOUTH [MASSACHUSETTS], JANUARY 15, 1745, CONCERNING THE REV. MR. GEORGE WHITEFIELD. (BOSTON, MA 1745).

[These ministers disapproved of Whitefield's itinerant ministry and his enthusiastic spirit. They believed the congregations were too loud at his meetings. The tone of this resolution was less combative].

Samuel Niles of Braintree, MA
Samuel Brown of Abington, MA
Daniel Perkins of Bridgewater, MA
John Taylor of Milton, MA
Jonathan Bowman of Dorchester, MA
John Fowle of Hingham, MA
Nehemiah Walter of Roxbury, MA
Nathaniel Walter of Roxbury, MA

Nathaniel Eells of Situate, MA
Ebenezer Gay of Hingham, MA
John Angier of Bridgewater, MA
Samuel Dunbar of Stoughton, MA
William Smith of Weymouth, MA
Philip Curtis of Stoughton, MA
James Allen of Brookline, MA

TESTIMONY OF AN ASSOCIATION CONVENED AT MARLBOROUGH, JANUARY 22, 1745, AND THAT OF A NUMBER OF MINISTERS IN THE COUNTY OF BRISTOL. (BOSTON, MA: 1745).

[This is a bitter and mean-spirited rebuke of the Great Awakening in general and of Whitefield in particular. The firmly rejected Whitefield's accusation that many New England ministers were unconverted men, and that Harvard and Yale colleges were unfaithful to the gospel].

John Prentice of Lancaster, MA

Israel Loring of Sudbury, MA

---

[2] Joseph Tracy, *The Great Awakening*, p. 346.

Significant New England Ministers who Publicly Did Not Support George Whitefield and/or the Awakening

Job Cushing of Shrewsbury, MA
William Cooke of Sudbury, MA
John Swift of Acton, MA
Ebenezer Morse of Shrewsbury, MA
Elisha Marsh of Narraganset, NH
John Mellen of Lancaster, MA
John Greenwood of Rehoboth, MA
Ebenezer White of Norton, MA
John Burt of Bristol, RI
John Gardner of Stow, MA
Nathan Stone of Southborough, MA
Aaron Smith of Marlborough, MA
Thomas Goss of Bolton, MA
Joseph Davis of Holden, MA
Joseph Avery of Norton, MA
David Turner of Rehoboth, MA
Solomon Townsend of Barrington, RI

SELECT BIBLIOGRAPHY

PRIMARY SOURCES

Ames, Nathaniel. *Almanacs for 1744 and 1765*. (Boston, MA: R&S Draper, Printers). Courtesy of the American Antiquarian Society, Worcester, MA.

Anonymous. *A Caveat against Unreasonable and Unscriptural Separations*. (Boston, MA: 1748).

Appleton, Nathaniel. *God, and not Ministers to Have the Glory of all Successes to the Preached Gospel*. (Boston: 1741).

Ashley, Jonathan. *The Great Christian Duty of Charity*. (Boston: 1742).

Babson, John J., editor. "Diary of Rev. Samuel Chandler." *Notes and Additions to the History of Gloucester*. (Salem, MA: 1841).

Ballantine, John. *Diary of Rev. John Ballantine*. (Worcester, MA: American Antiquarian Society, transcribed 1886).

Bamberg Cherry F., editor, *The Diary of Capt. Samuel Tillinghast of Warwick, Rhode Island, 1757-1766*. (Rhode Island Historical Society, 2000).

Barnard, John. *Autobiography of John Barnard*. Massachusetts Historical Society Collection, 3rd Series, vol. V (1856).

Bass, John. *A True Narrative of an Unhappy Contention in the Church at Ashford*, (Boston, MA: 1751).

Bentley, William. *The Diary of William Bentley*. (Salem, MA: Essex Institute, 1907).

"Benjamin Colman Papers." Massachusetts Historical Society.

Boston Evening Post.

Boston Gazette.

The Boston Post-Boy.

Boston Weekly Newsletter.

"Boyle's Journal of Occurrences in Boston." *The New England Historical and Genealogical Register*. (Boston, MA: 1930).

Bowen, Ashley. *The Journals of Ashley Bowen of Marblehead*. (Salem, MA: Peabody Museum, 1973).

Brekus, Catherine A. *Sarah Osborn's World: The Rise of Evangelical Christianity in Early America*. (New Haven, CT: Yale University Press, 2013).

A Brief Account of the Late Persecution and Barbarous Usage of the Methodists at Exeter. (Oxford, England: 1745).

A Brief Narrative of Some of the Brethren of the Second Church of Bradford. (Boston: 1746).

Broome, John D. editor. *Life, Ministry, and Journals of Hezekiah Smith, 1737-1805*. (Springfield, MO: Particular Baptist Press, 2004).

Burnham, Jonathan. *The Autobiography of Col. Jonathan Burnham of Salisbury, Massachusetts.* (Portsmouth, NH: S. Whidden, Printer, 1814).

Burt, Henry M. *The First Century of the History of Springfield, Massachusetts, the Official Records from 1636 to 1736.* (Springfield, MA: Henry M. Burt, Printer, 1898).

Canonicus. *A Letter to the Rev. George Whitefield.* (Boston, MA: 1743).

Canonicus. *A Second Letter to the Rev. Mr. George Whitefield.* (Boston, MA: 1745).

Chauncey, Charles. "Original Letters of Charles Chauncey." *The New England Historical and Genealogical Register.* (Vol. X, 1859).

Chauncey, Charles. *Seasonable Thoughts on the State of Religion in New England.* (Boston, MA: 1743).

The Christian History, (Boston: 1742-1744).

Cleveland, John. "To the Inhabitants of New England." *Essex Gazette.* April 1775.

Cleveland, Mary. "Journal of Mary Cleveland." *John Cleveland Papers.* (Salem, MA: Essex Institute Historical Folders).

Connecticut Gazette.

The Connecticut Journal and New Haven Post-Boy.

Cutler, William and Julia Cutler, editors. *Life, Journals, and Correspondence of Rev. Manasseh Cutler.* (Cincinnati, OH: Robert Clarke & Company, 1888).

Davenport, James. *The Rev. Mr. Davenport's Confession.* (Boston, MA: 1744).

Dean, John W. *Memoir of Rev. Michael Wigglesworth . . . .* (New York: Joel Munsell Printer, 1871).

The Declaration of the Rector and Tutors of Yale College in New Haven, against the Rev. Mr. George Whitefield . . . . (Boston, MA: 1745).

"Diary of Ebenezer Storer, 1749-1764." *Congregational Library and Archives.* https://www.congregational library.org/nehh/series 2/StorerEbenezer.

"Diary of John Whiting of Dedham, Massachusetts, 1743-1784." *The New England Historical and Genealogical Register.* (Boston, MA: Published by the Society. 1909).

"Diary of Rev. Jacob Eliot." *The Historical Magazine . . . Concerning the Antiquities, History and Biography of America.* (January 1869).

"Diary of Rev. Samuel Dexter." *The New England Historical and Genealogical Register.* (Boston, MA: Samuel G. Drake, Publisher, 1860).

Diary of Zaccheus Collins of Lynn, 1726-1769. (Original manuscript courtesy of the Peabody Essex Museum, Phillips Library, Rowley, MA).

Dow, George F., compiler. "Diary of Mrs. Mary (Vial) Holyoke, 1760-1800." *The Holyoke Diaries, 1709-1856.* (Salem, MA: The Essex Institute, 1911).

Early Records of the Town of Worcester. (Book II, 1740-1753: Worcester, MA: 1880).

Edwards, Jonathan. *A Faithful Narrative of the Surprising Work of God in the Conversion of many hundred Souls in Northampton, and the Neighboring Towns and Villages of New Hampshire . . . .* (Boston: 1738).

Edwards, Jonathan. *Letters and Personal Writings of Rev. Jonathan Edwards.* (New Haven, CT: Yale University Press), vol. 16.

Edwards, Jonathan. *A Sermon Preached in Portsmouth at the Ordination of Job Strong, June 28, 1749.* (Boston, MA: 1750).

Edwards, Jonathan. *Some Thoughts Concerning the Present Revival of Religion in New England, and the way in Which it ought to be Acknowledged and Promoted . . . .* (Boston: 1743).

Edwards, Jonathan. *The Great Christian Doctrine of Original Sin Defended: Evidence of its Truth Produced, and Arguments of the Contrary Answered.* (Stockbridge, MA: 1757).

Emerson, Joseph. *Diary Kept at the Siege of Louisburg, March 15-August 14, 1745.* (Cambridge, England: University Press, 1910).

Fiske, Nathan. *Rev. Nathan Fiske Papers, 1750-1799,* (Worcester, MA: American Antiquarian Society).

Fletcher, Reuben. *The Lamentable State of Religion in New England.* (Boston, 1772).

Fuller, Arthur. *An Historical Discourse Delivered in the New North Church, October 1, 1854.* (Boston, MA: Crosby, Nichols & Company, 1854).

Gee, Joshua. *A Letter to the Rev. Mr. Nathaniel Eells, Moderator of the Late Convention of Pastors in Boston.* (Boston, MA: 1743).

Gilmore, Evelyn L. *Christ Church, Gardiner, Maine: Antecedents and History.* (Gardner, ME: The Reporter-Journal Press, 1893).

Gorman, William M. editor. *The Works of Rev. David McGregor (MacGregore), 1710-1770.* (Westminster, MD: Heritage Books, 2009).

Heaton, Hannah. *The World of Hannah Heaton: The Diary of an Eighteenth Century New England Farm Woman.* Edited by Barbara E. Lacey. (1793: reprinted by Northern Illinois University Press, 2003).

Hempstead, Joshua. *Diary of Joshua Hempstead of New London, Connecticut.* (New London, CT: New London County Historical Society

Henchman, Nathaniel. *A Letter from the Rev. Nathaniel Henchman, Pastor of the First Church in Lynn, to the Rev. Stephen Chase, of Lynn End, giving his reasons for declining to admit the Rev. George Whitefield into His Pulpit.* (Boston, MA: 1744).

Henchman, Nathaniel. *A Letter to the Rev. Mr. William Hobby.* (Boston, MA: 1745).

Historical Collections of the Essex Institute. (Salem, MA).

Hopkins, Samuel. *The Works of Samuel Hopkins.* (Boston: Doctrinal Tract and Book Society, 1852).

Holyoke, Edward. *The Duty of Ministers of the Gospel to Guard against the Pharisaism and Sadduceeism of the Present Day.* (Boston, MA: 1741).

Holyoke, Edward. *The Testimony of the President, Professors, Tutors, and Hebrew Instructor of Harvard College in Cambridge against the Rev. Mr. George Whitefield.* (Boston, MA: 1744).

Hobby, William. *Self-Examination in its Necessity and Advantages Urged and Applied in Sunday Sermons.* (Boston, MA: S. Kneeland and T. Green, 1746).

Jewett, Frederic C. *History and Genealogy of the Jewetts in America.* (New York: The Grafton Press, 1908).

Judd, Jonathan. *Diary of Rev. Jonathan Judd, 1742-1801.* Courtesy of the First Congregational Church of Southampton, Massachusetts.

Karlsen, Carol and Laurie Crumpacker, editors. *The Journal of Esther Edwards Burr, 1754-1757.* (New Haven CT: Yale University Press, 1984).

A Letter to the Rev. Mr. William Hobby, a Pastor of a Church in Reading, being a Gentle and Necessary Correction of Him for His . . . Defense of the Itinerancy and the Conduct of the Rev. Mr. George Whitefield. (Boston, MA: 1745).

Letter to the Rev. Mr. William Hobby, Pastor of the First Church in Reading. (Boston, MA: 1745).

Letter from Rev. Jonathan Edwards to Rev. Ebenezer Wheelock, October 9, 1740. (History Room, Forbes Library, Northampton, MA).

Loring, Israel. *Journal of Israel Loring.* Unpublished Journal, Connecticut Historical Society Special Collections.

Loring, Israel. *The Journal of Rev. Israel Loring (1682-1772) of Sudbury, Massachusetts, Covering his Early Life and the Years 1704-1745.* L.P. Thomas, editor. (Sudbury, MA Public Library).

Lyon, Benjamin. *Diary of Benjamin Lyon, 1729-1769.* (Hartford, CT: Connecticut Historical Society).

MacSparron, James. *A Letter Book and Abstract of Out Services, 1743-1751.* (Boston, MA: Merrymount Press, 1899).

Jay, William, compiler. *Memoirs of the Life and Character of the Late Cornelius Winter.* (Philadelphia, PA: B. Redman, Printer, 1823).

Mather, Cotton. *Diary of Cotton Mather, 1681-1724.* (Boston, MA: Massachusetts Historical Society, 1911).

McClure, David and Elijah Parish. *Memoirs of the Rev. Eleazar Wheelock, Founder and President of Dartmouth College . . . .* (Newburyport, MA: Edward Little Printer, 1811).

"Memoir of the Rev. John Callender, A.M." *Collections of the Rhode Island Historical Society.* (Providence, RI, 1838).

Murray, John. *The Life of the Rev. John Murray, Preacher of Universal Salvation.* (Boston, MA: Universalist Publishing House, 1869).

Nelson, Dan. *A Burning and Shining Light: The Testimony and Witness of George Whitefield.* (Somis, CA: LifeSong Publishers, 2017).

The New England Historical and Genealogical Record.

New London Gazette.

Newport Mercury.

"Notes from the Rev. Samuel Cooper's Interleaved Almanacs of 1764 and 1769." *The New England Historical and Genealogical Register.* (Boston, MA: 1901).

Occum, Samson. *The Collected Writings of Samson Occum.* (Oxford, England: Oxford University Press, 2006).

Paine, Robert T. "Robert Treat Paine Papers." *Massachusetts Historical Society.* https://www.masshist.org/publications/rtpp/index.php/view/RTP1d196.

Parkman, Ebenezer. *The Diary of Ebenezer Parkman, 1754-1755.* (Worcester, MA: American Antiquarian Society, n.d.).

Parsons, Jonathan. *Freedom from Civil and Ecclesiastical Slavery.* (Newburyport, MA: 1774).

Parsons, Jonathan. *A Funeral-Sermon on the Death of Mr. George Whitefield.* (Portsmouth, NH: 1770).

Pickering, Theophilus. *Mr. Pickering's Letter to Mr. Whitefield . . . .* (Boston, MA: 1745).

Pickering, Theophilus. *Letters to the Rev. Mr. Nathaniel and Mr. Daniel Rogers of Ipswich.* (Boston, MA: 1742).

Pickman, Benjamin. *The Diary and Letters of Benjamin Pickman of Salem, Massachusetts, 1740-1819.* (Newport, RI: Southworth Press, 1929).

A Plain Narrative of the Proceedings which Caused the Separation of a Number of Aggrieved Brethren from Second Church in Ipswich. (Boston, MA: 1747).

"Plymouth Church Records." *Publications of the Colonial Society of Massachusetts.* (Boston, MA: Published by the Society, 1920).

Prince, Thomas. *The Christian History.* (Boston, MA: 1743).

The Providence Gazette.

The Result of a Council of Ten Churches, Convened at Exeter, January 31, 1743. (Boston: 1744).

The Sentiments and Resolution of an Association of Ministers Convened at Weymouth, January 15, 1745, Concerning the Rev. Mr. George Whitefield's Preaching in the New England Churches. (Boston, MA: 1745).

Shurtleff, William. *A Letter to those of His Brethren in the Ministry Who Refuse to Admit the Rev. Mr. George Whitefield into Their Pulpits.* (Boston, MA: 1745).

Some Reasons Given by the Western Association upon the Merrimack River, Why they Disapprove of the Rev. Mr. George Whitefield's Preaching in the New England Churches. (Boston, MA: 1745).

"Relation of Samuel Fayerweather, May 24, 1741." *Records of the First Church in Boston.* Colonial Society of Massachusetts, publications XXXIX-XL (Boston, A: 1961).

Reynolds, James B, Samuel Fisher, Henry B. Wright. *Two Centuries of Christian Activity at Yale.* (New York: G.P. Putnam's Sons, 1901).

Rowe, John. *Letters and Diaries of John Rowe, Boston Merchant, 1759-1762, 1764-1779.* (Boston, MA: W.B. Clarke & Company, 1903).

Second Congregational Church Records 1733-1834. (Newport Historical Society, Vol. 5).

Seccombe, Joseph. *Occasional Thoughts on the Influence of the Spirit with Seasonable Caution against Mistakes and Abuses.* (Boston, MA: 1742).

Seccombe, Joseph. *Reflections on Hypocrisy.* (Boston, MA: 1741).

Steere, Thomas. *History of the Town of Smithfield, from its Organization in 1731, to its Division, in 1871.* (Providence, RI: E.L. Freedman, Printer, 1881).

Stiles, Ezra. *Extracts from the Itineraries and other Miscellanies of Ezra Stiles, D.D. 1755-1794.* (New Haven, CT: Yale University Press, 1916).

Stiles, Ezra. *The Literary Diary of Ezra Stiles.* (New York: Charles Scribner's Sons, 1901).

Smith, Thomas. *Journal of the Rev. Thomas Smith.* (Portland, ME: Joseph E. Bailey, Printer, 1849).

Stone, Edwin M. *History of Beverly, Civil and Ecclesiastical.* (Boston, MA: J. Monroe & Company, 1843).

Tagney, Ronald A. *The World Turned Upside Down: Essex County during America's Turbulent Years, 1763-1790.* (West Newbury, MA: Essex County History, 1989).

The Testimony and Advice of an Assembly of Pastors and Churches in New England, at a Meeting in Boston, July 7, 1743, Occasioned by the Late and Happy Revival of Religion in the Land. (Boston, MA: 1743).

The Testimony and Advice of a Number of Laymen. (Boston, MA: 1743).

The Testimony and Advice of a Number of Pastors and Churches in New England, at a Meeting in Boston, July 7, 1743, Occasioned by the Late Happy Revivals of Religion in the Land. (Boston, MA: 1743).

The Testimony of an Association of Ministers Convened at Marlboro, Jan. 22, 1744-45, against the Rev. Mr. George Whitefield and His Conduct .... (Boston, 1745).

The Testimony of a Number of Ministers Convened at Taunton, in the County of Bristol, March 5, 1745, in Favor of the Rev. Mr. Whitefield, &c. Giving Reasons of their Inviting Him into their Pulpits .... (Boston, MA: 1745).

Tudor, John. *Deacon Tudor's Diary ... A Record of More or Less Important Events in Boston, from 1732 to 1793, by an Eyewitness.* (Boston, MA: Press of Wallace Spooner, 1896).

Wadsworth, Daniel. *Diary of Rev. Daniel Wadsworth, Seventh Pastor of the First Church of Christ in Hartford, Connecticut.* (Hartford, CT: Press of the Case, Lockwood & Brainard Company, 1894).

Webb, Jonathan. *The Great Concern of New England.* (Boston, MA: 1743).

Webster, Samuel. *A Winter Evening's Conversation Upon the Doctrine of Original Sin.* (Boston, MA: 1757).

Wheatley, Phillis. "On the Death of Rev. Mr. George Whitefield." (Boston: 1770). https://allpoetry.com/On-the-Death-of-Rev.-Mr.-George-Whitefield,-1770.

Wheelock, Eleazer. "Extracts from the Private Journal of the Rev. Eleazer Wheelock," in Joseph Tracy, *The Great Awakening: A History of the Revival of Religion in the Time of Edwards & Whitefield.* (1842: Carlisle, PA: Banner of Truth Trust, 1989).

Whitaker, Nathaniel. *A Funeral Sermon, on the Death of the Reverend George Whitefield . . . Preached in Salem on Wednesday the 27th of October Following, by Nathaniel Whitaker, Pastor of a Church of Christ in Salem.* (Salem, MA: 1770).

Whitefield, George. *George Whitefield's Journals.* (1751: reprinted by Banner of Truth Trust, Carlisle, PA: 1960).

Whitefield, George. *A Letter to the Reverend President and Professors . . . of Harvard College in Cambridge . . . .* (Boston, MA: 1745).

Whitefield, George. *Ten Sermons Preached on Important Subjects.* (Portsmouth, NH: Pierce & Larkin Printers, 1797).

Whitefield, George. *Works of George Whitefield.* (1771: reprinted by Quinta Press, Shropshire, England, 2000).

Wigglesworth, Edward. *A Letter to the Reverend Mr. George Whitefield, by way of Reply to His Answer to the College Testimony against Him . . . .* (Boston, MA: 1745).

Williams, Stephen. *Diary of Rev. Stephen Williams, Longmeadow, Massachusetts.* (Longmeadow, MA: Richard S. Storrs Library, 2011).

Williamson, William D. "Sketches of the Lives or Early Maine Ministers." *Maine Historical Society.* (Portland, ME: 1894).

SECONDARY SOURCES

Ahlstrom, Sidney E. *A Religious History of the American People.* (New Haven, CT: Yale University Press, 1972).

Allen, Charles E. *Rev. Jacob Bailey: His Character and Works.* (Lincoln County Historical Society, 1895).

Allen, Myron O. *The History of Wenham, Civil and Ecclesiastical.* (Boston, MA: Barfin & Chandler, 1860).

Andrews, John R. *George Whitefield: A Light Rising in Obscurity.* (1879: reprinted by Elibron Classics, London, England, 2005).

Andrews, William G. *A History of Christ Episcopal Church in Guilford, Connecticut . . . .* (Guilford, CT: The Echo Press, 1895).

Askew, Thomas A. and Peter W. Spellman. *The Churches and the American Experience.* (Grand Rapids, MI: Baker Book House, 1984).

Atkinson, Minnie. *A History of the First Religious Society in Newburyport, Massachusetts.* (Newburyport, MA: News Publishing Company, 1933).

Atwater, Edward E. *History of the Colony of New Haven . . . Connecticut.* (New Haven, CT: Printed for the Author, 1881).

Babson, John J. *History of Gloucester, Cape Ann, Massachusetts.* (Gloucester, MA: Proctor Brothers Printing, 1860).

Backus, Isaac. *A History of New England, with Particular Reference to the Denomination of Christians Called Baptists.* (Newton, MA: Backus Historical Society, 1871).

Bacon, Leonard. *Thirteen Historical Discourses, on the Completion of Two Hundred Years: From the Beginning of the First Church in New Haven.* (New Haven, CT: Durrie and Peck Publishers, 1839).

Bailey, Sarah L. *Historical Sketches of Andover, Massachusetts.* (Boston, MA: Houghton & Mifflin and Company, 1880).

Baker, Henry A. *History of Montville, Connecticut . . . 1640 to 1896.* (Hartford, CT: Press of the Case, Lockwood & Brainard Company, 1896).

Baptisms, Marriages, Burials, and List of Members Taken from the Church Records of the Rev. Ammi Ruhamah Robbins, First Minister of Norfolk, Connecticut, 1761-1813. (Norfolk, CT: 1910).

Barry, William. *A History of Framingham, Massachusetts . . . .* (Carlisle, PA: Applewood Books, 1847).

Bartlett, William S. *The Frontier Missionary: A Memoir of the Life of the Rev. Jacob Bailey.* (New York: Stanford and Sword, 1853).

Belcher, Joseph. *George Whitefield: A Biography with Special Reference to His Labors in America.* (New York: American Tract Society, 1857).

Belden, Albert D. *George Whitefield—The Awakener.* (London, England: Sampson, Low Marston and Company, 1930).

Bell, Charles H. *History of the Town of Exeter, New Hampshire.* (Exeter, NH: The Quarter-Millennial Year, 1888).

Bemis, Charles A. *History of the Town of Marlborough, Cheshire County, New Hampshire.* (Boston, MA: Press of George H. Ellis, 1881).

Bicknell, Thomas W. *History of the State of Rhode Island and Providence Plantations.* (New York: The American Historical Society, 1920).

Billings, Thomas H. *The Great Awakening.* (Salem, MA: Essex Institute, 1930).

Billingsley, A.S. *The Life of the Great Preacher, Rev. George Whitefield.* (Chicago, IL: J.S. Ziegler & Company, 1889).

Bissell, Frederic C. *Hebron, Connecticut Bicentennial, August 23 to 25, 1908.* (Hebron, CT: 1910).

Blaikie, Alexander. *A History of Presbyterianism in New England . . . .* (Boston, MA: Alexander Moore, Publisher).

Bonomi, Patricia. *Under the Cope of Heaven: Religion, Society, and Politics in Colonial America.* (New York: Oxford University Press, 2003).

Bourne, Edward E. *A History of Wells and Kennebunkport, from the earliest Settlement to the Year 1820.* (Portland, ME: B. Thurston Company, 1875).

Bowen, Clarence W. *Woodstock: An Historical Sketch.* (New York: G.P. Putnam's Sons, 1886).

Bradbury, Charles. *History of Kennebunk Port, from its First Discovery.* (Kennebunk, ME: James K. Remich, Printer, 1837).

Brewster, Charles. W. *Rambles about Portsmouth: Sketches of Persons, Localities, and Incidents of Two Centuries.* (Portsmouth, NH: C.W. Brewster & Son, Printer, 1859).

Brockway, Robert W. *A Wonderful Work of God: Puritanism and the Great Awakening in America . . . .* (Philadelphia, PA: Joseph M. Wilson, Publisher, 1857).

Brooks, Charles. *History of the Town of Medford, Middlesex County, Massachusetts . . . .* (Boston, MA: James M. Usher, Publisher, 1855).

Brown, Warren. *History of Hampton Falls, N.H.* (Concord, NH: The Rumford Press, 1918).

Budington, William I. *The History of First Church Charleston . . . .* (Boston, MA: Charles Tappan Printer, 1845).

Bushman, Richard. *The Great Awakening: Documents on the Revival of Religion, 1740-1745.* (Chapel Hill, NC: North Carolina Press, 1969).

Bushman, Richard L. *From Puritan to Yankee: Character and the Social Order in Connecticut, 1690-1765.* (Cambridge, MA: Harvard University Press, 1967).

Buzzell, John, editor. *The Life of Elder Benjamin Randall.* (Limerick, ME: Published by Hobbs, Woodman and Company, 1827).

Byington, Ezra H. *The Puritan in England and New England.* (Boston, MA: Roberts Brothers Printers, 1896).

Caldwell, Mark M. *George Whitefield: Preacher to Millions.* (Anderson, IN: The Warner Press, 1929).

Candee, Richard M. *Building Portsmouth: The Neighborhoods and Architecture of New Hampshire's Oldest City.* (Portsmouth, NH: Back Channel Press, 2006).

Cashin, Edward J. *Beloved Bethesda: A History of George Whitefield's Home for Boys, 1740-2000.* (Macon, GA: Mercer University Press, 2001).

Catalfo, Alfred. *The History of the Town of Rollingsford, New Hampshire, 1623-1973.* (Rollingsford, NH: New Hampshire Printers, 1973).

Caulkins, Frances M. *History of Norwich, Connecticut; from its Possession by the Indians to the Year 1866.* (Hartford, CT: Lockwood & Brainard Press, 1873).

Caulkins, Frances M. *History of New London, Connecticut* . . . . (New London, CT: Published by the Author, 1860).

Chaffin, William. *History of the Town of Easton, Massachusetts.* (Cambridge, MA: John Wilson & Sons Printers, 1866).

Chamberlain, Mellen. *A Documentary History of Chelsea . . . 1624-1824.* (Boston, MA: Massachusetts Historical Society, 1908).

Chandler, George. *The Chandler Family: The Descendants of William and Annis Chandler* . . . . (Worcester, MA: Press of Charles Hamilton, 1883).

Chase, George W. *The History of Haverhill, Massachusetts: from its Settlement, in 1640, to the Year 1860.* (Haverhill, MA: Published by the Author, 1861).

Chenoweth, Caroline V.D. *History of the Second Congregational Church and Society in Leicester, Massachusetts.* (Worcester, MA: Commonwealth Press, 1908).

Churchill, John W. *History of the First Church in Dunstable-Nashua, New Hampshire* . . . . (Boston, MA: The Fort Hill Press, 1918).

Clayton, W. Woodford. *History of York County, Maine: with Illustrations and Biographical Sketches.* (Philadelphia, PA: Everts & Peck Printing, 1880).

Coffin, Joshua. *A Sketch of the History of Newbury, Newburyport, and West Newbury.* (Boston, MA: Samuel G. Drake, Publisher, 1845).

Collections and Proceedings of the Maine Historical Society. (Portland, ME: Published by the Society, 1894).

Collections Historical and Miscellaneous, New Hampshire Historical Society. (Concord, NH: J.B. Moore, Publisher, 1823).

Collections of the Maine Historical Society and Proceedings. (Portland, ME: Published by the Society, 1893).

Collections of the Massachusetts Historical Society. (Boston, MA Printed by Phelps and Farnham, 1823).

Concise History of the First Church of Christ, in Ipswich, from its Formation in A.D. 1634, to A.D. 1862 . . . . (Boston, MA: Wright & Potter, Printers, 1862).

Corey, Deloraine P. *The History of Malden, Massachusetts, 1633-1785.* (Malden, MA: Printed by the Author, 1899).

Contributions to the Ecclesiastical History of Connecticut . . . . (New Haven, CT: William Kingsley Publisher, 1861).

Contributions to the Ecclesiastical History of Essex County, Massachusetts. (Boston, MA: Congregational Board of Publications, 1865).

Copeland, M.T. and E.C. Rogers. *The Saga of Cape Ann.* (Freeport, ME: The Bond Wheelwright Company, 1963).

Corey, Deloraine P. *The History of Malden, Massachusetts 1633-1785.* (Malden, MA: Published by the Author, 1899).

Corliss, Augustus. *Old Times: North Yarmouth, Maine.* (Somersworth, ME: New Hampshire Publishing Company, 1977).

Craig, Lawrence W. *A History of the South Church and Parish (Unitarian) and Universalist Church . . . in Portsmouth, New Hampshire.* (Portsmouth, NH: 1966).

Crane, Ellery B., editor. *Historic Homes and Institutions and Genealogical and Personal Memories of Worcester County, Massachusetts.* (New York: The Lewis Publishing Company, 1907).

Crisp Oliver D. and Douglas A. Sweeney. *After Jonathan Edwards: The Courses of New England Theology.* (New York: Oxford University Press, 2012).

Crissey, Theron W. *History of Norfolk, Litchfield County, Connecticut 1744-1900.* (Everett, MA: Massachusetts Publishing Company, 1900).

Currier, John J. *History of Beverly, Civil and Ecclesiastical.* (Boston, MA: J. Monroe and Company, 1843).

Currier, John J. *Old Newbury: Historical and Biographical Sketches.* (Newbury, MA: Damrell and Upham, 1896).

Cushing, James S. *The Genealogy of the Cushing Family . . . who Came to America in 1638.* (Montreal, Canada: Perrault Printing, 1905).

Cutter, William R., editor. *New England Families, Genealogical and Memorial.* (New York: Lewis Historical Publishing Company, 1913).

Dallimore, Arnold. *George Whitefield: The Life and Times of the Great Evangelist of the Eighteenth Century Revival.* (Carlisle, PA: Banner of Truth Trust, 1980).

Davis, Charles H.S. *History of Wallingford, Connecticut* .... (Meriden, CT: Published by the Author, 1870).

Davis, Emerson. *A Historical Sketch of Westfield.* (Westfield, MA: Joseph Root Publishers, 1826).

Davis, Felix G. and Grace S. Durfee. *The History of Amicable Congregational Church, 1746-1946.* (Tiverton, RI: 1946).

Dean, Benjamin A. *Annals of the Brentwood, N.H. Congregational Church and Parish.* (Boston, MA: Press of T.W. Riley, 1889).

Denison, Frederic. *Westerly, Rhode Island and its Witnesses: for Two Hundred and Fifty Years, 1626-1876.* (Providence, RI: Reid Publishers, 1876).

Dexter, Franklin B. *Historical Catalogue of the Members of the First Church of Christ in New Haven, Connecticut (Center Church), 1634-1914.* (New Haven, CT: 1914).

Dion, Frances. *Upon this Rock: A History of the Community Congregational Church, Greenland, New Hampshire.* (Portsmouth, NH: Strawberry Bank Print Shop, 1956).

Doggett, John. *A Sketch of the History of Attleboro* .... (Boston, MA: Press of Samuel Usher, 1894).

Dow, George F. *Two Centuries of Travel in Essex County, Massachusetts, 1605-1799.* (Topsfield, MA: Topsfield Historical Society, 1921).

Drake, Samuel A. *The Making of New England, 1580-1643.* (New York: Charles Scribner's Sons, 1886).

Dutton, Samuel W.S. *The History of North Church in New Haven* .... (New Haven, CT: A.H. Maltry Publisher, 1842).

Eaton, Lilley. *Genealogical History of the Town of Reading, Massachusetts* .... (Boston, MA: Alfred Mudge & Son, Printers, 1874).

Ellis, Theo W. *Manual of the First Church of Christ and Names of all the Members: from the Year 1735 to Nov. 1, 1885.* (Springfield, MA: Springfield Printing Company, 1885).

Emery. Samuel H. *The Ministry of Taunton.* (Boston, MA: John P. Jewett Publisher, 1853).

Ewell, John L. *The Story of Byfield: A New England Parish.* (Boston, MA: George W. Littleton, 1904).

Fassett, James H. *Early History of Nashua, New Hampshire* .... (Nashua, NH: Telegraph Publishing Company, 1915).

Felt, Joseph B. *Annals of Salem.* (Boston, MA: James Monroe and Company, 1945).

Felt, Joseph B. *History of Ipswich, Essex, and Hamilton.* (Cambridge, MA: Folston Printers, 1834).

The First Centenary of the North Church and Society in Salem, Massachusetts. (Salem, MA: Printed for the Society, 1873).

The First Church in Exeter, New Hampshire: 1638-1888. (Exeter, NH: Printed for the Parish, 1898).

First Church in Middleboro, Mass ... A Historical Account .... (Boston, MA: Published by the Church, 1854).

Fisher, George P. *Discourse Commemorative of the History of the Church of Christ in Yale College ... Preached in the College Chapel November 22, 1857.* (New Haven, CT: T.J. Stafford, Printer, 1857).

Fletcher, Edward H. *The Descendants of Robert Fletcher of Concord, Mass.* (Boston, MA: Printed for the Author, 1881).

Flint, Jacob. *Two Discourses Containing the History of the Church and Society in Cohasset* .... (Boston, MA: Munroe and Francis Publishers, 1822).

Folsom, George. *History of Saco and Biddeford; with Notices of other Early Settlements* .... (Saco, ME: Alex C. Putnam Printer, 1830).

Foster, Frank H. *A Genetic History of the New England Theology.* (Chicago, IL: The University of Chicago Press, 1907).

Fox, Charles J. *History of the Old Township of Dunstable: Including Nashua, Nashville, Hollis, Litchfield, and Merrimack, New Hampshire.* (Nashua, NH: Charles T. Gill, Publisher, 1846).

Frothingham, Richard Jr. *The History of Charleston, Massachusetts.* (Charleston, MA: Charles P. Emmond, Printer, 1845).

Fuess, Claude M. *Andover: Symbol of New England.* (Portland, ME: The Antheoeson Press, 1959).

Fuess, Claude M. *The Story of Essex County.* (New York: The American Historical Society, 1935).

Gage, Thomas and James Bradford. *The History of Rowley: Anciently Including Bradford, Boxford, and Georgetown.* (Boston, MA: Ferdinand Andrews Printer, 1840).

Gaustad, Edwin S. and Mark A. Noll, editors. *A Documentary History of Religion in America to 1877.* (Grand Rapids, MI: Eerdman's Publishing, 2003).

Gaustad, Edwin S. *The Great Awakening in New England.* (New York: Harper & Brothers, 1957).

Geake, Robert A. *A History of the Narragansett Tribe of Rhode Island.* (Charleston, SC: History Press, 2011).

Gibson, William and Thomas W. Smith. *George Whitefield: Tercentenary Essays.* (University of Whales Press, 2015.

Gillis, Jennifer B. *Life in Colonial Boston.* (Chicago, IL: Heinemann Library, 2003).

Gilles, John. *Memoirs of Rev. George Whitefield.* (1772: reprinted by Hunt & Noyes Publishers, Middletown, CT: 1836).

Gillespie, C. Bancroft, compiler. *An Historical Record and Pictorial Description of the Town of Meriden, Connecticut.* (Meriden, CT: Journal Publishing Company, 1906).

Gledstone, J.P. *George Whitefield: Supreme among Preachers.* (1900: reprinted by Ambassador Publications, Belfast, Ireland, 1998).

Gold, Theodore S. *Historical Records of the Town of Cornwall, Litchfield County, Connecticut.* (Hartford, CT: Case, Lockwood & Brainard Press, 1877).

Goodenough, Arthur. *The Clergy of Litchfield County* [Connecticut]. (Litchfield County University Club, 1909).

The Gospel Advocate . . . for the Year 1822. (Boston, MA: Joseph W. Ingram, Printer, 1822).

Gray, Edward. *William Gray of Salem, Merchant, with Biographical Sketches.* (Boston, MA: Houghton, Mifflin and Company, 1914).

Green, Samuel A. *The Natural History and the Topography of Groton, Massachusetts.* (Cambridge, MA: University Press, 1912).

Greven, Philip J. *Four Generations: population, Land and Family in Colonial Andover, Massachusetts.* (Ithica, NY: Cornell University Press, 1970).

Griffin, Edward M. *Old Brick: Charles Chauncey of Boston, 1705-1787.* (Minneapolis, MN: University of Minnesota Press, 1980).

Gurney. Caleb S. *Portsmouth, Historic and Picturesque . . . .* (Portsmouth, NH: Published by the Author, 1902).

Hammett, Charles E. *A Contribution to the Bibliography and Literature of Newport, R.I.* (Newport, RI: Published by the Author, 1887).

Hammett, Charles E. *A Sketch of the History of the Congregational Churches of Newport, Rhode Island, from the Records and Other Sources.* (Newport Historical Society, 1891.

Hammond, George and David C. Jones. *George Whitefield: Life, Context, and Legacy.* (Oxford University Press, 2016).

Harsha, D.A. *The Life of the Rev. George Whitefield and Rev. James Hervey.* (Albany, NY: Nursell Company, 1886).

Harlan, David. *The Clergy and the Great Awakening in New England.* (UMI Research Press, 1980).

Hawk, David. *The Colonial Experience.* (New York: MacMillan Publishing Company, 1885).

Haykin, Michael A.G. *George Whitefield.* (Grand Rapids, MI: EP Books, 2014).

Hazen, Azel W. *A Brief History of the First Church of Christ in Middletown, Connecticut, 1668-1918.* (Middletown, CT: Russell Library, 1918).

Henry, Stuart C. *George Whitefield: Wayfaring Witness.* (New York: Abington Press, 1957).

Hill, Hamilton A. *A History of the Old South Church (Third Church).* (Boston, MA: Riverdale Press, 1890).

Hill, John B. *Bi-Centennial of Old Dunstable . . . .* (Nashua, NH: E.H. Spalding Publisher, 1878).

An Historical Review: One Hundred and Fiftieth Anniversary of the First Church of Christ in Amherst, Massachusetts. (Amherst, MA: Amherst Record Press, 1890).

Historical Sketch, Articles of Faith, and Covenants of the Original Congregational Church, in Wrentham, Mass. (Boston, MA: S.N. Dickinson & Company Printers, 1845).

Historical Manual of the Congregational Church in Topsfield, Massachusetts, 1663-1907. (Topsfield, MA: Published by the Church, 1907).

History of the First Church in Marlborough (Congregational), United Church of Christ on the Occasion of its Three Hundred and Fiftieth Anniversary, 1666-2016. (Marlborough, MA: Printed by the First Church Congregational, 2017).

History of the First Congregational Church of Westfield, Mass. (Printed for the church, 1979).

History of Litchfield and an Account of its Centennial Celebration, 1895. (Augusta, ME: Kennebec Journal Printers, 1897).

History of Litchfield, Hillsborough County, New Hampshire. (Philadelphia, PA: J.W. Lewis & Company, 1885).

Hoffer, Peter C. *When Benjamin Franklin met the Reverend George Whitefield.* (Baltimore, MD: The Johns Hopkins University Press, 2011).

Hopkins, Samuel. *Memoirs of the Life of Mrs. Sarah Osborn, who Died at Newport, Rhode Island on the Second day of August, 1796 . . .* (Worcester, MA: Leonard Worcester, Printer, 1799).

Hovey, Horace C. *Origin and Annals of "Old South" Presbyterian Church and Parish in Newburyport, Mass., 1746-1896.* (Boston, MA: Damrell & Upham Printers, 1896).

Hudson, Alfred S. *The History of Sudbury, Massachusetts, 1638-1889.* (Published by the Town of Sudbury, 1889).

Hudson, David. *History of Jemima Wilkinson: a Preacheress of the Eighteenth Century.* (Geneva, NY: S.P. Hull, Printers, 1821).

Hudson, Charles. *History of the Town of Marlborough, Middlesex County, Massachusetts . . . .* (Boston, MA: T.R. Marvin & Sons, Publishers, 1862).

Hughes, Paul C., Anna Hughes, and Paul F. Hughes. *A Pleasant Abiding Place: A History of Greenland, New Hampshire.* (Greenland Historical Society, 2018).

Hunnewell, James F. *A Century of Town Life: A History of Charlestown, Massachusetts . . . .* (Boston, MA: Little, Brown & Company, 1888).

Hurd, D. Hamilton. *History of Bristol County, Massachusetts, with Biographical Sketches . . . .* (Philadelphia, PA: J.W. Lewis & Company, 1883).

Hurd, D. Hamilton. *History of Essex County, Massachusetts.* (Philadelphia, PA: J.W. Lewis & Company, 1888).

Hurd, D. Hamilton. *History of New London County, Connecticut, with Biographical Sketches . . . .* (Philadelphia, PA: J.W. Lewis & Company Printers, 1882).

Hurd, D. Hamilton. *History of Plymouth, Massachusetts, with Biographical Sketches . . . .* (Philadelphia, PA: J.W. Lewis & Company, 1884).

Hurd, D. Hamilton. *History of Rockingham and Strafford Counties, New Hampshire, with Biographical Sketches.* (Philadelphia, PA: J.W. Lewis & Company, 1882).

Jackson, Francis. *A History of the Early Settlement of Newton . . . Massachusetts . . . from 1639 to 1800.* (Boston, MA: Stacy and Richardson Printers, 1854).

Jedrey, Christopher M. *The World of John Cleveland of Ipswich, Massachusetts.* (New York: W.W. Norton & Company, 1979).

Johnstone, John. *Sketches of the Life and Labors of the Rev. George Whitefield.* (Edinburg, Scotland: General Assembly of the Free Church of Scotland, 1759).

Jones, Douglas J. *History of Newbury, Massachusetts, 1635-1902.* (Boston, MA: Dawcell and Upham, 1902).

Jones, Douglas L. *Villages and Seaports: Migration and Society in Eighteenth Century Massachusetts.* (Boston, MA: University of New England Press, 1981).

Johnson, Donald B. *Upton's Heritage: The History of a Massachusetts Town.* (Published by the Town of Upton, 1984).

Judd, Sylvester. *History of Hadley . . . , Massachusetts.* (Springfield, MA: H.R. Hunting & Company, 1905).

Katz, Stanley and John Murin, editors. *Colonial America; Histories in Politics and Social Development.* (New York: A.A. Knopf, Inc., 1983).

Kelley, Brooks M. *Yale: A History.* (New Haven, CT: Yale University Press, 1999).

The Kennebunkport Register, 1904. (Brunswick, ME: Published by H.E. Mitchell, 1904).

Kidd, Thomas S. *American Colonial History: Clashing Cultures and Faiths.* (New Haven, CT: Yale University Press, 2016).

Kidd, Thomas S. *The Great Awakening.* (New Haven, CT: Yale University Press, 2007).

Kimball, David T. *Sketch of the Ecclesiastical History of Ipswich . . . .* (Haverhill, MA: Printed at the Gazette and Patriot Office, 1823).

Kimball, Gertrude S. *Providence in Colonial Times.* (Boston: Houghton Mifflin Company, 1912).

Kingman, Bradford. *History of North Bridgewater, Plymouth County, Massachusetts.* (Boston, MA: Published by the Author, 1866).

Kingsley, James L. *A Sketch of the History of Yale College in Connecticut.* (Boston, MA: Printed by Perkins, Marvin & Company, 1835).

Kingsley, William L. *Contributions to the Ecclesiastical History of Connecticut.* (New haven, CT: W.L. Kingsley, Publisher, 1861).

Knight, Helen C. *Lady Huntington and Her Friends; or The Revival of the Work of God in the Days of Wesley, Whitefield . . . and others in the Last Century.* (New York: American Tract Society, 1853).

Labaree, Benjamin W. *Colonial Massachusetts: A History.* (Millwood, NJ: KTO Press, 1979).

Labaree, Benjamin W. *Patriots and Partisans: The Merchants of Newburyport, 1764-1815.* (New York: W.W. Norton & Company, 1975).

Lambert, Frank. *Inventing the Great Awakening.* (Princeton, NJ: Princeton University Press, 1999).

Lambet, Frank. *"Pedlar in Divinity" George Whitefield and the Trans-Atlantic Revivals, 1737-1770.* (Princeton, NJ: Princeton University Press, 1994).

Lampos, Jim and Michelle Pearson. *Remarkable Women of Old Lyme, Connecticut.* (Charleston, SC: The History Press, 2015).

Lamson, D.F. *History of the Town of Manchester, Massachusetts, 1645-1895.* (Manchester, MA: Printed by the Town, 1895).

Lawrence, H. Newman. *The Old Narragansett Church (St. Paul's) built A.D. 1707, a Constant Witness to Christ and His Church.* (Episcopal Diocese of Rhode Island, 1915).

Lawrence, Robert F. *The New Hampshire Churches: Comprising Histories of the Congregational and Presbyterian Churches in the State* .... (Claremont, NH: Claremont Manufactoring Company, 1856).

Leamon, James S. *The Rev. Jacob Bailey, Maine Loyalist: For God, King, Country, and Self.* (Amherst, MA: University of Massachusetts Press, 2012).

Lewis, Alonzo. *The History of Lynn, including Nahant.* (Boston, MA: 1844).

Lewis, Alonzo and James Newhall. *History of Lynn, Massachusetts.* (Boston, MA: 1865).

Lewis, Everett E. *Historical Sketch, First Congregational Church, Haddam, Connecticut.* (Middletown, CT: Pelton & King Printers, 1879).

Lincoln, William. *History of Worcester, Massachusetts, from its Earliest Settlement to September, 1836.* (Worcester, MA: Charles Hersey, Publisher, 1862).

Lockwood, John H. *A Sermon Commemorative of the Two Hundredth Anniversary of the First Congregational Church of Westfield, Mass.* (Westfield, MA: Clark & Story Printers, 1879).

Love, William D. *The Colonial History of Hartford.* (Hartford, CT: Centinel Press, 1974).

Macy, Clinton T. *A Brief History of St. Peter's Church* [Salem, MA]. (Published by the Church, 1958).

Mahaffey, Jerome D. *The Accidental Revolutionary: George Whitefield & the Creation of America.* (Waco, TX: Baylor University Press, 2011).

Mahaffey, Jerome D. *Preaching Politics: The Religious Rhetoric of George Whitefield.* (Waco, TX: Baylor University Press, 2007).

Mansfield, Stephen. *Forgotten Founding Father: The Heroic Legacy of George Whitefield.* (Nashville, TN: Highland Books, 2001).

Manual of the First Congregational Church of Great Barrington, Mass. (Cambridge, MA: Riverside Press, 1873).

Mary (Dodge) Cleveland Papers, Diary 1742-1762, (box 2, John Cleveland Papers, Essex Institute, Salem, Massachusetts).

Marty, Martin E. *Strangers in their Own Land: Five Hundred Years of Religion in America.* (New York: Penguin Books, 1984).

Manual of First Church of Malden, May 1878. (Boston, MA: Beacon Press, 1878).

Marvin, Carolyn. *Hanging Ruth Blay: An Eighteenth Century New Hampshire Tragedy.* (Charleston, SC: The History Press, 2010).

McConnell, Francis J. *Evangelicals, Revolutionists and Idealists.* (Port Washington, NY: Kennicat Press, 1942).

McLoughlin, William. *Rhode Island: A History.* (New York: W.W. Norton & Company, 1978).

McDuffee, Franklin. *History of the Town of Rochester, New Hampshire, from 1722 to 1890.* (Manchester, NH: John B. Clarke Company, 1892).

McKnight, Tim. *No Better Gospel: George Whitefield's Theology and Methodology of Evangelism.* (Timmonsville, SC: Seed Publishing Group, 2017).

The Metropolis of New England: Colonial Boston, 1630-1776. (Boston, MA: Massachusetts Historical Society, 1976).

Miller, Susan M. *George Whitefield: Clergyman and Scholar.* (Philadelphia: Chelsea House Publishers, 2001).

Mitchell, Nahum. *History of Bridgewater, Massachusetts.* (Bridgewater, MA: Henry T. Pratt, Publisher, 1897).

Mofford, Juliet H. *The History of North Parish Church in North Andover.* (Lawrence, MA: Naiman Press, 1975).

Moody, Charles C.P. *Biographical Sketches of the Moody Family* .... (Boston, MA: Samuel G. Drake, Publisher, 1847).

Morris, John. *Alone at Sea: Gloucester in the Age of Dorymen, 1623-1939.* (Beverly, MA: Commonwealth Editions, 2010).

Nash, Gilbert. *Historical Sketch of the Town of Weymouth, Massachusetts, 1622-1884.* (Weymouth, MA: Weymouth Historical Society, 1885).

Nelson, Dan. *A Burning and Shining Light: The Testimony and Witness of George Whitefield.* (Somis, CA: LifeSong Publishers, 2017).

Northend, Mary H. *Historic Homes of New England.* (Boston, MA: Little, Brown and Company, 1914).

Nissenbaum, Stephen. *The Great Awakening at Yale College.* (Belmont, CA: Wadsworth Publishing, 1972).

Norwalk after Two Hundred and Fifty Years. (Norwalk, CT: Norwalk Historical Society, 1901).

Nourse, Henry S. *History of the Town of Harvard, Massachusetts: 1732-1893.* (Harvard, MA: 1894).

Noyes, Harriett E. *A Memorial History of Hampstead, New Hampshire.* (Boston, MA: George B. Reed Publisher, 1903).

One Hundred and Fiftieth Anniversary 1748-1898 of the Congregational Church of East Hampton (Chatham,) Conn., November 30, 1898, (published by the church, 1898).

Orcutt, Samuel. *A History of the Old Town of Stratford . . . .* (New Haven, CT: Fairfield County Historical Society, 1886).

Osgood, Charles S. *Historical Sketch of Salem, 1626-1879.* (Salem, MA: Essex Institute, 1879).

Paige, Lucius R. *History of Cambridge, Massachusetts . . . 1630-1877.* (Boston, MA: H.O. Houghton & Company, 1877).

Parr, Jessica M. *Inventing George Whitefield: Race, Revivalism, and the Making of a Religious Icon.* (Jackson, MS: University of Mississippi Press, 2015).

Parker, Edward E. *The History of the City of Nashua, New Hampshire, from the Earliest Settlement of Old Dunstable to the Year 1895 . . . .* (Nashua, NH: Telegraph Publishing Company, 1897).

Parker, Edward E. *The History of Londonderry and Derry, New Hampshire.* (Boston, MA: Perkins & Whipple Publishers, 1851).

Parker, Edwin P. *History of the Second Congregational Church, Hartford, Connecticut.* (Hartford, CT: Belknap & Warfield Publishers, 1892).

Perley, Sidney. *The History of Boxford, Essex County, Massachusetts.* (Boxford, MA: Sidney Perley Printer, 1880).

Pettee, Julia. *The Rev. Jonathan Lee and His Eighteenth Century Parish: the Early History of Salisbury, Connecticut.* (Salisbury, CT: The Salisbury Association, 1957).

Philip, Robert. *The Life and Times of George Whitefield.* (1837: reprinted by Banner of Trust, Carlisle, PA: 2007).

Philips, James D. *The Life and Times of Richard Derby, Merchant of Salem, Massachusetts, 1712-1783.* (Cambridge, MA: Riverside Press, 1929).

Philips, James D. *Salem in the Eighteenth Century.* (Boston, MA: Houghton & Mifflin Company, 1937).

Pierce, Frederick C. *History of Grafton, Worcester County, Massachusetts . . . .* (Worcester, MA: Published by the author, 1879).

Pollock, John. *George Whitefield and the Great Awakening.* (Garden City, NJ: Doubleday & Company, 1972).

Pringle, James R. *History of the Town and City of Gloucester, Cape Ann, Massachusetts.* (Gloucester, MA: Published by the Author, 1892).

"Relation of Samuel Fayerweather, May 24, 1741." *Records of the First Church in Boston.* Colonial Society of Massachusetts, publications XXXIX-XL (Boston, A: 1961).

Read, Benjamin. *The History of Swanzey, New Hampshire, from 1734 to 1890.* (Salem, MA: The Salem Press and Publishing and Printing Company, 1892).

The Register of the Malden Historical Society, 1910-1911. (Lynn, MA: Frank S. Whitten, Printer, 1911).

Reynolds, James B. *Two Centuries of Christian Activity at Yale.* (New York: G.P. Putnam's Sons, 1901).

Ridlon, Gideon T. *Saco Valley Settlements and Families; Historical, Biographical . . . .* (Portland, ME: Published by the Author, 1895).

Roads, Samuel Jr. *The History and Traditions of Marblehead.* (Boston, MA: Houghton, Osgood & Company, 1880).

Robbins, Chandler. *A History of Second Church, or Old North, in Boston . . . .* (Boston, MA: Printed by John Wilson & Son, 1852).

Roberts, Richard O. *Whitefield in Print.* (Wheaton, IL: Richard Owen Roberts Publishers, 1988).

Robinson, David. *The Unitarians and the Universalists.* (Westport, CT: Greenwood Press, 1985).

Rockey, J.L. *History of New Haven County, Connecticut.* (New York: W.W. Preston & Company, 1892).

Ross, Marjorie D. *The Book of Boston, the Colonial Period, 1630-1775.* (New York: Hastings House Publishers, 1960).

Rothschild, Robert. *Two Brides for Apollo: The Life of Samuel Williams, 1743-1817.* (Bloomington, IN: iUniverse Press, 2009).

Rudd, Malcom D. *An Historical Sketch of Salisbury, Connecticut.* (New York: 1899).

Sanborn, Edwin D. *Churches of New Hampshire: An Historical Discourse . . . .* (Bristol, NH: R.W. Musgrove, Printer, 1876).

Sanford, Enoch. *History of Raynham, Massachusetts, from the First Settlement to the Present Time.* (Providence, RI: Hammond, Angel & Company Printers, 1870).

Sanford, Enoch. *History of the Town of Berkley, Massachusetts.* (New York: Kilbourne Thompkins Publisher, 1872).

Scales, John. *History of Strafford County, New Hampshire and Representative Citizens.* (Chicago, IL: Richmond-Arnold Publishing, 1914).

Schenck, Elizabeth H. *The History of Fairfield, Fairfield County, Connecticut, from 1700 to 1800.* (New York: Published by the Author, 1905).

Nigel Scotland. *George Whitefield: The First Transatlantic Revivalist.* (Oxford, England: Lion Hudson Publishers, 2019).

Scudder, Townsend. *Concord: An American Town.* (Boston, MA: Little, Brown and Company, 1947).

Sedgwick, Charles F. *General History of the Town of Sharon, Litchfield County, Connecticut . . . .* (Amenia, NY: Charles Walsh Printer and Publisher, 1877).

Seeman, Erik R. *Pious Persuasions: Laity and Clergy in Eighteenth Century New England.* (Baltimore, MD: Johns Hopkins University Press, 1999).

Sewett, Samuel. *The History of Woburn, Middlesex County, Massachusetts, from 1640 to the Year 1860.* (Boston, MA: Wiggin and Lunt Publishers, 1868).

Shattuck, Lemuel. *History of Concord, Middlesex County, Massachusetts . . . .* (Acton, MA: Russell, Odiorne, and Company, 1835).

Sherburne, Edward R. *Some Descendants of Henry and John Sherburne of Portsmouth, N.H.* (Boston, MA: The New England Historical and Genealogical Society, 1904).

Sibley, John L. *Biographical Sketches of Graduates of Harvard University.* (Cambridge, MA: C.W. Sever, Printer, 1881).

Simpson, Alan. *Puritanism in Old and New England.* (Chicago: University of Chicago Press, 1955).

Simpson, Richard V. *Historic Tales of Colonial Rhode Island . . . .* (Charleston, SC: The History Press, 2012).

Sloan, Douglas. *The Great Awakening and American Education.* (New York: Columbia University Press, 1973).

Smalley, E. *The Worcester Pulpit with Notices, Historical and Biographical.* (Boston, MA: Phillips, Sampson and Company, 1851).

Smith, Annie Morrill. *Morrill Kindred in America . . . .* (New York: The Lyons Genealogical Company, 1864).

Smith, Baxter Perry. *History of Dartmouth College.* (Boston, MA: Riverside Press, 1878).

Smith, C.P. *Yankees and God.* (New York: Hermitage House, 1954).

Smith, Chard P. *Brief History of Sharon*. (July 1949: Courtesy of the Sharon Connecticut Historical Society).

Smith, Helen Evertson. *Colonial Days and Ways*. (New York: The Century Company, 1900).

Smith, Isaac W. *History of the Town of Hampstead, N.H.* (Haverhill, MA: 1884).

Smith, Lisa. *The First Great Awakening in Colonial Newspapers: A Shifting Story*. (New York: Lexington Books, 2013).

Smith, Ralph D. *The History of Guilford, Connecticut: from its First Settlement in 1639*. (Albany, NY: J. Munsell, Printer, 1877).

Smith, Samuel F. *History of Newton, Massachusetts: Town and City, from its Earliest Settlement to the Present Time, 1630-1880*. (Boston, MA: American Logotype Company, 1880).

Snow, Caleb H. *A History of Boston, the Metropolis of Massachusetts* . . . . (Boston, MA: Munroe & Francis Printers, 1825).

Spofford, Jeremiah. *A Gazetteer of Massachusetts: Containing a General View of the State*. (Newburyport, MA: Charles Whipple, Publisher, 1828).

Sprague, William B. *Annals of the American Pulpit*. (New York: Robert Carter & Brothers, 1865).

Stackpole, Everett S. and Winthrop S. Meserve. *History of the Town of Durham, New Hampshire* . . . . (Durham, NH: Published by the Town, 1913).

Standard History of Essex County, Massachusetts. (Boston, MA: C.F. Jewett and Company, 1878).

Stark, Charles R. *Groton, Connecticut, 1705-1905*. (Stonington, CT: The Palmer Press, 1922).

Stein, Stephen J., editor. *Jonathan Edwards' Writings: Text, Context, Interpretation*. (Bloomington, IN: Indiana University Press, 1996).

Stiles, Henry R. *The History of Ancient Windsor, Connecticut*. (New York: Charles B. Norton Publisher, 1859).

Stiles, Henry R. *The History of Ancient Wethersfield, Connecticut* . . . . (New York: The Grafton Press, 1904).

Stone, Edwin M. *History of Beverly, Civil and Ecclesiastical*. (Boston, MA: J. Monroe and Company, 1843).

Stout, Harry S. *The Divine Dramatist: George Whitefield and the Rise of Modern Evangelicalism*. (Grand Rapids, MI: Eerdman's Publishing, 1991).

Stout, Harry S. *The New England Soul: Preaching and Religious Culture in Colonial New England*. (New York: Oxford University Press, 1986).

Streeter, James L. *Groton, Historical Bits and Pieces*. (Bloomington, IL: iUniverse Press, 2009).

Swayne, Josephine L. *The Story of Concord*. (Boston, MA: E.F. Worcester Press, 1906).

Sweet, William M. *Religion in Colonial America*. (New York: Charles Scribner's Sons, 1942).

Tapley, Harriet S. *St. Peter's Church in Salem, Massachusetts before the Revolution*. (Salem, MA: Essex Institute, 1944).

Tagney, Ronald N. *A County in Revolution: Essex County at the Dawn of Independence*. (Manchester, MA: Cricket Press, 1976).

Tagney, Ronald N. *The World Turned Upside Down: Essex County during America's Turbulent Years, 1763-1790*. (West Newbury, MA: Essex County History, 1989).

Taylor, Charles J. *History of Great Barrington, Massachusetts*. (Great Barrington, MA: Clark W. Bryan & Company, 1882).

Temple, J.H. *History of Framingham, Massachusetts* . . . , *1640-1880*. (printed by the Town of Framingham, 1887).

Temple, J.H. *History of North Brookfield, Massachusetts*. (Published by the Town of Brookfield, 1887).

Tracy, Joseph. *The Great Awakening*. (1842: reprinted by Banner of Truth Trust, Carlisle, PA: 1989).

Tiffany, Charles C. *History of Sharon, Connecticut*. (unpublished 1942: Courtesy of the Sharon Historical Society).

Trumbull, Benjamin. *A Complete History of Connecticut, Civil and Ecclesiastical* . . . . (Hartford, CT: Hudson & Goodwin Printers, 1797).

Turell, Ebenezer. *The Life and Character of the Reverend Benjamin Colman, D.D., late Pastor of a Church in Boston, New England, who Deceased August 29, 1747.* (Boston, MA: Rogers & Fowle Printers, 1749).

The Two Hundredth Anniversary of the First Congregational Church in Haddam, Connecticut. (Haddam, CT: 1902).

The Two Hundredth Anniversary of the Organization of the United Congregational Church, Little Compton, Rhode Island, September 7, 1904. (Little Compton, RI: 1904).

Tyerman, Luke. *The Life of the Rev. George Whitefield.* (New York: Anson D.F. Randolf & Company, 1877).

Vital Records of Grafton, Massachusetts, to the End of the Year 1849. (Worcester, MA: Franklin P. Rice Publisher, 1906).

Vose, James G. *Sketches of Congregationalism in Rhode Island* . . . . (New York: Burdett & Company, 1894).

Wadsworth, Joseph A.C. *The History of Halifax Congregational Church of Halifax, Massachusetts.* (Halifax, MA: 2008).

Wainwright, Charles E. *Tales from the Attic: A Celebration of the First 350 Years of the First Parish and Church in Beverly Massachusetts.* (Beverly, MA: Published by the First Church, Beverly, MA: 2017).

Wakeley, Joseph B. *Anecdotes of the Rev. George Whitefield, M.A.* (1772: reprinted by BiblioLife Reproductions, n.d.).

Wakeley, J.B. *The Prince of Pulpit Orators: A Portraiture of Rev. George Whitefield.* (New York: Carleton & Lanahan, 1871).

Walker, Williston. *The History of Congregationalism in the United States.* (New York: The Christian Literature Company, 1894).

Wall, Caleb A. *Reminiscences of Worcester from the Earliest Period, Historical and Genealogical* . . . . *(Worcester, MA: 1877).*

Walsh, Kenneth. *The Economic History of Newport, Rhode Island.* (Bloomington, IN: AuthorHouse Publishers, 2014).

Wells, Charles C. *New North Church: from Birth to Death in Early Boston.* (Oak Grove, IL: Chauncey Park Press, 2014).

Wells, Daniel and Ruben Wells. *A History of Hatfield, Massachusetts, 1660-1910.* (Springfield, MA: F.C.H. Gibbons, Printer, 1910).

Weston, Thomas. *History of the Town of Middleboro, Massachusetts.* (Boston, MA: Houghton, Mifflin and Company, 1906).

Wheeler, Richard A. *History of the First Congregational Church, Stonington, Connecticut, 1674-1874.* (Norwich, CT: T.H. Davis and Company, 1875).

Wieder, Lois M. *A Pleasant Land—A Goodly Heritage.* (Wethersfield, CT: First Church of Christ, 1986).

Wiley, Frederick L. *Life and Influence of the Rev. Benjamin Randall, Founder of the Free Will Baptist Denomination.* (Philadelphia, PA: American Baptist Publication Society, 1915).

Willey, George F. *Willey's Book of Nutfield: A History* . . . . (Derry Depot, NH: G.F. Willey Publisher, 1895).

Williams, Stephen. *The Genealogy and History of the Family of Williams in America* . . . . (1847: reprinted by the University of Wisconsin Press, 2008).

Williamson, William D. *The History of the State of Maine* . . . . (Hallowell, ME: Glazier, Masters, and Company, 1832).

Willis, William. *The History of Portland, from 1632 to 1864* . . . . (Portland, ME: Bailey & Noyes Printers, 1865).

Winiarski, Douglas L. *Darkness Falls on the Land of Light: Experiencing Religious Awakenings in Eighteenth-Century New England.* (Chapel Hill, NC: University of North Carolina Press, 2017).

Winsor, Justin. *History of the Town of Duxbury, Massachusetts* . . . . (Boston, MA: John Putnam Printer, 1849).

Winsor, Justin. *The Memorial History of Boston . . . , 1630-1880.* (Boston, MA: James R. Osgood & Company, 1882).

Wood, Benjamin. *A Centennial Address, Delivered at Upton, Mass., June 25, 1835.* (Boston: William Pierce, Publisher, 1835).

Wood, Nathan. *History of First Baptist Church, Boston, 1655-1899.* (Philadelphia, PA: American Baptist Society, 1899).

Worcester, Samuel T. *History of the Town of Hollis, New Hampshire, from its First Settlement to the Year 1879.* (Nashua, NH: Press of D.C. Moore, 1879).

ARTICLES AND SERMONS

"1740—Jonathan Edwards and the Great Awakening." *The Society of Colonial Wars in the State of Connecticut.* http://colonialwardct.org/1740_s.htm.

Beales, Ross W. Jr. editor. "Solomon Prentice's Narrative of the Great Awakening." *Proceedings of the Massachusetts Historical Society*, Vol. 83 (1971).

Biggs, Charles L. "When George Whitefield Came Through New Haven." Unpublished manuscript, Connecticut Historical Society.

Billings, Thomas H. "The Great Awakening." *Historical Collections of the Essex Institute.* (Salem, MA: Essex Institute, 1929).

Brauer, Jerald C. "Conversion: From Puritanism to Revivalism." *Journal of Religion.* vol. 58 (July 1978).

"Brief Memoirs and Notices of Prince's Subscribers." *The New England Historical and Genealogical Register.* (vol. 8, 1854).

Brown, Anne S. "Visions of Community in Eighteenth Century Essex County: Chebacco Parish and the Great Awakening." *Essex Institute Historical Collections*, CXXV (1989).

Chamberlain, Ava. "The Grand Sower of the Seed: Jonathan Edwards' Critique of George Whitefield." *The New England Quarterly.* vol. 70, No. 3 (September 1977).

"Church History, The United Church of Upton." http://www.unitedparishupton.org/about/church-history.html.

Clark, Elizabeth. "Canaan Falls Village Town History." *Town of Canaan, Connecticut.* https://www.canaanfallsvillage.org/history.

Clarke, M.L. "A Brief History of the First Parish Church in Medford, Massachusetts." http:www.uumedford.org.

Conforti, Joseph A. "Joseph Bellamy and the New Divinity Movement." *The New England Historical and Genealogical Register.* (Boston, MA: 1983).

"Devil's Footprint, Ipswich, Massachusetts," http://storiesfromipswich.org/2014/01/21/the-devils-footprint.

"Dr. Daniel Rogers." http://freepages.genealogy.rootsweb.ancestry.com.

"Dr. Mayhew, the First Unitarian Preacher in America." *The Monthly Repository of Theology and General Literature.* (Paternoster-Row, Great Britain, 1821).

"Early Records of Windsor, Connecticut." *The New England Historical and Genealogical Register.* (Boston, MA: 1851).

Gatgounis, George J. "How Did Harvard College Respond to the Great Awakening." *The Christian Observer*, March 2, 2014. https://christianobserver.org/how-did-harvard-college-respond-to-the-great-awakening.

Greenleaf, John. "Memoir of Rev. Jonathan Parsons." *American Quarterly Register.* Vol. xiv (November 1841).

"First Church, Cohasset, Massachusetts." http://www.firstparishcohasset.org/about/history.

"First Church Congregational." [Manchester, MA] http://www.firstparishchurch.org/about/our-history.

"First Congregational Church and Society in Brighton." http://oasis.lib.harvard.edu/oasis/deliver/~div00011.

"First Congregational Church-Our History." http://www.kitterypointucc.org/church-history.html.

Harlan, David C. "The Travail of Religious Moderation: Jonathan Dickman and the Great Awakening." *Journal of Presbyterian History.* Vol. 61 (1983), pp. 411-426.

"History of the Plymouth Church." http:www.plymouthchurchframingham.org /whoweare/history.

"The History of Your Congregation." *History of the Second Congregational Church, Hartford, Connecticut*. http://www.southchurchhartford.org/ourhistory/history/default.html.

Hughes, Paul. "Some Episodes in Greenland's Church History." *Annual Reports of the Town of Greenfield, New Hampshire, 2004.* (Greenland, NH: Published by the Town, 2004).

Labaree, Leonard. "George Whitefield comes to Middletown." *William and Mary Quarterly*. Vol. 7, no. 4 (October 1950).

Lang, Stephen J. and Mark A. Knoll. "Colonial New England: An Old Order, a New Awakening." *Christian History*. vol. 4, no. 4 (1985), pp. 8-10, 35.

Lawson, Kenneth E. "Who Founded Methodism? Wesley's Dependence upon Whitefield in the Eighteenth Century English Revival." *Reformation and Revival*. (Summer 1995), pp. 39-57.

"Letter from Rev. Arthur Brown." *The New England Historical and Genealogical Register*. (Boston, MA: Thomas Prince, Printer, 1852).

Loetsher, Frederick W. "Presbyterianism in Colonial New England." *Journal of the Presbyterian Historical Society*. Vol. XI, No. 3-4 (September /October 1921).

Loring, Amasa. "Rev. George Whitefield." *Old Times: A Magazine Devoted to the Preservation and Publication . . . of North Yarmouth, Maine*. (Somersworth, NH: New Hampshire Publications Company, 1977).

Minkema, Kenneth P. "A Great Awakening Conversion: The Relation of Samuel Belcher." *William and Mary Quarterly*. vol. 44 (January 1987), pp. 121-126.

"New North Religious Society." *Historical Notices of the New North Religious Society, Boston*. (Boston, MA: 1822).

Neilson, Larz, "The Fighting Parson," *Wilmington Town Crier*, October 19, 1983.

"Newport—History." http://www.city-data.com/us-cities/The-Northeast/Newport-History.html.

O'Brien, Susan. "A Trans-Atlantic Community of Saints: The Great Awakening and the First Evangelical Network, 1735-1755." *The American Historical Review*. vol. 91, no.4 (October 1986).

Partridge, Dennis. "Church History of Ashford, Connecticut." *Connecticut Genealogy*. https://connecticut genealogy.com/windham/church_history_of_ashford.htm.

"A Pants-Free Preacher Starts a Bonfire of the Vanities in New London." *New England Historical Society*. https://www.newenglandhistoricalsociety.com/a-pants-free-preacher-starts-a-bonfire-of-the-vanities-in-new-london.

Pappalardo, Wilma. "Reverend John Ballentine: A Profile of the Complete 18th Century Minister." Westfield Athenaeum—Westfield History Room, April 6, 1990).

Perley, M.V.B. "James Leslie of Topsfield." *The Historical Collections of the Topsfield Historical Society*. (Topsfield, MA: Published by the Society, 1915).

"A Quiet Country Town: 18th Century Medford." (Medford, Massachusetts Historical Society and Museum, 2016).

Rack, Henry O. "Religious Societies and the Origins of Methodism." *Journal of Ecclesiastical History*. vol. 38, no. 4 (October 1987), pp. 582-595.

"Rev. Samuel Haven Fathered Seventeen." http://www.seacoastnh.com/famous-people/link-free-or-die/rev-samuel-haven-fathered-17.

Reist, Irwin W. "John Wesley and George Whitefield: A Study in the Integrity of Two Theologies of Grace." *The Evangelical Quarterly*. vol. 47, no.1 (January-March 1975) pp. 26-40.

"The Rev. Thomas Bradbury, D.D." *The New England Historical and Genealogical Register*. (Boston, MA: 1873).

Russell, Eugene D. "Harvard College and Lynn in Colonial Times." *The Registrar of the Lynn Historical Society*, (Lynn, MA: 1912).

"Sarah Edwards on George Whitefield." *Banner of Truth*. https://banneroftruth.org/us/resources/articles/2012/sarah-edwards-on-george-whitefield.

Schmotter, James W. "Clerical Professionalism and the Great Awakening." *American Quarterly*. (Summer 1979).

Spofford, Ellen W. "Personal Sketches of Early Inhabitants of Georgetown, Mass." *Essex Institute Historical Collections*. (Salem, MA: Essex Institute, 1905).

Stout, Harry. "The Great Awakening in New England Considered: The New England Clergy." *Journal of Social History*. Vol. 8, No. 1 (Fall 1974).

Tapley, Harriet S. "St. Peter's Church in Salem before the Revolution." *Essex Institute Historical Collections*. (Vol. 80: 1944).

Toleman, Charles B. *An Historical Sermon Delivered in the First Church of Christ (of the Old Town of Brookfield) at West Brookfield, Mass. Sunday, September 18, 1910*. (Ware, MA: Ware River News Print, 1911).

"Town of Groton." http://www.groton-ct.gov/about/history.asp.

Walsh, James. "The Great Awakening in the First Congregational Church of Woodbury, Connecticut." *William and Mary Quarterly*. vol. 28 (1971), pp. 543-562.

Walsh, Thomas F. "Whitefield in Wethersfield." ww.weathersfieldhistory.org/articles/george-whitefield-the-billy-graham-of-colonial-america.

Warnock, Adrian. "George Whitefield Meets Jonathan Edwards." http://www.pathos.com/blogs/adrianwarnock/2009/11/george-whitefield-meets-jonathan.

Whiting, Lyman. *A Bi-Centennial Oration made in West Brookfield, July 4, 1860, at the Celebration of the Two Hundredth Anniversary of the Settlement of the Town of Brookfield*. (West Brookfield, MA: Thomas Morey, Printer, 1869).

Williamson, William D. "Sketches of the Lives of Early Maine Ministers." *Proceedings of the Maine Historical Society*. (Portland, ME: Published by the Society. Vol. iv, p. 321.

Willingham, W.F. "Religious Conversion in the Second Society of Windham, Connecticut, 1723-1743: a Case Study." *Societas*. vol.6 (1976), pp. 109-119.

Wood, Nathan. "History of First Baptist Church, Boston, MA." *Baptist History Homepage*. http://baptisthistoryhomepage.com/mass.boston.fbc.wood.4.html, (1899).

INDEX OF SIGNIFICANT PEOPLE

A

Hull Abbott 293, 347

Robert Abercrombie 253

Eliphalet Adams 277-279, 376

John Adams 34, 339

Joseph Adams 119, 194-195, 333, 492

Samuel Adams 69

Benjamin Allen 208-210, 492

Timothy Allen 278-279, 315

William Allen 60, 196, 338

Ames, Nathaniel 497

Nathaniel Ames 119, 408

Nathaniel Appleton 48, 71, 114, 153, 172, 349, 393, 492-494

Ashley, Jonathan 497

B

Isaac Backus 224, 320-321, 327, 347-348, 358, 377-378, 383, 502

Jacob Bailey 393-394, 502, 509

William Balch 318, 494

John Ballentine 87-88, 515

Jonathan Barber 403

Edward Barnard 220, 494

John Barnard 54, 65, 117, 174, 316, 410, 494, 497

Jonathan Barnard 149

Theodore Barnard 184

Thomas Barnard 116, 397, 494

Edward Bass 489

John Bass 315

James Bayley 161-162, 492

Joseph Bean 447-448

Jonathan Belcher 45, 47, 68, 75, 77-78, 260

Joseph Bellamy 410-411, 428, 481, 492, 514

William Bentley 313, 497

Edward Billings 260

Richard Billings 229

Samuel Bird 219-220, 239-240, 364-365

Ruth Blay 395, 509

Daniel Bliss 76, 147, 235, 244, 348, 351, 391-392, 401, 491

John Blunt 194, 492

Nicholas Bowes 172, 494

John Boyle 400

Benjamin Bradstreet 112, 178, 492

Simon Bradstreet 69, 293, 492

Robert Breck 89

Matthew Bridge 251, 351-352

Charles Brockwell 64

Peter Brockwell 116, 180

Arthur Brown 193, 515

John Browne 328

Aaron Burr 325-326

Isaac Burr 78-80

Mather Byles 49, 376

C

John Callender, Jr. 228

Othniel Campbell 230, 491

Henry Caner 107

Ezra Carpenter 245, 492

Joseph Champney 408

James Chandler 182, 455, 488, 491

Samuel Chandler 129-130, 201, 210, 310, 333, 344, 460, 462, 491, 497

Asa Chaplin 455

Stephen Chase 146, 157, 499

Charles Chauncey 116-117, 126, 136, 154, 158, 247, 290, 390, 409, 450, 493, 498, 506

Nathaniel Chauncey 101

Samuel Checkly 152

Edward Cheever 145-146, 175, 249-250

Thomas Cheever 142

Thomas Cheney 81

John Chipman 318-319, 408, 492

Nathaniel Clapp 34-37, 227, 305

Thomas Clapp 262, 268-269, 363-366, 378-380, 426

Peter Clark 55, 119, 247-248

Aaron Cleveland 101

John Cleveland 112-113, 119, 176, 180-181, 310-312, 316, 319-320, 333, 344, 364, 409, 412, 479, 498, 508-509

James Cogswell 381

Benjamin Coleman 31, 136-140

Sylvanus Conant 356, 358

Samuel Cook 172, 492, 494

William Cook 76-77

William Cooper 46, 68, 294-295, 400, 492

John Cotton 75, 164, 172, 403, 491, 494

Josiah Cotton 226-227, 492

Ward Cotton 57, 491

Josiah Crocker 167-168, 357-358, 491

Andrew Croswell 276-277

Caleb Cushing 174, 493

James Cushing 202, 220, 238, 494

Nathaniel Cutler 454

Timothy Cutler 46, 295, 350

D

Naphtali Daggett 363, 366, 378-379

Addington Davenport 46

James Davenport 108-109, 113, 126, 275, 277, 279

William Davidson 201, 218

Ebenezer Devotion 94

Samuel Dexter 74, 498

Moses Dickinson 108

James Diman 407-408, 491

E

Jonathan Edwards 14, 22, 30-31, 76, 81, 83-85, 87-89, 92-93, 95, 98-99, 102, 104, 115, 119, 123, 128, 135, 146, 154-155, 189, 193, 239, 248, 253-256, 258, 261-262, 265, 266-269, 276, 278, 280, 290, 319, 325, 347, 390, 392-393, 410-411, 425, 431, 438, 441-442, 459, 471, 477, 481, 492, 498-499, 504, 512, 514, 516, 518

Nathaniel Eells 267, 491, 493-494, 499

Andrew Eliot 243-244

Jacob Eliot 377, 498

Andrew Elliott 345-346, 350

Richard Elvins 212,-213

Daniel Emerson 236, 491

John Emerson 182-183, 187, 491

Joseph Emerson 65, 142, 175, 192, 451, 492

Nathaniel Emmons 448

F

Daniel Farrand 430-431

Timothy Farrar 402

Elijah Fish 353

Nathaniel Fisher 169

Jabez Fitch 130, 132, 193-194, 298

Henry Flynt 71, 153

Thomas Foxcroft 46, 136-137, 154, 295, 319, 492

John Foxe 371

Benjamin Franklin 11, 22, 287-289, 371, 375, 420, 507

G

Ezekiel Gavitt 266-267

Joshua Gee 47, 118, 247, 295, 319, 492

Gillman 201, 305, 356

Nicholas Gilman 201, 305, 339

David Goddard 80, 491

George Griswold 281

H

James Hale 315

Theophilus Hall 102

Howell Harris 123, 285, 300, 302

Asahel Hart 431

Elias Haven 171, 447, 491

Joseph Haven 203, 463

Samuel Haven 335-336, 464, 515

Hannah Heaton 270-271, 367, 499

Phineas Hemenway 236

Joshua Hempstead 276-277, 281, 499

Nathaniel Henchman 145-148, 157, 249-250, 499

Jedediah Hide 272-273

Jonathan Hillier 227

William Hobby 70, 146, 148, 223, 247, 250, 491, 499

Edward Holyoke 48, 71, 137, 153, 329, 349, 404, 413, 456

James Honeyman 34-35, 37, 305

Samuel Hopkins 104, 306, 327, 385, 411, 425, 439, 441-444, 448, 481, 499

John Hovey 210, 214, 492

Selina Huntington 418

J

Edward Jackson 149

Richard Jacques 178, 332

Samuel Jefferds 210, 215, 492

David Jewett 274, 277, 279, 376, 492

Jedediah Jewett 182, 187, 332, 343, 393-394, 397-398, 452, 473, 491

Jonathan Judd 256-257, 499

K

Bathsheba Kingsley 119

Daniel Kirtland 271, 273

L

Samuel Langdon 130, 132, 298, 303, 335, 463

Samuel Lankton 392

Jonathan Lee 426-427, 431, 510

Nathaniel Leonard 163-164, 293, 356, 492

James Leslie 461-462, 515

Isaac Lewis 379

James Lockwood 95, 97

Benjamin Lord 271-273, 360, 377, 492

Israel Loring 76-77, 147, 156, 347, 470, 495, 499, 500

Nicholas Loring 208-210, 492

Index of Significant People   515

John Lowell 61-62, 184, 187, 220, 493

Isaac Lyman 336, 392, 459, 463

Benjamin Lyon 406-407, 500

M

Thaddeus Maccarty 163

David MacGregor 202, 218, 235

James MacSparron 230-231

Amos Main 119, 202-204, 491

Alexander Malcolm 173-174

Alexander Malcom 54, 65

Daniel Marshall 262-263, 486, 487

Jonathan Marsh 95, 262

Cotton Mather 29-30, 47, 431, 434, 500

Jonathan Mayhew 294, 409

David McGregor 217-219, 499

James McSparran 306

Jonas Meriam 403, 462

Henry Messenger 170, 447

Jedediah Mills 103, 105-106, 269, 492

Samuel Moody 59, 64-65, 128, 142, 191-192, 210, 302-303, 336, 392, 459, 491

John Moorhead 143-144, 157, 480, 491

Isaac Morrill 396-397

Moses Morrill 210, 492

N

John Newmarch 302, 337

Samuel Niles 266, 494

John Norton 381

Joseph Noyes 269, 364-365

Sarah Noyes 452-453

O

Sampson Occum 381

Samson Occum 273, 378, 418, 500

John Odlin 196-198, 201, 304, 339-340

Woodbridge Odlin 197-198, 340

Sarah Osborn 36-37, 306, 327, 385, 444, 497, 507

John Owen 275-277, 492

P

Joseph Park 266-267

Ebenezer Parkman 47-48, 78, 246-247, 249, 305, 353-354, 358, 492, 500

David Parsons 258-259, 492

Jonathan Parsons 184, 220, 280-281, 303, 317, 331, 343, 394, 459, 467, 469, 473, 478, 487-488, 492, 514

Moses Parsons 112, 182-183, 316, 332, 344, 454, 488

Lucy Hidden Pearson 467

William Pepperell 64, 191, 192, 195, 302

Daniel Pierce 185, 193, 463, 470

James Pierpont 102, 269, 270

James Pike 119, 131, 195, 204, 207, 214, 491

Benjamin Pomeroy 275

John Porter 166, 491

Solomon Prentice 166-167, 248, 491, 514

Thomas Prentice 69-70, 294, 347, 492

Benjamin Prescott 55, 174, 235, 493

Roger Price 480

Thomas Prince 27, 46, 73-74, 112, 137, 159, 193, 314, 319, 491, 515

Daniel Putnam 223, 492

R

Benjamin Randall 227, 464-465, 481-482, 503, 513

Solomon Reed 351-353

Philemon Robbins 104, 271

Joseph Roberts 181

Ammi R. Robins 428

Daniel Rogers 200, 304-305, 339-340, 473, 488, 500, 514

John Rogers 56, 62, 112, 119, 132-133, 175-178, 180-181, 195-196, 207, 210, 214, 318, 463-464, 492

Nathaniel Rogers 133, 175-177, 186-187, 492

John Rowe 413, 455-456, 501

David Rowland 446

Samuel Russell 274

William Russell 98-99

S

Richard Salter 244

James Searing 228, 305, 359, 385, 441

Joseph Seccombe 115

John Seccomb 240-241, 491

Joseph Sewell 51, 72, 137, 141, 152, 159, 247, 295, 314, 319, 328, 491

John Shaw 165-167

Henry Sherburn 129-130, 190

William Shurtleff 58, 60, 130-131, 190-191, 193, 298, 335, 492

Aaron Smith 77-78, 249, 495

Cotton Smith 434

Hezekiah Smith 221, 468, 478, 497

Richard Smith 421, 423, 467, 472

Thomas Smith 186, 208-212, 214, 241, 392, 492, 501

Joseph Snow 227, 382-383, 445

John Sparhawk 55

Shubal Stearns 486-487

Mary Stedman 184

Benjamin Stevens 337

Abel Stiles 406

Ezra Stiles 385-386, 438-444, 476, 501

Solomon Stoddard 30-31

Ebenezer Storer 317, 498

Seth Storer 172, 494

Job Strong 319, 498

Josiah Swan 239-240

John Swift 247, 251, 495

T

Gilbert Tennent 36, 112, 124, 135, 247, 283, 296, 298

Peter Thatcher 451-452, 492

Gardner Thurston 441, 443, 445

Samuel Tillinghast 403, 497

Samuel Tobey 169, 491

William Tompson 213

Christopher Toppan 56-57, 61, 184-185

Jonathan Townsend 223

Nathaniel Trask 305, 339

Caleb Trowbridge 237, 260

Henry True 340-341

John Tucker 331

John Tudor 388, 470

Joshua Tufts 119, 238, 491

Ebenezer Turell 172, 299, 350-351, 391, 492, 494

U

John Usher 39

V

Samuel Veazie 162, 491

William Vinal 305-306, 359, 385, 441, 444

W

Daniel Wadsworth 96-98, 245, 446, 501

John Wales 168-169, 492

Nathaniel Walter 47, 141, 494

John Webb 31, 139-140, 157, 222, 235, 242-243, 295, 319, 345, 350, 491

Jonathan Webb 31, 46, 68, 328

Habijah Weld 170, 447, 492

Thomas Weld 248

William Welstead 50

Charles Wesley 18, 124, 285-286, 372, 418

John Wesley 42, 122, 124-125, 285-286, 301, 371-372, 417-419, 476, 515

Eleazer Wheelock 111, 114-115, 273, 347, 378, 410, 492, 501

Joseph Whipple 57, 493

David White 252

Elizabeth Edwards Whitefield 17

John White 24, 177-178, 187, 332, 491

Elnathan Whitman 362-363

Samuel Whittlesey, Junior 105

Samuel Whittlesey, Senior 101, 105

Edward Wigglesworth 153, 182, 329

Samuel Wigglesworth 181, 332, 491

Jabez Wight 271, 273

Jemima Wilkinson 482-483, 507

Samuel Willard 27

Chester Williams 83, 258, 492

Samuel Williams 392-393, 511

Stephen Williams 48, 73, 75, 83, 88, 261, 470, 472, 492, 502

Warham Williams 172, 494

William Williams 86-87, 172, 494

Cornelius Winter 419-421, 423, 500

Jeremiah Wise 195, 204-205, 207, 214, 492

Ebenezer Wright 108-109

Jabez Wright 492

Robert Wright 423-424

ABOUT THE AUTHOR

I AM A NATIVE NEW Englander. My father and my mother are the descendants of immigrants from England, the Azores, Nova Scotia, and Denmark, who settled in New Hampshire and Massachusetts.

I was born in New Hampshire and raised in North Andover, Massachusetts. After six years in the U.S. Army, I went back to school and graduated from Salem State College in Massachusetts. After marriage, my wife and I lived in southern New Hampshire. Were it not for pursuing higher education and a career in military service, I might never have left New England.

After graduation from Salem State College, I earned a M.A. degree from Bob Jones University; an M.A. and a M.Div. degree from Cincinnati Bible Seminary; and the D.S.T. degree from Bethany Theological Seminary. Later I earned a Ph.D. in United States History from Preston University. During these years I maintained my military status as a U.S. Army Reserve chaplain while serving as a pastor of a church on the north shore of Boston, in Beverly, Massachusetts. I published books and articles at this time, but was primarily a pastor and chaplain. After some years I went back to school to earn the Doctor of Ministry degree from Westminster Theological Seminary in Pennsylvania.

At the college level, I have taught courses in Theology, Church History, Chaplaincy, and American Church History. I authored several books and numerous articles on history and theology themes. After the September 11, 2001 attack on America, I was called from reserve status to active duty, and ministries shifted to the full-time Army chaplaincy for a career in military service.

I completed all Army Chaplain School training, and I am a graduate of the U.S. Air Force War College. While in the Army, I taught as an adjunct college professor of church history and theology for eleven years both in the United States and overseas. As an Army chaplain, I wrote four additional books and numerous articles on history and religious-military themes. The Army granted me the additional skill indicator (ASI) as a Historian.

I am retired from the U.S. Army after thirty-four-plus years of service, first as a common soldier and then as a chaplain. I retired with the rank of colonel. I have seen much of the world, but my heart, my family and my home are still in New England. I am currently an adjunct college professor and a writer on U.S. history and church history themes.

My roots in New England are deep. On my Dad's side and on my mother's side, I have New England genealogy that goes back to the seventeenth century. I had relatives in New England when Rev. George Whitefield traveled through the area on his various preaching tours between 1740-1770. I wonder if they ever heard him preach. I wonder what my distant relatives thought of this controversial itinerant preacher.

Ambassador International's mission is to magnify the Lord Jesus Christ and promote His Gospel through the written word.

We believe through the publication of Christian literature, Jesus Christ and His Word will be exalted, believers will be strengthened in their walk with Him, and the lost will be directed to Jesus Christ as the only way of salvation.

For more information about
AMBASSADOR INTERNATIONAL
please visit:

www.ambassador-international.com

Thank you for reading this book. Please consider leaving us a review on your favorite retailer's website, Goodreads or Bookbub, or our website.

More from Ambassador International

From their earliest arrival in America 350 years ago, the Scots-Irish left a lasting legacy. The history of the United States is interwoven with outstanding personalities from the Scots-Irish diaspora and the distinctive characteristics of a people who pushed the frontiers to new horizons. This comprehensive study of the Scots-Irish in America by Northern Ireland author Billy Kennedy has created a much greater awareness of the accomplishments and the durability of the hardy settlers and their families who moved to the New World during the eighteenth century and created a civilization out of a wilderness.

In *Worldchangers*, challenge your faith as you meet men and women from around the world who turned some of the darkest moments of history into transforming opportunities. Experience the true stories of Christians who lived the adventure of saying yes to a faithful God and be transported to unforgettable moments when ordinary people trusted God for things that seemed impossible and, as a result, changed the world for the better.

James Oglethorpe was a British aristocrat and philanthropist in the eighteenth century who pioneered prison reform in the United Kingdom before founding the state of Georgia as a classless society for poor people from England. He planned the town of Savannah as well as established a deep friendship with Native Americans. Oglethorpe refused to allow slavery in Georgia, despite strong opposition, and successfully defended Georgia from an attack by the Spanish in Florida. On his return to the UK, Oglethorpe became the senior general in the British army and supported the campaign to abolish slavery in the British Empire.

General James Oglethorpe: From Georgia to Cranham Hall highlights Oglethorpe's outstanding achievements, acknowledges some of his significant shortcomings, and offers reflection on his legacy both in Georgia and in the UK.

www.ingramcontent.com/pod-product-compliance
Lightning Source LLC
Chambersburg PA
CBHW060307240426
43661CB00059B/2685